The Rise of the Global South

The Rise of the Global South

*The Decline of Western Christendom
and the Rise of Majority World Christianity*

Elijah J. F. Kim

WIPF & STOCK · Eugene, Oregon

THE RISE OF THE GLOBAL SOUTH
The Decline of Western Christendom and the Rise of Majority World Christianity

Wipf & Stock
An Imprint of Wipf and Stock Publishers
199 W. 8th Ave., Suite 3
Eugene, OR 97401
www.wipfandstock.com

ISBN 13: 978-1-61097-970-2

Manufactured in the U.S.A.

For Amy, Shalom, and Samuel Kim

"Come, let us return to the LORD. He has torn us to pieces but he will heal us; he has injured us but he will bind up our wounds. After two days he will revive us; on the third day he will restore us, that we may live in his presence. Let us acknowledge the LORD; let us press on to acknowledge him. As surely as the sun rises, he will appear; he will come to us like the winter rains, like the spring rains that water the earth." (Hosea 6: 1–3)

And this gospel of the kingdom will be preached in the whole world as a testimony to all nations, and then the end will come. (Matthew 24:14)

After this I looked, and there before me was a great multitude that no one could count, from every nation, tribe, people and language, standing before the throne and before the Lamb. They were wearing white robes and were holding palm branches in their hands. And they cried out in a loud voice: "Salvation belongs to our God, who sits on the throne, and to the Lamb." (Revelation 7:9–10)

Contents

List of Tables *ix*
List of Charts *x*
List of Graphs *x*
List of Maps *xi*
Foreword *xiii*
Preface *xvii*
Introduction *xxiii*

1   Twenty-First Century Christianity 1

2   The Crisis of Christianity in Europe 42

3   What Is European Christianity? 80

4   Secularization in Europe 130

5   Revival Movements in Europe 178

6   American Awakenings and Revivals 239

7   The Secularization in the United States 305

8   Global Trends in Christianity 362

Bibliography 427
Subject/Name Index 457

List of Tables

Table 1.1   Renewalists by United Nations Region / 7

Table 1.2   Major Christian Traditions and Churches in Africa / 22

Table 1.3   Christians in Asia by region, 1910 and 2010 / 24

Table 1.4   Renewalists in Asia, 1910 and 2010 / 25

Table 1.5   Christianity in Asia / 26

Table 1.6   Renewalists in Latin America / 27

Table 1.7   Largest Renewalist Traditions by Adherents, 2010 / 28

Table 1.8   Largest Population of Independents / 37

Table 1.9   Adherents in Major Christian Traditions and Movements, 1910 and 2010 / 39

Table 1.1   Largest 25 of 201 Independent Traditions, 2010 / 40

Table 2.1   Belief in God in Great Britain and Northern Ireland, 1991 / 47

Table 2.2   Connection between denominational integration and different beliefs (Cramer's V^3) / 51

Table 2.3   Loyalists, returnees, and dropouts compared on beliefs and moral issues (as percentages) / 54

Table 2.4   Awareness of a presence or power compared with church attendance / 55

Table 2.5   International church activity by percentage of the adult population, 1990 / 58

Table 2.6   Total adult attendance in Great Britain, 1980–2000 / 70

Table 2.7   Adult Church Attendance in England, 1980–2000 / 71

Table 2.8   Frequency of Church Attendance, 1990 (%) / 73

Table 2.9   Church membership in Britain, 1900–2000 / 76

Table 2.10   Total UK church members / 76

Table 3.1   Christian symbols in a pagan setting / 108

Table 6.1   Belief in God in Great Britain and Northern Ireland, 1991, 2008 / 207

Table 6.2   Survey on Belief on God   / 249

Table 6.3   Religious Beliefs among Adults   / 250

Table 6.4   American and British Beliefs Contrasted   / 250

Table 6.5   Church-Related Behavior in the Last Seven Days   / 253

Table 6.6   Mainline Church Members, Evangelicals, and Catholics per 1,000 Church Members, 1940–1985 / 260

Table 8.1   1910 Largest Cities / 368

Table 8.2   Largest Urban Areas by Population 2010 / 372

List of Charts

Chart 8.1   Protestant Churches in Brazil / 421

List of Graphs

Graph 1.1   Christians by continent, 1910 and 2010 / 5

Graph 1.2   Fastest Renewlist Growth / 6

Graph 1.3   Percentage of all Christians in the Global South from AD 33–2010 / 17

Graph 1.4   Distribution of Christians by continent, 1920–2010 / 18

Graph 1.5   Waves of renewal, 2010 / 33

Graph 1.6   Christian Major Traditions—Percentage of Global Population, 1910 and 2010 / 38

Graph 2.1   Religious and spiritual beliefs / 52

Graph 2.2   Comparative Growth of World Religions, 1920–2000 / 60

Graph 2.3   Global Religious Change, 1920–2010 / 61

Graph 2.4   Religions by Global Adherents, 1920 and 2010 / 61

Graph 2.5   Global Religion by Proportion, 1920 and 2010 / 62

Graph 2.6   Adult Church Attendance in Britain, 1851–1989 / 66

Graph 2.7   Church Attendance in Britain, 1851–1989 / 67

Graph 2.8   Christian church membership, Britain, 1900–1990 / 75

Graph 6.1   Americans and British Belief in God by Percentage / 248

Graph 6.2   Percent Membership Change / 252

Graph 6.3   Rates of Religious Adherence, 1776–1980 / 255

Graph 6.4   Religious Adherents by Denomination, 1776
           and 1850 / 256

Graph 6.5   White Protestant Church Attendance, 1952–1968 / 258

Graph 6.6   Ratings of Honesty and Ethics of the Clergy / 262

Graph 8.1   Approximate Spread of Immigrants in the Past Fifty Years
           (Total 191 Million) / 375

Graph 8.2   International Migration, 2009 / 376

Graph 8.3   Percent of the Population by Race and Hispanic Origin,
           1990, 2000, 2025, and 2050 / 378

List of Maps

Map 1.1   Ratio of Muslims to Christians / 20

Map 1.2   Christians in Asia by Province, 2010 / 23

Map 1.3   Christians in Asia by country, 1910 / 24

Map 1.4   Renewalists in Latin America 2010 / 29

Map 2.1   Percentage Majority Religion by Province, 2010 / 63

Map 8.1   100 largest cities by religious adherence, 2010 / 373

Foreword

FEW SCHOLARS DISAGREE WITH the conclusion reached by Elijah Kim in this book that we are living through "one of the transforming moments in the history of religion worldwide," as Christianity is rising in the South.[1] Many scholars, like Elijah Kim, find and describe the decline of Christianity in the West. Calling it a pessimistic view, Philip Jenkins, professor of history and religious studies at Pennsylvania State University, did however discuss this matter in his book, *The Next Christendom: The Coming of Global Christianity* acknowledging that for over a century, the decline of religion has become a common Western thought. Other scholars like, Mark Hutchinson, chairman of the church history department at Southern Cross College in Australia, noted that "what many pundits thought was the death of the church in the 1960s through secularization was really its relocation and rebirth into the rest of the world."[2]

Ed Vitagliano highlights the 10/40 Window in his article: "The rebirth of Christianity" to show what he calls the "amazing progress of the gospel elsewhere." The growth of the church in the 10/40 Window is well documented. Between 1990 and 2005, the general population grew at only 1.5 percent annually, while the population of Christ followers grew at an amazing 5.4 percent per year![3] The annual growth rate of Christ followers inside the 10/40 Window was almost twice that of those outside the Window. Christ followers in the 10/40 Window

---

1. John McClosky, December 13, 2011, quoting Philip Jenkins whom he calls "perhaps the foremost historian of religious trends today." No pages. Online: http://www.holyspiritinteractive.net/columns/johnmccloskey/perspectives/14.asp.

2. Vitagliano, Ed, ed. *AFA Journal News.* No pages. Online: http://www.orthodoxytoday.org/articles4/VitaglianoChristianity.php.

3. Bryan Nicholson, Global Mapping International Memo of July 16, 2008 (Colorado Springs, CO, 2009) using Patrick Johnstone's data prepared for two upcoming publications, *The Future of World Evangelization* and *Operation World.*

nations increased from 2.5 percent of the population in 1990 to 4.7 percent in 2005.[4]

This is the new face of Christianity in 2012. Elijah Kim represents that face of emerging Christianity today. What is different to scholars from the West is that Elijah brings the vibrancy, fervency, and revival spirit with his own study as a respected scholar who has deliberated for extended periods in Europe and the United States. Elijah is a recognized scholar who has earned his right not only by earning a PhD, but also due to his studies in respected institutions and from esteemed scholars from the West. For this reason I believe the book will have a global impact on Christianity and academia.

Elijah also represents the spiritual vitality and revival fire of the Majority World. The conviction that he was to write this book came from a very personal call he received from God. Elijah relates how he received a mandate from God seven years ago to describe the present situation of Western Christianity and the rise of Majority World Christianity. He concluded that the problem of European Christianity is not systematic or religious but they have lost vitality in the church. The life of the church comes from the outpouring of the Holy Spirit. For me, that is revival and awakening. This decline and rise has shown me the contrast of the presence or absence of the Holy Spirit among God's people.

He arrives at his conclusions unlike most other scholars dealing with this topic who come from the West. "The vitality has always been interrelated with the revival fire. In my opinion North America is in the middle. It has the elements of the decline found in Europe but America is still contributing to the growth of global Christianity through Diaspora connection, multicultural elements, American globalization, and mission endeavors. The Majority World Christianity has manifested the primitive elements of the revival fire as we have seen in the early church models." Despite the dramatic demographic shifts in the number of Christians from the Minority World to the Majority World as brought out by Elijah Kim there are two realities to keep in mind. The first reality check relates to the fact that the major reason for the shift is the rapid population growth in the Majority World in comparison to the Minority World. The second relates to the use of the term Christian. The terms Christian and Christianity used

4. Ibid.

in the *Atlas of Global Christianity* referenced throughout this book is defined as "Followers of Jesus Christ of all kinds: all traditions and confessions, and all degrees of commitment." They include cultural Christians as well. The vast majority of Latin Americans would identify themselves as Christians by religion. For example take the country of Argentina. More than 89 percent or 36.3 million Argentineans identify themselves as Christians while 9 percent or 3.7 million are considered evangelicals according to the latest edition of Operation World.[5] Elijah chooses to use the term Majority World which defines the community in terms of what it is, rather than what it lacks which represents a more accurate, up to date, and descriptive picture than the terms developing countries, Third World, and the South. The term Majority World highlights the fact that these countries are indeed the majority of humankind.

One of the questions being asked by those from the West is whether missionaries from the East will repeat the same mistakes they made. For example one mission pastor who expressed this to me personally in a conversation wrote: "The Apostle Paul describes gospel partnership as 'striving side by side for the faith of the gospel'" (Phil 1:27). Missionaries sent from all points of the globe find themselves working near each other in cities and communities around the world. Sometimes, those diverse missionaries humbly work together, learning from one another and leveraging the individual and cultural strengths of each person. Too often those missionaries work in cultural isolation from one another. Westerners tend to perceive some Majority World missionaries as unwilling to listen to the painful lessons they have learned about paternalism, cultural pride, and the damage done to missionary families who sacrificed time with their children for the sake of the work. There is the perception that in their zeal and confidence, some Majority world missionaries are repeating the mistakes Western missionaries made in the 1950s. Being from the East does not make missionaries immune to missiological missteps. Often Majority World missionaries bring intense dedication, boldness, prayerfulness, and personal sacrifice to the missions community. These are qualities Western missionaries need. Western missionaries bring experience, balance, innovation, and diverse resources to the missions community. These are qualities Majority World missionaries

---

5. Mandryk, *Operation World*, 100.

need. Our challenge is to improve our ability to humbly collaborate side by side for the Gospel."[6]

What this book communicates is how important it is for those from the Minority World and those from the Majority World to learn from one another. The non-Western world needs to learn a lesson from the West in history, and the West should learn from the fervency of the Majority World. Elijah Kim has written a prophetic word to God's people for this season as Elijah the prophet spoke to his generation.

Luis Bush PhD,
International Facilitator of Transform World Connections
and
Servant Catalyst, 4/14 Window Movement

---

6. From an email from a missions pastor from a church in North America sent to the author of the foreword, dated 12th December 2011.

Preface

IT WAS THE MOST joyful time of my missionary journey walking in between the trash piles of the desolate slum village of the Philippines where no one bothered to stop by and foul odors and bugs of all sorts moved in and out between my toes. I had no idea of what was happening in the world, and there was no electricity or running water. It was there I held my wife's hand for prayer and preaching the gospel became the greatest joy. It was a time when the internet was developing rapidly but we did not have a computer, but the joy we had by giving our lives to Jesus for missions was indeed a time of true, deep joy. Without knowing any worldly news, we spent the days reading the Word, prayed freely, and deeply mediated on the Scriptures. During such deep times of prayer the Lord spoke clearly:

I will send you to Europe and show you many things.

- European Christianity is declining and decaying.

- Study the decline of Christianity in the West.

- Islam is rapidly rising as a force to oppose Christianity.

- You must research Islam.

- And the Majority World is experiencing a global Christian revival.

- You must research and study revival.

For me, hearing the voice of the Lord almost felt like a dream.

How could I study Islam here in the slums of the Philippines?

How could I, who cannot even earn a piece of bread for the day, go to Europe, a place I have only seen in movies?

Though I have traveled often the 40 Asian nations, I have not been to Latin America even once.

How would I study the Christian revival of the Southern Hemisphere?

Every time I prayed during the next 10 years, He kept guiding and speaking to me to study Christianity and Islam. As the Lord had spoken, European Christianity was in serious demise and decline when I visited England to see for myself. England was no different from the other European nations. I began to visit and research the churches that held weekend long revivals weekly and churches that made historical impacts throughout Europe. I counted 187 churches that I visited and researched, and by God's grace was able to meet many leaders there. Professor Hugh McLeod's lectures on the secularization of Europe greatly assisted me in understanding the decline and also British history as well. Lectures on Islam through professor Dr. David Thomas along with renowned Islamic scholars opened my eyes to realities of Islam in the world. The program, which was called the Interreligious Dialogue at Crowder Hall of the Church Missionary Society and the United College of the Ascension, provided me the worldviews that Europeans held in a religiously pluralistic society. Religious pluralism was a topic I only read about, but through occasional lectures and seminars at the University of Birmingham I was able to listen to lectures by Dr. John Hick on this topic firsthand. I felt holy anger greatly rise up within me while hearing what pluralism was doing to people. I could not agree even for a moment with the many roads promising salvation since Jesus alone is the only way to salvation to the Father.

I was able to study and research even more deeply concerning religious pluralism that rampantly displayed itself throughout all the spheres of society in Europe. Not only was I able to research the factors of secularization, but Pentecostal revival movements, postcolonialism, postmodernism, and inculturation were all studied in depth. As I read and researched on European church history, I began to see the often resurfacing disparity between Christendom and Christianity. I have written in depth about this in the book. As a student who experienced firsthand the revivals in Korea, the Philippines, and Asia, researching global Christianity in England was not just a time of study or research, but a precious and grace filled time of eye opening blessing. It was also a time of meeting God's precious people as well. Meeting global Christian leaders from Latin America, Africa, and Asia also allowed me to see and appreciate a bigger picture of global Christianity. I began to have a wider perception and a renewed lens on European awakenings and revivals as I learned more about European Christianity and revival history for two years at Birmingham Christian College. And seemingly without end, symposiums were held almost weekly by inviting global Christian leaders at United College of the Ascension, Crowder Hall, and the University of Birmingham. I felt the grace and favor of God through these precious meetings. After finishing my PhD program in England, I was led by the Lord to America.

After speaking with Professor Harvey Cox at Harvard Divinity School, I attended the various symposiums and seminars there and other educational institutions and researched on American Christianity. From there, I was able to fix my eyes not on the European continent but research from America's Christian scholarly perspective and materials especially from Andover Library and Yenching Library, which provided me great assistance during the journey. A year later, I was able to meet Dr. Douglas Hall of Boston's historical Emmanuel Gospel Center. This turned out to be an absolute blessing from God as I was able to get a hold of the most vital information and valuable material for my research. As I met international leaders in Boston and various church leaders including African American, Hispanic, Pan-Asian, and American, I was able to see the seriousness of secularization in the churches and felt a greater desire to see revival come again. By working together with Mission America Coalition's City Impact Roundtable's design team as a member, which works in every major city in America, establishing the Global Urban Ministerial Network, and by uniting the various networks and missional societies in America, Europe, and Latin America, a more clear and bigger picture of global Christian movement began to emerge.

I was then able to preach and teach on where the present day global church was heading, and what we must do in this present hour for the evangelization of the world as God opened doors in the Middle East, East Asia, Southeast Asia, Latin America, Europe, Africa, and North America and other nations. The two main reoccurring themes were "Revival" and "The Holy Spirit." All the major papers I wrote while traveling back and forth from Boston's several university libraries and seminars were in a dust pile due to the demands of busy ministry, but the calling and burden of global revival has led me once again to pick up my pen. As I read my previous edition of this book, I felt it would be better to rewrite it and as a result, new materials have come out. I have edited the book to make it more accessible.

In order to accomplish this task, David Moon spent several months with me meticulously going over the original draft. He sacrificed much in order to read every page together and to revise and edit literally every sentence. So first of all, I want to deeply thank David Moon the most. I also want to thank Mrs. Hyeyoung Park for recreating all the graphs and charts. I really want to thank Steve Kang for sacrificing so much for reading the drafts and helping me to edit this work. I also want to thank Deborah Beatty Mel for upgrading my work professionally through typesetting and final editorial work. I want to deeply thank her for all her sacrifice. It has always been a joy to me to communicate with Dr. Luis Bush as we often shared together about visions and strategies for global Christianity. I am so grateful to Dr. Bush for his worldwide vision for the evangelization. I am grateful to Dr. Todd Jonson for his generosity in allowing me to quote material from the "Atlas of Global Christianity."

Many people also prayed and gave in order to make this one book possible, in particular with my warmest gratitude to Mr. Frank Hahn and his family. As former director of the Vitality Project at the Emmanuel Gospel Center for several years, I would like to share my joy with the great staff there. My personal gratitude goes to colleagues Doug and Judy Hall and Jeff Bass, Emmanuel Gospel Center, Dr. Sang Bok Kim, Chairman of World Evangelical Alliance and Torch Trinity Graduate University, Dr. Wonsuk Ma, Executive Director of Oxford Center for Mission Studies, Bishop Thompson, Jubilee Christian Church, Dr. Roberto Miranda, Lion of Judah Congregation, Rev. Chris Mineau of Massachusetts Family Institute, Rev. Seungwook Kim, Hallelujah Community Church, Dr. Corrie de Boer, Asian Theological Seminary and Elijah International World Mission Institute, City Impact Roundtable colleagues such as Tom White, Phil Miglioratti, Jarvis Ward and Glenn Barth, Viju Abraham of Global Urban Ministry Network, Dr. Jonathan Bonk of Overseas Ministries Study Center and Yale Divinity School, Gregg Detwiler, Intercultural Ministries, Bishop Efraim Tendero of the Philippine Council of Evangelical Churches, leaders at the Manila International Mission Institute and Manila International Mission Conference including Dr. Anne Dyer, Dr. Andrew Kirk, Dr. Raju Abraham, Dr. Alex Philip, Dr. Robert Tuttle, Dr. Sadiri Joy Tira, Dr. Benjamin L. Moses, Dr. Shinjung Cha, Rev. Mark Anderson, Call2All, Dr. Tae-Yon Kim, Rev. John Rankin, Rev.

Daniel Ryu, the faithful staff at the Elijah Global Mission School especially my spiritual son Cristor Bernil, Vitality Project team members Bobby Bose, Brian Corcoran, Brandt Gillespie, Colleen Sherman, Linda Clark, and Dale Atlas, 'Prayer For Boston' ministers, David Hill and Tom Griffith, New England prayer leader, Jeff Marks, Professor Steve O'Malley of Asbury Theological Seminary and other professors, sincere intercessors, John Robb, International Prayer Council, prayer leaders in Canada, Mexico, Britain, India, and Europe and Asia, and numerous leaders from around the world who are not listed here. I want to thank you all for participating in this work.

I want to share the joy of finishing this book with my precious daughter Shalom, who stayed up with me to endure the disturbance of working deep into the late hours in order to finalize the drafts. I also want to share this accomplishment with my angelic spiritual partner and supporter, the most precious prize of my life, my wife, Rev. Amy Kim, and my adopted son Samuel who is like a stream of fresh water who gives me joy and makes me smile every time I face difficulty. I sincerely hope that he reads my confessions of love to him when he gets older. I want to deeply thank my parents, family, and brothers at A Grain of Wheat Church in the Philippines.

I have used more than 30,000 sheets of paper in the numerous drafts. My fingers have swollen from typing and starring at the computer screen for eighteen hours a day have hurt my eyes and body. However, to see the global church rising and waiting on God to send his revival was my motivation and as a result I have written these words with my sincerest prayers. I give all the glory to God alone who works day and night in order to revive His Church to bring one more soul into His Kingdom. To God be the Glory!

In the grace of Christ
Elijah Kim, PhD

Introduction

Recapturing the Twentieth Century Christianity

As WE ENTER THE twenty-first century, humanity is facing new challenges. The center of Christianity has moved from the West to non-Western regions. Shifts in theology, church, race, and culture are occurring, and the influence of Western theology is decreasing while non-Western theological themes and explorations are becoming dominant including contextualization, indigenization, and acculturation. The notion of what constitutes a mission field is also changing. Gone is the unidirectional model of Western nations sending missionaries to non-Western nations; churches of every nation, people, tribe, and language now act as missionaries, and the mission field of the church has become every corner of the earth (Rev 7:9–10).

The center of gravity of the Christian faith has shifted from the West to the non-West where the majority of the world's Christians now live. However, these geographic, racial, and quantitative changes do not necessarily mean that qualitative changes have occurred. The developing world, which is called the majority world, remains largely unchristian and unreached. Churches in non-Western regions still follow Western forms of worship, theology, and mission practices. Still, Christianity in developing nations is challenging the notion that Christianity is Western. Churches in majority world nations can emphasize different aspects of the gospel and focus on particular doctrines resulting in multiple forms of Christianity.

The greatest need for the global church is to unite and follow the Great Commission without being limited to one's native country or church denomination. Thus, we can see the need for church unity and for revival movements. Revival is an energizing force that leads to missions and evangelism. If the world's Christians still view Christianity as a Western religion, it is because they are still unable to discern the religious shifts happening all around. These shifts cannot always be seen through simple statistics and numerical measurements due to the complexity of global systems. Every nation has its religious, political, and historical landscape that impacts how Christianity can thrive there. An analysis of common factors within Christianity worldwide yields the following observations:

CHRISTIANITY'S CENTER MOVES TO THE NON-WEST

At the end of the twentieth century a remarkable growth of the church in Latin America, sub-Saharan Africa, China, India, Indonesia, the Philippines, and South Korea, among others can be seen. Christian growth has occurred in both developing and non-Western nations. While nation-state forms of Christianity (such as Lutheran, Anglican, and Dutch Reformed) have weakened in the West, African indigenous churches, South American grassroots churches, China's underground churches, house churches in India, and Indonesian independent churches are growing rapidly. Revivals prior to the twentieth century were led by whites, but twenty-first century revivals are being led by non-white, non-Western Christians. Even the churches that are growing in the West are often immigrant-led.

DEMANDS UPON CHRISTIAN LEADERSHIP
IN THE MAJORITY WORLD

Though there has been a decline of the Western church's influence, leadership from around the world in seminaries, denominations, and theological institutions is still predominantly Western. The World Council of Churches, World Evangelical Alliance, Lausanne Movement, and worldwide missionary organizations are still dominated by Westerners. Though Western Jesus Christ is in a quantitative fall, this does not reflect a qualitative decline in their leadership.

With both qualitative and quantitative growth, Christianity can impact a nation's political, social, and cultural foundations. This was the case in the West where Christianity has influenced national norms, social ethics, philosophy, ideology, politics, and the economy. Its decline will be felt in these spheres as well. It is highly ironic that European nations whose Christian influence has declined at home still lead global missionary and denominational organizations. On the other hand, the norms, ethics, and overall inculturation in the Global South have not been effectively penetrated by the various qualitative forms of Christianity from the West.

THE WESTERN CHURCH'S DECLINE AND ITS AFTERMATH

Decline began gradually during the Enlightenment when rationalism took center stage as the Western worldview. This began to influence theology, calling into question long-held beliefs such as the occurrence of miracles, the virgin birth of Jesus, the inerrancy of the Bible, salvation uniquely through Christianity, and Jesus Christ's resurrection and ascension. Unitarianism laid the foundation for liberal theology, which disavowed the traditional belief that salvation is available through Jesus Christ alone. At the same time, the Industrial Revolution and urbanization caused many people to leave their rural, farm-centered lifestyles and the parochial system that had ministered to them. New urban-ministry models struggled to meet the needs of the many migrants moving there. As the predominant worldview became highly individualistic, churches became a matter of individual choice. The separation of church and state also deprived the church of government support. Experiential faith began to be seen as irrational, especially to those influenced by Unitarian Universalism, which put a damper on the presence and expressions of the Holy Spirit.

HISTORICAL ANALYSIS OF THE RELATIONSHIP BETWEEN REVIVALS AND DECLINES

Two major historical trends working at cross purposes in the Western church are revival and secularization. Revival movements stoked spiritual awakening periodically since the time of the Reformation, including Puritanism and Pietism, the Great Awakenings, revival prayer movements, and the Holiness and Pentecostal movements. Many insights can be gleaned by comparing and contrasting Western revivals that enlarged evangelicalism with the non-Western church growth phenomenon if we can examine the theological, historical, and interdisciplinary nature of the church/society relationship. An opposite trend began in Europe: a secularism based upon human reason. Revival reenergized the church in Europe, and the Great Awakening led to many new believers in the

United States. Pentecostalism in the early twentieth century further spurred church growth in the United States as well as in the majority world. While secularization did not lead to a precipitous decline of the American church as it had in Europe, the American church would be wise to recognize the threat it poses.

The history of the church in Europe is marked by revivals and declines, described by historian Robin Gill as the "cyclical theory" of institutional religion.[7] However, this pattern no longer holds true; there has been a steady decline since the mid-twentieth century. Other forces including Eastern mysticism, Islam, the New Age movements, and Buddhism are growing rapidly. Most of the European churches experiencing growth are composed of non-Western immigrants. A majority of scholars agree that secularism is the primary cause of the decline of the church. Since the Enlightenment, human reason has taken the place of Christian belief as the touchstone for European society. This trend has negatively affected religious behaviors, values, worldviews, social norms, morals, ethics, institutional norms, and moral consciousness. As secular criticism and liberal thinking have increased in science and academia, belief in the supernatural was condemned, including beliefs in the virgin birth, the resurrection of Jesus after his death on the cross, and the afterlife. Even after secularization took hold in Europe after the Reformation, there was a brief revival. As secularization advanced over time, revivals and awakenings occurred to overcome some of the negative effects. The Pietism was one such revival that occurred at a time when denominational and religious wars had caused many to become cynical. Pietism emphasized reading the Word, praying in the Holy Spirit, and cultivating an individual relationship to Christ. These factors were also critical in non-Western revivals in Latin America, sub-Saharan Africa, China, India, and Indonesia, among others. Revivals outside the West also involve indigenization, contextualization, and inculturation.

Awakenings and revivals in the United States and Europe during the twentieth century inspired many missionaries who laid the foundation for revival worldwide. Revival led to increased efforts in literacy and medical services and the establishment of hospitals, nursing homes, and educational institutions. During the Great Awakening in the United States, numerous new Evangelical universities gradu-

---

7. Robin Gill, *Beyond Decline*, 67.

ated committed Christians whose influence was felt throughout society. More people volunteered for overseas missions, a sphere in which the United States played a major role. Likewise, the New York prayer revival that began before the Civil War brought great healing to the nation after the war ended. In Britain, many blessings with great social impact came as a result of revival movements: the abolition of slavery, child labor restrictions, recognition of women's rights, and the fight against the exploitation of workers were advanced by devout and godly Christians known as the Clapham Sect, led by William Wilberforce. Often, the same people leading revivals and awakenings were those responsible for advocating social transformation, such as Wilberforce, John Wesley, Jonathan Edwards, and Count Nicolaus Zinzendorf.

Following World War II, creeds, catechism, confessions, and faith itself were called into question as society moved away from authority and tradition, sexual freedom became commonplace, and liberal criticism of theology intensified. Church attendance began to decline in 1960s in a trend that has not been reversed. At the same time, however, in areas abandoned by most Western missionaries particularly by Europeans—sub-Saharan Africa, India, China, Indonesia, and Latin America—a revival of historic proportions was beginning. It is not an exaggeration to call the 1960s the decade of "invisible religious revolution." From that time, many Westerners began to prefer living life, building families, and forming societies and cultures apart from religion, especially Christianity. They began to rely on standards of morality alone, without religious moorings. Biblical standards of good and evil, Christian marriage, and Christian social values and norms were no longer the standard; human reason was now seen as the preferred source of morality and happiness. Such a development suggests that the seeds of de-Christianization had been planted well before the time when they began to flower in the 1960s.

ANOTHER CENTER OF THE WESTERN CHRISTIANITY: THE UNITED STATES

Traditionally, Europe was divided among the Roman Catholic, Eastern Orthodox, and Protestant churches. Making up the Protestant church were the Lutheran church of Scandinavia and Germany; the Presbyterian Church in Geneva, Switzerland, and the Netherlands; Scotland's Presbyterian Church; and the Anglican Church of England.

Most of these denominations became national churches. However, other Protestant groups were ostracized or persecuted, including Baptists, Puritans, Quakers, and Anabaptists. These groups emigrated to the United States seeking religious freedom and autonomy. Separated from Europe's cultural and political influences by the vast Atlantic Ocean, America provided an opportunity for these forms of Christianity to grow, and American Christianity grew to become a powerful Christian force.

The American Church successfully balanced revival and secularization, achieving a mixed worldview. American revival movements allowed their leaders, such as Jonathan Edwards, James McGready, Charles Finney, and D.L. Moody, to display global leadership and to leave a permanent mark in history. The opening of the Western frontier further fueled church growth. This national expansion motivated by the Manifest Destiny, inspired many American Christians to carry the momentum to mission fields overseas. Still, materialism, commercialism, rationalism, and the American ideology of individualism combined to create a form of secularization distinct from that of Europe. Then, Los Angeles's Azusa revival in 1906 provided the spark that ignited revivals throughout the world. Not only did the European denominations experience growth during this time, but also denominations in America such as the Baptists, certain Methodists, Christian and Missionary Alliance (C&MA), and Assemblies of God (AG) grew to become the world's largest Protestant denominations. Pentecostal churches had a worldwide impact unlike any other denomination, demonstrating the global impact of the American church.

THE LEADERSHIP OF THE AMERICAN CHURCH
IN THE TWENTIETH CENTURY

The patterns of Christian revival and decline in Europe and the United States are quite distinct. In contrast to Europe, where the church maintained a close relationship with the state for centuries, the United States produced a new religious culture that includes a variety of denominations, worldviews, and value systems. The American church has traditionally emphasized harmony and moderation, unlike in Europe, where the national church propagated its own particular doctrine. American Christianity has allowed opposing views to coexist by giving people choices to dwell in regions where particular views were emphasized. Arminianism and Calvinism also found their own regions of acceptance, and both beliefs grew as people chose to embrace one or the other. Americans chose to be tolerant of one another due to their shared value of freedom of choice.

A comparison of Christianity in Europe and in the United States will yield insights into the vitality of the faith. Revivals in America influenced the nation's social norms, values, education, policies, and culture. Unlike the European cycle of the rise and decline, revival in the United States had a consistently upward trend. American revival builds upon the Puritan awakening movement, the Great Awakenings, the New York prayer revival, the Holiness revival movements, and the Pentecostal movement. In particular, the missions focus of the second Great Awakening in the early 1800s, the 1857 New York prayer revival, the Moody Student Volunteer Movement and the Classical Pentecostal movement at the dawn of twentieth century has changed the world's religious landscape.

The Great Awakening and religious revival movements greatly influenced society and the state to adapt Christian norms, ethics, and worldview in education, family, government, and social life. Conversely, the Enlightenment and intellectual liberalism helped to speed up the process of secularization, modernization and industrialization. The impact of secularization in Europe was enhanced when revival movements dwindled and was no longer influencing social and individual activities of spiritual life. The caesaropapist church and state relationship in Europe mutually benefited from issues such as taxation, social protection, political agenda, and public education yet complicated issues gradually developed deteriorating the relationship. Paradoxically, those who led the separation of church and state in Europe in the eighteenth and nineteenth centuries declared that secularism would replace religion believing that societal norms, ethics, and values can exist without Christianity. This idea will be further explained in the following chapters. On the other hand, we will also see that the American church generated diverse denominations out of the separation of church and state.

THE DEFINITIVE PERIOD OF CHRISTIAN DECLINE IN EUROPE: THE 1960S

Scholars today are studying Great Britain as a case of Christian decline. After the Reformation, England displayed the compatibility of Catholicism and Protestantism. As the birthplace of evangelicalism, the cradle of missions, the seedbed of American Christianity, and the leader in overseas missions, Britain was the world's foremost Christian nation. However, the church began to collapse starting in the 1960s—an example of a phenomenon occurring throughout Europe. Church attendance in Europe today is far below many developing nations, and it has become a target of Islamic missions. Great Britain provides a microcosm to study present religious conditions throughout Europe. Although declining, Christianity until the 1950s was the most influential factor in England's society, but this position was lost in the 1960s.

One critical factor in this decline was that many British people ceased to trust Christian values and focused instead on trust in oneself. *Most* mainstream churches failed to remain relevant to people's lives as revolutionary changes upended social norms and values. At the same time, immigrants from former colonies—non-Christian nations—pulled public attitudes in a different direction. Traditional churches lost their far-reaching influence on people and eventually collapsed; secularism became the norm in European society.

The church's quantitative downhill fall was conclusive and rapid, affecting morality, social norms, and belief in the supernatural, especially resurrection and the afterlife. These changes reflected the individualistic attitude of Westerners and also a qualitative decline that had been happening quietly within the church prior to the 1960s.

Prior to the 1960s, there were at least hints of balance among worldviews, reflected in expressions such as "the sacred and the secular," "church and state," and "the world and Christianity." During this time, holiness was maintained in the churches. However, beginning in the 1960s, secular ideas and practices infiltrated the church. Churchgoers became attracted to secular influences, no longer seeing these values as tainted or evil, but acknowledging them as the norm. Churches even went so far as to accept Eastern religions and new religious movements, which became alternative religions for those whose hearts had already left the mainstream churches. More and more people sought spiritual fulfillment outside of the mainstream church.

After the two World Wars, many former British colonies achieved independence, spurring an influx of immigrants to Europe. Furthermore, in order to replace the many who had died on the battlefield, Europe supplemented its workforce with immigrants from the Caribbean, Africa, India, and Pakistan—a heterogeneous group that included Muslims and Pentecostals alike. Likewise, France, the Netherlands, and Spain experienced an influx. In Germany, most of the immigrant workforce consisted of Muslims from Turkey and other Islamic countries. However, over time, the minority population grew in number and influence. Islam in particular began to eclipse Christianity as the main religious power. Two forces, Islam and secularism, were working at cross purposes in Europe. Islam began to rise, impacting national economies, politics, and the education system, uprooting several hundred years of Christian heritage. Islam is now beginning to substitute pluralism, such that no European nation can create policies or welfare programs with Christian values or traditions.

THE UNITED STATES IN THE 1960s

The history of the United States includes upward and downward fluctuations with regard to the church. Awakenings and growth are followed by declines due to war, followed in turn by growth in the aftermath of conflict as awakenings again flourished. If the overall picture of the church in Europe is a downward slope, the United States displays upward curve. When the Puritans first arrived in America, church attendance was merely 10 percent, which later reached 36 percent in the 1900s, then 49 percent in the 1940s, and up to 60 percent in the 1960s. The Christian population grew from one-third of the entire United States population in 1900 to three-fifths in 1950. Nonetheless, America also experienced rapid Christian decline in the 1960s. Not only did European and American churches experience a wide decrease in Christianity, but this was also the first time when such a continuous decrease occurred. American churches experienced their maximum increase just prior to the 1960s, the culmination of a period of dynamic and productive growth that spanned from 1800s to the 1960s. Making this growth possible were five key factors: religious revival during the time of westward expansion, the holiness revival movement, immigration, the rise of religious organizations and groups, and religious freedom. However, the American church experienced a decline in the 1960s similar to that of Europe. The continuous growth of the previous 150 years was for the first time starting to wane. Not all Christian denominations declined during this time; liberal churches were in decline, but fundamentalist, Bible-centered, and Pentecostal/Charismatic churches all grew during this period.

Serious declines were seen in the Methodist, Lutheran, Congregational, Anglican, and Presbyterian churches, primarily because members no longer felt fulfilled during worship services and due to the compromise of the church to secular culture. Secularism, liberal theology, humanism, religious pluralism, and materialism contributed to the decline.

PHENOMENAL GROWTH OF CHRISTIANITY IN THE MAJORITY WORLD

The fall of Western Christianity and the revival of the faith in the majority world in the global south began after the end of colonialism and World War II. If the 1960s marks the start of continuous European and American Christian decline, many non-Western regions experienced pivotal events that led to growth, including China's Cultural Revolution, Christian revival in Islamic Indonesia, and the arrival of liberation theology in Latin America, making Bible reading permitted. Sub-Saharan Africa experienced a remarkable growth with native churches led by indigenous leaders. Church growth in the global south made up for almost all the losses in the West. Main contributors to this growth are Pentecostal denominations born at the beginning of the twentieth century and the Charismatic movement of the 1960s. Significantly, most churches that experienced rapid growth accepted such movements as coming from God. We can conclude that the main cause of church growth is due to this new movement of God: the Pentecostalism.

THE OPPOSING FORCES OF SECULARISM AND REVIVAL

Christianity initially developed within the Hellenic worldview, and the institutionalization of Christian power occurred within Western cultural structure. Thus, the Christian faith became disconnected from its Jewish roots. Constantine established a new paradigm to endure for more than a thousand years, the caesaropapist system resulted in the idea of Christendom not as Christianity but as a system which maintained a close collaboration between the state and church, at times in harmony and at others in tension, competition, or rivalry. The norm of Christendom justified mass killings through the inquisition or crusades, and unbearable persecutions against dissident groups such as Waldenses, Hussites, Huguenots, and Lollards, and many more occurred. The Reformation brought about necessary theological changes, but did not go far enough. British Episcopal and German Lutheran liturgy and church structure drew heavily on the traditions of Roman Catholicism which can be considered a "Re-form" from the formation of the medieval Catholic Church system, particularly the Constantinian Christendom model. Post-Reformation Renewal movements made deeper changes, including individual piety, the systematization of faith emphasized by the Methodist Church, the religious autonomy emphasized by Baptist churches, the baptism of the Spirit characteristic of the Holiness movement, and the manifestation of the Holy Spirit in the Pentecostal church. After the Reformation, it was impossible for any one denomination to represent the whole of Christianity.

Today, the Christian world can be divided into three categories. First is the liberal church, which underwent a great deal of secularization and subsequent decline. Many liberal churches deny the uniqueness of redemption through Jesus Christ as in Unitarian Universalism, deny miracles, doubt the reliability of the Bible, and created ecumenical movements that emphasize liberalism. Second, the evangelical church emphasizes the Bible, faith in Jesus Christ, and forgiveness through God's grace. Third, Pentecostal churches focus on the anointing and manifestations of the Holy Spirit. Throughout history, churches led by the Holy Spirit have seen conversions, salvation, and overflowing assurance.

THE RESTORATION OF ISRAEL AND JEWISH MISSIONS

The Jews of the diaspora after the destruction of Jerusalem in AD 70 became deeply disconnected from the Western church. Thus, the Gentile church has missed out on the abundance of blessings and promises given to Israel and a deep understanding the full scope of the saving grace accomplished by the Messiah. The Gentile church became institutionalized as the Roman Catholic Church and continued to live under these influences, which imbued much of its theology, liturgy, and doctrine. However, the reestablishment of Israel in 1948 inaugurated a new work in the history of God's harvest. Prophecies from the Old and New Testaments once considered insignificant have gained new importance in the church as renewed focus has been placed on uniting Jews and Gentiles as one in the body of Christ to see the salvation of all (Matt 24:1–2; Luke 21:24; Isa 66:7–8; Jer 32:37–41; Ezek 37:10–14; Dan 9:26; Amos 9:14–15; Mic 3:11–12).

SHARED RESPONSIBILITY FOR EVANGELISM

The seed of gospel planted by the early church is not confined to the Western world, but has spread globally. While massive revival is taking place in the non-Western church, the forces of Islam, Buddhism, and Hinduism are also strong. The church of the majority world, with its non-Western forms, now shares the responsibility to evangelize the rest of the world. To solve the common problems of humankind, the church will need to unite as it moves forward. Local churches will need to become healthy in their own regions and then come together as the body of Jesus Christ to advance the kingdom of God.

ISLAM AND CHRISTIANITY

The birth of Islam in AD 622 brought Christianity in North Africa and the Middle East to a standstill and then to destruction. The Crusades, mounted under the pretense of recovering the Holy Land, left a heritage of destruction and gave Christian the faith a bad name that has endured for generations among Muslims. Bearing this burden of historical injustice, the non-Western church now faces the challenge of missions to Muslims.

Islam has undergone the most impressive growth of all world religions. In contrast to the slower growth of Buddhism and Hinduism, Islam has grown more than 500 percent during the twentieth century and is now the world's second largest religion. Islam is the majority religion in North Africa, the Middle East, Central and Southeast Asia, Indonesia, and Malaysia. Due to immigration, Islam is growing rapidly in Europe and North America, just as a decline of Christianity is underway. Furthermore, Westerners living in traditionally Christian regions are converting to Islam.

RELIGIOUS PLURALISM

Liberal theologians such as religious pluralists often object to Christianity claiming it is exclusive. In contrast, liberalism urges reconciliation among Judaism, Islam, and Christianity, all of which worship the same God, and it advocates for harmony among Hinduism, Buddhism, and even shamanism, animism, and other religions because they all deal with the spiritual realm. Evangelicals have maintained a distance from proponents of religious pluralism, who focus on a so-called "god," by refusing to compromise on the uniqueness of the power of the gospel and the salvation through Jesus Christ.

Secularization is one of the main reasons for the decline of the Western church, and contributing to secularization is religious pluralism. In the eighteenth century in Europe, pluralism referred to a plurality of denominations within the Christian church. However, when non-Christian faiths began to influence the Western worldview, the notion of religious pluralism expanded. What began as a homogenous Christian pluralism now made room for the New Age Movement, Islam, Buddhism, and Hinduism, among others. As the church declined, these faiths, which came along with new immigrants, emerged as alternatives to Christianity. Among the theologians advocating for pluralism is John Hick, who shifted from a Christ-centered faith to a belief that there is more than one way to salvation. This represented a major change in the Western world. Now, rather than accepting that any one faith was superior, it became more common to compare religions because Westerners dismissed Christianity's unique ability to offer salvation.

Pluralism proposes historical relativism and views the most important challenge to be dialogue with faiths outside of Christianity, along with human liberation and social progressivism. It advocates that 'all classical religions are relative,' and that all religions need to deepen their understanding of each other through 'dialogue which brought about transcendental religious essence.' Pluralism sets forth the premise that all religions stand on an equal footing.

HUMANISM

A shift to a human-centered worldview is a major factor in Western Christianity's downfall. Revival movements throughout history have been characterized by experiential renewal during times of social and moral decline and indifference to faith. Such revivals occurred during the periods of the Enlightenment, rationalism, humanism, science, liberalism, existentialism, and postmodernism. There is a fundamental correlation between secular humanism and spiritual renewal movements, including the Reformation, Pietism, the first and second Great Awakenings, New York prayer revival movement, Holiness movement, Pentecostalism, and the charismatic movement. The revival movements, in turn, are countered by another wave of humanism, usually in a different form.

In the twentieth century, the dual forces of secularism and experience-centered revival became globalized from their Western origins. Secular, intellectual elements took center stage in the fields of education, culture, arts, government, the press, entertainment, and economics. Even educational institutions that had started through revival movements became disconnected from faith, and Christianity lost its dominance in government, the economy, and culture, becoming one religion among many. Emphasizing a Christian viewpoint was now seen as narrow-mindedness and intolerance. The Western world, having removed Christianity from a central position, gravitated toward Islam, New Age beliefs, Oriental mysticism, the occult, and hedonism.

CHANGE OF WORLDVIEW

The divine dignity and meaning given to humanity can only be realized when we acknowledge we are God's creation, made in God's image and likeness (Gen 1:26). Freedom and human rights are among the gracious blessings of Jesus Christ. Outside of Christ's salvation, these goals are human-centered rather than God-centered. While economic activity and abundant land can meet basic human needs, they cannot bring about heaven's blessings. All those living on earth who have moved away from their identity as bearers of God's image are drawn toward a human-centered worldview that focuses on the lower priorities of comfort and convenience.

1

Twenty-First Century Christianity

PENTECOSTALISM IS THE DOMINANT force in global Christianity today. By looking at the characteristics and trends of this movement of the Spirit, we can see how far it has come since its inception in the early twentieth century and the directions in which it is moving. In particular, we will look at the expansion of Global Christianity in the majority world. The Global South now has more Christians than the Global North and will play a significant role in shaping the future of the faith.

Worldwide, the growth of Christianity continued after World War II as majority nations were liberated from colonial powers. A great shift was underway: Christianity was decreasing in the West, but increasing in the Global South: Africa, Latin America, and Asia. The Pentecostal revivals of the early and mid-twentieth century mushroomed to a global scale, bringing hundreds of millions of souls to salvation in Jesus Christ. Today, those nations that follow the United States in numbers of missionaries sent out are not from the West, but include South Korea, India, Brazil, the Philippines, Indonesia, China, Nigeria, and Argentina.

In the 1960s, European and American churches encountered opposition from secularists, humanists, atheists, and others antagonistic to the gospel: free-sex and same-sex advocates, consumerism capitalists, theological and philosophical liberals, and religious pluralists. The Western churches could not mount an effective defense against these assaults and shrank, entering an era of post-Christianization. While the Western church lost power in the domains of politics, social authority, and education, these are not the greatest losses. Greater is the loss of the power and outpouring of the Holy Spirit.

1

The first church in Jerusalem was born from the outpouring of the Holy Spirit at Pentecost. The church flourished through the Spirit's power, which made possible divine healings and other miraculous signs. Not only in Jerusalem, but in other parts of the Roman Empire as well, manifestations of the Holy Spirit were seen as churches grew in the Middle East, Asia Minor, North Africa, and Mediterranean Europe. However, these spiritual experiences declined in the third and fourth centuries after since Emperor Constantine recognized Christianity and the church became institutionalized. The former vitality of the Spirit within Christian services and the spiritual lives of individuals gave way to a structured, institutional religious system rather than a living extension of the Holy Spirit.

For centuries, the church was governed by a hierarchical system, dogmatic discipline, clerical orders, and ritualized worship. Church and political structures became intertwined, and the church became a cultural commonality among European nations, where a monopoly of church and state was the norm. Rationalism by way of the Enlightenment led to the separation of secular and sacred, culminating in an erosion of shared Christian mores, ethics, morality, values, and worldviews. European churches began shrinking. American churches, while vital at first, began to show a downturn in the middle of the 1960s. Now, with the rise of Christianity in the Global South, the obvious question is: What's going on, and what's next?

GLOBAL CHANGES

As of 2010, the majority of Christians worldwide can no longer be found in the West, but in non-Western regions such as Africa, Latin America, and Asia. The greatest number of Christians reside in Asia, yet Asian Christians are not the majority in their own nations. Andrew Walls states:

> Once more the pattern of Christian advance appears as serial rather than progressive, withering at the centre, blossoming at the edges. The great event in the religious history of the twentieth century was the transformation of the demographic and cultural composition of Christianity brought about by the simultaneous processes of advance and recession. It means that the representative Christians, the Christian mainstream, now belong to Africa and Asia and Latin America, with intellectual and theological consequences still to be comprehended.[1]

1. Walls, "Christianity across Twenty Centuries," 48.

Christianity has transitioned on an axis from Jerusalem, to Europe, and to North America and is now turning in multiple directions to Latin America, Africa, and some countries in Asia today.

The Decline of the Global North

In medieval Western Europe, the Catholic Church sustained a homogenous religious predominance, while Eastern Europe was dominated by the Eastern Orthodox Church. These churches were not known for spiritual experiences, except for a few cases in monasteries and occasional ascetic movements. The Reformation was successful at reforming the systems and doctrines of Catholicism, but failed to restore the spiritual empowerment common in the early church. Smaller groups from Reformed traditions tried to rediscover the spiritual vitality of the first-century church, such as the Quakers, Moravians, Pietists, and Methodists. Free Reformed, Lutheran, Presbyterian, Anglican, and Congregational (early Puritan) churches did not have the same empowerment of the Holy Spirit as on the day of Pentecost. From institutionalization, the church found revitalization through the revivals and awakenings. Sometimes, there were schisms within the revival and awakening movements themselves, such as the Old Lights and New Lights among Congregationalists in the First Great Awakening, the New School and Old School and New Measure and Old Measure among Calvinist Presbyterians and the Reformed church in the second awakening, and the formation of new denominations such as the Quakers, Disciples of Christ, Methodists, Holiness churches, Church of God in Christ, Assemblies of God, and many more.

For many years, it was believed that "as the West goes, so goes Christianity." However, the opposite is true today. The West has been on a path of de-Christianization and loss of church influence in the social, communal, political, academic, and cultural spheres. At the same time, the majority world has been flourishing with phenomenal Christian growth. If people view Christianity from the European historical perspective, it is seen as inevitably declining. Many people perceive that the gospel spread from Jerusalem to the Mediterranean, Europe, North America, and then to Asia. But in fact, the gospel spread from Jerusalem in multiple directions: eastward to central Asia and China, southward to Ethiopia and North Africa, northward to Eastern Europe, and westward to Western Europe. Growth of non-Western Christianity has been happening throughout more than a thousand years of history, but the greatest growth has come in the latter half of twentieth century.

The Rise of the Global South

The twentieth-century decline of Christianity in the Global North is well recognized by Westerners, but the rise of Christianity in the Global South, particularly in majority nations, is not. Dynamic, vital Christian churches are found in many majority world nations while churches in Western nations struggle to survive with a dwindling number of members. The geography of Christianity has been changing dramatically, yet Western European Christian leaders, with a Eurocentric mentality, may not realize that the fastest-growing denominations come from non-European areas: sub-Saharan Africa, Latin America, and some countries in Asia. Churches in the West still maintain a prestigious position in global church leadership, theological institutions, church hierarchy, and allocation of resources. However, the inner spiritual life of Western churches has been diluted by liberal theology, religious pluralism, humanism, and secularism. In contrast, African Christianity has vital worship and Pentecostal manifestations, and Latin American Christianity has become Pentecostal in worship style, doctrine, and church systems. Still, the Western church clings to traditional worship, doctrines, and church systems. Why is Western Christianity so reluctant to change? Do we recognize properly the global state of Christianity? What about Christian traditions that have been marginalized globally over the centuries: Eastern Orthodox, Egyptian Coptic, Syrian Orthodox, Ethiopian Orthodox Tewahedo Church, and the Assyrian Church of the East?

In 1900, according to Dana Robert, 70.6 percent of the Christian population lived in the West. At the end of twentieth century, two-thirds of the Christian population is now in the developing world, with only 28 percent of the world's Christians found in Europe. The percentage of Christians living in North America did not change too greatly, but, notably, the number of Christians in Latin America and Africa now make up 43 percent of global Christian population.[2] More strikingly, according to *Atlas of Global Christianity*, in 1910, 80.9 percent of Christians lived in the Western hemisphere. This number was 10 percent higher than in 1900. In 2010, Western Christians make up 37.9 percent of the total. While Christianity in the Global South has

2. Robert, "The Great Commission: In an Age of Globalization," 13.

experienced tremendous growth, a significant decline has taken place in the Global North, including Europe and North America, in the last hundred years.[3]

GRAPH 1.1 CHRISTIANS BY CONTINENT, 1910 AND 2010

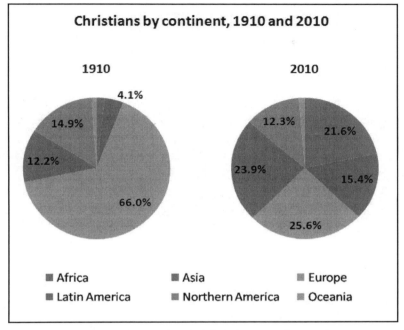

Source: Atlas of Global Christianity[4]

The Rise of Renewalists

At the beginning of the twentieth century, there were few Pentecostal churches with only a handful of members. Through the small beginnings of Classical Pentecostalism and then the Second Charismatic and Third Wave Renewal movements, Pentecostalism disseminated all over the globe.[5] Today, there are more than 600 million Pentecostal and Charismatic Christians—second only to Catholics. It is not an exaggeration when the twentieth century is called the Pentecostal

---

3. Johnson and Ross, *Atlas of Global Christianity*, 8.

4. Ibid., 8.

5. Pentecostal and Charismatic Churches are commonly referred to as PCC.

Century.[6] Churches from the Reformed tradition, including Lutheran, Anglican, Free Reformed, and Presbyterian, are now in the minority among Protestant denominations. Non-Reformed churches, including Methodist, Baptist, and Assemblies of God, represent the largest Christian denominations in the world. Johnson and Ross give the term *renewalists* to those who espouse classical Pentecostalism, the Charismatic movement, and the neo-charismatic movement: mostly independent and indigenous churches.[7]

For the last 100 years, Renewalists had one of the fastest growth rates among Christians: 15 to 17 percent. The number of Pentecostals and Charismatics was 614 million in 2010. In 1910, 91.5 percent of Pentecostals lived in Africa through the influence of the Azusa revival. By 2010, the largest number of renewalists can be found in Asia: 29.3 percent. Africa has 26.5 percent, followed by Latin America with 25.4 percent. North American renewalists make up only 12.9 percent.[8]

GRAPH 1.2 FASTEST RENEWLIST GROWTH

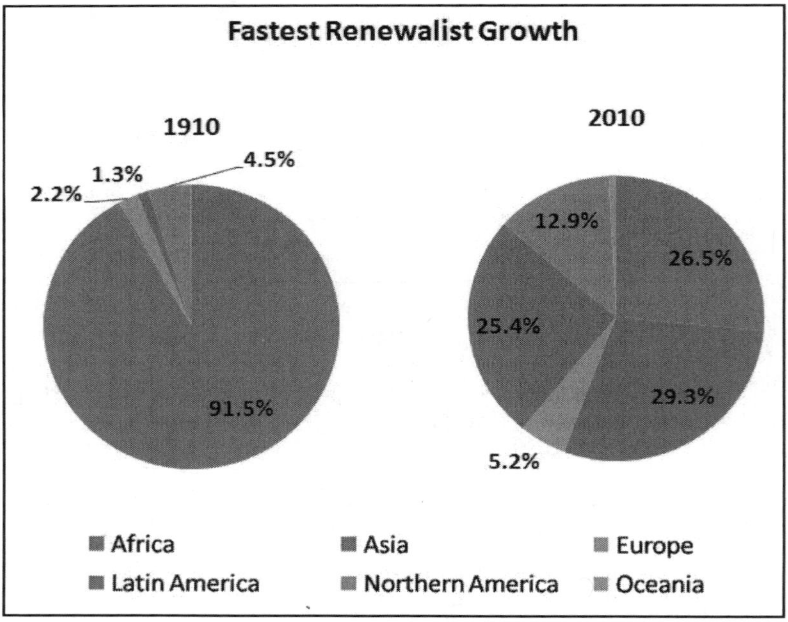

Source: Atlas of Global Christianity[9]

6. Sun, "Assemblies of God Theological Education in Asia Pacific," 227.
7. Johnson and Ross, *Atlas of Global Christianity*, 102.
8. Ibid., 102.
9. Ibid., 102

Looking at the number of renewalists by region, there are 179 million in Asia, 162 million in Latin America, 162 million in Africa, 79 million in North America, and only 31 million in Europe as of 2010.

TABLE 1.1 RENEWALISTS BY UNITED NATIONS REGION

	1910			2010			
	Population	Renewalists	%	Population	Renewalists	%	■ 1910 ■ 2010
Africa	124,228,000	1,101,000	0.9	1,032,012,000	162,664,000	15.8	
Eastern Africa	33,030,000	0	0.0	332,107,000	48,087,000	14.5	
Middle Africa	19,443,000	0	0.0	129,583,000	30,067,000	23.2	
Northern Africa	32,002,000	0	0.0	206,295,000	1,600,000	0.8	
Sothern Africa	6,819,000	989,000	14.5	56,592,000	24,177,000	42.7	
Western Africa	32,933,000	112,000	0.3	307,436,000	58,733,000	19.1	
Asia	1,028,265,000	5,800	0.0	4,166,308,000	179,624,000	4.3	
Eastern Asia	556,096,000	3,700	0.0	1,562,575,000	104,289,000	6.7	
South-central Asia	345,121,000	2,000	0.0	1,777,378,000	32,852,000	1.8	
South-eastern Asia	94,104,000	100	0.0	594,216,000	41,676,000	7	
Western Asia	32,944,000	0	0.0	232,139,000	807,000	0.3	
Europe	427,154,000	26,300	0.0	730,478,000	31,649,000	4.3	
Eastern Europe	178,184,000	600	0.0	290,755,000	10,044,000	3.5	
Northern Europe	61,474,000	2,200	0.0	98,352,000	9,133,000	9.3	
Sothern Europe	76,940,000	0	0.0	152,913,000	6,661,000	4.4	
Western Europe	110,556,000	23,500	0.0	188,457,000	5,810,000	3.1	
Latin America	78,269,000	15,300	0.0	593,696,000	156,117,000	26.3	
Caribbean	8,172,000	12,900	0.2	42,300,000	6,209,000	14.7	
Central America	20,777,000	700	0.0	153,657,000	24,228,000	15.8	
South America	49,320,000	1,700	0.0	397,739,000	125,680,000	31.6	
Northern America	94,689,000	54,400	0.1	348,575,000	79,067,000	22.7	
Oceania	7,192,000	500	0.0	35,491,000	4,889,000	13.8	
Australia/New Zealand	5,375,000	500	0.0	25,647,000	2,950,000	11.5	
Melanesia	1,596,000	0	0.0	8,589,000	1,758,000	20.5	
Micronesia	89,400	0	0.0	575,000	93,600	16.3	
Polynesia	131,000	0	0.0	680,000	87,000	12.8	
Global total	1,759,797,000	1,203,000	0.1	6,906,560,000	614,010,000	8.9	0% 25% 50%

©Edinburgh University Press, 2009

Source: Atlas of Global Christianity[10]

No previous movement has had the global impact of the Pentecostal/Charismatic movement in the twentieth century. In 2001 in Asia, 313 million people were Christians, among them 135 million Pentecostals/Charismatics, out of a total population of 3.7 billion. Of those, 5 percent are Pentecostals, 16 percent Charismatics, and 79 percent neo-Charismatics. Neo-Charismatics include 6.8 million Filipinos and 49.7 million Chinese independent/indigenous groups, apart from Christians belonging to the officially sanctioned Three-Self Patriotic Church in China. Neo-Charismatics number 16.6 million in India, 6.8 million in Indonesia, and 3.3 million in South Korea.[11] While the number of classical Pentecostals in Asia is great, they are the smallest of the three Pentecostal/Charismatic groupings.

10. Ibid., 103.

11. Barrett et al., *World Christian Encyclopedia*, 13.

The growth of evangelicals in Latin America in the twentieth century has been remarkable. In 1900, they were only 700,000, or 1 percent of the population, but by 2000, the number had risen to 55 million. In Latin America, Pentecostals are the fastest growing evangelical group with more than 32 million affiliates constituting 28 percent of the world's Pentecostals.[12] Latin American Pentecostalism has grown through local revivals that connected with historic Protestant churches or missionary agencies from overseas. More importantly, Pentecostals and Charismatics are in the same phase where Asian and African counterparts have experienced growth.[13]

In 1988, there were 11,000 variations among Pentecostal denominations and 3,000 independent Charismatic denominations in the world. These denominations far outnumber the 150 non-Pentecostal ecclesiastical confessions and include 8,000 ethno-linguistic cultures, which span 95 percent of the world's population. Included are Charismatic churches and fellowships as well as some charismatic Roman Catholics.[14] That same year, there were 332 million Pentecostals, 123 million Charismatics, and 28 million neo-Charismatics totaling 483 million. They include "pre-Pentecostals, quasi-Pentecostals, indigenous Pentecostals, isolated radio Pentecostals, post-Pentecostals, post-Charismatics, crypto-Charismatics, radio/TV Charismatics, independent Charismatics. Of these nine categories only the last two have been recognized up to now as genuine Pentecostal/Charismatics. But all of them are recognized as part of the Renewal."[15] The Global North has become the minority with whites representing 29 percent of the global Christian population. Globally one in three are Christian Renewalists, 66 percent from the developing world.[16] Jay Gary reports that there are 520 million Pentecostals and Charismatics.[17] Patrick Johnstone has found that there are 33,000 Pentecostal/Charismatic and independent renewal movements around the world. Whichever figures are used, it is clear that Pentecostals/Charismatics number

12. Johnstone and Mandryk, *Operation World*, 29–38.

13. Matviuk, "Pentecostal Leadership," 163.

14. Barrett, "The Twentieth-Century Pentecostal/Charismatic Renewal," 119.

15. Ibid., 119.

16. Ibid., 119.

17. Gary reports that Pentecostals/Charismatics comprise the second largest expression of Christianity, second only to Roman Catholicism. Gary, "Ten Global Trends in Religion."

more than half a billion.[18] The following shows that in 2010, the total number of Pentecostals/Charismatics was found to be 614 million, or 8.9 percent of the global population.[19]

At first, the Pentecostal revival movement did not have influence at the nationwide level and were struggling to convince denominations to accommodate Pentecostal characteristics. But later, when the second worldwide wave of neo-Pentecostalism broke out, there were many ripple effects on Catholic, Anglican, and Protestant denominations from the United States, Europe, Latin America, Africa, and Asia.

The Origins of Renewal

At the end of the nineteenth century, there was great expectation for world evangelization through vigorous missionary endeavors. However, few were expecting a new and different manifestation of the Holy Spirit. A.B. Simpson and the Holiness tradition focused on healing as one aspect of the Fourfold Gospel.[20] Still, experiences of miraculous healing were uncommon. As the twentieth century dawned, the beginnings of a great outpouring of the Holy Spirit were seen in humble places in several nations. This Pentecostal revival was similar to previous revivals and awakenings in several ways, but different as well.

The evangelical revivals came primarily from the Holiness movement, which emphasized the Holy Spirit, confession and repentance of sins, and sanctification of individual life. This tradition traced back to Methodist founders John Wesley and John Fletcher, who described three stages of one's faith journey: unconverted, converted, and entirely sanctified.[21] Later in the twentieth century, churches and leaders were divided in their theology of the second blessing. In the Holiness tradition, the second blessing is a process of entire sanctification, leading to perfection, that must be followed after conversion if a person is baptized with the Holy Ghost.[22] One step is not enough when a person has a conversion experience; a person is saved from sin through sever-

18. Johnstone and Mandryk, *Operation World*, 755. Barrett and Johnson, "Annual Statistical Table on Global Mission," 25.

19. Johnson and Ross, *Atlas of Global Christianity*, 103.

20. A.B. Simpson, founder of the Christian and Missionary Alliance denomination, summarized Jesus' roles as Savior, Sanctifier, Healer, and coming King.

21. Anderson, *An Introduction to Pentecostalism*, 25.

22. Spickard et al., *A Global History of Christianity*, 401.

al steps. Spickard states, "They did not think they would ever achieve perfection on this earth, but they were certain that God wanted them to try and that he would empower them to make progress."[23] They desired the baptism of the Holy Spirit to be increasingly sanctified.

The ways in which the Holy Spirit is manifested sets the Pentecostal revival apart from others: speaking in tongues, prophesying, and an urgent response to the missionary call. The Welsh revival in 1904 and 1905 provided ample proof of Holy Spirit baptism. Those who attended revivals were "singing in the Spirit (using ancient Welsh chants), simultaneous and loud prayer, revelatory visions and prophecy, all emphasizing the immediacy of God in the services and in personal experience."[24] The teachings of Evan Roberts on the baptism of the Holy Spirit paved the way for greater revivals not only in Wales, but worldwide.

The first distinctive Pentecostal manifestation is speaking in tongues, which was experienced by the early church, but only sporadically in subsequent centuries. Then, in Topeka, Kansas, in 1901, Charles Parham encouraged students from his Bethel Bible School to attempt to experience the Holy Spirit Baptism.[25] Agnes Ozman experienced speaking in tongues on January 1, 1901.[26] Parham later relocated to Houston, Texas, to do school ministry; there, William Seymour experienced the same Holy Spirit baptism. This innovative form of Christianity went on to become the greatest Christian renewal movement of the twentieth century.[27] The Pentecostal fire that William Seymour brought to Los Angeles shortly thereafter was no longer a local experience, but a national and international expansion of Christianity. Cox states:

> The fire from heaven descended on April 9, 1906, . . . at 214 North Bonnie Brae Avenue in Los Angeles. . . . But despite ridicule and opposition, the conflagration continued to expand as the sparks blew from ghetto to slum to rural hamlet, to St. Louis and New York, and then across the oceans to Europe and

23. Ibid., 396.

24. Anderson, *An Introduction to Pentecostalism*, 36.

25. Robertson, "The Roots of Azusa," lines 6–22.

26. Nichol, *The Pentecostals*, 3.

27. Protestant missions now comprises of a large percentage of Pentecostals exploding in various formats, especially in Africa, Latin America and Asia. Davies and Conway, *World Christianity*, 75–77.

Asia, Africa and South America. As the world approached the cusp of a new millennium, the fire was still spreading.[28]

People accepted the baptism in the Holy Spirit convinced that the prophecy of Joel cited by Peter in Acts 2 was fulfilled by the "latter rain" poured out to them in order to preach the gospel to the utmost parts of the world. Joseph Smale, a Baptist pastor, witnessed the Azusa revival. Another connection was made by Frank Bartleman who corresponded with Evan Roberts about the Pentecostal revival in Los Angeles.[29] People from Holiness traditions and from other denominations, from all racial and ethnic groups, flocked to the Apostolic Faith Mission on Azusa Street in Los Angeles. Most were poor and excluded from elite social circles. Ordinary people had become strong missionary advocates because they were empowered by the Holy Spirit. Healings, prophecies, and speaking in tongues were manifested day after day.[30] Those who experienced new kinds of Pentecostal revivals including Spirit baptism spread the phenomenon throughout major cities in the United States and around the world. At the turn of the twentieth century, according to Dayton, a vast network of Holiness groups, institutions and movements constituted "a sort of pre-Pentecostal tinderbox awaiting the spark that would set it off."[31] Pentecostal revivals provided enough adherents to shape a Pentecostal denomination, the Assemblies of God, in Hot Springs, Arkansas, in 1914,[32] and other Pentecostal denominations across the United States from 1906 to 1932.[33]

In the early twentieth century, the Pentecostal fire spread to Europe, South Africa, Australia, Chile and Brazil in Latin America, India, Korea, China, and many more nations. In England, the same fire of the Holy Spirit fell on the All Saint Church in Sunderland, where Jeffery Brothers delivered Pentecostal revival messages. Eventually, Pentecostal denominations formed, including Elim Church in 1915, Apostolic in 1918, and Assemblies of God in the United Kingdom in 1924.[34]

28. Cox, *Fire from Heaven*, 45–47.

29. Anderson, *An Introduction to Pentecostalism*, 36.

30. Spickard et al., *A Global History of Christianity*, 401.

31. Dayton, *Theological Roots of Pentecostalism*, 174.

32. A doctrinal issue threatened the existence of the newly formed Assemblies of God. Durasoff, *Bright Wind of the Spirit*, 79–80.

33. Chappell, "Healing Movements," 368.

34. Tidball, *Who Are the Evangelicals?*, 49.

CHRISTIANITY IN THE GLOBAL NORTH

Religion impacts both the social and personal spheres of life. Religion that is intertwined with the national government is vulnerable to the environment of holistic elements of society which religion stands for. The role of Christianity in the Western world is determined by how people perceive religion. Is it a belief system confined to personal matters? Yet, for more than a century, Christianity in the West has influenced social, political, cultural, economic, educational, and academic areas.

Europe

The process of secularization in Europe has been the subject of extensive study. Science has become a quasi-religion. Others deny the inevitability of secularization, citing religious practices and beliefs flourishing in different forms. As Michael Hill says, "In any discussion of the secularization controversy it is important to specify that the conclusion of the argument depends to a considerable extent on its basic premises: how we define secularization—and, perhaps even more fundamentally, how we define religion—largely determines whether or not such a process can be identified."[35]

In studying the decline of religion in Europe, it does not matter that the Christian church is on the decline or another religion is on the rise, but that we measure and quantify these trends. If we look at the church as an institutional entity, the decline in the number of church members and Sunday attendance can be called secularization. However, if "we define religion as some quantum of 'religiousness' within every individual, secularization would become impossible by definition and could only be used to refer to the changing content given to this universal feature of human psychology."[36]

Many of the scholars who have studied de-Christianization have overlooked the wave of Pentecostal and Charismatic renewal. Charismatic renewal does not nullify rationalism, but it has introduced a free style of worship that offers an alternative to formal, ritualized, liturgical worship that many have found devoid of meaning.[37] While state churches and established denominations in Europe are losing

35. Hill, *A Sociology of Religion*, 228.
36. Ibid., 228.
37. Dobbelaere, *Secularization*, 125.

adherents, in some cases, smaller and independent churches are growing, although they involve only a small percentage of the populace.
Robin Gill states, "some sociologists have argued that it is small self-
contained sects, which have built up barriers against a predominantly
secular society, that will be the only religious institutions to survive in
Britain in the future. . . . If religion survives it will only do so as the
pursuit of a tiny minority of the population."[38]

North America

North American influences have touched the entire globe, including
Pentecostal revivals, Charismatic movements, overseas missionary
endeavors, and natural ethno-linguistic connections between immigrants and their nations of origin. Stanley Burgess says, "Since the
beginning of this century, Christianity has witnessed the emergence of
two great renewal movements of the Spirit: the Pentecostal movement,
beginning in 1901, and the charismatic movement that developed several decades later. . . . The impact of these movements has changed
the face of Christianity around the world and ushered in a new era of
Christian spirituality."[39]

Before the twentieth century, North America experienced a zenith of religious revival. In the twentieth century, the region became
a source of powerful missions efforts that led to great revivals in sub-
Saharan Africa and Latin America.[40] Some of the most outstanding
leaders from Holiness, Trinitarian, and oneness Pentecostalism were
Charles H. Mason and Aimee Semple McPherson. Charismatic leaders included Episcopalian Dennis Bennett, faith healer Oral Roberts,
and Roman Catholic Leon-Joseph Cardinal Suenens. Contemporary
leaders include David Wilkerson, Ray H. Hughes, and many more.[41]

In spite of these positive aspects, the overall decline of Christianity
in North America is still a fact. Secularization, liberalism, humanism, materialism, atheism, and religious pluralism have substantially
weakened Christian churches and institutions.[42] The Christian faith
in some cases has been replaced by eastern religions and New Age

38. Gill, *Beyond Decline*, 66.
39. Burgess and McGee, *Dictionary*, 1.
40. Robinson and Smith, *Invading Secular Space*, 18.
41. Burgess and McGee, *Dictionary*, 1.
42. Guder et al., *Missional Church*, 1.

beliefs, and other cultic movements. Many Americans see religion as a marketplace of sorts, where one chooses what one likes. Practices such as transcendental meditation, yoga, sports, and sexuality have been put forth as replacements for faith.[43]

Today, religious events in North America impact the world because of the connections maintained by immigrant communities with their nations of origin. Cultural and ethno-linguistic groups in North America became a channel to their connections outside of North America. In the beginning of twentieth century, revivals in Wales, Northeast India, Southwest India, South Africa, Australia, China, and South Korea influenced the immediate vicinity and surrounding countries. In 1906, the revival at Azusa Street in Los Angeles drew awareness from all around the world because ethnic, cultural, and missional elements were at work. The Azusa revival spread to South Africa, Brazil, Chile, Northern Europe, and beyond. Henry May asks, "Was this really a revival of religion, or only a search for identity on the part of third generation immigrants or other-directed exurbanites?"[44] The influence of twentieth-century Pentecostal revival bears a closer look.

The Pentecostal revivals had a positive impact on church growth, but also had the negative effect of creating division. Schisms created several new denominations along racial, cultural, and ethnic lines. As the revivals dissipated, small differences among followers generated greater disputes about social, cultural, political, and doctrinal matters. Eventually, conflict arouse about racial leadership and institutional structure. Groups that joined the Azusa revival came from different streams of the late-nineteenth-century revival movements, including Wesleyan Holiness, Trinitarian, and Oneness. Leaders from different backgrounds brought different expectations for doctrine, church governance, and denominationalism. By the time of the World Wars, classical Pentecostals had formed denominations including the Assemblies of God, Church of God (Cleveland, Tennessee), and International Church of the Foursquare Gospel.

The picture we have of the American church in the postwar period is a mixed one. While European churches were dramatically declining, North America churches demonstrated both upward and downward trends. On one hand, the increase of religious adherents in the United States can be attributed to religious revivals like Azusa Street. On the

43. Marty, "Religion in America," 279.

44. May, "The Recovery of American Religious History," 75.

other hand, it can be argued that growth was not the result of the revivals because Christianity was already increasing at a steady rate. While revivals contributed to an upward trend after the wars, secularist trends were also at work in the realms of social norms, values, sexuality, religious beliefs, education, and worldviews. Glock and Stark conclude that "there has been a propensity neither towards greater religiousness nor towards greater secularization."[45] In the 1960s, according to Marty, "Fundamentalism was eclipsed by the secular theology, liberal civil rights and antiwar movements, the civil religion of the New Frontier, and Vatican II, but only momentarily, for it came back to new vogue-and with new force-during the late sixties.[46]

In the 1960s, the renewal now known as the Charismatic Movement began. During this time, some conservative churches became strong, yet liberal and mainline churches experienced decline. Marty explains, "In an apparently secular and certainly diffusive religious America, the 'strong' churches were paradoxically prospering, perhaps precisely because they were antimodern-absolutist, fanatic, conformist, highly committed to the group, rigidly disciplined, and zealous to proselytize."[47]

While spiritual renewal affected society, secular trends were also impacting social and spiritual life. In the 1970s, the Jesus movement and the hippie movement, with its characteristic sexual liberty, were both flourishing. The Catholic, Episcopal, and conservative mainline churches accepted Sprit Baptism, speaking in tongues, and other gifting. On the other hand, young people were experimenting with drugs, free sex, cults and the occult. As Marty puts it, "The Beautiful People were 'into' an alphabet of phenomena, from astrology to Zen."[48]

In the late twentieth century, megachurches began to arise while traditional, denominational churches were decreasing or remaining at a plateau. Ostwalt calls them megachurches, super churches, "full-service churches, seven-day-a-week churches, shopping-mall churches, and pastoral churches."[49] The megachurch trend has been strong in

---

45. Glock and Stark, *Religion and Society in Tension*, 68.
46. Marty, "Religion in America," 282.
47. Ibid., 282.
48. Ibid., 278.
49. Ostwalt, *Secular Steeples*, 57.

North America, but not in Europe. Ostwalt summarizes their influence, both negative and positive:

> At a time when mainline denominations are hurting and small churches are failing, some boast the megachurches are the fastest growing segment of the religious population in the United States. Others claim that the megachurch movement represents the future of the church in America and will lead to a major reform of American Christianity. At the same time, the movement is carving out a shaky foothold in Western Europe.[50]

Seeing only megachurches may give the impression that Christianity is flourishing. However, the church in North America is declining overall. Since the 1960s, virtually every church in North America has been influenced by the Pentecostal and charismatic movements. Mark Noll states, "Pentecostal worship has always been exuberant, spontaneous and subjective. Charismatic emphases include a stress on personal conversion, physical healing, speaking in tongues, participation in small group fellowships, and freshly written songs."[51] In the late twentieth century and early twenty-first, after unexpected spiritual experiences, the healing revival, and charismatic revivals, raised theological arguments and biblical hermeneutics from the theological doctrine of mainline denominations and the churches.[52]

Expectations for the future of the church in North America will vary depending on whether one focuses on the bright or dark side of the church.[53] The decline of Christianity does not mean the decline of religion, but a replacement of religious beliefs with other belief systems, such as the New Age and occult movements. Even the secularization thesis concedes that people in a secularized society can pursue religion as they so choose. Russello recognizes these new movements as "a retreat from the West's traditional heritage rather than an advance."[54] According to his analysis, "far from being a liberation of humanity from superstition, such movements cloak their adherents in a shroud of sentimentalism and pseudo-theology."[55]

50. Ibid., 57.
51. Noll, "Christianity in Northern America, 1910–2010," 191.
52. Hyatt, *2000 Years of Charismatic Christianity*, 168–193.
53. Jenkins, *The Next Christendom*, 8–9.
54. Russello, *Christianity and European Culture*, xviii.
55. Ibid., xviii.

CHRISTIANITY IN THE GLOBAL SOUTH

Crisis in Christian West became an opportunity for the non-Western world to become arising Christian power. According to Johnson and Chung, "By around 1950 Christianity's statistical centre of gravity crossed below 31.8° north latitude (Jerusalem) for the first time since the time of Christ."[56] In 1980, Christians in the Global South, including Latin America, Africa, Oceania, and Asia exceeded the number in the Global North for the first time in a thousand years. By 2100, Global South Christians are expected to number 2.8 billion, three times more than the Global North, which is expected to have 775 million Christians.[57]

GRAPH 1.3 PERCENTAGE OF ALL CHRISTIANS IN THE GLOBAL SOUTH FROM AD 33–2010

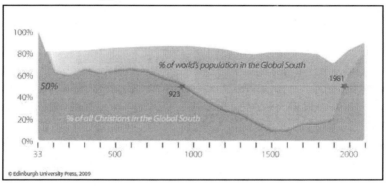

Source: Atlas of Global Christianity[58]

The Pentecostal and charismatic movements in North America have seen tremendous growth, but have remained in the minority. The situation is quite different in Latin America, Asia, and Africa, where Pentecostal and charismatic movements have grown even more significantly. Those who convert from non-Christian religions experience the baptism of the Holy Spirit. Through prayer meetings and Bible studies, believers experience healing and exorcism. Westmeier says that the transformation and spiritual outpourings happening in

---

56. Johnson and Chung, "Christianity's Centre of Gravity," 50.

57. Ibid., 50.

58. Ibid., 51.

Latin America can apply to others places around the world.[59] Church growth Korea, the Philippines, India, Chile, Guatemala, Brazil, and Argentina, among other nations, resulted from classical Pentecostal revival movements. Indian revivals in the Church Missionary Society and the Mar Thoma church in 1860, 1873, and 1895 predated the Azusa Street revival.[60]

Overall, the church in Europe and North America is on the decrease, in Africa, Latin America, and Asia it is rising, and in Oceania it is maintaining a plateau.

GRAPH 1.4 DISTRIBUTION OF CHRISTIANS BY CONTINENT, 1920–2010

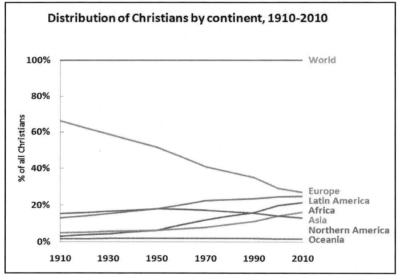

Source: Atlas of Global Christianity[61]

---

59. Westmeier states, "The basic thesis of this book is that changing social conditions brought about by migration, mechanization, and changes in individual lifestyles and family relationships have generated the need for a new religion. For many people, this new religion is the popular Evangelicalism they chose over traditional Roman Catholicism and Catholic piety." Westmeier, *Protestant Pentecostalism in Latin America*, 105.

60. George, "Pentecostal Beginnings in Travancore, South India," 215–221.

61. Johnson and Ross, *Atlas of Global Christianity*, 58.

Africa

Christianity is an integral part of Africa today. Hastings affirms, "Black Africa today is totally inconceivable apart from the presence of Christianity, a presence which a couple of generations ago could still be not unreasonably dismissed as fundamentally marginal and a mere subsidiary aspect of colonialism."[62] Christianity is growing extensively in Africa, particularly in sub-Saharan Africa. However, at the beginning of twentieth century, the Christian influence in Africa was minimal. In the north, the Muslim majority prevailed. In 1910, there were 11.7 million Christians in Africa while Muslims numbered 40 million. In 2010 Christianity increased 40-fold to more than 490 million while the number of Muslims grew tenfold to 418 million.[63]

The African church has its origins in the first century. The apostle Mark visited Egypt in AD 47, followed by Thomas later on. In the second century, the faith had spread to North Africa around Carthage, and by the fourth century had become dominant. However, most Christian churches dwindled or disappeared with the ascendance of Islam. Surviving churches include the Egyptian Coptic Church, the Ethiopian Orthodox Tewahedo Church, and the Church of the East. Christianity remained a minority religion in Africa until the Pentecostal and charismatic revivals.

In 1900, Muslims were the vast majority with four times as many adherents as Christianity: 34.5 million Muslims representing 32 percent of all Africans. At the end of the colonial era, in 1962, there were 60 million Christians and 145 million Muslims. Christians included 10 million Coptic and Ethiopian Orthodox, 23 million Protestants, and 27 million Catholics.[64] In 2000, the number of Christians grew dramatically to 380 million. The 2006 Pew Forum on Religion and Public Life study found that Pentecostals and Charismatics numbered 147 million.[65] Over a period of 110 years, from 1900 to 2010, Muslims increased 20-fold from 11 million to 234 million. The Christian population grew 70 times larger during the same period, from 7 million in 1900 to 490 million in 2010. Christians in sub-Saharan Africa make

---

62. Hastings, "Turning Points in Religious Studies," 208.

63. Johnson and Ross, *Atlas of Global Christianity*, 112.

64. Bonk, "Ecclesial Cartography and the Invisible Continent," No Pages.

65. Lugo and Cooperman, "Islam and Christianity in Sub-Saharan Africa," 1.

up 21 percent of the world's Christians. Muslims in Africa make up 15 percent of the world's Muslim.

Map 1.1 Ratio of Muslims to Christians

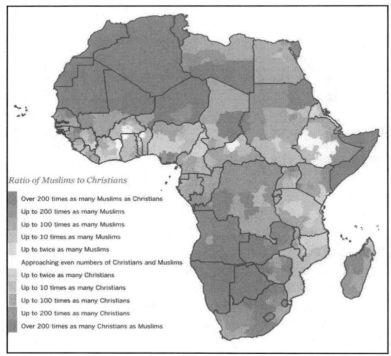

Source: Atlas of Global Christianity[66]

The most dynamic church growth in sub-Saharan Africa is due to the Pentecostal and Charismatic movements of the twentieth century. The churches founded during this time of revival were indigenous, independent, attuned to the supernatural, and diverse in geographic region, race, tribe, language, culture, and traditions. In 2001, there were 300 major ecclesiastical traditions with 33,820 denominations in 238 nations. Of all the denominations, independent denominations numbered 22,000 with 2 in 3 accounting for independent denominations.[67] Denominations and churches can be categorized into

66. Johnson and Ross, *Atlas of Global Christianity*, 113.

67. In the 2001 edition of the World Christian Encyclopedia, there were 22,000 Independent denominations, 9,000 Protestants, 1,600 Marginals, 781 Orthodox, 242 Roman Catholics, and 168 Anglican denominations. Barrett surveyed that Barrett,

five types: Episcopal, Presbyterian, congregational, charismatic, and Pentecostal.[68] The Episcopal category includes the Anglican, Catholic, and Orthodox churches. Lutheran, Reformed, and Methodist churches classified as the Presbyterian type. Autonomous churches belong to the congregational type, including Baptist and Congregational churches. If the focus of the church is on the leadership of the founder, Mugambi calls this a charismatic type church (a different focus than North America's Charismatic churches). Those churches that emphasize the work of the Holy Spirit are the Pentecostal type.[69]

Charismatic, Pentecostal, and some mainline churches in Africa practice Holy Spirit baptism and manifestations such as speaking in tongues, healing, miraculous signs, prophecy, resurrecting the dead, and deliverance. Pentecostals and Charismatics together accounted for 11 percent of Christians in Africa in 2000. This is much higher than in Asia and North America.

The fastest growing African churches are independent churches, called African-initiated churches or the African independent (indigenous) churches. The Roman Catholic, Orthodox, and Anglican churches are the largest in Africa in the twenty-first century, but most of the 100 largest denominations are independent churches that are Pentecostal and charismatic in nature.[70]

Kurian. Johnson, World Christian Encyclopedia, Volume 1, 16.

68. Mugambi, "Christianity in Africa," 112.

69. Ibid., 110.

70. Ibid., 112.

TABLE 1.2 MAJOR CHRISTIAN TRADITIONS
AND CHURCHES IN AFRICA

Major Christian traditions and churches in Africa

	1910	2010	Rate*		Denominations	
	Adherents	Adherents	1910-2010	2000-2010	Total	Average size
Anglicans (A)	443,000	50,866,000	4.86	2.68	41	1,241,000
Catholics (C)	2,153,000	169,495,000	4.46	2.85	60	345,000
Independents (I)	46,900	98,819,000	7.95	2.40	12,550	8,000
Marginals (M)	980	3,663,000	8.57	4.26	230	16,000
Orthodox (O)	5,431,000	48,286,000	2.21	2.27	90	510,000
Protestants (P)	2,177,000	137,207,000	4.23	2.87	1,930	71,000

*Rate - average annual growth rate, per cent per year, between dates specified
©Edinburgh University Press, 2009

*Rate = average annual growth rate, per cent per year, between dates specified.
Source: Atlas of Global Christianity[71]

Asia

In Asia, Christians are not in the majority, but their numbers have grown greatly. Still, this growth does not make Christianity a powerful political or religious force except in a few nations, including the Philippines, South Korea, Armenia, and Georgia, as well as some regions in India, China, Myanmar, and Indonesia. Noticeable Christian growth has occurred in Nepal and Cambodia since 1990. In the twentieth century, the number of Christians in Asia doubled, growing to make up 8.5 percent of Asians in 2010.[72]

71. Johnson and Ross, *Atlas of Global Christianity*, 112.
72. Ibid., 136.

MAP 1.2 CHRISTIANS IN ASIA BY PROVINCE, 2010

Source: Atlas of Global Christianity[73]

Pentecostal and charismatic churches in Asia have experienced phenomenal growth, which is attributed to the revivals and awakenings of the early twentieth century. Areas where significant growth has taken place—South Korea, Philippines, India, China, Indonesia, and Myanmar—all experienced revival in the early twentieth century. Among the revivals in Asia are the 1905 Mukti Mission of Pandita Sarasvati Ramabai in South India, the Khasi Hills in North India, and the 1907 Pyongyang Revival, which I call the Pentecost of Korea. These revivals all included repentance, conversion, Spirit baptisms, and life-changing experiences of rebirth, leading ultimately to the large Christian populations that we see today.[74]

There are a few Asian nations where the Christian population is the majority. The most Catholic country is the Philippines. In South Korea, 26 percent of the population is Protestant and 13 percent is Catholic. There are a significant number of Christians in Indonesia, the nation in Southeast Asia with the fastest Christian growth. Christians make up less than 10 percent of the population in China, India, Malaysia, Myanmar, Cambodia, Vietnam, Sri Lanka, Pakistan, and Mongolia. In general, there are small numbers of Christians in most Asian countries.

73. Ibid., 137.

74. Anderson, *An Introduction to Pentecostalism*, 36–38.

This does not mean that the growth rate was low, however. The World Christian Database, which includes Catholic, Orthodox, and Protestant churches, records only 22 million Christians in Asia in 1900.

MAP 1.3 CHRISTIANS IN ASIA BY COUNTRY, 1910

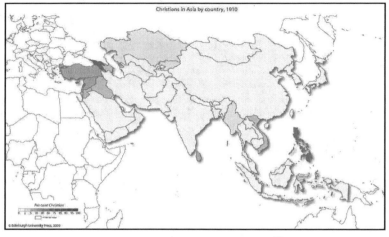

Source: Atlas of Global Christianity[75]

That number grew to 101 million in 1970, and to 351 million in 2005. In 2010, Christians accounted for 8.5 percent of the entire Asian population. Among Protestants, (including Anglican, indigenous, and independent churches), the number grew from 0.5 percent in 1900 to 6 percent in 2005. In 2010, there were 352 million Christians in Asia.[76]

TABLE 1.3 CHRISTIANS IN ASIA BY REGION, 1910 AND 2010

	1910			2010		
Christians in Asia by region, 1910 and 2010						
	Population	Christians	%	Population	Christians	%
Asia	1,028,265,000	25,123,000	2.4	4,166,308,000	352,239,000	8.5
Eastern Asia	556,096,000	2,288,000	0.4	1,562,575,000	140,012,000	9.0
South-central Asia	345,121,000	5,182,000	1.5	1,777,378,000	69,213,000	3.9
South-eastern Asia	94,104,000	10,124,000	10.8	594,216,000	129,700,000	21.8
Western Asia	32,944,000	7,529,000	22.9	232,139,000	13,315,000	5.7

©Edinburgh University Press, 2009

Source: *Atlas of Global Christianity*[77]

75. Johnson and Ross, *Atlas of Global Christianity*, 137.
76. Ibid., 136.
77. Ibid., 136.

Pentecostals and Charismatics represent a small percentage of the Asian population because the percentage of Christians overall is small. This contrasts with the significant percentage of Pentecostals and Charismatics (10 to 20 percent) in Latin America and Africa. Classical and neo-Pentecostal adherents made up 3.5 percent of Asians in 2005, or 138 million people.[78] Charismatics account for less than 1 percent of the population—25 million people. Pentecostals and Charismatics make up one third of Christian population in Asia. In 2010, Renewalists (classical Pentecostals, Charismatics, and neo-Charismatics) totaled 4.3 percent of the population, or 179 million.

TABLE 1.4 RENEWALISTS IN ASIA, 1910 AND 2010

	1910			2010		
	Population	Christians	%	Population	Christians	%
Asia	1,028,265,000	5,800	0.0	4,1666,308,000	179,624,000	4.3
Eastern Asia	556,096,000	3,700	0.0	1,562,575,000	104,289,000	6.7
South-central Asia	345,121,000	2,000	0.0	1,777,378,000	32,852,000	1.8
South-eastern Asia	94,104,000	100	0.0	594,216,000	41,676,000	7.0
Western Asia	32,944,000	0	0.0	232,139,000	807,000	0.3

Source: Atlas of Global Christianity[79]

78. Lugo, "Pentecostalism in Asia," 1.

79. Johnson and Ross, *Atlas of Global Christianity*, 102.

TABLE 1.5 CHRISTIANITY IN ASIA

	1900		1970		1990		2005	
	In millions	As % of total Population	In millions	As % of total Population	In millions	As % of total Population	In millions	As % of total Population
Catholics	11	1	51	2	91	3	124	3
Protestants, Anglicans and Independents	5	<1	44	2	155	5	240	6
Total Christians	22	2%	101	5%	249	8%	351	9%

Source: The PEW Forum on Religion and Public Life[80]

Latin America

Scholars have begun to study the rapid growth of the church in Latin America; David Stoll and David Martin have published books on this topic.[81] The Azusa revival in 1906 had a significant impact on evangelicalism in Brazil, Argentina, Chile, and other Latin American countries. Stoll and Martin found that this unprecedented church growth was the result of the Pentecostal and Charismatic revivals in the latter half of the twentieth century. Although Protestant churches began their missionary work early in the century, significant growth took place after 1950. Pentecostalism began to eclipse Catholicism as the primary expression of Christian faith in Latin America.[82] In 1910, evangelicals represented 1.1 percent of the population in Latin America and numbered 895,000. In 2010, evangelicals made up 8.1 percent of the population with 48,118,000 adherents.[83] The growth of Renewalists has been dramatic. Currently, Pentecostals and Charismatics account for 26.3 percent of the populace, three times more than evangelicals.

---

80. Lugo, "Pentecostalism in Asia," 1.
81. See Stoll, *Is Latin America Turning Protestant?* and Martin, *Tongues of Fire*.
82. Bidegain, "Christianity in Latin America," 174.
83. Johnson and Ross, *Atlas of Global Christianity*, 99.

In 1910, there were only 15,300 Renewalists, but this grew to 156 million by 2010.[84]

TABLE 1.6 RENEWALISTS IN LATIN AMERICA

1910			2010		
Population	Renewalists	%	Population	Renewalists	%
78,269,000	15,300	0.0	593,696,000	156,117,000	26.3

Source: *Atlas of Global Christianity*[85]

During the colonial era, events in Europe had implications for colonies abroad.[86] As Luther's Reformation threatened the Catholic Church in Europe, Spain and Portugal were the bastions of the Counter-Reformation. Any ideas viewed as heterodox by Roman Catholics were systematically eradicated in Europe and in Latin America. France and Britain revived colonial expansion efforts including both Catholic and Protestant missionaries. In 1493, Pope Alexander VI prevented conflict between Spain and Portugal by drawing a line down the map of the Atlantic, awarding discoveries to the west of the line to Spain and to the East to Portugal.[87] Within these colonial territories, Protestantism was seen as a heresy that threatened the ideological and political integrity of the colonies, which had been established with Catholic Christianity as a model.

The religion of Britain and France did not present an attractive option because it was seen as the religion of colonial imperialism.[88] Protestantism faced fanatical opposition to its efforts to establish missionary activities in Latin America during the Spanish colonial era, and this was also the case in many countries in Africa and Asia. Western Christianity encountered strong resistance until missionaries learned to better indigenize the Christian faith to allow for the expression of local cultures. Successful examples include the African Independent Church, Chinese house churches, and Charismatic-type churches in these regions.[89]

---

84. Ibid., 103.
85. Ibid., 103.
86. Read, *New Patterns of Church Growth in Brazil*, 11.
87. McManners, *The Oxford Illustrated History of Christianity*, 301–05.
88. Bastian, "Protestantism in Latin America," 314.
89. Read, *New Patterns of Church Growth in Brazil*, 11.

Church demographic figures have not changed greatly in Latin America over the past 100 years. In 1910, Christians accounted for 95.2 percent of the population; that figure had dropped slightly to 92.5 percent by 2010.[90] The largest Renewalist group in Latin America is Latin-rite Catholic, followed by the Brazilian/Portuguese Pentecostal group. These two groups total 149 million Renewalists.[91]

TABLE 1.7 LARGEST RENEWALIST TRADITIONS BY ADHERENTS, 2010

Largest Renewalist traditions by adherents, 2010

	Minor tradition	Adherents
1	Latin-rite Catholic	133,130,000
2	Baptist-Pentecostal or Keswick-Pentecostal	77,423,000
3	Chinese Charismatic	76,816,000
4	African Independent Pentecostal	23,548,000
5	African Independent Apostolic	18,737,000
6	Brazilian/Portuguese Pentecostal	16,636,000
7	White-led Charismatic	12,723,000
8	Chinese Neocharismatic	12,686,000
9	Holiness-Pentecostal: 3-crisis-experience	11,884,000
10	African Independent Neocharismatic	11,248,000

©Edinburgh University Press, 2009

Source: *Atlas of Global Christianity*[92]

Several denominations have huge churches in Brazil, Columbia, Guatemala, Chile, Argentina, Mexico, and more. For instance, the Brazilian Universal Church of the Reign of God (Igreja Universal do Reino de Deus) has more than three million followers. The Church of God Ministry of Jesus Christ International in Bogota, Colombia, has more than 500 congregations in several Latin American countries, the

90. Johnson and Ross, *Atlas of Global Christianity*, 176.
91. Ibid., 102.
92. Ibid., 102.

United States, Europe, and Japan.[93] One-fifth of the world's Pentecostals live in Brazil, making them proportionally the largest membership anywhere in the world. Stoll has made some impressive projections for the growth of Pentecostalism based upon the Protestant growth index between 1969 and 1985 in several Latin American countries and also accounting for "the typical fragmenting nature of Pentecostal churches."[94] Brazil alone has a Pentecostal community of at least 13,323,000.[95]

MAP 1.4 RENEWALISTS IN LATIN AMERICA 2010

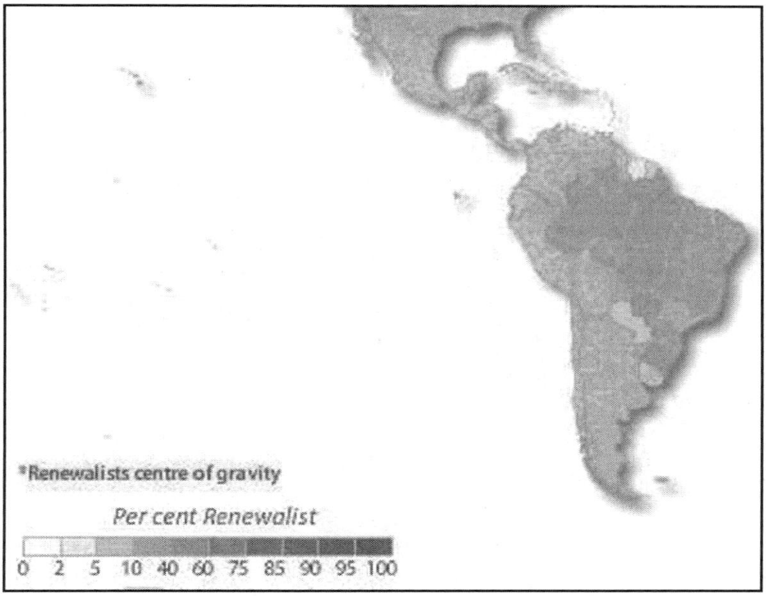

Source: Atlas of Global Christianity[96]

93. Martin, *Tongues of Fire*, 175.

94. Wagner states, "Pentecostals are either the largest church or the largest natural groupings of churches in Brazil, Argentina, Chile, Peru, Ecuador, Colombia, Panama, El Salvador, Honduras, and Mexico." Wagner, *Look Out! The Pentecostals Are Coming*, 26.

95. There were 13,523,000 Pentecostals and 39,524,000 Charismatics in Brazil in 2001. Johnstone and Mandryk, *Operation World*, 120.

96. Johnson and Ross, *Atlas of Global Christianity*, 102.

GLOBAL RENEWAL MOVEMENTS

Evangelicalism was propagated through revivals and awakenings until the late nineteenth century. In the twentieth century, while evangelicalism remains strong, it has been characterized increasingly by fragmentation. Rather than a few large denominations, there are alliances and clusters. Pentecostal and charismatic groups are counted among the worldwide community of evangelicals.

Classical Pentecostalism

The Pentecostal revivals of the twentieth century are indebted to the evangelical and Holiness revivals of the previous century. The terms *Pentecostal* and *charismatic* were not commonly used until the beginning of the twentieth century following the Azusa revival. The term *Pentecostal* invokes Acts 2 and is used to describe Christians willing to receive the baptism in the Holy Spirit. David Barrett describes Pentecostalism as:

> a Christian confession or ecclesiastical tradition holding the distinctive teaching that all Christians should seek a post-conversion religious experience called the baptism with the Holy Spirit, and that a Spirit-baptized believer may receive one or more of the supernatural gifts known in the early church: instantaneous sanctification, the ability to prophesy, practice divine healing, speak in tongues, *glossolalia*, and interpret tongues.[97]

Most American Pentecostal denominations accept the gift of speaking in tongues, or glossolalia, as initial evidence of Spirit baptism. The practice of speaking in tongues became one of the distinctive characteristics of classical Pentecostal churches such as the General Council of the Assemblies of God, the Church of God in Christ (COGIC), and the International Church of the Foursquare Gospel.[98]

In addition to Spirit baptism, Pentecostalism is characterized by a worship style that differs from mainline churches. Worship includes "speaking in tongues, prophesying, healings, exorcism, hand-clapping, uncoordinated praying aloud, running, jumping, falling,

97. Barrett et al., *World Christian Encyclopedia*, 669.
98. Johnstone and Mandryk, *Operation World*, 755–57.

dancing 'in the Spirit,' crying, and shouting with great exuberance."[99] Pentecostalism can be incorporated with a popular form and extensive notion, quite surprisingly against intellectualism and secularism, as an indicative of a spiritual embryo and emotional attraction coming from the segments of doctrinal and rational components. In other words, when Pentecostalism becomes a spiritual movement through empiricism there has always been the tendency to not conform to secularism that had intellectual, liberal, modernist contents but to follow the format of the popular religion and folk religiosity. Pentecostalism can include any denomination, grouping, independent church, or mission agency that shares these characteristics.

Pentecostalism has been growing significantly in the developing world, making up a larger portion of global Christianity while theological liberals have dwindled in number and influence. Overall, the numbers of Christians globally and the growth rate of the faith has remained constant, but the balance has shifted: more Christians live in developing nations now than in the West. Representatives from developing nations, who are classified mainly as Pentecostals, have gradually entered into leadership positions in the global church and mission organizations.

> The growth first of Pentecostalism, and later of a charismatic interest right across the denominational spectrum, has been as much a new feature of the last fifty years as the existence of the World Council [of Churches] itself. Of course this has had an ecumenical impact on its own as charismatic Christians have successfully lowered barriers across confessional boundaries, discovering one another in the Spirit.[100]

Revivals and awakenings built up the church, paving the way for the growth of evangelical Christianity. We should also remember the global influence of Dwight L. Moody; his Student Volunteer Movement for Foreign Mission had a great impact on the developing world through a renewed focus on missions.[101] The establishment of theological institutions also contributed to the expansion of Christianity by making it possible for young people to receive the training they

---

99. Eliade, *The Encyclopedia of Religion*, 230.

100. Briggs, "Beyond Membership," 317.

101. Clymer, *Protestant Missionaries in the Philippines*, 11–12.

need for mission work overseas, mainly from the United States, but also from Great Britain.[102]

Billy Sunday is considered an advocate of revivalism. A famous Major League baseball player who knew how to promote a game, Sunday used his fame to promote revival. He used his showmanship to encourage people to accept Jesus Christ as Savior during revival meetings. His approach was not theological or intellectual, but emotional and entertaining. According to Spickard, Sunday did not "know any more about theology than a jack-rabbit knows about ping-pong, but [he] is on [his] way to glory."[103] Billy Graham has brought millions of souls to Christ through his organized revival meetings, huge prayer rallies, evangelistic campaigns and crusades around the globe.

The missionary nature of Pentecostalism has meant that the movement has influenced Christianity on a global scale. From its modest beginnings, Pentecostalism has led to the birth of new denominations in the United States and non-Western countries. Developing nations are experiencing a renewal of faith while the state of the church has been unchanged or declining in most European countries. Previous revivals, while evangelical in nature, did not have Pentecostal characteristics.[104]

102. Blumhofer, *The Assemblies of God*, 109–13; Durasoff, *Bright Wind of the Spirit*, 78.

103. Spickard et al., *A Global History of Christianity*, 396.

104. Using *renewal* as a generic term seems to be appropriate for David Barrett, but I also use the term *Pentecostal* synonymously. Barrett says, "This survey views the Renewal in the Holy Spirit as one single cohesive movement into which a vast proliferation of all kinds of individuals and communities have been drawn in a whole range of different circumstances. This explains the massive babel of diversity evident today." Barrett, "The Twentieth-Century Pentecostal/Charismatic Renewal," 119.

GRAPH 1.5 WAVES OF RENEWAL, 2010

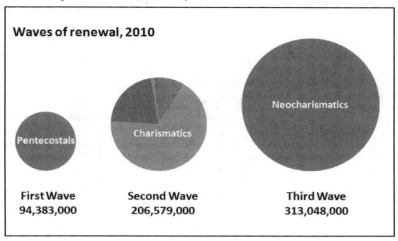

Source: Atlas of Global Christianity[105]

Charismatic Movement

The advent of Pentecostalism made waves in the theological and denominational order of the day. Those who accepted Pentecostal worship came to separate from traditional churches to form their own denominations, while those who rejected the movement remained in existing churches and sometimes became its opponents. Division took place not only along denominational lines, but also racial and ethnic ones. The early, classical Pentecostal churches eventually formed superstructures and became institutionalized. In the early years of the movement, Pentecostal followers were primarily low-income, working-class, people; as time went by, more middle-class followers were added.[106]

Classical Pentecostal revivals were seen in South Korea, Chile, Myanmar, Indonesia, Brazil, Vietnam, the Philippines, and South Africa in the early twentieth century, with more sporadic revivals in Europe, Oceania, and North America. Some of these movements grew rapidly while others started with great revivals but died out swiftly, such as in Japan, Germany, Denmark, France, Argentina, and Taiwan. Pentecostalism paved the way for a great outpouring of the Holy Spirit

105. Johnson and Ross, *Atlas of Global Christianity*, 102.

106. Spickard et al., *A Global History of Christianity*, 402.

throughout the world. As David Martin says, while the movement started in Los Angeles 1906, Pentecostalism ultimately "broke with the genealogy of the local past to create a genealogy of the universal future."[107]

In the 1960s came a second wave of the Pentecostal movement, known as the Charismatic Movement. Charismatics, like Pentecostals, believed in the outpouring of the Holy Spirit and affirmed that believers receive the Spirit of baptism as a distinctive work of grace. In contrast, Charismatics consider this a renewal of the baptism in the Spirit for those who have already been baptized with water and had a conversion experience. Some Charismatics affirmed that speaking in tongues, or glossolalia, provided initial evidence of the presence of the Spirit; others disagreed.[108]

While classical Pentecostal denominations and churches were growing, it was not until the Charismatic Movement that the impact was felt in existing churches. For example, Episcopal priest Dennis Bennett's widely read book *Nine O'clock in the Morning* described his encounter with the Holy Spirit. As more people came to accept Pentecostal doctrines and practices, great numbers of Protestants and Catholics received Spirit baptism. Lutheran minister Harald Bredesen used the term *charismatic* in 1962 to describe renewal in mainline churches.[109] During this time, it was common to see charismatic-style music, prayer, and liturgy incorporated into worship in many churches.[110] Timothy Tennent of Asbury Theological Seminary affirms:

> A second wave of Pentecostalism has swept through mainline Protestant, Roman Catholic, and Eastern Orthodox churches. This diverse background forced Pentecostals to embrace unity in spiritual terms, rather than in structural or doctrinal terms. This is why the word Pentecostal is frequently used both as an adjective and a noun in a way that is not generally found with terms such as Lutheran or Methodist. People can consider themselves to be Pentecostal Roman Catholics or Pentecostal Methodists without fear of contradiction.[111]

---

107. Martin, *Christian Language in the Secular City*, 70.

108. Eliade, *Encyclopedia of Religion*, 230.

109. Hocken, *Streams of Renewal*, 184.

110. Spickard et al., *A Global History of Christianity*, 402.

111. Tennent, *Invitation to World Mission*, 423–24.

Bernardo Campos states that "pentecostality [is] the universal experience that expresses the Pentecostal event—'*el acontecimiento Pentecostal*'—as the key event that characterizes the life of those who identify themselves with the historical Pentecostal revival."[112] The movement can also be found in Latin America where it has been growing at an accelerated rate, but with a twist. Political changes have led to a broad range of charismatic movements, including those that reflect the aspirations of ethnic groups, those that reflect certain regions or social classes, and those that accommodate diverse doctrinal, polity, and denominational emphases.[113]

The beginnings of charismatic renewal can be traced back to 1959 in Van Nuys, California, where Bennett and his parishioners experienced the baptism of the Holy Spirit and the gift of tongues.[114] Similar groups are now found elsewhere in the United States as well as in other countries, including France, South Africa, the Philippines, and Nicaragua.[115] David du Plessis's book *The Spirit Bade Me Go: An Astounding Move of God in the Denominational Churches*, proliferated across denominational boundaries in the United States as early as 1961. Covenant communities have also contributed to lay leadership, mostly among Catholics.[116]

For charismatic Catholics, the Vatican's permission for them to read the Bible had far-reaching effects.[117] Guidelines laid out after Vatican II envisioned *aggiornamento*, allowing lay Catholics to read the Bible in public mass and liturgies in their vernacular language. The *aggiornamento* allowed Bible-believing Christians and Catholics to bring their spiritual lives to new levels. The Catholic charismatic movement was a global phenomenon that included Bible studies and prayer meetings led by lay preachers, priests, and nuns.[118] Pope John Paul II was optimistic about the work and need of the Holy Spirit at the end of the second millennium in his *Dominumet Vivificantem (DV)*.[119]

---

112. Alvarez, "The South," 137–38.

113. Kärkkäinen, "Culture," 272.

114. Hocken, "A Survey of the Worldwide Charismatic Movement," 117.

115. Ibid., 132–33.

116. Hocken, "A Survey of the Worldwide Charismatic Movement," 117–18.

117. Wostyn, *Doing Ecclesiology*, 44–45.

118. Zaide, "The Centennial of Biblical Christianity," 32.

119. Joseph, *Paraclete*, 4.

Catholic Charismatics are recognized as "charismatic-equipped with gifts of service for the good of the church."[120]

Independent Churches

The term *independent church* can mean different things depending on who uses it. Roman Catholics and the Eastern Orthodox use this term for Protestants. Mainline Protestants use it to designate free churches and dissent groups such as Puritans, Baptists, and Quakers. Pentecostals use it to denote a third wave from the Pentecostal tradition. When Barrett began to classify independent church groups, they were first defined as "non-white indigenous" and then "crypto-Christian." These groups were located in the Southern hemisphere and were indigenous, autonomous, and independent of Western established churches and denominations. At the dawn of the twentieth century, 266 million people were Roman Catholic, 115 million were Orthodox, and 103 million were Protestant. At this time, the independent church group accounted for only 8 million people.[121] The number of independent churches seemed somewhat small. In 1910, most independent churches were from Polynesia and North America, at 15 percent 7.2 percent, respectively. Filipino independent churches accounted for over 2.1 million people. India, Switzerland, Jamaica, Austria, Tonga, and South Africa followed.[122]

---

120. Vatican II documents: Dogmatic Constitution on the Church "Lumen Gentium" #12; Decree on the Apostolate of the Laity, "Apostlicam Actuositatem" #13. Sin, *Guidelines*, 8–9.

121. Barrett, Johnson, and Crissing, "Missionmetrics 2008," 29. Barrett's statistics show 1.1 billion Roman Catholics, 386 million Protestants, and 252 million Orthodox. The Independent group is bigger than Protestants, with 423 million.

122. Gerloft and Akrong, "Independents, 1910–2010," 76–77.

TABLE 1.8 LARGEST POPULATION OF INDEPENDENTS

Largest population of Independents

Largest population

	1910	Independents	2010	Independents
1	USA	6,771,000	China	85,000,000
2	Philippines	2,184,000	USA	72,700,000
3	India	98,300	Nigeria	26,500,000
4	Switzerland	42,900	Brazil	21,330,000
5	Jamaica	23,000	Philippines	19,500,000
6	Austria	20,400	South Africa	19,050,000
7	Tonga	19,400	India	18,200,000
8	South Africa	18,400	DR Congo	15,132,000
9	Liberia	13,400	Indonesia	6,800,000
10	Japan	11,300	Kenya	6,720,000

©Edinburgh University Press, 2009

Source: *Atlas of Global Christianity*[123]

In 2010, the largest Christian group was the Roman Catholics with 50.4 percent of global Christian population. Protestants, the second largest group, had 6.1 percent, followed by the Independent church group with 5.3 percent and 369 million followers—not that much smaller than the Protestant group, which accounted for 419 million. Evangelicals had 3.8 percent, and Pentecostals claimed 8.9 percent, with 614 million adherents. Independent churches can either be classified as a major tradition or as a Pentecostal movement.

123. Ibid., 77.

GRAPH 1.6 CHRISTIAN MAJOR TRADITIONS—
PERCENTAGE OF GLOBAL POPULATION, 1910 AND 2010

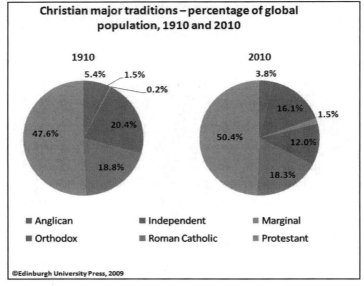

Source: Atlas of Global Christianity[124]

___

124. Johnson and Ross, *Atlas of Global Christianity*, 70.

TABLE 1.9 ADHERENTS IN MAJOR CHRISTIAN TRADITIONS AND
MOVEMENTS, 1910 AND 2010

Adherents in major Christian traditions and movements, 1910 & 2010						
	1910			2010		
Traditions	*Adherents*	*Global %*	*Christian %*	*Adherents*	*Global %*	*Christian %*
Anglicans	32,920,000	1.9	5.4	86,782,000	1.3	3.8
Independents	9,269,000	0.5	1.5	369,156,000	5.3	16.1
Marginals	1,070,000	0.1	0.2	34,912,000	0.5	1.5
Orthodox	124,923,000	7.1	20.4	274,447,000	4.0	12.0
Protestants	115,013,000	16.6	18.8	419,316,000	6.1	18.3
Roman Catholics	291,440,000	6.5	47.6	1,155,627,000	16.7	50.4
Movements						
Evangelists	80,192,000	4.6	13.1	263,464,000	3.8	11.5
Renewalists	1,203,000	0.1	0.2	614,010,000	8.9	26.8

*Rate - average annual growth rate, per cent per year, between dates specified

©Edinburgh University Press, 2009

Source: *Atlas of Global Christianity*[125]

In 2010, the largest independent churches came first from China, the
United States, Nigeria, and Brazil. The growth of independent churches in Africa and Asia is particularly catching one's attention. Johnson
states, "The 100-year Independent growth rate in Africa was nearly
four times greater than that of the general population."[126]

125. Ibid., 71.
126. Ibid., 78.

TABLE 1.10 LARGEST 25 OF 201 INDEPENDENT TRADITIONS, 2010

Largest 25 of 201 Independent traditions, 2010	
Minor tradition	*Members*
1 Chinese Charismatic	76,816,000
2 African Independent Pentecostal	23,548,000
3 Independent Baptist	21,555,000
4 African Independent Apostolic	18,737,000
5 Brazilian/Portuguese Pentecostal	16,636,000
6 White-led Charismatic	12,723,000
7 Chinese Neocharismatic	12,686,000
8 African Independent Neocharismatic	11,248,000
9 New Apostolic, Catholic Apostolic, Old Apostolic	10,940,000
10 Black American Pentecostal	9,880,000
11 Latin American Pentecostal	8,834,000
12 Independent Reformed, Presbyterian	8,355,000
13 Zionist African Independent	8,185,000
14 White-led Pentecostal	8,086,000
15 Independent Methodist	6,939,000
16 Filipino Neocharismatic	6,290,000
17 Reformed Catholic, retaining Catholic claims	6,123,000
18 Independent Disciple, Restorationist, Christian	4,740,000
19 Independent Fundamentalist	4,626,000
20 African Independent Charismatic	3,831,000
21 Hidden Hindu believers in Christ	3,824,000
22 Latin American grassroots	3,432,000
23 Conservative Catholic (schism ex Rome)	3,238,000
24 Indian Neocharismatic	3,041,000
25 African Neocharismatic of mixed traditions	2,834,000
©Edinburgh University Press, 2009	

Source: *Atlas of Global Christianity*[127]

Those who experience the gifts of the Holy Spirit from mainline Protestant churches are normally considered neo-Pentecostals, while Charismatics in the Catholic Church are referred to as Catholic Pentecostals or Charismatic Catholics. Accordingly, "'charismatic' by and large can be appropriate to all who experience baptism and other gifts of the Holy Spirit expressed in Paul's Epistle to the Corinthians."[128] In this respect, Charismatics are differentiated from classical Pentecostals in that Pentecostals hold their own denominations while Charismatics remain part of mainline denominations.[129]

127. Gerloft and Akrong, "Independents," 1678.
128. Kitano, "Spontaneous Ecumenicity," 11.
129. Wiegele, "Transforming Popular Catholicism," 4.

Pentecostal independent churches are identified with the third wave renewal movement, comparable to the second wave charismatic renewal, but the so-called "initial evidence" of glossolalia is not required.[130] Pentecostals and Charismatics are found mostly among nonwhites in Africa, Latin America, and Asia.[131] European evangelicals are more concerned with social issues and ecumenism while developing-world Christians, who are generally younger by age and in faith, seize the fundamental truths of Scripture and apply Pentecostal and charismatic principles to worship. Today, independent churches have become major movements in many parts of the world.

CONCLUSION: THE ROOTS OF THE GLOBAL SOUTH

Looking at global Christianity we have seen a great number of believers in Jesus are living in the Global South yet the diversity of the Global South Christianity is tremendous. Analyzing all of the Christian branches in the Global South challenge scholars and researchers to study why they are flourishing. This questions brings us to consider the origins and connectedness of the Global South Christianity into the where Christianity and existed in the global north. The author will explore the connections the Global North and South. We will first look at Christianity in Europe to start the investigation.

---

130. Johnstone and Mandryk, *Operation World*, 755.
131. Eliade, *Encyclopedia of Religion*, 230.

2

The Crisis of Christianity in Europe

THE LAST FEW CENTURIES have seen a major, fundamental shift in global Christianity. Whether people were aware of it or not, while Europe was spreading the faith to other nations, it was also abandoning its own Christian foundation. Passengers on the Titanic had assurance that the ship was the largest, safest, and strongest of its kind. Its makers called it unsinkable. But, as we know, the ship sank when it struck an iceberg. Similarly, Europe was once a leader in Christian missions, culture, church governance, traditions, and theology. Now, however, these areas are in decline. What caused this shift, and what is its significance?

THE CRISIS OF CHURCHES IN BRITAIN AND EUROPE

In the eighteenth and nineteenth century, Great Britain was a major player in the missionary endeavor in terms of theology, church power, and evangelicalism. At the dawn of the twentieth century, the greatest mission power was overtaken by American church that the nation led the world mission in promulgating the great expansion of Christianity in the global south. How did it happen that the great missionary country decline so greatly in the mid 1960s Great Britain began to fall with an ever decreasing number of Christian beliefs and practices looking at every situation in European nations the situation differed a lot from Britain. Let us explore to see what's happening in this time period in Great Britain and the rest of Europe.

Declining or De-Christianizing

Callum G. Brown's in-depth book, *The Death of Christian Britain*, states that "it took several centuries to convert Britain to Christianity, but it has taken less than forty years for the country to forsake it."[1] He fairly depicts the British church's general decline and affirms, "It is not especially novel to proclaim that the Christian churches are in decline in Britain. But what is new is the idea of the 'death of Christian Britain.'"[2] Undoubtedly, most mainline British churches have drastically dwindled in membership, faith practices, and social influence. Although newer and independent Pentecostal and charismatic churches have experienced sizeable growth, this has not counterbalanced the overall decline of the British church. Attendance is decreasing in every mainline Christian denomination, and the growth of newer, independent, and Pentecostal/charismatic churches has yet to permeate unchurched communities enough to result in a significant number of conversions. Halsey describes the situation aptly: "In short, though by no means outlandish from the European culture to which they belong, the British are to be seen and see themselves as a relatively unchurched, nationalistic, optimistic, satisfied, conservative, and moralistic people."[3]

The religious attitude of the majority of the Britons is an inconsistent one. They tend to have no church affiliation, yet occasionally attend worship on special occasions such as Easter and Christmas. They are indifferent toward established churches, yet seem to have a romantic affection for medieval and Victorian red-brick church buildings and sentimental hymns.[4] The role of Christianity in Britain has been denigrated to the point of marginalization, indicating that the church has become "seriously amiss," according to Robinson.[5] Whether one fully agrees that Christianity in Britain has reached the point of death, the decline of the faith in Britain and Europe is beyond dispute. The church's loss of influence in the social, religious, and political arenas

1. Brown, *The Death of Christian Britain*, 1. Alister McGrath agrees with Brown that the turning point came in the 1960s: "The loss of credibility did not date from the industrial era, nor the aftermath of either of the two world wars, but from a rupture of the centuries-long cycle of intergenerational transmission of the Christian faith. . . . It was at this time that the 'Death of God' movement erupted in the United States, gaining media attention. Titles such as Paul van Buren's *Secular Meaning of the Gospel* (1963) and Thomas J.J. Altizer's *Gospel of Christian Atheism* (1966) garnered headlines in a puzzled yet fascinated secular press." *The Future of Christianity*, 15.

2. Brown, *The Death of Christian Britain*, 1.

3. Halsey, "On Methods and Morals," 10.

4. Bruce, *Religion in Modern Britain*, 70.

5. Robinson and Smith, *Invading Secular Space*, 16–17.

has been documented by numerous scholars.[6] James Bentley's *Cry God for England*, Robin Gill's *Beyond Decline,* and Bruce's *Religion in Modern Britain* all vividly describe the present crisis of de-Christianization facing the British church.

Diminishing or Disappearing

The church's geographical presence in Europe is eroding as beautiful medieval and Victorian church buildings deteriorate or are converted to other purposes. This phenomenon is seen not only in urban areas, but also the countryside, where churches have traditionally been centers of influence. Church buildings have become Sikh temples, mosques, factories, pubs, townhouses, and offices. Even the final vestiges of the once-vibrant life of these churches—the exterior architectural markings—are now disappearing.[7] The leader of Great Britain's Roman Catholics, Cardinal Cormac Murphy O'Connor, affirms that "Christianity, as a sort of backdrop to people's lives and moral decisions—and to the government and social life of the country—has now almost been vanquished."[8] Os Guinness paints a bleak, but accurate, picture:

> Christianity is like the majestic ruins of an ancient cathedral from which stones are plundered for the construction of countless other buildings. Politicians quarry from her vocabulary, psychiatrists dip into its treasury of practices and symbols, and advertisers mimic the resonances of its acoustics. Each pillager uses just what is convenient. But the decisiveness and authority of any distinctive Christian truth are gone.[9]

An alternative scenario envisioned by liberal theologians is that Christianity will inevitably move in a multi-faith direction. Brown describes this trajectory: "[E]cumenism and church union introduce a new acknowledgement of the validity of religious experience and belief derived from other religious traditions."[10]

What are the roots of the decline of Christianity in the West? How is this decline related to the rise of rationalism and the Enlightenment's emphasis on human reasoning? How have social and economic dislocations caused by the Industrial Revolution and modernization af-

---

6. McLeod, *Secularisation in Western Europe*, 11.

7. Gibbs and Coffey, *Church Next*, 10.

8. Jackson, *Hope for the Church*, 62.

9. Guinness, *The Gravedigger File*, 212. Cf. Warren, *Being Human*, 29.

10. Brown, *The Death of Christian Britain*, 3.

fected Christianity's place in society? We will examine these questions in the following chapter.[11]

Most strikingly, it seems as if Great Britain, once the leading engine of modern overseas missions and the Great Awakening movements of the eighteenth and nineteenth centuries, is now spiritually exhausted. In fact, Britain is no longer considered a mission force, but rather a mission field, by most Christians.

A dramatic transformation of the geography of faith has taken place during the modern era. From the Medieval era to the nineteenth century, Christian ethics and values predominated in Western Europe due to the proximity of church and state in most nations. During the late nineteenth century and early twentieth centuries, however, Christianity lost its position of prominence and esteem. Yet, as this was happening, a small number of European Christian missionaries and emigrants spread the gospel to the rest of Europe and far beyond—throughout the world. This concurrent process of loss and gain left Europe having forfeited "its own self-confidence as the bearer of Christianity."[12] Consequently, in the social, political, and academic arenas, Christian doctrines, morals, beliefs, and practices came under attack.

During the past century, Christianity has grown speedily in Africa, Asia, and Latin America, collectively known as the Global South. In Europe, it has gradually lost its influence and conviction. The past three centuries saw Western missionaries venturing to non-Christian areas to bring the gospel to the native inhabitants of territories under colonial rule. Today, in a turnabout, Christians and missionaries from the Global South are making efforts to help their brothers and sisters in the Global North to reinvigorate the faith.[13]

THE CRISIS OF CHRISTIAN BELIEFS

The world can be divided into two major, distinct parts for the purpose of tracing the history of Christian beliefs and practices. During the

11. Brown states that "for most scholars, Christian religion in Britain, Europe and North America has been in almost constant decay for at least a century, and for some sociologists and historians for even longer—for between two hundred and five hundred years." Brown, *The Death of Christian Britain,* 3.

12. Chadwick, "Great Britain and Europe," 341.

13. The fastest growing churches in Europe, North America, and Australia/New Zealand are not in the traditional white churches but by African, Caribbean, Asian, and Latin American churches. All the growing churches have been in immigrant churches particularly in Europe. O'Sullivan, "Is Europe Losing Its Faith?," 1.

twentieth century, the Global North, especially Europe, abandoned the Christian faith in large numbers. In the Global South, especially Latin America, Africa, and many parts of Asia, millions of people embraced the Christian faith with open hearts. Examining the specific religious beliefs and practices of Christians the Global North and the Global South will give us important insights into the causes of this shift. As we will see, the connection between religious *beliefs* and *practices* is key.

Religious Belief

Historically, people who focused only on maintaining their traditional religious beliefs without practicing did not see themselves as religiously "active." Pierre Bréchon has observed that practice and belief are nevertheless closely linked: "[R]eligious practice without belief is rare, as is religious belief without practice." In his view, the practice of religion shapes one's belief system:

> Even if religious practice is only one aspect of religious integration, it is extremely significant. Church attendance indicates the degree of denominational integration, that is, the degree to which a denominational religious identity has been shaped. A regular churchgoer is likely to approve the system of belief of his denomination; his religious identity clearly depends on an institutional system. The intensity of religious participation indicates the sharing of a religious culture and likely affects moral and political values.[14]

At the same time, sociologists who study religion, as well as church historians, unanimously agree that Christians' beliefs are not affecting their practices as before. Steve Bruce describes this trend:

> Although not regarded with any great hostility, our churches are unpopular, their teachings are ignored by the vast majority of the population, their leaders no longer have the ears of our rulers, their efforts to glorify God are barely noticed, and their beliefs no longer inform the presuppositions of the wider culture. . . . Insofar as the supernatural or the spiritual is still to be found in the mainstream, it is in almost homoeopathic concentrations: so watered down as to be a shadow of its former self, nearly undetectable to the untrained eye.[15]

14. Bréchon, "Integration into Catholicism and Protestantism," 116.
15. Bruce, *Religion in Modern Britain*, 125.

Self-reported rates of belief in God differ greatly from rates of church attendance. In a 1995 survey, 65 percent of British people regarded themselves as Christians and also considered Great Britain to be a Christian nation.[16] However, the diminishing and downward curve of Christian affiliation had never stopped. According to David Voas and Rodney Ling in their 2008 report, only 50 percent identified themselves as Christian.[17] Another survey revealed that only 62 percent of the British believe in a Christian God and that the number of believers in a Universal God (i.e. a belief in some sort of supernatural power or higher being) was increasing. Survey participants were asked the same questions twice, reworded the second time. The results revealed that "only 50 percent believed in a Christian God. Of those, only half felt close to God, and almost a quarter felt 'not close at all.'"[18] In the British Social Attitudes survey shows that believers in a type of Christian dropped to only 17 percent.[19]

TABLE 2.1 BELIEF IN GOD IN GREAT BRITAIN
AND NORTHERN IRELAND, 1991

Response	Position	Britain (%) 1991	N. Ireland (%) 1991	Britain (%) 2010
I don't believe in God	1	10	1	18
I don't know whether there is a God, and I don't believe there is any way to find out	2	14	4	19
I don't believe in a personal God, but I do believe in a higher power of some kind	3	13	4	14

16. Those who believe in Triune God are described as "Christian" in this book. Brierley et al., *UK Christian Handbook*, 12.

17. Voas and Ling, "Religion in Britain and the United States," 67.

18. Bruce, *Religion in the Modern World*, 33.

19. Voas and Ling, "Religion in Britain and the United States," 68.

I find myself believing in God some of the time, but not at other	4	13	4	13
While I have doubts, I feel that I do believe in God	5	26	20	18
I know God really exists, and I have no doubts about it	6	23	57	17
I don't know/no answer	7	2	7	NA

Source: British *Social Attitudes Survey*, 1992[20]

As it can be seen the results of the survey show that a belief in God is steadily declining. The number of people who state a belief in God with no doubts was 23 percent in 1991. In 2011, that number has dropped to 17 percent. This number is shocking in comparison to the number of Americans who were asked the same question demonstrated 61 percent. This comparative study between British and Americans will be dealt in chapter six. The results of this survey support Grace Davie's view that the British have moved from "believing and belonging" to "believing without belonging." Although a high percentage of the British say they believe in God, only a few actually attend a church.[21] When we examine rates of church attendance, Britain is highly secularized compared to the United States, African Christian nations, and Latin American nations. Still, a greater percentage of the British population believes in God than in South Korea and the Philippines, nations that are experiencing rapid Christian revival. What is the reason for this lack of involvement, in spite of self-reported belief?

Over time, central Christian doctrines such as God as Creator, Jesus as Savior and the Son of God, and the existence of heaven and

20. These statistics are a combination of a 1992 BSA survey and the 2008 American Religious Identification Survey. Ibid., 66.

21. Davie, *Religion in Britain*, 2. Her central thesis is that church attendance has declined much faster than changes in belief, although she recognizes that residual belief is vaguer and less obviously shaped by a Christian understanding of the nature of God and of redemption. Many other Europeans also persist in their belief in God.

hell have been abandoned by many Europeans while anti-God senti-ments and nontraditional beliefs, once held by only a small number of people, have grown tremendously.[22] Other traditional Christian beliefs—such as the reality of miracles, the Virgin Birth, the bodily resurrection of Christ, the expectation of Christ's return, and the reali-ty of eternal damnation—are no longer widely held.[23] With the decline of mainstream Christian beliefs and practices has come "a very wide range of diffuse and privatized beliefs."[24] Changes can be observed not only among individuals, but also among mainline denominations:

> God is no longer seen as an actual person but as some sort of vague power or our own consciences. The Bible is no longer the word of God but a historical book with some useful ethical and moral guidelines for living. Miracles are explained away; either they did not really happen or they were natural phenomena misunderstand by ignorant peasants. Christ is no longer the Son of God but an exemplary prophet and teacher. Heaven and hell cease to be real places and become psychological states.[25]

Bruce describes the decline of Christian beliefs among the British:

> In Britain, generally less than a quarter of respondents in a variety of surveys claim "no religion." To be more specific, few people claim to be atheists or agnostics: in the 1991 British Social Attitudes (hereafter BSA) survey, 10 and 13 per cent re-spectively. However, the unbelievers are now more numerous than a decade earlier, when only 4 per cent identified them-selves as "atheists." In 1947, using the Gallup formula, only 6 percent said they "Don't really think there is any sort of spirit/ God or life force"; in 1968 it was 11 per cent.

Furthermore, the author of *Religion in the Modern World* also states:

22. Analysis of almost 100 surveys conducted from 1939 to 1996 showed "a sig-nificant erosion of belief in God. . . . Second, the most serious decline occurred in specifically Christian beliefs including belief in a personal God and belief in Jesus as the Son of God as well as traditional Christian teachings about the afterlife and the Bible. . . . Third, while traditional Christian beliefs changed markedly, non-traditional beliefs remained stable albeit among a minority of respondents." Bruce, *God Is Dead,* 71–72.

23. Bruce, *Religion in the Modern World,* 36.

24. Ibid., 58.

25. Ibid., 144.

> [T]he traditional Christian view of God as a person is now less popular than a very wide range of non-theistic visions of the supernatural. Between 1947 and 1987 the proportion of respondents who agreed that "There is a personal God" fell from 45 to 37 percent, while those who chose the option "There is some sort of spirit or vital force which controls life" increased from 39 to 42 percent. The various agnostic and atheistic positions increased in popularity from 16 to 21 percent. To take the central Christian claim, 71 per cent of Gallup respondents in 1951 agreed that "Jesus Christ is the Son of God." In 1965 it was 64 per cent and in 1982 it was only 43 percent. In a 1957 survey 54 per cent said they believed in life after death. In the BSA survey only 27 per cent made the same claim. Other traditional beliefs were similarly unpopular. Only 24 per cent of respondents said they believed in the Devil or in hell.[26]

A 2011 survey done by John Humphrys reveals a more gloomy picture of British religious life that "34% believed in a personal God or gods (ranging from 28% among the 18–34s to 42% of over-55s), 10% in some higher spiritual power, 19% in neither, with 29% unsure or agnostic."[27] Overlooking periodical tendency of British religious survey unveils how steadily British people are leaving from biblical principle and beliefs in the Bible. Seeing the decline of Christian religion in Britain gives us to draw our attention on the decline of European Christian beliefs and practices.

European Religious Belief

The decline of traditional Christian beliefs among the British has led to widespread secularization. In other European nations as well, a similar pattern has emerged. Fewer people claim to believe in a "personal" God or to hold traditional Christian beliefs such as life after death, humans having souls, hell, heaven, and sin.

26. Ibid., 33.
27. Fields, "British Religion in Numbers," lines 20–21.

TABLE 2.2 CONNECTION BETWEEN DENOMINATIONAL INTEGRATION
AND DIFFERENT BELIEFS (CRAMER'S V^3)[28]

Religious Beliefs	Integration into	
	Catholicism	Protestantism
Believe in God (yes/no)	0.43	0.42
Personal God or some sort of spirit or life force	0.29	0.27
God is important in his life (10 persons scale)	0.33	0.30
Believe in life after death (yes/no)	0.30	0.25
Believe in soul (yes/no)	0.31	0.27
Believe in the devil (yes/no)	0.26	0.21
Believe in hell (yes/no)	0.29	0.22
Believe in heaven (yes/no)	0.33	0.26
Believe in sin (yes/no)	0.32	0.27
Believe in the resurrection of the dead (yes/no)	0.35	0.29
Believe in reincarnation (yes/no)	0.10	0.09
Life is meaningful only because God exists	0.28	0.25
Death has a meaning only if you believe in God	0.26	0.20
Sorrow and suffering only have meaning if you believe in God	0.25	0.20
To be religious, non religious or a committed atheist	0.61	0.60
Religion gives comfort and strength	0.43	0.37
To take some moments of prayer, meditation or contemplation	0.34	0.29
Frequency of prayer to God	0.30	0.27

Source: "Integration into Catholicism and Protestantism"[29]

28. Bréchon, "Integration," Cramer's V^3 "is an index which measures the strength of the relationship between two qualitative variables. It ranges from 0 to 1. Coefficients betweens .20 and .30 correspond to the rather strong statistical connections for social phenomena," 118.

29. Ibid., 118.

European religious survey which was conducted in 2005 reveals on results of European religious or spiritual beliefs. That result of the survey shows that 78 percent answered believe in a God although a God in not exclusively Christian God but include Judeo-Christian Islam and a supreme being. Seventy seven percent believe in a spirit of life force. However, due to multiple answers available to the questions, Europeans replied that 61 percent of them "do not have religious or spiritual beliefs."[30]

GRAPH 2.1 RELIGIOUS AND SPIRITUAL BELIEFS

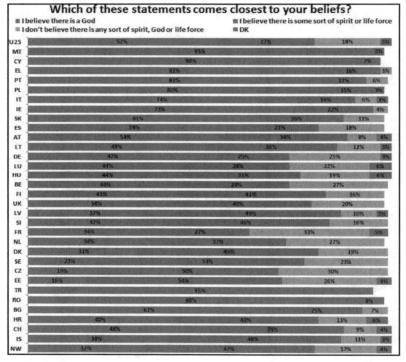

Source: European Commission: Social values, Science and Technology[31]

The survey shows that Mediterranean and eastern European countries where state church as Catholic or Orthodox is predominant have answered relatively high in beliefs in God. Highest rate of countries are Malta by 95 percent, Cyprus by 90 percent, Greece and Portugal by

30. Directorate General Research, *Social values, Science and Technology*, 8.
31. Ibid., 9.

81 percent, Poland by 80 percent, Italy 74 percent, and Ireland 73 percent.[32] A great number of Europeans, especially the young, no longer hold conventional religious beliefs. Among Christians, adherence to traditional beliefs is highly correlated with church attendance:

> Furthermore, the majority of those believing in a "personal God" attend a church service weekly. Those conceiving of God as a "spirit" or "life force" and those who "do not really know how to 'conceive' him" attend less frequently. Finally, people who doubt God's existence or do not believe in him are overwhelmingly not involved in a church. In Belgium, a person's conception of God is a better predictor of his or her participation in a church than vice versa.[33]

Table 2.2 also shows that beliefs closely align with denominational allegiance and religious practice. Belief in reincarnation received the lowest score; this non-Christian concept has its origins in Buddhism and Hinduism. However, even this relatively low rate of belief in reincarnation is evidence of a religious pluralism that has taken root in Europe.[34] Bréchon interprets this outcome as follows:

> Religious beliefs which move away from the traditional Christian milieu are not strongly congruent with integration into Catholicism and Protestantism. What is striking, however, is the (weak) link between belief in reincarnation and integration into Christianity. Belief in reincarnation is least common among committed atheists while churchgoers believe in reincarnation even (slightly) more than non-churchgoers. To many, reincarnation is not a well-defined belief, and many churchgoers claim to believe in both resurrection and reincarnation. Theologically speaking, of course, the two beliefs are considered to be antinomical.[35]

A 1993 survey measured religious beliefs among 645 Roman Catholics, including returnees and dropouts. This survey shows the membership pattern in Christian attendance according to the beliefs that either caused them stay or leave the church.

---

32. Ibid., 9–10.
33. Dobbelaere, "Church Involvement," 21.
34. Belgian Catholics accepted reincarnation at a rate of 20 percent. Ibid., 24.
35. Bréchon, "Integration into Catholicism and Protestantism," 118–19.

TABLE 2.3 LOYALISTS, RETURNEES, AND DROPOUTS COMPARED
ON BELIEFS AND MORAL ISSUES (AS PERCENTAGES)

	Loyalists (n=407)	Returnees (n=143)	Dropouts (n=95)
Believe in eternal life	89	88	48
Believe in the devil (Satan)	66	65	25
Morality index:			
Traditional	43	30	15
In-between	22	32	18
Alternative	35	38	67

Source: "When the Sacred Returns"[36]

Belief in eternal life and the devil are ranked higher among loyalists
and returnees, but these beliefs are held by relatively low percentages of
those no longer affiliated with any church activity. One of the findings
reveals that a reason for leaving the church is a decreased conviction
in the afterlife and a supernatural being, namely, God. The morality
index shows the same pattern. Among both Protestants and Catholics,
returnees and loyalists are very close in their beliefs in the afterlife
and the devil, but returnees hold a moral position between that of the
loyalists and the dropouts. The researchers conclude, "When viewed
in combination with their responses to the questions regarding eternal
life and the Devil, these once-lapsed Catholics seem to resemble their
never-lapsed Counterparts."[37]

Although the spread of the non-Christian worldview is evident,
many Europeans still feel allegiance to the established church in spite
of their nonadherence to traditional Christian beliefs and a lack of
regular observance of church practices. Dobbelaere points out this
irony:

> People, even those practicing regularly, "pick and choose"
> what to believe and what to practice. They no longer accept
> the "set menu" of their Church, and this is most clearly seen
> in a Church with authoritatively given beliefs, practices, and
> ethics, i.e. the Catholic Church.[38]

36. Hammond and Shibley, "When the Sacred Returns," 41.
37. Ibid., 41.
38. Dobbelaere, "Church Involvement," 23.

Religious beliefs are also closely interrelated with religious experiences. Acquaviva conducted a survey that compared people's church attendance with their sense of spiritual presence.

TABLE 2.4 AWARENESS OF A PRESENCE OR POWER COMPARED
WITH CHURCH ATTENDANCE

	Aware	Not Aware
Regular or occasional attendee	23	3
Seldom or never attend	42	24
Totals	65	27

Source: "Religious Experience and Practice"[39]

Fewer of those who regularly participate in religious activities and are aware of a power or presence are only 23 percent. Those who seldom or never attend church service show a surprisingly high rate of awareness at 42 percent.

Western Religious Belief

Americans have more religious experiences than the British: 45 percent compared to 33 percent, according to a 1985 Gallup poll.[40] A 2011 Gallup survey reveals 92 percent Americans believe in God[41] (The comparative survey between the British and American society will be dealt in chapter 6). Age differences also exist between the two nations, with more elderly people in the UK likely to have intense religious experiences, but both younger and older Americans reporting such experiences. The number of elderly people in Britain who participate in Christian services is declining; even the oldest attend only occasionally. In the United States, however, attendance patterns are similar for all age groups. Among survey respondents, 43 percent of the churched in America acknowledged a religious experience, but only 24 percent within the unchurched group.[42]

Centuries of Christian faith in Europe have not disappeared entirely. Disbelief in God, or any kind of spirit or life force, varied from about 20 percent in Denmark and Sweden to less than 1 percent

39. Acquaviva, "Some Reflections," 52.
40. Ibid., 52–53.
41. Newport, "More Than 9 in 10 Americans Continue to Believe in God," line 6.
42. Acquaviva, "Some Reflections," 53.

in Ireland. Most Europeans still believe in some form of spiritual or religious being, although belief in the Judeo-Christian God is diminishing. Europeans increasingly look to Eastern religions, the New Age movement, and cults to fill their spiritual hunger.[43]

The decline of Christian beliefs among the British and other Europeans has led to smaller numbers of people attending church. At the same time, more people claim to hold Christian beliefs than are involved in a church. There has been an insignificant, if any, rise in Christian beliefs in Europe since the Second World War—particularly in the belief of personal, creator God. A religious survey on belief in a Christian God in 1950s and 1990s divulges a plummeting decline from 31 percent to 43 percent. Furthermore, "In May 2000 the Opinion Research Business 2000 (ORB) survey found that number had further declined to 26 percent. The number of those explicitly saying they did not believe in God rose steadily from 2 percent in the 1950s to 27 percent in the 1990s."[44] It is not only the overall decline of belief in God but also the alarming rise of disbelief in God in British society.

When traditional Christian beliefs are watered down, there are fewer points of friction between faith and culture. The secularization hypothesis predicts the decline of religious beliefs resulting in the decline of religious attendance. The demise of religious beliefs and practices may allow openness towards other religions, the new age movements and eventually secular trends. If the secularization process is implemented in British society, Bruce envisages that "they [things that affect religious decline] remove the necessity for arguing with other religions. If hell is a psychological state, there is less necessity to argue about its nature and how to avoid it."[45]

The Scandinavian countries rank the lowest in Europe in church attendance and also in rates of Christian beliefs and practices. They have the lowest percentage of citizens who believe in a personal, creator God. Most Scandinavians are, at best, marginal members when it comes to organized Christian religion, and they rarely attend church worship services. Similarly, as many as half the residents of the Netherlands were classified as unchurched in a 1990 survey:

43. Halman and Riis, "Contemporary European Discourses," 12.
44. Bruce, *God Is Dead,* 71–72.
45. Bruce, *Religion in the Modern World,* 144.

> Apart from a large proportion of unchurched people, a relatively large proportion of the Dutch is strongly engaged in church activities. It seems as if, in the Netherlands, either one is engaged and thus a core or modal member, or one leaves the church and becomes unchurched.[46]

Looking at Europe as a whole, the north has grown more secularized than the south, with the exception of Ireland.[47] However, most European countries (Spain in particular) have shown not only steady decline in Christian beliefs and practices, but also overall decay in the category of personal religiosity.[48] Italians are an exception, displaying the opposite pattern.[49]

International Religious Belief

In Canada, Australia, and New Zealand as well, overall church influence, membership, and attendance rates have been on the decline for several decades.[50] It should be noted that, in Australia from 1955 to 1963, there was a modest religious boom affecting every denomination. Crusades and revival meetings fueled this increase.[51] In 1962, during this time of revival, one in two people sent his or her children to Sunday school, according to David Martin. However, only one in seven children attended Sunday school regularly just two years later.[52] Despite some national differences and short-term revivals, the clear overall trend in the mid-twentieth century was one of decline for Christianity in both Britain and much of the Western world.[53] Halman

46. Halman and Riis, "Contemporary European Discourses," 8–9.

47. Iceland is an exceptional case in Scandinavia, with a high level of Christian belief and practice. The highest levels of Catholic Church participation and beliefs are found among the Irish. See Ibid., 9–10.

48. Ibid., 10.

49. Italians have become more religious in the late twentieth century. In 1981, 28 percent of Italians believed in a personal God, and 67 percent in 1992. The researchers state that "Italian society resembles the overall European general decline in traditional institutional religiosity. . . . Apparently, Italians are becoming more and more religious not in the official, traditional, institutional way, but in a personal, unofficial way." Ibid., 10.

50. McLeod, *Religion and the People of Western Europe*, 37.

51. Brown, *The Death of Christian Britain*, 5.

52. This period, at least four in five seem to feel that Christianity should be passed on in these various ways to children. Martin, *A Sociology of English Religion*, 41–42.

53. Brown, *The Death of Christian Britain*, 5.

and Riis continue to report that most religious people in western Europe are the Irish while people in France and Denmark marked the "least religious people." In this respect, Halman and Riis conclude, "Apart from a (small) general decline in religiosity, no changes seem to have taken place in the rank ordering of European countries."[54]

Comparable figures for regular church attendance in all churches of all nations are difficult to obtain. The rate in the United States is 40 percent, while France has a rate of just 13 percent; 12.4 percent in France are Roman Catholics. Other nations report as follows:

TABLE 2.5 INTERNATIONAL CHURCH ACTIVITY BY PERCENTAGE OF THE ADULT POPULATION, 1990

Nation	Church attendance	Church members	Church community
	%	%	%
Finland	3	28	93
Denmark	4	23	94
Norway	5	32	95
Great Britain	10	14	65
French-Swiss	13	23	84
France	13	21	85
Spain	14	24	69
Australia	27	N/a	57
United States	40	N/a	70
South Africa	N/a	31	80

Source: Christian England[55]

With the decline in church attendance and Christian beliefs in Europe has come the demise of many religious establishments, known as the institutional crisis. In the case of Britain, older citizens tend to be more religious than younger ones. Even if the younger group becomes more religious as they age, Halman and Riis caution that this may result in "unofficial religiosity growing in society while official religiosity

54. Halman and Riis, "Contemporary European Discourses," 10–11.

55. Brierley, *Christian England,* 51. "Church Community" refers to British people who are not practicing or attending Christian service yet they feel they live in the boundaries of the Christian community called the church.

declines."[56] The reality of religious differences among generations has been verified by a number of surveys in Europe. The younger generations, comprised of who have not experienced the World Wars, appear to have less exposure to religious instruction at home and school. At the same time, they came of age in a more secularized society than their parents and grandparents. The lack of a religious foundation among younger Europeans has consequences:

> And although even young generations show increasing levels of this kind of unofficial or personal religiosity when they get older, the starting level of their religiosity is so low that they will never reach the levels of religiosity of the older generations. In other words, even unofficial religiosity is on the wane at the macro level, but increases at the individual level as people get older. . . . The religious decline seems to begin with a lack of primary religious socialization and primary religious role-models. The replacement of generations thus implies that society gradually becomes less and less religious.[57]

An analysis of history demonstrates a correlation between the decline of traditional Christian beliefs and the spread of the Enlightenment and modernism. Jenkins summarizes the situation as follows:

> In contemplating this shift to traditionalism, a historical analogy comes to mind. In eighteenth-century Europe and America, secular Enlightenment ideas made enormous progress among social elites. Few traditional bastions of Christian belief escaped attack. The Trinity, the divinity of Christ, the existence of hell, all fell into disfavor, while critical Bible scholarship undermined the familiar bases of faith.[58]

In marked contrast to Europe, Christianity has been growing exceedingly fast in parts of the non-Western world, such as in Africa, Asia, and Latin America. The so-called "third-world church" has demonstrated, and continues to demonstrate, tremendous growth and vigorous faith over the same time period when Western European churches experienced dramatic declines.[59] In the year 2000, roughly

---

56. Halman and Riis, "Contemporary European Discourses," 11.

57. Ibid., 11.

58. Jenkins, *The Next Christendom*, 9–10.

59. Robinson concurs that the worldwide church, excluding the Western church, "has demonstrated astonishing life and vigour in precisely the same period that the Western church has suffered reversal and decline." Robinson and Smith, *Invading Secular Space*, 17.

32.3 percent of the world's population was comprised of nominal Christians (that is, those who call themselves Christians), 19.2 percent Muslims, 13.7 percent Hindus, and 5.7 percent Buddhists. The following graph shows how the major world faiths have expanded since 1920"[60]

GRAPH 2.2 COMPARATIVE GROWTH OF WORLD RELIGIONS, 1920–2000

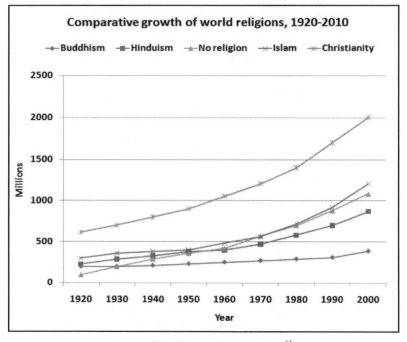

Source: "The Future of Christianity"[61]

David Barrett estimates that Muslims numbered more than one billion people, or 18 percent of the world's population in 1995 (figures for Islam include many who are simply nominal adherents). The third largest group, Hindus, numbered 777 million people, or 13 percent of the world's population. These three most common faiths account for three-fifths (59 percent) of the world's population. The following graphs show the numbers and trends of different faiths over the last century:

60. Muslims and Hindus have steadily increased their percentage of the world population, and Christianity and Buddhism show smaller percentages of adherents than in 1900. Unbelief has increased most of all. Taylor, "The Future of Christianity," 633–38.

61. Ibid., 633–637.

GRAPH 2.3 GLOBAL RELIGIOUS CHANGE, 1920–2010

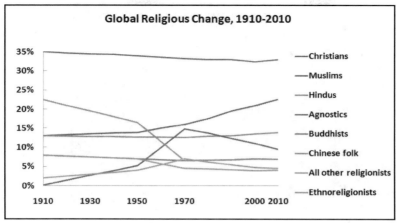

Source: *Atlas of Global Christianity*[62]

The number of Christians increased from 617 million in 1901 to 2.3 billion in 2010. The number of Muslims rose from 220 million in 1910 to 1.5 billion in 2010, and the Hindu population grew from 223 million in 1910 to 948 million in 2010.

GRAPH 2.4 RELIGIONS BY GLOBAL ADHERENTS, 1920 AND 2010

Religions by global adherents, 1910 and 2010						
	1910		**2010**		▪1910%	▪2010%
	Adherents	*%*	*Adherents*	*%*		
Christians	612,028,000	34.8	2,292,454,000	33.2		
Muslims	220,895,000	12.6	1,549,444,000	22.4		
Hindus	223,419,000	12.7	948,507,000	13.7		
Agnostics	3,367,000	0.2	639,852,000	9.3		
Buddhists	138,025,000	7.8	468,736,000	6.8		
Chinese folk	392,423,000	22.3	458,316,000	6.6		
Ethnoreligionists	135,181,000	7.7	261,429,000	3.8		
Atheists	243,000	0.0	138,532,000	2.0		
New Religionists	6,865,000	0.4	64,443,000	0.9		
Sikhs	3,232,000	0.2	24,591,000	0.4		
Jews	13,193,000	0.7	14,641,000	0.2		
Spiritists	324,000	0.0	13,978,000	0.2		
Daoists	437,000	0.0	9,017,000	0.1		
Baha'is	225,000	0.0	7,447,000	0.1		
Confucianists	760,000	0.0	6,461,000	0.1		
Jains	1,446,000	0.1	5,749,000	0.1		
Shintoists	7,613,000	0.4	2,782,000	0.0		
Zoroastrians	119,000	0.0	181,000	0.0		
Total population	1,759,797,000	100.0	6,906,560,000	100.0		

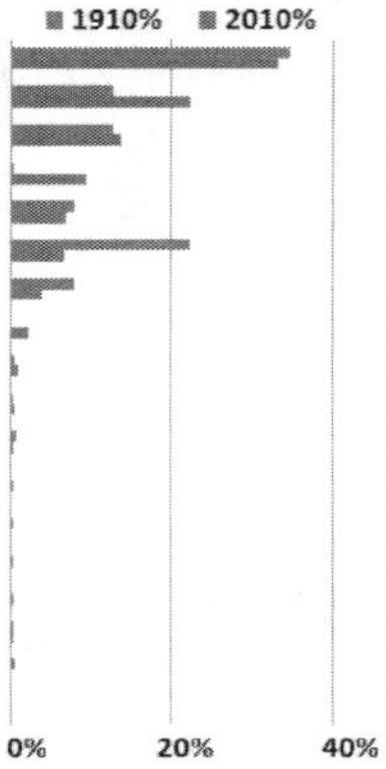

©Edinburgh University Press, 2009

Source: *Atlas of Global Christianity*[63]

62. Johnson and Ross, *Atlas of Global Christianity*, 6.
63. Ibid., 7.

GRAPH 2.5 GLOBAL RELIGION BY PROPORTION, 1920 AND 2010

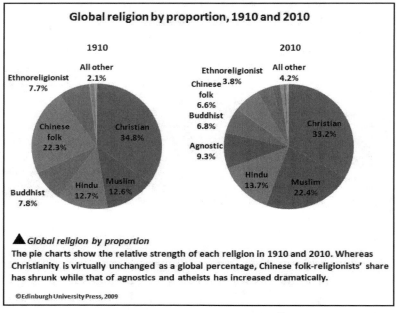

Global religion by proportion, 1910 and 2010

1910

Ethnoreligionist 7.7%
All other 2.1%
Chinese folk 22.3%
Christian 34.8%
Buddhist 7.8%
Hindu 12.7%
Muslim 12.6%

2010

Ethnoreligionist
Chinese folk 6.6%
Buddhist 6.8%
Agnostic 9.3%
All other 4.2%
Christian 33.2%
Hindu 13.7%
Muslim 22.4%
Chinese 3.8%

▲ *Global religion by proportion*
The pie charts show the relative strength of each religion in 1910 and 2010. Whereas Christianity is virtually unchanged as a global percentage, Chinese folk-religionists' share has shrunk while that of agnostics and atheists has increased dramatically.

©Edinburgh University Press, 2009

Source: *Atlas of Global Christianity*[64]

Christianity, Islam, and Hinduism are three major religions in the world today. But, as we know, the three groups are not distributed equally across the globe, but concentrated in certain geographical areas.[65] The following map shows the percentage of people in nations worldwide who adhere to various faiths:

64. Ibid., 6.
65. Brierley, *Future Church*, 31.

MAP 2.1 PERCENTAGE MAJORITY RELIGION BY PROVINCE, 2010

Religions by global adherents, 1910 and 2010						
	1910		**2010**		■ 1910%	■ 2010%
	Adherents	%	Adherents	%		
Christians	612,028,000	34.8	2,292,454,000	33.2		
Muslims	220,895,000	12.6	1,549,444,000	22.4		
Hindus	223,419,000	12.7	948,507,000	13.7		
Agnostics	3,367,000	0.2	639,852,000	9.3		
Buddhists	138,025,000	7.8	468,736,000	6.8		
Chinese folk	392,423,000	22.3	458,316,000	6.6		
Ethnoreligionists	135,181,000	7.7	261,429,000	3.8		
Atheists	243,000	0.0	138,532,000	2.0		
New Religionists	6,865,000	0.4	64,443,000	0.9		
Sikhs	3,232,000	0.2	24,591,000	0.4		
Jews	13,193,000	0.7	14,641,000	0.2		
Spiritists	324,000	0.0	13,978,000	0.2		
Daoists	437,000	0.0	9,017,000	0.1		
Baha'is	225,000	0.0	7,447,000	0.1		
Confucianists	760,000	0.0	6,461,000	0.1		
Jains	1,446,000	0.1	5,749,000	0.1		
Shintoists	7,613,000	0.4	2,782,000	0.0		
Zoroastrians	119,000	0.0	181,000	0.0		
Total population	1,759,797,000	100.0	6,906,560,000	100.0	0% 20% 40%	

©Edinburgh University Press, 2009

Source: *Atlas of Global Christianity*[66]

THE CRISIS OF CHURCH ATTENDANCE

If we look at church membership rates, we might suppose that the majority of Europeans are Christians, because these percentages are still high. Rates of church attendance and of following Christian practices, however, tell another story. Why this discrepancy?

1851 British Survey

Studying church attendance data will begin to give up a better idea of the religious practices of past centuries, and a number of church historians and sociologists of religion have attempted to do just that. Only fragmentary data is available from church rolls and records before 1851, both regionally and locally, with variations depending upon whether the church was an established, mainstream church or a smaller, newly formed body. The earliest available survey of church attendance is the Census of Religion in 1851, which used more reliable, scientific methods of polling. After analysis by contemporary scientists, the data shows that church attendance during this time of ranged between 40 to 60 percent of the entire British adult popula-

66. Johnson and Ross, *Atlas of Global Christianity*, 6–7.

tion.[67] Using this data, Robin Gill has determined that 56.9 percent of the population attended the Anglican Church and the Free Church, excluding Roman Catholics in Cumbria.[68]

Another obstacle to obtaining accurate church attendance figures is that fact that the same people attended church multiple times on any given Sunday. The 1851 census shows that the attendance rate in Scotland was 61 percent; in England and Wales, it was 58 percent of the adult population. Steve Bruce's analysis, which eliminates the double counting of multiple attendance, still shows that at least one-third of the population went to church on Sunday in 1851. In the same way if "double sitting" of the 1980s is considered among small evangelical denominations, the result would be "the same as the figure for attendees: in Scotland 17 per cent of the population, in Wales 13 percent, and in England 9 percent."[69]

Robin Gill has investigated Anglican Church attendance in fourteen adjacent parishes in north Northumberland as a case study, and his analysis confirms that Anglican Church attendance peaked in 1866 and declined thereafter.[70] He concludes that the overall decline has been in progress ever since the 1851 Census took place. Even dissenting denominations began to experience decline starting in the 1880s. Most church historians agree that church membership in Britain increased from 1800 until 1850. Steve Bruce's analysis on the decline of church membership in this time period indicates that "we could interpret that period of church membership growth as evidence that church adherence varies cyclically and hence that describing the overall pattern as one of decline is at worst mistaken and at best premature."[71] In this context, looking at the demise of church decline from the 1850s to today through the eyes

67. Bruce points out that the census in 1851 was derived from clergy estimates of how many people attended their churches on a particular Sunday. Bruce, *God Is Dead*, 63.

68. In the 1851 census, rural areas represent 44.5 percent, small towns 63.6 percent, and larger towns 63.7 percent for Church of England and Free Church attendance in Cumbria. Gill, *The Myth of the Empty Church*, 296.

69. "Double sitting" is when the same person is counted more than once for any given week's attendance record inflating the actual attendance number. For example, there were usually two Sunday services and a weekday service. Bruce, *Religion in the Modern World*, 30.

70. Gill, *The Myth of the Empty Church*, 35–38.

71. Bruce, *God Is Dead*, 67.

of the secularization process challenges scholars to overview the social, political, industrial, and urban factors and changes.

Changes in Attendance

Membership enrollment was not required for state churches, such as the Church of England and the Church of Scotland, during the eighteenth century. However, dissenting churches did require members to attain the status of "membership." It was common practice for state churches to minister to the entire population. They served the congregants by issuing baptismal, marriage, and burial certificates. Attendance was considered very important because it predicted an individual's likelihood of living out the practices of the faith. In contrast, Free Church members paid affiliation dues by attending the church of their choice during the late eighteenth and early nineteenth centuries.[72] The national churches no longer exercised strict control over their adherents. This trend became even more pronounced by the end of the twentieth century, when attending a church had become "a better index of attachment than membership. . . . [Most] churches gave membership very readily and were slow to revise rolls and hence many people remained nominal members while their active involvement withered."[73]

While church attendance in England and Wales was declining, attendance rates in America increased to 39 percent. American and British church attendance rates have been inversely correlated from 1851 onward. During the two World Wars, church attendance demonstrated radical cycles of increase and decrease. And, after the wars, the decline continued.[74] Callum Brown puts the peak point of British church attendance at 1904–1905. After this, British churches experienced a steady decline each decade between 1940 and 2000. The de-

---

72. In the British church system, prior to the Census of Religion, Free Church members paid affiliation dues that are different from religious taxation. The state church, the Church of England, could have collected tithe or religious tax as a tax duty collected from every citizen by the monarchy. The head of the church was the head of the Church of England. However, dissent or Free Churches, which did not have religious tax benefits from the monarchy, asked church members to pay tithe or their allegiance.

73. Bruce, *God Is Dead,* 67–68.

74. Gibbs and Coffey, *Church Next,* 17–18.

cade of steepest decline was the 1960s, and the year of steepest decline was 1963.[75]

GRAPH 2.6 ADULT CHURCH ATTENDANCE IN BRITAIN, 1851–1989

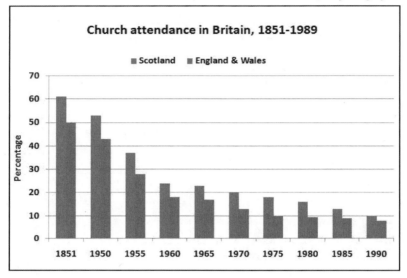

Source: "Secularisation: Now You See It, Now You Don't."[76]

Roman Catholic Mass attendance was not exceptional either, as it underwent a 28 percent decline over a ten-year period from 1851 to 1990. The Methodist rate of decline was similar at 26 percent. However, over the same period, under the same morally declining cultural conditions, Baptist churches grew by 2 percent, and new churches increased by an astonishing 38 percent. According to Brierley's analysis, churches in England describing themselves as evangelical have declined by a mere 3 percent, while Catholic churches have declined by 48 percent.[77]

75. Brown, *The Death of Christian Britain*, 7.

76. Hamilton, *Secularisation*, 28.

77. Croft, *Transforming Communities*, 24.

GRAPH 2.7 CHURCH ATTENDANCE IN BRITAIN, 1851–1989

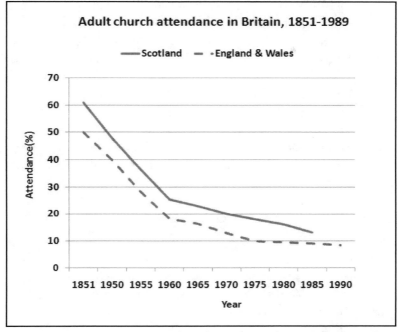

Adult church attendance in Britain, 1851-1989

Source: "Secularisation"[78]

Attendance and Membership

Historically, different church denominations have used different methods of measuring church attendance and enrollment. Bruce signifies this interpretation between attendance and membership;

> As far back as we have records, the Church of England and the Church of Scotland have had far more people on their rolls than have attended church. Nominal association is even greater for the Roman Catholic Church, which counts as Catholic anyone baptized as such. . . . Generally only the small and more sectarian Protestant churches have had more people in their congregations than on their books. According to a major 1984 census of the Scottish churches, only the small Baptist Church was attended by more people than claimed membership.[79]

78. Hamilton, *Secularisation*, 28.
79. Bruce, *Religion in the Modern World*, 29–30.

Recent surveys have shown that the Church of England is considered by the public to be the custodian of the nation's conscience and the last state church in Great Britain. But, in reality, only 3 percent of the British population regularly attends Anglican worship services.[80] Peter Brierley indicates that British church membership "has decreased from 7.5 million in 1980 to a projected total of 5.9 million by 2000, a decline of 21%." He also demonstrates, "only by 3% across a 20 year span in 1980 to 2000."[81] Bruce states the British church survey conducted by Peter Brierley in 1998 and indicated "7.5 percent of the adult population attended church. This represents a continuation of the trends previously found that the figures for his 1979 and 1989 censuses were respectively 12 and 10 percent."[82]

Sunday School

During the nineteenth and early twentieth centuries, even in the midst of a measurable decline in church attendance, many continued to have their children baptized and have them attend Sunday school or catechism classes. In this way, the majority of people identified themselves as adherents of one of the many Christian denominations. Consecrating marriages and paying tribute to deceased loved ones in the church was a common Christian practice, and the church was the primary authority of moral influence in society.[83] Above all, Christian education remained a powerful and influential enough tool to pass on the blessings of Christian faith from one generation to the next. The primary cause of religious blessings ceasing to flow in the twentieth century is the decline in Sunday school attendance. This is evident as contemporary European adults, who did not have enough church instruction during their own childhoods, are failing to bring foundational Christian values to their own homes as parents.

British children suffered as a result of missing Sunday school. However, in the public education system, where the voice of Christian education was already beginning to diminish, the 1944 Education Act instructed all students through high school to take part in daily prayer and collective worship, unless inhibited by their parents. Even though

---

80. Thomson, "Some Reflections," 375.
81. Brierley et al., *UK Christian Handbook*, 13.
82. Bruce, *God Is Dead*, 64.
83. McLeod, *Secularisation*, 7.

the emphasis on the uniqueness of salvation through Jesus was curtailed, it nevertheless provided some revival in the nation where there was dire need of Christian discipleship.[84]

Sunday Worship

During the eighteenth century, the majority of small village schools (and also a small number of public schools) were operated by parish clergy and required the elements of Christian education to be dominant in their curricula. As early as grammar school, pupils were encouraged to attain sound doctrine and good Christian character as the aim of both teachers and students.[85] Until the middle of the nineteenth century, most schools worked closely with their local churches, and, for that reason, many pupils and even their parents had to attend Sunday school in order to acquire a "secular" education. Whether schools were operated by voluntary societies or by churches, a considerable number of unchurched parents put their children in Sunday schools in order for them to learn the basics of Christian faith and to have access to education in general. Even during the early and mid-twentieth century, British pupils were accustomed to learning about the Christian faith daily. While it is not surprising that the elements of Christian education were minimized in public schools and many grammar schools, the fact that Christian education decreased dramatically in churches and Sunday schools during the second half of the twentieth century is cause for alarm. Attendance in Sunday school has dropped so dramatically that the youngest generations no longer have any Christian upbringing in their lives. Even in the public education arenas, people who are "wholly or mainly of a broadly Christian character" are no longer visible.[86] Instead, multifaith worship and education was implemented by the national 1988 Education Reform Act, which grouped the Christian God, the Muslims' Allah, the Hindu pantheon, and so on, all together into one cohort.[87] The fact that public schools are no longer solely Christian institutions, as during the nineteenth century, is not unique to England; it true in the United

---

84. Hull, "Can One Speak of God," 22–23.

85. Moorman, *A History,* 324–26.

86. Bruce, *God Is Dead,* 68–69.

87. Hull, "Can One Speak of God," 23–34.

States as well. Furthermore, the literary and scientific disciplines and institutions have been affected greatly by the secularization process.[88]

Now, fewer than 8 percent of the British population in 2000 say they attend Sunday worship on any given week, and less than a quarter of these are members of a church. Also, less than a tenth of all children go to a Sunday school, although membership numbers from churches account for twelve percent of population.[89] Brierley's findings indicate that church attendance in Britain has fallen from 10.9 percent of the adult population in 1980 to 8.2 percent by 2000.

TABLE 2.6 TOTAL ADULT ATTENDANCE IN GREAT BRITAIN, 1980–2000

Great Britain	1980	1985	1990	1995	2000
Total (millions)	4.77	4.51	4.38	3.98	3.79
% of Population	10.9%	10.1%	9.6%	8.7%	8.2%

Source: *UK Christian Handbook*[90]

The following table shows how this decline was experienced by different denominations. Catholic Church attendance plummeted more than 40 percent, from 1,601,400 in 1980 to 972,700 in 2000, in a mere twenty-year period. Attendance in the 1980s fell by 14 percent, and, in the 1990s, they fell further by 28 percent. The second largest denomination, the Church of England, saw attendance drop from 1,671,000 in 1979 to 980,000 in 1999—a fall of 24 percent in the 1980s and 23 percent in the 1990s. The United Reformed Church suffered a similar fate. Only smaller denominations, such as the Orthodox Church, grew from 10,000 to 25,000. Overall, attendance for these four churches over a period two decades fell from 3.9 million to 2.4 million members.

---

88. Russello, *Christianity and European Culture*, 28.

89 The attendance decline is even more pronounced, according to other statistics: "[A]s few as 3 per cent of people regularly attend church in some counties of England, and in most the non-churchgoers represent over 90 per cent of the population. Brown, *The Death of Christian Britain*, 3.

90. Brierley et al., *UK Christian Handbook*, 212.

TABLE 2.7 ADULT CHURCH ATTENDANCE IN ENGLAND, 1980–2000

England	1980	1985	1990	1995	2000
Anglican	968,000	920,900	917,600	854,000	831,800
Baptist	201,300	196,200	197,200	197,700	192,000
Catholic	1,601,400	1,424,200	1,346,400	1,100,800	972,700
Independent	164,200	176,500	179,700	184,900	190,000
Methodist	437,900	420,800	395,200	350,500	321,800
New churches	50,300	81,000	114,200	156,100	198,000
Orthodox	7,200	8,400	9,600	10,800	12,000
Pentecostal	147,200	152,400	164,700	171,900	179,000
United Reformed	139,000	121,400	104,100	97,900	91,500
Other Churches	97,700	81,400	83,000	75,700	73,000
Total	3,814,200	3,583,200	3,512,200	3,197,800	3,061,800
% of Adult	10.2%	9.3%	9.0%	8.1%	7.7%

Source: *UK Christian Handbook*[91]

While there were a few bright spots of growth, the overall trend is unmistakably downward. A 2010 BSA survey reveals 62 percent of the British never attend at religious service.[92] The decline of attendance has not taken place abruptly but gradually in most denominations through the mid-twentieth century onwards. Steve points out that "Methodist attendances fell dramatically: from 621,000 in 1979 to 379,700 attendances in 1999." The denominations experiencing growth were the Pentecostal and Baptist churches which have been growing slightly though their attendance is still in the minority of Protestant groups. Surprisingly, Bruce indicates, "the "new churches" grew over the same period from 64,000 to 230,000."[93] Though a few minority denominations saw increase the decline of the majority was so large that the growth of the minority denominations could not overturn the general decline.

91. Brierley et al., *UK Christian Handbook*, 212.
92. Voas and Ling, "Religion in Britain and the United States," 70.
93. Bruce, *God Is Dead*, 64.

Bruce goes on to state that for the first time in 1997, the Church of England attendance records signified that attendance dipped below one million for the first time since attendance records began in the mid nineteenth century.[94] In 1851 the population of Britain stood at 20 million with 60 percent of the population being Anglicans (approximately 12 million people). In comparison to Britain's 2011 population of 62.6 million it is astounding to see just one million Anglicans in attendance today.[95]

An examination of congregation sizes in England in the twenty-first century illustrates that the size of English churches are implausibly small in number. According to Steven Croft, churches that have 50 members or less account for 40 percent of British churches. Even when small churches were included, 64 percent of English churches have less than 100 members. If we up that threshold to 150 member churches, 75 percent of churches belong to this category. This means only 25 percent of churches have more than 150 members. In 1998, the median church membership in the Church of England was 60 and Methodist Church 61, respectively. He points out "44% of Anglican and 41% of Free Church churchgoers attend just 11% of the churches giving some indication of the importance of the larger churches to the denominations as a whole."[96]

As is in the case in Britain, young adults across Europe tend to be less involved in church practices and activities, with a growing number of them not having any church affiliation at all. According to data from the European Value Systems Study Group (EVSSG), a much higher number of practicing Catholics can be found than practicing Protestants. Dobbelaere states, "37 percent of Catholics and 9 percent of Protestants still went to church weekly. However, this does not mean that people who do not attend weekly have severed all ties with their church. Only one-third of the self-declared Protestants and a little more than one-fifth of the self-declared Catholics never go, whereas the others go occasionally."[97] The EVSSG figures reveal that

---

94. Ibid., 64–65.

95. This data is excerpt from United Kingdom Demographics Profile 2011. Date is conducted in July 2011. No pages. Indexmudi, "United Kingdom Demographics Profile 2011," line 1. Cf. Barrow, "What is the Population of Britain?," lines 24–28.

96. Croft, *Transforming Communities*, 52.

97. Dobbelaere, "Church Involvement and Secularisation," 20.

people between the ages of 18 and 35 represent about 20 percent of all non-church affiliation. In a similar pattern to that found in Britain, the older age groups had higher rates of church involvement throughout Europe. Ireland and Northern Ireland had the highest church attendance, and the Scandinavian countries checked in with the lowest rates. Dobbelaere comments that roughly 10 percent of people who came from Protestant regions, and from mixed regions of Protestants and Catholics, affirmed themselves as having no church connections whatsoever, whereas only 7 percent of those from Catholic regions claimed the same.[98]

TABLE 2.8 FREQUENCY OF CHURCH ATTENDANCE, 1990 (%)

	At least once a week	Once a month	Christmas, Easter, etc.	Once a year	Never
European Average	29	10	8	5	40
Catholic Countries					
Belgium	23	8	13	4	52
France	10	7	17	7	59
Ireland	81	7	6	1	5
Italy	40	13	23	4	19
Portugal	33	8	8	4	47
Spain	33	10	15	4	38
Mixed Countries					
Great Britain	13	10	12	8	56
West Germany	19	15	16	9	41
Netherlands	21	10	16	5	47
Lutheran Countries	Once a month or more				
Denmark	11				
Finland	—				
Iceland	9				
Norway	10				
Sweden	10				

98. Ibid., 21.

Source: What Europe Thinks[99]

Church attendance in Europe has dropped because European churches have undergone secularization in both their cultural and religious spheres.[100] In the chapters that follow, I will highlight the reasons behind this decline, especially secularization.

THE CRISIS OF CHURCH MEMBERSHIP

It will be helpful to begin with a definition of precisely what I mean by a "member" of a church or an organization. Briggs states that membership in any organization is characterized by "paying a subscription and very generally subscribing to its aims, without a daily commitment to fight for the issues with which the parent body is concerned."[101] When it comes to church membership, it is quite difficult to define what is meant by the similar and often overlapping terms "communicant," "affiliate," "baptized," or "registered." And, of course, membership should be distinguished from mere attendance. Based on my research, I will define a church member as one who has made a commitment to give financial contributions to one's church.[102]

Steve Bruce says, "With various adjustments to compensate for most differences within denominations, we can estimate the present proportion of the adult population of the United Kingdom which 'belongs' to the Christian churches as about 14 per cent, or 6.7 million people. Three-quarters of these are members of just three denominations: the Church of England, the Church of Scotland, and the Catholic Church."[103] Further, "Most people in Britain do not have any church affiliation or connection, no longer subscribe to the core beliefs of the religion that shaped their culture, and are rather suspicious of those who take religion 'too seriously' and who claimed to have 'got God'. Nonetheless, most people like the idea of religion and are quick and

---

99. Ashford and Timms, *What Europe Thinks*, 46, and Davie, "Europe: The Exception that Proves the Rule?" 69.

100. Ostwalt, *Secular Steeples*, 50.

101. Briggs, "Beyond Membership," 1.

102. For example, Anglican members are accounted based on electoral enrollment, but most other denominations count only those who have been baptized. Davie, *Religion in Britain*, 45–47.

103. Bruce, *Religion in Modern Britain*, 35.

open to have some religion taught to their children (though not keen enough to send them to Sunday school).[104]

GRAPH 2.8 CHRISTIAN CHURCH MEMBERSHIP, BRITAIN, 1900–1990

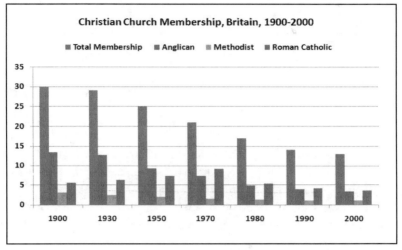

Sources: *Vision Building, UK Christian Handbook*[105]

Membership Survey

Brierley's research shows that the British Christian population grew slightly from the 1900s until the 1930s, when the nation's population grew slightly faster than church membership. Thus, there had been real Christian growth for four straight decades. This trend ceased in the 1940s, when there was no membership growth. Net church membership then declined beginning in the 1950s. Church membership never completely recovered from this dramatic fall, especially after the losses incurred in the 1960s. The reasons for the precipitous fall during this particular decade will be explained in detail in later chapters.

104. Ibid., 54.

105. Brierley, *Vision Building,* 49; Brierley et al., *UK Christian Handbook,* 28.

TABLE 2.9 CHURCH MEMBERSHIP IN BRITAIN, 1900–2000

Year	Members (000)	Population (000)	Members (as % of Population)
1900	8,664	32,237	27
1920	9,803	44,027	22
1940	10,017	47,769	21
1960	9,918	52,709	19
1980	7,529	56,353	13
2000	5,862	59,122	10

Source: *UK Christian Handbook*[106]

While a decline in membership seems to have affected all religious organizations in the UK, institutional Christian churches have suffered the largest decline while many non-Christian and smaller religions have seen an increase of members. Statistics from Brierley, combined with observations of institutional churches, Free Churches, non-Trinitarian churches, major non-Christian religions, and new religious movements, together show that religious membership fell from 8,646,464 to 8,172,993 between 1980 and 1995 in the UK. This is a drop of 473,471 or approximately 5.5 percent.[107]

TABLE 2.10 TOTAL UK CHURCH MEMBERS

Denomination	1970	1980	1990E	2000E
Anglican	2,548,000	2,154,000	1,824,000	1,551,000
Methodist	694,000	558,000	509,000	482,000
Baptist	295,000	240,000	244,000	255,000
Presbyterian	1,807,000	1,509,000	1,288,000	1,135,000
Other Churches	532,000	534,000	652,000	783,000
Catholic	2,715,000	2,343,000	1,949,000	1,657,000
Orthodox	193,000	209,000	232,000	252,000
Total	8,784,000	7,546,000	6,699,000	6,114,000
`Percentage	21%	17%	14%	13%

E=Estimated

Sources: *Vision Building, UK Christian Handbook*[108]

106. Brierley et al., *UK Christian Handbook* 1998/1999, 2.12, 4.10.2.
107. Lee, "Religion," 477–78.
108. Brierley, *Vision Building*, 49; Brierley et al., *UK Christian Handbook*, 2.8,

The table above shows that both the Anglican and Roman Catholic churches lost one million members between 1970 and 2000. This largely accounts for the rapid decrease in total British church membership from 8.8 million in 1970 to 6.1 million in 2000. The Methodist Church and other major historical denominations have also declined. In contrast, independent churches, including Pentecostal/charismatic churches and newer, smaller evangelical churches, have all grown in attendance and membership. However, their overall growth in numbers never made up for the decrease in involvement in the mainline churches. These newer, vibrant, and growing churches include African and West Indian churches, the independent churches of the House Church Movement, and other immigrant churches.[109] The United Reformed Church (URC) denomination declined so greatly that, in 1972, it merged with the Presbyterian Church of England and the majority of congregations in the Congregational Union of England and Wales. At the time of the merger, the URC had lost almost half of its membership.[110] British church attendance from 1970 to 2000 fell from 12 to 7.5 percent of the population. Sadly, this decline is the religious reality of the contemporary Western world.[111]

In the case of Scotland, the church has demonstrated a general decline. This includes most conservative and liberal Presbyterian congregations. The more liberal United Free Church shrank to less than half of its original size between 1956 and 1986. Furthermore, Bruce points out that the membership of the mainline Church of Scotland fell by 36 percent, and that the churches managing to maintain their membership were the two most conservative Presbyterian denominations: the Free Church and the Free Presbyterian Church. However, the stability of membership rates in these churches is attributed to a population shift of the Highlands and the Islands.[112]

From my personal observations of British churches, I have seen that most British people still express religious sentiments, but do so by staying away from places of worship. One will find a handful of gray-

---

2.10. *The author combined statistics from several sources. Therefore, the statistical numbers may be different from the original citation of the references.

109. Brierley, *Vision Building,* 49–50.

110. Brierley, *Christian England,* 43.

111. Bruce, *God Is Dead,* 64.

112. Bruce, *Religion in the Modern World,* 86–87.

haired citizens attending uninspiring liturgical worship services in most of the mainline churches I have visited, and, in Roman Catholic masses, disciples are silent regarding their faith, even dozing off during the program.

Overall Decline

While this is happening, every day throughout society, unchurched non-Christians live their lives without guidance on life's larger questions of meaning and purpose, like sheep without a shepherd. The small percentage of people who do attend church are disproportionately elderly, female, and conservative in their backgrounds and voting habits.[113] Many British citizens turn to the church during times of crisis.[114] However, other faiths, such as Islam, have been growing rapidly in popularity.[115] It is now accurate to say that there are more practicing Muslims than practicing Methodists in Europe. Many British and other Europeans are now attracted to Islam, the New Age movement, Native American spirituality, Druidism, Hinduism, Sikhism, and paganism.[116] Muslim and Hindu immigrant families, and perhaps Buddhists as well, tend to have higher than average birth rates. This fuels the growth of these faiths internally, while they also add to their numbers from the many citizens who have no prior church background or allegiance.[117]

It is alarming to see that statisticians now routinely predict the disappearance of churches. Major denominations from the Roman Catholic Church to the Church of Scotland struggle to recruit new clergy. Britain's leading church statistician, Peter Brierley, has warned that declining popular support will cause some denominations to completely disappear in this century. The Church of Scotland in 1997 even put a date on its own demise caused by membership loss—the year 2033.[118] If this rate of decline continues, many churches will pass a point of no return, unable to reproduce and maintain their build-

---

113. Davie, *Religion in Britain*, 2.

114. For example church plays a role at the three major life events of "hatching, matching and dispatching," i.e., birth, marriage and death. See Townroe, *Sociology*, 156–59.

115. Thomson, "Some Reflections," 375.

116. Coffey, *Church Next*, 22–23.

117. Ibid., 23.

118. Brown, *The Death of Christian Britain*, 4–5.

ings, clergy, and organizations for future generations. Steve Bruce paints the following bleak picture:

> The Church of England will by then be reduced to a trivial vol-untary association with a large portfolio of heritage property. Regular churchgoers will be too few to show up in representa-tive national survey samples. Perhaps then the critics of the secularization paradigm will recognize that, however convinc-ing our explanations of decline, decline is not a sociological myth.[119]

The statistics from Britain, and partially from Europe, needs proper interpretation behind the numbers. More than the number of the decline, we assume that religious decline may have not occurred accidentally but steadily with numerous social, individual and histori-cal interrelationships.

CONCLUSION: ARE WE HEADED FOR A POST-CHRISTIAN ERA?

Through a complex, interlocking chain of causal factors, state churches in Europe clearly have lost the privileged position that they enjoyed in the past. Secularization in Europe is rising as evangelical zeal grows colder and colder. The declines in membership and attendance cause much grief to the body of Christ.[120]

In the past, whenever the churches in Britain were in decline, there were a number of revivals, great awakenings, and new church move-ments that reinvigorated the Christian faith. This held true until the early twentieth century. After the World Wars, however, Christianity in Britain and Europe seems to have never fully recovered, but has continued to decline.

We can view these warning signs as either negative or positive, depending upon how we diagnose the present sickness of today's British and European churches. The next task should be to examine what Christians can do now to reach out to the present generation, and to prepare the way for possible near-future revivals.

119. Bruce, *God Is Dead,* 73–74.

120. Runia sees this trend stemming from the schism between the eastern and Western churches and from the Reformation, which produced many denominations. On the other hand, secularization has blurred denominational boundaries. Runia, "The Decline of Faith?" 198–217.

3

What Is European Christianity?

A PROPER UNDERSTANDING OF the origins of Christian traditions—
including Christmas, Easter, lent, mass, priestly vestments, and
the sacraments—is needed to understand the nature of the church and
the history of Christianity. And history tells us that pagan rites and the
Christian feasts and calendar have been blended since the inception
of Christendom, corrupting the church. Lewis asserts, "The prevailing
tendency to religious syncretism in the Roman empire paved the way
for corrupting Christianity by union with the State."[1] To identify the
essential elements of the church from its very beginnings, we will re-
visit the accumulated scholarship of the past centuries to see how the
church was born in Jerusalem, clothed with Hellenism, institutionalized in Rome, and lived out as a culture in Europe. The Christianity
that remains in Europe flows out of more than two millennia of history, including the construction of magnificent cathedrals and the
establishment of church hierarchy and a caesaropapist system. As we
now see European Christianity in decline, we must ask whether the
foundation of European Christian civilization is in fact biblical and
authentic, and what this means for Christianity in Europe today.

FORMATION OF CHRISTENDOM

Anton Wessels's shocking work, *Europe: Was It Ever Really Christian?*,
challenges the notion that Europe was properly evangelized during
the last two millennia, concluding that Europe needs to be evangelized for the first time, not re-evangelized.[2] A century ago, Hilaire

1. Lewis, *Paganism Surviving*, 91.

2. Wessels insists that the first Christianization of Western Europe around AD
750 was still an ongoing process as Christian churches struggled against pagan

Belloc asseverated Christian dominance in Europe by saying, "Europe is the faith and the faith is Europe."[3] "Europe has been nurtured by Christianity and must continue to be shaped by Christianity," affirms Duncan Forrester in quoting the declaration of Belloc: "Europe must return to the faith or she will perish."[4]

Was Europe ever truly Christianized? The official recognition of Christianity by Emperor Constantine marked the starting point of institutionalized Christianity in the early fourth century, which resulted in a massive sweep of conversions throughout the Roman Empire during the mid-fourth century. Prior to this, Christianity was accessible in some parts of the Roman Empire due to the presence of wealthy Roman Christians or upper-class patrons who gave their support. Roman social and political institutions in place at this time had evolved over a long period within the existing secular culture.[5]

The debate continues over which specific type of Christianity was implemented in Europe. It took considerable time over many centuries to reach the Barbarian European territories and kingdoms. Furthermore, the official, state-recognized Christianity that had gained supremacy developed into a massive sociopolitical institution over the centuries.

Christendom between Judaism and Paganism

The Christian church was born in Jerusalem, but institutionalized in Rome, placing it at the nexus of two incongruous cultures, Hellenism and Judaism, and within the irreconcilable religions of polytheism versus monotheism.[6] Roman authorities perceived early Christianity as a rebellious Jewish sect.[7] And, certainly, Christianity had grown out of Judaism.[8] But in the surrounding culture, cults, polytheism, Roman

---

superstition while northern Europe had not been reached until this time. Wessels, *Europe*, 1–16.

3. Belloc, *Europe and the Faith*, 2.

4. Forrester, "Christianity in Europe," 40.

5. Markus, "From Rome to the Barbarian Kingdoms," 62–63.

6. The recognition of Christianity by Constantine did not mean persecution ended, but it led the church to face paganism, which was "no more than a spongy mass of tolerance and tradition." MacMullen, *Christianity and Paganism*, 2.

7. Wilken, *The Christians as the Romans Saw Them*, 119.

8. Lyon, "Judaism and Christianity," 367.

pagan temples, Greek Platonism, and Manicheism were prevalent in the early fourth century. Above all, Caesar worship was practiced throughout the empire.[9] Jackson Shirley Case states, "one must admit that in childhood it [Christianity] was rocked in a Jewish cradle and that it grew to maturity in a gentile home. Its Jewish connections no one will dispute, but we must also remember that at an early date it was transferred to gentile lands."[10] Though the elements of paganism existed long before Christianity, the term *pagan* was coined by the emperor Theodosius I to distinguish Christians from non-Christians.[11]

During the earliest days of the church, the surrounding religious and cultural environment had profound effects as Christianity established its foundations. The effects of Greek culture were felt in many ways: "the process of 'Hellenization' is mysterious and obscure, not easily defined or demonstrated."[12] Taking a closer look at Greek beliefs of the time will help us understand how Christianity and Hellenism became intertwined.[13] One example is the cult of the Phrygian mother goddess, Cybele, and her consort, Attis, during the sixth and fourth century BC, respectively. According to Case in 204 BC, Romans began to honor and worship Cybele, giving her credit for saving the city from Carthaginian invaders. In the middle of the first century, Case states, with imperial patronage, an annual festival was established for the Cybele/Attis cult "in which the death of Attis, mourning for the dead god, and rejoicing at his resurrection constituted the prominent features of the ceremony."[14] Equivalent cults also sprung up elsewhere around the Mediterranean. The "Syrian Adonis was a prominent rival of Attis, and fostered almost identically the same type of religious belief and practice." The relation of Adonis became matrimonial to Aphrodite. Their story picks up the theme of "the death of the god, the mourning of the goddess, and Adonis' restoration to life,"[15] which bears an unmistakable resemblance to the story of the life, death, and resurrection of Jesus. When Paul preached in Syria and Cilicia, "the Adonis religion was

---

9. Wand, *A History of the Early Church*, 137.

10. Case, "Christianity and the Mystery Religions," 6.

11. Brown, "Constantine Invented Christianity," 9.

12. Gruen, *Heritage and Hellenism*, xiv.

13. Castleman, "Golgotha, Athens, and Jerusalem," 47.

14. Case, "Christianity and the Mystery Religions," 11.

15. Ibid., 12.

still thriving, its two chief centers of worship being Byblos in Syria and Paphos in Cyprus."[16] The Isis/Osiris/Serapis cults in Egypt expressed similar themes. Case says, "Isis and Osiris are familiar figures in the religion of ancient Egypt, and their relation to one another is similar to that of Cybele and Attis, or Aphrodite and Adonis."[17]

The church fathers after the apostolic age were well aware of the dangers of syncretism and tried to eradicate polytheism. However, believers were confronted during their daily lives with a variety of pagan religious practices. Tcherikover points out, "The Greeks were prepared to accept God of Israel into their Pantheon, but here they were faced with a riddle. The gods of Greece could easily compromise with the God of Israel, but He could not compromise with them."[18] He continues, "The Greeks neither knew, nor could they know, the peculiar character of the Jewish faith, the faith in one, unique God, Creator of the heavens and earth. . . . The Jews neither could nor did surrender this belief, for their entire national culture was based on it."[19]

In addition to aspects of polytheistic mystery religions, Greco-Roman philisophy became intermingled with Christian theology as church systems were being established.[20] Castleman points out, "the Church was able to accommodate the insights of philosophy into its own spiritual vision while rejecting the pantheons of gods in favour of its own monotheistic *theōria*. Moreover, Greco-Roman philosophy tended to reject the mythological gods and was therefore an unexpected ally."[21] Jewish communities were widespread throughout the Roman Empire with a diaspora network of merchants, traders, and synagogues. Emerton illustrates, "Jews had gone as merchants and men of science out from the narrow conditions of their little province into the larger horizons of the Hellenic culture. More spiritual in its original form than any other of the religions of the ancient

16. Ibid., 12.

17. "The name of Serapis, which displaces, or rather absorbs, that of Osiris, was introduced by Ptolemy I late in the third century B.C. when he virtually made this cult the official religion of Hellenistic Egypt. The genealogy of Serapis is very obscure, yet the cult of Isis-Serapis is essentially identical with that of the earlier Isis-Osiris, and the names of Osiris and Serapis are perpetuated side by side." Case, "Christianity and the Mystery Religions," 13.

18. Tcherikover, *Hellenistic Civilization and the Jews*, 374–75.

19. Ibid., 375.

20. Burckhardt, *The Age of Constantine the Great*, 136.

21. Castleman, "Golgotha, Athens, and Jerusalem," 71.

world, it lent itself more readily to purely speculative treatment."[22] In the context of dynamic reciprocal interaction between Judaism and Hellenism, Christianity entered into Roman Empire "as another type of a secondary oriental cult" with a salvific message.[23]

Before Christianity was recognized, there was no ecclesiastic institution, nor were church leaders willing to speak out in the midst of severe persecutions. When dissensions or arguments occurred in the New Testament church, they solved their differences without involving outside entities (Acts 15:1–29). The first systematic defense of authentic Christian faith was made by the Apostles to the Jerusalem Council (Acts 15), setting the stage for the coexistence of Jewish and Gentile Christians in their different cultural settings.

When Christianity was officially recognized by the Roman Empire, biblical feasts and early church practices such as Sabbath observance were adapted into the Roman system while Gentile customs, festivals, myths, and non-Christian religious elements began to infiltrate Christianity. Greco-Roman gods and goddesses, myths, cults, Roman imperial rituals, polytheistic holidays, and mystery religions were adapted to Christian theology, taking the forms of saint veneration, Mariology, Hellenistic Christian philosophy, rituals, feasts, and clerical hierarchy. Wand finds that "these cults were strong rivals of the Church on the institutional side. In their easy tolerance they were quite unlike Christianity, but they resembled it closely in so far as they were both individualist and universalist."[24] Most scholars agree that Christianity became blended and syncretized with elements from the Roman religious world.

One example of how Christianity adopted Greek philosophical concepts is the use of the word *Logos*.[25] Philo, a Hellenized Jew in

---

22. Emerton, "The Religious Environment of Early Christianity," 188–9. "The outcome was twofold: first a new religion, Christianity, as another type of a secondary oriental cult entering at once into competition and co-operation with the rest in the spiritualizing of religious thought and second, a new philosophy, which was to prove one of the most effective agencies in bringing men to a realization of the Christian message."

23. Ibid., 188.

24. Wand, *The Early Church*, 38.

25. Philo insists, "the Logos is an ambassador and suppliant, neither unbegotten nor begotten as are sensible things. . . . One of the roles of the logos . . . was that of God's architect, who put God's creative power into action in the material world." Freeman, *A.D. 381*, 61.

Alexandria, was a contemporary of Jesus and Paul. (He was twenty years older than Jesus, though there is no evidence that they knew one another.)[26] Emerton points to

> a system of thought which in place of the multitudinous deities
> of the ancient world put one single mediatory idea, the idea of
> the *Logos*, the utterance of God, the expression of divinity that
> was itself divine. It was an evolution eminently in harmony with
> the best traditions of Hebrew thought. It helped to retain the
> primary idea of the indivisibility of the divine being, while at the
> same time it mediated between the abstractness and remoteness
> of this absolute deity and the limitations of the human mind.[27]

Another case of interpretation of *Logos* is "law," developed by Heraklitus.[28] Nash points out that, even before Alexandrian Judaism was formed, "The Stoic distinction between λόγος ἐνδιάθετος (the word within the breast) and λόγος προφορικόσ (the word that goes forth from the breast) was merely a single detail of their system." Furthermore, the Apostle Paul's epistles attributed to keep intact the influence of Hellenistic thought and cultural modification.[29]

Emerton admires Philo for finding a way that lessened the array of Greek images of the divine, but "still left room for manifold encroachments upon the principle of unity." The concept of *Logos* incorporated the Hebrew idea of a single deity as well as Hellenic philosophical metaphors:

> The *Logos*, at once a divine reality and a result of human specula-
> tion, offered a way out of the ancient entanglements. Without any
> machinery of gods or demigods, this one sufficient Revealer of
> the divine plan was to enter vitally into every attempt to make
> Christianity acceptable to a polytheistically minded world.... The
> two lines of effort are only so many illustrations of that universal
> tendency towards a spiritualizing and rationalizing of religious
> conceptions which we are trying to make plain.[30]

The *Logos* described by Philo is God who rejects anthropomorphism on the one hand, but is also remote, "only condescending to

---

26. Philo visited Rome twenty years after the crucifixion of Jesus. Adeney, "New Testament Theology to Jewish Alexandrian Thought," 41.

27. Emerton, "The Religious Environment of Early Christianity," 189.

28. Nash, "The Idea of the Logos," 171.

29. Adeney, "The Relation of New Testament Theology," 43.

30. Emerton, "The Religious Environment of Early Christianity," 189.

reach out to the world through intermediate agencies—angels, powers, [*logoi*]—Jesus brings the idea of God down from the heavens, telling how he observes the fall of a sparrow and cares for the smallest things in his children's lives."[31]

Many early church fathers were deeply familiar with Greek philosophy and used it to express theological concepts; most prominent among them were Clement and Origen.[32] For Clement of Alexandria, "philosophy was provided to the Greeks by God as a preparation for the Christian Revelation in the same way that Judaism prepared the Jews for the Incarnation of the Word."[33] Clement claims,

> The Greek preparatory culture, therefore, with philosophy itself, is shown to have come down from God to men, not with a definite direction but in the way in which showers fall down on the good land, and on the dunghill, and on the houses. And similarly both the grass and the wheat sprout; and the figs and any other reckless trees grow on sepulchres. And things that grow, appear as a type of truths. For they enjoy the same influence of the rain. But they have not the same grace as those which spring up in rich soil, inasmuch as they are withered or plucked up. [34]

Other early church fathers such as Theophilus, Origen, Tertullian, and Justin Martyr rejected pagans gods as "idols . . . the works of men's hands and unclean demons." They cautioned that idols could align with "the intent of the fallen angels."[35] According to Castleman, Tertullian's view was that "The gods, it is claimed, simply do not exist but the worship offered them is perpetuated and diverted by the fallen angels and their demonic progeny away from God and towards themselves."[36]

Justin Martyr was one of the most influential at using Greek philosophical arguments to explain Christian theology in an intellectual

---

31. Adeney, "The Relation of New Testament Theology," 43.

32. Origen used his theology in a Platonic framework, while Clement taught at his school in Alexandria that "Jesus is the logos, the Word, incarnate," according to the Gospel of John. Freeman, *A.D. 381*, 35.

33. Castleman, "Golgotha, Athens, and Jerusalem," 74.

34. Clement of Alexandria, *The Stromata*, 1.7.

35. Castleman, "Golgotha, Athens, and Jerusalem," 70.

36. Ibid., 70–71. In Greek Castlemen explains "they are idols εἴδωλα), 'the works of men's hands and unclean demons (ἐργαχειρῶν ἀνθρῶπων και δαιμόνια ἀκάθαρτα).'"

way. Justin used *Logos* to show that Greek philosophy was "naturalized in Christian circles by the Prologue of the Fourth Gospel."[37] His work was "partly Biblical and partly apologetic,"[38] using Greek philosophy as a means of explaining the divinity of Jesus. Richardson states,

> The *Logos* being divine, and yet not the Father himself, accounts both for the divinity which Christians have found in Jesus, and by retrospect for the divine appearances in the Old Testament. The Reason [*Logos*] incarnate in Christ is also the diffused reason that speaks in every man (Justin is not deeply interested in the cosmic action of the *Logos*).[39]

Justin also states "what kind of being the prophetic Spirit is, in view of the fact that the *Logos* is also a Spirit, and the Spirit speaks through the prophets the Word of God."[40] Justin also believed that those who lived by reason could be credited with Christian faith: "He is the Word (Λόγος) of whom every race of men were partakers; and those who lived reasonably are Christians, even though they have been thought atheists; as, among the Greeks, Socrates and Heraclitus, and men like them. . . ."[41] For Justin, "while Plato and other Greek philosophers had not known Jesus, they had lived *kata logon*—'in accordance with the *logos*,' and were thereby, in some sense, 'Christians.'"[42] Identifying the *logos* with Jesus has been attempted not just by the early church fathers, but by modern scholars as well, and this connec-

37. Richardson, *Early Christian Fathers*, 161.

38. Richardson says, "The chief thing to remember about the word "logos" is that it means everything except a single word—speech, design, argument, reason—therefore God's thought, plan, utterance, and so on." Ibid., 161.

39. Ibid., 161–62.

40. Richardson explains, "Nor again does Justin bother to state precisely how the Spirit and the Logos are distinguished from the lesser angelic powers, who follow the Son (pre-eminently God's Angel), and who in one passage are named between him and the prophetic Spirit. Certainly Justin knows that God is the only Fashioner of the universe, who made it out of formless matter. But he seems to have no interest in where that came from. Perhaps he could conceive of nothing more nonexistent . . . Justin repeatedly refers to Christ as an Angel. . . . They [Justin and Trypho] just strongly disagreed over whether Jesus, who was disgracefully crucified, and who was called God by the Christians, could be that Angel. Clearly the assumptions which Justin and Trypho held in common (assumptions consistent with what is known of Jewish thought at this time) were of exceptional significance." Ibid., 226.

41. Justin Martyr, *First Apology of Justin*, ch. 46, lines 3–4.

42. Wright, "The Christian and Other Religions," 13.

tion led progressively to the church's adoption of Greek philosophy, and stoicism in particular.[43] Many such as Eusebius believed that *logos* is "the connecting link uniting God and Man."[44]

During the first century, Christianity achieved a synthesis of Jewish monotheism and Greco-Roman polytheism in its pluralistic cultural, philosophical and religious environment. Castleman finds that "Christianity was, for the most part, able to assimilate elements of Jewish and Gentile cultures valuable to itself without compromising its own structural and symbolic integrity."[45] Still, the church's cultural vocabulary was Greco-Roman until the fourth century. Even after Constantine, a Roman deity was identified with the Christian God.[46] Constantine was indentified as well as a Roman god "Sol Invictus, the Unconquered sun."[47] In AD 363, Themistius, a Roman imperial court orator, described the emperor Theodosius as the "true son of Zeus, raised up by Zeus, and sharing with Zeus his array of titles."[48]

Durant finds that "Christianity did not destroy paganism; it adopted it. The Greek mind, dying, came to a transmigrated life in the theology and the liturgy of the Church . . . the Greek mysteries passed down into the impressive mystery of the Mass. Other pagan cultures contributed to the syncretist result. . . . Christianity was the last great creation of the ancient pagan world."[49] Challenged to develop a new language of theology, dogma, and an ecclesiastical system, the church sought to maintain the assertion of salvation through Jesus Christ alone, but was also "able to correct and incorporate into itself the intellectual life of the Greco-Roman civilization and reconnect it to a revealed religious tradition."[50] In so doing, the church "would provide the Empire with the spiritual cohesion that it had lost. At the same time, Christianity was able to acknowledge its Jewish heritage without being bound by it and becoming simply another of the many Jewish

43. Lyon, "Judaism and Christianity," 370.

44. Baker, *Constantine The Great*, 304.

45. Castleman, "Golgotha, Athens, and Jerusalem," 78.

46. Freeman, *A.D. 381*, 46–47.

47. Roman emperors were labeled gods, with approval of the senate. Freeman indicates that the title of divus ("deified") was used as late as the sixth century. Ibid., 46–47. See also MacMullen, *Christianity and Paganism*, 35.

48. Freeman, *A.D. 381*, 12.

49. Durant, *Caesar and Christ*, 595.

50. Castleman, "Golgotha, Athens, and Jerusalem," 78.

sects."[51] While retaining its authentic salvific message, the church also assimilated rituals, feasts, and annual celebrations from Jewish and Greco-Roman religious traditions.

The Formation of Christendom

In considering Europe as a whole, Davie finds three foundational worldviews: Judeo-Christian monotheism, Greek rationalism, and Roman organization. In other words, Judeo-Christian monotheism merged with Greco-Roman civilization. The combined influence of these three worldviews shaped the history of the church in Europe, as well as playing a major part in forming "a way of life that we have come to recognize as European."[52] Thus, the history of Europe is inseparably intertwined with Christian history. European civilization and society have been imbued with Christian beliefs, ethics, values, and norms over many centuries. The legacy and heritage of European Christianity are "often considered the foundation of a common European identity uniting all European countries and their citizens."[53] The many denominations corresponding to regional, ethnic, cultural, and national identities tie back to a common Christian identity, offering an overarching connection among all European nations.

Emperor Constantine, who is "One of the most significant figures of early Church history remains shrouded in mystery. . . . [H]e ended the imperial persecutions of the Church and unified the declining Roman Empire."[54] In the 300s, with Constantine's conversion of Christianity, the civil state and the church became intermarried. Popescu concludes, "a religion which had been persecuted and considered a dangerous sect became *licita* [lawful] and was integrated into the life of the empire."[55] Sadly, this union had unintended negative consequences for generations to come.[56] Popescu concludes that the church of Rome was

> a false church that corrupted Biblical truth by its assimilation of paganism. Throughout the centuries, more and more unbiblical traditions, doctrines, rituals, etc. have been added.

51. Ibid., 78.

52. Davie, "Europe: The Exception that Proves the Rule?," 65–66.

53. Halman and Riis, "Contemporary European Discourses," 1.

54. Emperor Constantine's full name was Flavius Valerius Constantinus.

55. Popescu, "Constantine the Great," 86.

56. Baker, *Constantine The Great*, vii.

> Wherever the Church of Rome has spread, it has allowed the absorption of native pagan beliefs and practices, rather than teach pure Biblical truth and separation from paganism.[57]

In AD 312, Constantine defeated Maxentius at the battle of Milvian Bridge, and in AD 313 the Edict of Milan was declared.[58] Constantine ruled the western empire while co-emperor Licinius, his rival and brother-in-law, reigned in the East. The two met in Milan to discuss religious toleration.[59] The Edict of Milan has been called the "Magna Charta of religious liberty," signifying the equal status of Christianity and pagan religions. Imperial decree allowed Christians to worship without persecution: "With happy auspices . . . we decided to establish rules by which respect and reverence for the deity would be secured, to give the Christians and all others liberty to follow whatever worship they choose, so that whatsoever divine and heavenly powers exist might be enabled to show favour to us and to all who live under our authority."[60] Political and humanitarian benevolence also resulted from the edict. Constantine forbade theatrical performances, particularly gladiatorial combat, because for the first time they were perceived these activities as cruel, licentious, and idolatrous.[61] Constantine even regarded himself as the "thirteenth apostle" and the "bishop of bishops."[62]

The Edict of Milan heralded the beginning of the Catholic Church. Flick concludes that the edict gave the church "opportunity for public organization, thus paving the way for the Catholic hierarchy already begun."[63] The crown became a religious guardian instead of a persecutor of the church. Christians were free to worship, laws against Christians were repealed, Christian clergy members were "exempted from municipal and military duties (a privilege already granted to pagan priests and

---

57. Ibid., 2.

58. Freeman, *A.D. 381*, 38.

59. They met in 313 near Mediolnurn (modern day, Milan) to celebrate the marriage of Constantine's younger half-sister Constantia with Licinius. Constantine triumphed over Licinius in 323. Two years later, Nicene Council was held. Johnson, "Constantine the Great," 163.

60. Popescu, "Constantine the Great," 86.

61. McGiffert notes that most gladiators were from barbarian captives. "The Influence of Christianity," 33.

62. Brown, "Constantine Invented Christianity," 9.

63. Quoted in Willems, "Constantine and Christianity," 6–7.

Jewish rabbis), and Christian slaves were emancipated."[64] Additionally, "by 323 the pagan symbols of Jupiter, Apollo, Mars, and Hercules had disappeared from imperial coins. It is interesting to note that most of Constantine's decrees before A.D. 323 seem to be aimed at maintaining equality and toleration for Christianity."[65]

Constantine proceeded to integrate the religious and cultural spheres of the Roman Empire—a phenomenon never seen in Jewish tradition or the New Testament Church. The church was fully supported by the state and was faithful to the state. Constantine gained political support from the church and, in return, the church became a recipient of imperial protection as two institutions, the church and the empire, began to work hand in hand.[66] The state supported and participated in ecumenical councils, which established church hierarchy, rituals, liturgical prayers, and feasts. Imperial decree spurred the construction of church buildings and legitimated the killing of dissident Christians such as the Donatists in North Africa. Church buildings were erected where pagan worship centers had stood, resulting in the assimilation of aspects of paganism into Christian worship.[67] As Freeman states, "a pagan custom, the worship of gods through impressive buildings, was transferred successfully into Christianity."[68] Popescu says that Christian symbols prevalently spread. "[A] cross of precious stones appeared in his [Constantine's] private apartments, and in front of the portico of the palace the emperor was painted holding a cross and stepping on a dragon. The apogee was no doubt his request to receive the baptism and also, for the first time in history, Constantine as a defunct emperor was the subject of the Christians. The liberated Church considered its protector "equal to the apostles" and raised him among the saints."[69]

64. Ibid., 6–7

65. Ibid., 7.

66. Ibid., 7.

67. Freeman, *A.D. 381*, xii.

68 According to Freeman, "such display was completely alien to the Christian tradition, and the ascetic scholar Jerome must have spoken for many traditionalists when he complained that 'parchments are dyed purple, gold is melted into lettering, manuscripts are dressed up in jewels, while Christ lies at the door naked and dying.'" Ibid., 48.

69. Popescu, "Constantine the Great," 86–87.

Nonetheless, Constantine did not eradicate the pagan temple cults.[70] Furthermore, customs were adopted that had been foreign to the early church. Pagan clothing designs were incorporated into priestly robes and the "mosaic designs of churches."[71] As Burckhardt describes, "it was not long before priestly vestments and altar covers had whole stories embroidered upon them."[72]

Constantine played the role of religious leader with ecclesiastical support. This caesaropapist model was a carrot-and-stick relationship: religious support for the political agenda helped reduce unnecessary conflicts within the empire. Positioning himself to give political solutions in religious affairs, Constantine became the imperial guardian of the church, identifying himself as *episkpos pon ektoi* (bishop of external affairs), and, as such, "was engaged in the first big controversy to shake the unity of Christianity, Arianism."[73] In 325, the first ecumenical council convened at Nicaea under the emperor's leadership in response to growing heresies. The emperor "took his seat, too, in the midst of them, as an individual amongst many, dismissing his guards and soldiers and all whose duty was to defend his person."[74] In fact, he played the role of the head of the clergy: "from the beginning Constantine considered it his duty to keep dogmatic unity, as 'intestine strife within the Church of God is far more evil and dangerous than any kind of war or conflict.'"[75]

When conflicts or disputes occurred, ecumenical councils provided imperial and ecclesiastical solutions in the form of government-endorsed creeds, laws, and decrees. Constantine's participation in the councils Arles and Nicaea was significant: "In 325 at Nicaea, the world changed: the caesar participated in a meeting concerning the stability of the state, surrounded not by senators, but by bishops. The emperor gave patient audience to all alike and received every proposition with steadfast attention and by occasionally assisting the argument of each party in turn."[76] After the council, Arius was condemned as a heretic and expelled.

70. Freeman, *A.D. 381*, 38.

71. Burckhardt, *The Age of Constantine*, 223.

72. Ibid., 223.

73. Popescu, "Constantine the Great," 87.

74. Ibid. 87.

75. Ibid. 87.

76. Ibid. 87.

Likewise, Constantine convened at the Council at Arles to discuss Donatist dissidents. The council concluded with an edict against "Novatians, Valentinians, Marcionites and Paulines," labeling them as "haters and enemies of the truth and life." Ironically, the church that had until recently been the object of persecution was now persecuting dissident Christian groups.[77]

At Nicaea, theological and doctrinal issues raised by the Arian controversy were clarified, providing guidance for churches throughout the Roman Empire. The church was also challenged by Donatists in Africa and the Middle East, Ebionites in the Middle East, and Gnostics throughout the empire.[78] In Constantinople AD 381, the Niceo-Constantinopolitan Creed declared that the Holy Spirit shared in the divine nature of the Trinity.[79] During the ecumenical council in Ephesus in AD 431, Nestorius raised the issue of the dual nature of Jesus.[80] This necessitated a fourth ecumenical council in Chalcedon in AD 451.[81]

The swiftness of the conversion of Rome to Christianity and the methods that brought it about are still the subjects of debate. During the time of Constantine, Christians were still a minority: "By this point in time, there were some six million believers in the Empire, around ten percent of [the] total population."[82] Yet, Christianity had

77. Ibid. 87.

78. In 325, the Athanasian Creed affirmed divinity of Jesus and of the Holy Spirit. The council in AD 381 declared the Holy Spirit to be equal with God the Father and God the Son. Gibbon, *The Decline and Fall*, 311–45.

79. The Niceo-Constanopolitan Creed emphatically states, "We believe in the Holy Spirit, the Lord, the giver of life, who proceeds from the Father [and the Son], who with the Father and the Son is worshiped and glorified, who has spoken by the prophets" (English Liturgical translation). Anderson, "Nicene Creed," lines 15–18.

80. Theological debate between Nestorius and Theodosius brought about the Nestorian Schism, giving rise to the Nestorian Church.

81. The Chalcedon Council focused on the issue of monophysitism, a belief that Jesus has only one nature. Eutyches insisted that Christ has one nature of combined divinity and humanity, not two natures.

82. Haykin, "Constantine and His Revolution," 5. It is difficult to obtain accurate demographic data on the Christian population in the fourth century. Jacob Burckhardt states, "According to Stöaudlin, Christians comprised half the entire population, Matter a fifth, Gibbon a twentieth, and La Bastie believes a twelfth, which is perhaps nearest to the truth. More precisely, we may conjecture that for the West the proportion was a fifteenth, and for the East a tenth." Burckhardt, *The Age of Constantine the Great*, 124. According to Freeman, the western part of the empire,

institutional power and eventually developed into a politically and socioeconomically privileged class. However, most of Europe was left unevangelized during this time, including the Barbarian kingdoms, which were only nominally converted at best. Only Christian institutions (including monasteries), and not necessarily groups of dedicated believers, became state-recognized churches. Such churches had the goal of extending themselves not only by evangelizing the common people, but also by baptizing kings and rulers and then canonizing them as national saints.[83]

Nonetheless, the post-Constantine era marked the opening of European Christendom in which society, politics, and communities established the principle of civil unity through public Christian profession. Even in Byzantine cultures, where Hellenistic influences still reigned, a unified group identity was established for more than a thousand years through Christian norms and values.[84] After the post-Constantine era, Christendom underwent another shift during the time of Charlemagne. The close link of *Pax Romana* (Roman peace) and *Romanitas* (Roman culture and society) with Christianity eventually became inseparable throughout Europe.[85] Forrester affirms the strongly Christian flavor of European identity, which defended "itself against infidels without and within." Being European meant being Christian, and being Christian meant being European.[86]

Christianity in Europe had a shape distinct from that of the faith in other parts of the world in that European civilization was formed around Christianity. A common religious worldview was shared by most Europeans, affecting cultural and spiritual identity.[87] Even though Christendom was not confined to Europe, the norms, values, worldviews, and morality of European societies were accountable to the local and national ecclesiastical hierarchy. This shared value sys-

---

which he calls the Latin-speaking west, represented only 2 percent of Christians in AD 300. Freeman, *A.D. 381*, 40.

83. Markus, "From Rome to the Barbarian Kingdoms," 63–72.

84. Russello, *Christianity and European Culture*, 36–37.

85. The military power of the Roman Empire maintained and had kept a "reinforced peace" through the Pax Romana and provided Roman roads covering most districts enabling easier travel for soldiers, traders, and missionaries. Adeney, "From Christ to Constantine," 2.

86. Forrester, "Christianity in Europe," 36–37.

87. Russello, *Christianity and European Culture*, 23.

tem stayed in place for more than a thousand years, through political shifts, revolutions, and redrawn national boundaries. In the last two centuries, however, dramatic de-Christianization has occurred.

Pagan-Christian Feasts

Christianity can be viewed as a living organism. At the macro level, Christian culture nourishes the individual, the community, and society. While Christianity was present in early Europe, cultural forces and pagan practices prevented the faith from penetrating beyond the upper strata.[88] Stark points out the rather incomplete way in which Christians evangelized Europe, stating that "the Christianity that prevailed in Europe was an elaborate patchwork of state churches that settled for the allegiance of the elite and for imposing official requirements for conformity, but that made little sustained effort to Christianize the peasant masses."[89] As a result, for centuries, preexisting pagan cults and ancient religious rituals were widely practiced and elements were incorporated into Christianity.

It is important to distinguish between the terms *Christianity* and *Christendom*. Christendom was formed during the time of Constantine, became institutionalized through political power, and incorporated pagan religious elements. Christendom concerns art, culture, education, government, religious rituals, festivals, and social life. Christianity originated in Jerusalem, but Christendom originated in Rome. Jevons says, "Primitive Christianity, originating as it did in Palestine, stands aloof from Hellenism, uninfluenced by Graeco-Roman culture. It did not seek at first to operate on or through literature."[90] One of the earliest existing records of Christian worship dates from AD 112, when Roman governor Pliny observed that Christians were celebrating worship and communion in their own way. "They were accustomed to meet on a fixed day before dawn, to sing antiphonally a hymn to Christ, . . . but not to commit acts of fraud, theft or adultery, not to falsify their word, not to refuse to return a deposit of called upon to do so."[91] Later, Christians adopted the form of Greco-Roman literature for new purposes: "A Christian literature which had been in prepara-

88. Ibid., 24.
89. Stark, "Secularization, R.I.P.," 9–10.
90. Jevons, "Hellenism and Christianity," 182.
91. Cultural Research Service, "The Pagan Saviours," 9.

tion now broke like a flood into the empty channel of the century and in a short space surpassed in volume all that has survived from the world of pagan writers."[92]

Christendom is inseparable from Greco-Roman culture and civilization, while the church in Jerusalem had relied on the empowerment of the Holy Spirit and the leading of the apostles for evangelism, worship, literature, philosophy, communion, and governance. Nash states, "if primitive Christianity, cut off from Graeco-Roman culture (or sheltered from it?) made no appeal at first to *literati* or philosophers, if it ignored or was ignorant of philosophy and literature, it was because its message was to the heart rather than to the mind, to the religious consciousness of the individual."[93]

The Jerusalem church held that the head of the church was Jesus Christ and that the Holy Spirit indwelled all believers. But the church in Rome instituted ecumenical councils instead of listening to the Holy Spirit and blended church activities with pagan practices and cultic elements. Existing religions around the Mediterranean had a variety of regional worship practices. In Greece there were Demeter and Dionysus as well as the Eleusinian and Orphic mysteries. Cybele and Attis were venerated in Asia Minor, Isis and Osiris (also known as Serapis) in Egypt, Adonis in Syria and Palestine, and Mithras in Persia. Nash explains, "The earlier Greek mystery religions were state religions in the sense that they attained the status of a public or civil cult and served a national or public function. The later non-Greek mysteries were personal, private, and individualistic."[94]

As the gospel gradually reached every part of the Roman Empire during the second and third centuries, Christian practices took the place of pagan rituals and Hellenistic elements in many ways. Dobschütz agrees, "from the time of Constantine the process of Hellenization went on a larger scale, and more quickly."[95] Temples of healing gods were supplanted by patron saints of the church and many Christians practiced "charms, amulets and so on."[96] Dobschütz states,

---

92. Burckhardt, *The Age of Constantine*, 218.

93. Jevons, "Hellenism and Christianity," 182.

94. Nash, "Influenced by Pagan Religions?," 1.

95. Dobschütz, "Christianity and Hellenism," 263.

96. Ibid., 263.

> Two views oppose one another. The one looks upon this development as a desirable progress. It was necessary; for Christianity could reach its fullest success only by becoming a speculative system of religion and a developed civilization. The other complains that the change altered woefully the essence of Christianity. It ceased to be pure religion when it gave itself to the Greek spirit and Greek culture. [97]

Two conflicts led Jews to disconnect from gentile Christian communities: the destruction of Jerusalem in AD 69–70 and the Bar Kochba rebellion in AD 132–135. Even in the second century, great differences were found between Christians in the east and the west in the Roman Empire.

Burckhardt's research has revealed that more than three hundred deities were worshipped through mystery religions during this time.[98] "While a tendency toward eclecticism or synthesis developed after A.D. 300, each of the mystery cults was a separate and distinct religion during the century that saw the birth of the Christian church."[99] The assimilation of practices from cults and pagan religions started during the Constantine era, and the Hellenization of Christianity contributed substantially to the formation of Christendom.

Dobschütz's view is that Christendom was formed in three steps. First, Christianity tried to impose "itself upon Hellenism with all its vigor; in the *second*, Hellenism tries to absorb the new religion; in the *third*, Christianity, organized as a church, comes back to itself, establishes a religious compromise between the Gospel and Hellenism, and enters the circle of Hellenistic civilization. Each period covers, roughly speaking, about a century."[100] In the end, Christendom came to affect theology, creeds, arts, and apologetics, and Hellenism became a foundation for philosophical formulations such as Christology,[101] moral standards,[102] Christian education, and visual arts, including catacomb paintings, iconography, and fine arts.[103] Hellenism became the means

---

97. Ibid., 264.

98. Burckhardt, *The Age of the Constantine*, 162.

99. Nash, "Was the New Testament Influenced by Pagan Religions?," 1.

100. Dobschütz, "Christianity and Hellenism," 250.

101. Ibid., 257.

102. Ibid., 260.

103. Ibid., 261.

by which the Christian faith was codified in dogma, literature, and theology in the formation of Christendom.[104]

Cultural continuity made it easier for society to adopt the new Christian religious movement. Burckhardt states, "the Christians in their belief . . . partly of Judaizing and partly of popular origin, run parallel with the pagans."[105] Pre-Roman and pagan religious and folkloric elements absorbed during this time contributed to popular Catholicism in the Middle Ages.[106] People are more willing to adopt a new religion to the extent that it remains in cultural continuity with familiar religious conventions.[107] Greek mythology, Mediterranean and German cults, Babylonian religion, Greek philosophy, and religious festivals of the Roman Empire were all present in the Mediterranean world before it was Christianized. Whether intentionally or not, official recognition of Christianity by Constantine allowed existing practices to be modified and branded as Christian. Latourette agrees that

> the culture of the area [the Mediterranean] was a mixture of pre-Christian and Christian elements and had only partially—except for small minorities only slightly—conformed to Christian ideals. In the contact with the civilization of the Mediterranean the inherited customs and institutions of the invaders tended to disintegrate, with a decline in the traditional forms of social control and in morals.[108]

Burckhardt points out that the "mixture of gods was in itself well calculated to prepare the ground for a new religion. It denationalized the divine and made it universal; it crushed Greek and Roman pride in their old native cults."[109]

What of the origins of Christian feasts, the church calendar, mass, church hierarchy, and sacraments—did they emerge from Jewish tradition or the New Testament church? A document known as the *Liber Generationis* (Liberian Catalogue) from AD 354, along

---

104. Ibid., 259.

105. Burckhardt, *The Age of Constantine*, 207.

106. MacMullen defines the term folkloric as describing "a distinction between the beliefs and practices of the majority. The masses, the populous, vulgus, lower classes, uneducated, the simple or unlettered or however they might be labelled, as opposed to some dominant minority." MacMullen, *Christianity and Paganism*, 76.

107. Stark, *The Rise of Christianity*, 137.

108. Latourette, "Christianity Through the Ages," lines 57–59.

109. Burckhardt, *The Age of Constantine*, 214.

with other documents called the "D(omimi) N(ostri) Constanti VII IDV AUG" written between 337 and 361,[110] showed that Christian festivals and holidays were being observed in Rome.[111] Hurlbut states that, in AD 405, "images of saints and martyrs began to appear in the churches, at first as memorials, then in succession revered, adored, and worshipped. The adoration of the Virgin Mary was substituted for the worship of Venus and Diana."[112] Great transformations took place after the Edict of Milan.

Before Constantine's reign, a weekly holy day was not celebrated. Rome chose Sunday instead of Saturday to differentiate the Christian day of rest from the Jewish Sabbath. Jewish rebellions had led the empire to uproot the Jewish population; both Vespasian and Hadrian ordered the Jews to leave Rome. Also, Jewish believers observed different rites than Gentile Christians, including feasts and worship traditions. While Jewish believers met on the Sabbath, they observed Jewish times of prayer and religious meetings in the Jerusalem temple. The destruction of Jerusalem in AD 70 left Christians with no place to meet.

As Jewish and Gentile believers became disconnected from each other, Sabbath observance and the Hebrew calendar were eclipsed by the Roman calendar. This change occurred gradually in the eastern part of the empire, but rapidly in the west. Sunday as the Sabbath was promoted not only by Roman authorities, but also by some of the early church fathers, who saw Sunday Sabbath observance as a way of distancing the church from Judaizing influences.

The origins of Christmas are also less than pure. The holiday stems from both Saturnalia (a licentious December feast for the Roman harvest god, Saturn), as well as the pagan Germanic Yule festival of northern Europe, which was originally celebrated from late December to early January. Christians ultimately designated December 25 to commemorate of the birth of Jesus, which coincided with the birthday of the god Sol Invictus and the winter solstice.[113]

110. Another document belonging to Ambrose, De Virg. 3.1, was recently discovered. Ambrose's theological issue of virginity was expressed in his writings *De virginibus* and *De Virginitate*. Laughton, *Virginity Discourse*, 80–81.

111. *Pagan City*, 232.

112. Hurlbut, *Story of the Christian Church*, 73.

113. The deposito martyrum, a document commemorating Christian martyrs completed in AD 336, contains the first reference to Christmas, "natus Christus in Betleeem Iudeae." Curran, *Pagan City*, 229.

As the calendar shifted, Christian celebrations of Easter and Pentecost became disconnected from the Jewish dates for Passover, Pentecost, and Shavuot.[114] The Jewish Passover date of Nisan 14 was ultimately replaced by Easter Sunday.[115] Further, Easter celebrations incorporated elements of Germanic spring fertility rites from eastern and central Europe.[116]

Freke and Gandy point out that "Each mystery religion taught its own version of the myth of the dying and resurrecting Godman, who was known by different names in different places."[117] Among the best-known deities of this type are "Demeter and Dionysus (or Bacchus) in Greece, Cybele and Attis in Phrygia, Mithra in Persia, Ishtar and Tammuz in Babylonia, Atargatis and Hadad in Cilicia, Ashtart and Esh-mun [or Adon]—the Aphrodite and Adonis of the Greeks—in Syria, and Isis, Osiris, and Serapis in Egypt."[118]

Zukeran has found that the Greek Dionysius and Egyptian Osiris had a counterpart in the Zoroastrian god Mithra, whose death and resurrection was commemorated and who was called the "son of god" and "light of the world" by adherents.[119] Mithra is said to have been born on December 25 and resurrected three days after being buried. Mithra was originally venerated in the eastern parts of Asia Minor; when Alexander the Great invaded Persia, the belief spread to Rome. The story of the nativity in Luke 2 resembles "the astrological tradition of the Magi associated with Mithraism."[120] The midnight ceremonies on December 25 in Rome marks Mithra's birth date, which bear an unmistakable resemblance to Christmas: "The temples are lit up. Priests in white robes stand at the altar. Boys burn incense. The congregation is here to celebrate the birth of their Lord God. But Jesus Christ is not the name on their lips—when he was born this was already an ancient ceremony. It commemorates the sun god Mithras."[121] Seeing the re-

---

114. The feasts of Trumpets (Rosh Hashanah), Atonement (Yom Kippur), and Tabernacles (Sukkot) were no longer kept by Christians.

115. Bacchiocchi, *From Sabbath to Sunday*, 198–200.

116. Bamaiyi, "The Effect of Syncretism," 6.

117. Freke and Gandy, *The Laughing Jesus*, 55–56.

118. Case, "Christianity and the Mystery Religions," 9–10.

119. Zukeran, "Pagan Connection," 1.

120. Cultural Research Service, "The Pagan Saviours," 9.

121. Ibid., 4.

semblance to pagan activities, "We must examine the preoccupations of the early pagan cults and try to assess whether some of those too may have rubbed off on early Christian belief."[122]

A death-and-resurrection story from the Hellenic world is that of Cybele, the mother goddess, who fell in love with a young Phrygian shepherd named Attis.[123] In similar fashion, veneration of this couple expanded throughout the empire via the Roman "army, trade, and the circulation of slaves" to "the Balkan countries, up the valley of the Danube . . . down the Rhine valley" and even to Britain, Italy, France, and Spain.[124] In the first century Roman world, a variety of death-and-resurrection myths were available to be conflated with the story of the death and resurrection of Jesus.[125] Pagan rituals and celebrations continued even into the Middle Ages and beyond. MacMullen affirms,

> Libanius, faithful heathen, and John Chrysostom describe the kalends [first day of the Roman month] celebrations as presided over by the gods, among whom, as late as the second half of the sixth century, Malalas speaks of Janus and Saturn paraded through the streets of a Lydian city. In the capital, the merrymaking involved monks, clergy, even bishops along with the highest secular and military officials; cross-dressing, too, and dancing and masks, some of which survive from the thirteenth-century palace. . . . In the west in this and later periods the participants dressed up in masks representing Saturn also, along with Jupiter, Hercules, Diana, and, evidently, Cernunnos, favorite deer-headed deity among Celtic populations of northern Italy, Spain, Gaul, or Britain. . . . Boniface in [AD] 742 reports and decries the annual parading, singing, shouts, and loaded banquet tables in the open squares of Rome around Saint Peter's itself, on the traditional date and "according to pagan custom;' "by heathen ritual."[126]

122. Ibid., 5.

123. Zukeran, "Pagan Connection," 5.

124. Emerton states, "In the whole of Greece there has so far been found but one positively authentic Mithraitic shrine, and that is at the Piraeus, the harbor of Athens, a place famous in antiquity, as it is today, for the conglomeration of nationalities that made up its population." Emerton, "The Religious Environment of Early Christianity", 198.

125. Cultural Research Service, "The Pagan Saviours," 7.

126. MacMullen, *Christianity and Paganism*, 37.

MacMullen points out that pagan influences were present in "ceremony, gesture, symbol, terminology, myth, or allusion. Original in paganism, naturalized among Christians. . . . Otherwise they could not have persisted among Christians."[127]

Pagan Rituals in Medieval Christendom

Many scholars have studied aspects of the history of the church in Europe, including analyses of art, rituals, theology, liturgy, poetry, architecture, music, painting, sculpture, law, inquisitions, crusades, and the relationship of politics, society, and religion. The expansion of European Christendom included civic life, the practice of faith, and, to some extent, evangelization of local populations, as well as the absorption of preexisting pagan practices from newly assimilated areas into Christianity. Curran states, "the pagan elements in the [pagan-Christian] celebrations were 'neutralized', before being replaced by explicitly Christian practices." He finds that the essential "rejection of the pagan character of the traditional commemorations was the refusal of Constantine to ascend the Capitol in either 312 or 315."[128] Johansen stresses, "The transition from paganism to Christianity is a complex process which happens at different times in different places."[129] MacMullen explains that the Christians "had almost no special language of gestures or symbols in which to express their feelings or their wishes . . . such as pagan[s] had developed. . . . Christians had none to turn to; but pagans did, and resorted to them constantly."[130] The great schism between the west and the east drove western Christianity to try to extend its territory to the far-flung people groups of Europe, including Britons and Nordic people.[131]

Recent scholarship has explored prehistoric religious practices that were absorbed by Christianity and survived, as well as literary expressions of religion throughout history. For instance, Lewis Spence has demonstrated that a large number of ancient religious beliefs and practices are connected with modern Western Christianity.[132]

127. Ibid., 148.

128. Curran, *Pagan City*, 220.

129. Johansen, "From Paganism to Christianity," 1.

130. MacMullen, *Christianity & Paganism*, 150.

131. Latourette, *A History of Christianity*, 350–352.

132. Among relevant works by Spence are *The Mysteries of Britain, Boadicea,*

These ancient practices were modified and even superimposed upon Christianity as "higher elements," taking a variety of forms in different nations and regions. The religious practices of the common people were devalued by the ruling class so the official religious establishment could maintain its dominance. These so-called higher ideas and practices added no real value to the development of the faith.

Pagan beliefs and practices from ancient Europe were integrated with Christianity, modifying and reshaping it. For instance, as Bruce Reed illustrates, many Western Catholics place St. Christopher's medals in their cars or around their necks for safety. The medieval church also altered existing pagan religious places for Christian purposes. Pagan rites were converted into baptism and Christian festivals such as Christmas and Easter. Reed stresses, "The introduction of Christianity into Britain was consolidated by the early missionaries taking over the existing pagan sanctuaries such as Iona and Lindisfarne."[133]

While Christianity adopted pagan practices, conversely, many who merely appropriated Christian symbols into their lives gradually developed subjective interpretations based more on nature and non-Christian religions than on the symbols' true meanings. Pagan artifacts and practices took on more modern forms, as did superstitious beliefs. Such beliefs began to "emerge openly from the caves and hollows of the minds of the general mass of the people, and the old symbols got new meanings, so that for example to wear a cross today is not necessarily to intend any Christian significance."[134]

Even in the Middle Ages, we can see the continuous growth of pagan activities. Christendom was an amalgam of pagan elements, Jewish roots, and the theology of Greco-Roman philosophies. Christendom expanded and came to dominate Northern, Eastern, and Western Europe.[135] In doing so, it took on Germanic, Gothic, Slavic, Celtic, Nordic, and Anglo-Saxon flavors in the folk Catholicism of the various ethnic communities. In the Greek Orthodox Church of the time, Lalonde identifies "a penchant for views, churches, saints, cults, and rites of Byzantine and early modern Greek Orthodox religion as

---

Legendary London, The History and Origins of Druidism, and *Mysteries of Celtic Britain.*

133. Reed, *The Dynamics of Religion,* 104.

134. Ibid., 105.

135. Bamaiyi, "The Effect of Syncretism," 5.

replications of real or supposed pagan Greek counterparts."[136] Lalonde examines the healing rituals in the Church of Agia Marina Theseiou in Athens to see if there is a connection to ancient pagan practices such as "gods, heroes, nymphs, cults, and shrines of the Classical Greeks."[137] Among his findings is that "[T]he patron saint of childbirth in the Eastern Church, was the logical successor to the ancient fertility cult of the Hyakinthid Nymphs," although there is no connection to the Agia Marina. Even so, a great deal of evidence points to an intermingling of pagan rituals and Christian practice.[138] Lalonde found that the "changing [of] garments of sick children also fits into a large pattern of religious rite that is so common," and which is likely a "direct continuity from ancient prototypes" of pagan rituals.[139]

Another example of pagan-Christian syncretism is found in Greece, where popular religious shrines were converted into way stations for Christian pilgrims traveling to Jerusalem. This was the case with the shrine in the beautiful village of Panayia on the island of Tinos. Popular religion in Greece, as well as on the Iberian Peninsula and in other Catholic countries, was more focused on external practices than on one's internal state. As Dubisch says, religious practices were naturally more in tune "with the public and communal than with the interior or the mystic."[140]

In Ireland in the fifth century, "Christian and early pagan/Celtic traditions became fused [fostering] the creation of a unique Christian culture that reached its fullest development during the Medieval Age."[141] Archeological finds and ancient works of art confirm that Celtic pagan polytheistic rites—such as honoring the dead through symbols or portraying the head of the deceased—were still practiced. The first missionaries in Ireland delivered "a dualistic faith based on the conflict between good and evil,"[142] proclaiming that believed people can be saved "through the acceptance of Jesus Christ, a martyred god,"[143]

---

136. Lalonde, "Pagan Cult to Christian Ritual," 91.

137. Ibid., 92.

138. Ibid., 97–98.

139. Ibid., 114.

140. Dubisch, "Pilgrimage and Popular Religion," 113–36.

141. Hutchinson, "The Pagan Influences," 1.

142. Ibid., 3.

143. Ibid., 3.

a contrast with the warrior ideal celebrated in Celtic culture. The first Irish believers worshipped secretly "in house churches and interred their dead in abandoned salt caves."[144] Retaining pagan cultural elements made it easier for the Irish to adopt the Christian faith:

> Christianity was able to advance quickly in Ireland, not only because of the power of Christ's message, but also because of the use of art to educate the people. The policies of the Christian leadership that permitted the Irish to retain many facets of their pagan culture was [sic] also a contributing factor. Christians connected Irish mythology with Christian scripture; the heroes of old worked with the Christian saints to bring about early Irish Christianity.[145]

In France, Charlemagne massacred rebellious Saxons for twenty years in his desire to impose Christianity on them. In 772, he "was determined to bring the Saxons into his realm and . . . reduced much of the region to ostensible submission. As part of the process of integration under his rule, he insisted upon baptism,"[146] which was strenuously opposed by the Saxons. Once subdued, the Saxons' pagan practices became syncretized with Catholic rituals and sacraments.

In Britain, evidence of pagan religious practices can be found in the stories of King Arthur and the Holy Grail, which mentions the feast of Pentecost. Hernandez explains, "As sung in a familiar fourteenth century English ballad, it was in 'the merrie, merrie month of May' that the Pentecost story became the basis for festivities capable of holding pre-Christian fertility traditions alongside the annual Christian commemoration of God's outpouring of the Holy Spirit nine days after the Ascension of Christ."[147] The feast of the Advent, also known as the "forty days of St. Martin" before Christmas, is well observed to this day.[148] In the twelfth century, adding to Advent was the celebration of the Twelve Days of Christmas from December 25 to January 6. According to Bamaiyi,

144. Ibid., 3.

145. Ibid., 6.

146. Latourette, *A History of Christianity*, vol. 1, 350.

147. Hernandez, "Re-Discovering," 13–14.

148. The feast of St. Martin of Tours begins November 11 and lasts until Christmas.

> By the High Middle Ages, the holiday had become so promi-
> nent that chroniclers routinely noted where various magnates
> celebrated Christmas. . . . The Yule boar was a common feature
> of medieval Christmas feasts. . . . Various writers of the time
> condemned caroling as lewd, indicating that the unruly tradi-
> tions of Saturnalia and Yule may have continued in this form.
> "Misrule"—drunkenness, promiscuity, gambling—was also an
> important aspect of the festival. In England, gifts were exchanged
> on New Year's Day, and there was special Christmas ale.[149]

Pagan fertility rituals have been perpetuated by blending with the
Christian celebration of Pentecost. Hernandez, by studying the writings of poets and minstrels, has observed different symbolic aspects of
Pentecost celebrations. "Pentecost green" symbolized nature, and red
indicated the Holy Spirit. Hernandez concludes that "over time, these
folk-myths and stories, and the feast days marking their annual passage, became assimilated alongside Christian conceptions about May
Day celebrations, the Virgin Mary, and the Feast of Pentecost."[150]

Ninth- and tenth-century missions to Scandinavia, especially
Denmark and Sweden, replicated the pattern of Christendom in
which secular and ecclesiastical power works together to Christianize
in a top-down approach.[151] When the residents accepted Christianity,
many preexisting pagan customs persisted, as archeological investiga-
tions of Viking burial sites have shown.[152] This includes the Viking
custom that "all the dead should be burned, and put on the funeral
pyre with all their possessions."[153] Christianity "did not destroy previous belief systems such as Slavic paganism, but rather transformed
them."[154] The Slavic pagan god Perun (the counterpart to Germanic
Thor) was venerated long after the conversion into Christianity,
eventually being conflated with the prophet Elijah.[155] Draskoczy has
found that pagan burial rituals of Odin, the god of death, continued
to be observed, as well as "tree-worship, animal veneration, and rock

---

149. Bamaiyi, "The Effect of Syncretism," 18.

150. Hernandez, "Re-Discovering," 14–15.

151. Latourette, *A History of Christianity*, vol. 1. 385–86.

152. Richard, "Pagan and Christians," 383.

153. Ibid., 391–92.

154. Draskoczy, "Amalgam of Allegiance," 96.

155. Ibid., 100.

magic."[156] The tale of Odin resembles the story of Jesus: he was crucified "on a tree where he hung for nine days and was fed vinegar and pierced with a spear" and resurrected for the redemption of sinners.[157] The cult of saints was connected with death, since its true purpose was to "join Heaven and Earth at the grave of a dead human being."[158]

Latourette provides examples of how Scandinavia paid the price of peace (i.e. they reluctantly accepted Christian baptism), resulting in the baptism of Saxons. Many Europeans converted to Christianity because of the decisions of their rulers. Once the king declared that Christianity was the religion of the kingdom, his subjects had no choice but to follow, or at least appear to. Pagan temples were destroyed, and practitioners of witchcraft, shamans, and magicians were slain.[159] In Norway, Olaf Haraldsson tried to adopt Christian principles, "proscribing paganism and customs which were contrary to Christian morals.[160]

Scandinavian religious practice in the eleventh century, including human sacrifice, was centered in the luxurious temple at Uppsala, Sweden. For the sake of converting the population to Christianity, missionaries allowed Christ and the various saints (especially Olaf) to supplant those previously in the pagan pantheon. This kind of conversion merely involves changing one set of gods for another with Christian modifications—a superficial conversion that allowed native pagan traditions to persist in Christianized forms. Stark affirms that primitive Christian faith was "never deep enough in northern Europe to generate much mass attendance, nor deep enough to survive changes into the religious affiliation of their political leaders during the Reformation, sometimes back and forth across denominational lines."[161] Archeological finds show that Christian rituals were intertwined with pagan rituals in Ireland, Scotland, and England as well as Scandinavia.

---

156. Ibid., 97.
157. Ibid., 98–99.
158. Ibid., 100.
159. Latourette, *A History of Christianity*, vol. 1, 385–88.
160. Ibid., 388.
161. Stark, "Secularization, R.I.P.," 10–11.

TABLE 3.1 CHRISTIAN SYMBOLS IN A PAGAN SETTING

Artifact	Dating	Origin	Symbolic Function
Bronze hanging bowl	Merovingian Viking	Ireland	For ritual washing hands
Gold filigree pointer	AD 850–900		Personification of Jesus*
Tating ware pottery	AD 770–850	Rhine region	Liturgical wine containers**
Reticella bowls	AD 700–800	England	?
Claw beakers	AD 550–600	England (Kent?)	Pagan drinking cult
Gold foiled funnel beaker	AD 750–850	Rhineland	Christian chalices
Gold Foil figures	AD 500–900	Scandinavian	Pagan Cult

*Personification of Jesus (Alfred's Jewel); wisdom, for turning pages in holy manuscripts; emblem of the king's (wise?) rule.
** Liturgical wine containers or for holding water for ritual hand washing
Source: "Paganism to Christianity"[162]

Bruce defines pre-Reformation Christianity as, in essence, a mix of three prevalent medieval beliefs and practices: a church that performed official religious duties on behalf of the people, a widely diffused yet shallow Christian faith, and a pervasive, superstitious belief in the supernatural. One modern historian believes that the decline of Christianity actually began immediately following the Reformation, for formal involvement in organized religion declined when the legal and political balance was upset.[163] The prestige and power of organized, official Christianity in the medieval era fell after the Reformation. Beliefs in the supernatural diminished gradually over the centuries, but traces nonetheless remain today throughout Europe.

Folk Catholicism

Such popular, yet non-supernatural, Christianity is more prevalent in Roman Catholic and Orthodox churches, which emphasize sacramental symbols, than in Protestant churches. The Roman Catholic

162. Johansen, "Paganism to Christianity," 8.
163. Bruce, *Religion in Modern Britain*, 42.

form of "elite Christianity" was the prevailing form practiced by the majority of Europe's educated, upper middle class. This same group of Western and Western-educated people was influenced over the centuries by the Enlightenment, rationalism, and secularization. Moral and functional values of the faith are emphasized while mystical, symbolic, and festive dimensions are downplayed. As Dubisch and Stark see it, a popular religion emphasizing the latter would be classified as a rather "low" form of Christianity.[164]

The aggressive expansion of Christianity in the Iberian countries, particularly Spain, was fueled equally by religious zeal and colonial avarice, resulting in a nominally Christian Iberia at best. In this respect, 1492 marks the pinnacle of European Christendom, when Columbus sailed across the Atlantic and paved the way for the European expansion of Christendom in the New World.[165] However, the gospel that took root in Spain and Portugal was, in my opinion, not a pure form of Christianity, but folk Catholicism. Spanish folk Christianity was the result of Spanish religious imagination and superstitions amalgamating with the diverse forms of Catholicism in Iberia—primarily Roman Catholicism, whose grip on the nation was strong enough to prevail through the upheavals of the Reformation. Furthermore, the Spanish church was not unaffected by the doubt aroused by the Age of Reason throughout Europe. Subjugated by the Moors for more than six centuries, Spain and Portugal—accustomed to the idea of totalitarian faith—imposed on Latin America and the Philippines a Christendom that was largely medieval in nature. The church was synonymous with the state, and the cross ruled alongside the sword. Such circumstances facilitated the rapid implementation of Christianity in newly discovered colonial territories.[166]

The religious atmosphere of Spain in the sixteenth century reflected a rather complex religious heritage. Among peasants and those of the lower social stratum, Christianity, magic, and ancient non-

---

164. Eliade, *The Encyclopedia of Religion*, vol. 11, 440.

165. In 1493, Pope Alexander VI pronounced his Bull Inter Caetera, dividing the world between Spain and Portugal. According to Forrester, this allowed the two crowns "exclusive right of trade and conquest and duties of evangelization on the two sides of a line drawn west of the Azores and Cape Verde Islands (and moved westward in 1494, enabling Portugal to colonise Brazil)." Forrester, "Christianity in Europe," 37.

166. Maggay, "Towards Sensitive Engagement," 362.

Christian traditions merged, creating rich syncretistic traditions.[167] Such folk religion, inherited from the Middle Ages, was deeply inscribed in the popular consciousness and was exported to Spanish colonies in the New World, including Latin America, the Far East, and the Philippines.[168] State-sanctioned Catholicism imposed by Spanish colonial authorities, in cooperation with clergy and friars, was further adapted by native populations in the New World. Indigenous people combined some of their traditional beliefs and practices with the newly arrived Iberian Catholicism. As a result, an anti-Reformation religious spirit known as "folk Catholicism" came into existence.[169]

Missionaries accompanying the Conquistadors began making converts and by the seventeenth century Christianity (Catholicism) was firmly established in Latin America. The task was made easier by the lack of a single, unifying indigenous religion. The friars who now replaced the native shamans rendered Catholicism more attractive by adapting many pagan beliefs and rituals while impressing the people with a combination of religious flamboyance and mysticism. Aside from the dominant Marian cults, most Spanish villages after the Council of Trent had their "own church, sacred relics, and attending priest, specialized saints, centered cult, thaumaturgical crucifixes, and powerful relics."[170]

Social scientists have distinguished official Catholicism from folk Catholicism. Official Catholicism is defined as "a set of beliefs, rituals and practices which are held, approved, prescribed, required and maintained as normative by ecclesiastical authority." Folk Catholicism, on the other hand, "includes elements at times viewed as harmless, that can yet be condemned by Church authorities, which are all nonetheless derived from and sanctioned by the community where it is believed and practiced, as an expression of human needs and longings."[171] Folk Catholicism has endured because it provides a way for human beings

---

167. Ruiz, *Spanish Society, 1400–1600*, 234.

168. Ruiz cites "the daily regimen of men aboard one of the king's galleons making the biannual crossing of the Atlantic. Sailors of the sixteenth and seventeenth centuries could not be accused of excessive religiosity or great spiritual sensibility." Ibid., 236.

169. Phelan, *The Hispanization of the Philippines*, 72.

170. Ruiz, *Spanish Society, 1400–1600*, 235.

171. Hunt et al., *Sociology in the Philippine Setting*, 257.

to perceive spiritual reality and to understand their place in the world. Its rituals provide commonalities that promote social cohesion.[172]

Folk Catholicism allows its adherents to express spiritual emotions while shaping a sense of identity among them. Vestiges of animism and superstition may be present, but, nonetheless, Folk Catholicism provides a sense of direction as well as personal and communal identity. Folk Catholicism constitutes a sort of "Catholic underworld" with its own logic and worldview. It presents a coherent, if largely unarticulated, description of the general order of existence, which orients the lives of those who practice it. It also provides practical solutions to the questions and problems of everyday life and immediate spiritual needs. For instance, Catholics were able to experience healing and spiritual life by practicing novena prayer, passion plays, penitence, buying of indulgences, and all souls day.

While folk Catholics might adhere to the doctrines and rituals of official Catholicism, they often modify them to suit local needs and their environment, and sometimes syncretize them with native animistic beliefs and practices.[173] Official Catholicism retains its ecclesiastical system over the region, but there is still ample room for traditional belief systems to persist. This double structure explains how Catholic beliefs seep into traditional animistic worldviews.[174]

Spanish friars and priests proselytized native populations to typical Iberian Catholicism. Still, animistic traditions were too deep-seated to be completely eliminated, and many Catholic theological beliefs were transformed, reinterpreted, changed, acculturated, indigenized, contextualized, and, to some extent, syncretized.[175] Throughout its history, Western Christianity has not been completely victorious over folk and popular religious beliefs of the native people groups to which it has been introduced. Rather, it has had a history of struggle, assimilation, harmony, compromise, transformation, opposition, and even surrender when folk and popular religion confronts the established church or the hierarchical, institutionalized church.

New folk and popular religious movements have often arisen in Europe to challenge established churches. These new movements

---

172. Beltran, *The Christology of the Inarticulate*, 5.

173. Ibid., 5.

174. Diesto, "The Effects of Colonial Mentality," 44–45.

175. Hunt et al., *Sociology in the Philippine Setting*, 255–56.

have developed into churches, sects, and sometimes cults. Some later disappeared or greatly diminished, such as the Waldensian, Albigenes, Anabaptist, and Jansenism movements.[176] Others developed into institutionalized churches, including the Quakers, Methodists, Assemblies of God, Foursquare Church, and Church of God, which are now established Protestant denominations.[177] Loosely held Christian belief was drastically weakened during the Enlightenment and in many places was replaced by secularism. Following is a sketch of this process of decline during four time periods: post-Reformation, modern, postwar, and postmodern.

In pre-Reformation Europe, practices of magic and popular folk beliefs had worked their way into the established Medieval Church and become prevalent.[178] Religion during this period was pervaded by a sense of mystery, such that many people, including a considerable number of unbelievers, went on pilgrimages with relics, prayed with the rosary, and even paid religious taxes. Lewis Spence, in his careful study of Celtic mystics and pagan practices in the British Isles, finds that "Irish Druidic superstition long survived and is by no means defunct. . . . There are numerous instances of folk-beliefs in the efficacy of certain stones, for example the Stones of Speculation, from which it was thought fire could be drawn."[179] For example, a medieval Catholic tradition called the All Saints' Day, was simply a continuation of the pagan Samhain, celebrated to sanctify the spirits of the dead.[180] In the British Isles, ancient mystical and occult traditions mixed with Christian rituals. Chrétien de Troyes' *The Story of the Grail* also provides evidence of the continued existence of such traditions over an extended period.[181] This combination of Catholic mysticism and ancient cultic practices pervaded the lives of the common people.[182]

Folk religion seems to be more prevalent in Catholic countries than in Protestant ones. Throughout Ireland, the Iberian countries, and southern Europe, the Catholic faith has mixed with popular folk beliefs and practices, and this amalgam is used to convey cultural

176. Knox, *Enthusiasm*, 1–8, 75–78.

177. Roy M. Anker's research connects popular religious movements to Christian Science. Anker, *Self-Help*, 1–10.

178. Bruce, *Religion in the Modern World*, 56.

179. Spence, *Mysteries of Celtic Britain*, 228.

180. Ibid., 229.

181. Ibid., 234–40.

182. Bruce, *Religion in the Modern World*, 54.

norms. Catholics often stay limited within the boundaries of the official church for ceremonies and services, but, in their private lives, espouse both institutional and folk beliefs that are often at odds with one another.[183]

MODERN CHRISTIANITY

British society and the British church, which was born out of Reformation in the sixteenth century, had adopted the idea of Christendom, with church and state authority overlapping. The whole society was seen as being under God and, as much as possible, under the church as well.[184] However, during the Enlightenment, the Christian faith and church practices came under the influence of secular culture. Bob Jackson points to "a steady, creeping secularization of society stemming from the shift from the Industrial Revolution, which brought about the shift from settled rural living to a more fluid and impersonal urban life" in the nineteenth century.[185] Industrialization and the growth of scientific knowledge both led to secularization, which marked the beginning of an overall religious decline.

REFORMATION OF REASON

Christendom was seen as one body in the minds of Europeans when medieval Catholicism dominated. Then, European Christianity was forever altered by the Reformation, which broke that body into Catholic and Protestant pieces. The rule of the institutional Catholic Church met with defeat in Britain when Henry VIII overruled the decisions of the ecclesiastical hierarchy and established the Church of England. Still, British society as a whole could scarcely be called secular, as Christian ideals and norms continued to influence the people in all aspects of their daily lives.[186]

In spite of the English Reformation, dissent was hardly recognized by Catholic authorities in continental Europe. In England, Scotland, and the Netherlands, a considerable number of breakaway groups launched "free churches" that were independent of the rule of the state. Where Reformed churches established themselves as the

183. Brandes, "Conclusion," 185–99.
184. Warren, *Being Human, Being Church*, 27–28.
185. Jackson, *Hope for the Church*, 61.
186. Squires, "The Significance of Religion in British Politics," 82.

majority, a large Catholic minority still remained. This was the case in the Netherlands, while Catholics remained the dominant group in Ireland. Though significant conversion efforts were made by English rulers to bring Catholics into English Protestantism, this aim was not fully achieved.[187]

In 1689, the Toleration Act was passed by Parliament to initiate a rule within the Anglican Church which would guarantee the establishment of Protestantism. Even so, "no congregation, Anglican or nonconformist, was allowed to meet without first having been certified by the Bishop of the Diocese or the Archdeacon of the Archdeaconry within whose province the congregation fell."[188] At the same time, Presbyterianism was established separately by law in Scotland.[189] The Toleration Act was a turning point in Britain's modern religious history. Three groups—the official institution of the Church of England, unofficial ecclesiastical institutions, and secularism—had been vying for the attention of a fourth group, the single largest in the country: "those who had no such settled religion conviction."[190] This legislation permitted the freedom of worship to some extent in the Trinitarian Protestant Churches, but only some concessions were applicable for the nonconformists. In contrast, the Blasphemy Act of 1698 established punishments and imprisonment, in some cases even death, for nonconformists, until its repeal in 1813.[191]

The decline of Christianity accelerated during the post-Reformation period, when the Enlightenment and the Industrial Revolution led to widespread secularization. From the Enlightenment onward, secular and intellectual powers began to voice their own ideologies and passions, all antagonistic to the church.[192] Gerald Russello concludes that

> the consequences of this denial of spiritual reality have become clear. Europe is faced with a number of serious problems, both physical and cultural. Economic agreements cannot substitute

187. McLeod, *Religion and the People of Western Europe*, v.

188. Squires, "The Significance of Religion in British Politics," 83.

189. McManners, "Enlightenment," 267–71.

190. With the Toleration Act, the state gave up its attempts to force Anglicanism on the whole population through compulsory church attendance and the persecution of rival denominations. McLeod, "The Privatization of Religion," 4.

191. Squires, "The Significance of Religion in British Politics," 83.

192. Russello, *Christianity and European Culture*, xvii.

> for cultural unity, nor can the ignorance of a millennium of common history be overcome by political arrangements . . . Europe is possible only with Christianity, for it is a spiritual unity rather than a political one.[193]

Dawson also points out that, after the eighteenth century, it is questionable to link Christian civilization or culture to the Medieval Christendom model. Christian ideals and norms no longer held their prominent place throughout Europe.[194] The late eighteenth and nineteenth centuries also saw tremendous growth in missions. Overseas missionaries from the Western world proclaimed the gospel mostly in their own colonial sphere. This gospel proclaimed differed drastically depending upon whether the missionaries came from Catholic or Protestant nations. British, Dutch, and American missionaries who proclaimed evangelical Christianity were unexposed to Iberian Catholicism in its folk-influenced form, which had been brought to the New World, including Latin America, Asia, and Africa. Nevertheless, from the viewpoint of the native populations, Christian expansion in non-Western nations was perceived as a unified effort to advance Western civilization and to advocate for the superiority of European culture.[195]

Enlightenment

In continental Europe and the British Isles, the Enlightenment wave spread through entire societies through education, accelerating secularization from the eighteenth century to the twentieth. Reason replaced divine revelation as the touchstone of truth and came to be viewed as a superior worldview. In academia, reason gave a buoyant but false hope that it could replace religion as a source of answers.[196] New scientific disciplines such as sociology, anthropology, and psychology applied logic and reason in a widening arena.[197] A hallmark of secularization occurred in 1778, when arguments against Christianity by Voltaire and Rousseau were published. The following generations

---

193. Ibid., xvii.
194. Ibid., xvii.
195. Russello, *Christianity and European Culture*, 19–20.
196. Hadden "Desacralizing Secularization Theory," 5.
197. Ibid., 3.

of academics, including Comte and Freud, considered the Christian faith to be nothing more than superstition or "infantile illusions."[198]

As Hadden points out, tension began to grow dramatically during this period between religious authorities and the emerging new order of reason. Even before Charles Darwin's *Origin of Species* was published, philosophers hypothesized that the world evolved in a series of progressive stages, similar to Darwin's theory of evolution. The traditional Christian worldview seemed antiquated in comparison, and the ecclesiastical establishment appeared to be "standing as an obstacle to progress." During the French Revolution, not only were secular powers targeted for overthrow, but also the ecclesiastical establishment that legitimated and collaborated with the monarchy.[199]

Also during this period, the solidarity of the religious culture of Western Europe was forever altered by the birth of Protestantism.[200] Protestant faith provided a healthy balance with the newly rising influence of the Enlightenment. Believers who experienced the knowledge of God could apply reason to these real experiences; thus, they came to be known as "people of experimental religion." Derek Tidball concludes:

> The doctrine of assurance, which bound evangelicalism together, was certainly something to be experienced. Reason had its place and was not to be undervalued in favour of enthusiasm and feelings. Rational, scriptural evidence was given as a basis for faith. Religion and science were not in conflict with one another. Natural theology was an aid to belief.[201]

In the Iberian Peninsula, the church was predominantly Catholic and even more conservative than in France and Italy. The Nordic countries were mostly Lutheran, and, in many parts of Germany, a mixed population of Protestants and Catholics coexisted. In France, the minority Protestant Huguenots were persecuted during the sixteenth and seventeenth centuries, causing many to flee to neighboring countries such as the Netherlands, Switzerland, and England.[202] Even

198. McManners, "Enlightenment," 281–83.

199. Hadden, "Desacralizing Secularization Theory," 5.

200. Bruce, *Religion in the Modern World*, 237.

201. Tidball, *Who Are the Evangelicals?*, 36–37.

202. Today, regular church attendance in France (mainly Catholics) has fallen to 6 to 8 percent the population. See Johnstone and Mandryk, *Operation World*, 254–57.

in these countries, which allowed some degree of religious freedom, dissenters suffered considerable discrimination. "The lives of the great majority of the people were closely bound up with the official churches."[203]

In the late nineteenth century, after the Enlightenment and the French Revolution, new schools of thought emerged that were strongly opposed to the church: humanism, atheism, anarchism, radicalism, communism, socialism, and secularism. The Catholic Church in its staunch opposition to these changes became their central opponent, particularity in France, but also throughout central Europe. Reason and science were used to oppose religious mystery, including folklores, supernatural beliefs, superstitions, and ignorance. The church declared that anyone who adopted this new order was now an enemy of the church, such as those who supported anticlericalism.[204]

As a result, the church itself became a polarizing force in Western Europe, separating Christians and non-Christians, clericals and anticlericals, conformists and nonconformists. Secular thought was the new foundation not only for intellectuals and the middle class, but also for the masses and in educational institutions. More and more people became marginalized from the religious establishment. Instead of being a unifying force, the religious establishment "became instead a major basis for the distinctive identity of specific communities, classes, factions in a divided society. Many people found their loyalty to their churches intensified in the process."[205]

The diminished role of Christian culture in most of Western Europe is noteworthy in that, though it had gained a tremendous amount of ground during the past several centuries, these gains quickly disappeared within the latter half of the twentieth century.[206] David Martin claims that the relatively high church attendance in Victorian Britain may have been influenced by nonreligious factors. In the nineteenth century, church attendance was a sign of middle-class respectability. Many Victorians may have attended church to be seen rather than to express deep religious convictions. Martin emphasizes that social changes and non-religious factors may have affected the

203. McLeod, *Religion and the People of Western Europe*, v.
204. Hadden, "Desacralizing Secularization Theory," 5–6.
205. McLeod, *Religion and the People of Western Europe*, v.
206. Russello, *Christianity and European Culture*, 20.

lives of modern people to link with privatization, cultural differentiation, mobility, and anonymity in the Western world. This situation is
similar to other European countries such as France, Australia, New
Zealand, Canada, and Russia.[207]

Some sociologists argue that a decline in institutional religion
cannot be interpreted as a decline in religious belief and commitment.
Religion today may be expressed in different venues because it has
become increasingly privatized; people develop their beliefs and relationships with God and see religious institutions as less important.[208]
Robin Gill points out that Christian decline has led to "disastrous
anti-intellectualism" among the British churches. Some dominant
models of evangelism are far too simplistic to be effective and further contribute to the churches' reputation as anti-intellectual.[209] He
insists that many Christians who would not have "satisfied university
entrance for themselves, marginalize their own academic theologians,
and must expect to occupy less than [a] central role in an educated
and thinking society."[210] The decline of evangelicalism and religious
enthusiasm are major causes of "more open acceptance" to so-called
"religious toleration," which ultimately paved the way for secularization in British society.[211]

207. David Martin describes a vivid interaction between conformist and nonconformist mindset. He provides many results of his data collected on dissenting
groups in the late nineteenth to twentieth century. His work gives a general picture
of English church decline stating that it did not happen by a single factor but by
a combination of social, economic, political, and industrial factors. See Martin's *A
General Theory of Secularization*.

208. Lee, "Religion," 479.

209. Gill says that "a society becomes better educated simplistic evangelism cannot be an adequate response to decline." See Gill, *Beyond Decline*, 2–3.

210. Ibid., 6.

211. Wheeler-Barclay observes that, throughout the latter half of the eighteenth
century, the Scottish church, like the Church of England, had been dominated by
a group of latitudinarian clerics who opposed all forms of religious "enthusiasm"
as dangers to social order and civic peace. Closely allied with the leading thinkers
of the Scottish Enlightenment and deeply imbued with its ethos, these "moderate"
theologians stressed the harmony between reason and revelation and the importance
of a practical expression of faith through conformity with the ethical teachings of
the gospels. From about 1800, however, moderate influence in the church entered a
period of gradual but steady decline in the face of a gathering evangelical reaction.
Ibid., 2–3.

POSTWAR CHRISTIANITY

The decline of Christianity is a long process involving a series of opposing forces throughout history. Still, certain junctures have been critical turning points along the way.

Decline of Religion

An important turning point in Christian Europe becoming non-Christian was the middle of the twentieth century. The decline of the British Church accelerated in the 1960s, according to Brown:

> For a thousand years, Christianity penetrated deeply into the lives of the people, enduring Reformation, Enlightenment and industrial revolution by adapting to each new social and cultural context that arose. Then, really quite suddenly in 1963, something very profound ruptured the character of the nation and its people, sending organised Christianity on a downward spiral to the margins of social significance.[212]

The critical issue of secularization thesis has always been interrelated with the year 1851, the first time a national census was conducted in Britain. Through the census a glimpse of religious behavior and activity from 1851 onwards could be studied. The statistics and tendencies of the social changes, industrialization, migration, and economic changes displayed were very critical. Hugh McLeod's work *The Religious Crisis of the 1960s* draws on this decline of Christendom. He talks about ecumenism, aggiornamento, affluence, coming of the new worlds, gender and the crisis of the church. This normative transformation of the decline of the churches not only affected British society but also Europe, North America, and even Oceania. The people of this period underwent the effects of liberal theology, ecumenical movements, the rise of the younger generations, request of Catholic reform to the Vatican, the dropping out of many churches, and believing without belonging.[213]

212. Brown explains, "In unprecedented numbers, the British people since the 1960s have stopped going to church. . . . Since then, a formerly religious people have entirely forsaken organised Christianity in a sudden plunge into a truly secular condition." Brown, *The Death of Christian Britain*, 1.

213. Hugh McLeod's views on historical secularization have provided insight, inspiration, and accurate analysis on the historical secularization of the West. McLeod, *The Religious Crisis of the 1960s*, 60–82.

Without a doubt, Christianity's influence in Britain and Europe spun into a steep decline in the twentieth century. The year 1850 can be considered the high point of Christian influence. At this time, most British citizens went to church, and children were brought up with Christian ethical teachings. During the first half of the twentieth century, however, the trend turned downward. Steve Bruce gives a glimpse of British Christianity in the 1930s: Church attendance dropped significantly lower than in the nineteenth century, a considerable number of British did not go to church, only some children attended Sunday school, and Christian teachings and morality were no longer included in school curriculums. Christian guidelines no longer remained a staple in politics, public affairs, and media; rather, religious pluralism prevailed as the social norm. Bruce affirms this rapid religious transformation, stating that "it would indeed be a miracle if Christian ideas remained as popular as they were in the 1950s."[214]

The effects of gradual secularization of the previous three hundred years were realized in every aspect of religious and social life in the 1960s, and the transformation was concurrent in virtually all Western European nations. Previously, secularization had progressed differently in different nations. Secularization had gained ground from 1880 to 1930. Brown also agrees with McLeod that secularization spread "with Berlin in advance of London, and London in advance of New York" and expanding to other major cities around the Western world. [215]

Throughout Europe, the effects of de-Christianization and moribund churches are now common sights as the influence of the church in public and personal life grows smaller.[216] The decline of Christian norms, values, and beliefs, coupled with the rise of postmodernism and materialism, has impacted the British and Western Europeans politically, psychologically, and culturally.[217] Even European architecture is being transformed as medieval cathedrals and Victorian red-brick church buildings are converted to other uses: pubs, mosques,

---

214. Bruce, *God Is Dead*, 71.

215. Brown, "The Secularisation Decade," 29–30.

216. Today, a secular and non-Christian environment affects all spheres of public and personal life in Europe. See Runia, "The Decline of Faith?," 197–98.

217. Kaase and Newton, *Beliefs in Government*, 63.

warehouses, offices, factories, apartments, and even Sikh temples.[218] Robinson describes that the state of the Western church had fallen dramatically.[219] Scholars agree that the decline of British and European churches began in 1850 and took a turn for the worse during the 1950s and 1960s, following the two World Wars. The precise point at which this decline began, and the reasons behind it, constitute a bigger mystery—one into which we will now delve.

Since the 1960s, the decline of official, mainline denominations has been pronounced while popular forms of religious beliefs, images, and practices that imitate other forms of the supernatural, apart from the traditional Christian faith, have risen. Bruce describes them as "amorphous and idiosyncratic and have few, if any, behavioral consequences."[220] Ecclesiastical hypochondria is one result of decline. Churches continually take their own pulse and temperature, using data not merely to determine the presence or absence of the kingdom of heaven, but also to determine the state of God's health![221]

Clergy and churches are responding to this decline by adopting secular solutions, which ironically contributes further to the problem.[222] Church authorities are constantly dealing with the disposal of church buildings by selling them off as carpet showrooms or for conversion to residential units, while older cathedrals and ministers survive by transforming churches into heritage sites for historical/religious tourism to raise funds, rather than using them for worship.[223]

218. Gibbs and Coffey, *Church Next*, 10.

219. "Despite the fact that most cities in Europe have skylines that still feature church spires and city centers whose roads lead to large and beautiful cathedrals, the situation of the church is worrying and getting worse. It is claimed that less than 1% of the population attends church in Copenhagen and that under 5% of the population attends church in most Scandinavian countries. Even though the figures for church attendance in Catholic southern Europe are not yet as low as for Protestant northern Europe, there is a dramatic drop in attendance which so far shows no sign of slowing. Even in the Catholic Republic of Ireland, the cultural dominance of the Catholic Church is being severely challenged with attendance at Mass declining significantly." Robinson and Smith, *Invading Secular Space*, 20.

220. Bruce, *Religion in Modern Britain*, 71.

221. Morris sees church membership as a barometer of the kingdom of heaven. If membership increases, the kingdom is at hand; if it declines, it is tarrying. Bentley, *Cry God for England*, 20–21.

222. Gill, *Beyond Decline*, 120–36.

223. Brown, *Death of Christian Britain*, 4.

The decreased social influence of Christianity along with a loss of intellectual confidence in Christian doctrine has contributed to the decline in total church attendance since the 1950s and 1960s.[224] There has also been a decline of folk religion in Britain.[225]

Belief in the supernatural, particularly the Bible's accounts of miracles, Christ being the Son of God, and the existence of heaven and hell, is declining among the British. As belief in the miraculous has waned, so too has agreement with Christianity's claim of possessing the one and only truth.[226] The roots of such trends can be found in the biblical criticism and rationalism of the nineteenth century.[227]

1950s

Many scholars have identified the separation of church and state as the factor precipitating the decline of the church. The union of the two had formed a cultural, social, communal, and geographical identity during medieval times. When this was broken, so was the common European identity. The medieval solidarity of the Catholic Church was replaced by an array of different denominations in Western Europe—Anglican, Presbyterian, and Lutheran, among others. Ecclesiastical power declined and secular society came to dominate during the Enlightenment and the Industrial Revolution.[228] Some from the upper social classes became nostalgic for a Catholic monopoly and painted the past in rosy tones. Dobbelaere points out this tendency: "the more sophisticated versions of this fairy story select certain features of Catholicism which happen to be empirically coexistent from the eleventh to the thirteenth century and use these as a definition of religion. The selective elements are the temporal power of the Church, extreme asceticism, realism in philosophy, and ecclesiastical dominance in the sphere of artistic patronage and learning."[229]

---

224. The 1930s were a time nominal Christianity was very acceptable. People would be "church people" but not necessarily believe all that the church taught. Many older people do not have clear scriptural theology even if they have had a great deal of church-going experience. Brierley, *Vision Building*, 54–55.

225. Jackson, *Hope for the Church*, 59.

226. Bruce, *Religion in Modern Britain*, 15–18.

227. Broadbent, *The Pilgrim Church*, 388–93.

228. Dobbelaere, *Secularization*, 46.

229. Ibid., 46.

Even in the late Victorian period, it was rather inaccurate to state that the majority of the British were committed Christians, although churchgoing was at its peak. Between 1942 and 1960, church membership, attendance, and Christian beliefs were all growing, along with conservatism and popular Protestantism.[230] The Victorian period is usually mentioned as the historical peak before Christianity began to decline in Europe, with the World Wars as an interim during which decline continued "unabated."[231] Brown agrees, pointing out comparisons between Britain and the United States during the Victorian era. As America's "popular religiosity and institutional church strength not only continued to grow but also earlier denominationalism gave way to a vigorous and inclusive religious culture which—as in Britain—nurtured conservatism and traditional values, whilst church membership *per capita* grew faster than at any time since the recording of statistics began in 1890."[232]

Christianity has risen and fallen in a slow cyclical pattern in Britain throughout the centuries, but, in the 1950s and 1960s, its decline was greater than the total decline of the previous hundred years—and the numbers have never recovered. In contrast, the church in the United States saw its religious peak in the 1940s and 1950s. British and European churches underwent dramatic changes in the mid-1960s. According to Dobbelaere:

> In the last decennia the number of people who believe in God and life after death has also fallen, and in several countries even the rites of passage are being celebrated by fewer and fewer people. Wilson reports, and other studies could be cited in confirmation, that the number of religious vocations is also sharply declining, which is very indicative of the declining social significance of the churches. More and more people are becoming aware of these developments, since the figures are published and commented upon in the daily newspapers and on radio and television.[233]

230. Brown, *The Death of Christian Britain*, 5.

231. Alister refers to the Victorian period as a time "before Europe transferred the secularization of its intellectuals to popular culture as a whole." McGrath, *The Future of Christianity*, 28.

232. Brown, *The Death of Christian Britain*, 5.

233. Dobbelaere, *Secularization*, 140–41.

According to statistics analyzed by Brown, in the 1950s, society had moved considerably far from the Christian beliefs and mores common in the 1900s, but would move even further by 2004.[234] He explains, "Religion mattered and mattered deeply in British society as a whole in the 1950s. But it started to stop mattering in 1960s. Something happened to change those statistics of church connection and activity, statistics which had moved up and down only for over a hundred years, but which very suddenly plunged."[235]

The 1950s was a time of religious complacency. The prestige and position obtained by the church during the Victorian era falsely projected a stable future for mainline denominations, as the church and state still coexisted harmoniously. After the Worlds Wars, however, mainline churches were unwilling or unable to maintain *regular* contact with the majority of the British, especially the working class.[236] According to Davie, "there was a growing awareness that the urbanized and industrialized parts of the country were increasingly slipping away from the churches' influence. The effectiveness of the churches in many working-class areas was hardly reassuring in 1950s."[237]

1960s

The 1960s represent another historical turning point in the decline of Christianity. For religious sociologists, church historians, and even secular phenomenologists, no period in Christian history is as important as the 1960s. According to Brown, the 1960s transformed "the way in which British culture narrates religion." During this decade, British society underwent more secularization than over the previous four centuries combined. Brown asserts, "Never before had all of the numerical indicators of popular religiosity fallen simultaneously, and never before had their declension been so steep."[238] Churches encountered waves of social change, religious indifference, and revolutionary sexual attitudes never seen before. A considerable number of immigrants from former British colonies imported non-Christian beliefs, from Hinduism and Islam to a new type of Afro-Caribbean

234. Brown, *The Death of Christian Britain*, 6–7.
235. Ibid., 7.
236. Davie, *Religion in Britain Since 1945*, 42–43.
237. Ibid., 32–33.
238. Brown, "The Secularisation Decade," 30.

Christianity, creating a religiously pluralistic society in a very short time. The Christian faith no longer held a monopoly in social and political spheres, and the longstanding traditional Christian communal life disintegrated.[239]

The decline of the 1960s was unprecedented in that trends in European Christianity showed only downward cyclical patterns without any signs of upward growth. This marked the beginning of the permanent decline of Christianity in Europe. The decline of the 1960s accounts for two main historical events: the terminal decline of most mainline denominations and the permanent decline of the traditional and religious cultural milieu to which most British had been accustomed for almost two millennia. This decline was present in most parts of British society.

Though this downward trend began in the 1960s, it has slackened in the late twentieth century, mitigating people's concern about the effects of de-Christianization. In the United States, several cities and suburban areas have also experienced a decline resembling that of Europe, and American churches will certainly follow the European pattern of decline if they do not try to bring forth a new vitality.[240] As church and state were disintegrated post-Enlightenment, reason has replaced the divine as a basis for thought and action, and freedom has replaced the sacred as our highest ideal. According to McLeod, a wide-ranging spirit of rebellion arose "against the various official churches that had emerged triumphant from the turmoil of the Reformation and Counter-Reformation, [leading to] the consequent breakdown of the religious unity that had been imposed."[241]

In her article "Church Involvement and Secularization," Dobbelaere utilizes Stoetzel's four types of European religious affiliations in the nine nations covered by the European Value Study Group (EVSG): dominantly Catholic (Spain, Italy, and Eire), predominantly Protestant (Denmark, Great Britain, and Northern Ireland), religiously mixed (western Germany), and the laicized region (France, Belgium, and the Netherlands), where those who have no religious affiliation form a sizeable percentage of the population.[242] The number of ac-

239. Davie, *Religion in Britain*, 33.

240. Robinson and Smith, *Invading Secular Space*, 23–24.

241. McLeod, *Religion and the People of Western Europe*, v.

242. Dobbelaere, "Church Involvement and Secularization," 19; Davie, *Religion in*

tive Catholics is at a record low despite a relatively high number of people who identify themselves as Catholic in France and Belgium—a result of the momentous fall that occurred in the late 1960s and early 1970s. This is also true in the Netherlands. Thus this record-breaking decline affects almost all Western European countries, Catholic or Protestant.[243]

Critical Decades

Church attendance declined drastically beginning in the 1960s, and every sphere of people's lives became increasingly secular. Norms, values, laws, customs, and communal life principles were based on secularism.[244] This momentous decline affected protestant and Catholic churches alike throughout Europe during the 1960s and 1970s. Davie states that "membership figures, together with almost any other indicator of religiosity in the 1960s, reveal all too clearly the churches' continuing inability to stem the growth of religious indifference in Britain." One example cited is John A.T. Robinson's *Honest to God*, a 1963 book that undermines the traditional concept of the Christian God.[245]

Adrian Hastings agrees that "the crisis of 1960s was a crisis of secularization."[246] He states that the most important Catholic ecclesiastical event of the century took place in the 1960s, when the Vatican Council's principal constitutions and decrees were pronounced: "It so greatly changed the character of by far the largest communion of Christendom (and by and large, in a direction which we may describe not too unfairly as one of "Protestantization"), that no one has been left unaffected."[247]

Davie further accentuates that the 1960s represented a pivotal moment: "Taken to extremes, policies which break down too many barriers between the sacred and the secular can be dangerous, for they

---

Britain since 1945, 13.

243. Dobbelaere, "Church Involvement and Secularization," 19–20.

244. O'Sullivan, "Is Europe Losing Its Faith?," 2.

245. Davie, *Religion in Britain*, 34.

246. Hastings points out that the term "'secularization' should not be need to be disputed that in many ways something fairly caked 'secularization' was proceeding extremely rapidly – all the statistics point to it." Hastings, *A History of English Christianity*, 585–586.

247. Ibid., 525.

leave the sacred in a vulnerable position." What Davie points out is that British people had lost a sense of reverence to the sacred because the sacred is no longer functioning as a religious authority among the common British. As a result the church inevitably followed the pattern of the secular rather than the sacred. She states that "the process of secularization, many would argue, has penetrated the churches themselves [but] never more so than in the 1960s."[248]

Other seismic changes during the 1960s include a growing moral pluralism and the implementation of new laws reflecting nontraditional, non-Christian sexual ethics. According to McLeod, laws that were once "justified as an expression of Christian moral principles have been replaced by others founded on the recognition of current moral pluralism, and usually taking the form of a compromise between the demands of the various concerned lobbies."[249] One example of this shift is the number of divorces granted in Britain. From 1961 to 1981, the number of divorces per year jumped from 27,000 to 159,000. This can be contrasted to 3,000 divorces in 1921 and a mere 700 in 1911.[250]

Apart from revolutionary social changes, the rise of religious and moral pluralism, and widespread secularism in Britain, the 1960s also saw the advent of new religious movements (NRMs) as Christianity declined. As Davie points out, the influx of NRMs "became a focus of public as well as religious attention, as at least some (though never all that many) people looked outside the mainline churches for spiritual satisfaction."[251] NRMs benefitted from the changing social and religious landscape, and "were standing 'in some degree of protest against the dominant traditions of society and rejecting prevailing patterns of belief and conduct,'" flourishing as a result. Alongside NRMs, newer and younger house churches emerged during this decade and "began to multiply in response to a somewhat similar demand among Christians (usually evangelicals) for a great distinctiveness in Church life."[252] Davie points out that the rise of NRMs and cults, though they

248. Davie, *Religion in Britain*, 35.

249. The liberalizing Obscene Publication Act in 1959, the legalization of homosexual acts and abortions in 1967, and the Divorce Law Reform Act in 1969 are a few examples. McLeod, "The Privatization of Religion in Modern England," 15–16.

250. A 1988 estimate predicts that one-third of current marriages in Britain are likely to end in divorce. Abercrombie et al., *Contemporary British Society*, 290–98.

251. Davie, *Religion in Britain*, 36–37.

252. Ibid., 36–37.

appeared to have affected a minority of the population, represent a symptom of a larger problem. The decline of the established church has not shattered "religious belief but it has rendered such belief vulnerable to all kinds of external pressures. Nominal Christianity provides a rich seedbed for alternative versions of the sacred."[253]

In the 1970s, many immigrant communities, by this time a significant and visible feature of many British cities, chose to retain their own forms and styles of religious life, resisting pressures to adapt to British ways of thought, including its understated religiosity.[254] As a result, a nominal form of Christianity remained dominant while foreign religions and even cults continued to grow.[255]

The 1980s (known as the Thatcher decade, for Prime Minister Margaret Thatcher) need to be examined separately. In the 1990s, British society is often described as being consumerist, displaying ambivalence regarding the sacred. Religious organizations responded to popular trends by marketing products ranging from books to events, some with greater success than others. The few who rejected consumerism and materialism altogether perceived the sacred as the different, and ultimately better, way of life, but did not spread their faith actively.[256]

The 1960s left the religious landscape in Britain transformed as non-Christian values in the social, family, ecclesiastical, and sexual spheres created a religiously pluralistic society.[257]

CONCLUSION: WAS EUROPE EVER CHRISTIANIZED?

As we indicated, the total decline of Christianity and church membership in Europe, particularly in Britain, has been constantly downward, resulting in a church that has a relatively large number of elderly people. In fact, 25 percent of adults attending church are sixty-five years of age or older. This age group represents only 19 percent of the total population.[258] Christian churches have diminished not only in

253. Ibid., 43.

254. Ibid., 37.

255. Ibid., 38.

256. Ibid., 38–41.

257. Brown, *The Death of Christian Britain*, 8.

258. Some churches and parachurch organizations are enjoying a boom in their legacy income due to deaths of elderly people. Brierley, *Vision Building*, 52–54.

size and number, but also in their own moral standing. Churches were once a guardian of moral standards. Now, however, confidence in the integrity of church leaders is challenged almost weekly by scandals reported in the news media.[259]

A lack of participation in the life of the church leads to the erosion of a distinctively Christian convictions and behavior among the British.[260] It is likely that many individuals who adhere partially to Christian beliefs and whose behavior is in part directed by their faith are not formally registered as church members.[261] Colin Morris optimistically comments on the decline: "some would say that these statistics prove that the Church is on the way out. Others would say that the Church is losing an awful lot of accumulated fat and might be a leaner, maybe even hungrier, but a healthier institution as a consequence."[262] He continues, by stating that if churches are "reduced in numbers" and, as what James Bentley diagnoses, become "leaner and hungrier, perhaps more convinced, more committed—then maybe it will ask how churches can serve the Kingdom of God."[263]

The decline of European Christianity didn't take place instantly but over an extended period of time. By observing the the decline of Christendom, and analyzing and understanding the flawed practices of Christianity in European history, we can see that Christians will greatly benefit by seeking the revival pattern of the Bible, especially the one in the Book of Acts.

---

259. Brown, *Death of Christian Britain*, 4.

260. Jackson points out that not attending church leads to a drop in Christian behavior, saying, "my basic contention is that, with no gathered church, the wider influence of the Christian faith on the attitudes, beliefs and behaviour of people is bound to fall." Jackson, *Hope for the Church*, 60.

261. Lee, "Religion," 479.

262. This interview with Colin Morris by Bentley appears in Bentley, *Cry God for England*, 20.

263. Ibid., 21.

4

Secularization in Europe

WITH THE RISE OF the modern era has come a decline in Christianity in Western Europe, as exemplified by Britain. In this chapter, we will examine how secularism has affected different aspects of European society and how social scientists have viewed this phenomenon. We will also examine the question of whether secularization is inevitable as a society matures, touching on issues from the time periods of Constantine to the twenty-first century.

As the decline of Christianity has become a main focus of socio-religious studies, various theories on the subject have arisen, called secularization, secularism, religious humanism, laicism, sacralization, privatization, disenchantment, differentiation, de-Christianization, desacralization, and post-secularization.[1] All have the one common focus: the decline of religion in society. Historically speaking, there have been three major eras: the medieval age with its monopoly of church and state; the Reformation and Enlightenment, when there was a separation of church and state; and the twentieth century and beyond, with a decline of religious authority and power. The anticipated future state of Christianity in the West looks implausibly gloomy. As Anthony F. C. Wallace states, "The evolutionary future of religion is extinction. . . . Belief in supernatural powers is doomed to die out, all over the world, as the result of the increasing adequacy and diffusion of scientific knowledge."[2]

---

1. Costa, "Secularization and Sacralization," 2.
2. Quoted in Gorski and Altinordu, "After Secularization?," 56.

GENEALOGY OF SECULARIZATION

The ecclesiastical and secular histories of Europe are intimately intertwined. In academia, the origins and developments of science, intellectualism, metaphysics, and theology are explained through assumptions about religion and the secular disciplines. One major assumption is known as the *secularization thesis*, which proposes that the decline of religion is inevitable as societies advance and mature.

The terms secular, secularism, and secularization

The term *secular* derives from the Latin word *saeculum* (century, age, era, or epoch), and it has come to mean *world* in the same sense as the Greek *kosmos* and *aiōn* in the Vulgate.[3] In particular, *aiōn* indicates the "temporal as distinguished from the eternal and to this world."[4] Generally speaking, it connotes a worldview that excludes the supernatural and the sacred, but it can also mean *materialism* in the sense of focusing on the physical rather than the spiritual.[5]

The Hebrew equivalent to *saeculum* is *olam hazeh*, which communicates the idea of the reign of God in this world through the coming of the messianic age, which will make it possible for us to join the world to come, *olam haba*. In this context, the Catholic Church advocates that this world must be governed by the church, particularly through the Pope, who is considered the vicar of Jesus Christ. In the fourth and fifth centuries, *saeculum* was understood not only as *age*, but also *world* with the extended idea of the spirit of an age. The word *saeculum* appeared in Latin Catholic prayers (*sæcula sæculorum*) indicating "unending time," "forever and ever," or "the world out there."[6] Augustine and the early church fathers used *saeculum* to express the idea of this world or this time as opposed to the world to come. Gorski and Altinordu note that the antonym of *saeculum* "was not the religious realm, but the *eschaton*—the end of time at the moment of Christ's return."[7]

---

3. Neill, *Dictionary of the Christian World Mission*, 545–47.

4. Prosman, *The Postmodern Condition*, 35.

5. Loetscher, *Encyclopedia of Religious Knowledge*, 1009.

6. Swatos and Christiano, "Secularization Theory," 211–12.

7. Gorski and Altinordu, "After Secularization?," 60.

We can see that the concept of *saeculum* not only refers to the present time, but contains an expectation of the coming age. As Prosman puts it, *secular* is the "time of the world, as opposed to God's time: eternity. . . . The time of this world was not the time of God, but this did not make it meaningless. Far from that, the time of the world was *kairotic*."[8] The Jewish understanding of the time of the world refers to the coming of the Messiah—the so-called messianic age that will complete all other time. In this sense, as Prosman articulates, "The secular is not divine, but it is meaningful as it takes place between meaningful events such as creation, incarnation and the last judgment."[9]

In the Hebrew concept, according to David Castelli, "This world, moreover, is not considered to be the real life, but as compared to the life to come, it is the vestibule or ante-room, through which we pass to the banquet-hall, and we are exhorted to prepare ourselves in the olam hazeh, in order to be admitted to the olam haba. . . . [O]ne hour of bliss in the future world is worth more than the whole of our present life."[10] The concept of two worlds, this world and the world to come, is related to the messianic age. John J. Parsons points out, "the resurrection of the dead is considered the end of the world, whereas the coming of the Messiah . . . was to be followed by a national revival ushering in the Messianic age."[11] The Messianic age stands at the intersection of the present and future ages, each of which is indefinite, but not infinite, in duration.[12]

The church also conceived of a duality, but not a temporal one, as Prosman describes:

> In the early Church emerged a duality of sacred and secular in which the sacred, monastic life was regarded as superior. The clergy was concerned with eternal things, whereas the laity was concerned with temporal affairs. Jerome, for example, wrote on the *duo genera christianorum*. So the distinction between

---

8. Prosman, *The Postmodern Condition*, 45. "Kairos in Greek is an experience of time as qualified, more than mere durative time (chronos)."

9. Ibid., 45.

10. Castelli, "Rabbinical Literature," 319–20.

11. Ibid., 336. The Messianic age is known as *Yemot HaMashiach*.

12. Parsons says that one major question is "whether the Torah, understood here to refer to the various *mitzvoth* found in the writings of Moses, will abide as 'everlasting' commandments, or whether the conditions of the world win be so transformed that they win no longer apply." Parsons, "Olam HaTorah," 7.

worldly and sacred affairs was developed within the Church of the West. The distinction was not a rigid duality but over time it grew more and more complex, for example in the class of the rulers. "The kings of the Middle Ages were not strictly secular but neither were they clerical. They were anointed, but had no religious tasks." [13]

The secular, in the Catholic Church, was contrasted with the activities of clergy "such as priests and monks [who] have turned away from the secular to live closer to eternity." [14] Prosman states, "In the Middle Ages, the concept of secularization functioned most explicitly in canonical law. . . . A priest could live either in a monastery or in 'the world.' The transfer from the monastery to the world was referred to as secularization in canonical law." [15] The secular clergy were those who returned to the world from the monasteries, while others remained apart.

Still, the two realms can not be fully separated. John Keane points out:

> The Christianisation narrative, the tale of the conquering of the temporal world by the spiritual, has reappeared under modern conditions, in mirror-image form, in the doctrine of the secularisation of the world. . . . there is a strong tendency to dogmatise secularism by supposing its long-term victory over the process of Christianisation. [16]

The relationship "between civil and ecclesiastical law, lands, and possessions" [17] was negotiated through the implementation of canonical law. Costa states there was a reciprocal understanding of the "expropriation—by the State—of property belonging to the Catholic Church" which is different from the property of the feudal lords. [18] Prosman notes that "The Carolingian kings [of seventh-century France], when they took on the protection of the Church, received taxes and land in exchange." [19]

13. Prosman, *The Postmodern Condition*, 35.

14. Ibid., 45.

15. Ibid., 35.

16. Keane, "Secularism?," 5.

17. Swatos and Christiano, "Secularization Theory," 211–12.

18. Costa, "Secularization and Sacralization," 6.

19. Prosman, *The Postmodern Condition*, 35.

The concept of secularization took on a spatial connotation during the Middle Ages, when it described

> a monk's renunciation of the rule of his order, his exit from the monastery, his return to the world, and more specifically to his transfer to the worldly or secular clergy that ministered to the laity. Importantly, a secularized priest retained traces of his monastic past: He was required to wear the emblem of his order. . . . This layer adds both a spatial and an individual dimension to the concept: spatial, insofar as the sacred space of the monastery is opposed to the profane space of the world; and individual, insofar as the departure of the monk implies a loss of heart or commitment, if not of belief itself. It also anticipates another common figure in secularization theory: the notion that secularized realms still bear religious traces.[20]

From this point on, the concept of secularization has come to mean a separation from or a rejection of religion. In the nineteenth century, George Jacob Holyoake stated that secularists sought a "world order and moral program of individual action that would address human problems without the use of supernatural explanations."[21] A contemporary of Holyoake, Charles Bradlaugh, used the term *secularism* to describe the Christian practice of asking church authorities to be disconnected from political affairs. Secularists, too, expressed the need for certain areas to be separated from Christianity. Keane indicates, "morality is concerned with the well-being of human beings in the present life, to the exclusion of all considerations, drawn from belief in God and the afterlife."[22] Swatos and Christiano indicate that the term secular "already had an ambiguous, but increasingly negative, use by the time it was adapted into social science."[23] In *The Reasoner*, Holyoake declared his disbelief in God and urged others to join him in following worldly life principles that do not presume a belief in God and the afterlife, which he promoted as a better social order. Holyoake states, "[S]ecularism is not an argument against Christianity, it is one independent of it. It does not question the pretensions of Christianity; it advances others."[24]

20. Gorski and Altinordu, "After Secularization?," 60.
21. Swatos and Christiano, "Secularization Theory," 211–12.
22. Keane, "Secularism?," 7.
23. Swatos and Christiano, "Secularization Theory," 211–12.
24. Knight, "Secularism," lines 74–75.

The term *secular* has now come to convey ideas and norms that do not recognize the existence of God and salvation through Christ Jesus. *Secularization* expresses the idea that church has lost its power and that a worldview without reference to God has gained ascendency over the sacred. Secularism is a two-sided coin. On the positive side, it promotes "social progress and the amelioration of material conditions for the working classes."[25] The negative side is a dismissive attitude toward Christianity.

Looking at the French term for *secularism, laicization* (from *laïcité*) has two attributes. Jean-Paul Willaime asserts that

> on the political plane, it refers to a general principle of neutrality towards any and all belief systems or "worldviews" (*Weltanschauungen*). This would include the principle of respective independence between government and religion. On the philosophical plane, it refers to secular, non-religious, worldviews conceived as an alternative to religious beliefs.[26]

Willaime says "the notion of *secularization* is not as extensive as *laïcité*, whereas *secularism*, depending on nuances, may go further."[27] Hence, Willaime suggests *laïcité* has an etymological connection to *laïque* in which it usually denotes the denigration of religion. He proposes three different meanings for *laïcité* including "(1) secularism as non-sectarian neutrality of the state (Secular State); (2) secularism as a secular worldview alternative to religious beliefs; and (3) secularism as an ideology opposing religion and denouncing its misdeeds and deleterious effects (one speaks of 'laicism' in this case)."[28] In addition, Willaime says of *laïcité*; "laicity as a cause for the emancipation of public institutions and individuals from any religious influence is a notion that appears to be more operative in Catholic countries than in Protestant ones. Laicity, in this case, appears as a movement of emancipation reacting against the control and influence that the Catholic Church once exercized within and over some civil societies."[29] He gives various usages of the term *laïcité*:

---

25. The idea of secularism put forth by Holyoake evolved later into extreme atheism by F.L. Cross. *Oxford Dictionary of the Christian Church*, 1236.

26. Willaime, "Secularism at the European level," 2.

27. Ibid., 2.

28. Ibid., 2.

29. Ibid., 3.

The secularization (*laïcisation*)of French society is not the secularization (*sécularisation*) of German society. They are two different processes in the political neutralization of religions: the Catholic or post-Catholic process is effected through separation rather, while the Protestant one proceeds more by interiorizing and absorbing elements [that were] initially religious."[30]

As Western Christianity declined, advocates of secularization sought to replace religion with secular alternatives. Prosman suggests looking at both religion and reason when considering secularization: "The notion of secularization has served exactly this goal; to envisage the complexity involved in, on the one hand, the modern divide between the age of faith and the age of reason, and on the other hand, the great extent to which the religious is still present in modernity and postmodernity."[31]

Whenever the term *secular* is used, it evokes its antonym, *sacred*. Philip Sheldrake clarifies that

"[T]he sacred" is "wholly other" than the mundane and separated from everyday action and experience. . . . the manifestations of the sacred (hierophanies) take place in ordinary objects or locations or a human incarnation of the divine, there is no continuity with the ordinary. What is manifested is "something of a wholly different order, a reality that does not belong to our world."[32]

Emile Durkheim asserts that the sacred is an essential component of religion.[33] Durkheim theorizes that religion originated from solidarity and communal awareness in primitive society.[34] He defines religion as "a unified system of beliefs and practices relating to sacred things, that is to say, things set apart and forbidden—beliefs and practices which unite into one single moral community called a

---

30. Quotation from Professor Jean-Marc Ferry, philosopher at the Free University in Brussels. Ibid., 2–3.

31. Prosman, *The Postmodern Condition*, 32.

32. Sheldrake, "Placing the Sacred," 243.

33. Antolinez, "Primal Religion," 95–96.

34. George Adams explains that, in Durkheim's theory, primitive mechanical solidarity is supplanted more and more by a solidarity based on symbols. Adams, "The Interpretation of Religion," 302–03.

Church, all those who adhere to them."[35] The forbidden is called *profane* in contrast to a temple that is consecrated and considered holy.[36] Expounding on Durkheim's definition, Geertz states that every religion is a cognitive system that becomes a culturally constituted belief system of tenets that are commonly held to be true.[37] Stewart Guthrie sees a continuity between religious and secular belief systems, "since all models, religious or secular, depend on logic—there is no fundamental disjunction between religious and nonreligious modes of thought, despite their differences in content. The relation of religious to nonreligious thought is one of similarity of form and continuity of substance."[38] Religion that originated from a belief in the supernatural and the sacred would logically diminish when modern concepts can explain phenomena previously attributed to the supernatural. As many scholars like Durkheim and Comte anticipated, non-supernatural and non-transcendental elements comprise a new type of religion. Comte saw humanism as a new type of religion, while Durkheim saw that social power would be the substitute of old religion.

The term *secularization* has been used to assess the future of religion in general and also to express the decline of belief in the supernatural and the sacred as religious faiths lose their influence.[39] Throughout much of European history, Christian and secular forces have been intertwined in individual lives and in communal society. Church and state together formed a politico-ecclesiastical hierarchy, Christian ethics served as a check and balance for economic activity, and individuals usually held a belief in the afterlife.

Butterfield points out, "the condition of culture tended to favor the idea of the secular State, the notion of a capitalistic enterprise, and the principle of the emancipation of the individual."[40] Paul M. Zulehner, dean of the theology department at Vienna Catholic University, claims that the religious state is not as irreligious as previously thought, but

35. Durkheim, *The Elementary Forms of the Religious Life*, 47. See also Pickering, *Durkheim on Religion*, 123.

36. Hulbert, "Profanity," 70.

37. I do not think that a religious system as a cognitive is always true, but I do agree that every religious system could be explained by a cognitive system. See Alexander, "A Biofunctional Theory of Religion," 546.

38. Guthrie, "A Cognitive Theory of Religion," 181.

39. Stark and Bainbridge, *The Future of Religion*, 429.

40. Butterfield, "England in the Eighteenth Century," 6.

points out that "We are observing a boom in religious yearning and at the same time a shrinking process of the churches."[41] He concludes that "The Church have secularized themselves."[42] External forces have certainly played a role in the decline of the church, but secularizing forces within the church, and within individual Christians, are also at work.

Christendom and Secularization

Christendom—the unified church/state structure that ruled Europe for centuries—can trace its beginnings to Constantine's Edict of AD 313 (see chapter 3).[43] The process of secularization and its effects were not exposed until the Reformation, and the type of secularization observed after the Reformation was very different than the Catholic idea of secularization following clerical service. This process of decoupling church from state extracted more life from European Christendom within a century than all of its history combined, even from nations with all-encompassing Christian cultures.[44] Ideologies, worldviews, norms, values, and morality drew heavily upon the primarily Christian European culture before the Reformation; European nations had become superficially Christianized. David Martin states that Europe was considered "a unity by virtue of having possessed one Caesar and one God, i.e., by virtue of Rome." The combination of political and religious powers originated with Constantine, who adopted as his symbol the cross with the rising sun after supposedly seeing in a vision the words, "*hoc signo vince*" ("In this sign conquer").[45] Abraham Kuyper interprets Constantine's conversion as a sign of recognition of the kingship of Jesus. Kyuper states,

> When the first contest eventuated in this that the emperor bowed to Jesus, then . . . the kingship of Christ began to be triumphant in society. . . . The kingship of Christ from this time on stood as a direction-giving power above the imperial

41. Quoted in O'Sullivan, "Is Europe Losing Its Faith?," lines 12–13.

42. Ibid., 2.

43. Robinson and Smith, *Invading Secular Space*, 48–49.

44. Jenkins argues that medieval Europeans referred to the era as "Christendom," the *Res Publica Christiana*, that served as "a true overarching unity and a focus of loyalty." Jenkins, *The Next Christendom*, 10.

45. Murray, "Christendom and Post-Christendom," 1.

power, which, in order to strengthen its influence, tried for an ever increasingly close integration with the kingship of Jesus. . . . When in the fourth century persecution ceased and the imperial power evinced a readiness to accommodate itself to Jesus, the basic victory became apparent. . . . This principal victory continued on during the entire course of the long period known as the Middle Ages. [46]

Through the propagation of religious symbols, Constantine was able to unite political and ecclesiastical constituents in a structure that would impact Europe for more than a thousand years. Murray describes the process: "In the following decades it seemed like revival— massive church growth, wonderful new church buildings, changes in laws and customs, church leaders taking on political and social roles, Constantine ruling as a Christian emperor. . . . Christianity had become the state religion, the only legal religion, and it was pagans who were being persecuted."[47]

It is evident that New Testament church vitality was not predominant in post-Constantine Christianity. The difference between the New Testament church and Constantine Christianity is that in the post-Constantine church we saw only a few who converted voluntarily and received compulsory baptism.[48] After the formation of Christendom by the joining of politics and the ecclesiastical system, all citizens became Christians by birth except the Jewish population. Murray points to the "development of a 'sacral society,' where there was no effective distinction between sacred and secular, where religion and politics were inter-twined." He identifies the characteristics of this arrangement:

- The definition of "orthodoxy" as the common belief, determined by socially powerful clerics supported by the state;

- The imposition of a supposedly "Christian morality" on the entire population (although normally Old Testament moral standards were applied);

- A political and religious division of the world into "Christendom" and "heathendom";

46. Ibid., 3.
47. Ibid., 1–2.
48. Ibid., 3.

- The defense of Christianity by legal sanctions to restrain heresy, immorality and schism, and by warfare to protect or extend Christendom;

- A hierarchical ecclesiastical system, based on a diocesan and parish arrangement, which was analogous to the state hierarchy and was buttressed by state support;

- A generic distinction between clergy and laity, and the relegation of the laity to a largely passive role;

- Obligatory church attendance, with penalties for non-compliance;

- The practice of infant baptism as the symbol of obligatory incorporation into this Christian society;

- The imposition of obligatory tithes to fund this system.[49]

The caesaropapist model could be characterized by tension or by harmony between the church and the state. Murray states, "The form of this partnership might vary, with either partner dominant, or with a balance of power existing between them. There are examples from the fourth century onwards both of emperors presiding over church councils and of emperors doing penance imposed by bishops. Throughout the medieval period, power struggles between popes and emperors resulted in one or other holding sway for a time."[50] The Catholic Church progressively assumed more and more political power, resulting in secularization and corruption. Church became a primarily political mechanism. Murray states, "The church provided religious legitimation for state activities; the state provided secular force to back up ecclesiastical decisions."[51]

Since the earliest days of the Christian faith, salvation through Jesus Christ has been a priority. However, when the church functioned as an ecclesiastical system within Christendom, with power over politics, art, public life, and culture, unthinkable tragedies occurred. The proper relationship between church and state has been addressed by prominent early Christian theologians, including Augustine. He distinguished "the 'historia gentium' [history of Gentiles] and the history of salvation. For Augustine the sacred and secular history are

49. Ibid., 2.
50. Ibid., 3.
51. Ibid., 3.

two different narratives."[52] Sacred history can impact the secular if redemptive and prophetic accomplishments are achieved, such as the Christianization of the Roman Empire.

On the other hand, Eusebius saw the history of the Roman Empire as part of the sacred because of the Christian victory over the secular empire. Prosman sates, "Augustine reacted against this idea of a realization of salvation through the Roman empire. Eusebius of Caesarea saw the reign and conversion of Constantine as a part of God's plan for uniting humanity. The Eusebian scheme interpreted the empire in theological terms as an image of Christ's kingdom and the emperor as a representation of the divine logos."[53]

In the *City of God*, Augustine paints a picture of salvific actions possible through the Catholic Church on earth.[54] Christians live in the secular world as pilgrims, Augustine describes, constantly in a state of "spiritual warfare . . . moving from death to life. . . . either attuned more and more to the reign of the sacred or ever more grimly and stubbornly attached to the glamorous evil of the 'falsely autonomous' secular. . . . there is no "neutral halting point or 'place of stillness' between the two." [55] A tension is inherent between the matters of the world and spiritual matters. Trainor says further:

> [I]n this spiritual battle fought between these everlasting poles (in effect, the "sacred" and the "satanic") of social and political life, there is no respite. The City of God is socially and politically victorious where secular rule is subject to the reign of the sacred, and where there is what we might call an "Augustinian equilibrium," that is, where the focus of the empirical state (government, ruling authority) on temporal matters under God's reign and guidance is balanced and complemented by the focus of the church on spiritual matters under Christ's reign and overlordship. Likewise, the City of God is victorious where God's eternal (sacred) righteousness informs human (secular) justice. [56]

In this respect, Augustine was the person who gave theological legitimacy for the church's involvement in ruling over the secular

52. Prosman, *The Postmodern Condition*, 34.
53. Ibid., 34.
54. Ibid., 34–35.
55. Trainor, "Augustine's 'Sacred Reign—Secular Rule,'" 2.
56. Ibid., 2.

world. *The City of God* introduces "a Christian idea of 'the sacred' with *sanctuary* which implies not merely special places but an image of protection and *refuge* from what is other."[57] Trainor illustrates, "For Augustine, the 'secular' is truly itself (and truly authoritative and legitimate) when it is oriented to the 'sacred,' its divine origin and end."[58] Therefore, when "the sacred (God) 'reigns,' presides and uplifts, whereas the secular authority (government) 'rules,' commands and punishes" the world is ruled by the sacred instrument which is the church and Christendom acted as the Kingdom on earth.[59]

Sadly, Christendom ruled in sacred and secular arenas in a corrupted fashion. Brian Trainor asserts, "the kind of grounding and legitimating role once performed by the 'sacred' for the 'secular' in the Christendom era is just as crucial and necessary in the West today . . . the church is more widely acknowledged as having a special role to play in remedying the current 'truth deficit'/ 'justification deficit' in the West and in providing a 'sacred' solution to the current Western crisis of legitimacy."[60]

Philip Sheldrake paints a picture of how Augustine saw the human city: "the earthly city is marked by a 'lust for domination'. . . . Again, the true 'city' for Augustine was the community of believers destined to become the City of God. He was rightly suspicious of any attempt by even Christian Emperors to suggest that their commonwealth was the perfect politics let alone the Kingdom of God on earth."[61] If the church involves itself with the concerns of individual souls, the church then has a relationship with individual lives. Individual and public matters are played out in the secular world. Augustine distinguishes between "'earthly city' (the *civitas terrena*, realm of sin) and the political realities of society and city."[62] Sheldrake explains,

> The secular sphere, for example the city, is a neutral "space" where the spiritual reality of "the city of God" and the counter-spiritual reality of "the earthly city" co-exist and contend, like the wheat and tares, until the end of time. Augustine, while

57. Sheldrake, "Placing the Sacred," 246.

58. Trainor, "Augustine's 'Sacred Reign—Secular Rule,'" 1.

59. Ibid., 1–2.

60. Trainor, "Augustine's 'Sacred Reign—Secular Rule,'" 1.

61. Sheldrake, "Placing the Sacred," 246.

62. Ibid., 246.

far from indifferent to the moral foundations of places like the city, defended a legitimate place for the secular realm within a Christian interpretation of the world as the theatre of God's action. Indeed, some commentators suggest that the vocation of the human city—socially and architecturally—is to strive to become a trace of the *civitas Dei*. According to this view, while Augustine was neither city planner nor political theorist, he effectively redeemed an urban culture in crisis by using the city as his image of heaven. [63]

Augustine's heavenly city cannot stand unless the sacred has an appropriate role in the earthly city. Therefore, the secular rule must coincide with divine reign. Prosman asserts, "it is *intrinsically* spiritual/sacred, or at least intrinsically oriented to the spiritual/sacred, so that to regard 'spiritual rule' and 'secular rule' as separate and distinct and in such a way that one might be deemed to be higher or lower than the other, is to separate the inseparable."[64] Sadly, theology and dogma have been incorrectly interpreted and, as a result, the Caesaropapist collaboration has resulted in improper condemnations, inquisitions, monopoly, crusades, and massacres.[65]

Trainor agrees with Augustine's position that the sacred should reign and the secular rule, because the sacred holds up Christian morality while the secular executes its laws in the public sphere. Anticipating the negative, Trainor points out, "when this fails to occur and a government blatantly fails to do as it ought, this is because the secular is in revolt against its own sacred origin and end, that is, an actual, empirical 'existential' government is in revolt against its own 'truth,' its true being or essence."[66]

In the fourth to eight centuries, The Carolingian formula (two there are by whom the church is rule)[67] was developed where papal and political areas are ruled by the church. In the eleventh century, Gregorian Reform clarified the role of church and state, but affirmed that "'spiritual rule' must have primacy over or be acknowledged as higher than 'secular rule' would—viewed in terms of this conception—be acceptable if by 'spiritual rule' was meant 'sacred reign' or 'spiritual

63. Ibid., 246.

64. Trainor, "Augustine's 'Sacred Reign—Secular Rule,'" 4.

65. Ibid., 4–5.

66. Ibid., 4.

67. Ibid., 5.

reign,' for king and bishop are both subject in their respective realms to this 'reign from above' and both need to be informed, guided and enriched by the eternal font of righteousness."[68]

The Gregorian Reform came in response to a power struggle between pope and emperor in the Holy Roman Empire, known as the investiture controversy, during the eleventh and twelfth centuries The *Dictatus Papae Gregorii VII* called "for a far-reaching *Libertas Ecclesiae* ['freedom of the church'] and the desacralization of the emperor."[69] This struggle originated from a disagreement about "the lay investiture of bishops and abbots."[70] Prosman explains, "Prelates held land and often exercised secular as well as ecclesiastical functions. For this reason, lay lords had a great interest in their appointment. Pope Gregory VII condemned lay investiture[.] (1075) After his condemnation he disputed with emperor Henry IV (1056–1106) whether the pope or the emperor should dominate the Church."[71] This dispute between the pope and secular kings and rulers was ongoing in Medieval Europe. In the late thirteenth century, the norm of collaboration spiritual and temporal secular power substantiated that the clergy can cover the monasteries and secular parishes in England. John Keane points out that "the adjective 'secular' (from the Latin *saecularis*) was first used in English, often with negative connotations, to distinguish clergy living and working in the wider medieval world from 'religious' clergy who lived in monastic seclusion."[72]

From its position of power, the Catholic Church carried out inquisitions and crusades, killing thousands. The church exercised power through "'the secular arm' (from the Latin *brachium seculare*) of civil power invoked by the Church to punish offenders"—a close collaboration between the church and state. At the same time, a clergy member who ministered in secular parishes was referred to as a "'secular abbot,' a person who was the beneficiary of the title of abbot and enjoyed part of the revenues, but who was himself neither a monk nor entitled to exercise the functions of an abbot."[73] This system within

68. Ibid., 5.

69. Prosman, *The Postmodern Condition*, 35.

70. Ibid., 35.

71. Ibid., 35.

72. Keane, "Secularism?," 6.

73. Ibid., 6.

Christendom led to injustices and abuses of power: persecution, crusades, indulgences, and inquisitions. The Reformation was not a sudden movement led by a few, but the culmination of the efforts of numerous forerunners who read the Bible and took courageous steps to practice the truth they discovered. Murray states that in the pre-Reformation era, those who read the Bible "began to ask whether it was the Christendom system itself that was the root of the problem, rather than a particular issue. And once they reached the decision that the Christendom system was suspect, they became deeply suspicious that the Bible was being misinterpreted to legitimate this system. It was as if they were now looking at the Bible through a different lens from the Christendom churches."[74]

A critical impetus for the Reformation was that the Catholic Church tried to enforce power over all areas of life, both sacred and secular. In the fourteenth century, "William of Ockham and John Wycliffe . . . strengthened this sense of the word secular by distinguishing institutions concerned with civil, lay and temporal matters from others which were clearly religious or 'spiritual.'"[75] The church and state had a relationship characterized by both tension and cooperation.

Reformation

A nonviolent revolution—the rise of secularism—transformed the face of European history in a magnitude comparable to the recognition of Christianity within the Roman Empire by Constantine. Gradually yet consistently, after the Reformation, the Christianity that had once unified Europe became fragmented; with Protestant and Catholic blocks, state church and Free Church blocks, and conformist and nonconformist blocks. In the public sphere, many nations remained dominantly Christian until the nineteenth century. At the micro level, however, individuals began to be affected by macro-level secularized norms, ideas, and worldviews. Most individuals retained Christian practices only superficially, causing the faith to erode and leading to a complete loss of Christian faith for the majority of the people by the mid-twentieth century, a hundred years later.[76]

74. Murray, "Christendom and Post-Christendom," 7.

75. Keane, "Secularism?," 6.

76. Russello, *Christianity and European Culture*, 8–9.

Medieval Christendom began to crumble at the hands of reform-ists and was eventually divided into several major denominations. This process not only challenged the errors of the Catholic Church, but also created gaps in European society for secular values to penetrate. Most aspects of politics, social norms, and values remained Christian, despite differences among Christian blocs. Secularization accelerated not because of a societal loss of interest in the faith, but because of the church's loss of interest in society. Social movements such as the Enlightenment, the French Revolution, and the Industrial Revolution gave people an alternative view of religion: that it was extraneous or irrelevant to their daily lives.[77]

Church and state no longer held a monopoly on culture as the Reformation made room for secular values to seep into society and shape individuals, eventually causing medieval Christendom to dis-integrate.[78] Generally speaking, secularization was more extensive in the north than in the south, and its effects were more powerful in Protestant than in the Catholic churches. Halman and Pettersson state, "The extensive, dogmatic, collective creed of the Catholic church is assumed to impose a stronger collective identity upon its members." Secularization took different paths depending upon the social and cultural setting of each affected nation.[79]

Reformers Martin Luther and John Calvin both insisted on the separation of church and state.[80] In many nations, the crown was trans-ferred from Catholic to Protestant rulers. Until freedom of religion was decreed in each country, wars between Catholic and Protestant nations took place. While not perfect, the Reformation broke the powerful collaboration between the sacred and the secular. In addi-tion, Prosman states, "Luther writes that the distinction between the world and the Church is not dissolved, but that the Church should not be concerned with worldly power, rather with humility. In this sense, the intention of the Reformation was not to immunize the secular

---

77. Ibid., 9.

78. Jenkins states that in "post-Christendom" there is no longer "any connection between religion and political order" in this century. Jenkins, *The Next Christendom*, 10–11.

79. Halman and Pettersson, "Differential Patterns of Secularization in Europe," 29–30.

80. The Reformation opposed the Catholic system and declared the priesthood all believers.

realm from the sacred, as many (in the line of Weber) interpret the Reformation, as itself an agent of secularization."[81] Keane points out, "these originally neutral or negative connotations of 'the secular' as the temporal domain of 'the worldly' not subject directly to religious rule—the domain of the non-ecclesiastical, non-religious, or non-sacred—[was] weakened. . . . '[S]ecularisation' connoted a process of reducing the influence of religion, as when the term was used in legal and ecclesiastical circles to describe the transfer of religious institutions or property to lay ownership or temporal use."[82]

The nations where Catholicism remained dominant experienced fewer aftershocks from the Reformation, but felt the impact of the French Revolution. Supporters of the Revolution, according to Bruce, considered the church and its followers as anti-revolutionary: "the old regime, the social elite against the forces of social reform."[83] These states had been greatly segregated between rural Catholics and urban, industrialized secularists since the late eighteenth century. Secularists were often needlessly regarded as anticlerical. Even nations where Catholic domination of the state remained intact could no longer remain complacent, but now had to consider an equally powerful enemy: the monopoly of a communist society and socialist government over the state. The Catholic-dominant nations of France, Italy, Spain, and Portugal were divided into two groups: the traditionally committed Catholics and the exceedingly secularized communists and socialists.[84]

The Reformation not only brought about the fall of medieval Christendom in Catholic countries, but also fed anticlericalism and antisupernaturalism, accelerating secularization even in Protestant countries such as Britain, the Scandinavian countries, and the United States. Anticlericalism, which arose in Catholic countries from minority Protestants who resisted the hierarchy of Rome, ultimately led to secularization within the Catholic Church as well.[85]

81. Prosman, *The Postmodern Condition*, 36–37.

82. Keane, "Secularism?," 6.

83. Bruce, *Religion in the Modern World*, 59.

84. Ibid., 59–60.

85. Protestantism in the nineteenth century, Chadwick argues, facilitated secularization because "some of the leading French anticlericals were neither atheist nor agnostic but Protestant." Chadwick, *The Secularization of the European Mind*, 107–39.

Enlightenment

One of greatest challenges to Christianity in European history came from the Enlightenment, which changed the relationship between natural science and religion. Previously, metaphysics and theology had overruled secular scientific disciplines through church authority. Now, in the place of theology, human reason became the dominant force. The intellectual and spiritual influence of Christianity over society in Europe dwindled steadily through the nineteenth and twentieth centuries. Some of the schools of thought to emerge during the Age of Enlightenment included continental rationalism, British empiricism, and European deism. Prominent enlightenment thinkers included John Locke, David Hume, François-Marie Arouet (Voltaire), Jean-Jacques Rousseau, Auguste Comte, Karl Marx, and Emmanuel Kant.[86] The impact of the Enlightenment spread to intellectuals in various fields. It is well known that Karl Marx envisaged that the "the world of the future would be a world without religion," while Thomas Jefferson supposed that "human enlightenment would be accompanied by a rational form of religious knowledge and experience."[87]

The Enlightenment marked the birth of modernity as human reason took the place of religious faith at the center of society's value system. However, the Enlightenment had different expressions throughout Europe in the context of religious and political disputes. As Jean-Marc Ferry states, "Let us say that French Enlightenment would have centered on the State and the political sphere; Scottish Enlightenment, more so on markets and civil society; Prussian Enlightenment, on scholarship (*Université*) and culture."[88] In the case of France, Prosman indicates, the Enlightenment interconnected with the progress of "secularization as *laïcization*, with a strong antireligious tainting, [which] is typical for the French Enlightenment.[89] The German case of the Enlightenment is much more religious than that of the French, which generated the philosophical concept of religious liberation. Prosman notes, "German philosophy, most notably the philosophy of G. W. F. Hegel, amounts to a 'secularized Christianity.'

---

86. Brown, *Christianity and Western Thought*," 285.

87. Editorial introduction, "After Secularization," 5.

88. Willaime quoted from Jean-Marc Ferry's work. Willaime, "Secularism at the European level," 2–3.

89. Prosman, *The Postmodern Condition*, 39.

In the philosophy of Hegel, the term secularization, or *Säkularisierung* does not occur. Instead, the term *Verweltlichung* is frequently used."[90]

Crawford points out that antisupernaturalism produced "a lessening of societal expectation that appeals to the supernatural." He states, "Although the disappearance of witchcraft prosecutions, the popularity of the writings of Enlightenment thinkers, and the interest the educated had in scientific experimentation reflected a lessening of expectation of supernatural intervention in daily life, eighteenth-century British and Americans were still highly religious."[91] Beyond their views of the supernatural, there were differences among Protestants. For example, national elites who were mostly conformist were confronted by socialists and liberals who were dissidents of the state and supported Free Church elements.[92]

According to Northcott, the birth of the modern scientific perspective, "in which God is increasingly excluded as part of the meaning and plausibility structure of the modern *weltanschauung* [worldview]" paralleled the development of the individualistic worldview together with the Enlightenment.[93] Wilson emphasizes the effects of secularization, stating, "The rapid acceleration of the process of rationalization and secularization had the effect, markedly in the early decades of the twentieth century, and even more emphatically after the Second World War, of rendering [the church's] institutional structure increasingly

90. "The term *Verweltlichung* as a legitimate translation of *sécularisation* makes clear that the concept is, at least in part, rooted in Christendom. Scholars who define secularization in this sense tend to stress the historical continuity of Christianity and Modernity and hold that the latter is always dependent for its sustenance on its Christian substrate. Vergote, for instance, speaks of secularization as '. . . a cultural and religious phenomenon.' He asserts that secularization is product of a Western, Christian civilization. He even ascribes to secularization a certain historical necessity." Prosman, *The Postmodern Condition*, 39.

91. Crawford relates this secularization into trans-Atlantic regions, England and New England, seeing that "decline in the practical influence of the clergy over public policy and social behavior and growth of indifference of civil authorities to the promoting of religious uniformity and performance of religious duties" was inevitable. There is no doubt that clergy influence over secular political bodies dropped significantly in the eighteenth century on both sides of the Atlantic. Crawford, "Origins of the Eighteenth-Century Evangelical Revival," 376–77.

92. Bruce, *Religion in the Modern World*, 60.

93. Northcott, *The Church and Secularization*, 12.

hollow."[94] As the influence of the church decreases, Wilson anticipates, industrialization will accelerate rationalism and even secularization.

The catastrophic effects of secularization—the loss of a unified Christian identity and the destruction of Christian communal life that gave the European people social comfort and stability—are hard to miss. Instead of unity, a middle-of-the-road uncertainty began to permeate social life and identity for Europeans.[95] The advent of industrial and modern society has been the starting point for most studies of secularization because this was the point when the significance of ecclesiastical power declined in people's religious lives due to the loss of Christian identity. This was the case in Great Britain.[96]

Historians have developed two major theories of religion in Britain from 1800 to 1963. The first is that industrialization, by migrating to urban areas, lived in crowded living conditions that rendered myths and religious practices impractical.[97] The second theory posits that the working-class people in urban areas had been estranged from established religion and were, therefore, on the forefront of secularization.[98] Bryan Wilson believes that individualism accelerated the process: "a propensity of individual life rather than collective or public life scarcely mulls over the elements of the supernatural with regard to a person's usual life."[99]

Rural areas were not left untouched by the changes of the modern age. Brown points to "the growth of machines, rationality, class division, and dissenting churches as well as the supposed decline of primitive husbandry, superstition, and harmonious social relations." A combination of powerful forces, "modernization, pluralization, urbanization, and Enlightenment rationality," reduced the need for

94. According to Wilson, "The institutionalised forms of the church differed according to the historical relationship of church and state: thus it took on a different character in Britain and Scandinavia, with their established state churches, from that found in France and Belgium, where the state emerged as the secular arm, in some respects parallel to, and in other respects almost in rivalry with, if not in opposition to, the church." Wilson, "New Images of Christian Community," 572–73.

95. Russello, *Christianity and European Culture*, 178.

96. Wilson points out that, with the supernatural playing less of a part in people's lives, interpretation of the supernatural becomes less and less relevant and the institutionalized church is marginalized. Wilson, *Religion in a Secular Society*, 25–28

97. Cox, *The Secular City*, 1.

98. Brown, *The Death of Christian Britain*, 8–9.

99. Bentley, *Cry God for England*, 4.

individuals to seek out the church to give meaning to their lives.[100] Most historians and sociologists agree that "British industrial society was already 'secular' before it had hardly begun."[101] Northcutt observes that urban living "reduce[s] humanity's sense of dependence on the creator as man becomes master of his own environment, time, and mental space for awareness of the divine, fostered in prayer, silence or meditation, shrinks rapidly, while increasing activities in business, leisure, entertainment and the culture of consumerism tend in their turn to increase irreligiosity."[102]

Church and State

The principal impact of secularization was the dismantling of the monopoly between the church and state. As a consequence, many functions formerly performed by religion were transferred to components of secular society. The authority of religion diminished while the role of modern, secular society increased. However, religion does not decline irreversibly. More powerful outpourings of the Holy Spirit will revitalize churches and individuals around the world in the form of revivals and awakenings. Because the European and American cases differ, secularization and revivals in Europe and America will be addressed separately.

After the Reformation in Europe, several revolutions (The Thirty Year's War in central Europe, Peasants' War) took place in the public and private sectors.[103] The divide between Catholic and Protestant and the relationship between church and state were changing. This environment gave rise to modernity, a school of thought that rejects belief in the supernatural and religious authority over public and individual arenas. During this time period, Prosman suggests, "Secularity cannot be convincingly thought of as residual ideas, which, like individualism and mutual benefit, would simply remain once the religious and metaphysical plumage had been done away with. To speak of secularization as an imaginary, does justice to the fact that humans are actively shaping the social world in which they live."[104]

100. Brown, *The Death of Christian Britain*, 10.

101. Ibid., 10.

102. Northcott, *The Church and Secularization*, 12.

103. Kreis, "Europe in the Age of Religious Wars," lines 50–62.

104. Prosman, *The Postmodern Condition*, 41–42.

Through his investigation of British matrimonial statistics from 1844 to 1904, Owen Chadwick found that "through the Victorian age, England grew much more secular."[105] Church historian Hugh McLeod identifies the post-1789 period as the time when segregation of the religious and non-religious began, ultimately resulting in separate groups of Christians and non-Christians, clericals and nonclericals, conformists and nonconformists. The nineteenth century has been called both a time of secularization and a golden period of revivals and awakening movements, which we will discuss in chapter 5.

The wellspring of dissenting or free churches emerging from revival movements furthered the social and cultural alienation from the established church, and faith no longer offered social unity for Europeans. At the same time, society became more divided as people found a stronger connection to various communities and social classes and to particular churches or denominations.[106] Religious attitudes once common to particular classes and communities inexorably dwindled, bringing religious adherents not in the traditional medieval way of Catholic predominance, but, chosen freely by the individual, to a church or denomination seated deeply within the secularized society of Western Europe.[107]

As the Enlightenment, the French Revolution, and the Industrial Revolution transformed European society, they brought both social and economic progress as well as secularization. Social developments that gave people from the lowest social levels the ability to improve their lives also resulted in secularized norms and a secular culture that became alien to Christianity.[108] The impact of secularization in Europe was influenced by the decline of the Roman Empire and the Holy Roman Empire and the increasing predominance of individual nation states. Joseph II and Friedrich II in Germany closed hundreds of monasteries and nullified the authority of clerical principalities. Prosman rightly points out that "[t]he secularizations can be regarded as symptoms of the emergence of a secular sphere, which no longer

---

105. Bentley agrees with Owen and Wilson that "religious activity will become more and more manifestly a leisure activity, an expression of purely personal, almost idiosyncratic interests, which others will simply tolerate." See Bentley, *Cry God for England*, 4.

106. McLeod, *Religion and the People of Western Europe*, 1–35.

107. Lechner, "The Case against Secularization," 1108.

108. Russello, *Christianity and European Culture*, 11–12.

tolerates the existence of a clerical power parallel to the nation state. This process has two components: In the first place the emergence of the nation state and in the second place the independence of political rule from religious institutions."[109]

In 1789, France, which was leading the way in secularization, decreed a stop to "feudal privileges and Church taxes." In 1790, the Catholic Church had to agree to close all orders. During the time of the French Revolution, says Prosman, "secularization became a central, political doctrine functioning in civil law." A similar secularization process took place in the Netherlands as church properties were confiscated and returned to the state.[110] In 1795, similar decrees in France and the Netherlands were implemented just after the peace treaty of Basel between France and Prussia was signed. From the early nineteenth century in Germany, Prosman asserts,

> [S]ecularization thus became a political doctrine that entirely rearranged the relation of the Church and the state. From now on the state took a position of neutrality in religious affairs. Nevertheless, in Bavaria for example, a predominantly Catholic area, the Church preserved certain privileges. In the whole of Germany, in the first decades of the 19th Century, the dioceses and archbishoprics were drastically reorganized. The protestant denominations were also reorganized according to the territorial principle. [111]

As properties of the church are returned to the secular government, "the discourse of republican politics develops, the term [secularization] is used to establish the autonomy of government at the expense of the Church and takes place against the background of a changed, religious landscape that is decisively shaped by the Reformation."[112]

Another aspect of secularization is the educational system. In Medieval Europe, most educational institutions were operated by the church. Davenport notes that the norm was for people to profess "a particular set of religious teachings and practices, and to worship in a particular institution. In such a society, they would be required to train their children in this faith, and forbidden to profess and prac-

109. Prosman, *The Postmodern Condition,* 37–38.
110. Ibid., 37.
111. Ibid., 38.
112. Ibid., 38.

tice faith in other incompatible religions. This is the strongest sense of 'establishment,' involving abridgement of *free exercise* and *freedom of religious expression*."[113] As part of secularization, many religious educational institutions were converted to secular use. In the public sector, Prosman states, "secularization has received a connotation that exceeds the context of canonical and public law. . . . it [secularization] is unmistakably directed toward a banishing of religion from the public sphere and the establishment of not only an autonomous polity, but also an autonomous, religiously neutral educational system."[114]

SOCIORELIGIOUS SECULARIZATION

During the Enlightenment in the eighteenth century, reason became the pivotal element of Western society rather than faith. Also contributing to the decline of Christianity were the events of the Restoration period in English history. The term *secularization* has been used differently by denominations, secularists, sociologists, and theologians. In medieval Europe, secularization meant the return of priests and monks to secular ministry from monasteries. In the case of the Germans, secularization often connotes the connection between Christianity and the Enlightenment. Dissident groups used the term to indicate the separation of established church from the state. Above all, the term was used to describe the collapse of western Christianity in the 1960s.[115] Prosman indicates, "The secular rationale on its turn guarantees neutrality and objectivity, to be preferred over religious prejudices. Philosopher of law Scheltens asserts that 'the secular provides a space where one can argue following no particular view of life but in a universal mode and on a purely human basis.'"[116]

Secularization and Christianity

In 1660, the Restoration period, when King Charles was returned to the throne after the republican Commonwealth period, led to the depoliticization and demystification of Christianity, as illustrated by the popular Anglican tracts *The Reasonableness of Christianity* and

113. Davenport, "Religion in the Public Sphere," 293.
114. Prosman, *The Postmodern Condition*, 38.
115. Ibid., 10.
116. Ibid., 10–11.

Christianity Not Mysterious. Science, literature, politics, and the arts became more secularized after this point. John Morrill observes:

> This dilution of religious energies, this breakdown of a world-view dominated by religious imperatives, can be seen in literature and in science. Restoration theatre differs from Jacobean not in its vulgarity or even in its triviality so much as in its secularism. Metaphysical poetry, which rooted religious experience in the natural world, gave way to a religious poetry either more cerebral and coolly rational, or else more ethereal and other-worldly.[117]

In 1710, Thomas Woolston predicted that Christianity would vanish around 1900 because the social influence of modernity was about to exceed that of Christianity. In the late eighteenth century, Voltaire envisaged that Christianity would come to an end within fifty years.[118] In France in the nineteenth century, Auguste Comte founded the discipline of sociology and the doctrine of positivism. He hypothesized that all society must endure three stages of development: the religious or theological stage, when religious and superstitious beliefs dominate; then the metaphysical stage, where philosophy takes center stage; and finally the positive stage. Comte suggested in his four-volume work *Système de politique positive* (1851–1854) that we would soon see a "religion of humanity" instead of Christianity. Comte foresaw a time when faith in humanity would displace faith in the sacred or supernatural—an idea espoused for many years afterward by humanist intellectuals—and he created his own concept of God, a deist concept, different from the Christian God, and discredited Christianity as an ambiguous religion.[119]

Comte saw the theological or religious stage of society as outdated. During the new age, which he called the positive stage, science alone would play an essential role, supplanting belief in the supernatural as the foundation for moral judgments and pushing religion into obscurity. Only at the positive stage would humans have their ultimate guide.[120] Comte did not predict when this transition would occur.[121] However, he did not expect the advent of positivism to lead imme-

117. Morrill, "The Stuarts," 347.
118. Stark, "Secularization, R.I.P.," 1.
119. Costa, "Secularization and sacralization," 2.
120. Lee, *Religion*, 469.
121. Stark, "Secularization, R.I.P.," 1.

diately to a "society without religion."[122] In Costa's view, "secularization as an irreversible evolution of magical mythical religion forms, towards a first stage of 'laicism' of thought."[123] Marx Weber offers a different standpoint; he "introduces us to a new perspective, by identifying secularization to 'disenchantment of the world,' which implies a growing distance and an emancipation of the political-economic spheres, from justifications of a religious nature, that is an emancipation of economic matters, from the influence of religion-centered moral values systems."[124]

Friedrich Engels similarly anticipated that religion soon would be dissolved by the socialist revolution, although he did not project a date by which he expected this to occur.[125] G. Holyoake followed Comte's idea when he advocated secularism in 1851. Other intellectuals and philosophers joined Comte and Holyoake in challenging Christianity with the proposition that humanity's outlook should be focused on the human being rather than on a divine being and that the mythical and superstitious elements of Christianity should be abandoned. Other proponents of secularization included Max Weber, Émile Durkheim, Talcott Parsons, Peter Berger, Bryan Wilson, and David Martin.[126] In the early twentieth century, Weber referred to modernization as the cause of the world's disenchantment. Sigmund Freud predicted that religious illusions, which he called neurotic illusions, would come to an end on the therapist's couch.[127] Anthony Wallace affirmed that "belief in supernatural powers is doomed to die out, all over the world."[128]

A number of theorists have focused on the contrasting results of the Reformation in Europe in the Protestant north and the Catholic south. Ernst Troeltsch, Max Weber, and Robert Merton have developed socioreligious theories to describe "the results of the Protestant Reformation for the modernization of Europe."[129] Of all the theorists, Weber hits the mark most precisely. Secularization theory consists of

122. Hadden, "Towards Desacralizing Secularization Theory," 590.

123. Costa, "Secularization and Sacralization," 2.

124. Ibid., 2.

125. Stark, "Secularization, R.I.P.", 1.

126. Bruce, *Religion in the Modern World*, 6.

127. Stark, "Secularization, R.I.P.", 1.

128. Ibid., 2.

129. Lechner, "The Case against Secularization," 1104.

a coherent body of empirical generalizations resting on fundamental premises developed by Weber. According to Riis, secularization was born during the Reformation, when Protestant ethics and norms challenged many followers to involve themselves in this world. An advocate of the modern spirit of capitalism, Weber stated that Protestants were urged to view work as a divine calling and profits from their labors both as a rightfully earned reward and as a way of salvation for the afterlife.

Weber prompted social scientists to consider the causes and effects of modernization, secularization, and Christian ethics with his work *The Protestant Ethic and the Spirit of Capitalism.*[130] In general, modernization included phenomena such as bureaucratization, industrialization, rationalism, mobility, socialization, functional differentiation, and urbanization, all of which contributed to the disengagement of modern people from religious organizations.[131] Weber describes the changes brought about by a societal focus on reason as religion loses political relevance.[132]

Weber saw rationalism as the view that human knowledge accumulated through science can explain all of the world's phenomena, displacing supernatural explanations with naturalistic ones. According to Swatos and Christiano, Weber described this as "*Entzauberung*—a word usually translated *disenchantment*, though perhaps more accurately rendered de-magi-fication or de-myster-ization. For Weber, disenchantment is not a denial of belief in the old mysteries of religion but rather a reduction of the notion of the mystery because knowledge gained from science and sociology, such as "human reason, ingenuity, and the products of technology" can be superior over the mysteries.[133] Weber's work afforded "a comprehensive set of conceptual tools for an ongoing analysis of modern society."[134] As modernization progressed, cultural norms shifted to deemphasize the place of the supernatural and the sacred in people's lives, causing them to become increasingly disaffected.[135]

---

130. Riis, "Religion and the Spirit of Capitalism," 22.

131. Dobbelaere, *Secularization*, 143.

132. Costa, "Secularization and Sacralization," 3.

133. Swatos and Christiano, "Secularization Theory," 212–13.

134. Hadden, "Towards Desacralizing Secularization Theory," 588.

135. Dobbelaere points to countercultural trends promoted in 1960s, particularly

Modernization

The forces of secularization were wide-ranging, affecting many intellectual and scientific disciplines. The Enlightenment gave rise to modernity with its secularized worldview. Auguste Comte, Max Weber, and Émile Durkheim anticipated the decline of religion as science continued to demystify phenomena previously attributed to the supernatural, though their opinions vary in their details. However, the secularization theory is not a single voice, but many. Though the predictions of the decline of religion diverge, many scholars say that the decline of religious authority, religious institutions, and the practice of faith are inevitable.

This predicted demise has not played out in history, however. Peter Berger emphasizes

> that the theory of secularization, which predicted that modernity would bring about the total secularization of society, has crumbled down and that experience shows that what modernity has brought about is not the age of secularization, but just the opposite, that is, an age marked by the expansion and the penetration of religiousness, in which religious pluralism is the key in a global world.[136]

The advent of secularization, which undermined the Christian identity that Europeans for centuries had held even more strongly than their national identity, is connected with the rise of modern industrial urban society in the 1800s. The decline of the social significance of the organized church was clearly evident in Britain. Northcott points out that the significance of religion had diminished in the lives of the working people, and eventually in the majority of the population, even before the nineteenth century. This led to the decline of practical religious activities such as church attendance and rites of passage.[137] Still, C. Wright Mills proposed that religion would survive in the private sphere of life. According to Hadden,

> Once the world was filled with the sacred in thought, practice, and institutional form. After the Reformation and the Renaissance, the forces of modernization swept across the globe and secularization, a corollary historical process, loos-

among the younger generation. *Secularization*, 143.

136. Berger, quoted in Costa, "Secularization and Sacralization," 7.

137. Northcott, *The Church and Secularisation*, 11.

ened the dominance of the sacred. In due course, the sacred shall disappear altogether except, possibly, in the private realm.[138]

In 1969, Peter Berger also articulated the thesis that modernization unavoidably leads to a decline of religion both in society and in the minds of individuals. In the modernist view, religion is a human enterprise that constructs a sacred cosmos to keep chaos at bay through a variety of cosmogony myths. He predicts that religion, "by virtue of being an ongoing human production, is continuously confronted with the disordering forces of human existence."[139] Hence, in his view, the decline or death of religion is inevitable. As he sees it, "the power of religion depends upon the credibility of the banners it puts in the hands of men as they stand before death, or more accurately, as they walk, inevitably, toward it."[140] As society progresses, he predicts that religion is sure to lose a significant role in European society over the next thousand years. Writing thirty years later, in 1999, he admitted that his earlier prediction was incorrect and readjusted his opinion, stating that religious institutions have lost power and influence in many places, yet religion has persisted in the lives of individuals, sometimes taking on new institutional forms and asserting itself through new and zealous movements.[141]

Religious or Irreligious

The loss of Christian influence in Western Europe has been studied by many.[142] Most scholars believe that the processes of secularization began during the modern, industrial era when Christianity was no longer able to maintain its dominance because it could not defend itself against the challenges of rationalism. In David Martin's thesis of

138. Hadden tried to translate Talcott Parson's 555-page tome, *The Social System.* In this work, Mills's secularization theory was introduced. Hadden's translation of Mills's work was quoted here. Hadden, "Towards Desacralizing Secularization Theory," 598.

139. Berger, *The Sacred Canopy,* 25–28.

140. Ibid., 44–51.

141. According to Berger, religiously identified institutions may play social or political roles even when very few people espouse the religion that the institutions represent. Berger, *The Desecularization of the World,* 2–5.

142. McLeod, *The Decline of Christendom in Western Europe,* 13–14.

secularization in 1960, he claimed that the secularization process had already taken place in Western Europe.[143]

In 1970, Wilson wrote about the effects of rationality on religion, stating that rational empirical inquiry itself is challenged when verifying the assertions of Western religious systems. Religious beliefs have been weakened by rationality because the belief in creation largely has been abandoned by Westerners. Propositions that go beyond the empirical remain questionable and vulnerable when subjected to rational tests. Rational religious people have to first test their beliefs by verifying their internal logic. Then, their beliefs are tested by the scientific methods in their respective cultures. In Western societies, he says, "where the social and physical milieu are increasingly dominated by formally rational prescriptions, that most religious believers maintain beliefs and undertake acts that reveal some degree of inconsistency."[144] With the rise of secularization, there is a "transfer of property, power, activities, and both manifest and latent functions, from institutions with a supernaturalist frame of reference to (often new) institutions operating according to empirical, rational, pragmatic criteria."[145] He highlights that the idea of salvation can be discovered within the universal religions when one religious system is no longer functioning to accomplish the will of God in society. Acquaviva sees the possibility that society could discard religion rationally "without taking account of the cost of all this in terms of the emotional support which men need in order to live."[146]

Secularization has been a long process, with some resulting phenomena appearing only recently. Its specific manifestations depend upon each historical/cultural context, the conceptions of the supernatural that were previously held, and the institutions in which they were enshrined.[147] The role of religion in a person's life will depend upon the role that person fills in a dominantly secular society. With religion no longer compulsory, its propositions must stand in a free

---

143. Martin, *A Sociology of English Religion*, 67–68; Gill, *The "Empty" Church Revisited*, 67–68.

144. Wilson, *Rationality*, xiv–xv.

145. Wilson, *Religion in Sociological Perspective*, 11–26, 148–53.

146. Acquaviva, "Some Reflections," 47.

147. Wilson, *Religion in Sociological Perspective*, 151.

market of ideas or die out.[148] Wilson points out that, according to Halman and Pettersson, "the secularization thesis focuses not on the decline of religious practice and belief *per se*, but on their diminishing *significance* for the social system. Clearly, decline in practice and belief might be part of such lost significance, but the decline which matters is decline in their importance, not necessarily, even if usually, decline in their appearance."[149]

Decline of Religion

The theory that secularization is inevitable as societies mature is controversial. Evidence for or against the veracity of this theory often cites the decline of ecclesiastic influence in public and private life and reduced levels of Christian belief, membership, and attendance—not just one facet of religious activity, but many. The societal and individual levels of secularization have been presented. How does the long-term trend of the decline of beliefs, church membership, and attendance connect to secularization? Dobbelaere suggests the three dimensions:

> Secularization occurs when religious authority structures decline in their ability to control societal-level institutions, meso-level organizations, and individual level beliefs and be- haviours. Most advocates of the ideas of secularization make such a distinction in macro-, meso-, and micro-level. At the societal level, secularization refers to the declining capacity of religion to exercise authority over other institutional spheres. Secularization at the organizational level may be understood as the religious authority's declining control over organizational resources within the religious sphere. And secularization at the individual level may be understood as the decrease in the extent to which individual actions are subject to religious control.[150]

Halman and Riis identify two levels of secularization, macro and meso levels, which manifest the effects of secularization distinctively through a differentiation between institutional spheres at the macro level, and through an internal secularization at the meso level. While organizations at these two levels may adapt and find new, secular ways

148. Dobbelaere, "Church Involvement and Secularization," 24.
149. Laermans and Wilson, *The Secularization Thesis*, 63.
150. Dobbelaere, "Church Involvement and Secularization," 48–49.

of operating in contemporary society, at the micro level, secularization could manifest itself "in the form of declines in church membership or church allegiance, in accepting prescribed beliefs, in participating in rituals, or in accepting the ethical standards prescribed by religious authorities."[151] On the micro level, Berger shows that societal and cultural segments become detached from religious institutional supremacy.

Jose Casanova describes three steps in the secularization process. The first is differentiation, when non-Christian or secular spheres of life become independent from the Christian faith. Second, individual secularization becomes privatization, a process through which religious beliefs and practices at the individual level declines. Lastly, faith is relegated to the private sphere; there is no more religious functioning in public life and no more influence on society and the public sphere because individuals in society are able to freely choose their lives. This final stage is also described as the "marginalization of religion to a privatized sphere."[152]

Dobbelaere sees secularization as a five-step process. The first is "differentiation of religious roles and institutions. Here religious and secular structures pull apart from each other." Second comes "demand for clarification of the boundary between religious and secular issues. Priesthoods are established and congregations gather, but the separation of religious and secular issues often takes longer than the separation of religious and secular structures." The third step involves the "development of generalized beliefs and values that transcend the potential conflict between the larger society and its component parts." An set of symbols are developed constituting a civil "religion"—for example, Sukarno's *Pancasila*, five general principles derived from Hinduism and Islam used to unify the Indonesian state. The fourth step involves "minority and idiosyncratic definitions-of-the-situation: groups and institutions, minorities and elites, struggle to extend or to limit the scope of the sacred in public life." Political agents become increasingly secularized while an increasing number of individuals and groups defend their rights on religious grounds. The fifth and final

---

151. Halman and Riis, "Contemporary European Discourses on Religion and Morality," 3.

152. Casanova, *Public Religion in the Modern World*, 7–10, 20–39, 211–234.

step is the "separation of individual from corporate life."[153] On one hand, there is a tendency toward limiting the sacred to the private sphere; on the other, a religious culture tends to expand the scope of the sacred to all areas.

Writing in 1967, Thomas Luckmann defined his relatively new terminology of societal secularization as "a process in which autonomous institutional 'ideologies' replaced, within their own domain, an overarching and transcendent universe of norms." Therefore, the church was shunted to the fringes of modern industrial societies.[154]

Peter Berger defines secularization this way:

> By secularization we mean the process by which sectors of society and culture are removed from the domination of religious institutions and symbols. . . . [W]hen we speak of society and institution in modern western history, secularization manifests itself in the evacuation by the Christian churches of areas previously under their control or influence—as in the separation of church and state, or in the expropriation of church lands, or in the emancipation of education from ecclesiastical authority. . . . [W]e imply that secularization is more than a social-structural process. It affects the totality of cultural life and of ideation, and may be observed in the decline of religious content in the arts, in philosophy, in literature and, most important of all, in the rise of science as an autonomous, thoroughly secular perspective on the world.[155]

Secularization in the American context is different than that which occurred in Europe. According to American theorists including Rodney Stark, Roger Finke, and Laurence Iannaconne, the dwindling religious institutions and the weakening social significance of religion does not take place in the same way, or even with the same speed, throughout all parts of Europe.[156] We will explore the American situation in chapter 7.

Lechner writes that sociological studies of religion "only elaborated in more systematic terms what was a common perspective shared by the majority of intellectuals."[157] He stresses that seculariza-

153. Dobbelaere, *Secularization*, 74.

154. Ibid., 29.

155. Berger, *The Sacred Canopy*, 107.

156. Halman and Pettersson, "Differential Patterns," 53–54.

157. Lechner, "The Case against Secularization," 1103.

tion does not necessarily equate to the decline of religiousness among modern people. Even contemporary people are, in many ways, "more 'religious' than they were in the past; in any case, religious revivals are bound to occur; religious beliefs and symbolism do not disappear but simply change in form."[158]

Mark Chaves also secularization in the declining scope of religious authority:

> This proposed focus on religious authority (1) is more consistent with recent developments in social theory than is a preoccupation with "religion"; (2) draws on and develops what is best in the secularization literature; (3) reclaims a neglected Weberian insight concerning the sociological analysis of religion; and (4) suggests new and promising directions for empirical investigations of religion in industrial societies. . . . Hence, understanding secularization as declining religious authority avoids the theoretical cul-de-sacs . . . within which too much contemporary sociology of religion flounders.[159]

Chaves argues that secularization occurs when "religion "ceases to be significant in the working of the social system," a process by which it "has lost its presidency over other institutions.""[160] He voices the importance of maintaining "a distinction between religion's influence and the mere existence of religious beliefs and sentiments among individuals."[161]

The decline of religious authority and influence includes "values, leaders, and institutions over individual behavior, social institutions, and public discourse."[162] However, Hugh McLeod emphasizes that this decline of religious authority may not mean the end of Christendom. He says, "Christianity is not equivalent to or dependent on the maintenance of Christendom, and . . . those who reject Christianity do not necessarily replace it with a purely secular world-view."[163] Even though religious beliefs and practices are declining, McLeod believes, "Christendom was a social order in which, regardless of individual

158. Ibid., 1104.
159. Chaves, "Secularization as Declining Religious Authority," 750.
160. Ibid., 752.
161. Ibid., 752.
162. Gorski and Altinordu, "After Secularization?," 58.
163. McLeod, *The Religious Crisis*, 265.

belief, Christian language, rites, moral teachings, and personnel were part of the taken-for-granted environment." McLeod still anticipates a bright future for Christianity, "[a]s Christianity lost a large part of its privileged position, the options in matters of belief, life-path, or 'spirituality' were open to a degree that they had not been for centuries."[164] Clearly, the decline of traditional Christendom does not mean the demise of Christianity, as we are seeing phenomenal growth in Pentecostal and charismatic churches in the Global South and in Eastern and Western Europe.

INDIVIDUAL SECULARIZATION

Secularization generally describes the wane of religious institutions in Britain and Europe. Yet, spirituality, newly risen sects, and new forms of religion are stirring the hearts of modern Europeans. We have moved into an era when Christian values and beliefs no longer underpin society as a whole.[165]

Belief or Unbelief

During the early Victorian era, nearly all members of the Church of England, including many Methodists, believed that the state ought to establish a church.[166] After the French Revolution, however, most of the important social and demographic upheavals associated with industrialization had already created, for example, squalid living conditions and exploitation by industrialists. These problems aroused a passionate response among Methodists and dissenting evangelists, shifting their view regarding who should establish the church.

In this historical context, modernization played a critical role in marginalizing Christianity. Secularization has long been included among the consequences of modernization, along with industrialization, urbanization, and rationalism. Modernization, as Stark points out, "is a long, linear, upward curve, and secularization is assumed to trace the reciprocal of this curve, to be a long, linear, downward curve."[167] The process of modernization is still occurring in Western

---

164. Ibid., 265.
165. Jackson, *Hope for the Church*, 56.
166. Chadwick, *The Victorian Church*, 476–78.
167. Stark, "Secularization, R.I.P.", 1.

Europe and in other developed nations, which are considered to be in the postmodern period. Stark finds that "secularization is at least 'ongoing' to the extent that a significant downward trend in religiousness can be seen."[168]

In the late nineteenth century, the combination of Darwinism and biblical criticism diminished the authority of the Bible among many believers, and an all-sided attack on Puritanism was undertaken in Britain and other parts of Europe.[169] As a result, belief in the essential doctrines of Christianity—incarnation, crucifixion, bodily resurrection, ascension, and second coming of Jesus Christ, heaven and hell, and the last judgment—faded along with attendance in mainline churches. Belief in the biblical account of creation and the authority of Scripture declined, while an increasing number of British believed in the theory of evolution, even among Christians. To hold the Christian truth as the sole truth was no longer acceptable in society, and relativism and religious pluralism prevailed among most British Christians.[170]

Unbelief in conventional Christian truths increased as a consequence of rationalism, and people now felt free from conventional religion and metaphysics. Many intellectuals renounced conventional Christian beliefs, stating that doctrines and mystical beliefs seen to be unscientific ultimately would be swept away. Secularists project the development and progress of a secular civilization. Leslie Stephen, an influential thinker, shook the British church when he abandoned his Christian faith and Anglican orders in 1875. A year later, he published *A History of English Thought into the Clear Light of the Day*, which had a powerful impact over both intellectuals and common people. Other intellectuals such as John Stuart Mill, Thomas Henry Huxley, and Sigmund Freud also criticized the core of Christian truth. The antagonists did not outnumber Christians, yet their influence was far greater than their numbers.[171]

---

168. Ibid., 1–2.

169. McLeod, "The Privatization of Religion," 4–6.

170. Lee, "Religion," 488.

171. For instance, thirty secular societies were active in the London alone between 1837 and 1866, and they recruited members under the banners of secularism, materialism, free inquiry, and free thought. Ellis, "The Intellectual Challenge," 48–51.

Privatization

The disintegration of the monopoly of the church began the process of secularization, which was accelerated by the Enlightenment. Studies in the sociology of religion have found that a decline of religious authority had occurred rather than a decline of religion itself. In this regard, the change can be described as a shift from a focus on institutional religion to individualistic religion.[172] Costa, referring to Hervieu-Léger's idea, says that the "loss of relevance affecting religious institutions is linked not only to the processes of greater individuation and pluralism, but also to the change of the State's position and role."[173] The predominance of the individual allows modern people to live in a religiously pluralistic society where their choice of faith and practice is according to their preference.[174] Multiple choices in the religious marketplace resulted in detraditionalization as well. Houtman and Aupers state, "As external and authoritative sources of meaning and identity lose their grip on individuals, the range of biographical and life-styles choices nevertheless widens considerably."[175]

Other problems associated with secularization affect not the external world of society, but the internal, private lives of individuals. Traditional Christian ethics and disciplined lifestyles became less and less acceptable. Many Christians became exposed to and affected by unbiblical practices such as premarital sex, adultery, abortion, cheating on taxes, and materialism. Bruce also points out the identical divorce rates of both Christians and non-Christians, since "they had the same increasingly liberal moral and ethical standards."[176]

Christianity no longer holds the societal dominance of the past, and its institutions have declined, yet it still has an impact on individual private lives. Berger and Luckmann suggest that privatization actually paved the way for a new type of religion.[177] Secularization, as it played out within "the historical experience of Western Europe,"

172. Costa, "Secularization and Sacralization," 9.

173. Ibid., 9.

174. Ibid., 8–9.

175. Houtman and Aupers, "The Spiritual Turn," 308.

176. Bruce, *Religion in the Modern World*, 146.

177. Berger and Luckmann, *The Social Construction of Reality*, 1–18. Halman and Riis state that privatization coincides with Durkheim's view about "the eventual formation of the 'cult of man.'" Durkheim, *The Elementary Forms of the Religious Life*, 23–35.

transformed faith into a primarily individual rather than institutional phenomenon.[178] The rationalist view propagated during the modern and postmodern periods discouraged people from automatically accepting the teachings, worldview, and values of traditional ecclesiastical institutions.[179]

Secularization has led to the separation of public and private religious life in Europe. Christian public policies had lost their influence on the beliefs adopted by individuals. The decline of individual religious values, norms, church attendance, and membership was felt in both the private and public spheres, yet the largest decline of religious influence occurred in the public sphere. Secularization on the societal level is somewhat ascribable to secularist public policy, while the decline of Christian beliefs and practices can be attributed to a possible ratification of secularization at the individual level, as observed by sociologists of religion who propagate their own doctrines.[180] The privatization of religion as an aspect of secularization is evidence of the existence of an underlying traditional, unifying, and transcendent Christian belief system in Europe alongside fast-paced social change. Europeans attempted to seek religion as a channel for a transcendent experience of spirituality.[181]

In this sense, in Europe, Christian ethics and norms are no longer influential over secular institutions, the public sphere, economics, and politics.[182] Religion has stopped playing any part in public life and does not even attempt to influence how politicians make decisions and how individuals in society choose to live their lives.[183] Alienation of the working class was already visible in the early nineteenth century. According to Dobbelaere,

> The churches were mostly linked to the middle and upper classes through financial dependence and its paternalist social ideology, and the lower classes were attracted to the opposition. Socialism was gaining a hold over the working class at the end of the 19th century, and in most European countries, the socialist leaders and activists were atheists. The secular-

178. Halman and Riis, "Contemporary European Discourses," 3.

179. Halman and Pettersson, "Differential Patterns," 49.

180. Dobbelaere, *Secularization*, 39.

181. Halman and Pettersson, "Differential Patterns," 17–25.

182. Ibid., 50.

183. Brown, *The Death of Christian Britain*, 12.

ist policy of the socialist parties alienated the workers from the churches. But in the early 19th century, the involvement of the Catholic Church in the old order and the alienation of the working class from local political and Christian traditions had already stimulated the working class in some countries to abandon the church and to move to the left politically. Radical liberalism and socialism manifestly estranged the workers from the churches. Indeed, the workers were already latently alienated from them.[184]

From early 1900s up to the 1960s, as faith gradually became privatized, the numbers of convinced unbelievers and non-Christian religious groups continued to grow.[185] Increasingly, the privatization of religion became evident in the home and the family. For example, tithing has decreased in churches and keeping the Sabbath has become less of a priority.[186] Significantly, elements of secularism also infiltrated the church as churches attempted to bridge the cultural gap with the public by adopting secular concepts such as the commercialization of the church, adopting secular management skills into church administration, and the promotion of church attendance as a means of appeasing people's consciences. Ostwalt comments that "churches might employ many strategies to bridge the gap, but in the final analysis, the results are the introduction of secular elements, categories, and standards into Christian worship and theology."[187]

Spirituality

Folk and popular religions continue to be practiced, particularly in Iberian countries. These beliefs and practices are often referred to as spirituality. Has Christianity ever reached a high degree of spirituality from the top level all the way down? Has any folk or popular spirituality or religion ever reached the level of an organized religion or been labeled mistakenly as a legitimate Christian religion? Lechner's answer is twofold: that there is "no good evidence that a high level of spirituality has generally been reached by the mass of mankind in past times," yet, at the same time, people's lives "were necessarily well integrated by religion."[188]

184. Dobbelaere, *Secularization*, 39.

185. McLeod, "The Privatization of Religion in Modern England," 6–7.

186. Brierley, *Vision Building*, 56–57.

187 Ostwalt, *Secular Steeples*, 62.

188. Lechner, "The Case against Secularization," 1106–07.

With European Christianity, the dynamic spiritual encounters and religious experiences of ordinary people are often ignored, whether intentionally or unintentionally, by the dominant Catholic hierarchy and even Protestant religious establishments. The vitality of early Christianity was never found in European religious institutions, though its vigor and empowerment were rediscovered through awakening movements such as the Waldenses, Anabaptists, Huguenots, Quakers, and Moravians. The Methodist movements and the Great Awakenings marking the start of modern evangelicalism occurred concurrently with modernization and secularization following the Enlightenment and French Revolution. Hadden observes that "the expectation that religion would vanish, either quickly or gradually, fits well with the evolutionary model of modernization, which attempted to account for the transition of human societies from simple to complex forms. But beneath the theoretical statement is a silent prescriptive assertion that this is good."[189]

The model presented by secular advocates, that secularization with modernization is a blueprint that naturally leads to the decline of institutionalized or organized religion, is partially derived from a partisan view. Any movement, such as modernization, has both negative and positive aspects. The fact that most sociologists of religion ignore the religion part of their discipline today is still reasonable within a modern worldview.[190] This is the reason why I am investigating the connection between evangelicalism and Pentecostalism and the rise of Christianity in the developing world today. North America has shown both the rise of evangelicalism and Pentecostalism in demonstrating a new and fresh growth of Christianity, yet mainline denominations continue to be negatively affected by secularization and modernization. In this sense, Steve Bruce perceives the Charismatic movement in the 1970s as a "significant injection of supernaturalism" accompanied by gifts of the Holy Spirit such as "speaking in tongues, healing, and prophesying."[191] Hadden correctly states that the "[s]ecularization theory will be radically revised or relegated to the category of a marginally useful heuristic pedagogical device, not unlike the theory of 'demographic transition.' The secular is not going to disappear from the modern cultures, any more than the sacred. But if secularization

189. Hadden, "Towards Desacralizing Secularization Theory," 607.

190. Lechner, "The Case against Secularization," 1106–07.

191. Bruce, *Secularization*, 14.

is to be a useful construct for analyzing a historical process, it will have to be significantly refined."[192] Popular secularization theories seem to fit neatly within the European context, though they need to be reevaluated in the case of North America and in the cases of many developing nations as well.

THE POST-SECULAR AGE

Several historical and theological perspectives attempt to explain secularization. Medieval Christendom combined the secular aand the sacred in order to set the stage for the Reformation, a historically decisive moment of division between the two. If modernity originated during the Enlightenment, secularization may also have its roots in that time. The latest trends will help us to perceive, as Jürgen Habermas insists, that we are now entering a post-secular age.[193] To postmodern ears, the terms postmodernism, postcolonialism, and postseculariza-tion are contemporaries of a postsecular conjecture. As John Caputo said, "If the word postmodern were not overused as it is now, its most worthwhile definition would be postsecular."[194]

Postmodern Secularity

Human reason had become a central focus during the process of secularization, and the philosophers and others envisioned the dis-appearance of belief in the supernatural and the decline of religion. Many projected that humanism would replace religion, stating that "postmodernism is the achievement of secularity. . . . Secularity is one of the key values of modernity and sometimes it is even seen as iden-tical with the history of the West."[195] Often, philosophers emphasize that modernity, with reason at its center, releases people from religion and tradition: "Religion and tradition are undermined 'by the reflex-ivity of modern social life, which stands in direct opposition to it.'"[196] Prosman asks whether, "[i]n postmodernity, doubts are cast on the autonomy and self-sufficiency of reason. What are the consequences

192. Hadden, "Towards Desacralizing Secularization Theory,"

193. Gorski and Altinordu, "After Secularization?," 56.

194. John Caputo, quoted in Prosman, *The Postmodern Condition and the Meaning of Secularity*, 3.

195. Ibid., 3.

196. Ibid., 3–4.

of this shift from a modern to a postmodern account of rationality for the concept of secularity?"[197] In the postmodern world, reason does not stand alone. Many people still believe that the supernatural exists, and religion still plays a role among postmodern people.

In fact, religion is not following a uniformly downward trend in the twenty-first century. Jeffery Stout argues that "secularism is not the end of Christianity, nor is it a sign of the godless nature of the West. Rather, we should think of secularism as the latest expression of Christian religion."[198] Empirically, we see signs of revival in the church. Evangelical and Pentecostal church growth in the Global South has contradicted theories of secularization. Many secularization scholars are seeking alternative hypotheses, suggesting that secularization is not the decline of religion itself, but the decline of religious authority. We can fairly say that the postmodern era is experiencing a return of religion.

Prosman proposes that theories of secularization were used to show "a certain legitimation to contingent history."[199] He distinguishes "a meaning of secularity" between "an ontological sense" and "a political sense."[200] He explains,

> Ontological secularity concerns the (relative) autonomy of the world and the human capacity to know this world. . . . The emergence of a scientific attitude in modernity changed the relation of man and world. In the place of speculative knowledge of reality, rational thought concerns the inner nature and regularity of the world. Implied here is that the relation to the world changes from an experience of belonging to the world to an experience of mastering the world."[201]

Secularization Thesis in a Post-Secular Age

Many assumptions have been made about our trajectory toward a secularized society through age of reason, the decline of religion, and the existential significance of individuals. Callum G. Brown and Michael Snape point out, that the study of secularization "crops up in all sorts

---

197. Ibid., 4.

198. Smith, *A Short History of Secularism*, 2.

199. Prosman, "The Postmodern Condition and the Meaning of Secularity," 4.

200. Ibid., 4.

201. Ibid., 4–5.

of disciplines, bandied about by scholars of diverse interests."[202] John Davenport affirms that the secularization thesis was wrong, stating that "belief in them [human beings] will fade away in the face of rational objections and be replaced by forms of reason—scientific and reflective—that do not rely on any alleged revelational source, or even on western-style belief in a personal God in general."[203] Looking back in history, we can see that religion has declined risen. When the decline reaches its nadir, historically, another revival takes place. God is still alive in the deepest places of spiritual discouragement.[204] Costa states that, while we live in a postmodern society, "religion does not tend to disappear, and, on the other hand, that the privatization process of religion, is not caused by secularization, but results from the actual historical ways in which the process has developed in each place."[205]

Davenport explains in his theory of secularization that "no matter how religion waxes or wanes in actual history, modern reason and natural science will eventually provide a secure and complete foundation for knowledge of the natural world, morality, the nature of life, and human society, based on *a priori* and empirical sources available to us without any theistic implications."[206] He argues the effectiveness of another secularization thesis, which he calls critical mythography.

Mircea Eliade, Romanian historian of religion, developed theories about the derivation and growth of religious beliefs and practices from mystical origins such as religious symbols and rituals. He calls this mythography, and indicates that it can aid in social evolution to experience transcendental elements of religion. He also points to the derivation of mysterious empiricism through the symbols, rituals, and religious myths that can lead people to the belief in the after life.[207]

Keenan advances a new theory of religion for the post-secular world, religion as a chain memory. He sees "religion as 'an ideological, practical and symbolic system through which consciousness, both individual and collective, of belonging to a particular chain of belief is constituted, maintained, developed and controlled.'"[208] His primary

202. Brown and Snape, *Conceptualising Secularisation*, 1.

203. Davenport, "Religion in the Public Sphere," 289.

204. Keenan, "Post-Secular Sociology," 282–83.

205. Costa, "Secularization and Sacralization," 7.

206. Davenport, "Religion in the Public Sphere," 291.

207. Rennie, "Sacred in the Profane," 204.

208. Keenan, "Post-Secular Sociology," 282–83.

idea is that the deinstitutionalization of religion and departure from traditions corrodes the potency of "communal ligatures of historical identity."[209] He explains, "Modernity effects a 'redistribution in the sphere of believing'. . . for great civilizational traditions of faith, small surrogate memories are substituted, for instance, through fan-based sporting associations, ethnic religions, utopian fellowships, telethons and other varieties of 'elective' fraternities and sororities."[210] In addition, Keenan states that "Hervieu-Léger's carefully modulated and thought-provoking take on 'the expulsion of memory from society' carries a strong tone of latent lament for the passing of the putatively religious ancestral ways of faith, by contrast with which the postmodern compensatory efforts to 'reinvent' memory chains adequate to the 'post-traditional' contexts in which we find ourselves *nolens volens* appear shallow and hollow."[211]

> Chaves articulated a "new differentiation theory" to explain why different social spheres have stronger or weaker connections to religion. Chaves builds upon Parsons's "influential formulation of differentiation" which posited increasing separation from religion as "a paradigm of evolutionary change."[212] He makes adjustments in four key areas:
>
> 1. The assumption of a master trend towards differentiation in all spheres is dropped;
>
> 2. The "functionalist fallacy"—by which we infer that extant institutions meet some legitimate societal need merely because they exist—is avoided;
>
> 3. The requirement for value integration is dropped, replaced by the idea that societal integration is achieved via institutional arrangements whereby functional spheres refrain from "producing insoluble problems" for other spheres;
>
> 4. Rather than identifying the ends of one or another societal sphere, say the state or the economy, with the ends of the society as a whole, new differentiation theory understands no single sector as necessarily primary in the

---

209. Ibid., 282.
210. Ibid., 282.
211. Ibid., 282.
212. Chaves, "Secularization as Declining Religious Authority," 751.

sense of gathering within itself the essential goals of the entire society.[213]

A renewal of religious faith in a post-secular age is called re-enchantment. This brings, as Costa asserts, "a 'sacralization of the world' insofar as the sacred, the mystery, is expressed outside the orbit of these experts. Re-enchantment that has many expressions in the life of societies implies different inquiries and may have a higher or lower degree of connection to the institutional sphere."[214]

Christianity in Post-secular Historical Context

Secular history is not always purely secular, but can be interrelated with redemptive history. Secular affairs have often been closely linked with ecclesiastic authorities historically. Areas where the two overlap include the caesaropapist monopoly, religious tolerance, the Reformation, the Enlightenment, rationalism, and modernization. "[T]he currently emerging post-secular state—the 'post' in 'post-secular' here meaning after and against the '*only* secular' or 'secular *against* the sacred' state—resembles, or is beginning to resemble to a significant degree, the 'Christendom state' which acknowledged God as its origin and end, and God's truth revealed in scripture as a 'sacred lamp unto its secular feet.'"[215]

When church and state were united, Christianity was the official religion. After the Reformation, the relationship between conformity and non-conformity, the established church and dissenters, secular and sacred, and eventually Christians and non-Christians, became pluralistic. When Christianity plays its role as a culture, religion becomes a cultural religion. However, cultural religion is subject to cultural secularization, *cultural laïcité*, as well. For instance in the eighteenth century in Britain, according to Jonathan Sheehan, the Enlightenment gave citizens the intellectual ability to convince others to abandon their traditional cultural Christianity, yet civil society was still influenced by Christianity as a cultural religion.[216] In Germany, as L. L. Bernard states, "The dominant German religion . . . was only inciden-

---

213. Ibid., 751.

214. Costa, "Secularization and Sacralization," 12.

215. Trainor, "Augustine's 'Sacred Reign—Secular Rule,'" 1.

216. Sheehan, "Enlightenment, Religion, and the Enigma of Secularization," 1069.

tally theological, but was primarily that of national aggrandizement—a politico-socio-economic religion—and it exhibited as many signs of intolerance and coercion in behalf of its 'Kultur [culture]' as did the theological or monotheistic religion of the Jews and other peoples in like stages of development."[217] A secularized religion functions as a social system to integrate culture and humanities.[218] Popular religion can omit certain elements and retain others, abandoning beliefs related to the supernatural as reason increases.[219]

As for the economy, capitalism functions as a form of secularized Calvinism.[220] When Christianity no longer holds power, a religiously pluralistic society requires a civil religion capable of existing harmoniously with other religions. As European Christianity has adapted to a religiously pluralistic context in a post-secular age, Europeans are also being attracted to non-Christian faiths. At the same time, American society is entering not only a secular stage, but a post-secular stage as well.[221] The history of secularization calls for a theological, sociological, and historical assessment of the "cross-national variability and historical contingency of most secularization processes," not only in Europe, but also all around the world.[222] Gorski and Altinordu state this kind of comparative study "has led some scholars to call for a fuller historicization of the secularization debate."[223]

CONCLUSION: IS REVIVAL POSSIBLE IN A SECULAR EUROPE?

Unquestionably, secularization was facilitated by the Reformation, French Revolution, and Industrial Revolution through modernization and rationalism. The declining curve of Christian beliefs and practices has caused many sociologists and intellectuals to agree that this is proof of the death of Christianity in the West. Christianity in Europe has dwindled in societal, public, and private life.

---

217. Bernard, "Religion and Theology," 72–73.
218. Prosman, *The Postmodern Condition*, 8.
219. Bruce, *Secularization*, 91.
220. Ibid., 7.
221. Merlini, "A Post-Secular World?," 118.
222. Gorski and Altinordu, "After Secularization?," 59.
223. Ibid., 59.

In spite of the decline of Christian influence in society, there have also been times of rejuvenation of Christianity in Europe. David Martin was the first to discard the thesis that secularization is inevitable. Theories of secularization have too often been used to justify the process of moving away from the spiritual. "A general theory [secularization] can be stated for society within a Christian ambit . . . and subsequently be qualified for other societies, just as secularization itself was exported with a modification to other societies."[224] Martin insisted that secularization may eventually enter a state of universal process for the industrial society, with components of several secularization stages. In addition, it is difficult to find a broad-spectrum consensus on when the shift occurred from a society in which traditional religions dominated the lives of humans to one in which the liberty and choices are present in secular society.[225] Peter Berger confirms some changes, inaccuracies, and misconceptions of the secularization thesis in his interview with the *Christian Century*:

> I think what I and most other sociologists of religion wrote in the 1960s about secularization was a mistake. Our underlying argument was that secularization and modernity go hand in hand. With more modernization comes more secularization. It wasn't a crazy theory. There was some evidence for it. But I think it's basically wrong. Most of the world today is certainly not secular. It's very religious. So is the U.S. The one exception to this is Western Europe.[226]

Charles Taylor takes issue with all theories of secularization. He does not believe that a decline in religious beliefs and practices is occurring, but that secular theorists have erred by omitting the spiritual dynamics and manifestations of the Holy Spirit.[227] In the next chapter, we will examine the revitalization of the Christian faith in Europe and the rise of religion in the developing world. Here, we see trends that point in the opposite direction of those predicted by theories of secularization.

224. Martin, *A General Theory of Secularization*, 2.
225. Ibid., 2–3.
226. Berger, "Epistemological Modesty," lines 122–25.
227. Taylor, *A Secular Age*, 534–35.

5

Revival Movements in Europe

THE PATTERN OF RISE and fall of Christianity in both the Global North and the Global South (that is, the developed world and the developing world) exhibits an irony: revivals and awakenings are almost always followed by secularization. Christianity has been growing at a phenomenal rate throughout the Global South in recent centuries, as Europe's has simultaneously been decreasing. Secularism has come to dominate Western European public affairs, norms, thoughts, values, social life, and religion. Religious domination of the past through the state church monopolies are long gone. Ecclesiastical initiatives, Christian morality and ethics, mediating functions of Christian faith, and the sacred and mysterious are no longer considered mainstream. The secularization thesis—the idea that religion will necessarily be abandoned as a society matures—was widely accepted, and many scholars saw no further need for religion, the only discipline that deals with spirituality and the afterlife.

Secularism then led to humanism, which placed humans at the center of every value system and worldview. This runs counter to the biblical worldview, which maintains that there is indeed another world, that all things were created by God for God's purposes, and that the two worlds are undividable and should be harmonized for God's soteriological and redemptive purposes. Eventually, secularization shaped religion in the private lives of individuals and, in an environment of modernization and rationalism, profoundly influenced Western philosophy, intellectualism, and culture. The process quickly advanced in Europe following the Enlightenment, French Revolution, and Industrial Revolution.

Then, a significantly new type of Christianity called evangelical-ism, emerged from the ashes of state churches, reshaping the religious geography of Western Europe. Protestant revivals and awakenings broke out in Britain and North America until the late nineteenth century, while the Catholic hierarchy moderately modified doctrinal positions in order to adapt to a more secularized world.

In the European nations where Christianity had never held a monopoly, growth in attendance and membership reached historic levels. Pentecostal and charismatic revivals in Germany, the Netherlands, Britain, and Scotland reshaped the face of world Christianity. In this chapter, we will examine and analyze the momentous revivals and awakenings that gave birth to evangelicalism, as well as consider concurrent social and religious phenomena during this remarkable time.

WHAT IS REVIVAL?

We have observed the critical issues of secularization in Europe but that study requires us to explore other aspects of spiritual awakenings and revivals that transformed communities and the nation. Certain secular trends and worldviews inevitably effaced the religious influence of nations where secularization was not yet the major influential player in their societies. If spiritual awakenings broke out among individuals or churches, such empiricism usually outlived former indoctrinations and church programs. Once the fire of God was kindled, it was engraved for future generations to see and study. Revival stories are recorded in the Bible, but the revival patterns recorded in the Scriptures that the Churches in Jerusalem, Antioch, and Ephesus experienced serve as the best patterns. Revivals broke out even during the Dark Ages intermittently. This book will not go over all the revivals in history but examine a few cases such as the Waldensians, Lollards, Hussites, and Savonarola. This chapter does not intend to describe the Reformation's historical significance *per se* but rather draw a grandeur picture of the spiritual awakenings and revivals in Europe. Therefore, rather than resummarize the story of the Reformation, revivals in the medieval age and Pietism and Wesleyan revivals in post-Reformation will be dealt with here.

Definition on Revivals and Awakenings

Methodist revivals and great awakenings in the United Kingdom and United States were essential to the emergence of evangelical Christianity. Before secularization, European Christians lived and thought within the traditions of the Catholic, Orthodox, and Reformed churches. Revivals and awakenings brought in vast numbers of followers from the major traditions who would reshape the face of Christianity.

The term *revival* implies bringing something back to life after a decline. The first usage of the term in a religious context occurred in New England by Cotton Mather in his work "Magnalia Christi Americana" in 1702. Here the term revival describes a state of "general awakening that brought by vitality, life of eternity, and vividness among traditional and nominal believers at the time.[1] Iain Murray described *revival* and *revivalism* as "the change coming in the 1820s from the older order of revival as a surprising work of God (in Edwards's words) undergirded by solid Calvinistic theology to the new view of revivals and revivalism as the organized series of meetings supported by emotional appeals and generally Arminian theology."[2] The term *revivalist* is defined as "one who conducts religious revivals."[3] None of these terms defined revival as a week of meetings, an evangelistic enterprise, or merely a social action or event. Nonetheless, some scholars have used these terms in this way.[4] George Smith accurately defines revival as "a work of grace affected by the Spirit of God on the souls of men."[5] Mark Stibbe defines that a "revival is a season ordained by God in which the Holy Spirit awakens the Church to evangelize the lost, and the lost to their dire need of Jesus Christ."[6]

1. Cotton Mather, *Magnalia Christi Americana*, 344.

2. Calhoun, *Reformation & Modern Church History*, 1–2.

3. Merriam-Webster, "Revivalist," line 1.

4. Orr, *Re-Study*, ii.

5. George Smith gave the first definition of revival during the Fourth Great Awakening in his three- volume *History of Wesleyan Methodism*, published in 1862, with a fourteen-page chapter on "Its Revivals."

6. He continues, "The distinguishing characteristic of revival is the way in which the Holy Spirit brings thousands of unbelievers to a place of profound conviction of sin. Revivals therefore involve a manifestation of the power of God in the community as well as in the church. They occur when God sweeps through a region in great power, causing believers and unbelievers to be impacted by the personality of

The *Oxford Dictionary of the Christian Church* calls revivalism "a type of religious worship and practices centering in on evangelical revivals, or outbursts of mass religious fervor, and stimulated by intensive preaching and prayer meetings."[7] This obviates the notion that the word *revivalism* originated on the American frontier, an idea not common to evangelical Christians until the 1850s.[8] Revivalism, a term first used in 1830, refers to Protestant evangelists, particularly a band of professional itinerant preachers, who tried to pass on the dynamic and vital Christian gospel to other communities and help usher forth a spiritual and religious experience of the new birth, or conversion, including salvation, regeneration, and sanctification. In this sense, revivals reinvigorate the spiritual lives of nominal Christians while awakenings transform the norms and values of non-Christians through conversion.[9]

An *awakening* is something that, "stir[s] into life and energy . . . from a state of inactivity, to be invigorated with new life . . . to excite from a state resembling sleep, as from death . . . to put into new life . . . to awake the dormant faculties . . . the act of rousing from sleep or inactivity; specifically, a revival of religion, impulses, etc."[10] This definition correlates in some degree with a more specific term, *evangelical awakening*, meaning the conversion of an unbeliever from an inactive state of religion to a life of faith following confession and repentance. On the other hand, the term *awakening* began to be used during periods of sociopolitical and cultural unrest characterized by trauma, anxiety, religious and spiritual isolation, a loss of influence from religious establishments, and an ambiguous vision and direction on the part of church and political leaders.[11] The Great Awakenings along with their subsequent revivals served

---

Jesus Christ. As such, revival cannot be worked up on earth; they must come down from heaven." Stibbe, *Revival*, 14.

7. The *Oxford Dictionary of the Christian Church* indicates that the occurrence of revival movements started with "the Methodist Movement of the 18th cent., where, under the Wesleys, G. Whitefield, and others, it was regularly encountered. Some bodies, e.g., the Salvation Army, make revivalism the principal element of all their worship," 1162.

8. Gabriel, *Religion and Learning at Yale*, 75; Fish, *Handbook of Revivals*, 105.

9. McLoughlin, *Revivals, Awakenings, and Reform*, xiii.

10. Webster, *Webster's Unabridged Dictionary*, 130.

11. McLoughlin, *Revivals, Awakenings, and Reform*, 2.

to work against the social deterioration and religious aloofness associated with this social climate. They instead revitalized, by means of large- and small-scale gatherings, religious fervor and enthusiasm in nations where secularism had penetrated deeply into every phase of social life.[12]

While the term *revival* is found more frequently in European contexts, the term *awakening* is used in the United States to define an archetype of enthusiastic American religious movements. The British and others who identify themselves as dissenters or Free Church believers of biblical principles and a highly disciplined Christian life, brought their values to the British colonies in America, allowing great awakenings to spread throughout all Christian denominations and to form a new American Christian culture.[13] The term *revival* in a religious sense connotes a lethargic Christian spirituality being brought back to life through a conversion experience and the personal assurance of salvation in Christ Jesus, either within or outside of the state church. For example, John Wesley and his colleagues—who were part of the Church of England—accentuated fundamental Reformation principles in their evangelical revival movements during the eighteenth century.[14]

The work of the Holy Spirit and Revival

J. Edwin Orr makes the point that evangelical awakenings are brought about by the Holy Spirit, who birthed the early church at Pentecost and made it possible to reach people all over the Middle East, Asia Minor, and even Europe. Even in the eighteenth and nineteenth centuries, numerous awakenings affected communities and churches throughout the West.[15] This historical illustration shows us what an awakening is—the conversion of unbelievers with no prior spiritual life—while revival is the renewal of religious life for the previously active believer.

The notion of revivalism as a series of meetings or evangelistic efforts historically developed from two main traditions. Jonathan Edwards defined revival as the sovereign work of God, with little con-

12. Ibid., 2.
13. Ibid., 1.
14. Armstrong, *The Church of England*, 49.
15. Orr, *Evangelical Awakenings*, vi.

tribution from man: a Calvinistic viewpoint. Charles Finney regarded revival as largely the effort of man: an Arminian view. Prior to the 1830s, the word *revival* was used to describe only "a sudden and unexpected outpouring of the Holy Spirit in which more are converted in one week than in one decade."[16] Edwards describes this type of revival in Northampton, Massachusetts, from 1734 to 1735 in *A Faithful Narrative of the Surprising Work of God*:

> And the work of conversion was carried on in a most astonishing manner, and increased more and more; souls did as it were come by flocks to Jesus Christ. From day to day for many months together, might be seen evident instances of sinners brought out of darkness into marvellous light, and delivered out of an horrible pit, and from the miry clay, and set upon a rock, with a new song of praise to God in their mouths.

This work of God, as it was carried on, and the number of true saints multiplied, soon made a glorious alteration in the town: so that in the spring and summer following, anno 1735, the town seemed to be full of the presence of God: it never was so full of love, nor of joy, and yet so full of distress, as it was then. There were remarkable tokens of God's presence in almost every house. It was a time of joy in families on account of salvation being brought to them; parents rejoicing over their children as new born, and husbands over their wives, and wives over their husbands. The doings of God were then seen in His sanctuary, God's day was a delight, and His tabernacles were amiable. Our public assemblies were then beautiful: the congregation was alive in God's service, every one earnestly intent on the public worship, every hearer eager to drink in the words of the minister as they came from his mouth; the assembly in general were, from time to time, in tears while the word was preached; some weeping with sorrow and distress, others with joy and love, others with pity and concern for the souls of their neighbors.[17]

V. Raymond Edman says that "revival, the gentle breathing of God's Spirit upon the dry bones of a dead orthodoxy or of a defiant godlessness, became a whirlwind in the ministry of Finney."[18] While

---

16. Jonathan Edwards, who witnessed revival in the 1730s and 1740s, likened it to tornadoes. See Murray, *Revival and Revivalism*, 19.

17. Edwards, *A Faithful Narrative of the Surprising Work of God*, §1.

18. Edman, *Finney on Revival*, 72.

the Holy Spirit provided the spark for revival, Finney saw human effort as playing a significant role in fanning the flames.

According to Charles Haddon Spurgeon, "To be revived is a blessing which can only be enjoyed by those who have some degree of life. Those who have no spiritual life are not, and cannot be, in the strictest sense of the term, subjects of a revival. . . . *A true revival is to be looked for in the church of God.*"[19] In this manner, the power of the Holy Spirit transformed individual lives in giving his fullness in order to equip the saint to fulfill his great commission. Dr. Heman Humphrey emphatically avows, "A genuine revival is the fruit or effect of a supernatural Divine influence, which restores the joy of God's salvation to backsliding Christians, startles the dead in trespasses and sins, convinces them of their lost and perishing condition, and makes them willing in the day of God's power."[20] Stibbe points out that the purpose of revival is the salvation of sinners. Duncan Campbell says, "The Church has often been evangelical without being evangelistic!"[21] The church can hold true to cardinal biblical beliefs, yet neglect the imperative of the Great Commission to reach out to share the gospel with others. For that reason, God sends his Holy Spirit to awaken the church to evangelize to the lost, and awaken the lost to their need of salvation through Jesus Christ.

Revivals in the Early Church

The advent of the Holy Spirit in Jerusalem gave birth to the church of Jesus Christ. The life of the church comes from the indwelling presence of the Holy Spirit, who gives power and authority to believers to testify that Jesus is Savior and Lord. Gerhard Uhlhorn affirms, "Witnesses who are above suspicion leave no room for doubt that the miraculous powers of the Apostolic age continued to operate at least into the third century."[22] Those leaning towards conventional reformed theological standpoints view that no miraculous signs and wonders took place

---

19. In other words, revival begins when the church of God spills over into the world. Spurgeon, "The Sword and the Trowel," lines 21–24, 28.

20. Humphrey, *Revival Sketches and Manuel*, 13.

21. Duncan Campbell's word is quoted in Stibbe's book. Stibbe, *Revival*, 18.

22. Uhlhorn, *Conflict of Christianity with Heathenism*, 169. Cf. Gordon, *The Ministry of Healing*, 155–159.

in the second and third centuries, even as Uhlhorn finds evidence of *charismata* during the post-apostolic era.[23]

Throughout history, revivals initiated by the outpouring of the Holy Spirit have occurred in various locations following the patterns of the New Testament churches. Revival has occurred in different places through the humble prayers of ordinary people, during the second and third centuries, and even during medieval times, when Bible reading was prohibited.

The message of salvation preached by the apostles drew people to Christianity in large numbers in the Roman Empire. Conversions were followed by miraculous signs and wonders from the Holy Spirit. New Christians were challenged to believe in Jesus and to live as witnesses, not only through evangelism, but also by enduring horrendous persecutions. In fact, revivals in the early church prepared believers for the trials they would face, making personal the imagery of metal being refined through extreme flame in order to be stronger in Christ.

The Holy Spirit is the origin of all revivals and awakenings. Most revivals resemble the New Testament pattern of the Jerusalem church in Acts: the Holy Spirit baptizes with fire, resulting in conversion by repentance, discipleship, corporate prayer, house fellowship, and vigorous evangelism. By the second century, however, manifestations of the Holy Spirit were very infrequent; many believed they had ceased. By the third century, the church had become institutionalized, and worship services became inflexible liturgy. Over the centuries, the institutionalized Catholic Church continued to conduct services in Latin, making it incomprehensible to the common people. It was as if the church had forgotten the fact that the Holy Spirit is one of three persons of the Holy Trinity and, in the Old Testament, was often called the Spirit of God. Jesus was incarnated by the Holy Spirit and ministered through the Holy Spirit, referring repeatedly to the "Spirit," "Counselor," and "Paraclete."

The early church focused not on the work of the Holy Spirit, but on indoctrination, institutionalization, and the sacraments. In due course, the belief that direct manifestations of the Holy Spirit no longer occurred constrained church leaders to ignore the Spirit in church practice despite their Trinitarian theology. God the Father and God

23. Benjamin Warfield insists on the cessation of the charismata. Warfield, *Counterfeit Miracles*, 3–15.

the Son were the focus of early church father's epistles, but the Holy Spirit was only mentioned in benedictions or sacraments. The theological debates of the time on the Arian heresy emphasized that God the Father and God the Son are one, yet Jesus identified the Spirit as being of a different nature from the Son.[24]

While defining the dual nature of Jesus as God and human, Athanasius attempted to clarify the nature of Holy Spirit as well.[25] Athanasius's writings on the Trinity represented the agreement of the ecumenical councils where the Nicene Creed [26] and the Apostles' Creed[27] were formulated indicating that the Holy Spirit was defined as the substance of the Godhead.[28] Thus the Holy Spirit was considered as equal (*homoousios, not homoiousios*) to God the Father and God the Son in the Council of Constantinople in 381.[29] In this same year, Theodosius decreed an *epistula* [(meaning 'letter' in Greek)] indicat-

24. Arius insists that the logos was the minister of creation more than man. The logos is the Son but Jesus was less than the Father. He indicates, "Christ is the Logos incarnate, Christ is capable of change and suffering, Therefore the Logos is capable of change and not equal to God." Wand, *The Early Church*, 149–50. Arius denied the deity of Jesus, saying he was not God the Son, but merely human. Therefore, he was condemned by Athanasius and Western church as a heretic. Arius states that "Christ was neither eternal nor identical with God. God is immutable; the Son is changeable. God is perfect; the Son progresses toward perfection." Hardy, "Athanasius' Writing on Arianism," 1.

25. Krueger says, "The conclusion is drawn that the doctrine of the Trinity leaves no loophole for tritheism. Each of the three persons is fully God and Lord. But one cannot deduce from this that there are therefore three Gods and three Lords. The Triune God, Father, Son and Holy Ghost, is one God." Krueger, "Origin and Terminology," 5.

26. The Nicene Creed was declared by the first ecumenical council in 325. In Latin, it was called *Symbolum Nicaenum* meaning the creed or profession of faith. In Greek, Συμβολον τῆς Πίστεως means 'the symbol of faith.'

27. After the Nicene council, the Trinity as God the Father, God the Son and God the Spirit was clearly indicated in the Apostles' Creed. The Latin name of the Apostles' Creed is *Symbolum Apostolorum* or *Symbolum Apostolicum,* meaning "Symbol of the Apostles." The Apostle creed began to spread from fifth century although Bishop Ambrose mentioned it as the "Creed of the Apostles" in 390.

28. The term *homoousios* is used as the same or equal substance of the Godhead. The term homoiousios, meaning 'similar,' created some confusion in defining the Holy Trinity. Freeman, *A.D. 381*, 58. Cf. Burckhardt, *The Age of Constantine*, 312.

29. There is a distinction between the Nicene and Constantinople councils in the definition of the trinity, which divided western Catholics and eastern Orthodox in theology. Freeman, *A.D. 381*, xix.

ing "the only acceptable form Christianity centered on a Trinity."[30] These creeds established a foundation for "a standard for all instruction in the faith."[31] The Athanasian Creed indicates that the Holy Spirit is distinct from God the Father and God the Son, but does not explicitly detail how. During the Ecumenical Council in Ephesus in AD 431, Nestorius raised the issue on the disunity of the two natures of Jesus.[32] The theological issue on the 'incarnation' necessitated the fourth ecumenical Council in Chalcedon in AD 451.[33] Not long after the death of the apostles, miracles, signs and healings were performed extremely infrequently. In 165, Justin Martyr confessed,

> But "Jesus," His name as man and Saviour, has also significance . . . for the destruction of the demons. . . . For numberless demoniacs throughout the whole world, and in your city, many of our Christian men exorcising them in the name of Jesus Christ, who was crucified under Pontius Pilate, have healed and do heal, rendering helpless and driving the possessing devils out of the men, though they could not be cured by all the other exorcists, and those who used incantations and drugs. [34]

In the second century, only a few theologians paid attention to the Holy Spirit. One of them was the Bishop of Lugdunum, Irenaeus, who was born in Smyrna and schooled under Polycarp. In *Adversus Haereses* (Against Heresies), he defended the Christian faith against Gnosticism. He encouraged Christians to use spiritual gifts: "In like manner we do also hear many brethren in the Church, who possess prophetic gifts, and who through the Spirit speak all kinds of languages, and bring to light for the general benefit the hidden things of men, and declare the mysteries of God, . . . they being spiritual because they partake of the Spirit."[35] Furthermore, through the spiritual gifts, we can freely minister to others:

30. Ibid., 1.

31. Burnaby, *The Belief of Christendom*, 6–7.

32. Theological debate between Nestorius and Theodosius brought about the Nestorian Schism birthing the Nestorian Church or the Church of the East. Nestorius did not attend the council but sent Cyril in his place.

33. The Chalcedon Council heavily rested on the issue of monophisics. Eutyches insisted that Christ has one nature of divinity and humanity, not as two natures, an argument called monophysitism (monos (single) and phsis (nature)).

34. Justin Martyr, *The Second Apology*, §6.

35. Irenaeus, *Against Heresies*, §1.

> Wherefore, also, those who are in truth His disciples, receiv-
> ing grace from Him, do in His name perform [miracles] . . .
> according to the gift which each one has received from Him.
> For some do certainly and truly drive out devils, so that those
> who have thus been cleansed from evil spirits frequently both
> believe [in Christ], and join themselves to the Church. Others
> have foreknowledge of things to come: they see visions, and
> utter prophetic expressions. Others still, heal the sick by laying
> their hands upon them, and they are made whole. Yea, more-
> over, as I have said, the dead even have been raised up, and
> remained among us for many years. And what shall I more
> say? It is not possible to name the number of the gifts which
> the Church, [scattered] throughout the whole world, has re-
> ceived from God, in the name of Jesus Christ. . . . For as she
> has received freely from God, freely also does she minister [to
> others].[36]

Tertullian spoke on the issue of the Holy Spirit:

> For what kind of (supposition) is it, that, while the devil is al-
> ways operating and adding daily to the ingenuities of iniquity,
> the work of God should either have ceased, or else have de-
> sisted from advancing? Whereas the reason why the Lord sent
> the Paraclete was, that, since human mediocrity was unable to
> take in all things at once, discipline should, little by little, be
> directed, and ordained, and carried on to perfection, by that
> Vicar of the Lord, the Holy Spirit. [37]

Tertullian's understanding of the Holy Spirit came out of his personal observations of the Spirit's work, "The clerk of one of them who
was liable to be thrown upon the ground by an evil spirit was set free
from his affliction, as was also the relative of another, and the little
boy of a third. How many men of rank (to say nothing of the common
people) have been delivered from devils and healed of diseases!"[38] In
spite of their theological shortcomings, Tertullian and the early church
fathers understood and focused their views on the outpouring of the
Holy Spirit.

---

36. Ibid., §4.
37. Tertullian, "On the Veiling of Virgins," lines 12–15.
38. Tertullian, *Ad Scapulam*, §4.

REVIVALS IN THE MIDDLE AGES

The early church was persecuted by the Roman Empire until its official recognition by Constantine. Ironically, in the post-Constantine era, sincere believers who did not acquiesce to the structure, liturgy, and governance of the institutional church were persecuted by church authorities. According to Adam Jones, Catholics duplicated the pattern of mass killings during the Middle Ages in following the way the pagan Roman Empire murdered Christians. He states "This period produced onslaughts such as the crusades: religious sanctified campaigns against "unbelievers," whether in France (the Albigensian crusade against Cathar heretics), Germany (against Jews), or Holy Land of the Middle East."[39] Professor David Plaisted calculated the number of people who were killed by the Catholic authority by means of crusades, inquisitions, and religious persecutions and killings. He estimates that "20 million [were] killed in the Holy Land and surrounding areas during the crusades, 1 million Waldenses, 1 million Albigenses, at least 18 million witches and others killed during steady state persecution of heretics in Europe from 1100 to 1600."[40] However, more fell victim with 10 million killed in the Thirty Years' War, several millions in the Huguenot wars, and 15 million Protestants killed between 1518 and 1548. More importantly are the 50 million Protestants who were killed after the Reformation particularly during counter-Reformation. As Plaisted suggests, if 45–50 million were killed during the Middle Ages, the total is at least 100 million killed by religious persecution in Europe alone.[41]

Plaisted's statistics on persecution against Bible believing Christians demonstrates how Catholicism condemned Christians as heretics and murdered a great number of innocent lives. The Fourth Lateran Council in 1215, led by Pope Innocent III, laid a foundation for true believers to be condemned as heretics. Under his leadership, numerous Waldensians and other Bible believers were massacred.[42] True believers in the Bible were labeled as radical or secret sectarian

---

39. Jones, *Genocide*, 5

40. Plaisted, *Lost Records*, 235.

41. Plaisted quoted the data from Middleton and estimates between 114 million and 150 million including American Indians numbering 50 million were killed. Ibid., 235.

42. Kreis, *Heretics, Heresies, and the Church*, §27.

believers. They were not pagan or Gnostic, but defied the Vatican and were thus condemned as heretics and excommunicated. They encountered persecution, inquisitions, crusades, and torture that impelled them to live in deplorable conditions if they did not conform to the Catholic Church.

Revival Characteristics

Were manifestations of the Holy Spirit part of the medieval European revival movements? Revivals seek to recover what the church lost in departing from the revival pattern of the Book of Acts. This brings us to an examination of the revival pattern in the medieval European church. During the Middle Ages, Christianity continued to expand within Europe, but manifestations of the Holy Spirit were rare. The hierarchy of the Catholic Church dominated both the secular and sacred, which contributed to the expansion of Christendom, but precluded the power and organic functioning of a dynamic, Spirit-filled church. When revival came, it was single-sided: the Bible played a key role, but miraculous signs, healings, and other manifestations of the Spirit were not apparent.

In the twelfth to fourteenth centuries, reform-minded preachers such as Peter Waldo and John Wycliffe brought messages on repentance and imitating Christ in accordance with the gospels. With Bible reading forbidden at this time by papal order, Bible translation and reading in Latin or in vernacular languages became a focal point. Inevitably, Catholic authorities sought to silence these wandering preachers. As early as AD 1030, a number of them were martyred at the stake, not renouncing their beliefs even in the face of death. Later, reformers including Martin Luther and John Calvin advocated a reliance on Scripture alone. Reading the Bible was made possible through the ministry of translation, undertaken by Christian leaders who faced enormous opposition from the Catholic Church. Can a little pebble break a large mountain? Revival movements that seemed like little pebbles at the time have been vindicated by history for shaking the mountain of the Catholic Church and eventually breaking its monopoly. The Bible translation work of the Waldensians, and Lollards gave a fresh breath to a spiritually stifling medieval church. The main reason for the evangelical revivals is the acute spiritual hunger of the common people, which was not being met until they had access to the truth of the gospel.

The Catholic Church reacted violently toward sectarian groups, mounting crusades, inquisitions, papal orders, excommunications, and massacres justified as a holy war against infidels. "These holy wars were sometimes directed against monarchs and other rulers, sometimes against cities, at other times against heretics like the Albigenses, or against the heathen in the north and northeast of Europe."[43] As Islam spread, formerly Christian areas including the Byzantine Empire and Iberian Peninsula came under Muslim influence. In response, Catholic leader Jacques de Vitry traveled to southern France and preached between 1211 and 1213, bringing the New Testament message to Eastern orthodox groups and Muslims.[44] These people lived in the Languedoc region, where the heretical Cathar movement was influential. However, this region was known as the place of the monastic revival in the early tenth century. In due course several monasteries like St-Pins-de-Thomière and the monastery of Lezat were established.[45] These believers, who retained an identity separate from Catharism, began to realize that the fundamental problems of the Catholic Church stemmed from its hierarchy, corrupted parochialism, and ossified liturgy. They sought the truth in the Bible and tried to translate some portions of New Testament, the book of Psalms, and others into their language. Seeing these Bible-believing Christians as true forerunners of the Reformation, Wylie finds that the Reformation's "cradle would be placed not in Germany but in the south of France.[46] The most prominent of these Bible believers lived in the city of Albi.[47] This bible reading movement primarily attracted the common people, but also drew distinguished nobles including Raymond Earl of Toulouse and Raymond Earl of Foxe.[48]

These believers were condemned for rejecting Mary worship, infallibility of the Pope, clericalism, and saint veneration, among other reasons. However, the predominant reason was that they translated

43. Munro, "The Popes and the Crusades," 352.

44. Johns, "Christianity and Islam," 182.

45. Costen, *The Cathars and the Albigensian Crusade*, 19.

46. Ibid., 33.

47. Kurian, *Nelson's Dictionary of Christianity*, 14.

48. Forbush, *Book of Martyrs*, 45.

the Bible into local languages and read it when the Catholic Church did not allow either of these activities. Thus, we can say that the history of the medieval church is the history of religious warfare between the followers of Bible reading and followers of papal authority. It is well known that the Catholic Church banned the masses from reading or to reproducing the Bible. Philipp Schaff points out, "In 1199 Innocent III, writing to the diocese of Metz where the Scriptures were being used by heretics, declared that as by the old law, the beast touching the holy mount was to be stoned to death, so simple and uneducated men were not to touch the Bible or venture to preach its doctrines."[49]

In 1215, Innocent III declared that whoever attempted to translate the Bible into their languages "shall be seized for trial and penalties, who engage in the translation of the sacred volumes [the Bible], or who hold secret conventicles, or who assume the office of preaching without the authority of their superiors; against whom process shall be commenced, without any permission of appeal."[50] In 1229, the Council of Toulouse outlawed the possession or reading of the Bible by laypeople.[51]

M'Crie describes the search for Bible believers during this time as a collaborative effort of bishops and the national army: "one priest and two or three laics, who should engage upon oath to make a rigorous search after all heretics and their abettors, and for this purpose should visit every house from the garret to the cellar, together with all subterraneous places where they might conceal themselves"[52] In 1234, the Council of Tarragona "ordered all vernacular versions to be brought to the Bishop to be burned."[53] Using force to assert its authority, "The Church defined and condemned the heresy, and the State punished it by the sword, using carnal force against spiritual offenses."[54] Intolerance for dissenting beliefs resulted in disastrous killings. Schaff states, "The great and good St. Augustine was the first among the fathers who formulated the very principle of persecution by his famous misinterpretation of 'Compel them to enter in.' Innocent III, who inspired the

---

49. Schaff, *History of the Christian Church,* vol. VI, 722–3.

50. Callender, *Illustrations of Popery,* 387.

51. Allix, *"Ecclesiastical History,"* 213.

52. M'Crie, *History of the Reformation in Spain,* 82.

53. Simms, *Bible from the Beginning,* 162.

54. Schaff, *"The Development of Religious Freedom,"* 351–52.

horrible crusade against the Albigenses and Waldenses, was one of the purest, as well as ablest, among popes."[55]

Central to their condemnation was the issue of Bible translation. These persecuted groups are considered forerunners of the Reformation: radical Christians. Ahlstrom observes, "Christian radicalism, of course, is as old as the Church. The gospel is a radical message. . . . In the Middle Ages much of this potential radicalism was channeled into the monastic and mendicant orders and the lay brotherhoods associated with or similar to them. There were also signs of it among the Waldensians, the Lollards of England, and the Hussites."[56]

Waldensian Revival

In the darkest time of medieval Europe, the tiny flame of the Waldenses kindled one of brightest revivals in Europe. Revival historian William Allen acclaims that "[w]here they live, 'there is not a rock that is not a monument, not a meadow that has not seen an execution, not a village that does not register its martyrs.' In the twentieth century they experienced a revival which resulted in great evangelistic activities."[57] From their communities in the southwestern Alps, Pyrenean France, Northeastern Germany, and the extreme south of Italy, they expanded their reach into other parts of Europe.[58] They traveled together from town to town with small groups led by lay preachers to share the gospel message.[59]

As with other revival movements, this one had missionary characteristics. Allen states, "All were missionaries, and preached in the houses, streets, and market places. . . . The sect spread with extraordinary rapidity, and extended from Arragon [Aragon] to Pomerania and Bohemia, though most numerous in the south of France's Alsace, and in the mountain districts of Savoy; Switzerland and Northern Italy."[60]

Cameron finds that "they were largely orthodox in most of their beliefs; and they were opposed to the authority and pretensions of the

---

55. Ibid., 354.

56. Ahlstrom, *A Religious History of the American People*, 81.

57. Allen, *History of Revivals*, 9.

58. Cameron, *Waldenses*, 1.

59. A small group leader was called a *barba* and was cared for by Waldensian members.

60. W. Allen quotes C. Allen. Allen, *The History of Revivals*, 10.

Western Church."[61] Most Waldensians lived in the Alps and Pyrenees, especially in the Alpine valleys of the Piedmont near Turin, which borders northern Italy, Switzerland, and southern France. A great number lived in francophone areas from the late twelfth century to the sixteenth century.[62] During the Reformation, many joined Calvinist or Reformed churches. "Elsewhere in Europe they were either subsumed into another movement in the great religious upheavals of the sixteenth century, or had already disappeared before then."[63]

The Waldenses were led by Peter Waldo (or Valdo)[64] and were known as the "Poor Men of Lyons" or the "Poor in Spirit."[65] Latourette says that "they resembled the movement which Francis of Assisi was to inaugurate three decades or so later."[66] This movement prepared the way for later revivals among the diaspora Waldenses in Bohemia, the Moravians, and John Wesley's Methodism.[67] The Waldensians read the Bible, especially the New Testament that had been translated into their language, Romaunt, with copies made by hand.[68] They rejected Catholic ecclesiastical authority.[69] They memorized large sections of the Bible and went to villages two by two, "preaching, simply clad, barefoot or wearing sandals" in order to share the gospel.[70]

Waldensian beliefs and practices crossed from Catholicism to Protestantism, reflecting Waldo's personal experiences. His "dilemma . . . highlights the predicament of lay people at this stage in the de-

61. Cameron, *Waldenses*, 1.

62. "The Waldenses of the later middle ages had no very precise idea of their own origins. Some believed their movement to be as old as the apostles; some thought that it dated from the fourth century, in the time of Pope Sylvester I (314–35). Years later, some Protestant apologists tried to argue for a similarly ancient origin, at least as far back as the ninth century and possibly before." Ibid., 11.

63. Ibid., 1.

64. See Anonymous, *Universal Chronicle*; Poitiers, *Life of Pope Alexander III*; Cameron, *Waldenses*, 11; and Brown, *Heresies*, 262.

65. Strayer, *The Albigensian Crusades*, 36.

66. Latourette, *A History of Christianity*, 451.

67. Knox, *Enthusiasm*, 76.

68. Blackburn, *History of the Christian Church*, 309–10.

69. More recourse, cf. *A History of the Christian Church* (Waldenses) by William Jones (1831), *History of the Ancient Churches of Piedmont and Albigenses* by Pierre Allix (1690), *A History of the Waldenses* by J.A. Wylie (1860), and *A History of the Ancient Christians of the Valleys of the Alps* by Perrin (1847).

70. Latourette, *A History of Christianity*, 452.

velopment of medieval Christianity. One could seek the 'perfect' way of celibacy, monastic renunciation, or ordination early in life; or one could seek the 'unperfect' way of marriage, involvement in the lay world, business and property."[71] Waldensian allegiance to Catholic churches differed by region, but it is clear that they tried to obtain clerical approval in the early stages of the movement. After the Catholic authorities expressed their disapproval, "the Waldenses also routinely denounced the clergy as a sink of vice, and rejected its claim to control access to the means of grace. The clergy, for its turn, regarded the Waldenses as a menace, and pursued them with a vigour which never relented and occasionally erupted into mass persecution."[72]

In medieval times, the Catholic authority allowed only the Latin Vulgate translation of the Bible to be used. Waldo asked two priest friends to translate some pieces of the New Testament into the vernacular. He then committed them to memory and proceeded to have most of the New Testament, Psalms, and other parts of the Old Testament translated as well. Waldo "then undertook the task of making the Scriptures available to the public in those 'vulgar' [local language of southern France] translations."[73] The influence of these translations was profound and wide-ranging.

Waldo, a wealthy man, can be compared to the rich young ruler in the gospels (Matt 19, Mark 10). Waldo's life was moved in 1173 when he heard St Alexis, "a fifth century Roman patrician who had left a wealthy bride for a life of mendicancy and almsgiving in Syria." Cameron states that Waldo "went to ask the local theologians which was the most "certain and perfect" way to reach God.'" In searching the story of the young rich man it led Waldo to follow what Jesus asked the rich man, "If you wish to be perfect, go and sell everything that you possess."[74]

He went on to give up his property for the poor and to live like a beggar, following a New Testament model of communal life and sharing or divesting oneself of possessions for the sake of following Jesus Christ.[75] His advocacy of Bible reading and translation represented

71. Cameron, *Waldenses*, 14.
72. Ibid., 2.
73. Brown, *Heresies*, 262.
74. Cameron, *Waldenses*, 12.
75. Latourette, *A History of Christianity*, 451.

a threat to Catholic authorities and resulted in inquisitions against people who had New Testaments in their possession. The Catholic authorities declared that "No man must presume to receive or assist heretics, nor in buying or selling have any thing to do with them, that being thus deprived of the comforts of humanity, they may be compelled to repent of the error of their way."[76]

Despite papal opposition, Waldo encouraged people to follow biblical standards in their lives. This led to persecution and massacre of thousands of Waldensians. Many left the Piedmont area and spread to other places. Around the same time, Hugo Speroni, consul in Piacenza, and his followers rejected Catholic rites and sacraments such as "baptism, penance, and the eucharist, and sought to replace them with a spiritual communion with the word; and sought been a kind of anticipation of the early Quakers, stressing both simplicity of life and intimate, personal fellowship with God through the Word."[77]

In following Peter Waldo, Waldensians spread the gospel message all over neighboring regions. Michal Costen says that a great number of lay Waldensian preachers with empty hands lived by alms, "learnt long tracts from the vernacular Bible by heart and this training formed the basis of preaching which was aimed primarily at calling their hearers to repentance."[78] Before the war in 1209, the Waldensians were divided into two groups, the Italian and the French groups. Costen states, "The Italian group survived to become the Waldensians of modern time, while the French group found themselves caught up in the struggle against the Cathars."[79]

Eventually, "The persecution of the Waldensians only ended in the 17th Century when Oliver Cromwell of England intervened vigorously on their behalf. The Waldensians survive in Northern Italy to this day – the oldest Protestant church in the world."[80] Protestant denominations such the Mennonites and Baptists claim that their churches share a historical relationship with the Waldensians.[81] Although most

---

76. Ouseley, *A Short Defense of the Old Religion*, 221.
77. Brown, *Heresies*, 262.
78. Costen, *The Cathars and the Albigensian Crusade*, 56.
79. Ibid., 57.
80. Hammond, "The Reformation," lines 24–26.
81. Orchard, *A Concise History of the Baptists*, 199.

of them were ultimately martyred, their followers numbered about 800,000 in Europe in 1315.[82]

The Waldensians were in alignment with the upcoming reform movements of the Reformation, Pietism, and Wesleyan Methodism. "They contend for the lively hope which they have in God through Christ—for the regeneration and interior revival by faith, hope, and charity—for the merits of Jesus Christ, and the all sufficiency of his grace and righteousness."[83] Cameron describes their interactions with other Waldensian Christian communities and Hussites in Germany and Eastern Europe in the fifteenth century. In the following century, the Waldensians in the southwestern Alps corresponded together through literary exchange. According to Cameron, "Constantly exposed to Catholic rites and preaching, Waldensian followers seem to have found it very hard to stay at a logically consistent distance from the majority religious culture. Supposedly hostile to the cult of the saints or the service of the dead, they may be found nevertheless to have participated in these alongside the Catholics at least some of the time."[84] The Waldensian influence and boldness in sharing the Gospel of Jesus truly prepared the coming age of the Reformation.

The Lollards and John Wycliffe

Edward Cheyney illustrates the distinctiveness of the Lollards who prepared another dimension of the English Reformation. The Lollards were, as Cheyney says, "A group of bold, earnest, enthusiastic men in the first flush of an assertion of independent judgment and of the world's need of moral reform nevertheless abjured their beliefs, acknowledged the authority of the Church, and conformed themselves to its behests almost as soon as they were bidden to do so by its accredited officials."[85] John Wycliffe, the leader of the Lollards, was called the precursor of the English Proto-Protestant movement and "morning star" of the Reformation in the late fourteenth century. F.F. Bruce gives him the title *doctor evangelicus* for his adherence to the Bible above any other authority.[86] His belief in the power of the word of God drove

82. Knox, *Enthusiasm*, 84.

83. D'Aubigne, "History of the Reformation," 1.128.

84. Cameron, *Waldenses*, 3.

85. Cheyney, "The Recantations of the Early Lollards," 423.

86. Bruce, "John Wycliffe and the English Bible," 3.

him to advocate reforms and oppose papal authority through his ferocious but Bible centered lifestyle. F.F. Bruce describes John Wycliffe as having "The highest form of ministry in his eyes was the preaching of the Word: he ranked it emphatically higher than the celebration of the eucharist. The office of the priesthood, he maintained, could not be discharged without a knowledge of Holy Scripture; and that knowledge should be communicated to others. Holy preaching came next after holy living."[87]

As with the Waldensians, Bible translation was central to the Lollards' appeal to common people of the time. In 1382, Wycliffe translated the Vulgate into English; this was the Lollard Bible or the Wycliffe Bible. The Lollard movement was first condemned as a heresy in British history and believed to be the teachings of John Wycliffe, which were first employed by an Irish Cistercian monk named Henry Crumpe.[88] The term *Lollard* took on a negative connotation, indicating a person who was against the Church: "knights who hankered after Church property, dissatisfied tenants of an oppressive abbey, parishioners who refused to pay tithes, and apocalyptic visionaries."[89] In 1382, the Archbishop of Canterbury utilized *lollards* to denounce Wycliffe and his followers.[90] According to Crompton, "He [Crumpe] chose to call them [Wycliffe and fellows] *Lollards,* and was as a consequence suspended from all academic exercise and from preaching in the university, on the grounds that he had, thereby, caused a disturbance of

87. Wycliffe defended the word of God in his "Treatise on the Truth of Holy Scripture" (*De veritate sacrae scripturae*) in 1378. Ibid., 3.

88. Crompton, "Leicestershire Lollards," 11. In Old Dutch, *lollen* or *lullen* meant "sing," "mutter," or "chant." In Latin, *lolium* means "tares" indicating a "mumbler or babbler of prayers"; Kurian, *Nelson's Dictionary of Christianity*, 419. Repeatedly through Christian history, new movements arose seeking to embody the full, uncompromising Christian life. During the twelfth century, the new monastic order of the Cistercians, from Citeaux (Latin Cistercium) in what is now northeastern France. In general, the Cistercians conformed to the Benedictine pattern, but they had a rule of much stricter poverty. They established their monasteries far from other human habitation, where the monks, aided by lay brothers, cleared the land and erected their buildings by hand. The churches were austere, and they observed the rule of silence except in their common worship and for necessary communication. In contrast to many monasteries, which recruited boys dedicated to them in childhood and reared within their walls, the Cistercians would admit no novice below the age of sixteen and thus sought to assure an intelligent personal commitment.

89. Crompton, "Leicestershire Lollards," 11.

90. Kurian, *Nelson's Dictionary*, 419.

the peace.[91]" Haddock says, "Lollardy was essentially a religious re-form movement but one whose tenets held ramifications for the entire structure of English society."[92]

While heresy and inquisitions were common in continental Europe at the time, they were new to the British Isles, as Catholic ho-mogeneity had remained essentially unchallenged. In the fourteenth century, however, "Ecclesiastical revolt, radical religious ideas, and even actual heresy were showing themselves in several parts of the country and in various classes of society."[93] Wycliffe, like other revival leaders of the Middle Ages, was focused on the Bible as his source of authority, which led him to reject Catholicism's "indulgences, pil-grimages, transubstantiation, clerical celibacy, royal confession, the church's temporal power, prayers for the dead, images, and ecclesiasti-cal hierarchy."[94] He saw the church's wealth as evidence of corruption and was adamant to confiscate the property of the church and to allow the common people to read the Bible. He objected to the belief in tran-substantiation (that the bread and wine in mass literally transforms into the body of Christ) and denied that priests must be intermedi-aries between God and his people.[95] Wycliffe and his followers also protested the civil service of the clergy, who made up one in three members of the House of the Lords and nobility, insisting that the church should not rule over "its temporal power and [secular govern-mental] position."[96] Cheyney states, "scarcely would you see two men on the road but one of them was a disciple of Wycliffe."[97] The Pope condemned Wycliffe as a heretic in 1377.

Wycliffe spent his time divided between the University of Oxford and the parish; his ideas became fodder for Lollard preachers, and "the potential danger posed by unlicensed and uncontrolled evangelisers whose teachings would reveal to all the disparity between Biblical teaching and orthodox Church practice, was quickly realised by the

91. Crompton, "Leicestershire Lollards," 11.

92. Haddock, "The Lollards and Social and Religious Reform," 67.

93. Cheyney, "The Recantations of the Early Lollards," 423.

94. Kurian, *Nelson's Dictionary*, 419.

95. Haddock, "The Lollards and Social and Religious Reform," 67.

96. Ibid., 67–68.

97. Cheyney, "The Recantations of the Early Lollards," 427.

Church."[98] Haddock shares an instance in 1381: "[T]here was a certain company of the sect and doctrines of Wycliffe which conspired like a secret fraternity and arranged to travel around the whole of England preaching the beliefs taught by Wycliffe. . . . If they had not encountered resistance to their plans, they would have destroyed the entire kingdom within two years."[99]

At Queens College, Oxford, Wycliffe first translated the four gospels, then the rest of the New Testament and a portion of the Old Testament, into English. His friend Nicholas of Hereford translated the other parts of Old Testament, and John Purvey assisted in the translation work as well. The translation of the whole Bible was completed in 1384. Further revision was later conducted by John Purvey and others in 1388 and 1395 to what became known as the Wycliffe Bible.[100] This translation greatly influenced not only his generation, but subsequent generations as well. The common people, who could not understand Latin masses, said that Latin was used because "the clergy wanted to make the laity as ignorant as themselves."[101]

Wycliffe's objections to Catholicism became influential in Scotland and among the Hussites in Bohemia.[102] In 1382, he enjoyed the support of Robert Rigge, chancellor of the University of Oxford, as well as academicians and theologians such as Nicholas of Hereford.[103] Even so, Cheyney states, "disseminating, as they did, translations of parts of the Bible into English; preaching in the church-yards, the market-places, and the open roads; developing a more emotional and more popular religious life, they must have formed a distinctly new and disturbing influence, quite apart from the heretical views which they probably held and expressed."[104]

Inevitably, Wycliffe and his followers met with resistance from the Catholic Church and persecution that resulted in many early leaders renouncing their beliefs. Cheyney testifies that "the whole of the

98. Haddock, "The Lollards and Social and Religious Reform," 70.

99. Ibid., 70.

100. ExLibris, "English Dissenters: Lollards," lines 10–59.

101. Haddock, "The Lollards and Social and Religious Reform," 71. This was a move by the clergy to maintain their class difference from the common people.

102. Cross, The Oxford Dictionary, 819.

103. Cheyney, "The Recantations of the Early Lollards," 423–24.

104. Ibid., 425.

first generation of the Lollards recanted."[105] For example, John Purvey had been imprisoned for nearly twenty years for his work translating the Word. An accusation of heresy against Purvey was "brought before a council of the province of Canterbury at St. Paul's in London, on the 29th of, 1400."[106] There, Purvey testified in Latin and was forced to renounce Wycliffe's teachings at St. Paul's Cross. Another forerunner of the Reformation, William Tyndale claimed to identify with the dissent movement of the Lollards. According to Donald D. Smeeton's painstaking research, "I find in all ages that men have resisted their doctrine with the scripture, and have suffered death by the hundred thousands in resisting their doctrine."[107] After Wycliffe's death, more severe persecutions took place, such as the burning of the Lollards during the rule of Henry IV in 1401. The Lollards became part of Protestantism after the English Reformation.[108]

Medieval Revival Luminaries

Translating the Bible was risky business, and opposition to the Catholic Church could lead to torture, disappearance, and martyrdom. Meyer states, "The tenet which makes the Bible the seat of authority in matters of faith and practice worked as a leaven in Christendom long before the day of Luther and of Calvin." People who read the Bible and began to live according to the world of God were met with severe persecution from the Catholic Church. Between the ninth and twelfth centuries, Bible believing Christian movements were led by "Ajobard of Lyons, the Pére Hyacinthe of Louis the Pious' cycle, and of the bold commentator Claudius of Turin, or, later on, the revolutionary reform movements, headed by Peter of Bruys, Henry of Lausanne and Arnold of Brescia."[109]

In the medieval age, while Tanchelm and Henry of Lausanne fought against the Catholic Church, Peter Bruys became one of the earliest leaders of the Reformation, rejecting images, infant baptism, "Eucharist, church buildings, ecclesiastical ceremonies, prayer for

105. Ibid., 423.

106. Ibid., 431.

107. Smeeton, *Lollard Themes in the Reformation Theology of William Tyndale*, 77.

108. Cheyney, "The Recantations of the Early Lollards," 419.

109. Meyer, "The Formal Principle of the Reformation," 31.

the dead and the veneration of the cross."[110] Whenever revivals occurred, the ripple effects were felt throughout Europe. John Wycliffe's Bible translation inspired reform-minded people to pursue the task of translating into their own languages; one of these remarkable works was accomplished in Bohemia.

A century before Wycliffe, Waldensian expatriates victimized due to their attempts at Bible translation wandered all over Europe. Some crossed into Bohemia, rekindling spiritual fire in the Moravian community.[111] In 1315, "there were 80,000 true Christians in Bohemia alone," an incredible figure.[112] Almost seventy years later, King Richard II of England married Anne, queen of Bohemia, in 1382, and Anne sent Wycliffe's writings to Bohemia. John Milic, archdeacon of the cathedral in Prague, spoke courageously against the sins of the Catholic Church, declaring that the "Antichrist has come" through the church's corruption. He was imprisoned, as were other preachers including Conrad Stickna and Matthew of Janov, who spoke out against the exploitations of the church and felt the sting of backlash.

During this time, Jan Hus, at age 34, began to minister as rector of Prague University. Wycliffe's colleagues, the Lollards, introduced him to Wycliffe's writings and Bible translation. Hus translated treatises and Wycliffe's sermons into Czech and began to criticize Catholic superstitious practices, indulgences, and idol worship. Like Wycliffe, Hus was at first protected by the crown, the university, and nobles from the Pope, who tried to close all churches, leaving even marriages and funeral services unavailable.

In 1405, Pope Innocent VII ordered Hus not to propagate the teachings of Wycliffe and issued a condemnation of forty-five of Wycliffe's articles. Hus refused to obey and thus lost his clerical position. Then, the archbishop condemned the activities of the Lollards in Bohemia, accusing them of instigating ecclesiastical disturbances. Pope Alexander V in 1409 issued a papal bull outlawing Wycliffe's teachings. By the time of the general church council of 1414, Hus was accused of heresy and jailed without a proper trial. Even in the harsh conditions of his captivity, he wrote apologetic tracts and letters.

---

110. Latourette, *A History of Christianity*, 449–50.
111. Allen, *History of Revivals of Religion*, 9.
112. Knox, *Enthusiasm*, 84.

Finally, after a sham trial, Hus was burned at the stake in 1415. His death galvanized a group of militarized opponents to the Holy Roman Empire. Hammond states, "Remarkably these vastly outnumbered Hussites repelled six crusades against them. These Hussites fought under Hus's motto: "truth conquers." They proved that one could take on the Holy Roman Empire—and survive!"[113] Hus anticipated that there would be someone bold who can reform the corrupted Catholic Church. His words foreshadowed the Reformation a hundred years later; when Martin Luther read the writing of Hus, he declared loudly, ""Ja, Ich bin ein Hussite" or "I am a Hussite!""[114]

Girolamo Savonarola of Florence was another forerunner of Martin Luther, preaching against the corruption and ungodly life of Christians at that time. According to Villari, "Wonderful was the effect of Savonarola's preaching on the corrupt and pagan society of Florence. His natural, spontaneous heart stirring eloquence, with its exalted imagery and outbursts of righteous indignation, was entirely unprecedented in that era of pedantry and the simulation of the classic oratory."[115] William Allen says further,

> The Prior's preaching confounded his foes, for it completely changed the aspect of the city. The women cast off their jewels and dressed simply; young profligates were transformed into sober, religious men, the churches were filled with people at prayer, and the Bible was diligently read. The fame of this marvellous preacher was now extending throughout the world by means of his printed sermons. Even the Sultan of Turkey commanded them to be translated into Turkish for his own study. Of course, the individual aim of Savonarola was simply to be the regenerator of religion. [116]

Savonarola indicted the corrupt church in one sermon after another. "With fiery oratory, Savonarola likened the Roman hierarchy to the 'wood, hay and stubble' that the Apostle Paul had warned the first century Church about: 'This is the new church, no longer built of living stones; but of sticks, namely, of Christians dry as tinder for the

---

113. Hammond, "The Reformation," lines 65–66.
114. Hill, "Martin Luther," lines 52–53.
115. Villari, *Life and Times of Girolamo Savonarola*, 11–12.
116. Allen, *History of Revivals of Religion*, 11.

fires of hell."[117] Pope Alexander VI labeled him a heretic and had him burned at the stake in 1498.

EVANGELICAL REVIVALS IN THE POST-REFORMATION

After a long period of spiritual decline in the state churches, awakenings and revivals began to emerge in response to spiritual hunger. Reform movements such as that of the Quakers led to evangelicalism, a new movement marked by a focus on Scripture, a personal relationship with Christ, and activism to combat social evils. Many new denominations were founded and the modern overseas missions movement took shape.

In Europe, the same Reformation passion that led to questions about dogma and ecclesiastical institutions—and paved the way for schisms in Britain, Germany, Netherlands, France, and other nations— also brought revival. Evangelical and Pietist movements emphasized spiritual experience, conversion, and individual commitment. Dissent groups such as Puritans, Anabaptists, and Baptists also refused to recognize the organized religious establishment, stating that it was only a counterpart to the secular government.[118] Though the established church was recognized by the crown, the dissent churches usually did not recognize the established church's authority over the secular. Christian revival groups including the Waldensians, and Anabaptists before the Reformation, followed by the Quakers, Pietists, and Puritans afterward, left their mark on many parts of Europe.[119]

REFORMATION AND REVIVALS

Martin Luther startled Europe through his torching fire for Reformation in 1517. The Reformation was indeed revival itself. In fact, Humphrey says the Reformation was "no less than a wide-spread and glorious revival" on a gigantic level.[120] What's more, he states, the

117. Villari, *Life and Times of Girolamo Savonarola*, 183.

118. Labaree, "The Conservative Attitude," 332.

119. For example, the influences of the Waldensian movement are found in France, Germany, East Europe, and Alpine regions, evoking the spirit of the early church. Blackwell, "The Plain Truth about the Waldensians," 3–6.

120. Humphrey points out that Reformation "was the reappearance of the divine economy in carrying forward the work of redemption." Humphrey, "Revival Sketches," 27.

Reformation "was an outpouring of the Spirit, under which the mountains flowed down at His presence; it was a conveying power that was acknowledged by tribes and nations."[121] After a long period of decline for the state churches, spiritual awakenings and revivals began to spring up amid a context of spiritual hunger. Early reform movements began with the Presbyterians, Puritans, Quakers, Pietists, Methodists, and Baptists and developed until their influence was felt throughout Europe. Revival led to evangelicalism: a new Christian movement marked by a focus on Scripture, fostering a personal relationship with Christ, and activism to combat social evils. Many new denominations were founded during this time, and the modern overseas missions movement took shape.

In Europe during the Reformation, the same religious passion that led to questions about dogmatized Christian doctrines and ecclesiastical institutions—and paved the way for schisms in Britain, Germany, Netherlands, France, and other nations—also brought revival. Evangelical revivals and Pietist movements emphasized spiritual experience, conversion, and individual commitment. Not only the Pietists, but also dissent groups such as Puritans, Anabaptists, and Baptists refused to recognize the organized religious establishment, stating that it was only a counterpart to the secular government.[122]

Evangelical Revivals

Seeing the Reformation in terms of historical and genealogical roots even before its inception, the spiritual empowerment of the reformation was closely connected with both the pre-Reformation and Post-Reformation movements. In other words, the Albigenisan and Waldensian revivals had connected with the Huguenots, Moravians, Baptists and Presbyterians. The Lollards had connected to the Reformation directly through the Moravians. The Reformation would not have happened unless pre-Reformation spiritual revivals had taken place. Heretics who were condemned by Catholics, namely the Waldensians, Huguenots, Hussites, Anabaptists, and Lollards, were the forefront advocates of true revivals for the Reformation. Walther states, "It [the Reformation] was not a new religion that came there in the 16th century; "their aim was merely to maintain the old one

121. Ibid., 28.
122. Labaree, "The Conservative Attitude," 332.

which was theirs for a long time.""[123] Dr. Lloyd-Jones also pinpoints, all revivals in history have one thing in common, "The Spirit of God came upon him and it lead to a revival in his area. It was the same thing exactly."[124] Lloyd Jones points out those revivals played a great role in reformed theology.[125]

Thomas J. Nettles asserts that "the most poignant displays of reformation come at times of great theological, moral, spiritual, and ecclesiological declension in the church."[126] We should not neglect how greatly the key revival movements in the Middle Ages paved the way for true Reformation as a revival movement.[127] The spiritual reformation was already transforming numerous lives during this time.[128] Nettles suggests three points of revivals, reformation doctrine, experiential application and extension of revival experience in the Reformation movement involved.[129] In this sense, the Reformation must be considered the greatest spiritual awakening in history in reshaping the entire Western world. John Calvin, an heir of the Huguenots, believed that "tears and prayers are our weapons."[130] There were already a considerable number of mighty prayer warriors even in the time of John Calvin. When Calvin passed away, there were 1,200 Calvinist congregations with two million Calvinist Christians occupying 10 percent of the French population.[131]

123. Walther, *Albigenses and Waldenses*, 182.

124. Lloyd-Jones, *Revival*, 98.

125. Haykin states, "Now, what is so striking about Lloyd-Jones's survey of revival from the history of the church is how large a place revivals have occupied in the Reformed tradition. In fact, Lloyd-Jones asserts that one of the main reasons why revivals have not been prominent in this century is due to the fact that the final half of the nineteenth century witnessed a widespread turning away from Reformed theology which continued unabated until the late 1940s." Haykin, "Calvinism and Revival," 2.

126. Nettles, "A Better Way," 24.

127. Ibid., 25.

128. Ibid., 26.

129. Ibid., 29–30. Nettles suggests three points as "the presence of reformation doctrine, either preached, read, or otherwise known; the experiential application of that doctrine accompanied by loving but careful investigation of that experience; and the extension of such an experience to a large number of people."

130. Calhoun, "Reformation & Modern Church History," 2.

131. Haykin, "*Calvinism and Revival*," 3.

Post Reformation, spiritual transformations occurred through several revival movements such as Puritanism and Presbyterianism in Scotland, Ireland, and England and eventually the United States.[132] William Couper depicts the Scottish revival, "The Reformation was Scotland's first great religious awakening—an awakening all the more thorough because of the people's deep sleep throughout the preceding centuries."[133] Scottish revivals were led by John Knox in mid-1500s leading the Scottish yearning for revivals where "the breath of the Spirit of God passed, awakening a nation to newness of life. . . . he [Knox] found everywhere the fuel gathered, needing only a spark to set it ablaze."[134] In 1596, the General Assembly of the Church of Scotland in Edinburgh stated that the signs of a revival manifested how deeply ministers conceded "their repentant hearts and spiritual passion back to their synods and parishes."[135]

Revivals followed with the leadership of John Welch, son-in-law of John Knox who sought revival in fasting and prayer, and Robert Bruce, a successor to John Knox at the Kirk in Edinburgh in the 1590s.[136] Keith E. Beebe asserts that the revival fire burst into flame among the Scottish Presbyterian Church when John Davison preached: "As the Holy Spirit pierces their hearts with razor-sharp conviction, John Davidson concludes his message, steps down from the pulpit, and quietly returns to his seat. With downcast eyes and heaviness of heart, the assembled leaders silently reflect upon their lives and ministry." We can only imagine how deeply the Spirit of the Lord touched the people at that time. Beebe gives a glimpse of their experience, "As the minutes pass, a growing sense of God's presence and holiness intensifies, and a spirit of deep repentance breaks in upon them, disrupting their silence. Suddenly loud sighs and groans

132. Humphrey, "Revival Sketches," 28.

133. Couper, *Scotland Saw His Glory*, 11–12.

134. Beebe, "Presbyterian and Revival," 2.

135. Ibid., 3.

136. Beebe sates, "Not only was the Presbyterian tradition birthed in a revival, it was nurtured in revival as well. God's work of awakening persons to their need of the Savior became a continual point of focus for the newly established Scottish Presbyterians, and an integral part of their identity, piety, and practice. Two pastoral leaders in particular, John Welch and Robert Bruce, were instrumental in fanning the flame of evangelical piety within the fledgling Scottish Presbyterian movement." Ibid., 2.

reverberate throughout the Cathedral . . . in tearful sobbing, melting under profound conviction of their sin."[137]

Beebe emphasizes the vital role Presbyterian Churches played in forming the Presbyterian revivals in the English-speaking world. Beebe states, Presbyterian Church in general, "was virtually birthed and nurtured in a period of intense spiritual awakening." This revival spread from Scotland to Ireland and British America.[138] With David Dickson, what Thomas M'Crie calls as "the principle of the revival,"[139] "the power of godliness did advance from one place to another" in Scotland from Stewarton in 1625 lasting until 1630.[140] Several revivals eventually grew larger as John Livingston ignited a revival flame in which the Holy Spirit manifested itself in the Kirk of Shotts in 1630.[141] It was the first of June 1630, when the service was about to come to an end, "the audience, and even the preacher himself, were affected with a deep, unusual awe, melting their hearts and subduing their minds, stripping off inveterate prejudices, awakening the impenitent, producing conviction in the hardened, bowing down the stubborn, and imparting to many an enlightened Christian a large increase of grace and spirituality."[142] In fact, an outstanding revival fire broke out through Spirit filled ministers from Scotland like "Brice Glendenning, Ridge, Blair," and more in the province of Ulster, Ireland unlike any spiritual awakening before 1625.[143] Religious turmoil in the British political transitions affected the Church in Scotland when Charles II tried to revert the British churches after the death of Oliver Cromwell in 1660. When Charles II regained his power, he abandoned the support for the Presbyterian and Covenantal Churches in Scotland resulting in the death of thousands while at the same time 400 churches converted to the Episcopal system.[144] A continuous revival was carried on by covenanters and Presbyterians in the midst of serious persecutions, es-

---

137. Beebe, "Touched By The Fire," 1, 1–8.

138. Ibid., 1–2.

139. David Dickson was former professor of Moral Philosophy of the University of Glasgow. His ministry at Stewarton played a pivotal role for significant revival between 1625 and 1630. M'Crie, *The Revival at Stewarton*, 415.

140. Humphrey, *Revival Sketches*, 30.

141. Ibid., 31.

142. Humphrey, 31–32.

143. Ibid., 33.

144. Love, *Scottish Covenanter Stories*, xiii–xiv.

pecially during the "Killing Time" between 1684 to 1685.[145] However, during the twenty eight years of persecution in the late sixteenth and seventeenth centuries in Scotland, John Howie (1735–1793) reports, "18,000 people . . . suffered death, 1700 were shipped to the plantations" and thousands killed and vanished in different locations.[146]

The Quaker revival which occurred after the English Reformation was initiated by George Fox. He encountered the Holy Spirit and began to challenge his followers to seek the same experience stating, "I was to bring people off from all their own ways, to Christ, the new and living Way, and to know the Spirit of Truth in the inward parts, and to be led thereby."[147] This revival accentuated the experience of an "inner light" from the Holy Spirit—claimed to be superior to the didactic interpretations of Scripture by the Catholic Church—and also emphasized encountering the holy presence of the Lord. One early writer described manifestations of the Spirit as trembling and shaking, occasionally accompanied by jerking, spasms, crying, fainting, seeing visions, prophesying, and speaking in tongues.[148] For the first forty years of the Quaker movement, the Quakers numbered fifty to sixty thousand in England alone.[149]

In early seventeenth century England, Puritan preachers emphasized that their nation was moving away from the past foundation of Christian faith and practice, and that this marked the beginning of an apocalyptic period. They predicted that God would judge the nation for its vices and corruption, the evil and malice of its kings, the extravagance of the aristocrats, and the heretical doctrines and opinions of bishops. The Puritans objected to the sin entrenched in their social institutions. After Britain's defeat of the Spanish, Britain entered a golden age and rise as a world power. This paved the road for social sins to permeate into the British colonies in America because the crown wanted to manipulate the British American colonies as a way of obtaining wealth and power for themselves. According to McLoughlin, "Puritanism provided a congenial 'new light' on what this meant for

145. Ibid., xv-xvi.

146. Howie, *The Scots Worthies*, 626.

147. Allen, *Revivals of Religion*, 22.

148. The official name of the Quaker denomination is the Society of Friends. The nickname *Quaker* was first given by Justice Bennet in 1650 when George Fox told him to tremble before the Word of the Lord. Cross, *Oxford Dictionary*, 529, 1130.

149. Allen, *Revivals of Religion*, 23.

England's God-ordained future greatness."[150] Puritanism gained an audience among the gentry and middle class after 1610.[151] On the other hand, some Puritans left England and sought greater religious freedom in the New England colonies, referring to themselves as the Puritanical in British America.[152]

In 1662, led by Laud and Jefferies, persecutions against the Puritans were executed by the Crown and Church of England called the Act of Uniformity. Within it was found the Five Mile Act. It affected two thousand pastors in which they were banned from preaching beyond five miles from their churches. Humphrey reports that "instead of crushing and silencing the witnesses, the pent-up fire broke out even in their sufferings and imprisonments into a flame that was to enlighten and bless all coming generations."[153] He further indicates, "Among the noble band of confessors we find the names of Bunyan, Baxter, Owen, Bishop Hopkins, Flavel, Alleine, Howe, and others, who have not been surpassed in any age for talents, for theological learning, for deep Christian experience, and for the valiant defense of "the faith once delivered to the saints.""[154]

A few years later, a constitutional crisis led to civil war and the revolution of 1688, which restricted royal power and held the monarchy responsible to Parliament. As a result of the religious and political disputes of the previous century, the Hanoverians (the royal family) objected to the social and political growth of a dissident religious movement in the early eighteenth century.[155] In 1689, religious toleration was implemented. Between 1640 and 1750, a remarkable revival broke out among the Calvinist Baptist churches in Britain. In 1640 only 7 Baptist churches existed but the number swelled to 100 in 1689 and 220 in 1715.[156] A century later, the French Revolution dissolved the absolute power of the monarchy and aristocracy, and colonial rev-

150. McLoughlin, *Revivals, Awakenings, and Reform*, 26.

151. Ibid., 28.

152. Ibid., 33.

153. Humphrey, *Revival Sketches*, 40.

154. Ibid., 40–41.

155. Elliott-Binns, *The Early Evangelicals*, 85.

156. Haykin, "Calvinism and Revival," 9–10.

olutions took place in the North American colonies of both England and Spain.[157]

In the seventeenth century, a great deal of medieval religious tradition remained in society and in the royal courts. Butterfield states that "persecution, scholasticism, the idea of the crusade or the Holy League, the predominance of Aristotle and the veneration for antiquity had still been important in the life of western Europe."[158] King James's reign paved the way for the Reformation with its focus on public decency, ethics, and order.[159] In the eighteenth century, religious enthusiasm and Puritan piety sprung up in an environment of renewal. The evangelical revival was able to thrive in new forms and styles under the Tudors and Stuarts, but Puritanism increased its influence in line with the denominations using the Book of Common Prayer.[160] For this reason, the Puritans' social and religious stance was very close to Anglicanism; only about 10 percent was revolutionary.[161] A shared sense of frustration and spiritual hunger led to revivals with results beyond all expectations. Studies on revivals and awakenings point out that they were preceded by a time of vanishing spiritual vitality and lukewarm church experiences.

Revivals in Continental Europe

Then, God began a vibrant and dynamic work in Europe. Pietism restored Christian vitality and experiential piety following the Reformation.[162] During the second half of the seventeenth century, Pietism led to renewal among the Lutheran and Reformed churches in Germany, Holland, Switzerland, and parts of Central Europe. At the start of the eighteenth century, before the Methodist revival, the people of Britain and British America were exposed to German Pietism

157. Pirouet, "Modern Missions," 1.

158. Butterfield, "England in the Eighteenth Century," 4–5.

159. Strong, *The Story of Britain*, 224.

160. Crawford, "Evangelical Revival," 374.

161. McLoughlin, *Revivals, Awakenings, and Reform*, 34.

162. In England, the success of the Methodist revival movement was based on more than simply offering religious services to the working poor who had been neglected by the established church. Methodists attracted hearers because they provided what the Church of England did not: "a vital, experiential religion, for the assurance of sins personally forgiven, and of salvation presently granted." Crawford, "Evangelical Revival," 372–73.

through Philipp Jakob Spener, the chaplain of Queen Anne's consort, the Lutheran Prince George of Denmark.[163] Considered the father of the Pietist movement, Spener was a Lutheran minister who encountered much resistance from his church, especially by those who ascribed to Lutheran orthodoxy. On a visit to Switzerland, Spencer was greatly influenced by French pietist Jean de Labadie; he experienced a powerful religious transformation. Consequently, he felt challenged to revive his peers within the Lutheran Church and, in 1675, he published a manifesto entitled *Pia Desideria* (*The Piety We Desire*) while in Frankfurt.[164] Eventually, a group of devotees and cohorts grew in Württemberg. Between 1680 and 1720, Pietists in Württemberg led a reform movement within the Lutheran Church, sharing their possessions and setting in motion the German Pietist movement.[165]

Another influential Pietist was August Hermann Francke, professor of theology at the University of Halle and leader of the Pietist movement in Germany. His writings strongly influenced a number of English Christian leaders, "including Griffith Jones, founder of the Welsh catechistic schools; Sir John Phillips, Jones's sponsor and philanthropic backer of the Oxford Methodists; Howell Harris, a founder of Welsh Calvinist Methodism; and dissenters Isaac Watts and Philip Doddridge." Even in New England, "Cotton Mather corresponded with Francke over many years about a scheme to use a basic, orthodox piety to unite the faithful remnant of true believers in preparation for Christ's Second Coming. Jonathan Edwards was well aware of Francke's work as well."[166] Francke advocated inward spiritual renewal, vigorous lay involvement in the church, and the practical application of the Bible by believers while holding a negative opinion of institutionalized ecclesiastical authorities.[167] In 1691, he moved to Berlin and became rector of the Nikolaikirche. Among his new supporters was elector of Brandenburg, who would become King Frederick I of Prussia in 1701.[168] Under his leadership, the University of Halle was established

163. Ibid., 383.

164. Cross, *Oxford Dictionary*, 1279–80.

165. Lehmann, "'Community' and 'Work,'" 81.

166. Crawford, "Evangelical Revival," 383–84.

167. Noll, *The Rise of Evangelicalism*, 17–18.

168. Francke and a number of followers were known as the Guilds of Piety, from which came the term Pietism. Walsh, *Dictionary of Christian Biography*, 1075.

in 1694 and continued to expand.[169] German Pietism provided fodder for the upcoming revival movement in Britain through their strong convictions and spiritual disciplines. Davies notes their "intensely personal devotion to God in Christ, the striving towards holy love, the groups which practice fellowship in the Spirit rather than in formal acts of worship, without neglecting the 'means of grace,' the desire to make known the love of Christ to those who have passed it by, and, most plainly, the hymns."[170] This pietism facilitated the emergence of evangelicalism in Britain and America, setting a pattern of vitality to revive the Reformation.

The Pietist movement was spread further by Nicolaus von Zinzendorf, a graduate of the University of Halle. In 1727, after an outpouring of the Holy Spirit, von Zinzendorf founded a community at Herrnhut, Germany, commonly called the Moravian movement, or Moravian Brethren. He held religious gatherings at his home for Protestant emigrants of the Bohemian Brethren, bringing together the spiritual legacy of the suppressed Hussite Unity of the Brethren (Unitas Fratrum) and Christians of central European countries. Everyday a group of men and women gathered at the prayer tower for 24/7 prayer, an incessant prayer meeting that lasted for a hundred years thereafter.[171] Due to the more visible influence of the Wesleyans, the contributions of the Moravians to revival have not always been fully recognized. Zinzendorf established a movement emphasizing lay leadership starting at Herrnhut, where followers surrendered denominational allegiances and gave up much of their property to participate in communal life. Pietism is noteworthy because it cut across denominational and confessional lines, enhancing revival and awakening movements in many Protestant denominations.

Some of the oppressed Protestants in central Europe, due to tensions and religious conflicts with Catholicism, found themselves spiritually hungry and urgently longing for revival.[172] British and British Americans were also hopeful for spiritual awakenings after being tested by religious strife and crisis. Many eagerly desired the outpouring of the Spirit and the conversion experiences that John

169. Cross, *Oxford Dictionary*, 1279–80.
170. Davies, *Methodism*, 21.
171. Walsh, *Dictionary of Christian Biography*, 1163–64.
172. Crawford, " Evangelical Revival," 391.

and Charles Wesley, George Whitefield, and Jonathan Edwards had experienced.[173]

The first Moravians came to England in 1728, but did not attract a large number of followers due to the austerity of their lifestyles. William Whiston attempted to initiate this new type of communal Christian faith, working at first within the Church of England and enjoying some success. Elliott-Binns notes that they "strove to work closely with it [the Church of England], and even elected the saintly Bishop Wilson of Sodor and Man to their synod"; correspondence dating from 1737 partially verifies their efforts.[174]

The German Pietists were a major influence on John Wesley at the time of his conversion. The Moravians he had met after a trans-atlantic trip to Georgia between 1735 and 1737 made a profound impression. He subsequently embarked on other spiritual pilgrimages in central Europe, including trips to Moravian communities at Herrnhut, Saxony in 1738. He also reached out to Moravian missionary Peter Böhler, leader of Fetter Lane Society in London for spiritual guidance. German Pietism paved the way for spiritual revival for Wesley on the other side of the Atlantic, greatly expanding Methodism and amplifying the effects of the awakenings throughout the region in the 1720s.[175] Revivalists in Britain and New England were filled with millennial hope, taking their lead from the Pietist movements of Central Europe.[176]

John Calvin inherited the religious enthusiasm of Southern France. Centering on Toulouse in southern France, 20,000 Protestants resided there in 1562. Daniel Walther's painstaking research cites Jean Carbonnier's *Le manifeste des Camisards* (1703) stating people lived in Cévennes practicing "the same religion for several centuries before the Reformation."[177] During this time there were 2 million Huguenots, roughly one in three among the French population. Between 1567 and 1573, 22,000 Protestants were murdered of the 100,000 residents in the Low Countries in France. Severe persecutions dispersed them to countries like "Belgium, Austria, Spain, Italy" and also the Americas

173. Ibid., 391–92.

174. Elliott-Binns, *The Early Evangelicals*, 118–19.

175. Crawford, "Evangelical Revival," 383.

176. Ibid., 391.

177. Walther, *Albigenses and Waldenses*, 182.

and other Catholic countries.[178] During 1680 and 1690, around 20,000 to 50,000 Huguenots entered Great Britain alone.[179] Also during that time, 160,000 French Huguenots including children escaped from the ferocious persecution of Louis XIV who invalidated the Edict of Nantes, a decree to allow free worship of Protestants by Henry IV in 1598.[180] In the midst of the persecutions and hardships faced by the Christians, John Taylor reports that in the late seventeenth century in the Cévennes region, the Holy Spirit descended among prayer revival meetings of Huguenot peasants in which they experienced "violent weeping and convulsions."[181]

Eighteenth Century Revivals

In the late eighteenth century, churches in Britain were at low ebb. Dr. Macfarlan describes, "The old styles of preaching was being fast laid aside, and cold formal addresses, verging towards a kind of Socinianism, were becoming fashionable."[182] However, England had its own unobtrusive Anglican style of Pietistic religious societies emphasizing a high-class, devout, and respectable religious setting. Later, Pietism reached the Reformed Churches as well.[183] Great Britain's Christianity was mainly comprised of the Church of England, but also included the Church of Scotland as well as dissenting communities, mostly Methodists, Congregationalists, and Baptists. Concurrently, the Great Awakening, which involved the Wesleys and George Whitefield, was breaking out in the thirteen colonies, chiefly through churches of the Reformed tradition.

In 1718, a short-lived revival occurred in Lakenheath in Suffolk, England. It was followed by a more impactful revival in Wales, which Elliott-Binns calls the "breeding-ground of revivals."[184] In the early seventeenth century, just before Griffith Jones, Howell Harris, Daniel Rowland and William Williams torched the revival fire in Wales, the British Isles experienced revival movements through George

---

178. Hammond, *The Reformation*

179. Butler, *The Huguenots in America*, 3.

180. Ibid., 1.

181. Taylor, *The Go-Between God*, 219.

182. Humphrey, *Revival Sketches*, 46.

183. Latourette, *A History of Christianity*, 1018–19.

184. Elliott-Binns, *The Early Evangelicals*, 118.

Whitefield and John Wesley.[185] The Great Awakening, through the work of Jonathan Edwards, began in 1733 in America and extended its influence to the Wales and Scotland in 1740.[186] The Independent Church was instituted in this area between 1715 and 1772, though some of them disappeared. Although it had a relatively small number of members, this dissenting church retained doctrine open to the influence of evangelical revival movements. It later became fertile soil to revive the old Puritan emphases in a new setting.[187]

In pre-industrial England, established churches were friendly and accepting to lower-class members, within a vertical structure that placed Protestant dissenters in the middle, flanked by Anglicans.[188] Imagine a triangle structure with the low class at the bottom (such as Anglican peasants and farmers) and at the top the crown and the top ranking established church leaders. In the middle of this triangle would sit the dissenters that included Puritans, Baptists, Quakers, and Presbyterians. Surprisingly, the number of Church of England dissidents decreased even as revival grew. Many project the disappearance of the dissent as having occurred within a generation, according to Elliott-Binns. In 1742 William Grimshaw discovered four deserted places once used for religious gatherings, including "Presbyterian chapels and a Quaker meeting-house which was only used once in the year,"[189] in Haworth. The hunger for revival from different Christian groups, including those within the Churches of England and Scotland as well as other less-organized groups, resulted in the foundation of new dissent groups.[190] Also in 1742, Rev. W. McCulloch and George Whitefield led a great revival

185. Allen, *Revivals of Religion*, 24.

186. The beginnings of the eighteenth-century revival can be traced back to Griffith Jones in 1709, and itinerant preacher Howell Harris was a forerunner of the Methodist revivalists. The revival in Scotland in 1740 was remarkable, according to Elliott-Binns, because "among those who were there converted was probably William Darney, who later founded many societies in East Lancashire and the West Riding of Yorkshire and exercised great influence over William Grimshaw." Elliott-Binns, *The Early Evangelicals*, 118.

187. Turner, *Conflict and Reconciliation*, 6.

188. Ibid., 5.

189. Elliott-Binn, *The Early Evangelicals*, 118.

190. John Wesley lamented the fragmentation of the Christian community during this period when "one of his preachers became an Independent minister in 1753: 'Did God design that this light should be hidden under a bushel in a little obscure dissenting meeting-house?'" Ibid., 109.

movement in Cambuslang. Whitefield delivered the message to twenty thousand people in an open-air service. Whitefield's diary stated, "you might have seen thousands bathed in tears, some at the same time wringing their hands, others almost swooning, and others crying out and mourning over a pierced Savior."[191]

Intense religious/political clashes between Protestants and Catholics at the beginning of the eighteenth century had "left in England a recurring politico-ecclesiastical 'No-Popery' complex."[192] A decaying dissident church already existed at this time and religious pluralism was gaining strength such that the Church of England could no longer retain a monopoly as the nation's religious establishment. Beginning in 1772, dissident groups drew followers through itinerant preaching and other evangelistic efforts. As a result of popular evangelicalism, dissent groups intensely attracted the artisan groups, a group similar to the Methodists who began as a lower class group but moved up to the middle class, but existing on a larger scale.[193] Dissent groups were nonconformist by nature and attracted only 6 percent of the population.[194] While Methodist preachers were welcomed in dissenting congregations, the Church of England locked their doors to them. Methodists preached in open areas such as the marketplace, prison cell, poor villages, and public plaza. The established churches realized that the phenomenal growth of Methodist meetings were inevitable so the authority distanced themselves from their meetings and remained neutral. As Crawford puts it, "Anti-Methodist rioting is a measure of the impotence of legal remedies to silence conforming clergymen."[195]

The impact of the 1750 revival was more significant among Protestants than Roman Catholics or Eastern Orthodox Christians. The Methodist movement benefited from social changes and revival

191. Finney, *Revival Lectures*, 25.

192. Butterfield, "England in the Eighteenth Century," 5.

193. Turner, *Conflict and Reconciliation*, 8.

194. Crawford states that "Dissenting revivalists would have had a relatively small audience and, restricted to licensed places of worship, could not have taken their message into the highways and fields. In contrast, ordained Anglican clergy had a large potential audience, both active and nominal Anglicans, willing to hear them, and there were few legal steps opponents could take to prevent conforming clergymen from preaching." Crawford, "Evangelical Revival," 392.

195. Ibid., 392.

movements, growing to become England's second largest dissenting group next to Puritans.[196] John Wesley believed the mighty power of the Holy Spirit including healing and miracles could be manifested in his time. Guy Duffiled and Nathaniel Cleave quote Wesley's diary, "one of the chaise-horses was on a sudden so lame . . . . I knew no remedy but prayer. Immediately the lameness was gone, and he went just he did before."[197] Methodist movements were followed by spiritual transformations and manifestations seeing its height between 1750 and 1815. The key of the Methodist revival is derived from the ministry of soul winning, or in modern terms 'evangelism focused.'[198] With a strong emphasis on evangelism, Methodism also began to expand to different forms up to the nineteenth and twentieth centuries.[199]

The Methodists expanded tremendously into the Holiness denominations branching out not only in Britain but also in America. Privileges long enjoyed by Anglican clergy, their unparalleled representation in many social arenas, overarching from the "squire to parson alliance,"[200] and its authority dating from the Medieval Church and extending even after the Reformation, were now under attack. David Hempton points out that the weakened Church of England "was in no position to resist a dramatic upsurge in undenominational itinerant preaching and cottage-based religion which even the various Methodist connections struggled hard to keep under control."[201] According to Crawford, a sizeable number of High Church Anglicans also adopted Wesleyan itinerant preaching and revival meetings, from the "discipleship of William Law's High Church precisianism to membership within the Methodist fold" in mid-eighteenth century.[202]

---

196. Turner, *Conflict and Reconciliation*, 8.

197. This happened on September 2, 1781 according to Wesley's diary. Duffield and Cleave, *Foundations of Pentecostal Theology*, 390.

198. Oswald Smith emphasizes the work of evangelism quoting John Wesley, "You have nothing to do but to save souls. . . . but save as many souls as you can; to bring as many sinners as you possibly can to repentance, and with all your power to build them up in that holiness, without which they cannot see the Lord." Smith, *The Revival We Need*, 25.

199. Latourette, *A History of Christianity*, 1022.

200. The squire to parson alliance means the time from the Medieval Church to the Post Reformation.

201. Hempton, *The Religion of the People*, 7.

202. Crawford, "Evangelical Revival," 372.

Nineteenth Century Revivals

History shows that, when church falls into lethargy, revivals tend to break out in unexpected ways. This was the case during the early eighteenth century. Immorality was rampant in society and faith seemed a ridiculous proposition in the eyes of many Europeans. In Norway's history no person could compare with Hans Nielsen Hauge, (1771–1824) who led the national awakening in terms of social, economic, spiritual, educational and church transformation and revivals between 1796 and 1804 among the common people. His influence can still be felt in that nation today.[203] His ministry was similar to the works of John Wesley and George Whitefield in Norway.[204] On 5 April 1796, Hauge encountered the Holy Spirit in a way that not only changed his life but also the history of Norway. Alison Stibbe states, "I began to consider that examining Hauge as a 'Spirit inspired' prophet and his message as 'Spirit inspired' prophecy might be an original avenue of enquiry worth pursuing."[205] At about the same time as Hauge, Paavo Ruotsalainen, Carl Olof Rosenius, and Wilhelm Beck critically influenced Finland, Sweden, and Denmark with great revival movements which brought an amazing national transformation.[206] Due to the Napoleonic War in Western Europe in the early nineteenth century, revivals did not break out until Robert Haldane ignited the revival flames in Geneva, causing a "chain reaction" throughout Europe. The European revivals had such a powerful impact that its effects were felt in Cape Town in 1809 through the leading of Dr. Helperus Ritzema.[207]

Then, from 1780 to 1830, Methodism grew tremendously. The growth rate was variable, slowing after this eighty-year phase because of domestic and overseas migration, political disputes, and ecclesiastical transformations like education and social lift and among the Methodist communities. Moreover, Irish Methodism did not grow as rapidly as English Methodism. According to Hempton, "The most convincing explanation for that pattern is not that Methodism offered a convincing religious vehicle for counter-revolutionary forces, but that it supplied the means by which England's confessional state was

203. Stibbe, *Hans Nielsen Hauge*, 18.

204. Orr, *Re-Study*, 12.

205. Ibid, 19.

206. Walker, *Standing Fast in Freedom History* , 4.

207. Orr, *Re-Study*, 12.

eroded from within, while at the same time it was being challenged from without by pressure from Roman Catholics in Ireland."[208] A powerful outpouring of the Holy Spirit caused a theological controversy, yet it led Edward Erving to experience speaking in tongue for the first time on April 30, 1831. His ministry influenced hundreds experience revival fire and *glossolalia* until the end of the nineteenth century.[209]

Nonetheless, in the period of the revival, the number of evangelicals grew considerably. Between one-eighth and one-quarter of clergymen were evangelical.[210] The Methodist revival spurred growth not only in the Methodist community, but also in the state church and other dissident groups as well. While the generation immediately following the revival backed away from its radical vitality, it retained an admiration for the strength of the autonomy of the revival. Leadership disputes put the Methodists to the test between the late 1840s and early 1850s, a time when they were experiencing extensive development. Even so, the growth in membership and attendance among Methodists surpassed all other nonconformist churches combined during the Industrial Revolution.[211] Passionate spiritual enthusiasm and frequent meetings were typical of the period. When Charles Finney's *Lectures on the Revivals of Religion* was circulated in Britain in 1839, religious leaders adopted his methods, skills, and messages to promote repentance and conversions. Finney's work fueled renewed evangelistic campaigns, which brought James Caughey, one of the most notable evangelist of the eighteenth century in the US, Canada, and Britain and contemporary to Charles Finney, from the United States and further strengthened Methodist churches in the 1840s.[212]

Across the Atlantic, as a result of the Laymen's Prayer Revival in 1857–1861 in the United States (particularly the revival in 1859), a revival movement began. Upon hearing of the American revival, 100,000

208. Hempton, *The Religion of the People*, 9.

209. Andrew L. Drummond reports that a Mrs. Cardale uttered "with great solemnity . . . snag in the Spirit." Drummond testified to several incidences of speaking in tongues in Erving's ministry. He goes on to say, "Friday I spent with Irving in the region of the supernatural. Understand that the 'gift of tongues' is here also." Drummond, *Edward Irving and His Circle*, 153, 168.

210. For instance, Tidball reports that three of their number became bishops: Henry Ryder in 1815, Charles Sumner in 1826, and John Sumner in 1828. Tidball, *Who Are the Evangelicals?* 38.

211. Hempton, *The Religion of the People*, 9.

212. James Caughey, *Honest Christianity*, 5–6.

converts were made all over Great Britain and Ireland. This revival also had a great impact in Wales, Northern Ireland, and Scotland where a visit from Charles Finney created spiritual momentum. The revival was characterized by prayer, physical responses to the Holy Spirit, conviction of sin, and a multitude of conversions. In 1859, a significant outpouring of the Holy Spirit transformed lives in Ireland leading to massive conversions, life changing experiences, Bible reading, fast growth of churches, and active involvements in mission.[213] John Weir reported that revival looked like "the coming spiritual flood; . . . like angels' visits . . . the torrent-flood of God's mercy".[214] In England, it had less of an impact, but elsewhere, it encouraged believers to redouble their efforts at evangelism.[215]

A revitalized Christian community convened at the first Keswick Convention in 1875, including both Anglican and independent churches. Many evangelicals at this time focused on developing inner holiness rather than on outward spiritual manifestations. The focus of the convention was "the promotion of Practical Holiness," providing a new form of social entertainment. By this it means that these spiritual revival services were used as an avenue of entertainment and relaxation spiritually.[216] The enthusiasm of the revival was felt during the convention through speakers, including Charles Finney and his colleague Asa Mahan, and women were active participants.

Other contributions from Americans to the British revival movement included the publication of W. E. Boardman's *The Higher Christian Life* in 1858 and the constant visits of Phoebe Palmer and Robert and Hannah Pearsall Smith.[217] From 1873 to 1875, D.L. Moody's visits fed revivals in Scotland and England. He preached to an audience of more than 2.5 million people during just four months of evangelistic campaigning in London and other places in Britain. His preaching, along with the folk songs of his coworker Ira D. Sankey, left deep impressions on all at the University of Cambridge. Moody's visits were both impactful and quite memorable in the development of

213. John Weir, *The Ulster Awakening*, 29 .

214. Quoted from David Adams's *Revival at Ahoghill: Its Narrative and Nature* in John Weir, *Irish Revivals*, 25.

215. Towns and Porter, *The Ten Greatest Revivals Ever*, 124–26.

216. Cross, *Oxford Dictionary*, 764.

217. Tidball, *Who Are the Evangelicals?*, 46.

interdenominational evangelistic campaigns that continued well into the twentieth century.[218]

EUROPEAN EVANGELICALISM

Europe, once the stronghold of global Christianity, saw the faith decline and its effect diminish throughout Western society. Evangelicalism then revitalized Europe and North America with one of the most successful forms of religion anywhere during the eighteenth and early nineteenth centuries. Evangelicalism stressed the authority of Scripture, but also emphasized the importance of Christian experience and social action, despite the fact that these two elements created considerable tension for the church.[219]

Evangelical Orthodoxy

Bebbington has identified the so-called "biblical experientialism of evangelicals," which was biased against inherited institutions. This idea, that God must be experienced personally, permeated intellectual, political, social and economic life as well as principles of conduct for the self and others, a search for social healing, and individual holy living.[220] Bebbington names four essential elements of evangelicalism in the United Kingdom: conventionalism, activism, Biblicism, and crucicentricism.[221]

Davies identifies the dominant characteristics of Methodism in the eighteenth century: a positive acceptance of the cardinal doctrines of the Christian faith, the personal relationship with God by the heart, empirical implication of the doctrine of the Holy Spirit, a holy personal and social life in Christ, individual commitment to the gospel, a generous concern for the spiritual welfare of the poor and margin-

218. Ibid., 45.

219. Bebbington emphasizes that the Bible remained authoritative so that evangelicals could share a confidence in the Bible as they worked out their faith in active experience. Furthermore, experience with God could accommodate human reason, traditions, and hierarchies. Bebbington, "Evangelical Social Influence," 129–30.

220. Bebbington points out that evangelicals could consult the Bible to find out the ultimate realities about the experience of Christ so that these could be integrated into their lives. Ibid., 130.

221. Crucicentrism is the focus on the cross as the atoning work of Christ as the redemptive act of God. Calver, *Hope for the Future*, 199.

alized, and lay partnership ministry.[222] This is a marked contrast to ecclesiastical institutions which, during the process of secularization, showed little or no evidence of members having personal relationships with God through the Holy Spirit. Liturgies and dogma had already been established as custom in the minds of Europeans, even after the Reformation.

We can trace the beginnings of evangelicalism to the Reformation and the emergence of dissent groups, out of which separatist and Puritan churches were formed. In the seventeenth century, great change and progress was taking place in the political atmosphere of geographic areas around the English Channel, particularly in places where Protestantism was dominant: the Netherlands, England, and the Protestant part of France. Through colonial expansionism by the Western European powers, society was being altered through the discovery of the New World and through the establishment of the East India Company and the Bank of Amsterdam.[223] At the end of the century, religious enthusiasm fueled by the Reformation weakened in Europe, and church involvement sunk to lower levels than in past centuries.[224] A causal link between the religious decline and the events of the eighteenth century seems reasonable upon historical analysis.[225]

As Western European societies became more secularized starting in the eighteenth century, evangelicalism picked up the mantle dropped by the mainline churches and brought people, including the marginalized working class, into God's kingdom through the vitality of the Christian gospel of salvation. In other words, evangelicalism became a powerhouse of the Christian church in the Western world. Alister McGrath points out that evangelicalism moved from its humble beginnings to become mainstream denominations of the new Western Christianity:

> Evangelicalism, once regarded as marginal, has now become mainline, and it can no longer be dismissed as an insignificant sideshow, sectarian tendency or irrelevance. It has moved from the wings to center stage, displacing others once regarded as

222. Davies, *Methodism*, 11–12.

223. Butterfield, "England in the Eighteenth Century," 3.

224. Butterfield also accentuates the religious tendency of the century in with the churches were located not in the strongest place to encounter "the challenge of science at a turning-point in the history of civilization." Ibid., 5–6.

225. Tidball, *Who Are the Evangelicals?*, 32.

mainline, who consequently feel deeply threatened and alienated. Its commitment to evangelism has resulted in numerical
growth, where some other variants of Christianity are suffering from severe contraction.[226]

Protestant awakenings all shared typical Protestant beliefs: the
authority of the Scriptures, salvation by faith alone, and the priesthood of all believers. They made much of one's personal religious experience, of new birth through trust in Christ, of utmost commitment
to him, and of faith in what God had accomplished through the incarnation, the cross, and the resurrection. Awakenings were intensely
missions-oriented, emphasizing evangelism.[227] Martin Luther was the
first person to utilize the word *evangelical* to describe Christians who
emphasized justification by faith alone and the words of the Bible as
the only measure of God's authority, in contrast to Roman Catholic
traditions, hierarchy, and belief in infallibility of the pope.[228] The term
evangelical as we know it today was born during the revival movement
of the eighteenth century in Britain, which, in turn, stemmed from the
Pietist movement in continental Europe.[229]

Evangelicalism and Pietism

Evangelicalism was heavily influenced by Pietism from Central
Europe, which conveyed its religious and political energy to both the
British and American revivals. The writings of German Pietists had
an influence on evangelicals and revivalists in England and America
similar to that of the Moravians on English Methodist leaders. Michael
Crawford comments, "There was no similar, face-to-face influence on
New England's evangelicals, but they as well as the English certainly
knew of the major political and religious events of Central Europe.
Both English and American evangelicals interpreted those events in
the terms of the apocalyptic struggle."[230]

Pietism, then, paved the way for the expansion of the gospel in
two ways. First, it sowed the seeds of evangelicalism in the transatlantic colonies, and, second, Pietism ushered in a new antiseculariza-

226. McGrath, *Evangelicalism and the Future of Christianity*, 17.
227. Latourette, *A History of Christianity*, 1019.
228. Synan, "Evangelicalism," 613.
229. Noll, *The Rise of Evangelicalism*, 17.
230. Crawford, "Evangelical Revival," 391.

tion sentiment in Central Europe. The emotional aspects of Pietism, Crawford notes, fascinated "ministers frustrated by an inability to halt secularization in their societies, to combat anticlericalism successfully, or to effect any lasting improvement in prevailing moral standards."[231] During this century, secularization became the hallmark of society and penetrated even into ecclesiastical institutions. The zeal of the Reformation at times introduced other frustrations, especially failures of Christian unity. As much as theological and moral skepticism and cynicism were gaining ground in society, Pietism still gained its followers' confidence in the assurance of salvation, new birth by the Holy Spirit, and personal experience with Christ. This led them to follow high moral standards and to seek to live with religious fervor rather than adopting a secularized worldview. This movement, which undoubtedly drew inspiration from Catholic mysticism, highlighted the personal experience with the Holy Spirit and one's relationship with Him—which was not the religious norm at the time. O'Brien points out the importance of the merger between Puritanism and Pietism: "The real significance of the mid-eighteenth-century revivals was not their wondrous spontaneity or their primary role in the formation of national consciousness, but rather their combining of traditional Puritan practices with fresh evangelical techniques and attitudes."[232]

The Enlightenment exerted its influence on European social, cultural, intellectual, and religious domains, and the French Revolution acted as a catalyst in transforming Western European societies. Hempton states that "the Revolution altered forever the terms on which religious establishments, the chief device on which the nations of the West had relied for Christianizing the people, must work."[233] As the French Revolution drove the Western European religious institutions to abandon the prestige they had held since the Middle Ages, secularization and revival competed for the hearts of British citizens, compelling them to choose either the secularized and weakened religious institutions or an unfamiliar, young, evangelical Christianity. Hempton says, "One was of religion as the formulary of an established society, its statement of faith in itself; the other as a catastrophic conversion of the individual, a miraculous shaking off of secret burdens."[234]

231. Ibid., 384.

232. O'Brien, "A Transatlantic Community," 815.

233. Hempton, "Evangelicalism and Reform," 17.

234. Hempton, *Methodism and Politics*, 23.

Popular Evangelicalism

The shape of the Protestant church today is undeniably the result of the revivals and great awakenings in North America. Contemporary evangelicalism was born out of the revivals that incorporated elements from low-church Anglicanism, high-church Anglican piety, medieval Catholic asceticism, and Moravian Pietism from Halle and Herrnhut. All of these contributed to John Wesley's Methodist movement in Britain.[235] After the birth of Methodism, revival movements in 1815 set the stage for further expansion of the movement in the nineteenth century.[236] Hempton praises the historical contributions of evangelicalism in Britain:

> As every evangelical school boy/girl knows, Methodism saved England from revolution; the Clapham Sect, with William Wilberforce to the fore, secured the end of the slave trade and of colonial slavery; evangelical sobriety cleaned up a dissolute nation and contributed the work discipline and moral earnestness which lay at the heart of England's "greatness" in the Victorian period; and evangelism supplied the religious zeal which fought back the secularising dynamics of the eighteenth-century Enlightenment and secured the central place of religion in British society until at least the First World War.[237]

In *The Methodist Revolution*, Bernard Semmel states John Wesley and his followers practiced quintessential popular religious forms in adjusting themselves to Enlightenment liberalism though at the first stage they opposed the Enlightenment and Reason.[238] Semmel emphasized how deep Wesley was acquainted with the Enlightenment. "We must note the very considerable links between Wesleyan Arminianism and Enlightenment Liberalism. Wesley found himself most fully in the Enlightenment tradition in his concern for the principle of religious tolerance."[239] Wesley adopted the rationalism of the Enlightenment concerning religious toleration. He had no affinity for persecution or violence, and desired that everyone, perceived by Wesley as people alienated from God, must be saved. John Wesley attempted to be a me-

---

235. Neill, *A History of Christian Missions*, 213.

236. Latourette, *A History of Christianity*, 1018.

237. Hempton, *Methodism and Politics*, 17–18.

238. Semmel, *The Methodist Revolution*, 4.

239. Ibid., 88.

diator between traditional Calvinism and Arminian Protestantism.[240] Hempton believes that Wesley's "strenuous advocacy of the abolition of slavery, and his doctrines of perfection and assurance . . . could be seen as theological expressions of Enlightenment optimism and empiricism."[241]

The popular Methodist movement in which evangelicalism has its roots played a major role in bringing about social, political, and economic transformations that enabled English society to embrace a new pattern of religion. Methodism steadily increased its power and number over the Church of England at the end of the eighteenth century and, according to Hempton, "may be seen more as an expression of social radicalism than as a reinforcement of *ancien regime* control."[242] He says further:

> Popular evangelicalism did not create the free-born English-men, nor did it single-handedly create the English capacity for disciplined protest, but through Methodism and the connex-ional system it offered a vibrant religious vehicle for both to operate outside the confines of the Established Church with-out seriously destabilizing the British state in the era of the French Revolution.[243]

Nevertheless, the impact of the Wesleyan Methodist Church and other smaller Methodist Churches movements linking arms was sub-stantial during the eighteenth-century awakening in Britain. Christian awakening reached England, Scotland, Wales, and Ireland.[244] Further, Calvinist evangelicalism varied greatly from the Church of England, enabling Calvinist dissent groups to also experience conversion and this unconstrained stream of Puritanism that were once con-cealed from them. Puritan renewals paved the way for revival even before Wesley's "heart-warming" at Aldersgate in May 1738. George Whitefield, a Calvinist, brought revival through charismatic itinerant preaching to crowds in North America. Follow-up disciple build-ing, however, fell to the next generation of Whitefield's followers.[245]

240. Ibid., 8–9, 12–13.

241. Hempton, *Methodism and Politics*, 23.

242. Hempton, *The Religion of the People*, 8.

243. Ibid., 8–9.

244. Latourette, *A History of Christianity*, 1029.

245. Turner, *Conflict and Reconciliation*, 7.

Wesley, on the other hand, was both an enthusiast and a rationalist, using methodical application (hence the term *Methodism*). He integrated evangelistic zeal into his rational system. According to Turner, this system brought a counter-Enlightenment spirit and included a "concern for pastoral care, the endeavor to do good and to foster more personal religion, concern for education, missions, and Bible study."[246] Even the Moravians were able to attract high-church Anglicans and "to make more palatable doctrines which might otherwise have been dismissed brusquely as enthusiasm or worse."[247]

Fittingly adopting a Moravian distinction, the Methodists gained many converts in areas where patriarchal influences were dominant, including freehold parishes, industrial towns, mining areas, marketplaces, and urban regions. Hempton contends that the Primitive Methodists[248] transformed the ways of "an older paternalistic, hierarchic and integrated society" and launched a new and enthusiastic expression of faith that energetically spread through more expressive and "populist forms of religion." He affirms that "The result was a mixture of class and cultural conflict which reflected the economic and social structure of the area and led to the growth of an agricultural trade unionism almost entirely under Methodist leadership."[249]

The extraordinary capabilities of leaders such as the charismatic Whitefield and the organizationally gifted and enthusiastic John Wesley resulted in substantial numbers of followers. Their teachings such as the new birth, conversion, repentance, and sanctification "were not the introduction of a new theology that set the Revival in motion but a new and powerful presentation of some basic teachings of the Reformed tradition."[250]

246. Ibid., 7.

247. Ibid., 7.

248. According to Turner, the major evangelical revival that shaped English Methodism was the beginning point of the evangelical mainstream which is equivalent to the Second Great Awakening of the United States. This major revival movement took place between 1810 to the early 1900s. During this time the Primitive Methodist Church was birthed to adopt evangelistic evangelism different from the early Methodist movement. The critical camp meeting that rekindled the fire occurred at Mow Cop May 31, 1807. This revival disseminated into other regions and religious societies. This became to be known as the Primitive Methodist Movement. Ibid., 82–88.

249. Hempton, *The Religion of the People*, 7.

250. Crawford, "Evangelical Revival," 379.

Evangelicalism and Denominationalism

The awakening spread across denominational and national boundaries, drawing adherents into collaboration to accomplish common objectives: advancing religious education through Sunday school, efforts to benefit youth and students, the abolition of slavery, promoting international peace, temperance or prohibition of alcoholic beverages, and spreading the gospel to other nations and social groups. Then, in the twentieth century, the Ecumenical Movement began with evangelicals who had experienced the revivals and awakenings, eventually reaching far beyond this group to mainstream Protestants, eastern and other non-Protestant denominations, and even representatives of the Roman Catholic Church.[251]

Although the awakening involved Christians regardless of denominational affiliation, it also gave rise to new denominations and greatly strengthened existing ones as well. Among the new denominations were several branches of Methodists, Baptists, Congregationalists, Disciples of Christ, and scores of smaller bodies. Such groups were not territorial, as were most of the Lutheran, Reformed, and Church of England congregations. Hardly ever did they win the allegiance of all or even the majority of the inhabitants of a particular geographic area, or even have such a goal. They were in many ways similar to the various religious orders within the Roman Catholic Church: conscious of being one branch within the larger Christian church, and in this case, within Protestantism.[252] As an example, Davies characterizes Methodism as "a religion which prefers personal converse with God to institutional forms and authority; a concern to bring the truth to simple people; a stress on holiness; a reaffirmation of the doctrine of the Holy Spirit; a semi-lay Church Order; and all of this combined with orthodoxy.[253]

By the end of the eighteenth century, Methodism had influenced the English way of life extensively, including ethics, morality, and communal life. Secularization and industrialization reduced evangelistic efforts to some degree in the final third of the century, although Methodists continued to expand in mining areas, urban communities,

251. Latourette, *A History of Christianity*, 1019–20.

252. Ibid., 1020.

253. Davies, *Methodism*, 15.

and industrial regions.[254] The social status of Methodists accelerated rapidly and continued to do so as their adherents and church influence grew. The census of 1851 demonstrated that Methodists were not only working-class urban workers, but a large number of them now represented the middle class in their lifestyles and social involvement.[255]

In many places, revival movements created far-reaching impact by distributing devotional literature, supporting overseas missionaries, establishing nurseries and schools for poor children, providing materials and social services by means of voluntary Christian agencies, and building Christian dispensaries and hospitals. Moreover, theological convictions of spiritual holiness and the practice of revivalism itself continued to spread like wildfire by the frequent communications and travels of itinerant preachers throughout the transatlantic region.[256] The success of the evangelical movement could be measured by quantitative church growth, an updated worship style, numerous church plants by itinerant preachers and lay leaders, and the provision of much-needed social work for the community.[257]

The great awakenings and revivals of the nineteenth century, with their enormous spiritual and social contributions, revitalized deteriorating churches and launched new denominations including Methodism, the Salvation Army, Holiness churches, and many others. These movements also prompted mainline churches to grow and embrace evangelical characteristics. Similar revival movements can indeed occur again, and can become the inspiration for another great and new revival in the twenty-first century.[258] All in all, the awakening greatly strengthened what might be called the extreme fringes of Protestantism while also bringing new vigor to Lutheran, Reformed, and Anglican bodies. It especially stimulated the growth of the denominations furthest removed from the Catholic tradition, such as the Congregationalists, Baptists, and Methodists.[259]

254. Ibid., 22–23.

255. Birtwhistle, "Methodist Missions," 132.

256. O'Brien, "A Transatlantic Community," 813.

257. Calver, Hope for the Future, 199.

258. Gill, Beyond Decline, 69.

259. Latourette, A History of Christianity, 1020.

THE EFFECTS OF REVIVAL AND EVANGELICALISM

One of the most conspicuous facts of the eighteenth-century revival movement was that it did not appeal to the elite or ruling class, but mostly to the poor and to common people, as its appeal was primarily emotional. The impact on the religious enthusiasm of this cohort was a remarkable contrast to the skepticism, cynicism, and antagonism toward Christianity promoted by the forces of secularization among the elite and intellectuals, who viewed Christianity as a mysterious religious practice filled with superstitions and its adherents as un-reasonable fanatics. Secular elites tended to view organized religion as exploiting the illiterate. Regardless, revivalist preachers paved the way for great numbers of the poor to hear the Christian gospel and to respond with enthusiasm.[260]

Spiritual versus Rational

The "Protestant crisis" of secularism can be traced back to the 1730s. Concurrently, revival movements were being set in motion and inter-national revival connections were forming even in the midst of religious and social tides of anti-Protestant sentiment. Political upheavals in con-tinental Europe stemming from the expansion of Protestant territories, especially in Catholic countries, caused British and American authorities to pay close attention to several renewal and revival movements. In the early eighteenth century, just before the 1730s, some political positions held by Protestants did return to Catholicism. In one example cited by Crawford, "the Reformed house in the Palatinate had died out and had been succeeded by a Catholic branch."[261] But, on balance, the effects of revivals and awakenings in the transatlantic region were quite remark-able. As a result of the revival, Edwin Err reports, between 1740 and 1800, a momentous church growth took shape among non-conformist churches. Churches went from 27 to an astounding 926 and temporary chapels also sprang up from 506 to 3,491.[262]

The eighteenth century revivals carried widespread ramifications throughout Western Europe. Individuals from all denominations

260. Elliott-Binns, *The Early Evangelicals*, 56.

261. Crawford, "Evangelical Revival," 390. According to Crawford, in the eigh-teenth century some Protestant rulers accepted Catholicism dwindling Protestant numbers.

262. Orr, *Re-Study*, 4.

were transformed by personal confession in Christ, commitment to God, and reliance on the Holy Spirit. These experiences motivated overseas missionary work and related efforts to share the gospel so that others might also have the joy of salvation. Those touched by the revival worked to eradicate slavery, reform child labor laws, and fight discrimination against those at the lower end of the social ladder. The expanding revival drew public attention for its spiritual vigor and for the involvement of laypeople. The revivals' domino effect created a glowing optimism and caused the decline of conventional social authorities, the rigid Anglican hierarchy, and the values of individualism and secularization.[263]

As Elliott-Binns points out, the revival in the eighteenth century "came as a breath from the Spirit of God into a hopeless and fainting world [that] can only be accounted for, from a human point of view, by that instinct for God which never quite dies away in the hearts of men." In the late eighteenth century, revivals took place in several separate and distinct regions.[264] Once the reformers renewed a focus on Scripture, sacrament, and discipline in the church, the Pietists, Moravians, and evangelicals emphasized the importance of the Christian cell group—a small group that meets for prayer, Bible study, and mutual edification.[265] Evangelical revivals after the Reformation, according to John Munsey Turner, were like tributaries "flowing into a common stream, each stressing those doctrines of the Holy Sprit and the cross which the Age of Reason had pushed to the periphery of spirituality."[266]

The eighteenth century, the Age of Reason, was also the time when a great renewal of religion of the heart took place, including Pietism in Germany, the Great Awakening in America, Anglican evangelicalism, and the Methodism of John Wesley and his followers. We must note that Wesley should be considered within the rich context of an exuberant time of revival, for, as Turner puts it, "simple chronology disposes of the stereotype of the whole Revival as a chain-reaction

263. Ibid., 374.

264. The spread of revival in the mid- nineteenth century was due in part to news of revivals circulated widely by newspapers. This, as Elliott-Binns points out, "might stimulate similar movements; but this cannot account for their rise in the eighteenth century." Elliott-Binns, *The Early Evangelicals*, 117.

265. Turner, *Conflict and Reconciliation*, 7.

266. Ibid., 7.

from the Aldersgate Street experience and of John Wesley as a solitary Moses striking the rock of petrified Anglicanism to release a sudden stream of revival."[267]

Evangelism and Mission Oriented

Reaching the common people was a passion shared by lay preachers of the eighteenth century revival. Itinerant lay preachers "now found a vent for their oratorical talents along more mundane channels, such as fervently haranguing groups of unofficial strikers."[268] Working people took the opportunity of the revival to increase their social status, a change that would last for generations to come. Revival meeting also brought entertainment and amusing news to the working class in a way quite similar to modern times.[269]

Evangelical revival movements in England attracted more urban working people than in rural areas, where traditional ecclesiastical institutions still had a great deal of influence over the community. Crawford believes the attraction for urban people was that "it rescued them from "anomie and social insecurity" created by separation from the intimate relationships and moral oversight of the common-field village community."[270] Evangelicals provided clear instructions for a new life and offered a powerful conversion experience that established religious communities could not or did not provide. In the evangelical church, people had "the feeling of belonging to a cohesive social group, of being integrated into a complex network of primary relationships," ultimately enhancing their lives.[271] Hugh Price states:

> We Christians, when we unite our forces, are simply irresistible. Let us, then, in the name of God and humanity, combine heartily to abolish Slavery, Drunkenness, Lust, Gambling, Ignorance, Pauperism, Mammonism, and War. After that is done, we shall not have much difficulty in settling all our theological and ecclesiastical differences.[272]

---

267. Ibid., 6–7.

268. Elliott-Binns, *The Early Evangelicals*, 13–14.

269. Ibid., 13.

270. Crawford, "Evangelical Revival," 367.

271. Ibid., 367–68.

272. Quoted in Turner, "Methodism in England," 310.

The Pietist movement in Central Europe had a similar impact, providing the first evangelism encounter and powerful spiritual experience for many. In general, during the seventeenth and eighteenth centuries, the people who felt the effects of the revival most keenly were from the state churches: the Lutheran Church, the Church of England, and minority dissenting group, such as the Baptists and Puritans.[273] Virtually all overseas missionary work during this period was attributable to the Pietist movement or the revival movement through leaders such as Nicolas Zinzendorf, John Wesley, and George Whitefield. In 1732, early German Pietist Zinzendorf began missionary voyages from Dresden to the Virgin Islands, Greenland, South Africa, Jamaica, and the North American Indians.[274] His commitment is captured in his words: "I have one passion. It is He and He alone."[275]

In the eighteenth century, as a result of the evangelical revivals and great awakenings in Britain, North America, Germany, and the Nordic countries, overseas Protestant missions took shape alongside European imperialistic colonialism. The revivals produced renewed growth in individual commitment to Christ, social action growing out of a biblical worldview, and interest in the geographical advance of Christianity. Christian missions reached out to prisoners and cared for orphans and children living on the streets. Biblically motivated political action attempted to amend or constitute the rights of workers, limit children's working hours, improve working environments through acts of Parliament, abolish the slave trade, and end slavery altogether. Eventually, missions would attempt to contextualize Western Christianity into the non-Western World.[276]

The revival movement of the nineteenth and early twentieth centuries started in the transatlantic region and gradually moved into the other English-speaking countries, such as South Africa, Canada, Australia, and New Zealand. Latourette notes that "Spain and Portugal, Roman Catholic lands, had led in the expansion of Europe between 1500 and 1750, but after 1750 it was through peoples that are often called Anglo-Saxon that this expansion was chiefly accomplished."[277]

273. Pirouet, "Modern Missions," 2.

274. Pettifer and Bradley, *Missionaries*, 18.

275. Ibid., 19.

276. Pirouet, "Modern Missions," 1–2.

277. Latourette, *A History of Christianity*, 1021.

Iberian Catholicism had been exported with its Iberian folk Catholic characteristics and then mixed with the native culture and its folk religious practices to create a new type of Catholicism—an inculturated or indigenized Catholicism. Likewise, when evangelical Christianity expanded, it retained an Anglo-Saxon flavor. During the colonial period, many Protestant characteristics reflected traits adopted or modified from Anglo-Saxon evangelicalism and Anglo-American civilization.

One of the most phenomenal results of the revival was the formation of the highest number of new mission agencies in Christian history, which occurred between the eighteenth and nineteenth centuries. In the nineteenth century, international revival movements emerged in Germany and in different parts of Europe. In the 1830s, a revival broke out in Geneva and made its way to the French Protestants. As a result, Switzerland, France, and Norway became involved in overseas missionary work during this period. In the same era in Norway, Hans Nielson Hauge initiated a revival among several national churches in close collaboration with the Norwegian state church, but still maintaining independence. [278]

Some of the most noticeable Protestant overseas mission organizations began in the late seventeenth century. They include the Society for the Propagation of the Gospel (SPG) in New England, the Society for Promoting Christian Knowledge, the Society for the Propagation of the Gospel in Foreign Parts, the (Scottish) Society for Propagating Christian Knowledge, and Moravian missionary efforts. Since its inception, Moravian missionaries shared the Gospel in "Labrador, North America, South America, South Africa, Asia, Australia," and other parts of the world representing the largest mission movement in the eighteenth to early nineteenth centuries. [279] The 1790s and the opening years of the nineteenth century have generally been acknowledged as the beginning of the Protestant foreign missionary enterprise. [280] Even John Wesley was sent out by the SPG in 1737 to Savannah and Atlanta to reach out to the new settlers. [281] As we consider the effects of the revival in the first half of the eighteenth century, it is also fitting to honor the preparations made for revival by patrons of charity schools such

278. Neill, *A History of Christian Missions*, 213–14.
279. Allen, Revivals of Religion, 16.
280. Latourette, *A History of Christianity*, 1032.
281. O'Connor, *Three Centuries of Mission*, 41–42.

as the Society for the Propagation of Christian Knowledge (SPCK), the Welsh-speaking charity schools established by Griffith Jones, the Societies for Reformation of Manners, and the Anglican religious societies in Britain.[282]

Evangelical sentiments and motives stemming from the revival movement became the catalyst for enthusiastic overseas missions efforts. In 1791, the father of modern missions, William Carey, founded the Baptist Missionary Society. Three years later, the London Missionary Society was established as an interdenominational agency, though its inception was through the Congregation Church. In 1796, the Scottish Missionary Society, Glasgow Missionary Society, and Church Missionary Society (CMS) were some of most powerful mission organizations formed, primarily supported by evangelical Anglican organizations including the Clapham sect, led by William Wilberforce. Between the years 1817 and 1818, the Wesleyan Methodist Missionary Society was formed.[283] The CMS sent out a great number of missionaries whose efforts drew both negative and positive reactions, primarily due to the fact that colonial conquests usually accompanied missionary advances. Ward and Stanley rightfully proclaim that "the Gospel was not the possession of the missionaries, nor could they dictate how the Gospel would be received and understood."[284] In the same way, Methodist missionary zeal was not restricted to the British and American territories, but expanded globally, prompting John Wesley to say, "I look upon all the world as my parish."[285]

Revivals also greatly influenced the Christian student movement, starting with one prayer union at Oxford University in 1850. Evangelicals organized a student group at Cambridge in 1877 called the Cambridge Inter-Collegiate Christian Union. D. L. Moody conducted an evangelistic campaign at Cambridge in 1878, which resulted in the conversion of C. T. Studd, who later labored in China as a missionary and organized the Worldwide Evangelization Crusade.[286] Overseas and domestic missions were not considered to be matters of denominational expansion or of expanding profits for nations or busi-

282. Crawford, "Evangelical Revival," 371.

283. Latourette, *A History of Christianity*, 1032–33.

284. Ward and Stanley, *The Church Mission Society*, 2–3.

285. Birtwhistle, "Methodist Missions," 1.

286. Quoted in Cross, *Oxford Dictionary*, 1297.

nesses. Overseas mission work was compelled by voluntary religious zeal to reach out to other nations with a message of salvation. The evaluation by scholars such as Ward points out the critical tension that "Christian missions can never be isolated either from the great game of European politics, or from the political systems local to the area where they are to operate."[287]

One example is the Church of Uganda (Anglican), formed as a result of the Keswick Convention and the work of the CMS. The East African Revival movement in the 1920s led by the Balokole movement also credited its success partially to the Keswick Convention. Shortly thereafter, the Cambridge Inter-Collegiate Christian Union was formed, in which missionaries Joe Church and Stanley Smith joined forces to further the Christian transformation of individual lives by contextualizing the gospel from the African standpoint. Amos Kasibante summarizes their principal message as "repentance, public confession, and belief in the efficacy of the Blood of the lamb, in washing a person clean of sin."[288]

The remarkable overseas missionary work of the eighteenth century, it can be argued, initiated the discovery and formation of the New World and the transformed the rest of Europe. The reverberations of the 1789 French Revolution lasted all the way up until 1914, when the First World War began.[289] The eighteenth century has been viewed as the European century, during which a Christian Europe was able to enforce its will and ideas on the whole of the inhabited world. The European way of Christianity has been inseparably linked with the expansion of imperialistic secular European civilization as global commerce and missionary activities advanced in tandem.[290]

Many postmodern scholars fault missionary endeavors of the church as imperialistic, reflecting a Western superiority complex that led to abuse of native populations, especially during the twentieth and twenty-first centuries. Missiologists Julian Pettifer and Richard Bradley define this association of missions with Western imperialism as "one of the unfortunate accidents of history."[291]

---

287. Ward, "Missions in Their Global Context," 108.

288. Kasibante, "Beyond Revival," 363–64.

289. Neill, *A History of Christian Missions,* 207.

290. Ibid., 207.

291. Pettifer and Bradley, *Missionaries,* 19.

But if the association has become an embarrassment in recent years for many Christians, for the spread of Christianity it has been anything but unfortunate. The nineteenth century missionaries, like their predecessors, had few qualms about using the arteries of empire to further their own spiritual ambitions.

CONCLUSION: REVIVING FOR REVIVAL

Revivals in Europe were not a one time event. It has always created a domino effect where denominations, churches, parachurch organizations, and even overseas mission agencies directly and indirectly were interconnected in terms of exchanging their ideas and influences. The revival in Jerusalem spread all over the Roman Empire. The revival in Italy affected France, Austria, Germany, and Czech. The revival in Britain affected the nations in Central Europe all the way to America. The Scandinavian revivals influenced other European nations. Revivals are like ripple effects that also create positive side effects such as sound evangelicalism. Unfortunately, however, revivals are always remembered in the ruins, museums, books, and archives of history. Descendants of revivals are succeeded through the revivals movements in which they have become institutionalized denominations such as Methodists or parachurch organizations such as the Moravian missions. On the other hand, even today there are places where the previous revivals are being awakened again as God's people start to yearn for revival fire.

6

American Awakenings and Revivals

JUST AS REVIVAL MOVEMENTS have been the vital factor in the rise of evangelicalism in Britain and Europe, great awakenings have spurred the rise of American evangelicalism, the Holiness movement, and Christian fundamentalism. Moreover, Pentecostal revivals in the United States in the early twentieth century greatly contributed to the expansion of Christianity in the developing world, the Global South. If secularization is one of the chief causes of the decline of religious establishments in Europe, the same question should be asked about the North America. The two have similar revival roots, even though the effects of secularization have been comparatively different. By examining the correlation of the North America's religious landscape with its particularities, we will draw the origins and developments of North American revivals and Great Awakenings in order to more accurately compare the European and American situations. Such differences between the religious situations of Britain and the United States call for sound study, beginning with description, exploration, and investigation of the historical and sociological factors and the reasons behind them.

In examining these two contrasting situations, we will see the rise of Christian beliefs and practices in one nation and not the other, but we must also examine other religious and cultural elements. The cycles of increasing and decreasing church attendance in the United States show a very different pattern than in Europe. The rise of Christian America begins with Puritanism, the Great Awakenings, evangelical revivals, Holiness movements, and the Pentecostal movement, which are also all distinctively American. In chapter 7, we will examine the process of secularization in North America, particularly in the United States.

THE RELIGIOUS TAPESTRY IN NORTH AMERICA

The contemporary church in America has a more dynamic, vigorous, and proactive stance than that of Europe. One wonders why European churches have declined so significantly while the American church is still at the peak of church attendance and doctrinal strength. Two-thirds of American adults participate in the Christian faith, despite the fact that there is no state church. The United States is still one of the most religiously attentive and participating countries in the world even though secular movements such as religious humanism, same sex marriage, secularism, and atheism have crept into American society in public and private arenas. America is considered "the most God-believing and religion-adhering, fundamentalist, and religiously traditional country in Christendom," with a few exceptional cases such as Ireland and Poland.[1]

A Religious Paradox in North America

Christianity in the United States is unlike that of Europe in that there has been no longtime close association of church and state. Instead of a religious monopoly, there has been an unofficial, broader relationship between the church and culture where religious pluralism could flourish.[2] Douglas J. Hall of McGill University in Canada states that this unofficial presence of Christianity has led to an informal Christianization of society. Hall believes that the influence of the Christian faith in North America "has been far more effective and enduring than any other form of Christian establishment known to history." He goes on to say that "the old, legal establishments of Europe, existing today as mere vestiges of the past, could be set aside easily enough when the arrangement was no longer useful or particularly meaningful."[3]

However, in a religious paradox, the North American church holds the ongoing attractiveness of the sacred in a decidedly secularized community. Peter Berger points out that "Religion occupies a conspicuous place in American society, is accorded considerable social prestige, and appears to be a matter of active interest to large

1. Putnam quotes from Seymour Lipset's "Comment on Luckmann," 187. Putnam, *Bowling Alone*, 65.

2. Guder et al., *Missional Church*, 48.

3. Hall, *Confessing the Faith*, 196.

numbers of people."[4] Therefore, widespread Christian influence—not propagated by Judeo-Christian institutions, but the religious culture itself, what Berger calls "a cultural religion"—has been embraced by most Americans. The cultural religion, the counterpart of America to the state religion in Europe, can endorse a "solemn ratification" to moral and political values. Hence, it is easy to affix the cultural religion to politics and government at every level and receive support from the civil government on moral and economic issues. Berger states:

> The religious denominations, whatever else they may believe or practice, are carriers of this cultural religion. Affiliation with a religious denomination thus becomes *ipso facto* an act of allegiance to the common political creed. Disaffiliation, in turn, renders an individual not only religiously but also politically suspect.[5]

Prevalent American cultural religion produced widespread impressions of Christian beliefs, worldviews, values, ethics, and norms that did not emerge from by a single church or denomination, but from numerous denominations holding onto a universal ecclesiology mainly stemming from either Calvinism or Arminianism. Hence, the cultural religion shared across the broad religious landscape can be redefined as the American "Christian culture" or "churched culture," according to Guder.[6]

Secularization and modernization greatly affected American society as well, though the reactions were quite different from those in Europe. In the United States, none of the European state churches—such as the Lutheran, Anglican, Reformed, or even Roman Catholic—has been in a dominant position or attracted a majority of the populace. In Europe, nonstate churches—such as Baptist, Methodist, Holiness, Pentecostal, and Charismatic—all have the highest number of members in Europe. This fact corroborates the possibility that these denominations, which are also the largest in other parts of the world, particularly in the Global South, do have ties to their American counterparts. The denominations that grew out of the awakenings and revival movements in the United States sent a great number of missionaries abroad. In 1910, one-third of all missionaries in the world

4. Berger, *The Noise of Solemn Assemblies*, 31.

5. Ibid., 63.

6. Guder et al., *Missional Church*, 48.

were sent from North American churches. In 2010, the proportion of missionaries sent from the United States is roughly the same, with a total of 115,000 Americans involved in missions.[7]

Some argue that the figures displaying the rise of Christianity in America are inaccurate, since today's rise in attendance and membership does not add up to the previously higher percentage of religious participation among America's population. Some argue that the long-term growth tendency of the American religious landscape was already in place and did not gain additional benefits from the awakenings and revivals, especially because churches in North America have been more affected by secularization. Glock and Stark, however, believe that "there has been a propensity neither towards greater religiousness nor towards greater secularization."[8] Overall, there has been an upward trend of American church growth over the past three centuries, and statistics show that revival movements contributed tremendously to this growth.[9] This long-term growth of Christianity demonstrates that America indeed regards itself as a Christian nation until the Second World War.[10] We will now consider the religious beliefs and practices of common Americans and the contributions of the Great Awakenings and revivals in order to contrast their effects to those of secularism.

The Dynamic Religious Context in America

In the mid-nineteenth century, most Americans considered their nation to be a Protestant nation chosen by God in order to bring the gospel to the world. President Woodrow Wilson claimed that "America was born a Christian nation for the purpose of exemplifying to the nations of the world the principles of righteousness found in the Word of God."[11] While his claim does not compel Americans to confess Christianity as the one true faith, it does demonstrate the nation's legacy of Puritanism and the spiritual inheritance of the Great Awakening and revivals. The Supreme Court recognized the

---

7. Johnson and Ross, *Atlas of Global Christianity 1910–2010*, 263.

8. Glock and Stark, *Religion and Society in Tension*, 68.

9. Ibid., 72–73.

10. Marty, *The Modern Schism*, 109–10.

11. The president's address "The Bible and Progress" was delivered in Denver, Colorado on May 7, 1911. Woodbridge et al., *The Gospel in America*, 207.

United States as a Christian nation in 1931.[12] As did President Wilson, Franklin Delano Roosevelt expressed that the United States as "the lasting concord between men and nations, founded, on the principles of Christianity."[13]

> One hundred years before the statement by the Supreme Court[14], Frenchman Alexis de Tocqueville visited America for ten months and admired its flourishing spirit of Christianity. Christianity has therefore retained a strong hold on the public mind in America . . . in the United States, Christian sects are infinitely diversified and perpetually modified; but Christianity itself is an established and irresistible fact, which no one undertakes either to attack or defend. The Americans, having admitted the principal doctrines of the Christian religion without inquiry, are obliged to accept in like manner a great number of moral truths originating in it and connected with it.[15]

Of democracy in America, he wrote, "It is difficult to know from Americans' discourses, whether the principal object of religion is to produce eternal felicity in the other world, or prosperity in this."[16] Furthermore, Americans in their daily lives demonstrated Christian practices more than did the Europeans, with the exceptions of Catholic-dominant Ireland and Poland. The American Protestant identity was also evident in the concept of Manifest Destiny and in the notion that the United States was a nation for "God's special design and Purpose," displaying the "Providence of God" to justify her religious, civil and national expansion within the North American territory and beyond.[17] For instance, as Smith and others have highlighted,

12. In 1931 the US Supreme Court declared in *US v. MacIntosh* 283 U.S. 605, it was declared that "We [America] is a Christian people according to one another the equal right of religious freedom and acknowledging with reverence the duty of obedience to the will of God."

13. This claim was made when Roosevelt and British Prime Minister Winston Churchill met for a mid-Atlantic warship summit in 1931. DeMar, *America's Christian Heritage*, 8.

14. See the US Supreme Court's decision *Church of the Holy Trinity vs. U.S.* 143 U.S. 457. These, and many other matters which might be noticed, add a volume of unofficial declarations to the mass of organic utterances that this is a Christian nation.

15. Tocqueville, *Democracy in America*, 6–7.

16. Quoted in Fishwick, *Great Awakenings*, 39.

17. Woodbridge et al., *The Gospel in America*, 207.

many nineteenth century evangelicals thought that the United States was not only "blessed by God and destined to become the kingdom of heaven on earth," but also existed to bless other nations by bringing the Christian gospel and the strengths of its civilization. In 1866, a report on missions by the Southern Baptist Convention stated, "America is the radiating center whence high and ennobling influences beam upon the world; and we are enlightening mankind in bringing the radiance of our own piety."[18] In 1870, Methodist bishop Matthew Simpson, speaking in Chicago to a British audience, stated that "God is making our land a kind of central spot for the whole earth. The eyes of the world are upon us."[19]

The prevalence of Christianity in American society created a Protestant version of medieval Christendom that is still evident in the United States today. Marsden points out, "Christian principles held the nation together by providing a solid base of morality in the citizenry."[20] Congress, Senate sessions, and even presidential inaugurations commence with Christian prayer by chaplains or ministers. Even though religious freedom and the separation of church and state are the law of the land, Christian principles instilled by the Puritan fathers and reinforced by awakenings and revivals have penetrated individual values, social life, culture, and the practice of democracy.[21] Yount notes that "although secular humanists identity religion with superstition, they nevertheless retain and promote the values founded on faith."[22]

Consequently, as historian George Marsden states, evangelical Protestants regarded their Christian faith as "the normative American creed. . . . the nineteenth century had been marked by successive advances of evangelicalism, the American nation, and hence the Kingdom of God."[23] American Protestantism has influenced every sphere of American life, including law, education, social norms and values,

---

18. Handy, *A Christian America*, 67.

19. Edward Thomas, a Methodist coworker of Simpson's, affirmed that America will be a numerous nation "without an adulterer, or a swearer, or a Sabbath-breaker, or an ingrate, or an apostate, or a backslider, or a slanderer; hundreds thousands of homes without a prodigal, a quarrel, or a heart-burn, a bitter tear." Ibid., 80.

20. Marsden, *Understanding Fundamentalism*, 10.

21. Gallup and Lindsay, *Surveying the Religious Landscape*, 120.

22. Yount, *The Future of Christian Faith*, 22.

23. Marsden, *Fundamentalism and American Culture*, 11.

virtue, and culture.[24] This older order of American Protestantism, Marsden says, "was based on the interrelationship of faith, science, the Bible, morality, and civilization."[25]

Nonetheless, until the twentieth century, the concept of America as a Protestant nation was clearly remembered among most American mindsets. However, from the twentieth century non-Protestant religious groups migrated into the United States and gained power influencing society to be a religiously pluralistic one. Through the great awakenings, this dominantly Protestant nation became one of the most vigorous, religiously pluralistic countries in the world.[26]

Christian Beliefs in the United States

North Americans have high levels of religious belief and practice, according to numerous surveys: "Americans and Canadians believe in God, pray regularly, and consider themselves religious."[27] If the British tend to display habits of "believing without belonging," then the Americans appear to be much more "believing with belonging." While Americans express their faith and belong to churches more than the British, they still participate at low levels in actual ministry of the church. Religious pluralism, individualism, and privatization of religion have increased in North America; Guder and others affirm that "religion fits into North American secularism in a remarkable synthesis that the student of religious behavior finds fascinating. But for the Christian who takes the gospel of Jesus Christ seriously, this religiosity is a weighty challenge."[28]

The contrast between British and North American religious practice is marked. The legacy of Puritanism and evangelical awakenings is still evident among Americans, but no longer dominant among the British since the last century. The research of Gallup and Lindsay has shown that the percentage of American citizens who identify themselves as evangelicals is four times as great as among the British.[29]

24. DeMar, *America's Christian Heritage*, 7.

25. Marsden, *Fundamentalism and American Culture*, 17.

26. LaHaye, *Faith of Our Founding Fathers*, 70.

27. Guder et al., *Missional Church*, 1.

28. Ibid., 1.

29. Just 17 percent of British adults regard religion as "very important," compared to 57 percent of Americans. Gallup and Lindsay, *Surveying the Religious Landscape*, 122.

Their 1998 poll on religious affiliation showed that seven out of ten adults are church or synagogue members and two out of five adults go to church or synagogue weekly—three times the rates in Britain.[30] A total of 96 percent of Americans believe in God, compared to 70 percent of Canadians and 61 percent of the British.[31] A 1996 Barna study showed that around 85 percent of Americans still agree that the Christian faith or another religious belief system is productive for society, while only 13 percent believe that atheists contribute to improve society.[32] The majority of Americans still hold a conventional view of God; in 2006, 71 percent believed in the existence of a God who is omniscient, omnipresent, and the creator of the universe. A year later, the rate was 66 percent, described as "the lowest percentage in more than twenty years of similar surveys."[33]

The high percentage of Americans who believe in God has hardly changed in the last fifty years. In a 1999 national Gallup poll, 95 percent of American adults said that they personally believe in God, while only 5 percent upheld atheism.[34] Britain's rate of 62 percent is considerably lower.[35] In a 2001 survey, 76.5 percent of Americans identified themselves as Christian. This includes Catholics, who comprise 24.5 percent of the total population. A decade earlier, in 1990, 86.2 percent of Americans claimed to be Christian.[36] According to the 2011 British Humanist Association (BHA) survey, in 2001 70 percent of the British population responded as Christians. Surprisingly, in a March 2011 survey conducted by YouGov on behalf of the BHA, only 53 percent responded as being Christian, and 39 percent as having no religion.

---

30. Ibid., 11–15.

31. Ibid., 119.

32. Yount, *The Future of Christian Faith in America*, 22–23.

33. Barna Group, "Barna's Annual Tracking Study," lines 22–33.

34. Because of America's growing religious pluralism, the expressed belief in God is not just Christian, but includes other faiths as well. Ninety-five percent of adults believe in God or a universal spirit. A Gallup survey in 1947 showed that 96 percent of Americans believed in God personally—virtually the same rate as in 1999 (95 percent). Gallup and Lindsay, *Surveying the Religious Landscape*, 2, 21–25.

35. Glock and Stark, *Christian Beliefs and Anti-Semitism*, 4.

36. Kosmin, Mayer, and Keysar, *American Religious Identification Survey*, 12.

Less than 48 percent of those who responded as Christians believed that Jesus was a real person who died on the cross.[37]

TABLE 6.1 BELIEF IN GOD IN GREAT BRITAIN AND NORTHERN IRELAND, 1991, 2008

	Britain (%), 1991	N. Ireland (%), 1991	UK (%) 1994	US (%) 2008
I don't believe in God.	10	1	N/C	2.3
I don't know whether there is a God, and I don't believe there is any way to find out	14	4	5	4.3
I don't believe in a personal God, but I do believe in a higher power of some kind.	13	4	10	12.1
I find myself believing in God some of the time, but not at other times.	13	4	N/C	N/C
While I have doubts, I feel that I do believe in God.	26	20	20	5.7
I know God really exists, and I have no doubts about it.	23	57	64	69.5
I don't know / no answer	2	7	1	6.1

Source: British Social Attitudes Survey (1992), National Opinion Research Center (NORC), 1994. American Religious Survey 2008[38]

37. British Humanist Association, "Religion and Belief," lines 19–31.

38. Humphrys, "Survey Results."

GRAPH 6.1 AMERICANS AND BRITISH BELIEF IN GOD BY
PERCENTAGE

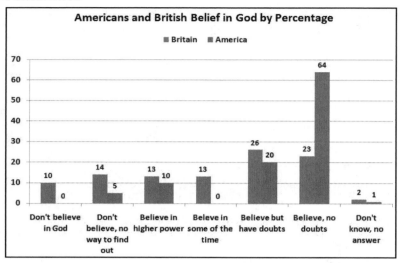

Source: British Social Survey, 1992; National Opinion Research Center, 1994.

A 2011 Gallup survey reveals 92 percent of respondents state a belief in God.[39] According to 1980 and 1995 Gallup surveys, in the transatlantic countries, the highest-ranked belief was the belief in God, which was 96 percent in the United States and 70 percent in Canada. Great Britain ranked the lowest with 61 percent. The majority of Americans identified themselves with Judeo-Christian religions (80 percent).[40] Since its inception in 1944, the Gallup survey has asked the same question "Do you believe in God?" and the results remain high. Although 2011 shows the lowest since its inception, it is still an amazing 92 percent. Past results have been 96 percent in 1994, 94 percent in 1947, and 98 percent in 1953, 1954, 1965, and 1967. However, this number includes liberals, agnostics and sympathizers who said "yes" but their answers come from their belief in a higher power or a supreme being or answered yes but have doubts. The Gallup survey reports that "the percentages of Americans who say they believe in God without doubts or as separate from a universal spirit have ranged from 73% to 86%."[41]

39. Newport, "More Than 9 in 10 Americans Continue to Believe in God," line 5.

40. Gallup and Lindsay, *Surveying the Religious Landscape*, 21.

41. According to Gallup poll in 2011, it appeared so high in belief in God. Also it

TABLE 6.2 SURVEY ON BELIEF ON GOD

Which of the following statements comes closest to your belief about God – you believe in God, you don't believe in God, but you do believe in a universal or higher power, or you don't believe in either?				
	Believe In God	Believe in Universal spirit	Don't believe in either	Other (vol.)	No Opinion
2010 May 3-6	80%	12%	6%	1%	1%
(vol.) = Volunteered response					
GALLUP					

*Volunteered response

Source: Gallup Survey 2011[42]

More Americans believed in heaven than in hell, while the majority asserted the existence of both places. However, the percentage who believed in heaven, hell, and the devil was lower than those who believed in God. Almost eight in ten American adults believed in the existence of heaven, while only six in ten Canadian adults and one in two British upheld this belief. Likewise, six in ten American adults believed in hell, while a little more than half of Canadians and one in four British believed in hell. Belief in reincarnation did not exhibit great differences.[43]

indicates, "The percentages who more definitively say there is no God are generally 6 percent or 7 percent across these questions, similar to the 7 percent or 8 percent who do not believe in God in the questions asked this year. This suggests that most Americans do believe in God, but when given the opportunity to express some uncertainty, a modest percentage opt to do so." Gallup, "More Than 9 in 10 Americans Continue to Believe in God". Newport, "More Than 9 in 10 Americans Continue to Believe in God," lines 83–85.

42. The question in full was "Do you believe in God, you don't believe in God, but you do believe in a universal spirit or higher power, or you don't believe in either?" Ibid., lines 86–90.

43. Gallup and Lindsay, *Surveying the Religious Landscape*, 120–21.

TABLE 6.3 RELIGIOUS BELIEFS AMONG ADULTS

	Canada (%)	Great Britain (%)	United States (%)
God or universal spirit or life force	70	61	96
Heaven	61	50	78
Hell	54	24	60
The devil	57	24	55
Reincarnation	33	26	27

Source: *Surveying the Religious Landscape*[44]

TABLE 6.4 AMERICAN AND BRITISH BELIEFS CONTRASTED

	Great Britain (%)	United States (%)
Believe Jesus Christ is . . .		
God or Son of God	46	84
Just a man, another religious leader	34	9
Just a story	9	1
Other/Not sure	11	6
Membership		
Roman Catholic	14	28
Church of England/Episcopalian	54	2
Church of Scotland/Presbyterian	6	5
Other	12	58
None	14	7
Religion's influence is . . .		
Increasing	12	27
Decreasing	73	63
Remaining about the same	10	5
Ever pray	59	88
Went to church in last seven days	12	27

Source: Surveying the Religious Landscape[45]

44. Ibid., 122.
45. Ibid., 123.

Belief in Jesus Christ as the Son of God in the United States is almost double the rate in Britain. Only 46 percent of the British responded yes, compared to 84 percent of Americans. Thirty-four percent of the British viewed Jesus as having been only a man or religious leader, while only 9 percent of Americans upheld this view.[46] Contrasts were not as great when it came to opinions about the influence of religion. Sixty three percent of Americans considered religion's role to be decreasing, while 73 percent of the British felt this way. Only 27 percent of Americans believed the influence of religion to be increasing, yet, for the British, that number was even lower at 12 percent. Eighty-one percent of Americans regarded themselves as being religious compared to 58 percent among the British.[47] Although the percentage of Americans who claim to have religious beliefs and practices is considerably higher than among the British and most other Europeans, those higher figures do not always portray the reality of the religious lives of ordinary Americans.

Church Attendance and Membership

Church attendance in the United States is greater than in Britain, with 43 percent of Americans attending on a weekly basis compared to only 14 percent of the British. Twenty-three percent of the British attend a church service at least monthly.[48] David Yount points to a paradox of the relationship between church attendance and actual membership, in which membership rose while attendance diminished. He points to sources showing that only 19.6 percent of Protestants and 28 percent of Catholics go to church on a weekly basis.[49] According to a 2009 Barna poll, 43 percent of Americans attended a religious service on a weekly basis. A National Congregations Survey and the US Congregational Life Survey revealed that 40 percent of Americans (around 118 million people) attend a Christian worship service on a weekly basis. The question arose whether the church attendance number had been an exaggeration because Kirk Hadway and Penny Marler demonstrated

---

46. Ibid., 124.

47. Ibid., 124.

48. Ibid., 124.

49. Yount, *The Future of Christian Faith in America*, 63.

that only 20.4 percent of the population attends weekly service, only half of Gallup's figure.[50]

GRAPH 6.2 PERCENT MEMBERSHIP CHANGE

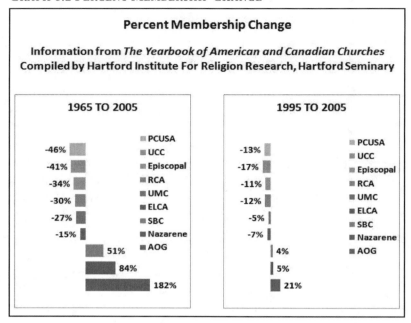

Source: Percent Membership Change; The Yearbook of American and Canadian Churches, Hartford Institute For Religion Research, Hartford Seminary.[51]

50. Hartford Institute, "How many people go to church each Sunday?," lines 2–6.

51. Ibid., lines 107–117.

TABLE 6.5 CHURCH-RELATED BEHAVIOR IN THE LAST SEVEN DAYS

Behavior in past seven days	2003 (%)	2002 (%)	2001 (%)	2000 (%)	1999 (%)	1998 (%)	1997 (%)
Attended a religious service	43	43	42	40	41	43	43
Attended Sunday school class	20	25	19	19	19	23	23
Participated in small group	20	18	16	17	18	18	18
Volunteered to help at church	21	24	20	21	24	25	24
Read from the Bible, other than while at church	39	42	37	40	36	38	36
Prayed to God	82	81	82	83	NA	80	NA
Shared faith in Christ, past year	22	23	24	24	23	21	26
Born-again Christian	38	40	41	41	40	39	43

Source: Barna poll "Tracking of Religious Behavior"[52]

Only 17 percent of the populace had a church affiliation on the eve of the American Revolution. This number grew to one in three during the Civil War and dramatically increased to two in three by 1980.[53] Two different studies measuring the average number of members in each Protestant church showed that number to be 75 in 1776 and 91.5

52. Barna Group, "America's Faith Is Changing," lines 152–161.
53. Yount, *The Future of Christian Faith in America*, 63.

in 1890.[54] However, Yount states that many of the small churches were "dying at the rate of fifty every week in America."[55]

Since the 1960s, mainline denominations have seen their membership and attendance diminish after two hundred years of growth while many evangelical and Pentecostal churches have sustained their growth. A 2003 Barna poll indicated that those who stay at home on Sundays disproportionately Baby Boomers, 69 percent of whom sleep in on the Sabbath, followed by young adults eighteen to thirty years old, two-thirds of who shun congregational worship altogether.[56]

> Although the vast majority of Americans continue to believe in God, pray regularly, and identify a religious preference, only a minority now worship together regularly. What of the others? Their religious life, whether fervent or lackadaisical, is almost exclusively private and personal. Like Thomas Paine, their minds are their church.[57]

Still, America's church attendance continually and gradually rose to 62 percent in 1980.[58] Statistics from the last two centuries from several denominations clearly show that major denominations declined during the eighteenth century while Methodists and Baptists added to their numbers considerably during the first half of the nineteenth century.

A 2001 survey revealed that one in two (52 percent) of American adults are Protestant, one in four (24.5 percent) are Catholic, and 14.1 percent have no religious affiliations. The numbers of Jews and Muslims were still quite small: Jews at 1.3 percent and Muslims at 0.5 percent.[59] These figures probably differ by small degrees today, but nonetheless, Protestantism was and is the most dominant American religion by far.

54. Finke and Stark, *The Churching of America*, 24, 26.

55. Yount, *The Future of Christian Faith in America*, 29.

56. Ibid., 63.

57. Ibid., 63.

58. According to Finke and Stark, a dramatic rise in church adherence—up to 37 percent— followed the Civil War. They found a remarkable decline of adherence in the South due to immense dislocation. "The rate then began to rise once more, and by 1906 slightly more than half of the U.S. population was churched. Adherence rates reached 56 percent by 1926. Since then the rate has been rather stable although inching upwards. By 1980 church adherence was about 62 percent." Finke and Stark, *The Churching of America*, 15.

59. Kosmin et al., *American Religious Identification Survey*, 8.

GRAPH 6.3 RATES OF RELIGIOUS ADHERENCE, 1776–1980

Rates of Religious Adherence, 1776-1980

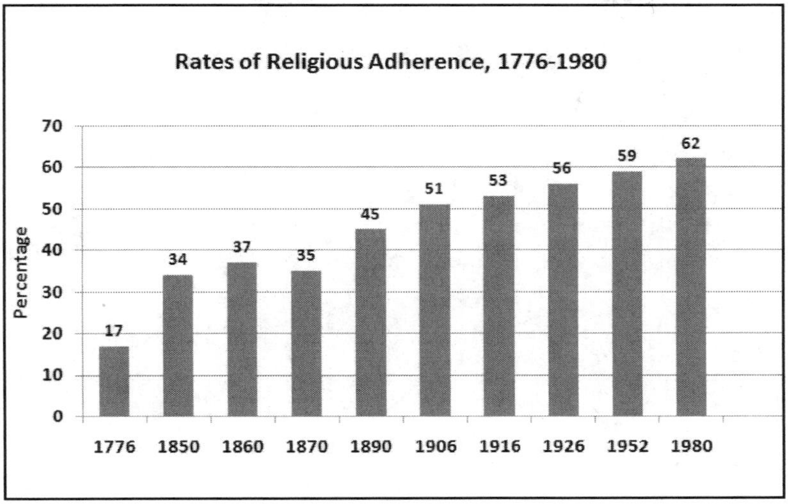

Source: *The Churching of America*[60]

Protestant denominations in the United States have grown in recent years, continuing an upward trend for evangelicals. Most historically mainstream and more traditional Protestant denominations have declined in attendance, with the exception of Baptist churches. Yount has found that "this slippage is not necessarily an indication of a permanent rejection of faith and practice, however, but of a shift favoring evangelical and Pentecostal churches, and nondenominational megachurches."[61] In other words, there has been a transfer of membership from mainline churches to younger and newer churches and denominations—unlike in Europe, where state churches maintained their numerical dominance. The smaller European denominations, such as the Baptist, Methodist, and Presbyterian churches, were instead the mainline churches in the United States. In 1776, three denominations—Congregational, Episcopal, and Presbyterian—represented 55 percent of all Americans.

Finke and Stark, citing the work of Ezra Stiles, describe the rise of one denomination and the fall of another in the United States from 1761 to 1860. Congregationalists in British America were seven million strong in 1761, while fewer than 400,000 were Baptists. A hundred

60. Finke and Stark, *The Churching of America*, 16.
61. Yount, *The Future of Christian Faith in America*, 28.

years later, in 1860, Congregationalists comprised fewer than 500,000 members while Baptists represented almost two million.[62] Hempton identifies the remarkable growth of other older mainline denominations from 1776 to 1850. Methodism began humbly in 1776, with only 2.5 percent of the populace being members, but went on to experience incredible growth by 1850 to 34.2 percent of the population—more than twice the number of Presbyterians, Congregationalists, and Episcopalians combined. During the 1840s, Methodist growth was fueled by 10,000 itinerant preachers and lay leaders.[63]

GRAPH 6.4 RELIGIOUS ADHERENTS BY DENOMINATION, 1776 AND 1850

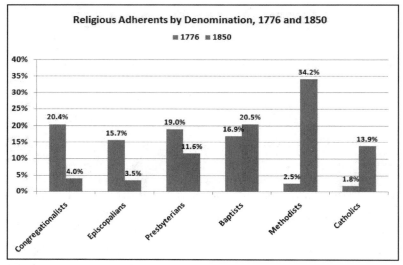

Source: The Churching of America[64]

Over the course of the eighteenth and nineteenth centuries, older mainline denominations declined as a result of their inability to overcome the social circumstances of their time, while the other denominations welcomed and benefited from the great awakenings and received substantial numbers of newcomers into their churches not by way of denominational legacy, but by the experience of conversion. Many newly arrived immigrants from Europe added to congre-

62. Finke and Stark, *The Churching of America*, 54.
63. Hempton, *The Religion of the People*, 9.
64. Finke and Stark, *The Churching of America*, 55.

gational numbers as well, especially among Catholics. Church growth through conversion led to phenomenal growth in the so-called minor denominations such as Methodists and Baptists, which later became mainline churches in the United States. In 1790, according to Mark Noll, only 10 percent of Americans professed to belong to such minor denominational churches, but this number grew very rapidly by means of camp meetings and revivals.[65] The growth of the Methodist church was most impressive. As Finke and Stark indicate, from 1776 to 1850, the denomination grew to more than 2.6 million members. Roughly one in three mainline churches was Methodist during this period; 13,302 Methodist churches were planted in just 74 years.[66]

Fishwick pinpoints, by 1900, 36 percent of Americans were Christians, and by 1940 and 1955, the numbers swelled to 49 and 60 percent, respectively.[67] After this dramatic growth, some decline followed. The 1960s was the decade worst for British religious decline as well as for mainline American churches, representing the first decade of overall church decline in American history. But while American Christianity is still flourishing—mainly evangelicalism, including fundamentalism—the European decline has not been reversed.

Dean M. Kelley of the National Council of Churches has documented the decline experienced by American mainline churches beginning in the late 1960s, including the American Baptist Convention, United Presbyterian Church USA, Presbyterian Church USA, United Methodist Church (including Evangelical United Brethren), Episcopal Church, and United Church of Christ.[68] Kelly graphs his findings and describes the plunge of membership in the sixties, saying the "strong upward curve weakens, falters, and tilts downward like a spent skyrocket."[69] At the same time, evangelical, Pentecostal, and fundamentalist churches began to increase after the decline of mainline churches.[70] Liberal theology and secularism are seen as

65. Noll, *The Scandal of the Evangelical Mind*, 63.

66. Finke and Stark, *The Churching of America*, 56.

67. Fishwick, *Great Awakenings*, 106–07.

68. Kelly asserts, "In the latter years of the 1960s, something remarkable happened in the United States: for the first time in the nation's history most of the major church groups stopped growing and began to shrink." Kelley, *Why Conservative Churches Are Growing*, 1–11.

69. Ibid., 2.

70. Fishwick, *Great Awakenings*, 1.

the main reasons for the decline. Three denominations—the United Church of Christ, United Methodist Church, and United Presbyterian Church—displayed the greatest loss of membership in the 1960s.[71] The most dramatic decline of white Protestant churches occurred in 1964; previous years showed a steady increase from 1952 through the early 1960s. After this decline, white Protestant church attendance never fully recovered.[72]

GRAPH 6.5 WHITE PROTESTANT CHURCH ATTENDANCE, 1952–1968

White Protestant Church Attendance, 1952–1968

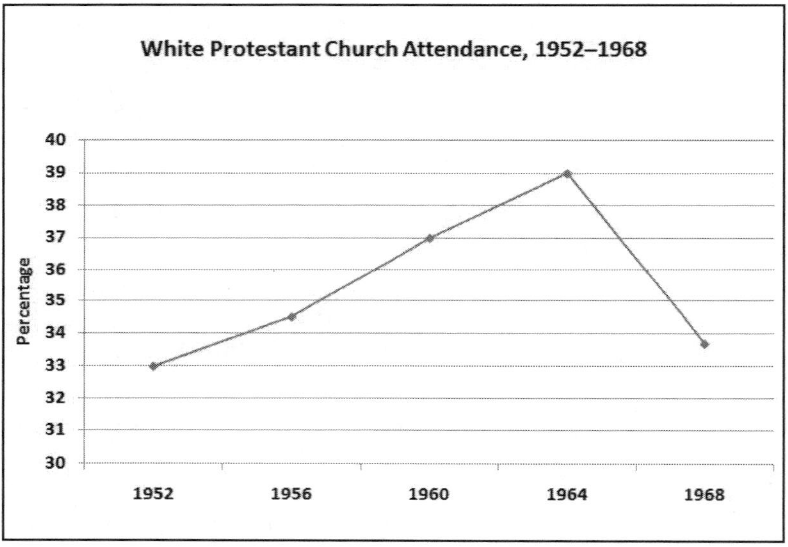

Source: "The Efficacy of Demographic Theories of Religious Change"[73]

Smaller and younger churches have been overtaking older mainline churches since 1776:

> Consider that the Church of God in Christ (3.7 million members) is already substantially larger than the United Church of Christ (1.7 million), the Presbyterian Church, USA (2.9 million), the Episcopal Church (2.4 million), and the American Baptist Churches in the U.S.A. (1.6 million). The Assemblies of God now number 2.2 million and the Churches of Christ enroll 1.6 million. As for the Latter-day Saints, their American

71. Hoge and Roozen, *Understanding Church Growth and Decline*, 17.

72. Roozen, "The Efficacy of Demographic Theories of Religious Change," 131–32.

73. Ibid., 132.

membership now trails only that of the Roman Catholics, Southern Baptists, United Methodists, and the newly merged Evangelical Lutheran Church in America.[74]

Despite significant efforts to reach the unchurched in the last decade of the twentieth century, the Episcopal Church saw a significant decline in membership. Yount points to "clashes over abortion, women priests, the ordination of gay clergy, and revisions of the prayer book and hymnal [which] are diversions from any church's agenda."[75]

Most mainline churches had been growing until 1960, as Edwin Scott Gaustad illustrates in his painstaking work *Historical Atlas of Religion in America*. From 1800 to 1960, "American religion presents for the most part, a picture of ruddy health: confident, vigorous, prolific, and on the move." He describes that the expansion of religion numerically and geographically as "dramatic" and "epic." Gaustad lists the five factors contributing to church growth: (1) the national occupation of the West in the nineteenth century with its religious revivals and numerous church plantings; (2) the second great awakening in the East, gaining many new converts through the efforts of Charles Finney, Dwight L. Moody, and Billy Graham; (3) westward immigration; (4) the rise of new religious groups; and (5) new measures of evangelism and religious freedom.[76] Other denominations enjoying growth during this century included the Southern Baptist Convention, Assemblies of God, Churches of God, Pentecostal and Holiness groups, and many other evangelicals. Other non-Christian religious groups also grew rapidly over the same period.[77] Until the mid-1960s, "the churches now called mainline Protestant tended to grow with every census or survey."[78] Liberal mainline churches declined in nineteenth and twentieth centuries.[79]

---

74. Finke and Stark, *The Churching of America*, 237.

75. Yount, *The Future of Christian Faith in America*, 33.

76. Gaustad, *Historical Atlas of Religion*, 37–55.

77. Ibid., 113–16.

78. Finke and Stark, *The Churching of America*, 247.

79. Ibid., 245–47.

TABLE 6.6 MAINLINE CHURCH MEMBERS, EVANGELICALS, AND
CATHOLICS PER 1,000 CHURCH MEMBERS, 1940–1985

Denomination	1940	1960	1985	Percentage loss or gain
Mainline				
United Methodist	124.7	93.0	64.3	−48
Presbyterian, USA	41.7	36.4	21.3	−49
Episcopal	30.9	28.6	19.2	−38
Christian (Disciples)	25.7	15.7	7.8	−70
United Church of Christ (Congregational)	26.5	19.6	11.8	−56
Evangelicals				
Southern Baptist	76.7	85.0	101.3	+32
Assemblies of God	3.1	4.4	14.6	+371
Church of the Nazarene	2.6	2.7	3.7	+42
Church of God (Cleveland, Tennessee)	1.0	1.5	3.6	+260
Roman Catholics	330.0	367.9	368.4	+12

Source: The Churching of America[80]

The main reason for the decline of mainline churches—including the Methodist, Congregationalist, Episcopalian, and Presbyterian churches—was their compromise with secular culture, a move made to appease adherents no longer content with existing church services.[81] This issue will be discussed further in the next chapter. After World War II, most churches increased in membership as "the American economy was growing rapidly and because the so-called baby boom was significantly adding to the population of young families who were joining the churches in record numbers."[82] Overall evangelical Protestants had been growing significantly in the nineteenth century up to the Second World War. Sectarian and New Religious Movements, like the New Age Movement, hippies, Mormons, and transcendent meditation (TM) made inroads into American society. Evangelicals

80. Ibid., 248.
81. Ibid., 246.
82. Wuthnow, The Crisis in the Churches, 5.

and fundamentalists increased political participation while membership of Protestant mainline denominations and Catholic churches
were declining. While immigration had been fueling church growth,
many immigrants were poor, making it difficult for them to support
their churches financially. Their offerings, Wuthnow says, were important "because the churches were an alternative to government—*free*
institutions that would not survive unless people supported them."[83]

Protestant denominational variety in America provided a religious marketplace where individuals could choose a church based
upon preference.[84] The lack of an official state church contributed
to the diversity of the religious marketplace, which is noticeable in
every aspect of American religious life. Robert Wuthnow comments, "Although they professed belief in the same Lord, Protestants
and Catholics were jealous competitors, and Lutherans, Baptists,
Methodists, and Presbyterians all struggled to keep their respective
denominations flourishing."[85] Rival churches and denominations
competed with one another in order to attract backsliders or dropouts
from other churches. Yount states that, "with doctrinal differences
less a matter of contention than in centuries past, the challenge is to
ensure that the individual faith of Americans is founded on more than
mere sentiment, that it transforms us, and that it compels us to serve
others."[86]

Even though mainline churches were declining in membership,
the reliability and integrity of many of the churches and Christian institutions did not diminish for another fifty years. Six in ten Americans
remained loyal to their denominations. Gallup and Lindsay reported
that "the church or organized religion has consistently ranked at the
top of the list of sixteen key American institutions." A majority of
American adults express more trust in Christian churches than in
other secular institutions.

A 1999 Gallup survey reported that people readily show respect
toward clergy members and ministers and think of them as highly
ethical and reliable people. Almost six in ten Americans valued the
"honesty and ethical standards" of clergy members or ministers as

83. Ibid., 10.
84. Yount, *The Future of Christian Faith in America*, 34.
85. Wuthnow, *The Crisis in the Churches*, 10–11.
86. Yount, *The Future of Christian Faith in America*, 34–35.

"very high or high."[87] Despite the high percentage of belief in God by Americans only a few Americans want to join the clergy. In one instance, the sharp decline of respect to the Catholic priest in the US in the recent decades shows that Americans have paid much less respect to clergy than in the past. Therefore, the 2009 Gallup survey reveals that number had dropped to 50 percent, the lowest in the 32 year period.[88]

GRAPH 6.6 RATINGS OF HONESTY AND ETHICS OF THE CLERGY

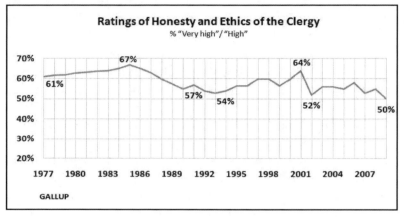

Source: *Gallup Survey 2011*[89]

According to the article posted on September 2011 titled "Americans have lost faith in religious leaders and church attendance" Professor Chaves indicated that Americans "between 1973 and 2008, the percentage of people with "great confidence" in religious leaders declined from 35 percent to less than 25 percent. He also found that two-thirds of Americans say they would prefer religious leaders to stay out of politics."[90] In many respects, Christianity in the United States remains quite strong. Polls have stated that the United States is one of

87. Gallup and Lindsay, *Surveying the Religious Landscape*, 120.

88. Jones, "U.S. Clergy, Bankers See New Lows in Honesty/Ethics Ratings," lines 3–10.

89. Newport, "More Than 9 in 10 Americans Continue to Believe in God," lines 1–10.

90. According to Chaves one of the elements that causing a loss of confidence in the clergy was the sex abuse scandal in the Roman Catholic Church in the Boston area in the early 2000s. Chaves, *Americans Have Lost Faith in Religious Leaders and Church Attendance*, lines 29–44.

the "most religiously committed nations of the world."[91] Even with the decline of mainline churches since 1960, emerging charismatic, independent, and Pentecostal churches have powerfully filled the gap.

PURITAN FOUNDATIONS IN CHRISTIAN AMERICA

An examination of the differences and similarities between European and North American Christianity will shed light on the reasons why secularization led to such dramatic declines of the church in Europe. Surveys and polls consistently find that American Christian beliefs and practices rank higher than Europe in all categories.

The Real Foundations of America

American Christian culture and tradition is rooted in the nation's Puritan heritage, a branch of the Reformation tradition that also revitalized evangelical Christianity and was reinvigorated by the Great Awakenings.[92] Not only the Puritans in New England, but also the Anglicans in early Virginia, Calvinists from the Netherlands who settled in New York and New Jersey, and the Scottish/Irish of Pennsylvania brought Reformed traditions to early British America.[93] Common beliefs included "salvation by faith, having only the Bible as the authoritative Word of God, not based upon the interpretation of the Catholic Church or Pope. Only such beliefs could be said to have been of the 'Puritan Reformation spirit.'"[94] Despite a shared Reformation spirit in the seventeenth century, Britain and the United States diverged as the American church was shaped by American democracy, Christian political idealism, Christian culture, and fervent missions.[95]

In the sixteenth and seventeenth centuries, the discovery of the New World, the counterreformation, and religious and international

91. Gallup and Lindsay, *Surveying the Religious Landscape*, 120.

92. Noll et al., *The Search for Christian America*, 28.

93. Woodbridge points out that early settlers used the principles articulated in Calvin's *Institutes of the Christian Religion*. The textbook used in William Ames's The Marrow of Theology class at Harvard proves this connection. Woodbridge et al., *The Gospel in America*, 23.

94. Ibid., 22–23.

95. Ibid., 23.

wars caused many Europeans to migrate to other places.[96] Even though the political framework had changed in many of the nations of Europe, state churches were still recognized as the only legitimate religious establishments. Smaller groups that disagreed with the established church and chose to break away became known as "the dissent," and were considered to be heretics or troublesome sectarians.

Over the course of the seventeenth century, the zeal of the dissenters had mostly burned out in Britain and Europe. "Many of the leading zealots had suffered martyrdom or exile and their remaining followers were either forced to accept the authority of the dominant churches or had been granted a modicum of toleration."[97] Religious minority groups, including the Huguenots, Puritans, and Quakers, sought havens of religious settlements in places such as Holland, England, and eventually the New World, where they were able to establish a majority presence around their respective settlements. As Labaree puts it, they "were able to organize a state church to suit themselves" in the New World America.[98]

Puritanism emerged in England in the early seventeenth century. The Puritans believed that their nation was God's ordained instrument for ushering in a fresh type of new light for the Christian faith during a dark time.[99] The term *puritan* originally was used pejoratively to refer to social eccentrics who ardently sought to purify the religious establishment. Later, it came to describe a much wider spectrum of pious religious activities.[100] Puritans held strict views not only on matters of religious piety, but also on social, economic, and political affairs, and later involved themselves in Parliament.[101] As mentioned in the previous chapters, after 1610, Puritan beliefs and values spread to broader audiences, including the gentry and the middle class of England.[102] Those who did not agree to conform to the Church of England were exiled to Holland in 1608 and resettled in the New World in America

---

96. Labaree, "The Conservative Attitude toward the Great Awakening," 332.

97. Ibid., 332.

98. Ibid., 332–33.

99. McLoughlin, *Revivals, Awakenings, and Reform*, 26.

100. Carden, *Puritan Christianity in America*, 21.

101. Ibid., 22.

102. McLoughlin, *Revivals, Awakenings, and Reform*, 28.

in 1620.[103] In 1625, when Charles I was enthroned, circumstances for the Puritans changed for the worse as the monarchy began to favor Anglo-Catholics.[104] More Puritans and dissenters emigrated to the New World, seeking and finding larger land areas along the East Coast with abundant natural resources and vast farmlands. Puritan colonists were not too numerous at first; their religious legacy and influence rather than their numbers had a long-lasting impact as further waves of migration followed.[105]

Today, the Puritan or Puritan-like church and Puritan ideal society have come to be known as the Puritan theocracy of the nation's first two hundred years of history.[106] Today's growing churches, including evangelical and Pentecostal churches, owe their beginnings to American Calvinistic Puritanism and pietism, which provided the fertile soil for the development of the nineteenth century revivals.[107] The early Puritan settlers gave shape to the essential American identity through their belief that they were given by God's providence a manifest destiny to construct this new nation for his kingdom. Mark Noll points out that this identity encouraged Americans to regard their nation as a moral example to the rest of the world, and as a place of "safe haven, big brother, world policeman, and exemplar of the democratic ideal of freedom and rights."[108]

Puritanism in New World

Puritans favored a congregational form of church governance—an autonomous church government formed by members, without any central hierarchal interference from official, denominational religious institutions or leaders. Carden indicates that this was a major reason for their break with the Church of England:

> The most puristic of the dissenters found this system preferable to any other but also found it unlikely to work in the existing Anglican Church. These dissenters, known as Brownists or Separatists, gave up on the Church of England, separated

103. Carden, *Puritan Christianity in America*, 24.

104. Ibid., 24.

105. Guder et al., *Missional Church*, 33.

106. Gallup Jr. and Lindsay, *Surveying the Religious Landscape,* 119.

107. Marsden, *Fundamentalism and American Culture*, 7.

108. Guder et al., *Missional Church*, 33.

themselves from it, and often worshiped in secret. It was such
a group, better known today as the Pilgrims, which founded
Plymouth in New England in 1620.[109]

The foundations of Puritanism were pure, biblical, evangelical
preaching and genuine piety. These characteristics provided a universal bond for Puritans in the New World, for both majority Anglicans
and minority dissenting groups.[110] Many religious dissenters who
were being alienated from their own countries settled in Pennsylvania,
Georgia, New England, and other colonies, where they enjoyed religious
freedom. Michel de Crévecoeur, renowned French visitor to America
in 1782, said, "If any new sect spring up in Europe, it may happen that
many of its professors will come and settle in America. As they bring
their zeal with them, they are at liberty to make converts."[111]

Puritanism has influenced generation after generation of
American life and thought. Johnson states, "Any inventory of the
elements that have gone into the making of the 'American mind'
would have to commence with Puritanism."[112] John Winthrop, the
first governor of Massachusetts Bay colony, drafted a religious, social,
and political covenant of Christian charity on board the ship bringing him over.[113] His ideas, delivered as sermons between April and
June of 1630, outlined a biblical theocracy that would establish a great
Christian society.[114] Winthrop declared, "We must consider that we
shall be a city upon a hill. The eyes of all people are upon us, so that if
we deal falsely with our God in this work we have undertaken, and so
cause Him to withdraw His present help from us, we shall be made a
story and a byword through the world."[115] Cotton Mather drew from
and further developed the idea of a new society. Sacvan Bercovitch
states that the early Puritans indeed founded and established "new

109. Carden, *Puritan Christianity in America*, 23.

110. Ibid., 23.

111. Quoted in Fishwick, *Great Awakenings*, xii.

112. Miller and Johnson, *The Puritans*, 1.

113. Noll et al., *The Search for Christian America*, 33.

114. Bercovitch describes this event as a covenant with God by the passengers of
the *Arbella*. They made a promise before God, and "He to them, to protect, assist, and
favor them above any other community on earth. But at their slightest shortcoming,
for neglecting the 'least' of their duties, He would turn in wrath against them and be
revenged." Bercovitch, *The American Jeremiad*, 3.

115. Yount, *The Future of Christian Faith in America*, 9.

promised land" set aside by God "for His new chosen people as the site for a new heaven and a new earth."[116]

The Puritan vision was to establish a society that would shine as "a city on a hill," "an elect nation," "a chosen people," and "God's New Israel."[117] Building such a society gave Puritans sound theological thoughts in the divergent contours of English society, putting their practice into action rationally and systematically through the influence of Presbyterian, Lutheran, and Reformed churches established in different parts of the New World. Smith points out that, despite the presence of religious diversity, Puritan theology was dominant in the churches of New England and also highly influential in the "Congregational, Presbyterian, Dutch Reformed, and Lutheran churches, as well as to some extent in many of the dissident groups, including the Baptists."[118] These ideas extended their reach, along with political idealism and democracy, across the country.[119] Noll and others portray the three centuries of Puritan influence as follows:

> At least partially for such reasons Puritan conceptions long remained major influences in America. In the most influential American churches Puritan categories were commonplace until the mid-nineteenth century. Except for a number of remarkable southern politicians, almost every prominent American thinker before World War I was either born in New England or educated there. As late as the early decades of the twentieth century, many American literary figures were still wrestling with the vestiges of the Puritan heritage. And even more pervasive than such influences on American ideas was the Puritan impact on American values. While Puritanism could not claim to have single-handedly shaped the American conscience, it certainly helped define its most distinctive traits.[120]

McLoughlin summarizes the difference between Christianity in America and Europe: "The millennial hopes of the colonialists, their pietistic perfectionism, their belief in further light and a higher law, their commitment to freedom of conscience and separation of church

---

116. Bercovitch, *The American Jeremiad*, 8–9.

117. Woodbridge et al., *The Gospel in America*, 125, 207.

118. LaHaye, *Faith of Our Founding Fathers*, 71.

119. Smith, "The Expansion of New England," 83–84.

120. Noll et al., *The Search for Christian America*, 29.

and state, and above all, their profound sense of individual piety made Americans different."[121]

Puritanism and Pietism

In Britain and in colonial America, Pietism influenced Protestants by stressing inner spiritual experience that worked itself out as a passion for lay-led missionary outreach. This movement created the environment for the revivals and awakenings that evangelized their regions and even other part of the world.[122] The revitalization movement sparked by Puritanism in the transatlantic region shook the traditional monopoly of church and state and ushered in "changes beyond the comprehension of the old structure." The revival "offered a new code of beliefs and values more harmonious with experiential needs. The Calvinistic was the necessary complement to the rise of bourgeois capitalism."[123] This is because the Calvinistic view is that occupation and work are a divine blessing by God. If Christians labor hard for profit and income they could contribute to the economic blessings and daily bread.

In the 1720s, John Wesley led the evangelistic revivals in Britain and America. Anton Wilhelm Boehm, the chaplain of Queen Anne's consort the Lutheran Prince George of Denmark, shared this spiritual enthusiasm through ties with Protestants of all denominations by translating the German writings of August Hermann Francke and certain works of German Pietists into English.[124] Once translated, Francke's writings made an impact in Britain and New England. Massachusetts Puritan minister Cotton Mather exchanged letters with Francke concerning fundamental Christian values and orthodox piety in uniting Christians to prepare for the second coming of Christ. Theologian and missionary Jonathan Edwards was aware of Francke's work as well.[125]

The high number of Europeans migrating to New England from 1701 to 1730 contributed to the rise of the awakening in the

---

121. McLoughlin, *Revivals, Awakenings, and Reform*, 26.
122. Pirouet, *Christianity Worldwide*, 2.
123. McLoughlin, *Revivals, Awakenings, and Reform*, 28.
124. Crawford, "Origins of the Eighteenth-Century Evangelical Revival," 383.
125. Ibid., 383–84.

New World during the Enlightenment.[126] Though rationalism reacted so vividly to the spiritual movements in different ways, Jonathan Edwards was called a man of spirituality and at the same time a man of rationality. In the 1720s, the Dutch Reformed Church of New York and many ministers in the mid-Atlantic colonies heard about Pietism in Germany. One of them, Theodore Frelinghuysen, was a gifted and ardent young preacher who challenged his congregation to a deeper inner spiritual experience.[127] Gilbert Tennent, another revivalist, both experienced and brought much spiritual awakening among Reformed churches. In the following decade, a series of revivals broke out predominantly in New England, including areas in and around Northampton, Massachusetts, stirred by the powerful sermons and charismatic personality of Jonathan Edwards.[128]

German pietism extensively spread Wesleyan revivals not only in Britain, but to an even greater extent in the New World, particularly in New England, through the influence of Philipp Jakob Spener and Augustus Hermann Francke. Before 1740, thousands of German Pietists migrated to America, particularly to Pennsylvania.[129] In England and New England, evangelical leaders advocated outreach to the common people with continental Europe's pietistic passion.[130] From Nova Scotia to Georgia, people experienced evangelical revivals.[131] By the mid-eighteenth century, formal and informal correspondence crisscrossed the Atlantic, leading to improvements in civil and legal welfare in the New World due to the easier availability in communication and making it possible to share revival news with likeminded believers.[132]

The transatlantic revivals correlated with the political crisis concerning Protestantism such as the persecution of Pietists in England and Europe. Puritans and Pietists sought a new religious haven moving away from the political and religious turmoil in their home lands.

---

126. Ibid., 363.

127. Mullin, "North America," 422–23.

128. Woodbridge et al., *The Gospel in America*, 139.

129. Labaree, "The Conservative Attitude toward the Great Awakening," 333.

130. Crawford, "Origins of the Eighteenth-Century Evangelical Revival," 379–80.

131. Mullin, "North America," 423.

132. O'Brien, "A Transatlantic Community of Saints," 815.

At the inception of the revivals, many had been longing for divine intervention in their individual, social, political, and religious lives because they were well aware that their faith was lukewarm. It is because after almost a hundred years after settling in the New World, the puritans had lost the original vision and purpose of establishing a Christian nation according to their founder's declaration. In Britain, the powerful message and the committed lifestyles of itinerant preachers met this desire for revival. Preachers presented the doctrines of regeneration, repentance, conversion, new life, and spiritual experiences through the Holy Spirit in their passionate advancement of the gospel. News spread quickly about the revivals, piquing interest in other regions. Transatlantic correspondence helped the movement to spread throughout Protestant denominations. Printed materials were used to pave the way for itinerant preachers by providing them critical information about the potential audiences so they could best prepare for the revival. Itinerant preachers also transmitted their exemplary preaching methods to other leaders, and soon local ministers and revivalists reproduced the same great results in their respective ministries.[133]

THE GREAT AWAKENINGS

Defining revivals and awakenings was attempted in the previous chapter. Looking at the historical events of the awakenings and revivals may be described differently at the hands of historians. Most people do not distinguish between revivals and awakenings because they view them as synonymous. In the author's views as indicated in the previous chapter, revivals are referred as more local and regional events in a country while awakenings are referred as events occurring between countries and continents. In this respect, Puritan movements in Britain and British America can be called Puritan Awakenings. The First and Second Awakenings occurred on both sides of the Atlantic. The New York prayer revivals influenced America and even Northern Ireland and some parts of Britain, yet the scale of impact was unlike the two awakenings. Numerous students and scholars of revivals and awakenings have labeled certain events as the Third and Fourth Great Awakenings but from the viewpoint of this book the Third and Fourth Awakenings will be referred to through the works of other specifically

133. Crawford, "Origins of the Eighteenth-Century Evangelical Revival," 388.

mentioned authors. However, there are no awakenings that can compare to the First and Second Awakenings and their cross-continental impact over societies, individuals, and norms.

The First Great Awakening

The Puritans, who laid the foundation of American Christian identity, as well as the Pietists, espoused religious reformation, but did not seek political change. Later on, however, those involved in the Great Awakenings advocated sociopolitical change as well as an outgrowth of their spiritual experience of personal salvation.[134] As new religious traditions arose from the Great Awakening, divisions appeared among the Puritans—groups known as the Old Lights and New Lights. The Old Lights opposed the Awakening while the New Lights embraced it and later became known as evangelicals. The New Lights encouraged their followers to repent, put their faith in Jesus Christ, and become active in purifying their churches through a call to regeneration and conversion. Old Lights were greatly alarmed about the possible disintegration of traditional Puritan New England society.[135] There were also divisions among the New Lights themselves. Some wanted to completely reshape all traditional churches. Others were more moderate and sought revivals within existing religious establishments; one example is Jonathan Edwards. Still others were traditional Calvinists who valued the movement, but were also afraid that it undermined their establishments. Some Old Lights separated themselves completely from any hints of the Great Awakening.[136]

In addition to shared cultural and religious traditions of Puritanism and Pietism, England and New England were influenced in the same way by the rationalism of the Enlightenment, making the intellectual and cultural starting points of evangelical revivals in these two nations very similar. The revivals that swept over Britain were not confined to one place and did not originate with one single person, but encompassed the Calvinist Methodists, Anglican evangelicals, nonconformists in England, and active revivalists in the Church of Scotland.[137] Revival in other European nations, such as Holland and

134. Noll et al. *The Search for Christian America*, 125.
135. Ibid., 60.
136. Ibid., 59–60.
137. Calvinistic Methodists are mostly coming from the Presbyterian Church

Scandinavia, was shared by their kindred in New England and the mid-Atlantic colonies as well.

The tremendous impact of the Great Awakening in the British colonies was also felt in the British Isles.[138] International connections between England and New England developed into a "close-knit communal life and mutual dependence" which was a means of trans-Atlantic communication.[139] Labaree describes the environment before the Awakenings as follows:

> But broadly speaking, religion and religious differences were no longer the vital factors they had been; religious fervor became the exception rather than the rule. Great preachers no longer trumpeted a call to crusade for the faith, and when lesser men tried to sound the clarion, they were seldom heard above the chorus of more secular appeals to interest and attention. Among the churches of both Europe and America, self-complacency tended to supplant inquiry after truth; in religious observance, habit succeeded spirituality; and among worshippers, apathy too often replaced self-sacrifice and zeal. Protestant Christianity seemed to have lost its militant spirit; worldliness and indifference had crept in to corrupt, if not destroy, the true essence of Christian faith.[140]

During the second quarter of the eighteenth century, the evangelical revivals in England and Great Awakenings of New England both benefited from a transatlantic exchange that strengthened both movements. While there was only a limited dependency of social structure and systems between New England and England, there were many social similarities: quest for better land, economic changes, and upward social mobility.[141]

---

from Wales. It is a unique denomination of the Presbyterian order originating from Wales yet is Calvinistic in theology.

138. O'Brien, "A Transatlantic Community of Saints," 816.

139. As individuals lost some of the security of traditional paternalistic society, they were forced to become more self-reliant, self-disciplined, and individualistic. People found themselves economically more competitive while continuing to believe in the more cooperative ideals of the past. The perception of the disjunction of behavior and values created psychological tension. Crawford, "Origins of the Eighteenth-Century Evangelical Revival," 369.

140. Labaree, "The Conservative Attitude toward the Great Awakening," 332–33.

141. Crawford, "Origins of the Eighteenth-Century Evangelical Revival," 368.

Not only were these men reacting to the same rationalist currents of thought that threatened the bases of belief in orthodox Protestant Christianity, building on the same Puritan-Pietist cultural tradition and being influenced by the same contemporary Pietist movements from the European continent, but they also were directly influencing each other through their writings, correspondence, and personal contacts.[142]

At the same time, piety was resurging among the oppressed Protestants of Central Europe. Contact between Central European Pietists, British, and Americans increased dramatically in the 1730s, due largely to the evangelical preachers frequently ministering in the Church of England. Many Central Europeans converted in the middle and late 1730s, appearing as a portent that God intended to revive piety in Britain and America as well. As the moral crisis in Europe grew increasingly grave, seizing the revival opportunity appeared all the more pressing and as a must for the society and individuals alike.[143] During the 1720s, Pietism had been introduced in Central Europe by Theodore Frelinghuysen, who acknowledged the experiential dimensions of the Christian faith rather than formalism. He began to minister to the Dutch Reformed church in Raritan, New Jersey, with the same Pietist approach: "as he warned his parishioners with increasingly pointed language that formal religiosity by itself would not save them from the wrath to come, his preaching created a stir. He called upon his people to seek a warmhearted relationship with God rather than a cold alliance."[144] Such a spiritual challenge to parishioners paved the way for another greater revival movement, this time by his close neighbor and Presbyterian minister Gilbert Tennent of New Brunswick, who had advocated repentance and regeneration not only in his church, but also to the entire surrounding region.[145]

Most of the people affected by the revivals on both sides of the Atlantic lived in close-knit agricultural communities.[146] The majority were either peasants or the disinherited who banded together in rural areas or lived in urban enclaves of outcasts. Crawford points

142. Ibid., 386–87.
143. Ibid., 393–94.
144. Woodbridge et al., *The Gospel in America*, 28.
145. Ibid., 28.
146. Crawford, "Origins of the Eighteenth-Century Evangelical Revival," 363.

out that they were "slaves, servants, and the impoverished."[147] The revivals brought a renewed sense of optimism to this community. Doctrines focused on repentance, forgiveness of sin, regeneration, holy life, salvation by faith, and experiential Christian life with God. Large religious gatherings featured "itinerant preachers; lay exhorters; open and communal expression of emotion, sometimes companied by convulsions and faintings; religious societies for pious consultation, prayer, and psalm singing; and mass conversions."[148] Revivalists such as George Whitefield, Jonathan Edwards, John Wesley, Charles Finney, and D.L. Moody furthered the movement.[149] Prior to the early eighteenth century, revivals were regional or local, but in the 1730s, the phenomenon became international.[150]

In addition to the movement's well-known leaders, the awakenings of the 1730s had a strong lay leadership component. Using similar worship styles, messages, and revival methods, lay leaders appealed to emotion in order to capture the hearts and attention of ordinary citizens.[151] The awareness of sinfulness and eagerness for spiritual renewal among the people provided a great conduit for the revival.[152] Prayer meetings, Bible reading, and personal exhortation services during the week were regularly conducted, beginning in Northampton with Jonathan Edwards. Consequently, the gospel of Jesus reached out to convert and transform the "the downtrodden and the despised."[153]

Much like that of John Wesley, the dramatic conversion experience of Edwards during his time at Yale College compelled him to preach individual repentance, regeneration, and the confession of sins. As a result of his stirring messages, a great number of people were converted.[154] This type of genuine conversion consistently produced

147. Ibid., 370.

148. Ibid., 363–64.

149. Hambrick-Stowe, *Charles G. Finney and the Spirit of American Evangelicalism,* 228–29.

150. Crawford, "Origins of the Eighteenth-Century Evangelical Revival," 397.

151. Ibid., 375–76.

152. Ibid., 365.

153. Edwards succeeded pastorate from grandfather Solomon Stoddard in a Congregational church in Northampton, Massachusetts. Noll et al., *The Search for Christian America,* 52.

154. According to Dobson and others point out, "He stated that there entered his soul 'a sense of the glory of the divine being' while he was reading the Pauline ascrip-

through Edwards's ministry in the Connecticut Valley grew to become a major regional awakening from 1734 to 1735. This movement further intensified the success of revivals in Britain and America during the late 1730s via correspondence, itinerant preaching, and the easy availability of printed materials such as evangelical magazines, sermons, and journals.[155] In 1737, Edwards published *A Faithful Narrative of the Surprising Work of God in the Conversion of Many Hundred Souls*, relating the Connecticut Valley Awakening of 1734–1735. The book was printed in Britain by Isaac Watts and dissenting minister John Guyse. John Wesley read the book in 1738 and from then on greatly longed for a similar revival in Britain.[156]

The similarities among the revivals of 1735 to 1750 within Congregationalism in New England, evangelicalism in England, the Reformed Church in New York and New Jersey, and Presbyterianism and the Cambuslang Work in Scotland have been identified and seen as evidence of the leading of the Holy Spirit.[157] The movement is known as the First Great Awakening. These traditions shared the Westminster Confession as their standard statement of faith and expressed the same degree of interest in spiritual revivals and awakenings. It is no surprise that Edwards communicated with his friends in Scotland frequently. Transatlantic correspondence among ministers about theological questions, the nature of piety, and the various practices of revival were common. O'Brien states that correspondence included "The circulation of devotional literature, recommendations for suitable reading, the collection of money for missionary work, and the provision of hospitality."[158] George Whitefield and John Wesley often visited the thirteen colonies to stoke the flames of revival across the ocean. O'Brien continues, "Once in place, the contacts proved useful to the ministers in other ways."[159]

The influence of brothers Robert and James Alexander Haldane in Scotland and continental Europe is also noteworthy. Thomas and

tion: 'Now unto the King eternal, immortal, invisible, the only wise God, be honour and glory for ever and ever. Amen' (1 Tim. 1:17)." Dobson et al., *The Fundamentalist Phenomenon*, 33.

155. Crawford, "Origins of the Eighteenth-Century Evangelical Revival," 397.
156. Ibid., 386–87.
157. O'Brien, "A Transatlantic Community of Saints," 811.
158. Ibid., 811.
159. Ibid., 813.

Alexander Campbell greatly contributed to revival in different areas of the British colonies in America, and Howell Harris was prominent in Wales.[160] For the most part, the Great Awakenings in America developed a new and vital type of Christianity while mainstream Christianity in Europe was languishing. Several national catastrophes struck American communities in 1739 and 1740 which, as Crawford points out, created even more urgency for revival: "[from] epidemics of diphtheria and scarlet fever that struck down thousands in New England, New York, and New Jersey during the latter half of the 1730s, to the sudden curtailment of paper money in Massachusetts in 1739, and to the outbreak of war with Spain that same year, events . . . aggravated anxiety and increased desire for religious solace."[161]

According to McLoughlin, "the cultural system during the Great Awakenings needed to be transformed in order to overcome jarring disjunctions between norms and experience, old beliefs and new realities, dying patterns and emerging patterns of behavior."[162] While this was happening in America, Europe's piety was diminishing. Revivalists and itinerant preachers in New England continued to focus on Reformation principles including justification by faith alone and the individual conversion experience. These values had been stressed by sixteenth century Puritanism, but spiritual coldness had grown over the years in American society and churches. However, a foundation of Reformation piety remained in preparation for great awakenings to come.[163] McLoughlin highlights the positive aspects of these times of transformation: "Great awakenings are not periods of social neurosis (though they begin in times of cultural confusion). They are times of revitalization. They are therapeutic and cathartic, not pathological."[164] The downfall of the Puritan ideal of a pure American Christianity led first to religious despair, and then to hope for a new revival.[165]

---

160. Latourette, *A History of Christianity*, 1022.

161. Crawford, "Origins of the Eighteenth-Century Evangelical Revival," 387–88.

162. McLoughlin, *Revivals, Awakenings, and Reform*, 11.

163. Crawford, "Origins of the Eighteenth-Century Evangelical Revival," 373–74.

164. McLoughlin, *Revivals, Awakenings, and Reform*, 2.

165. Although "a Puritan conception of society" based on tied collaboration of church and state was not refereed to as evil, American Christians understood that a monopoly of church and state by the Puritans had its detriments. Noll et al., *The Search for Christian America*, 60.

The Great Awakening in 1740 created a spirit of American independence and patriotism from Great Britain as well as a spirit of
freedom in Christ from religious or political tyranny.[166] In this respect,
the Great Awakenings and the American Revolution can be labeled
the two most significant events in American history. The revival
movement created space in the hearts and minds of Americans for
the Christian ideal of forming a new nation that would advance the
kingdom of God. According to John Price:

> The history of God's relationship with America is truly remark-
> able. Our Lord has intimately involved himself in our nation's
> history and thus has been instrumental in the establishment
> and growth of a free and vibrant country. America has expe-
> rienced four major, national revivals or awakenings . . . .God
> used the national repentance to turn his Body of believers back
> to him so that he could strengthen them for a coming, major
> national trial or difficulty. Finally, God used each of the four
> instances of national repentance to open wide the eyes and
> hearts of his people, who then took affirmative action to alter
> the social conditions of their time.[167]

The early settlement in the New World during the seventeenth
century had created not only British colonies, but also the first dissent Christian communities, including those of Quakers, Baptists,
Congregationalists, and Puritans. Starting in the middle of eighteenth
century, awakenings took place about every fifty years to revitalize the
faith. The first awakening led to the "creation of the American republic
[which] led to the solidification of the Union and the rise of Jacksonian
participatory democracy."[168] George Whitefield and Jonathan Edwards
led the people toward a personal conversion to Jesus Christ through

166. Ibid., 49.

167. Price, *America at the Crossroads*, 184.

168. McLoughlin notes the same parallels between the awakenings and political
developments. The "colonialists, after the First Awakening, first defeated the French
and Indians and then threw off the corrupt king and Parliament. The Americans,
after the Second Awakening, first eliminated the Indians and Mexicans and British
from the West and then attacked those who would secede from the covenant in
order to uphold black slavery. At the height of their Third Awakening, Americans
stopped attacking big business and turned against 'the Hun' to save the world for
democracy; the war against Nazism was simply a continuation of that effort. From
our Fourth Great Awakening we may expect a similar crusade, unless the new light
of this revitalization drastically alters the millenarian concept of manifest destiny."
McLoughlin, *Revivals, Awakenings, and Reform*, 11.

several massive gatherings where the spirit of Puritanism was revitalized among Congregationalists, Presbyterians, and others located around the eastern seaboard, mainly New England. The Methodists emerged and began to establish themselves in the South. The second awakening then was kindled on the frontier and engrossed the West through camp meetings and itinerant preaching, led by Francis Asbury. "A host of poorly educated preachers, black and white, were involved," according to Fishwick, who further points out that this awakening, "like almost everything else, was changed forever by the Civil War."[169] A new revival, different from the second awakening, emerged under the leadership of preacher Charles Finney, who brought the movement out of the rural frontier and into cities, including New York and the New England area. In addition, D.L. Moody led a powerful and experiential Christianity that formed in the new urban, industrial America, resulting in the birth of the Holiness Movement.

I personally believe there were two Great Awakenings in American history. However, McLoughlin believes that there were four. My understanding is that the first awakening included the time period of Jonathan Edwards (early to mid-eighteenth century), and the second awakening encompassed the time periods of James McGready and Timothy Dwight (late eighteenth to early nineteenth century). McLoughlin categorizes the Holiness revival as the third awakening and the fourth as having begun with the Jesus Movement. Though I do not personally agree with him, McLoughlin believes the "Third Awakening led to the rejection of unregulated capitalistic exploitation and the beginning of the welfare state; and our Fourth Awakening appears headed toward a rejection of unregulated exploitation of humankind and of nature and toward a series of regional and international consortiums for the conservation and optional use of the world's resources."[170] The third awakening occurred during a massive influx of immigrants from non-Protestant European countries such as Ireland, Italy, and nations in eastern and southern Europe. This awakening, Fishwick points out, "leveled off during the McKinley era and the Spanish-American War."[171]

169. Fishwick, *Great Awakenings*, 2–3.
170. McLoughlin, *Revivals, Awakenings, and Reform*, 11.
171. Fishwick, *Great Awakenings*, 3.

The great awakenings played a large role in confronting America's developing social problems that were brought about by the revolution and expansion of society, including civil strife, immigration, and industrialization. These profound social changes caused many to long for healing and spiritual revival.[172] The Puritan idea of a unified society in New England was no longer seen as viable; the great awakenings ended expectations for a Puritan society and state. Revivalists of this period did not intend to replace Puritan ideals, but focused instead on the spiritual vitality of believers. As a consequence they took up Puritan social idealism and values for themselves in order to focus on the spiritual movement.[173] During and following the Great Awakenings, Puritanism declined due to changes that established Christian society according to the biblical vision of kingdom of God for society had already departed from that vision for a hundred years. Therefore, renewal movements sought the outpouring of the Holy Spirit in order for the Congregationalists, Reformed church members, and Presbyterians to experience different spiritual dynamics and a new conversion experience. McLoughlin finds that the awakenings "revitalized the Baptists, Methodists, Campbellites, Disciple of Christ, and Progressive, Liberal Protestants."[174]

Beginnings of Revival

It is helpful to investigate the specific reasons for the onset of revival and awakening movements in England and New England, particularly in the 1730s and 1740s. During this time, rational and philosophical questions were calling into question traditional Christian beliefs and doctrine as well as on the authority of the Bible in Protestant countries. At the same time, the Catholic Church was making advances in the heartland of Protestantism.

The real beginning of the Methodist revival can be dated to "the devotional religious societies in the 1670s in London," which prepared the way for the revival of the 1730s: "London and Bristol supplied a framework for colonization by the Moravians, Whitefield, and the Wesleys."[175] British and American citizens reacted more strongly than

172. Gaustad, *A Religious History of America*, 228.
173. Noll et al., *The Search for Christian America*, 60–61.
174. McLoughlin, *Revivals, Awakenings, and Reform*, 22.
175. Rack, "Survival and Revival," 2–3.

did other Europeans to the evangelical messages of the revivalists and itinerant preachers. The Protestants of these two nations vigilantly guarded their hearts and honored key Christian doctrines including repentance, new birth, forgiveness, holy life, and hope in Christ, in contrast to those whose religious life was dry and formal, based in religious institutions that did not satisfy spiritual hunger or speak to the anxious hearts of believers. Revival presented an open door "for anxious persons [to] reaffirm their attachment to the ideal and to rediscover some of the reassurance of the tightly knit, loving, Christian community, despite changed circumstances" in the transatlantic region, especially for Britain and North America.[176] In other words, the great awakening in the United States paved the way for rekindling a sense of harmony and unity, for the nation again to be considered a cohesive unit, and for the people to feel free within their land.[177]

On either side of the Atlantic, few had a greater impact than George Whitefield, considered one of the greatest preachers not only of the eighteenth century, but all of Christian history. He began his work in Britain and eventually traveled to America with his powerful campaigns. After his conversion experience in the spring of 1735, he made his initial evangelistic journey while a student at Oxford. Previously, a revival had taken place in Rowland, Wales, in 1734 and 1735, leaving participants with a strong conviction of sin. Almost simultaneously, the great awakening was sparked by Jonathan Edwards in Northampton, Massachusetts.[178] The most vigorous stage of the great awakening in the thirteen colonies was ushered in by Whitefield, who continued to visit the region from 1739 until his death in 1770. His zeal for traveling caused the revival movement to spread widely.[179] Through itinerant preaching, Whitefield saw great success in the British colonies in 1739 and 1740.[180]

After his conversion (which occurred some years before the Wesleys'), Whitefield visited colonial Georgia for first time as a missionary commissioned by the Society for the Propagation of the

---

176. Crawford, "Origins of the Eighteenth-Century Evangelical Revival," 374–75.

177. McLoughlin, *Revivals, Awakenings, and Reform*, 1.

178. Bebbington, *Evangelicalism in Modern Britain*, 20.

179. O'Brien, "A Transatlantic Community of Saints," 816–17.

180. Whitefield discovered a revival already set in motion when he landed in the British colonies in 1738. Bebbington, *Evangelicalism in Modern Britain*, 20–21.

Gospel.[181] He had intended to conduct a few itinerant preaching tours to raise funds for Protestant refugees from Salzburg as well as for an orphanage. However, his preaching had a formidable evangelistic impact wherever he went, touching the spiritually hungry and inspiring sinners to turn to Christ for forgiveness.[182] Whitefield's dramatic rhetoric drew large audiences from Georgia to Maine. He emphasized repentance from personal sin, spiritual rebirth, and salvation in a desire to awaken those who belonged to established churches but lived a superficial Christian life.[183] In the winter of 1740, Jonathan Edwards welcomed Whitefield to New England, where revival had been sparked by Edwards in 1734 and reached its zenith through Whitefield's ministry in 1742. This revival continued all the way up to the Revolutionary War.[184]

The public response to Whitefield and other revivalists was enormous. Audiences were counted in the hundreds, thousands, and, at times, more than thirty thousand, such as at a gathering on Boston Common.[185] His evangelistic campaigns were not limited to any single denomination, but were always interdenominational, gaining the nickname "New Light" or "New Side." Labaree states, "To many men the revival seemed not merely an awakening but something approaching a religious revolution as well."[186] However, Whitefield was extremely critical of the unspiritual clergy and professed church leaders. As he visited Harvard and Yale, he stated that these places exemplified the phrase "Light is become darkness." Although hundreds repented and became regenerated in the places where Whitefield preached, many local clergy maintained a dry legalism.[187] Non-Anglicans, such as the Congregationalists and Presbyterians of New England, were astonished to hear about the salvation ushered in through Whitefield, an Anglican minister. This effectively erased hostility toward the Church of England, which had been pervasive in the northern colonies.

181. Ditchfield, *The Evangelical Revival*, 59.

182. Labaree, "The Conservative Attitude toward the Great Awakening," 333–34.

183. McLoughlin, *Revivals, Awakenings, and Reform*, 61.

184. The continuation of the revival depended on its acceptance or rejection by established clergy. Dobson et al., *The Fundamentalist Phenomenon*, 33–34.

185. Mullin, "North America," 423.

186. Labaree, "The Conservative Attitude toward the Great Awakening," 334–35.

187. Finke and Stark, *The Churching of America*, 51.

Crawford mentions that the revival meeting in Boston came about when many prominent leaders[188] gathered and took the requisite action that New England might have a share in the Revival under way elsewhere: they invited Whitefield to visit New England."[189]

In due course, Whitefield went not only to the principal cities and towns in the British Isles, but also to Georgia, Philadelphia, New York, New Jersey, and New England. He opened the way for the great awakening to grow into a transatlantic, regional, and urban revival phenomenon through his constant correspondence with his friends.[190] Friends such as Jonathan Edwards, Theodore Jacbous Frelinghuysen, the Gilbert Tennent, and many others were influenced by Whitefield's example, as Labarre points out, "many of them making up for what they lacked of his eloquence and personal magnetism by carrying to extremes their emotional appeal and their attack on hostile critics."[191] Connections made by Whitefield as he traveled influenced many friends and leaders who further spread the revival. Impressions of the revivals and meetings were recorded in his journals and letters sent to hundreds of other revivalists, ministers, and laypeople.[192]

O'Brien points out that, in addition to Whitefield, ministers who generated correspondence included "[Benjamin] Colman, and Thomas Prince, Sr., of New England; James Robe, William McCulloch, John M'Laurin, and John Erskine of Scotland; and English ministers Watts" and Doddridge. Interconnecting them with one another through correspondence helped them become a "close-knit group. . . . The contacts between the Scottish revivalists and their American counterparts are the most impressive set of bilateral relations in the revival, since they did not rely on any single figure and involved some relatively obscure individuals."[193]

---

188. These leaders were Benjamin Colman, William Cooper, Thomas Foxcroft, and Thomas Prince who were prominent Boston area preachers in the late 1600s and early 1700s. Thomas Prince was a prominent clergyman and historian who completed the comprehensive. Prince and Hale, *A Chronological History of New England.* xv-xvi, xiv-xv.

189. Crawford, "Origins of the Eighteenth-Century Evangelical Revival," 392–93.

190. Carwardine, "The Second Great Awakening in the Urban Centers," 328.

191. Labaree, "The Conservative Attitude toward the Great Awakening," 333–34.

192. O'Brien, "A Transatlantic Community of Saints," 816–17.

193. Ibid., 819.

Whitefield kept in touch with others who truly understood his revival movement, including ministers, lay evangelists, financial backers, and printers such as John Lewis and Howell Harris in Wales, Samuel Mason in London, Daniel Henchman in Boston, Thomas Noble in New York, Samuel Hazard in Philadelphia, and Ann Dutton in Huntingdonshire, England.[194] "He had crossed the Atlantic thirteen times in the course of a thirty-three-year career in which he preached, on the average, eight or nine times a week (a total of over 15,000 occasions)."[195] John Gillies's 1754 two-volume "Historical Collection of Accounts of Revival" published and characterized "the eighteenth-century revival as broad and sweeping, careless of national and church boundaries, and evangelical in character."[196] For instance, Whitefield befriended Gilbert Tennent in New Jersey in 1739 as well as Jonathan Edwards in 1740. Crawford notes that, "through friendships, corre-spondence, the exchange of pamphlets, and the printing of news of the revivals in religious periodicals in London, Glasgow, Edinburgh, and Boston, the revivalists influenced, encouraged, and taught one another and united the revival movements throughout the British Empire."[197]

This great awakening is known as the Frontier Revival. It origi-nated primarily in rural New England and was brought to the next level Jonathan Edwards through his book *A Faithful Narrative of the Surprising Work of God* and several evangelistic campaigns. The book made an impression on John Wesley by assuring him of Christ's aton-ing sacrifice; later, Wesley embarked on an itinerant preaching min-istry in the same manner as Whitefield. Noll believes that Jonathan Edwards is rightly considered the "greatest evangelical mind in America in large measure because his thought was driven by the pro-

194. Ibid., 819–20.

195. His transatlantic preaching travels included seven journeys to America and fourteen to Scotland. Noll et al., *The Search for Christian America*, 48.

196. John Gillies said, "the world is still sleeping "its sleep of death." It has been a slumber of many generations; -sometimes deeper, sometimes lighter,-yet still a slumber like that of the tomb, as if destined to continue till the last trumpet sound; and then there shall be no more sleep." Gillies states that the revival came out of the state of death and slumber. The wake up call from the outpouring of the Holy Spirit transformed thousands of souls to come to Jesus Christ. Bob Jones University, "John Gillies' Historical Collections of Accounts of Revival," lines 8–13. Cf. O'Brien, "A Transatlantic Community of Saints," 814.

197. Crawford, "Origins of the Eighteenth-Century Evangelical Revival," 386–87.

foundest truths of evangelical Protestantism."[198] Initially, the revival was local in scale, but it grew to have great repercussions throughout New England. Isaac Watts, a British hymn composer, comments that "never did we hear or read, since the first ages of Christianity, [of] any event of this kind so surprising as the present narrative has set before us."[199] Edwards's ministry launched soul-winning campaigns from his church to others and spurred new types of spiritual awakenings in 1734 and 1735.[200] Almost twenty years later, continuous regional revivals and awakenings arose in England between 1761 and 1763, and then in New England in 1763 and 1764,[201] followed by another awakening in Virginia between 1775 and 1776.[202]

The Second Great Awakening

After the First Awakening swept over many regions in North America, institutional and denominational churches were weakened and the influence of mainline denominations, primarily the Congregational church, was reduced (including in its position as the official church of New England). On the other hand, the emerging Methodist Church and existing Baptist churches grew dramatically with an influx of converts from the Second Awakening in the early nineteenth century.

The Second Great Awakening reshaped American religious life in many ways. Its style, forms of worship, and manifestations were different from those of the first awakening. Gatherings were not limited to traditional church buildings, but were held in "open fields, crude cabins, neoclassical churches, and remodeled theatres."[203] Some revivals were unplanned while others were thoroughly planned and promoted. According to Gaustad, "Some were characterized by emotional excesses (fainting, shouting, jumping), while others were sober and restrained. Some occurred under the leadership of a spectacular

---

198. Noll, *The Scandal of the Evangelical Mind*, 60.

199. Quoted in Mullin, "North America," 423.

200. The Congregational church in Northampton in which Jonathan Edwards then ministered gained approximately three hundred converts through his evangelistic efforts in neighboring towns. Woodbridge et al., *The Gospel in America*, 139–40.

201. Riss, *A Survey of 20th-Century Revival Movements*, 11.

202. Riis portrays this awakening as "the greatest revival of religion he had ever seen." Ibid., 11–12.

203. Gaustad, *A Religious History of America*, 150.

itinerant evangelist, while others emerged from a quiet countryside."[204] This phase of revivalism, Hammond points out, was considered the "voluntary church syndrome," characterized by "religious freedom, the competitiveness and commercialization of religious organizations and the privatization of faith. . . . Though not uniquely Protestant, this voluntary church syndrome was felt first and most deeply in Protestantism."[205]

The First Great Awakening initiated the repentance and regeneration movement, and the Second Great Awakening resulted in the unparalleled growth of many denominations, which also reflected demographic changes during this time. In 1800, the early phase of the Second Great Awakening, Marty notes that rural citizens outnumbered the urban population in a ratio of 15 to 1. At the start of the 1830s, that had diminished to 10.5 to 1. In 1820, the population of the country was 9.6 million; by 1860, it had grown to more than 31 million. "America did not yet look crowded to the people of the 1860s—the frontier appeared to be limitless. But citizens and especially immigrants had begun to converge on the burgeoning cities."[206] Demographic changes helped to bring growth to the Methodist Church, the most successful religious movement of the Second Great Awakening in the United States. Led by Francis Asbury and Peter Cartwright, the Methodist Church went from 15,000 followers in 1784 to just under one million in 1830; it became the largest denomination in the country by 1844.[207] "The Baptists doubled in number from 1802 until 1812 and the Presbyterians grew from 18,000 in 1807 to almost 250,000 in 1835. That this growth was not due to immigration is evident in view of the British interference with European migrations into North America during the Napoleonic wars until 1815."[208]

A significant revival occurred in 1787 at Hampden-Sydney College, which became the center of a "great interdenominational awakening which marked the final triumph of evangelical Christianity

204. Ibid., 149–50.

205. Hammond, *The Protestant Presence in Twentieth-Century America*, 43–44.

206. Marty, *The Modern Schism*, 118. By the middle of the century, that ratio decreased to 5 to 1.

207. Dobson et al., *The Fundamentalist Phenomenon*, 36.

208. Riss, *A Survey of 20th-Century Revival Movements in North America*, 14.

in Virginia."[209] The awakening began under college President John Blair Smith and later spread to New England, the mid-Atlantic states, the South, and the frontier under leaders such as Timothy Dwight (who was the president of Yale College and the grandson of Jonathan Edwards) and frontier revivalists such as James McGready and W. Barton Stone.[210] McGready, a Presbyterian revivalist, led frontier camp meetings in Kentucky and Tennessee.[211] In 1796, Dwight gave the baccalaureate sermon "The Nature and Danger of Infidel Philosophy," which became an archetype of student involvement and brought revival to a great number of students at Yale. The Second Great Awakening promoted national unity through the founding of voluntary nationwide societies, mission agencies, Bible societies, and temperance and anti-slavery movements.

In 1802, the awakening gained enough ground that "one-third of the students turned from the infidelity that formerly reigned throughout the entire student body due to influence of the French Enlightenment."[212] This revival generated new phenomena such as communitarianism, millenarianism, ministries led by lay leadership, revival advocacy, evangelists, and secessions from the mainline denominations. Particularly from 1787 to 1830, campus revivalism spread as many revivalists emphasized the need for Christian education and founded more than six hundred colleges to train the next generation for God's work and mission.[213] In 1808, for instance, Andover Theological Seminary (now known as Andover Newton Theological School) was founded to promote evangelical theology against the increase of Unitarianism among many Congregational churches in New England.[214]

In 1800, Presbyterian minister James McGready and his associates William Hodges and John Bankin led an event with possibly the greatest impact of the second awakening. On the American frontier, they led four days of revival meetings with about five hundred people. These newly born revivalists in turn spread spiritual renewal through-

209. Ibid., 12.

210. Noll, *The Scandal of the Evangelical Mind*, 62.

211. Dobson et al., *The Fundamentalist Phenomenon*, 36.

212. Orr, *Campus Aflame*, 25–30.

213. Ibid., 31.

214. Dobson et al., *The Fundamentalist Phenomenon*, 36.

out the frontier.[215] The awakening gained more followers in the South, from "Kentucky to Tennessee, North and South Carolina, western Virginia, and Georgia."[216] In 1800 to 1801, the manifestation of the Holy Spirit made a tremendous impact at the University of Georgia. As Riis portrays, "they swooned away and lay for hours in the straw prepared for those 'smitten of the Lord,' . . . or they shouted and talked in unknown tongues."[217] Wherever camp meetings were held, people gathered together for several days with enthusiastic singing, crying, and dancing before and after the preaching. The emotionally depressed were delivered, while confessing their sins, shrieking, and speaking in tongues. Fishwick says that "people fell to the ground like men slain in battle."[218] This revival movement in the South can be traced to the beginning of Methodism, although the Baptist revival was also influential. By the late eighteenth century, Francis Asbury[219] initiated a new Methodist revival movement in Brunswick County, Virginia.[220]

Francis Asbury is considered the father of American Methodism and was what Fishwick calls the "greatest white preacher of this period, and one of the most popular in modern times."[221] The Methodist awakening began in the 1770s when Asbury only had a few hundred followers and four preachers to assist. While Calvinist thought prevailed in the East and the North, Asbury concentrated his efforts in the South, leading to rapid growth of the Methodist Church. Methodists numbered 214,000 members with more than 2,000 ministers by the time of Asbury's death in 1816.[222] In the 1840s, lay preachers and itinerants numbered more than 10,000, driving the fastest church growth

215. Riis, *A Survey of 20th-Century Revival Movements*, 12–13.

216. Ibid., 13.

217. Ibid., 13–14.

218. During the time of the revival a traditional Native American dance called "stomp dancing" was practiced. Fishwick, *Great Awakenings*, 22.

219. Dobson et al., *The Fundamentalist Phenomenon*, 35.

220. Riis, *A Survey of 20th-Century Revival Movements in North America*, 12–14.

221. Francis Asbury was a central figure in Methodism's itinerant preaching and revival promotion. He suffered from "saddle sores, boils, bronchitis, rheumatism, and ulcers as he crossed what he called 'my Alps, the Appalachians' 40 times." Fishwick, *Great Awakenings*, 23.

222. Before his departure to the next world, Asbury said, "I look back upon a martyr's life of toil, and privation, and pain; I am ready for a martyr's death." Ibid., 23–24.

movement between the American Revolution and the Civil War. Methodists occupied only 2.5 percent of the Christian population in 1776, but had grown to 34.3 percent in 1850. Their number in 1850 was a little less than double that of the Presbyterians, Congregationalists, and Episcopalians combined.[223] This growth was more remarkable than Methodist growth in Britain. Geographically, the South was still considered a non-Christian area compared to the East and North. Kenneth Latourette describes the nation at the time:

> The country was new, virile, and hopeful, and the western frontier was being rapidly settled. It was predominantly rural. Like the Baptists, the Methodist preachers were usually men from the people, with slight education, and, speaking the language of ordinary folk, were able to reach them. Moreover, Arminian in the theology and not holding to the doctrine of election as did Presbyterians, Congregationalists, and many Baptists; the Methodists proclaimed the love of God for all and that all might repent and be saved.[224]

Denominational competition between Methodist and Baptists in winning souls by itinerant preaching, along with the marketing emphasis of religious establishments, may have driven more apparent growth in America than in Britain. Furthermore, "while the emotional heat of American Methodism remained hotter for longer than its British sister movement, Americans were also better (and still remain so) at presenting popular religion as a form of mass entertainment without the same neurotic fear of vulgarity and disorder that obsessed British Christians of all denominations in the nineteenth century."[225] Hempton summarizes the consequences of American Methodist growth:

> Nathan Hatch's recent attempt to assess the significance of American Methodism in four propositions could therefore, with minor modifications, be applied with equal validity to England. In both countries Methodist reconstruction of the church along voluntary lines contributed to a more pluralistic and competitive religious environment; equally, in both countries, Methodism was able to construct a vernacular religiosity which could appeal, at least in the short term, both to those who were at the raw edges of social change and to those who

223. Hempton, *The Religion of the People*, 9.
224. Latourette, *A History of Christianity*, 1039.
225. Hempton, *The Religion of the People*, 15–16.

stood to profit from it. Finally, Methodism, as the sheer complexity and variety of its political expressions in England and the United States clearly demonstrate, was an infinitely flexible and adaptable religious species. Not only were Methodists to be found supporting each of the main political parties in both countries in the 1830s and 1840s (though the majority was democrat in the United States and liberal in England), but the various pressures thrown up by anti-Catholicism, legal disabilities, moral reformism and social, ethnic and denominational competition produced a rich mosaic of political allegiances.[226]

Reverberations of the second awakening were felt in central and western New York State from 1820 until 1825. Revivalist Asahel Nettleton led revivals in 1821 in Connecticut, Massachusetts, and many other places. Of the many prominent evangelists of the spiritual movements, Charles Grandison Finney was most prominent in bringing the work of the Holy Spirit throughout America, beginning from New York in 1830.[227] As a young lawyer, he experienced Spirit baptism at the age of twenty-nine and immediately began evangelistic work in an attempt to win every sinner in his village. In 1824, he became a Presbyterian minister who rejected the Calvinistic belief of salvation of the elect and instead adopted the Arminian view of the importance of soul winning. In 1835, be became president of the new Oberlin College.[228] Finney is seen as a key figure in the Holiness Movement and as the father of modern evangelism.[229] His influence was felt in both frontier revival and in evangelism in growing urban areas in order to win as many souls as possible. Using his empirical experience, Finney affirmed that the conversion of the individual cannot be accomplished as a miracle without work.[230] Finney and his colleagues led urban-centered revival movements that took a populist approach toward culture.[231] His publication of *Lectures on Revivals of*

226. Ibid., 16.

227. Riss, *A Survey of 20th-Century Revival Movements in North America*, 14.

228. Gaustad, *A Religious History of America*, 150.

229. Dobson et al., *The Fundamentalist Phenomenon*, 37.

230. See James 2:26. Here "work" means deeds. Fishwick, *Great Awakenings*, 28–29.

231. Ibid., 30. Finney used "new measures" to draw more people and "prayed in colloquial, common, and "vulgar" language." Finney popularized those means to attract masses and was eventually attacked for using those methods. Christian History, "Charles Finney," lines 16–24.

Religion had a lasting influence, and he suggested a comprehensive principle of revival based on his experience, suggesting a method that could organize or even cause a religious revival.[232] Not only did his life become the model for the professional minister and evangelist, but his principles, tactics, methods, and teachings on revival also greatly influenced many pastors and leaders worldwide.

> He talked right to the people—spoke of "skinning the uncon-verted shepherds" of the flock. Older pastors, noting how he filled churches, began to listen and use some of his tactics. Combining various "laws of the mind," Finney's method be-came archetypal for those who followed: (1) direct, exciting, colloquial preaching; (2) protracted meetings given over to preaching, prayer, and counsel from sunrise to midnight, with all other business in town closed down; (3) anxious seats at public meetings for the convicted sinners who could be singled out for special attention; (4) public prayer for the conversion of individuals by name; (5) demand for immediate decision; (6) special meetings for the anxious [those considering a Christian commitment]; (7) extensive publicity; (8) bands of lined per-sonnel workers; (9) emotional music; and (10) the support of resident clergy.[233]

The Finney revival movement, with its perfectionist elements, was resisted by Presbyterian minister Lyman Beecher, but he even-tually changed his mind and later incorporated Finney's ideas into his own revival. He continued and even further developed Finney-style revivalism in New Haven, Boston, and Ohio.[234] Charles Finney spearheaded a new type of revivalism that reinvigorated the faith after a period of decline between 1842 and 1857. The decline was due to increased material prosperity, Millerite millennial predictions, and tensions arising from the antislavery movement. William Miller pre-dicted that the Second Coming of Christ would occur in 1843, and later revised the time to 1844. When the second advent of Christ did not happen, many turned away from their churches.[235] Furthermore,

232. Gaustad, *A Religious History of America*, 150.

233. Fishwick, *Great Awakenings*, 29.

234. Gaustad, *A Religious History of America*, 151.

235. This mistaken prophecy generated "the Great Disappointment" for those who believed and anticipated the advent of Christ. By the 1830s, adherents of mil-lennialism were found in virtually every major denomination.

the issue of slavery and its abolition created tensions and eventually led to divisions in the church and in the nation itself.

Prayer and Holiness Revivals

In the 1840s, revivals occurred internationally throughout Europe and America. Major reawakening events took place in Heemstede, Netherlands, through the leadership of Nicolaas Beets. In 1844, more revivals took place in Mötlingen, Germany, through Johann Christoph Blumhardt. Through Jacob Knapp led revivals in Baltimore, New Haven, Hartford, and Boston.[236]

In 1857, a worldwide awakening began with a humble prayer meeting led by Jeremiah C. Lanphier, a merchant who longed for a spiritual revival in the Dutch North Church of Fulton in New York. This prayer meeting grew from six people to thousands and gaining nationwide influence.[237] In 1857, the revival of New York spread to Hamilton, Ontario, where "more than 300 people were converted within a few days. . . . By January of 1858, twenty prayer meetings patterned after the Fulton Street meeting sprang up in New York City, and newspapers began covering "The Progress of the Revival" on a daily basis."[238]

The Ulster Revival was sparked when two Irish Presbyterian ministers went to New York City and joined the revival meetings at Fulton Street in 1858. They eventually asked the congregation to intercede for their synod of five hundred congregations in Ireland, and revival subsequently spread throughout that nation. In the same way, James Adamson visited America and observed the awakening and its miraculous outpouring of the Holy Spirit. Upon returning home to South Africa, he challenged the congregation at a conference of the Dutch Reformed Church in Worcester, South Africa, in 1860. There he addressed "the rise and progress of the revival in the United States," and, as a result, "the village of Worcester was powerfully affected by the rising tide of blessing, and, for a time at least, strange scenes were witnessed, which an outsider, unacquainted with the workings of the Spirit of God, would have called undiluted fanaticism."[239]

---

236. Riss, *A Survey of 20th-Century Revival Movements in North America*, 14.
237. Ibid., 14–15.
238. Ibid., 15.
239. Ibid., 15.

By 1890, the frontier mission had ended, but a new awakening was soon to emerge—not from the countryside, but within urban areas. Church growth and massive revival meetings were seen in large urban areas and small towns, including "New York, Chicago, Boston, Albany, Buffalo, Cincinnati, Richmond and many more" around the time of the Civil War.[240] Awakenings and national political events are closely correlated. For instance, the second awakening produced a spirit of unity between the eastern seaboard and western frontiers such as Kentucky, Tennessee, southern Ohio, and Indiana. The Third Great Awakening began around 1858, often referred to as the wonder year or miracle year (*annus mirabilis*), which was characterized by an urban-centered awakening and democratic principles.[241] The Third Great Awakening appeared as "an apparently spontaneous outbreak of religious excitement in a region (ideally a nation, but more than likely a circuit or locality) which resulted in a large number of conversions over a relatively short period of time [through] protracted meetings, lay activity and physical manifestations of conversion."[242]

The American Civil War between 1861 and 1865 generated a sense of social, religious, cultural, and intellectual crisis that undid many of the positive aspects of Christian revival:

> Within a generation, the cities had mushroomed; older churches no longer seemed able to preserve a vital witness in those cities; immigration brought vast numbers of new Americans and great problems of social cohesion; mammoth factories sprang up, and their owners achieved unrivaled influence in public life; freed slaves were forced back into inhumane conditions in the South and allowed a mere subsistence in the North; the Bible came increasingly under attack as a largely irrelevant, mythological book; and new views in biology challenged both divine creation and the uniqueness of the human species. [243]

Dwight L. Moody began his ministry as the prayer revival of 1859 was waning. In 1860, he committed himself to Christ to work entirely for the promotion of revival.[244] He led another style of revival

240. Fishwick, *Great Awakenings*, 27–28.

241. McLoughlin, *Revivals, Awakenings, and Reform*, 1.

242. Holmes, *Religious Revivals in Britain and Ireland*, xx.

243. Noll, *The Scandal of the Evangelical Mind*, 106.

244. Moody began his career as shoe clerk in Boston, where he attended the Congregational Church after being moved by a Sunday school teacher at the age

from 1865 until his death.[245] One of the most prominent preachers of his time, Moody organized the annual evangelical meetings, revival meetings, mission services, and special services on a regular basis. He planned and promoted activities that featured itinerant evangelists and lay preachers.[246] Marsden differentiates Moody from others, stating that he "was not a sensationalist evangelist like Charles Finney or the forthcoming Billy Sunday. . . . [H]e contributed tremendously not only toward revivalism but also to Christian education and philanthropic activities. His preaching was so popular and attractive that it drew the deep attention of the audience with his homey and sentimental style of storytelling."[247] Gaustad points out that "the theme seemed more plausible [and] the message more winsome when presented in the quiet, restrained, homey manner that Moody regularly employed. . . . [N]o hysterics were countenanced, no excesses of emotion encouraged. A simple gospel, simply presented was for many enough."[248] His revival campaigns were conducted from the mid-1870s until his death in 1899. Reeves appreciates that Moody had "a good mind, a winning personality, a solid command of Scripture, and a zealous faith."[249]

Moody stoked the fire of revival in Britain when he visited with his singing coworker Ira Sankey. Before their evangelistic tour, local revivals took place in South Wales in 1871. Then, Moody and Sankey brought revival to Scotland and Ireland in 1873 and continued the movement throughout England until 1875. When they returned to America, their influence was greater than before.[250] Their massive evangelistic campaigns were warmly welcomed in Philadelphia, New York City, Chicago, and Boston.[251]

---

of 18. This experience compelled him to start Sunday school ministries in Chicago after he left Boston in 1856. He shared the gospel tracts and tried to construct church buildings for caring and evangelizing discouraged and dispossessed people in Chicago. Ibid., 229–30.

245. Riss, *A Survey of 20th-Century Revival Movements in North America*, 16.

246. Holmes, *Religious Revivals in Britain and Ireland*, xx.

247. Marsden, *Understanding Fundamentalism and Evangelicalism*, 21.

248. Gaustad, *A Religious History of America*, 230.

249. Reeves, *The Empty Church*, 99.

250. Marsden, *Understanding Fundamentalism and Evangelicalism*, 21.

251. Riss, *A Survey of 20th-Century Revival Movements in North America*, 16.

Marsden describes Moody's message with the "Three R's": "Ruin by Sin, Redemption by Christ, and Regeneration by the Holy Ghost."[252] His primary concern was winning souls for Christ's sake. "I look upon this world as a wrecked vessel. . . . God has given me a lifeboat and said to me, 'Moody, save all you can.'"[253] Moody's teaching and influences shaped "individualistic, culture-denying, soul-rescuing Christianity."[254] His ministry emphasized "personal conversion" to the Christian faith and following a "strict moral code that condemned, among other things, drunkenness, Sabbath breaking, theater attendance, and 'telling vile stories.'"[255] The period of Moody was considered a time of great evangelistic activity, which included unprecedented outpouring of the Holy Spirit through the emerging Holiness Movement.[256] Marsden sees the Holiness Movement arising from the heritage of the Second Awakening with its focus on prayer revival and from Moody's evangelistic campaigns.[257]

The great awakenings led to a worldwide expansion of Baptist, Methodist, and Holiness churches as well as mission agencies in many parts of the British Empire. American revival influences were different in that they emphasized personal conversion and sanctification (or moral perfection), adopting biblical literalism. The Holiness movement originated from Methodism, but Holiness movement advocates emphasized the "second blessing" teaching yet a few Methodists leaders denounced this theology.[258] Holiness groups grew through camp meetings, revivals, itinerant evangelism, and preaching. Between 1895 and 1905, more than twenty Holiness denominations were founded, including the Church of God (Cleveland), the Church of God (1886),

---

252. Marsden, *Fundamentalism and American Culture*, 7.

253. Ibid., 21.

254. Ibid., 7.

255. Reeves, *The Empty Church*, 99.

256. Riss, *A Survey of 20th-Century Revival Movements*, 16.

257. Marsden, *Understanding Fundamentalism and Evangelicalism*, 21–22.

258. As a result of the differing opinions on the second blessing a new group called the Christian Union in North Carolina experienced a revival in 1896 accompanied by speaking in tongues by 130 people. The Church of God in Cleveland recognized that their denomination had historical connections to the 1896 revival. The Church of God (1886), the Christian and Missionary Alliance (1887), the Church of Nazarene (1895), and the Pilgrim Holiness Church (1897) have historical connections to the 1896 revival as well. Anderson, *An Introduction to Pentecostalism*, 27.

the Christian and Missionary Alliance (1887), the Church of the Nazarene (1895) and the Pilgrim Holiness Church (1897).[259] This was part of the overall growth of Christianity in the United States, Canada, Australia, and New Zealand. With the largest growth in the economy, population, and political power, the influence of these nations expanded exponentially.

THE EFFECTS OF THE GREAT AWAKENING

The great awakenings were spurred when evangelists and itinerant preachers spoke to the spiritual desires of ordinary people. The simultaneous spiritual revivals in the transatlantic region, particularly those in England and New England, were similar culturally and socially: "As religious culture evolved in Great Britain, New England shared in that evolution, borrowing, imitating, and adapting."[260] Before the turn of twentieth century, the great awakenings had formed a new type of American religious culture that would endure for centuries to come.

The first awakening was met with resistance both from the traditional denominations within which it had originated and from those outside those denominations, but it brought a fresh and ardent response and an emotional experience among followers.

> It set the example for the emotional outbursts which were to characterize many later revivals in this country, and it marked the beginnings of the evangelistic spirit which was destined to play an important part in the subsequent growth of American Protestantism and which became a significant feature of nineteenth-century American culture. Distressed at the spiritual dullness which had overtaken much of the population and crept into the churches, many sincere Christians welcomed the revival. At the same time many other equally sincere adherents of all denominations bitterly opposed it. They looked upon its emotionalism as a dangerous innovation and could see, in its tendency to upset the peace and order of the churches, only the hand of the Evil One.[261]

259. Ibid., 27.

260. Crawford, "Origins of the Eighteenth-Century Evangelical Revival," 379–80.

261. Labaree, "The Conservative Attitude toward the Great Awakening," 331.

The great awakenings shaped popular religious movements and the culture itself. Most Americans began to identify themselves with the so-called cultural religion, characterized by new transformations through popular religious patterns. Even though the popular and folk religion received negative reactions, positive reactions existed as well. Folk religion "sustains a healthy relationship with environmental and social change."[262] In other words, folk religion gets along with changes in the culture and adapts to social changes. Most evangelists, especially itinerants, conveyed an uncomplicated message that resulted in the strengthening of Christian America in the eighteenth and nineteenth centuries. Even in the twentieth century, preachers who employed such popular forms attracted large crowds: "Billy Sunday and Billy Graham, Oral Roberts and Kenneth Copeland, Jimmy Swaggart and Jerry Falwell, John Stott and Martyn Lloyd-Jones.[263]

Popular Religion

Throughout American history, the church has been shaped by the great awakenings, which also had a major impact on political, social, and economic events such as independence, the American Enlightenment, Civil War, and movements for suffrage, the abolition of slavery, and civil rights. As new, popular forms of religious revival began to grow, a disparity developed between European and American religious cultures. In the United States, everyday citizens committed themselves to the Christian gospel because they were able to overcome the self-consciousness of many Americans who viewed themselves undeserving of salvation. Choosing to accept the faith regardless of social class helped Americans develop an identity of democratic individualism and self-worth.[264] In the transatlantic region, the church of the seventeenth century had been utterly transformed by late nineteenth century. The rise of new Christian denominations— while not so significant in Europe, except in Britain—had changed the Christian landscape markedly in the United States following the revivals and awakenings. The largest denominations of the Puritan era, including the Presbyterians, Episcopalians, Lutherans, and other mainline churches, were outstripped by the relatively younger denom-

262. McLoughlin, *Revivals, Awakenings, and Reform*, 2.
263. Noll, *The Scandal of the Evangelical Mind*, 61–62.
264. Ibid., 62.

inations including Methodists, Baptists, and the Holiness churches. The Baptists and Methodists displayed the most proficient and effective adaptation of a democratic church system. Hempton ascribes the popularity of religion in the United States to the democratic and populist nature of new denominations:

> The popular religious movements of the early republic, in their refusal to defer to the clergy and learned theologians and in their willingness to take the religious experiences of ordinary people at face value, articulated a profoundly democratic spirit. The rise of popular religious culture of print, the place of origin of which shifted from eastern seaboard cities to west of the Alleghenies, together with the widespread dissemination of personal stories of transforming religious experiences, further contributed to the notion that the religion of the people no longer depended on clerical mediation.[265]

The missionary zeal exhibited by D.L. Moody—a desire to win as many souls as possible from among the unreached—was also seen in the overseas missionary movement during this time. According to Marsden:

> Many Protestants since the Civil War were losing confidence in social solutions to the world's problems. One sign of this shift was the increasing popularity of premillennialism, which emphasized that the world would not be improved until Jesus personally came again and set up his kingdom on earth. Moody and all his closest associates preached such doctrines. Their premillennialism, however, did not lead to complacency. Rather, it impelled them to more vigorous missionary and evangelistic efforts ("save all you can"). Moody himself established centers out of which such work radiated. In Chicago he adopted in 1886 a Bible Institute (later called Moody Bible Institute) to train laymen for evangelistic efforts. More important at the time were his Northfield Conferences, held near his Massachusetts home. Out of these grew one of the largest missionary efforts of the era, the Student Volunteer Movement founded in 1886. Thousands of students during the subsequent years pledged themselves to lives of missionary work. The motto of SVM well summarized Moody's own goals: "The evangelization of the world in this generation."[266]

265. Hempton, *The Religion of the People*, 9–10.
266. Marsden, *Understanding Fundamentalism and Evangelicalism*, 22.

The new popular religious culture and evangelicalism placed the United States in the forefront of the world missions movement. While young believers committed themselves to overseas mission, evangelicals responded to God's call for believers to share the gospel abroad. Gallup and Lindsey point out that "the economic and religious peculiarities of this country do not halt the ever-increasing engagement of Americans with international society. . . . In light of this trend toward globalization, it will be interesting to see if and how America's religious faith and fervor will shape society as the United States embraces the increasing global constituents in the twenty-first century."[267] Hambrick and Stowe firmly state "however integral evangelicalism was to the culture of the United States, and whatever distinctively American traits it had acquired by the antebellum period, it remained in a significant sense an international phenomenon."[268] In spite of instances of intentional and selfish promotion of popular culture, the missions movement during this period saw success, and the active, experiential, and individualistic character of the great awakenings was embedded in the message as it was disseminated overseas.[269]

Overseas Mission

The Great Awakenings shaped American religious lifestyles not only at home, but also abroad as Christianity expanded. The traditional model of parish priests and pastors was replaced by evangelists and itinerants, which had proven to be a far more effective evangelism tool for both the churched and unchurched. Villagers, farmers, and urban dwellers responded to a straightforward, individual, and popular approach. Evangelists such as Jonathan Edwards, George Whitefield, Francis Asbury, Charles Finney, and D.L. Moody emphasized the need for immediate repentance, regeneration, and baptism in the Holy Spirit. "What they did do was to plant the seeds of individualism and immediatism that would eventually exert a profound effect on Christian thinking."[270]

267. Gallup and Lindsay, *Surveying the Religious Landscape*, 120.

268. Hambrick-Stowe, *Charles G. Finney and the Spirit of American Evangelicalism*, 228.

269. Noll, *The Scandal of the Evangelical Mind*, 63–64.

270. Ibid., 61.

The diverse religious visions of the early colonial period were ultimately undermined by this new evangelical understanding. Likewise the new spirit of evangelical awakening quickened an interest in missions, and along with this a concern to spread the message to the outcasts of the colonial social order. David Brainerd (1718–47), son-in-law of Jonathan Edwards, began a mission to Native Americans. He had a fruitful ministry to the Native Americans in New Jersey and Pennsylvania. Of greater importance, the message began to spread to the African slave community. The issue of the evangelization of the slave community had been a thorny one, and before the middle of the century the few efforts at Christianization had been under the auspices of colonial Anglicans. But the new message found favour among African-Americans, and increasingly the message of a heartfelt gospel became the common piety of both blacks and whites.[271]

The great awakenings shaped home and overseas missions in direct and indirect ways. Latourette states, "Anglo-Saxon Christianity in part reflected the abounding vigour in other ranges of British and North American achievement, and its forms were to some extent determined and its expansion made possible by them. . . . In turn, the other phases of Anglo-American civilization were moulded, several of them profoundly, by the revived Christianity."[272] Anglo-American overseas missions constituted the leading missions force from 1815 to 1914. Latourette referred to it as "the great century" of Christian missions. Marsden says that American missions abroad "from 1890 to World War I was the golden age of Protestant missions."[273] Latourette further says that, "if the vitality of a religion is measured by its ability to give rise to new expressions, then the Protestantism which emerged from the revival was one of the most potent forms of religion that mankind has known."[274] Marsden describes the influence of the United States on worldwide missions:

> In the eighteenth century, the booming of missionary societies occurred soon following the revival movements in Britain. This became true of American overseas mission movements as well, since the origins of the missionary movement derived

271. Mullin, "North America," 424.

272. Latourette, *A History of Christianity*, 1021.

273. Marsden, *Understanding Fundamentalism and Evangelicalism*, 23.

274. Latourette, *A History of Christianity*, 1021–22.

from the great awakenings.[275] Eventually, between 1890 and early nineteenth century, American missionary zeal and fervor proliferated to such a great degree that it established Protestant churches in many unreached parts throughout world. Hence, American Christianity sheltered the worldwide evangelical community, including the church governments of overseas missions, Sunday schools, voluntary Christian organizations such as YMCA and YWCA, Bible societies, and philanthropic agencies. Most parachurch agencies and mission organizations collaborated with different denominations and "continued to provide the leading edge in organizing spiritual impulses" even until the postwar era.[276]

Evangelicalism

The great awakenings also led to the emergence of evangelicalism in Britain, which resulted in the founding of new educational institutions. Renewed evangelicals took control of many seminaries and divinity schools, and the new colleges and universities trained missionaries and their sponsors. Smith concludes that "evangelical Protestantism was basking in the luster of wave upon wave of successful revivals and awakenings-from those of Jonathan Edwards to Charles Finney that had and was converting enormous numbers of previously unchurched Americans into the evangelical Protestant camp."[277] The awakenings called their many newcomers to be faithful saints and urged dying churches to be revived through evangelism and inspiring worship services. The awakenings "had a great impact on colonial culture as a whole, providing new models of public speaking, new motives for public action, and new concern for public responsibility."[278]

The effects of the awakenings persisted in the form of new religious life patterns for many Americans. Whitefield exemplified the itinerant preaching lifestyle, preaching not in formal, ritual settings in church buildings, but in places where people congregated. This itinerant style of preaching penetrated America for more than two centuries.[279] Noll and others explain: "his form of public speaking, and the

275. Pirouet, "Christianity Worldwide," 1–2.
276. Marsden, *Understanding Fundamentalism and Evangelicalism*, 23.
277. Smith et al., *American Evangelicalism*, 3.
278. Noll et al., *The Search for Christian America*, 52.
279. Finke and Stark, *The Churching of America*, 51.

implicit message of his ministry concerning leadership, constituted a powerful stimulus to a more democratic life."[280] The remarkable growth of Baptists and Methodists was facilitated by Whitefield:

> Many of those brought shivering and trembling to salvation by Whitefield ended up in Baptist congregations, causing a sudden spurt of growth that carried them past the Episcopalians to become the third largest American denomination by 1776. Not only did many of Whitefield's converts end up Baptists, but his revival methods also took root among the Baptists and subsequently were adopted by the sect movement developing within the Church of England, the Wesley brothers. . . . [Whitefield] was in many ways the man who did most to launch the Methodist movement in America."[281]

Methodism was the most prominent common factor in the revivals on both sides of the Atlantic, drawing from a variety of denominations including Scottish/Irish Presbyterianism, English/Welsh dissent Calvinism, and even Anglicanism. In the dawn of the nineteenth century, one of greatest factors in spreading revivalism, particularly in Methodist revivalism, was the pervasive use of camp meetings for soul winning. It is right to say that "the earlier and more wholehearted flowering of teetotalism in America presented an opportunity for temperance revivalism that Britain did not at that stage offer."[282]

Revivalism and great awakenings in Britain and America planted the seeds of evangelicalism, with great similarities, yet distinctive flavors. Christian Smith states that contemporary

> American evangelicalism enjoys a religious vitality measured sociologically—that surpasses every other major Christian tradition in the country. . . . Whether gauged by belief orthodoxy, salience of faith, robustness of belief, church attendance, participation in social and religious mission, or membership recruitment and retention, the conclusion is the same: American evangelicalism is thriving.[283]

American evangelicalism absorbed a much more diverse stream of religious elements, including the Reformation, Puritanism, and

---

280. Noll et al., *The Search for Christian America*, 55.
281. Finke and Stark, *The Churching of America*, 51.
282. Carwardine, *Trans-Atlantic Revivalism*, 44–45.
283. Smith, "American Evangelicalism Embattled," 225.

Pietism, compared to its European counterpart. These influences shaped its emphasis on religious freedom, political independence, social change, industrial revolution, and picking and choosing of the European Enlightenment.[284] O'Brien asserts that "The real significance of the mid-eighteenth-century revivals was not their wondrous spontaneity or their primary role in the formation of national consciousness, but rather their combining of traditional Puritan practices with fresh evangelical techniques and attitudes."[285] Evangelicalism was an amalgamation "that played a major part, and perhaps the most creative part, in the systematic development of evangelicalism."[286] American evangelicalism nourished the emergence of fundamentalism in the late nineteenth through the early twentieth centuries and eventually birthed Pentecostalism. Carwardine compares the renewal movements on the two continents:

> If American evangelicals were socially and ecclesiastically more powerful than the British, if that power gave them a greater confidence, if that confidence was translated at times into a seemingly boundless optimism for the future of America as God's chosen country, and if the foundation of these attitudes was a revivalism more deeply rooted and far-flung than anything Britain could offer, British and American evangelicals nevertheless saw themselves as branches of the same closely knit family. The contagious element in revivalism, seen so clearly locally, operated at a transatlantic level, too. In the late 1820s and early 1830s, in the late 1830s and early 1840s, and again in the late 1850s, both British and American evangelical churches experienced a significantly quickened rate of growth.[287]

Although evangelicalism paved the way for fundamentalism, which manifested a much narrower and more conservative form of American Protestantism mainly led by Southern Baptists, evangelicalism encompassed a much broader spectrum. According to Marsden,

> [E]vangelicalism today includes any Christians traditional enough to affirm the basic beliefs of the old nineteenth-century evangelical consensus. The essential evangelical beliefs include

284. Noll, *The Scandal of the Evangelical Mind*, 59, 76.

285. O'Brien, "A Transatlantic Community of Saints," 815.

286. Ibid., 815.

287. Carwardine, *Trans-Atlantic Revivalism*, 198.

(1) the Reformation doctrine of the final authority of the Bible, (2) the real historical character of God's saving work recorded in Scripture, (3) salvation to eternal life based on the redemptive work of Christ, (4) the importance of evangelism and missions, and (5) the importance of a spiritually transformed life. By this account evangelicalism includes striking diversities: holiness churches, pentecostals, traditionalist Methodists, all sorts of Baptists, Presbyterians, black churches in all these traditions, fundamentalists, pietist groups, Reformed and Lutheran confessionalists, Anabaptists such as Mennonites, Churches of Christ, Christians, and some Episcopalians, to name only some of the most prominent types. In recent decades, opinion surveys that test for evangelical beliefs typically find somewhere around fifty million Americans who fit the definition.[288]

Thus, Christian faith in the United States did not come to identify itself with the term *Christendom*, but rather with the term *Christianity*. Revivals and Awakenings shaped the faith differently in the United States than in Europe. Likewise, secularization in America advanced differently than secularization in Europe.

Several events in Europe fueled emigration of religious dissenters to the New World. The Revolution of 1688 in England prompted mass migrations. An exodus of French Huguenots had occurred three years prior, in 1685, after several political events that reversed the Edict of Nantes, which had protected religious dissenters in France.[289] German Pietists arrived in Pennsylvania a short time after that.[290]

CONCLUSION: FLAMING THE REVIVAL FOR THE GLOBAL VILLAGE

The "where the West goes, the world goes" mentality has to change. During the past several centuries the entire geography and tapestry of Christianity has been so profoundly reshaped through the cross of American religion. Christianity gained the name as a civilization of world religion in Europe. Now Christianity has become an

288. Marsden, *Understanding Fundamentalism and Evangelicalism*, 4–5.

289. In 1685, Louis XIV of France annulled the Edict of Nantes, signed by his father in 1598 to grant religious, civil, and political liberties to the Protestant Huguenots. Louis XIV sought to drive the Huguenots out of France because he viewed them as wealthy merchants and skilled craftsmen who posed a threat to the monarch.

290. Labaree, "The Conservative Attitude toward the Great Awakening," 332–33.

Americanized faith due to the gravity shifting from Europe to America. When Europe lost its ecclesiastical power in the public and private sectors America began a new adventure to form her destiny into a new breed of Christianity. European Christianity is a culture, and a culture is Christian wherein customs, norms, and the union of church and state and beliefs and practices of Christian doctrine had been widely exercised amongst cultural Christians. However, Europe dismissed non-state churches and did not give dissenting groups a peaceful stay, causing them to depart for America. Therefore, such groups who escaped from the religious wars, persecution, or social rejection led the religious minorities to the new land in America and instituted their ideology within a theocracy to develop a biblical society, the Puritan America. The first and second awakenings paved the land to be evangelized through repentance. Further, the prayer revival in New York led the people to a prayer centered revival that swept over the continents, challenging and transforming the common folks. The holiness revival encouraged the pursuit of sanctification with the fourfold gospel. Furthermore, America laid ground the way to another greater and wider revival. The mission mandate of America was to light a fire from the Azusa Street to ignite a worldwide revival fire referred to as the Pentecostal revival. The whole world began to hear about the Pentecostal and Charismatic explosions. Now we can see the impact of America in terms of revivals and awakenings. However, America began to fight several new fights against the secular waves wherein religious humanism, secularism, liberal education, evolution theory, and same sex advocates began to devour the very places where revival and awakening took place, diminishing the witness of the Christian gospel. We will explore the counterattack of secular trends that have affected America in the next chapter.

7

The Secularization in the United States

WITH CHRISTIANITY EMBEDDED IN institutional systems, Europe has never been a solely sacred society. The faith has gone through cycles of peak and decline. Today, the European church faces decreasing attendance and diminishing ecclesiastical powers over secular society. Many scholars point to social, religious, and political complexities as reasons for secularization, de-Christianization, de-evangelization, or post-Christianization in Europe. This process has looked quite different in Europe than in the United States.

Secularization in the United States has been a gradual process more subtle than in Europe. Separation of church and state has always been in the nation's constitution, but for centuries, a basis of shared Judeo-Christian values was shared by virtually all citizens. The development of liberal theology, which questioned Christian core beliefs, led to humanism, which rejected them entirely and replaced God with human reason as the object of faith. The penetration of humanism into educational institutions and other social arenas led to church decline. However, the failure of material wealth to give meaning to life has left the nation ripe for revival.

THE NATURE OF SECULARIZATION IN THE UNITED STATES

Is secularization happening in the United States? American churches are still thriving in terms of church attendance, membership, beliefs, and practices, but the outer appearance does not tell the whole story; cultural, social, and intellectual forces antagonistic to Christianity have grown up alongside the awakening movements. The peak of American Christianity came in the beginning of the twentieth century as a result of the nineteenth century's awakenings. While noting the early twentieth-century American church's numerical strength, Henry Steele Commager notes that its theology had become secularized.

> Certainly by every test but that of influence the church had never been stronger than it was at the opening of the twentieth century, and its strength increased steadily. . . . The typical Protestant of the twentieth century inherited his religion as he did his politics, though rather more casually, and was quite unable to explain the differences between denominations. . . . That it was supported is clear, and whatever the spiritual quality American Christianity, the material and quantitative standards were high. There were forty-two million church members in 1916, fifty-five million in 1926, and seventy-two million in 1942. . . . The increase in wealth and in social activities was even more impressive; the churches, of necessity, borrowed the techniques of big business, and bishops were often chosen for their administrative talents rather than for their spiritual qualities. Never before had the church been materially more powerful or spiritually less effective.[1]

The spiritual strength of the church was compromised when, having become materially prosperous, the church was no longer able to be accountable for the sacred predicament over society. In other words, the church itself became secularized and unable to enlighten church members on eternal life, spiritual life, and holiness. When the church and clergy lost their ability to spiritually impact the community, the church went into a process of the "steady secularization."[2]

Following the great awakenings in the United States, churches experienced numerical and material prosperity. Younger churches were on track to become worldwide denominations while established mainline churches declined steadily starting from the nineteenth century. However, a decisive turning point for declining mainline denominations occurred in the 1960s—the same decade when European churches also entered an irretrievable decline. Would the American church also experience a definitive demise of religious authority over social issues?

The major reason for the decline of American mainline churches is that the church itself has become secularized. Despite high numbers of churchgoers, the church's teachings are often seen as irrelevant to

---

1. Commager, *The American Mind*, 166–67.
2. Hudson, *The Great Tradition of the American Churches*, 22–23.

public and private life. Secularization has permeated the life of church as well as the plurality of denominations in the United States. Wilson states there is an "absence of substantial ideological distinctions among at least most of the Protestant denominations." "Religion in America is characterized by its secularity."[3] Thus, American churches, like those of Europe, display different aspects of secularization.

The earlier enthusiasm of a flourishing Protestantism in the United States had left a vivid impression over European visitors, such as Alexis de Tocqueville in the 1830s, who commented on the faithfulness of the American people in contrast to the attitudes of Europeans as mentioned in the previous chapters. However, America had already in fact entered the secular stage in many spheres at the societal level. The religious landscape in the United States in the nineteenth and twentieth centuries has ranged from the religious and spiritual movements of primitive Christianity to a pervasive cynicism, humanism, liberalism, and secularism in the academia. At the same time, Europe started to see different types of secularization that had already pervaded in the mid-twentieth century. When their book was published in 1967, Herman and Anthony J. Wiener anticipated that there will be "increasingly Sensate cultures" that they described as "empirical, this-worldly, secular, humanistic, pragmatic, utilitarian, contractual, epicurean or hedonistic, and the like."[4] This secularization process is quite beyond our belief because until the 1960s, overall church membership and attendance was at its peak. Casanova gives this glimpse to use the debatable standpoints between Bauer and Marx, "Marx uses this evidence in his essay "On the Jewish Question" against Bruno Bauer to argue that since America is both the example of "perfect disestablishment" and "the land of religiosity par excellence," it follows that Bauer's proposal of political emancipation of the state from religion cannot be the solution to full human emancipation." Casanova insists that their arguments provoked to consider the secularization process through, amongst others, modernity, "industrialization, urbanization, scientific education, and other areas."[5]

As mentioned earlier, De Tocqueville's visit to the United States was during the peak of its spiritual and religious devotion. Perhaps he

3. Wilson, "Religion and the Churches in Contemporary America," 73.

4. Kahn and Wiener, *The Year 2000*, 7, 48.

5. Casanova, *Public Religions in the Modern World*, 27.

did not anticipate what would happen in 100 years because he experienced an American society that was greatly religiously ardent and spiritually self-motivated. Many believe that the period of secularization kicks in after the period of spiritual growth and then revival starts to wane. What are the causes of secularization in American churches and are American churches following the European pattern of secularization? Acquaviva laments,

> One might maintain the [secularization] thesis that in industrial society, the sacred and the religious tend more and more to become a sort of unexpressed potentiality instead of the active, manifest elements that they were until relatively recently. . . . From the religious point of view, humanity has entered a long night that will become darker and darker with the passing of the generations, and of which no end can yet be seen. It is a night in which there seems to be no place for a conception of God, or for a sense of the sacred, and ancient ways of giving a significance to our own existence, of confronting life and death, are becoming increasingly untenable.[6]

Most scholars agree that the United States is much more religious than Britain or Europe, but the analyses of the decline of European Christianity and the rise of the American church vary widely. There are two cases of secularization in the West, the European case, which has displayed demise in religion and the other is the American pattern that does not necessarily indicate a decline of religion. Casanova states, "we need to explain the lasting convincing power of the secularization paradigm in the face of overwhelming contrary evidence."[7] Overlooking the reality of irresistible evidences of American history and how greatly and deeply society and religion have become pretentious by secularization, this chapter will lead readers to explore the trajectory of secularization in North America.

HISTORICAL SECULARIZATION

Religion can be a spiritual and emotional experience, and can also serve social functions. If the spiritual aspect vanishes, it can remain as an organization addressing social action only. Hudson gives an illustration from Equity, New Hampshire, where religion "has largely ceased to

6. Acquaviva, *The Decline of the Sacred in Industrial Society*, 200.
7. Casanova, *Public Religions in the Modern World*, 28–29.

be a fact of spiritual experience, and the visible church flourished on condition of providing for the social needs of the community."[8] In this context, religion can work closely with secular systems, culture, values, and politics. The salvific mission becomes secondary to the social service role.[9] When the spirituality of religion diminishes, the social function of the church becomes more dominant—a process of secularization. As we have seen, in Europe after the Reformation, the church/state monopoly was broken in many Protestant nations at a time when the Protestant system was not as strong as its Catholic counterpart, opening opportunities for the onset of secularization.[10]

The Secular in Puritan Era

Throughout Europe's history, the relationship between church and state shaped the nature and verve of Christianity. Casanova observes, "If the universalist claims of the church as a salvation organization were undermined by the religious pluralism introduced by the Reformation, its monopolist compulsory character was undermined by the rise of a modern secular state which progressively was able to concentrate and monopolize the means of violence and coercion within its territory."[11] While church decline and secularization coincided in Europe, the American experience took a different tack.

European secularization often took violent forms, including revolutions and religious persecution. However, in the New World, Americanized Christianity included secular elements imported from Europe that would ultimately lead to a new and more subtle type of secularization.[12] In England, secularization occurred gradually and without separating the church and state. The church maintained its position as a guardian of the monarch and the king or queen as the head of the church.[13] Christian idealism had formed American civil religion through Puritanism and Pietism. The Great Awakenings propagated the faith throughout American culture and thought with an impact that has lasted for several centuries. However, secularism,

8. Hudson, *The Great Tradition of the American Churches*, 23.

9. Ibid., 22–23.

10. Ostwalt, *Secular Steeples*, 10–11.

11. Casanova, *Public Religions in the Modern World*, 22.

12. Mead, *The Lively Experiment*, 2.

13. Russello, *Christianity and European Culture*, 24.

atheism, deism, skepticism, humanism, liberalism, and modernism have all made headway in academia and among many religious leaders. The founding of the nation included elements of both faith and secularism.

> Given such uneven foundations, it is not surprising that America's later and more secularized culture accentuated the Puritans' paradoxical traits [of faith and rationalism]. Secularization certainly does not correct the fundamental design. Sometimes it may inadvertently improve it, but such alterations are both accidental and haphazard. The unevenness remains, sometimes more spectacular or even grotesque. Such conclusions apply to the subject of the long-range Puritan contributions to American principles of government—certainly a focal point for the persistent and popular arguments that America had genuine Christian foundations.[14]

In seventeenth century New England, Puritanism codified and preserved orthodoxy with a strict, rationalistic approach. The contrasting elements of faith and rationalism produced two tendencies: a spiritual hunger, which paved the way for the great awakenings, and a scientific approach to matters in the world and to religious doctrine.[15] To American culture, "the Puritans bequeathed . . . the conflict between reason and intuition, between the head and the heart, between realism and idealism."[16] A Puritan and Pietistic heritage enabled individuals to grasp the religious the experiences of the great awakenings: repentance, conversion, regeneration, and spiritual renewal. However, a sizeable cohort held to rationalism without a spiritual inclination, among them Unitarians, humanists, and even skeptics. McLoughlin affirms:

> Yet, at the same time, the Puritans were heirs of humanism, and their faith in human reason led them "to accentuate the element of rationalism." On the one hand the Puritans distrusted "the affections," emotions, passions, "enthusiasm"; but on the other they urged men to "strive for an inward communication with the force that controls the world." The Puritan longed for the mystical wonder and beauty of communion with God's Spirit and at the same time checked himself [themselves] against visions, arguing that God gave man reason in order to distinguish

14. Noll et al., *The Search for Christian America*, 38–39.

15. Miller and Johnson, *Puritans: A Sourcebook of Their Writings*, 3.

16. McLoughlin, *Revivals, Awakenings, and Reform*, 41.

truth from hallucination. In short, the Puritans managed to hold in delicate but firm balance the idealism of Platonic thought (or the mysticism of the saints) and the realism of Aristotelian thought (or the skepticism of the humanist).[17]

The Puritan settlers of New England formed a rationalistic approach to religious life and social ethics. At the same time, Roger Williams opposed the Puritan establishment and established a new settlement in Rhode Island. Other dissenting groups included the Quakers, led by William Penn in Pennsylvania; Presbyterians of the Dutch Reformed church in New York and New Jersey; Baptists and Methodists in the South; and others. The great awakenings boosted church growth and spiritual fervor within these different religious traditions. A considerable number of Catholic settlers also found their way to the United States from England, Ireland, Italy, Poland, France, and Spain. During the seventeenth and eighteenth centuries, new settlers from Europe generally practiced religious tolerance despite their different backgrounds. They were dissenters and religiously recluse groups such as Quakers, Moravians, Baptists, Jews, and Catholics fleeing from religious persecution by the established church in their homelands. Mead states, "Religiously, then, what was unique about this American—this "new man" after 1787—was his practice of religious freedom."[18] Though a polarization between enthusiasm and rationalism existed, by now a form of separation of church and state in the Puritan era was indeed geared to accept the acclimatization of European secular waves into a form of Americanization of secularization.

The Secular in the Antebellum Era

Even though the thirteen colonies were able to maintain denominational and ethnic homogeneity in Puritan era, it could still be referred to as a Protestant British America. However in the antebellum American era, Protestant preponderance was no longer in effect but rather had rapidly heterogeneously evolved maintaining non-Protestant traditions. This is because European immigrants flooded into the United States, bringing non-Protestant traditions such as Catholicism and Orthodoxy. Beyond religious differences, however, common Christian ideas that had shaped the young nation remained intact. Later, non-

17. Ibid., 41–42.
18. Mead, *The Lively Experiment*, 3.

Christian and atheistic or worldviews antagonistic to Christianity were propagated during the Enlightenment, especially in Scotland.[19] Christian and secular worldviews interacted to shape the religious foundations of the United States.[20] During the American Revolution Americans generally responded to this conflict not by taking sides, but by maintaining a middle position and avoiding extremes. Some ardent secularists, like Thomas Jefferson and James Madison, advocated removing religious influence from shared aspects of everyday life such as education, and politics.[21] American Christianity adapted and flourished in an increasingly secularized environment. Although Christianity was not an official, state-sanctioned faith, it filled the role of a *de facto* religious establishment by dominating many aspects of society, culture, and politics during the American Revolution.[22] Therefore, it is difficult to draw a bright line between the sacred and the secular in American society.

Even if the Puritan awakening of the seventeenth century and the great awakening of the eighteenth century had shaped the young nation, intellectual rationalism as well as religious zeal helped set the tone for the practice of faith the United States. The census of 1776 revealed that only 17 percent of the population attended church, but norms and worldviews were highly Christianized. Hitchcock states, "If the elite group of founding fathers had been representative of public opinion in 1789, America would have developed as a secular nation."[23] Nonetheless, the effects of the awakenings and secular public policy making proceeded together. The steady and moderate growth of church attendance and membership provides a counterexample to the secularization thesis that describes the experience of most of Europe.[24]

Observing the loss of influence of the church in Europe and the growth of Christianity in the United States, one could conclude that America is less secularized than Europe. However, secular aspects have penetrated the church in the United States, especially consumerism and a free-market worldview. We would not affirm America is still

19. Noll, *The Scandal of the Evangelical Mind*, 86–87.

20. LaHaye, *Faith of Our Founding Fathers*, 16.

21. Ibid., 16.

22. Hall, *Confessing the Faith*, 229.

23. Hitchcock, *What Is Secular Humanism?*, 52.

24. Stark, "Secularization, R.I.P.," 5.

a strong Christian nation. According to Bruce in seeing the American case, "As this basic change involves replacing the other-worldly with the mundane, there seems no obvious reason not to regard it as secularization."[25]

Some would look to statistics, while measuring just a small sampling of American religious beliefs and practices, and allege that American religious involvement exceeds that of all European nations, except Ireland and Poland. However Ostwalt states, "Although American intellectual life demonstrated some of the same secularizing tendencies in the eighteenth century as European intellectual life, the twentieth century seems to suggest that religion in America is more vital than ever and perhaps an even more important component in American society than secular aspects like politics."[26] The mere fact that the American attitude on religion is diverse and complicated shows that Americans give matters of faith serious consideration.

The Secular and Dissociation

A fundamental difference between Europe and America is that "America never had . . . an absolutist state and its ecclesiastical counterpart, a caesaropapist state church."[27] The one exception was in colonial New England when the Congregational church filled this role. European national churches enjoyed the support of the elites, but did not necessarily connect with ordinary citizens or popular culture. On the contrary, in the United States, the dissociation of church and state enabled Christian vitality to flourish with the great awakenings. While government sanction protects official state churches from competition, the opposite is true in the United States. The dissociation of church and state in Europe propelled religious bodies into a marketplace where they need to attract people without having governmental assistance and religious taxation. Ostwalt states that "religion has found itself in the position of wooing its clients for allegiance, often against rival suitors as diverse as Friday night dates and Sunday afternoon football games."[28]

In Europe, Baptists, Quakers, Puritans, and Methodists have been labeled sects, dissenters, or cults within their state churches. I believe

25. Bruce, *Religion in the Modern World*, 147.
26. Ostwalt, *Secular Steeples*, 21.
27. Casanova, *Public Religions in the Modern World*, 29.
28. Ostwalt, *Secular Steeples*, 22.

that denominationalism is almost identical to the European "church" category in the United States: "The most distinctive American contribution to Christianity has been the development of denominational pluralism, which is a qualitatively different phenomenon from the European dichotomy of church and sect, and an elaboration of the limited non-conformist denominationalism of eighteenth-century England."[29] Casanova points out, "In the absence of state churches, the *raison d'être* of nonconformist sects disappears as well, and all religious bodies, churches as well as sects, turn into denominations."[30] His analysis is as follows:

> It should have been evident to Europeans as well, had they looked at the striking differences within Europe itself between, on one hand, Catholic Ireland and Catholic Poland, which never had a caesaropapist state church, and, on the other, Catholic France and Catholic Spain. Besides, consistently throughout Europe, nonestablished churches and sects in most countries have been able to survive the secularizing trends better than has the established church. It is not so much the minority versus majority status that explains the difference but the presence or absence of establishment. One may say that it was the very attempt to preserve and prolong Christendom in every nation-state and thus to resist modern functional differentiation that nearly destroyed the churches in Europe.[31]

While there was no European-style association between church and state in the United States, a sense of unity and shared values still underlay the American mindset.

Church and State Relationship

Hitchcock finds that, "By the time of the American Revolution, virtually all the colonies on the continent had at least a quasi-official church"[32]—an unstable allegiance between church and government. The birth of the new nation coincided with the pinnacle of the European Enlightenment, and this greatly affected the writing of the nation's constitution and views on religious freedom. The United States Constitution was composed on the basis of human reason, not divine

29. Wilson, "Religion and the Churches in Contemporary America," 73.

30. Casanova, *Public Religions in the Modern World*, 29.

31. Ibid., 29.

32. Hitchcock, *What Is Secular Humanism?*, 49.

revelation. Hitchcock states, "There were thus certain paradoxes in the spirit of the new nation. The Declaration of Independence forthrightly acknowledged dependence on God; the Constitution did not mention him. America was in some ways a very religious nation, but, especially among its leaders, this religion was often ambiguous."[33]

American denominational pluralism was devised not to favor a church or denomination, but to treat them all equally. Now, "In an increasingly secular world, denominational pluralism as an appropriate religious pattern of organization has been diffused to most other English speaking countries."[34] The constitutional separation of church and state laid essential groundwork for the secularization that followed in the United States. European secularization had developed outside of the domains of established religion, such as during the Enlightenment and later the French Revolution. In the American case, the lines were not drawn this way. Among the supporters of the American Revolution were those who had resisted the infidelity of the Enlightenment and the revolution in France. Others perceived this European secular wave as anti-Christian.[35] American Christians, who were synonymously called patriots, attempted to identify Christian principles within the political agenda that emerged as American democracy was being formed. Noll and others state:

> Then in the early years of the United States, most Christian bodies took the basically secular principles of the American Revolution as the guiding light for organizing churches, interpreting the Bible, and expressing the Christian faith. This process of baptizing political philosophies into the Christian faith was a precarious one. Certainly some of the features of the political philosophy of the American Revolution were commendable from a Christian point of view. But just as certainly they did not deserve to be equated with Christianity or permitted to dictate church structure, interpretations of Scripture, or expressions of the Christian faith. How, then, are we as modern Christians to evaluate our predecessors who seemed to have forgotten that Christianity existed before the creation of American democracy?[36]

33. Ibid., 50.

34. Wilson, "Religion and the Churches in Contemporary America," 73.

35. Noll, *The Search*, 20.

36. Ibid., 20.

Incorporating Christian principles into the Constitution, political system, and democracy, while resisting the urge to take denominational sides, generated an American style of religion.

THE CHURCH IN A SECULAR STATE

If European secularization is marked by the demise of the authority of religion in society, American secularization is the "process of making religion more worldly" and "a contemporary growing irrelevance of religion."[37] American Christianity is more likely to adapt to secular society than to transform it. The significance of religion in society today is far behind that of the awakenings, and many Americans believe that Christianity is losing ground in society and culture unlike before. Ostwalt says "secular worldviews often compete directly with religious ways of understanding reality."[38] Casanova claims, "America is the exception that confirms the European rule, the corollary being that the European rule does not need to be questioned."[39] American Christianity seems to have "lost its saltiness" through internal secularization.

To measure secularization in the United States, it is important to scrutinize the combination of the sacred and the secular within the church more than the process of church decline that has been seen in Europe. Borrowing Peter Burger's term "sacred canopy," Ostwalt calls the American case a "secular canopy . . . where secular and popular trends often dictate ecclesiastical strategy."[40] The decline of religious authority shows that society has become more secular in Europe. Oswalt asserts, "if secularization means entanglement with secular and popular culture, then the church in the United States seems to be more defined by secular society. We should not make this an either-or definition of secularization but adopt a definition broad enough to include both trends of secularization."[41] The United States church competes for survival in a religious free market. This has led to the decline of mainline churches as people joined new evangelical, Pentecostal, and charismatic churches.[42] European secularization coincided with

---

37. Ostwalt, *Secular Steeples*, 8.
38. Ibid., 9.
39. Casanova, *Public Religions in the Modern World*, 28.
40. Ostwalt, *Secular Steeples*, 50. See Peter L. Berger's book, *The Sacred Canopy*.
41. Ibid., 50.
42. O'Sullivan, *Parish Alive*, 2.

the decline of the ecclesiastical body. "From independence to the present, American Protestantism has gone through three consecutive processes of disestablishment."[43]

Separation between Church and State

Throughout European history, church and state have been intertwined since the medieval era. As Moore says, "Brief reflections about European history leave us dazed by the various patterns of conflict and accommodation that have marked the interaction between those who have ruled churches and those who have ruled states."[44] After the Enlightenment and French Revolution, the degree of separation of the church from its former prestige in the secular realm has been seen as the evidence of European secularization. Once the church began to dissociate from the state, this separation made an enormous impact over society to such a degree that a loss of control and power of ecclesiastical authority was bound to occur in Europe.[45] However, when the United States codified separation of church and state in the constitution, the intention was not to suppress religion, but to allow its free exercise. They "learned something from the turmoil of the European past and . . . have written a Constitution that took politics out of religion and religion out of politics."[46] European visitor James Bryce observed that Americans long for religious freedom and peace in their young nation.[47]

While there were some state churches in the American colonial period, independence from England brought a fresh start to the church/state relationship. Regarding the Anglican Church in the mid-Atlantic, it quickly lost support of Virginia's taxes, and other southern states; the Congregational Church in Massachusetts and Connecticut was slightly more resilient, but eventually met the same fate.[48] The separation of church and state does not mean that public

43. Casanova, *Public Religions in the Modern World*, 135.

44. Moore, *Selling God*, 67.

45. Hudson, *The Great Tradition of the American Churches*, 32–33.

46. Moore, *Selling God*, 67.

47. Hudson emphasized the importance of religious freedom for Americans and quoted Bryce as saying that this "was the general sense of religious peace pervading the country." Hudson, *The Great Tradition of the American Churches*, 34.

48. Virginia strongly opposed supporting a religious establishment and refuted the general assessment in 1786. James Madison proposed a bill that was a legal separation of church and state, which clearly noted equal religious liberty. "South

support for the church was withdrawn; rather, as Robert Calhoon indicates, the young nation provided governmental support to all types of Christian churches by means of tax in "South Carolina, Maryland, Massachusetts, New Hampshire, and Connecticut (individuals could contribute to churches of their own choice or to a general assessment fund for distribution to all approved clergy) and [conducted] religious tests for office-holding (only Christians in Pennsylvania and Delaware and only Protestants in North Carolina, Maryland, Georgia, and New Jersey)."[49]

Americans evaluated their churches not as a ruling powerhouse or dominant authority over politics, norms, and ethics, as was often observed in Europe, but as a spiritual lighthouse to guide society in the context of revivalism.[50] They believed the church must be separate, autonomous, and independent from political influences: "not patronized by the civil power, nor restrained by law" for the sake of people and nation.[51]

> The state, for its part, being a democracy, will necessarily reflect the spiritual and ethical principles of its citizens. So far from thinking their commonwealth godless, the Americans conceive that the religious character of a government consists in nothing but the religious belief of individual citizens, and the conformity of their conduct to that belief. They deem the general acceptance of Christianity to be one of the main sources of their national prosperity, and their nation a special object of the Divine favour.[52]

In framing the American constitution, Madison and Jefferson believed that the nation should apply religious liberty to every individual—creating, as Jefferson called it, a wall of separation between church and state. Separation was necessary because "the sanctity of private judgment was the ultimate source of virtue in a republic and therefore 'the opinions of men are not the object of civil government nor under

---

Carolina followed suit in its 1790 constitution, but until 1818 in Connecticut and 1833 in Massachusetts was the Congregationalist establishment finally abolished." Calhoon, "Separation of Church and State," 272.

49. Ibid., 272.

50. Hudson, *The Great Tradition of the American Churches*, 33.

51. Ibid., 33.

52. Ibid., 33.

its jurisdiction.'"[53] The separation of church and state in Europe was viewed negatively, as it hastened secularization, but was welcomed in the United States. Evangelicals including Baptist pastor Isaac Backus, from New England, "saw separation as a guarantee that the United States would be a Christian republic in which churches would be free from political influence and hence fully open to the leading of the Holy Spirit."[54] Still, political statements throughout American history have been imbued with Christian vocabulary. In his first inaugural address in 1829, President Andrew Jackson said, "man can become more and more endowed with divinity; and as he does he becomes more God-like in his character and capable of governing himself. . . . Let us go on elevating our people, perfecting our institutions, until democracy shall reach such a point of perfection that we can acclaim with truth that the voice of the people is the voice of God."[55]

The issue on the separation of church and state in the young and new America seemed quite different from the case in France, in that America's founding philosophy and ideology in formulating the Constitution expressed the equality of freedom and religion. The French Revolution brought down the monarchy and also the union of church and state and their ability to implement secular governments especially now that there would be no religious interference from Catholic ecclesiastical authority. In American case, the Constitution gives liberty to choose their own denomination yet in the public sphere the common idea deeply seeped into Christian norms and values.

Disestablishment in the American Revolution

By the second great awakening, evangelical churches had emerged and grown strong. Casanova proposes that, since the 1830s, evangelical Protestantism functioned as the American civil religion.[56] American churches continued to grow because there was a spirit of denominational prestige. Casanova states "the homogenization of the main Protestant denominations made possible the launching of a

53. Calhoon, "Separation of Church and State," 272.

54. Backus insisted that Christian religion should be "prior to all states and kingdoms in the world and therefore could not in its nature be the subject of human laws." Ibid., 272.

55. Quoted in Casanova, *Public Religions in the Modern World*, 140.

56. Ibid., 140.

transdenominational evangelical crusade to 'Christianize' the people, the social order, and the republic."[57] In a critical observation based on her experience in Cincinnati from 1827 to 1831, novelist Frances Trollope wrote, "a religious tyranny may be exerted very effectually without the aid of the government, in a way much more oppressive than the paying of tithe, and without obtaining any of the salutary decorum which I presume no one will deny is the result of an established mode of worship. . . . Church and State hobble along, side by side, notwithstanding their boasted independence."[58] The monopoly held by European religious establishments for centuries created a sense of hostility against the church in Europe. However, religious freedom, equality, democracy, and individualism paved the way for Americans to help their denominations flourish. Hudson concludes, in the 1830s, American religious freedom and the separation of church and state were securely retained. He saw that "secular politics "gives the enemy less occasion to blaspheme than he is apt to have in Europe," and the person who becomes disaffected with his church does not become hostile to religion but simply joins some other denomination in which he feels more at home." Hudson concludes, "A heritage of colonial days, derived from the new conception of the church worked out among the English Puritans and finding initial expression in Rhode Island and Pennsylvania, the principle of separation of church and state had commended itself to a majority of Americans by the end of the colonial period."[59]

Hudson states:

> The national government was restrained at this point, but the states were not. And an establishment of religion—with each taxpayer assigning his rates to the church of his choice—did linger on for a generation in three of the New England states. But long before the adoption of the Fourteenth Amendment in 1868 imposed the restrictions of the First Amendment upon state governments, the principle of separation had been incorporated in the constitutions of the individual states and was taken for granted by everyone. Roughly by 1830s the complete

57. Ibid., 136.
58. Moore, *Selling God*, 67–68.
59. Hudson, *The Great Tradition of the American Churches*, 37–38.

separation of church and state had become an unquestioned postulate of all Americans.[60]

Even with disestablishment, Christianity maintained a strong position in the public sphere. De Tocqueville observed this between 1831–32 and, two years later so did Francis Grund, an Austrian visitor who was a naturalized American citizen. He wrote that religious beliefs and practices of Americans are meticulously interrelated with the private and public areas of social and moral activities. He even says that every sphere of American life was closely intertwined with the legislation. Most laws had been aligned with Christian principles and doctrines so that the government would be able to implement the very essence of the Christian principle.

> "[H]er inhabitants were distinguished for the simplicity of their manners and the high moral rectitude of their character; they were a highly *civilized* people . . . It was of the utmost importance for the safety of the government, which at that time was only an *experiment*, that the people should retain their simple habits, until age should have given strength to the constitution, and accustomed the people readily to submit to the newly-instituted authorities . . . The habits and morals of a people are the surest guarantee of the continuance of any government; they are the life and essence of its existence, without which the constitution is but a dead letter."[61]

Religion, affirmed Grund, "presides over their councils, aids in the execution of the laws, and adds to the dignity of the judges."[62] Even though the separation of church and state took effect in the 1840s, they were informally and unofficially interconnected.[63] After the Civil War, as the process of the second disestablishment of the nineteenth century was underway, a great transition took place based on geography: the North and the South, liberal and evangelical, respectively.[64] Casanova points out this regard:

60. Ibid., 27–28.

61. Grund, *The Americans in their Moral, Social, and Political Relations*, 11–12

62. Hudson, *The Great Tradition of the American Churches*, 39.

63. Moore, *Selling God*, 67.

64. The second disestablishment can be traced to the time of the Civil War. The new wave of non-Protestants from Europe contributed to the largely urban settlement in contrast to the previous pattern of rural living. Industrialization rapidly spread in many urban sectors allowing the people's lives to economically improve.

Defeat and victory in the Civil War only reinforced the divergent trends. Old time religion in the South became even more suspicious of worldly entanglements, finding theological justification for such a position in the tradition of strict Baptist separation of church and state. Victorious Yankee Protestantism, by contrast, became ever more committed to the postmillennial faith in the progressive realization of the millennium and in the manifest destiny of Christian America. As the second disestablishment proceeded apace, however, the conservative wing of northern evangelical Protestantism began to waver and to lose faith in urban, industrial America. The turnaround from postmillennialism to premillennialism and from social reform to rescue mission, which is noticeable in urban revivalism from Charles Grandison Finney to Dwight L. Moody, is the best indication of a transformation that prepared the ground for the emergence of fundamentalism.[65]

However, the actual process of secularization did not initiate with the Revolution, but with the Civil War. This period was called the *second establishment*. Casanova states that secularization took place through "higher education and the loss of Protestant cultural hegemony over the public sphere of American civil society."[66] As a result of the second Great Awakening and evangelical revivals, new colleges and universities established and promulgated the traditional Christian gospel while old colleges and universities were under the influence of secularism, liberalism, and social Darwinism. Additionally, antebellum America had undergone rapid social changes through industrialization and urbanization, which eventually transformed the religious geography of the nation as well. Casanova continues to argue on the secularization process in various areas:

> The new industrial society needed new institutions of higher learning. The traditional Protestant colleges and universities shed or marginalized their divinity schools, their original nuclei, as they entered upon the modern process of academic and

---

This phenomenon paved the way for individualistic approach of the religion in public life causing religion to become very private providing the idea that the church and state needed to be separated. The "Civil war and reconstruction created the structural conditions for the rapid process of capitalist industrialization and urbanization that radically and irrevocably altered antebellum American society." Casanova, *Public Religions in the Modern World*, 37.

65. Ibid., 139.

66. Ibid., 137.

scientific specialization. The opening up of public lands for state land-grant colleges speeded up the process. The natural sciences, particularly Darwinism, the newly emerging social sciences, and the cultural-historical sciences with their new epistemologies and critical methods of interpretation presented explanations of nature, society, and human culture that were often in conflict with established Protestant worldviews.[67]

Outwardly, there was no apparent support or political agenda for the church coming from the state by means of the constitution, political system, or governmental structure. Inwardly, however, there had been a strong sense of close interrelationship between church and state in antebellum America. As secular thought and philosophy in the forms of liberalism, rationalism, Darwinism, social science, and new learning from Europe began to permeate education and worldviews among ordinary Americans, it paved the way for secularization.

Process of Disestablishment in America

As in Britain, secularization in the United States took place through social and economic transformations such as industrialization, urbanization, and modernization. The rapid influx of non-Protestants was also significant as Catholic and eastern Orthodox immigrants reduced Protestant influence. In the late nineteenth century Catholics comprised the single largest Christian body. Immigrants began to shape the American religious landscape; cities and towns that were entry points for immigrants and destinations for migrants from rural areas became unchurched or non-Protestant in character. Large cities and industrial urban areas were in great need of the Christian gospel, but, ironically, it was not the evangelicals, but the liberal Christians who attempted to reach out through the social gospel movement. Still, social gospel ministry "would have to compete not only with sinful resistance but with secular and non-Protestant movements and organizations."[68]

In Europe, historical secularization marked the wane of ecclesiastical power and a loss of prestige and influence for national churches. In the United States, starting after the Civil War, many Protestant denominations—including Presbyterians, Methodist, Baptists, Episcopalians (Anglicans), and Congregationalists—segregated themselves between

67. Ibid., 137–38.
68. Ibid., 138.

blacks and whites, north and south, and even east and west. Casanova states, "at the time of the Civil War, the South was 90 percent Protestant. Furthermore, southern Protestantism was 90 percent Baptist and Methodist. Paradoxically, defeat in the Civil War allowed white southern evangelical Protestantism to remain the established civil religion of the South until the "recent third disestablishment."[69]

Casanova perceives that the third disestablishment came out of the rise of American fundamentalism that was a reaction to the social scientific, spiritual, and resource mobilization of the early and mid twentieth century.[70] American Protestantism includes four chief traditions: Puritan Calvinism, an independent Baptist church, Scottish Presbyterianism, and Wesleyan Methodism.[71] Congregationalism had declined significantly by the nineteenth century, and new denominations such as Methodism and other Holiness churches filled the gaps, altering the nation's religious makeup in the west and south. The steady growth of the Baptist Church advanced its position in the south and west significantly. From the 1830s, critical theological differences had led to official denominational segregation of the Presbyterian, Baptist, and Methodist denominations between the north and south. Casanova illustrates:

> As southern evangelicalism progressively repressed its original impulse to condemn the "evil" institution of slavery, accommodated itself resignedly to worldly realities, and finally learned to lend Christian justification to the system of slavery,

69. Ibid., 138.

70. Ibid., 145–66.

71. The essence of the American religious establishment originated from New England Puritan Calvinism along with covenant theology and postmillennialism. They believed that this theology inclines to transform the new world in America and accomplished their vision for God's kingdom. The Reformed theology from Princeton Seminary attributed to the intellectual rationalistic approach of society. On the other hand the Free Church traditions such as the dissenting, separatists Baptists tended to be "antinomian," "radical sectarian," and "anti-establishmentarian" when they were still the minority. In the nineteenth century when the new denominations (Methodism and Baptists in particular) gained more power the Methodist movement was able to contribute to the new idea of church establishment that seemed to be evangelical, pragmatic, and very individualistic. Particularly the spiritual movement along with the Wesleyan holiness movement in the U. S. was able to assist individuals in the sanctification process for all who partook of this belief. Casanova says "Methodism blended best with life on the frontier and with the spirit of the age." Ibid., 138–39.

it also lost the impulse to transform the world and became ever more otherworldly, concentrating on the all-important business of saving white and black souls. Burdened by "bad faith," southern evangelicalism never manifested as unequivocally as its northern counterpart a postmillennial faith in impulse progress.[72]

Adaptation to the secular culture led to internal secularization among the large Protestant denominations in the US and Britain. For instance, in Britain, industrialization, urbanization, and the rationalism of the Enlightenment paved the way for secularization within the Church of England. As a reaction, the Methodist movement emerged and began to flourish. In the course of time, however, the Methodist church assimilated to secular culture. This had two effects: the emergence of the Holiness Movement and a boost in sectarian movements such as the independent and individualistic church movements. Older mainline denominations were inevitably replaced by newer and younger churches and denominations, as Bainbridge points out, "In principle, this cycle could continue forever, constantly renewing Protestantism with vigorous, new movements that gradually ossify, only to be replaced in turn by their more vigorous offspring. This is a picture of Christianity running in place, as it were. The movements within Christianity move, but Christianity as a whole does not."[73]

Hence, the rise of fundamentalism in the twentieth century was closely interrelated with the second disestablishment that allowed "a modern antimodernist reaction" resulting in secularization of education and public life.[74] Emerging liberal Protestant thinkers and theologians disconnected evangelical Christian moral codes from public life. Casanova points out that "Militant fundamentalism fought its battles on three fronts: against the liberal-modernist heresies within the northern evangelical denominations, against the teaching of Darwinism in the public schools, and against 'rum and Romanism' in urban America."[75]

In the late nineteenth and early twentieth centuries in America, two opposing forces clashed. Evangelicals sought to declare the United

72. Ibid., 139.

73. Bainbridge, *The Sociology of Religious Movements*, 405.

74. Casanova, *Public Religions in the Modern World*, 140.

75. Ibid., 140–41.

States Christian nation, including religious observance, Christian teaching in educational institutions, and Christian influences on judicial rulings and legislation, while liberals and modernists tried to execute the "rationalist idea of a secular state."[76] According to Calhoon,

> In one category of cases, the courts have steadily and severely restricted the power of the state to compel pious behavior or foster religious observance by proscribing Sunday "blue laws," ordinances against blasphemy, compulsory school prayer, voluntary released time for religious training in the public schools, and religious test oaths. The outlawing of religious discrimination in public life and the marketplace, demanded by Jewish organizations in the 1930s and 1940s, prepared the way for similar attacks on racial and sexual injustice in the 1950s, 1960s, and 1970s.[77]

Eventually, the evangelical camp lost much influence in the judiciary. Some sociologists of religion see this as a corollary of the secularization thesis—the decline of religious influence in the public sphere. According to Ostwalt, at the critical point of the secularization process, the "enlightenment, science, or other social institutions" may replace religion or make "religion irrelevant or less relevant" by allowing more freedom of humanity. He insists, "This predominantly sociological view of religion is one that many contemporary religious organizations have taken to heart in their attempts to be more relevant to their constituents. Nevertheless, some contemporary sociologists challenged the view but now seem content that religion is not destined to disappear."[78] It is impossible to insist that individuals adhere to religious duty and principles in the public arena. So, as society pursued secular and liberal ideas, the byproducts of this pursuit resulted in the decline of the Christian faith among young people in the mid-twentieth century.

SECULARIZATION AND AWAKENINGS

During the "Age of Reason" in America since 1794, the nation began to construct the intellectual pathways that would facilitate secularization among academics, religious leaders, and intellectuals, a process

76. Calhoon, "Separation of Church and State", 272.

77. Ibid., 272–73.

78. Ostwalt, *Secular Steeples*, 2.

similar to that which weakened Puritanism in the eighteenth century. Mark Noll states, "The Age of Faith of Luther, Calvin, and Cromwell gave way to the Age of Reason of Newton, Locke, and Linnaeus. With the pejorative term 'enthusiasm,' many sneered at religious fervor."[79] He goes on to claim:

> Reason emerged from the shadows of Calvinist mistrust of that fallen faculty to shine as the beacon of the Enlightenment. Trust of reason led to faith in science, which now endeavored to bare nature's secrets on heaven and earth and even uncover the laws of morality, economics, and politics. As Puritanism lost momentum, many young New Englanders adopted the latest religious fashions arriving practically daily from England, particularly those at the cutting edge of the Enlightenment like Arminianism (which denied predestination), Latitudinarianism (which emphasized morality over creed), Unitarianism (which rejected the divinity of Christ), and Deism (which taught a passive God in a machine-universe). Moreover, New England itself had changed. It had grown too populated, too contentious, too wealthy, and too worldly. Or at least, so it appeared to some.[80]

The reason-centered life had begun to proscribe the spirit-centered life. The Great Awakenings and revivals nurtured a vibrant spiritual life among believers who had been Christianized with formal, nominal, liturgical beliefs and practices without spiritual experience. When the religion becomes a way of life, it affects people's interest to be irreligious and anti-spiritual. Religion becomes a duty of habitual practices rather than one's personal faith convictions. Reason, given by God for godly use, became divorced from faith and produced the Enlightenment, secularism, liberalism, modernity, and humanism. The arm of secularization reaches all rational people.

The Enlightenment and Great Awakenings

In the New World, particularly on American soil, the Enlightenment did not represent a religious movement, but an intellectual one with implications on an enormous scale. Casanova states that "The state and scientific culture . . . could serve as plausible independent variables, since church-state relations and the scientific worldviews carried by the

79. Stoll, *Protestantism, Capitalism, and Nature in America*, 78.

80. Stoll, *Is Latin America Turning Protestant?*, 78.

Enlightenment were significantly different in Europe and America."[81] Under the influence of the Enlightenment, separation of church and state increased and theology was rationalized so that Europe's church-centered society became one centered in human reason.

In Britain and Europe, the Enlightenment fundamentally re-shaped the relationship of church and society, which had been inter-woven. The same Enlightenment had an impact on American society in very different ways. British evangelicalism, including Methodism and Anglicanism, incorporated some functions of reason into their revival movements in positive ways. This prevented the strong secular rationalization during the Enlightenment that was seen in France and in central Europe, in which evangelical and spiritual elements were disdained and discarded.

The Enlightenment in Europe deeply affected the church, includ-ing state ecclesiastical establishments that had modified, adopted, and even recreated secular culture. Reason became the center not only of human thought, sciences, arts, literature, and philosophy, but also of theology and religion. The Enlightenment fostered "the belief that all human beings can attain here on earth a state of perfection hitherto in the West thought to be possible only for Christians in a state of grace, and for them only after death."[82] In the case in the United States, "The faith in reason, progress, and democracy was blended with the Calvinist emphasis on work and prosperity and tempered with a strong sense of transcendent values."[83] The American founding fathers had applied rationality to society and even to theological hermeneutics, at the same time retaining religious enthusiasm.[84]

Those affected by the Great Awakenings reacted differently to the Enlightenment than did theological liberals.[85] Mark Noll calls Jonathan Edwards not only an evangelist of the first great awakening, but also as an "enlightened" evangelical. While the French Enlightenment hastened secularization, Edwards and his successors in the United States utilized the reason of the Enlightenment to make use of phi-

---

81. Casanova, *Public Religions in the Modern World*, 28–29.

82. Crane Brinton, quoted in Yount, *The Future of Christian Faith in America*, 66.

83. Sydney E. Ahlstrom, quoted in Sturtevant, says, "The wines of the Enlighten-ment were sipped with cautious moderation." Sturtevant, *Popular Uprisings*, 90–91.

84. Yount, *The Future of Christian Faith in America*, 66.

85. May, "The Problem of the American Enlightenment," 118.

losophy, theology, history, literature, politics, science, and fine arts to Christian ends. "This evangelical embrace of the Enlightenment at the turn of the eighteenth century still remains extraordinarily important nearly two centuries later because habits of mind that the evangelical Enlightenment encouraged have continued to influence contemporary evangelical life. . . . [T]he most important were a particular kind of commitment to objective truth and a particular 'scientific' approach to the Bible."[86]

In Europe, Enlightenment rationality challenged the mystery of the sacred; in Britain and America, however, revivalists challenged rationality with revivals and spiritual awakenings. The positive use of Enlightenment principles was promoted by revivalists such as John Wesley, Jonathan Edwards, and many more. The Enlightenment in America had played in juxtaposition. According to Turner, "The early history of Methodism is almost unintelligible without some knowledge of the trends in English life in the eighteenth century, the world of the Age of Reason and the Age of Revival, which both diverge and curiously run together, so that Jonathan Edwards, in America, could preach sermons like "sinners in the hand of an angry God" and propound the philosophy of John Locke with equal conviction."[87]

The interaction between revivalists and intellectuals of the Enlightenment can be seen in three historical phases. The first phase, which May calls "New Learning at Yale from 1714," lasted until the Revolution.[88] The second phase was retaliatory against Christianity and was characterized by Ethan Allen's *Reason: the Only Oracle of Man*.[89] May calls the third phase, from 1800 to 1815, "defeat and absorption." As in Europe, the Enlightenment claimed to bring liberation from the Christian faith. However, Enlightenment principles were perceived differently by Americans, as May says: "the Enlightenment consists of all those who believe two propositions: first, that the present age is more enlightened than the past; and second, that we understand nature and man best through the use of our natural faculties."[90]

---

86. Noll, *The Scandal of the Evangelical Mind*, 83.

87. Turner, *Conflict and Reconciliation*, 1.

88. May, "The Problem of the American Enlightenment," 121.

89. Ibid., 121.

90. May, *The Enlightenment in America*, xiv.

May has identified four types Enlightenment in the United States: moderate, skeptical, revolutionary, and didactic. Moderate Enlightenment, which occurred in the mid-eighteenth century, is essentially synonymous with the "rational enlightenment" epitomized by Isaac Newton and John Locke.[91] The second type, skeptical Enlightenment, was developed by David Hume in Britain and by Voltaire, who was called its grand master in France around 1750. May asserts, "Its dogmas were usually elliptically stated and often mere negations, but if it was pursued systematically it issued either in the systematic epistemological skepticism of Hume or the systematic materialism of Holbach."[92] The third type, revolutionary Enlightenment, claimed "the belief in the possibility of constructing a new heaven and earth out of the destruction of the old. It had its beginnings with Rousseau and its culmination in (after 1780) Paine and Godwin."[93] According to May, the fourth Enlightenment began before the middle of eighteenth century in Scotland and was called the didactic Enlightenment, but was also known as the Scottish Enlightenment. This school of thought "tried to save from what it saw as the debacle of the Enlightenment the intelligible universe, clear and certain moral judgments, and progress."[94] Its most significant impact would not be achieved in Scotland, but in America.

According to Noll, there are three generations of American thinkers comprised of Francis Hutcheson, Thomas Reid, Adam Smith, and Dugald Stewart, who piloted the rationalist approach to social and moral areas with the Enlightenment perspective.[95] This was a modified form of the Scottish Enlightenment, developed over five decades on American soil.[96] To understand the American evangelical enlightenment, we must remember its European counterpart. After the first great awakening but before the second, in the 1780s and 1790s, Christianity was at a low point due to Enlightenment influences. Nonetheless, the United States demonstrated a relatively young and strong Christian identity.[97] Mark Noll states,

91. Noll, *The Scandal of the Evangelical Mind*, 84; May, xiv.
92. May, *The Problem of American Enlightenment*, xvi.
93. Ibid., xvi.
94. Ibid.
95. Noll, *The Scandal of the Evangelical Mind*, 84.
96. Ibid., 85.
97. Marty, *The Modern Schism*, 109–10.

Evangelical adoption of the didactic Enlightenment was one
of the measures that made evangelical Protestantism so dy-
namically powerful in the early history of the United States.
Had evangelicals not done so, their fate would probably have
been like the fate of Europe's established churches, which, as
they continued to rely on tradition and hierarchy, increasingly lost touch with ordinary people and eventually forfeited
their once-dominant place in Europe's intellectual life. It was,
in its own terms, a tremendous achievement for American
evangelicals to save both the reputation of the gospel and their
own influence within society. That achievement should not be
taken lightly. Unfortunately, however, the successful alliance
of evangelicals with main currents of American culture left a
weak intellectual legacy.[98]

Enlightenment ideas are at the foundation of the concepts articulated in the Constitution and the structure of the nation established
during the mid- and late eighteenth century.[99] Still, in the United
States as in Europe, the ideas of the Enlightenment were not widely
circulated among the general population, but were confined to an elite
who identified themselves as theists, atheists, secularists, and later
Unitarians.[100] In the 1820s, the latter years of the second great awakening, the influence of the Enlightenment in the transatlantic region lost
some of its strength: "The Enlightenment influence did remain in certain respects and had significant long-term effects, but the public spirit
of the nation was definitely religious."[101] Secularization in the United
States took the form of a secular religion based on Enlightenment
principles as a counterpart to the great awakening. In this respect, the
Enlightenment achieved freethinking through human reason. Reeves
asserts, "In this religion, pride, rather than being the first of the seven
deadly sins, was the cornerstone. A certain measure of self-respect is,
of course, a healthy thing, but the emphasis here was on the glorifica-
tion of the self-one's intellect, self-sufficiency, and all-importance."[102]

Secularists with a rationalistic approach to human nature gained
ground in academia, society, and some churches, especially in the
Unitarian church. This secular religion was intended to free people from

98. Noll, *The Scandal of the Evangelical Mind*, 105.
99. Guder et al., *Missional Church*, 32.
100. Hitchcock , *What Is Secular Humanism?*, 52.
101. Ibid., 52.
102. Sturtevant, *Popular Uprisings*, 1840–1940, 71.

superstition: "They [rationalists] meant to free him from belief in, and responsibility to, a demanding God."[103] The attractiveness of a secular religion can be seen in the rise of human rights, in education without religious influence, in the establishment of the freedoms of religion and speech, and in the right to organize, such as the labor movement. As Reeves points out, the French revolution in 1789 "first introduced universal male suffrage on a national scale, planned a national system of public schools, and proclaimed the abolition of slavery."[104] He traces the roots of three secular religions, "the Enlightenment, Marxism, and science," to the evolution theory of Charles Darwin.[105]

Darwinism and Humanism

The publication of Charles Darwin's *Origin of Species* in 1859 exacerbated the divisions between the proponents of evangelical awakenings and advocates of secularism and "sparked an intellectual crisis for Christians that no educated person could ignore."[106] As Darwinian theories were introduced in schools, the fundamentals of biblical belief began to erode. Although there was no state-church system in the United States, Christian values were nonetheless rooted deeply in American culture. Darwin's revolutionary idea that human beings had evolved and were not the creation of God undermined this common foundation. Coupled with the teachings of academics who raised questions about the authority of the Bible, Darwinism led many Americans to believe that Christianity was unreliable and that Christian education was only for children.

> Darwinism focused the issue on the reliability of the first chapters of Genesis. But the wider issue was whether the Bible could be trusted at all. German higher criticism, questioning the historicity of many biblical accounts, had been developing for more than a generation, so that it was highly sophisticated by the time after the Civil War when it became widely known in America. It would be difficult to overstate the critical importance of the absolute integrity of the Bible to the nineteenth-century American evangelical's whole way of thinking. When

103. Yount, *The Future of Christian Faith in America*, 66.

104. Ibid., 77.

105. Ibid., 82–83.

106. Noll et al., *Christianity in America*, 283.

this cornerstone began to be shaken, major adjustments in the evangelical edifice had to be made from top to bottom.[107]

Secular trends among American intellectuals had been utilized in comparative religion and biblical criticism to undermine Christian values and worldviews in the early twentieth century. These secular trends were already making headway in the late nineteenth century. Social historian Arthur Schlesinger's 1933 book *The Rise of the City* documented how widely American society followed secular trends, particularly through the educational system. He states, "improvement of the educational system occurred at every point from top to bottom. Congress had evidenced its interest in 1867 . . . . gathering statistics, disseminating information and holding up the torch for the more backward commonwealths."[108] On the flip side, awakenings and revivals powerfully transformed lives in rural areas. The forces of revival and secularization were juxtaposed, particularly after Civil War. Schlesinger claimed that Darwinism impacted intellectuals starting in the late nineteenth century. Schlesinger describes, "Meantime philosophy itself could not remain indifferent to the scientific temper. Both here and abroad it tentatively reconsidered its technique and concepts in the light particularly of the Darwinism hypothesis and the new psychology. Within these limits, however, many winds of doctrine blew across the scene."[109]

In addition, a new wave of non-Protestant immigration and domestic migration to urban areas interacted with secularism to pull people away from the rural, church-centered life. These changes "also sometimes had the effect of inviting superficial solutions such as working to preserve Protestant respectability but at the expense of a prophetic Protestant message that would challenge, rather than simply confirm, the value systems that were coming to control American life."[110] An influx of non-Protestant and eventually non-Christian immigrants began in the 1830s, creating an atmosphere of religious tolerance and pluralism as the nation became more urbanized. Many of them were, according to Hitchcock, "at least nominally religious,

---

107. Ibid., 285.
108. Schlesinger, *The Rise of the City 1878–1898*, 161.
109. Ibid., 238.
110. Noll, *Eerdmans'*, 288.

and many were a great deal more than nominal." [111] Religious tolerance provided the space in which new immigrants could practice their Catholic, Orthodox, Jewish, or other beliefs. European immigrants brought along with them rationalism, urbanization, and industrialization, opening up the door for the United States to face the challenge of European secularization.

Many educational institutions followed the path of secularization and became detached from church influence. Starting in the 1870s, teachings on creation, society, and human nature were greatly altered by the Enlightenment, Darwin's evolution theory, and new academic disciplines including sociology and anthropology.[112] The traditional role of American Protestantism was called into question as many intellectuals portrayed religion as an illusion of unenlightened people. Darwinism came to dominate American intellectual life and some predicted that the downfall of Christianity was inevitable. This trend began to reshape theology as many scholars called into question the authority of the Bible. "The stories and eternal verities long accepted by Christians seemed to some to be products of a much simpler and less enlightened time."[113] Between the Civil War and World War II, American society experienced profound social changes such as urbanization, industrialization, and modernization, and intellectuals adopted liberal theology and scientism as much as Darwinism had widely attracted its advocates in the Academia. Cities grew as urban dwellers migrated initially from rural areas and then from abroad as the influx from Europe continued, drawn to cities by the promise of employment.[114] The progress of internal and external migration and communication provided easier accessibility to Darwinism and humanism in American society.

American Secularism

In the United States, two forces were at work. Awakenings and revivals led people to religious fervor, enthusiasm, emotion, and mysticism. On the other hand, secularism and rationalism led people away the mystery of the Christian faith and resulted in many becoming

111. Hitchcock, *What Is Secular Humansim?*, 53.

112. Marty, *The Modern Schism*, 117.

113. Sturtevant, *Popular Uprisings*, 91.

114. Hitchcock, *What Is Secular Humanism?*, 53–54.

Unitarians, theists, pluralists, secularists, and even religious atheists LaHaye classifies both theists and atheists within the "secularist" category. Some were "deists rather than atheists, proclaiming belief in a supreme being who created the earth and the human race but was no longer involved in His universe."[115] Unitarians, theists, atheists, pluralists, and secularists no longer believed in traditional biblical authority and salvation by faith.

Many contemporary advocates of secularization claim that the mystery and sacredness of religion will ultimately vanish because reason will subsume its function in society. Who is to arbitrate between mystery and lack of mystery? Secularists will be the ones to decide their roles, because they can motivate the secularization process.[116] Regarding the work of German theologian Friedrich Gogarten, Shiner states:

> In one of his major postwar works Gogarten applies this sec-ularization-secularism continuum to three phenomena which dominate much of our discussion of the contemporary situation: science, culture, and history. Since the question of history is at the center of this exposition of Gogarten's thought, it would be well to look briefly at the way the secularization-secularism pattern is applied to the meaning of history. We will see that Gogarten finds the pattern finally inadequate to the deepest opposition between Christian faith and the subject-centered orientation of modern man.[117]

If in Europe secularization occurred over a protracted period, in the United States, the permeation of secularism into every sphere of life was archetypal. Fishwick observes, "In Europe the confrontation between secularism and religion tends to be more explicit and well defined. . . . In the United States hostility or demonstrative indifference to religion is a minor and manageable force. America's secularism is found within the churches themselves."[118] Secularists outside the church are fewer in number than those inside the church who adapt secular ideas to religious life. Still, their societal and intellectual influence is greater than their numbers would suggest.[119] Marsden states:

---

115. LaHaye, *Faith of Our Founding Fathers*, 16.

116. Shiner, *The Secularization of History*, 165–66.

117. Ibid., 166.

118. Fishwick, *Great Awakenings*, 104–5.

119. Hitchcock, *What Is Secular Humanism?*, 115.

> Somewhat more remarkable is that the specifically Christian aspects of [American] heritage had not eroded more. In Europe during the same era the winds of frankly secular ideologies were blowing strongly, and one might have expected that America, the land of revolutionary liberal political ideals, might by now have adopted a genial democratic humanism, freed from explicitly Christian dogmas and institutions. The fact that America had not in the nineteenth century followed the course set in the eighteenth by leaders like Franklin and Jefferson was due largely to vigorous evangelical enterprise. The United States had not drifted religiously during the nineteenth century. It had been guided, even driven, by resourceful evangelical leaders who effectively channeled the powers of revivals and voluntary religious organizations to counter the forces of purely secular change.[120]

American Christians seemed to discard the ideas of secularism and hold to conservative Christian beliefs, including the authority of the Bible, redemption by Jesus, and the coming judgment.[121] Nevertheless, secularists had an influence on social and religious life disproportionate to their limited numbers because of their influential roles in journalism, academia, politics, and other social spheres. When confronted with secularist views, many Christian theologians and apologists have failed to make a vigorous defense of orthodox faith. Hitchcock's viewpoint seems justified: "Either the churches do not fully comprehend the problem and do not strongly oppose it, or, in some cases, the churches themselves are deeply affected by it. . . . Ironically, to a degree the churches themselves are primary vehicles by which secularism is spread."[122]

In America, secularization is not readily apparent; the church has been growing, unlike in Europe, which has experienced a steady decrease in churchgoers and the loss of significance of religious authority. Marsden points out that "compounding the massiveness of the crisis was simply a basic secularization of American culture. . . . [Gradually] various areas of American culture were drifting away from any real connections with religious influences.[123] Christian denominations in the United States began to conform in the twentieth century to secu-

---

120. Marsden, *Understanding Fundamentalism and Evangelicalism*, 11–12.
121. Sturtevant, *Popular Uprisings*, 99.
122. Hitchcock, *What Is Secular Humanism?*, 115.
123. Marsden, *Understanding Fundamentalism*, 14.

larism and, as Noll et al. point out, took on a moralist character. The Protestant doctrine of salvation by faith was modified to a secular version advocating salvation through works of righteousness, in which religion serves as functional morality. "Puritanism indeed helped foster such traditions, but in their secularized versions the offspring of the Puritan ethic turn out to be at best the works-righteousness of Pelagianism, of self-salvation, or even of simple secular moralism."[124]

As religious cynicism and liberalism gained ground in the twentieth century, influential scholars and theologians began to assault the authority of the Bible. Protestantism had traditionally relied on the Bible as an infallible, inerrant, unique, and authoritative source of God's special revelation. Now, it was being interrogated antagonistically by secularists. In addition, secularists attacked the authority of Protestantism that had functioned as American public and civil religion.[125] Smith highlights this transformation: "orthodox Protestantism's dominance of American public culture was increasingly giving way to a 'neutral,' 'rational' version of cultural discourse that left little room for the voice of religious authority."[126] Guder paints a grim picture, "The cries are certainly many and complex: diminishing numbers, clergy burnout, the loss of youth, the end of denominational loyalty, biblical illiteracy, divisions in the ranks, the electronic church and its various corruptions, the irrelevance of traditional forms of worship, the loss of genuine spirituality, and widespread confusion about both the purpose and the message of the church of Jesus Christ."[127]

American intellectualism, while not anti-Christian, has the tendency to oppose the idea of a biblical foundation as the basis for Christian values. Noll and others identified relativistic secularism as "a major cultural force in twentieth century America. Although not a unified movement or belief system, relativistic secularism involves a broad consensus of shared ideas that dominates American intellectual life, law, politics, and the media."[128] This school of thought is based not in Christian values, but in social forces:

124. Noll, *The Search*, 41.

125. Fowler et al., *A Rocky Mountain Sailor*, 5.

126. Ibid., 5–6. Smith argues that scholars from many academic circles began to view the Bible as "human writings full of myths and errors" the "Scottish common sense realism" fatally diluted.

127. Guder et al., *Missional Church*, 2.

128. Noll, *The Search*, 128.

Such social determinism is balanced by a fervent faith in the value of the freedom of each individual for equal opportunity creatively to develop his or her full potential. Societies, using their scientifically based understanding of human conditions, should organize so as to guarantee such equality of opportunity while maximizing personal freedom, especially freedom from material needs. Almost every major development in twentieth-century American life, good as well as bad, has reflected the dominance of this consensus world view.[129]

People who claimed secular ideas and human-centered worldviews as a replacement for Christianity expanded to include theists, atheists, free-sex advocates, and religious humanists. A common thread connecting them all is secularism.

Secularization and Revivalism

These changes raised concern among church leaders, as Hitchcock states, some of whom "worried from time to time about the secularization of society, but at almost any time down to 1945 religion appeared to be in a healthy state." The number of Christian churchgoers was increasing and the church ministry was vigorous despite trends toward the secular. Importantly, "Christian morality was almost universally accepted in principle and was taken as the appropriate guide to conduct."[130] Christian beliefs were so common even many nonchurched people confessed a belief in God, the Bible, and heaven and hell. The effects of the great awakenings were still evident as the church effectively met needs for spiritual renewal, religious experience, and even societal and individual aspirations such as security, wealth, and health. However, the church was now confronted with an urban, industrial society where people's needs had shifted. Previous spiritual movements had dealt with individual conversion and private Christian life, though they impacted the community with social issues such as abolition, temperance, equality in education, and Christian morality.[131]

Urban residents were more alienated from the church, which traditionally had occupied a more central place in rural communi-

---

129. Ibid., 128.
130. Hitchcock, *What Is Secular Humanism?*, 55.
131. Charles and Rodney, *A Rocky Mountain Sailor*, 5–6.

ties. According to Hitchcock, "technology leads man to believe that the solutions to all problems lie within his grasp; all he needs is to work harder and become yet more ingenious."[132] One might have expected the social, political, and economic insecurities of urban life to European-style secularization. However, church membership and attendance in the United States grew in both in urban and rural areas in the nineteenth and twentieth centuries due to the great awakenings, Holiness movement, and Pentecostalism. The people in urban areas in the United States seemed, Hitchcock points out, "as religious as any other group, and more than some."[133] Protestants and Catholics in America both flourished more in the United States than in Europe.

However, with urbanization, the American church organized its operations along the lines of secular rationalism. Wilson sates, "Traditional church organization has undergone steady modification, particularly in urban America, toward greater rationalization and extensive innovation, especially in ancillary agencies, and the evolution of central bureaucracy."[134] The American people credulously fell into tendencies of internal secularization of the church, taking the church without having traditional rituals to which European churches had long been accustomed in the midst of urbanization.

> The [secularization] process has not been without its critics, nor have the traditional parish organization and the ecological organization of the church. Perhaps because they are most completely insulated from the impact of secular society, traditional and received ritual procedures have experienced the least disturbance, although Europeans have sometimes commented that dignity, solemnity, and gentility were lacking in American liturgical performance.[135]

American religious tolerance made possible the development of religious sects including the Christian Science Church, Mormon Church, and Jehovah's Witnesses.[136] Europe has not seen significant increases in New Religious Movements (NRMs). In the United States, however, there has been a decline in mainline churches, a rise in new

---

132. Hitchcock, *What Is Secular Humanism?*, 54.

133. Ibid., 54.

134. Wilson, "Religion and the Churches in Contemporary America," 74.

135. Ibid., 74.

136. Hitchcock, *What Is Secular Humanism?*, 55.

religious movements, and new expressions of Christianity including the Pentecostal and charismatic movements in the twentieth century. "For years, every retreat from a vivid, active conception of the supernatural by major Christian bodies was greeted as another confirmation of the secularization thesis, [and all] contrary signs of continued religious vigor . . . were dismissed as one last hurrah—a dying gasp."[137]

Stark and Bainbridge describe secularization as "a self-limiting process that engenders revival (sect formation) and innovation (cult formation)."[138] As organized religious groups mature, "they not only lose their vigor but give rise to sects that revitalize the religious tradition in new organizations."[139] Religion does not disappear, but is reasserted by sects or offshoot organizations that take up the religious function.

In the United States, denominational pluralism created a competitive spirit that resulted in church attendance, Christian practices, and the invitation of newcomers at much higher rates than in Europe. However, the same free-market forces also led to the church becoming secularized. Churches took on aspects of popular culture in order to attract people. Intentionally or unintentionally, they often became caught up in secular concerns such as consumerism, marketing strategies, and intentional numerical growth.[140] Os Guinness observes, "the separation of church and state has never meant the separation of religion from public life but the fostering of a remarkable national vitality."[141] He adds:

> Not so much despite disestablishment [the separation of church and state] as because of it, the influence of diverse faiths on American society has become all the stronger for being indirect and unofficial. "Free exercise" in religion therefore precedes and parallels "free enterprise" in commerce. One is the child of disestablishment, the other of de-monopolization. Free enterprise makes it possible to compete freely in the marketplace but to do so in a "fair game" and on a "level playing field." Free exercise includes the right of a person or a group to

---

137. Finke and Stark, *The Churching of America*, 42.
138. Stark and Bainbridge, *The Future of Religion*, 429–30.
139. Finke and Stark, *The Churching of America*, 43.
140. Ostwalt, *Secular Steeples*, 22.
141. Guinness, "A World Safe for Diversity," 146.

compete freely in the world of ideas and to persuade others by the strength of arguments and the quality of lives.[142]

Secularization in the American church has been a qualitative type—an erosion of faith from within that results from the adoption of, contextualization to, and even competition with "popular culture and secular models of entertainment."[143] Ostwalt states, "In the absence of compulsion, the church had to attract, and in many cases it attracted by conforming to popular trends."[144] He cites the nineteenth century Social Gospel movement as an example, saying, "the Social Gospel proponents attempted to compete by adopting and revising the popular, secular worldview and thus competing with secular culture bolstered by sacred foundations."[145] However, Ostwalt argues, popularizing religion by conforming to market forces ultimately leads to secularization from within.

> In America, secularization is expressed through the church aligning itself with popular, secular cultural forms and becoming more like them. In Europe, secularization is expressed through the rejection of an elite institution by the populace; thus, attendance and religious fidelity are apparently lower than America. Secularization is taking place in opposite direction: the church is moving toward popular culture in America; popular culture is moving away from the church in Europe. With this scenario, one could even argue that America is the more thoroughly secularized society as its church becomes increasingly akin to popular and secular cultural forms.[146]

In Europe, the 1960s was the decade of the most rapid decline in church membership. In the United States, church involvement also declined, but in a different—and more rapid—fashion.[147] In 1960 Christianity in America experienced a great turmoil stemming from the fact that churches experienced an unprecedented revolution such

142. Ibid., 145–46.

143. Ostwalt, *Secular Steeples*, 49.

144. Ibid., 49.

145. Ibid., 49–50. The Social Gospel movement applied Christian principles to social problems such as inequality, racial tension, and child labor. Many believed that the Second Coming could not occur until humankind dispensed with these evils by human effort.

146. Ibid., 22.

147. Hitchcock, *What Is Secular Humanism?*, 57.

as that of the Baby Boomers generation who sought religions other than traditional Protestantism. The New Age Movement and oriental religions began to flourish through the growing number of non-European ethnic immigrants. As religious humanism, secularism, atheism and antagonism against the fundamental Christian beliefs grew, Protestant influence and Christian rights steadily weakened in public arenas, leading to a decline in membership of the mainline denominations and a new influx of sectarian, non-Christian groups such as social activists, same sex marriage advocates, religious humanists, and atheists. By the end of the late 1960s a new culture of television, pop music and birth control pills had permeated into American society while sexual freedom, same sex liberation and women's rights were strongly integrated into society. Therefore conservative evangelicals lost ground and evangelical morality was accused as detrimental and oppressive. Hitchcock sees a momentous transition 1965 and 1970:

> If America was still a predominantly religious society in the early 1960s, it went through a secularization process which was amazingly rapid. The process is not complete by any means. In some ways America remains a very religious nation. But common attitudes, and especially the kinds of attitudes which are regarded as respectable, underwent a swift change between 1965 and 1970. Although it was perhaps only a minority who were most affected, they were the trend-setters. They either had little interest in religion or were hostile to it. They either rejected traditional morality or were willing to compromise it endlessly. They contrived to place traditional religious belief on the permanent defensive.[148]

The United States and Europe have followed different roads toward secularization. In the midst of church growth, strength, and expansion, North America made a rapid transition to a secular mindset, rationalization of theology, separation of church and state, and internal secularization because secular trends accumulated during this period.

AMERICANIZED SECULARIZATION

In the beginning of twentieth century, humanists, liberals, and secularists took positions as professors in theological institutions and Christian

---

148. Ibid., 60.

colleges, popularizing their values among the students.[149] Secular and liberal ideas spread through media, newspaper, radio, television, and books. LaHaye says, "Secularists established the movie industry to influence the mind through entertainment, which is why in 1948 they were equipped to take over the new medium of television. . . . The secularizers assumed control of the law schools and slowly changed the nation's view of the Constitution, law, morality, the first amendment, and respect for God and [shopping] mall."[150]

Liberalism and Fundamentalism

Liberal theology began in Germany with deep roots in the Enlightenment and also, to some extent, the French Revolution. In France, the establishment of freedoms of speech, press, assembly, election, and religion caused the separation of church and state. Freedom of religion led to a liberal school of thought not bound by any religious creed or ecclesiastical hierarchy, but based solely on human reason. Later on in Germany, theologian Friedrich Schleiermacher applied these liberal ideas to Christian theology, leading to the establishment of liberal theology.[151] The use of human reason in judgment of the Bible became a predominant school of thought. Conventional Christian doctrines were reexamined in light of rationalism, and the authority of the Bible was questioned and often dismissed by liberal theologians in Germany and, later, in the United States. With conventional beliefs in the Bible eroding, conventional Christianity lost its influence over society and culture. While Christianity was strong in the United States compared to Europe, those who embraced the revivals and awakenings experienced opposition in the form of liberal theology.

The adaptation of the Enlightenment to an American context does not mean that theological disputes had ended between conservatives, who consider themselves moderate Calvinists, and liberals. From the Puritan era until the eighteenth century, the majority of Americans "were neither extreme theological Calvinists nor liberal Christians but rather Christian Pietists of generally Calvinistic inclinations."[152] Disputes in the eighteenth century were few, as most theologians from

---

149. LaHaye, *Faith of Our Founding Fathers*, 24.

150. Ibid., 27.

151. Hitchcock, *What Is Secular Humanism?*, 116–17.

152. May, "The Decline of Providence," 138–39.

the Congregational, Presbyterian, Reformed, Baptist, and even some Anglican churches were considered pietistic believers or moderate Calvinistic Christians. In the mid-eighteenth century, as revivals broke out, more people became familiar with conservative biblical theology. At the same time, liberal theology continued to make inroads among intellectuals.

European influences gained ground in the United States, including Lockean philosophy and Anglican latitudinarianism, especially among Congregational ministers in New England and Boston in particular.[153] In the nineteenth century, liberal theology made significant advances. The resulting differences between liberals and conservatives become more visible in public, in educational institutions, and among church ministers. Wuthnow observes, "the fracture line [between theological liberals and conservatives] can be found in the soil of American religion as far back as the years immediately after the Civil War."[154] This division applies not only to conservatives and liberals, but also between the eastern seaboard and western frontier, and between North and South. The rise of liberalism led to trends such as Unitarianism, religious humanism, skepticism, atheism, and deism. At the same time, revivals were producing sectarian and cultic movements.

Over the years, those churches that accepted liberal theology experienced dramatic declines. Evangelicals connected to the awakening movements saw church growth, but mainline churches declined when liberal theology was promoted, including biblical criticism, demythologization, scientism, and theological and social Darwinism. According to Smith, "Secularistic and rationalistic approaches to traditional Christian beliefs on incarnation, miracle, accuracy of the Bible, creation theory, and salvation and truth in Christianity were confronted with Darwinian evolutionists, Newtonian scientists, and liberal theologians."[155] Doubts about the authoritative nature of the Bible multiplied as the theory of evolution became mainstream.[156]

May says, "Within Protestantism a rather bland variety of theological liberalism was powerfully entrenched in the socially dominant

---

153. Ibid., 138.

154. Wuthnow, *The Struggle for America's Soul*, 26.

155. Fowler et al., *A Rocky Mountain Sailor*, 5.

156. Sturtevant, *Popular Uprisings*, 91–92.

churches."[157] While liberal theology gained adherents in churches, theological institutions, the political realm, science, and the academy, supporters of revival movements hailed from evangelicalism, conservatism, and fundamentalism. The two schools of thought challenged each other for justification: "Yet in the Protestant camp itself, liberalism was increasingly challenged by orthodox revivalism and militant religious conservatism. It would be hard to say whether more people were influenced by Henry Ward Beecher or Dwight L. Moody."[158] Moody aggressively rejected liberalism, promoting evangelical views throughout the nation and especially in the South, while liberals gained followers among Unitarians and Congregationalists, mostly on the eastern seaboard. Due to the awakenings, most evangelical American Christians throughout the country retained conventional Christian beliefs such as salvation by faith and the authority of the Bible.[159] Moody was outraged that theological liberalism was flourishing, which led him to strongly oppose formal education that allowed pupils to think in ungodly ways, especially Darwinism.[160]

The Modernity Debate

In the twentieth century, American evangelicalism took shape as a result of the Great Awakenings and revivals. It comprised of various denominations sharing common beliefs in the authority of Bible, salvation by faith, and second coming of Christ. These churches identified with the term *conservative Protestantism*. At the same time, the secularization process was affecting social, intellectual, political, religious, and cultural milieus. Still, in spite of vast differences among denominations, the nation remained functionally Protestant before a massive influx of Catholic immigrants from Europe began in the early twentieth century. The dominance of Protestant culture had led politicians to advocate Americanized Protestantism "as part of the coming worldwide social and political millennium."[161]

As the twentieth century entered, American Christianity was being pulled in two different directions. Spiritual revival movements provided

157. May, Ideas, *Faith, and Feelings*, 157.

158. Ibid., 157.

159. Sturtevant, *Popular Uprisings*, 100.

160. Ibid., 99.

161. May, Ideas, *Faith, and Feelings*, 157.

a foundation of American evangelicalism and Pentecostalism, leading ultimately to fundamentalism. Liberalism moved in the other direction, supported by a secular group who advocated a new way of thinking called *modernism*, which is rooted in "higher criticism, evolutionary philosophy, and rationalism" within liberal denominations and among secular intellectuals in theological institutions.[162] By the early twentieth century, liberal theologians already made up half of seminary faculty. Liberal thinkers gained adherents and media attention, but evangelicals, who were not as well organized, did not get as much attention: "Although there was great concern among conservative theologians over the extent and impact of the liberal movement, the conservatives had made no unified, organized effort to combat its influence."[163]

Conservatives began to realize the need for unity in the early twentieth century. Their confrontation with liberalism took place in three stages: the first controversies from 1900 to 1918, a peak between 1918 and 1925, and downfall between 1925 and 1930. During these stages, secularists and humanists cast doubt upon the evangelical principle of biblical inerrancy and infallibility. Evangelicals responded by articulating "fundamental" beliefs, including the immaculate conception, crucifixion, resurrection, ascension, and the second advent of Jesus Christ. Influenced by evolution theory, secularists raised questions about the truth of miracle stories and the canonicity of the Scriptures. Evangelical conservatives "published a series of twelve booklets in order to assert their theological standpoints . . . entitled *The Fundamentals: A Testimony of Truth*."[164]

Then, from 1918 to 1925, the confrontation's second stage was characterized by increasing unity among conservatives, and "[e]xposed to external threats, the Fundamentalists had minimized their differences and maximized their areas of agreement."[165] Several heated exchanges resulted in irreconcilable disagreements between liberals and conservatives. The first conference of conservatives, the Philadelphia Prophetic Convention, gathered five thousand people in May of 1918. This was the peak of the confrontation, made possible by the previous publication of *The Fundamentals*.[166]

162. Dobson et al., *The Fundamentalist Phenomenon*, 78.
163. Ibid., 47.
164. Ibid., 48.
165. Ibid., 50.
166. Ibid., 50.

The third stage of the confrontation was a long period of disagreement between the two groups, lasting from 1930 and 1980 in which "[n]either side had gained a clear-cut victory. The Liberalism that had been entrenched in the major denominations was still entrenched, and the onslaughts of Fundamentalism had not uprooted its influential position. Neither had Liberalism obliterated Fundamentalism."[167] Their differences drove them in opposite directions as the Great Depression of the late 1920s set in. After the World Wars, a new wave of evangelicals emerged. Dobson, Hindson, and Falwell observe, "To comprehend better the role and growth of Fundamentalism, one must be cognizant of both the role and growth of Liberalism and Evangelicalism."[168]

Previous generations of secularists and humanists did not agree with fundamental Christian doctrines, but the two sides were able to live together amicably. In the early twentieth century, the two camps were at war each other. Conservatives were able to unify by rallying around the five fundamental doctrines. The majority of conservatives left liberal educational institutions and denominations to maintain their doctrinal standpoints. After this "Great Exodus," conservatives did not embrace denominations as before, but acted more like independents. They built schools, seminaries, and church buildings with no pressure from previous denominations. Further, they established Christian media outlets, including radio stations and publications.[169] While there were some positive results—keeping Christian doctrine intact—there was a loss unity and cooperation with other Protestant churches. As they became more and more divergent, the churches themselves became counterproductive, causing the downfall of their own movement.[170]

Religious Liberalism

Religious liberalism provides room for secularization to erode cardinal Christian beliefs. *Liberalism* is derived from the Latin *liberalis*, meaning "of freedom." While religious liberalism does not identify itself with secularism, it has prepared a way for secularization to enter the churches. Hitchcock points out that "the most advanced religious

167. Ibid., 79.
168. Ibid., 79.
169. Ibid., 76.
170. Ibid., 76–77.

liberals now have an outlook on life not essentially different from secularists, and they want to convert the church to that same outlook. . . . They are apostles of unbelief, endlessly telling believers that they should no longer accept this or that teaching of Christianity."[171] As political liberalism gained supporters, their ideas were promoted in public. Hitchcock believes that political liberalism sprang from ideas in the religious realm, "Religious liberals permitted, and often actively promoted, the secularization of Western education, for example. They also acquiesced in the idea that church-state separation should logically mean the complete secularization of politics. They underestimated the degree of hostility to religion of some liberal governments, and they opposed organized political action by religious groups."[172]

At first, religious liberals attempted to apply the principles of democracy to church governance. However, when they began to apply this approach to the tenets of Christian belief, they displaced central church teachings. "They exalted individual human judgment to the point where it sometimes did not seem to matter whether the individual came to know truth, but merely whether free personal inquiry was exercised. Religious liberals tended to develop a spirit of resistance or hostility towards the very idea of religious orthodoxy and religious authority."[173]

Using the principle of democracy, liberals within the church gave ear to secularists and skeptics. LaHaye states, "The liberal habit of looking over the shoulder to see what the skeptics think has become a general surrender to secular authority. . . . The church is kept in a perpetual state of judgment before the world, repeatedly apologizing for its past errors and promising to do better in the future."[174] The secular and liberal viewpoints largely coincided. "Like their atheist friends, the deists [those who believe in the moral teachings, but not the divinity, of Jesus] had no use for Scripture, and consequently their major conclusions differed little from those of other secularists."[175] Hitchcock gives five points of similarity between secularism and liberalism:

171. Hitchcock, *What Is Secular Humanism?*, 129.

172. Ibid., 117.

173. Ibid., 117–18.

174. LaHaye, *Faith of Our Founding Fathers*, 16.

175. Ibid., 16.

1. Authoritative Christian documents, whether the Bible, historic creeds, or other statements, are either ignored as irrelevant or employed only to the degree that they seem to fit with current secular preoccupations.

2. Worship is regarded primarily as a human experience, not as a way of paying homage to God. Worship services (and sermons) are structured in such a way as to create a sense of community and belonging among the worshippers with little regard for the transcendental dimension of the action.

3. Christians are not encouraged to have a strong personal sense of their dependence on God's providence. God is thought not to intervene in the affairs of men, so that human problems are to be solved through human means only.

4. A personal sense of fulfillment or satisfaction is taken as the ultimate criterion of truth. Thus religious doctrines and practices are kept or discarded to the degree that they seem "meaningful" to the individual. The concept of objective religious truth is effectively denied. The purpose of religion is thought to be the achievement of a subjective sense of spiritual wellbeing by the individual.

5. All morality is provisional only. Many of the past moral teachings of the church, especially with regard to sex, are now seen as pernicious and deforming. Since personal "need" is the ultimate guide to conduct and since personal fulfillment is the chief aim of existence, the liberal Christian often leads a life at odds with traditional Christian morality.[176]

Rationalism and liberalism were working together to deny the existence of the supernatural, salvation through Jesus only, and the authority of the Bible.

Religious Humanism

The origin of humanism can be traced back to Classical Greece. This movement flourished during the Enlightenment and came to the New World with the first English settlers. At the core of humanism are a variety of sentiments, not all of them secular. Noll and his col-

176. Hitchcock, *What Is Secular Humanism?*, 130–31.

leagues point out that "Humanism, or faith in humanity, has been mixed with virtually every American religious heritage, including evangelicalism and fundamentalism. . . . [M]any Americans, including many evangelical Christian Americans, have tended to believe in the essential goodness of humanity, in the importance of believing in oneself, in self-help, and the ability of a free people to solve their own problems."[177] This combination of Christian tradition and humanism has often gone unnoticed.

However, the term *humanism* has been misused and has taken on negative connotations, in spite of the fact that Christianity has humanistic characteristics. The word became associated with secular humanists who attempted to attack Christianity. Hitchcock points out, "Christians ultimately trust in God, Humanists in themselves. . . . [I]t is unfortunate that religious believers have allowed non-believers to preempt the term for their own use. In the end, Christians are the true humanists."[178]

When Christian values were dominant in European intellectual spheres during the medieval era, divine knowledge—the so-called theology with metaphysical structure—was seen as superior to any human knowledge. During the Renaissance, a harmony developed between divine and human knowledge, evenly balancing the importance of human reason and divine revelation. However, with the Enlightenment, human reason came to be seen as superior to any knowledge, even divine knowledge. Eventually, secular humanists declared the independence of human knowledge from any Christian knowledge.[179] Trace states that "intellectuals gradually, subtly, but inexorably and with devastating effectiveness, have dismantled Christian doctrine and tradition, and even religious belief in general, in favor of putting the search for the ultimate truths into the hands of man."[180] If the Enlightenment in Europe led ultimately to secularization, the American Enlightenment led to secular humanism as humanistic values became separated from spiritual and evangelical movements. Yount states that "the Enlightenment planted a seed in America that

---

177. Noll, *The Search*, 127.
178. Hitchcock, *What Is Secular Humanism?*, 139.
179. Trace, *Christianity: Its Rise and Fall*, 10.
180. Ibid., 10–11.

would grow into secular humanism, forcing the churches to choose whether to accommodate pride as a virtue or to resist it as a vice."[181]

American liberal theology took root in educational and intellectual circles in the early twentieth century. Theologians Harry Emerson Fosdick and A. N. Wieman were two of its most well known proponents, espousing the scientific method for humanism's sake and ultimately abandoning humanism's religious roots. Olds affirms, "The religious humanists saw the Judeo-Christian tradition not as normative, but as merely one of several equally valuable traditions. To the humanists, the Jewish-Christian past was evidence of the evolutionary character of religion; it was not a norm for guiding the present, which should be guided by contemporary norms."[182] The advance of humanism seemed to fulfill August Comte's prediction of a future society in which Christianity, to him a belief system of superstition, would end and humanism would take over.

Positivist Frederick M. Gould first used the term *humanism* to describe a trust in human effort; it was later adopted by Unitarian John H. Dietrich, who is considered to be the father of religious humanism in America:

> The age-honored word, this "humanism," would be a good name for [Dietrich's] interpretation of religion in contrast to theism. Then, leaning confidently upon the background of Renaissance humanism, he drew certain elements of meaning from it and fused them with his own more social concept of this term. More and more Dietrich moved to a kind of "naturalistic humanism" and away from liberal theism. In this move, he was going beyond the arms of conventional Unitarianism.[183]

Humanism in the United States became one of the strongest agents of secularization. There are many types of humanism such as secular humanism, religious humanism, economic humanism, and intellectual humanism. Of these types, religious humanism became a strong substitute to Christianity. John H. Dietrich in 1929 articulated the humanist perspective in a sermon entitled "Religion without God" to his Minneapolis Unitarian congregation. Dietrich denied the infallibility of Scripture, the virgin birth and deity of Jesus, and the traditional

181. Yount, *The Future of Christian Faith in America*, 67.

182. Olds, *American Religious Humanism*, 25.

183. Olds, "John H. Dietrich," lines 145–51.

doctrine of atonement. Dietrich's goal was to implement the religion of humanity like Augusta Comte had declared, and the same idea of the Ethical Union of Britain (EUB). In fact, Dietrich was the Unitarian minister in 1913 who acknowledged the EUB's usage of "humanism" to express a non-theistic philosophy of religion to his congregation in Spokane, Washington. Furthermore, Dietrich manipulated Darwin's idea, the evolution theory, and even altered the Apostles' Creed according to the ideas of religious humanism. He was accused by his denomination as a heretic, leading to his resignation that opened up the path for him to advocate religious humanism.[184] Dietrich hoped to claim religious humanism as a replacement for orthodox Christianity. A 1918 book by Roy Wood Sellars of the University of Michigan, *The Next Step in Religion*, depicted humanism as the religion of the future. Sellars predicted the religion in the future will not play as before in the Christendom era because religions "supernaturalisms and distortions, religious demands have often been morbid and full of unnecessary friction. Religion has sought to thwart and refresh human nature rather than to guide and express. But a religion of human loyalty [religious humanism] can be kindly as well as exigent, mirth-loving as well as stern."[185] Ten years later, Sellars published *A Religion Coming of Age*, asserting that the Christian religion will no longer function but humanism will be the substitute of the mature religion.[186]

Religious humanists then organized a Humanist Fellowship, inaugurated in 1928. Most were scholars, ministers, and students from the University of Chicago. A journal called the *New Humanist* was published that same year. In 1933, Sellars began to draft a humanist manifesto, with help from Curtis W. Reese, Raymond Bragg, Edwin H. Wilson, and others. When published, it created a crucial challenge within and outside of the Humanists Fellowship.[187] The manifesto expresses certainty that the religious humanist movement will replace Christianity and other theistic religions, offering an alternative where the existence of God is no longer necessary. In this respect, religious humanism is similar to Far Eastern religions such as Buddhism and Confucianism, which do not depend on the belief in a divine being.

---

184. Evans, *Humanism and Religion*, 1–2.
185. Sellars, *The Next Step in Religion*, 216.
186. Ibid., 131–32.
187. Olds, *American Religious Humanism*, 20.

Sellars compared Far Eastern faiths with Near Eastern traditions, including Judaism, Christianity, Islam, and even Zoroastrianism, which all include the concepts of God, heaven and hell, and salvation: "to exclude the Far Eastern view by complete acceptance of the Near Eastern view is the height of religious provincialism; therefore, if the view of the Far East is accepted, humanism can make a legitimate claim to being a religion. Sellars concluded, 'I doubt that any other religious movement has as fine a foundation in method and knowledge.'"[188]

The manifesto declared traditional Christianity could be replaced because science offered enough knowledge to modern people to comprehend the universe more deeply than ever.[189] Most signers of the manifesto were intellectuals, religious leaders, professors, writers, and ministers. One of the most well-known signers was John Dewey, professor of philosophy at Columbia University. "Other important professors were J.A.C. Fagginger Auer of the Harvard Divinity School, A. Eustace Haydon, professor of comparative religions at the University of Chicago, Edwin A. Burtt, professor of philosophy at Cornell University, and John Herman Randall, Jr., professor of philosophy at Columbia University. One Reformed Jewish Rabbi, Jacob K. Weinstein, signed. Most of the ministers who signed had a Unitarian affiliation; among them were John H. Dietrich, Curtis W. Reese, and Charles Francis Potter."[190]

While the first manifesto in 1933 supported "traditional theism," the second manifesto, drafted in 1973 by Paul Kurtz with Edwin H. Wilson and signed by 120 others, renounced religion as a guideline.[191] Its influence extended beyond the religious arena to school, media, court, politics, and other aspects of public life. Humanism became known as essentially a religious faith, making claims as the ultimate source of value in the universe. In 2003, the American Humanist Association published Humanist Manifesto III:

> Humanism is a progressive philosophy of life that, without supernaturalism, affirms our ability and responsibility to lead ethical lives of personal fulfillment that aspire to the greater good of humanity.

188. Ibid., 24.
189. Ibid., 20.
190. Ibid., 23–24.
191. Noll, *The Search*, 127.

The lifestance of Humanism—guided by reason, inspired by compassion, and informed by experience—encourages us to live life well and fully. It evolved through the ages and continues to develop through the efforts of thoughtful people who recognize that values and ideals, however carefully wrought, are subject to change as our knowledge and understandings advance.

This document is part of an ongoing effort to manifest in clear and positive terms the conceptual boundaries of Humanism, not what we must believe but a consensus of what we do believe. It is in this sense that we affirm the following:

- Knowledge of the world is derived by observation, experimentation, and rational analysis. Humans are an integral part of nature, the result of unguided evolutionary change.

- Ethical values are derived from human need and interest as tested by experience.

- Life's fulfillment emerges from individual participation in the service of humane ideals.

- Humans are social by nature and find meaning in relationships.

- Working to benefit society maximizes individual happiness.[192]

Humanists are concerned for the well being of all, are committed to diversity, and respect those of differing yet humane views. We work to uphold the equal enjoyment of human rights and civil liberties in an open, secular society and maintain it is a civic duty to participate in the democratic process and a planetary duty to protect nature's integrity, diversity, and beauty in a secure, sustainable manner.

Thus engaged in the flow of life, we aspire to this vision with the informed conviction that humanity has the ability to progress toward its highest ideals. The responsibility for our lives and the kind of world in which we live is ours and ours alone.[193]

The American Humanist Association's primary beliefs run contrary to the basic tenets of Christianity.[194] August Comte declared the coming age of religious humanism as an eventual substitute to Christianity in Europe and America. They placed humans in the place

---

192. See the full text of the "Humanist Manifesto III."

193. American Humanist Association, "Humanist Manifesto III," 2003.

194. Trace, *Christianity: Its Rise and Fall*, 17.

of God and declared their liberty that goes beyond the providence of God. They attempted to disown the belief in salvation through Jesus Christ and even denied the Christian truth of the bible in their Humanist Manifesto. The secular trends, mainly through religious humanist, gained greater ground. The author does not agree with any of the points in the Humanist Manifesto so this statement was inserted to dispel alarms. The author believes in Jesus as the only Savior of the world and only the Bible contains the truth.

Secular Education

In most European countries from the Post Reformation period and before the nineteenth century, most schools were operated by Christian institutions and their clergies. Curriculum, worship, and chaplaincy were based on Christian principles and relied on ministers or priests. With secularization, European educational institutions no longer answered to ecclesiastical authorities. "Europe was secularized in the nineteenth century, first by the takeover of its colleges and universities, which had been until then largely religious in origin. Gradually European courts, government, media, and even clergy were secularized, which has made Europe so susceptible to socialism in one form or another."[195]

When the United States became independent, the Protestant faith of the Puritans and evangelicals dominated principles in the political, social, educational, and social realms. Whether they professed Christian faith or not, most people agreed with basic Christian beliefs. In New England, Christian principles were firmly established at its educational institutions. Fowler states that "Given its role as primary moral guardian of the nation, it is not surprising that nineteenth-century evangelicalism exerted much control over the American education system, private and public, at all levels."[196] Harvard and Yale played a dominant role: "In his volume on the colonial clergy of New England, Weis (1936) reported that of the 1,586 men who had ever served as pastor of a Congregational church, 1,507, or 95 percent, were college graduates. Of these more than 60 percent went to Harvard and 29 percent went to Yale."[197]

195. LaHaye, *Faith of Our Founding Fathers*, 27.
196. Fowler et al., *A Rocky Mountain Sailor*, 4.
197. Finke and Stark, *The Churching of America*, 45.

Jonathan Edwards, Timothy Dwight, Charles Finney, D.L. Moody, and many more spread the gospel through schools. On the other hand, secularism and liberalism were propagated through academic institutions and scholars. Harvard became a strong Unitarian force in the eighteenth century.[198] During the Second Great Awakening, evangelical leaders established Christian schools and colleges. Casanova states:

> [A] new synthesis of Calvinist faith, Scottish commonsense realism, and the evangelical religion of the heart became entrenched in one Protestant college after another and maintained its cultural hegemony over the "life of the mind" until the last quarter of the nineteenth century. . . . Through the public school, the common school, and the Sunday school movements, it encompassed the entire public realm of education and religious instruction, and it extended to the mass media and to societies and movements for moral and social reform. Indeed, evangelical societies established the framework for all forms of American voluntary societies and evangelical revivalism became the cradle of American social movements.[199]

Schools functioned as means of both liberalism and revivalism. Evangelical influence was also felt in American educational institutions. Smith points out the involvement of clergy in leadership positions: "University and college presidents, for example, at even the most prestigious schools, were, often not businessmen, but well-educated clergymen. University boards of trustees, too, typically contained many Protestant church leaders and clergymen."[200]

> Furthermore, college and university curricula typically reflected a Protestant worldview and epistemology, combining classical curriculum with orthodox Protestant theology and piety to train properly the future leaders of America's Christian civilization. At lower levels, too, education included generous doses of training in Christian belief, morals, and virtues. Indeed, public schools were believed to be the primary agency that could unify America under a common Protestant perspective.[201]

Over time, many schools adopted secular tendencies. Education, culture, arts, and media came to be dominated by secular ideas isolat-

198. Ibid., 45–6.
199. Casanova, *Public Religions in the Modern World*, 137.
200. Fowler et al., *A Rocky Mountain Sailor*, 4.
201. Ibid., 4.

ing Christian norms and faith. How did secular ideas penetrate these institutions, despite the fact that the United States had once been one of the most religious nations? LaHaye believes that "a minority of secularists control the lives of a predominantly religious people."[202]

Although the separation of church and state was written into the constitution, religious influence was strongly felt in educational institutions throughout the eighteenth and nineteenth centuries. Russello notes that "the complete secularization of public education is a relatively recent factor; so that its impact on American culture has only recently been fully realized."[203]

Christian clergy and organizations provided schools with both funds and students; hence, many schools declared denominational affiliations. LaHaye points out, "during the first century of the colonial period, all 126 colleges were established by some religious group or denomination."[204] This differed from the situation in Europe, where faculties comprised of independent scholars were in control. So, in the United States, the "religious purposes of the institutions were largely preserved until overwhelmed by the secularizing trends of the twentieth century."[205]

> Such a curriculum suited the triple objectives of imparting knowledge, training young minds, and preparing responsible leaders for a burgeoning society. The last decades of the nineteenth century would witness the rise of the new research-oriented, diversified, and secularizing forces of the university, which would overshadow the unitary Christian learning of the churchly colleges. Nevertheless, the old-style colleges were founded as avowedly Christian institutions and nurtured the ideal of mental and moral education for the whole person. As such, they contributed stability to a society in flux and perpetuated a noble tradition.[206]

After the Civil War, evangelical ministers took leadership positions in mainstream schools and colleges, giving these institutions "a distinctly evangelical and moral flavor in key courses on 'moral science,'

---

202. LaHaye, *Faith of Our Founding Fathers*, 23.

203. Russello, *Christianity and European Culture*, 24–25.

204. LaHaye, *Faith of Our Founding Fathers*, 23.

205. Askew, "The Founding Colleges," 225.

206. Ibid., 227.

'political 'economy,' or 'evidences of Christianity.'"[207] After this period, in the late nineteenth century, things began to change. Following a German scientific model, "whether it was economics, political science, sociology, psychology, or even history and literary criticism, had become a separate professional discipline."[208] Bible teaching was phased out as Darwinism and science-centered knowledge became ascendant. "Within hardly a generation, vast areas of American thought and academic life had been removed from all reference to Protestant or biblical considerations."[209] Disciplines such as skepticism, German higher criticism, and secular humanism appeared.[210] With secularization, the purpose of education shifted away from religion and toward humanistic ends. Young Christian students encountered more secularists, humanists, and atheists.

During the second great awakening, in the early nineteenth century, evangelical Christian churches and leaders established new educational institutions, since older schools had abandoned their Christian roots. The schools became a battleground for competing theologies. Older schools challenged the authority of the Bible while embracing rationalism and Darwinian evolution theory. Liberal theologians challenged traditional beliefs by using textual criticism, historical criticism, and higher criticism. Hitchcock observes that "controversies raged not only between religious believers and skeptical scientists but also within the churches themselves."[211] Older schools such as Harvard, Yale, and Princeton retained Unitarian and liberal theology while newer schools upheld evangelical and spiritual tendencies.[212]

According to Marty:

> After the terms were set at mid-century they were acted upon in the latter decades of the century, in the growth of pluralistic metropolises, the secularization of higher (and, much later, elementary) education, the acceptance of the scientific world view, the development of non-religious philosophy, and countless other realms. Even after the mid-century flowering,

207. Marsden, *Understanding Fundamentalism and Evangelicalism*, 14–15.
208. Ibid., 14–15.
209. Ibid., 15.
210. LaHaye, *Faith of Our Founding Fathers*, 23–24.
211. Hitchcock, *What is Secular Humanism?*, 118.
212. Ibid., 118.

Christians have expressed surprise and pride to find a major
literary figure working out of specifically Christian symbolic
frameworks or commitments. Never again did evangelical literature regain its place.[213]

With academia, the legal system, media, entertainment, and art
seemingly led by secularists, many evangelicals responded by withdrawing from secular world to preserve their values:

Secularism shows no sign of giving ups its hold in the public
schools where a deterministic humanism prevails as often as
not. The evangelical message seems to have made little impact
on the American legal system, which, for example, often treats
criminals and victims with equal callousness. Few Evangelicals
have contributed distinctly Christian insights to the cries of
energy and ecology or to the ongoing debate over the moral
strengths and weakness of the American economic and political systems.[214]

More recently, new ideas have emerged in Christian circles, such
as world evangelism promoted by Youth With A Mission and the
Lausanne Covenant promoting world evanglism. These movements
advocate that Christians make use of the educational system, media,
art, government, entertainment, and business for kingdom purposes.
There is no better time than the present to reassert the Christian faith
in these areas.

Modernization

We have seen that secularization has been closely linked with
urbanization, industrialization, and rationalism in Europe. When
reason became the central focus of society, beginning with the
Enlightenment, the role of religion has fluctuated. The decline of
European Christianity led to the development of the secularization
thesis—the hypothesis that the downfall of the church is inevitable as
society advances and as secular values, norms, and worldviews displace religious ones.

Secularization is strongly linked to modernity, which refers to
the post-medieval or post-traditional time. The time period of modernity can be defined as 1436 to 1789, and can be extended up to 1895

213. Marty, *The Modern Schism*, 140.

214. Woodbridge et al., *The Gospel in America*, 12.

or even to the 1970s. Many make the assumption that religion has been declining because it failed to make the transition from agrarian society to modern times. However, religion still has a powerful place in modernity as part of a modified way of life.[215]

Different concepts of transcendence are still alive in modernity, particularly in Latin America, Africa, and some countries in Asia, where belief in the supernatural has been maintained up to the present. Modernity can be either hostile or friendly to transcendence and religion, and many secularized countries in the third world have experienced religious revivals.

According to some interpreters, modern-day religious revival is a temporary throwback generated by discontent, and secularization will prevail in the long term, but in the meantime, religious people can be expected to cause trouble. Others view the contemporary revival as a rediscovery of something important from past American tradition. During much of the twentieth century, some historians argue, people were preoccupied with the pursuit of material comfort. Once that had been largely achieved, the inability of prosperity alone to provide meaning in life became apparent. The complacent 1950s were thus succeeded by the turbulent 1960s, a time when people explored everything from drugs to political activism in a desperate effort to discover meaning. Those explorations, too, produced little more than discontent. An increasing number of counterculture activists turned to religion. As the 1970s brought a more politically settled milieu, larger segments of the population began turning back to the churches and synagogues. The result was the increased concern about the public role of religion that became evident in the 1980s.[216]

The author tried to deal with the issues on religious humanism, secularism, and liberalism in postmodern American society, and about how deeply American society encountered great waves of secular trends. Nonetheless there are religious experiences and revivals still occurring in many places. Secularists and revivalists are constantly in a battle to win their cause Here I claim Jesus is the Savior and in order to bring souls to Christ Jesus, the church is needed, as well as Godly education and spiritual anointing. The world belongs to the Lord, and its systems, authorities, and powers belong to Him as well, but secularists continue

215. Casanova, *Public Religions in the Modern World*, 25–26.
216. Wuthnow, *The Struggle for America's Soul*, 46.

to block the Christian gospel. Recognizing the importance of transcendence as part of modern life helps us to see that secularization detracts people away from the Christian truth that makes us truly human.

CONCLUSION: WHERE IS AMERICA HEADING?

America was called a Christian nation in receiving her destiny for missions all over the world. The Manifest Destiny caught the eyes of Americans to respond to the divine calling, that they have to take up the burdens of others by sharing the grace and prosperity of her possessions with others. Until the early twentieth century, in the public and private sectors of education, senate and congress, presidential inaugurations, the Supreme Court, open plazas, and marketplaces, people swore by the Bible and prayers were offered, hymns sung, and open air services conducted that drew multitudes of common Americans to faith in Jesus Christ as Savior and the Lord. America's Christianization and civilization amazed visitors who commended that America was truly a Protestant nation. The country owed a lot of what it had become to the awakenings and revivals yet repaid all the graces by allowing secular trends. In the twenty-first century prayer at public school has become illegal, evangelism in public spheres is hardly ever proclaimed, same sex marriage has been gaining victory for gays and lesbians to freely pronounce their unholy marriage in churches, where traces of stories of revivals still remain. Tombstones and steeples of the oldest churches have converted into museums, and public common areas have become places for same sex marriage protesters and other ungodly activities. Itinerant preachers and evangelists passionately proclaimed "repent" and people sobbed and beat their hearts with repentant prayer. Now those stories only exist through the mouths of past generations. The evolution theory, freedom of religious humanism, liberation theology, free sex, sports addiction, and religious pluralism overarches every sphere of society in America. America is now neck deep in pornography, adulterous movies, scholarly books of skeptics and atheists, and humanists who declare that humans have become gods. Other counties are learning from America how to become more secularized and following in her tragic footseps. Where is America heading? Is America heading upwards towards an awakening or downwards into secularization?

8

Global Trends in Christianity

THROUGHOUT HISTORY, THE REVIVAL pattern of the Holy Spirit seen in Acts 2 can be observed at different times and in different places. This outpouring was seen among the Lollards, Waldenses, Quakers, Moravians, and Wesleyans, and during the awakenings, the New York Prayer Revival and the Holiness revivals. Most revivals before the twentieth century were located in the West, were white-centered, had denominational and sectarian connections, were culturally homogeneous, centered theologically on the New Testament, focused on domestic and overseas mission, originated among the common people, offered hope to the marginalized, adhered to evangelical doctrine and behavior, had a missional ecclesiology, and ultimately transformed society and religion. Then, in the twentieth century, revival had greater geographic, theological, and phenomenological diversity. Revival movements were racially and ethnically multifaceted, indigenous, and led by independent leadership. Looking to the future, we will explore key issues of the twentieth and twenty-first century global Christianity.

TRANSITION OF CHRISTIANITY GRAVITY

As we approach the end of the twentieth century and enter the twenty-first century, humanity is facing new kinds of challenges never previously faced. The center of Christianity and its history have moved from the West to the non-West. We are witnessing a shifting change in theology, church, race, and culture. The entire world's change is evident in that the influence of Western-centric theology is decreasing, and more and more non-Western theological themes and explorations are becoming the majority Christian worldview. The most notable change that has occurred during the last 2000 years of Christian history is the fact that the center-gravity and majority of the Christian faith has recently shifted from the West to the non-West, where the majority of the world's Christians now live. These geographic, racial, and quantitative changes do not necessarily mean that essential qualitative changes occurred as well within Christianity in the non-West.

Global Shifting

Throughout human history, the existence of God and his plan of salvation were revealed to and through Israel, and the opportunity of salvation came to the Gentiles on the day of Pentecost as seen in the book of Acts. The mighty descent of the Holy Spirit gave birth to a Jewish-centered church. The Apostle Paul was responsible for taking the church, which had a tendency to remain within the bounds of the Jewish community, to Europe and spreading the faith there, thereby shifting the central axis of faith from Israel to Europe. However, due to *institutionalization*, ecclesiasticism, and doctrinism, Europe experienced the Dark Ages.

The Reformed Church separated itself from the apostate Catholic Church to form a new type of church emphasizing Scripture, faith, and grace. The Reformation, centered on the word of God, was followed by the evangelical revivals and Holiness revival movements where godly living and repentance were emphasized. In the New World, the United States experienced two Great Awakening movements based on faith alone leading to repentance and renewal. The New York Prayer Revival that followed began through a simple daily prayer meeting where the strong anointing of the Holy Spirit resulted in numerous confessions and conversions. At the end of nineteenth century, the Holiness movement began with new illumination and the baptism of the Holy Spirit. Repentance became an important part of Christian life and theology, and the Azusa Street Revival revealed the pattern of the work of the Holy Spirit. This pattern became more and more non-Western as emphasis on the gifts of the Holy Spirit increased.

There are many benefits of examining the similarities and differences between the Western revival that enlarged the evangelical camp and the non-Western church growth phenomenon. Each movement in its context can teach us something about the church/society relationship when we examine theological and historical factors.

The Jews of the diaspora after the destruction of Jerusalem lived disconnected from the Western church. This was a missed opportunity for the Gentile church, which failed to tap in to the blessings and promises given to Israel and to deeply understand the full scope of the saving work accomplished by the Messiah. The Gentile church, as a result of the institutionalization of the Roman Catholic Church, continued to operate under the influence of Hellenism, adopting its metaphysical structure and even much of its theology, liturgy, and doctrine. However, the reestablishment of the nation of Israel in 1945 became the starting point of a new work in the history of God's harvest, where fulfilled and yet-to-be-fulfilled prophecies once forgotten or considered insignificant came to light in the church. A new focus was placed on the need to unite Jews and Gentiles as One New Man in the body of Christ and to see the salvation of all mankind.

The seed of gospel planted by the early church is not only growing in the Western world, but now has also spread throughout the entire world. Christianity is experiencing a revival, but so also are Islam, Buddhism, and Hinduism. Developing-world Christianity in the Global South that simply reflects Western forms of the faith does not exist; today's Christianity is not under the influence of the traditional Western denominations. Instead, all believers share the responsibility for world evangelization, which can only be accomplished with the help of the whole Body of Christ: healthy local churches in every region that can contribute to the kingdom of God.

Christianity, which began in the Middle East, shifted to the West and underwent institutionalization. With the birth of Islam in 622, Christianity in North Africa and the Middle East came to a virtual standstill, followed by destruction. Under the pretense of recovering the Holy Land, the Crusades in the Middle Ages left a bloody legacy that caused Muslims to see Christianity as destructive. Carrying the burden of unsettled historical hurts from these wars, the non-Western church faces the new challenge of missions to Muslims. Now is a pivotal time when the nontraditional, non-Western church can take the lead in a new missions model for Islam.

Islam has undergone the most impressive growth of all world religions. Islam threatens Christianity by positioning itself as its replacement. Islam has become the majority religion in North Africa, the Middle East, central Asia, Indonesia, and Malaysia. Due to immigration, Islam is growing in Europe and North America at the same time Christianity is declining. Furthermore, Westerners living in Christian regions are converting to Islam in great numbers. Islam is expanding its influence and power over Western Christianity and has become the world's second largest religion.

Religious pluralism objects to the elevation of one faith over another. It urges reconciliation among Judaism, Islam, and Christianity, all of which worship the same God, and it urges unification among Hinduism, Buddhism, and even shamanism, animism, and general religions, which all share the same spiritual realm. The focus of religious pluralism is on this so-called "god." Evangelicals maintain a certain distance from religious pluralism due to the uniqueness of the power of the gospel and the salvation through Jesus Christ.

The process of secularization is one of the main reasons behind the decline of the Western church in the Global North, and pluralism has played an important role in secularization. Europe's religious structure was such that the national church became the conformist church, while minority denominations became known as dissents and the Free Church; faiths outside of Christianity were completely excluded. Therefore pluralism, which first emerged after the Enlightenment in the eighteenth century, originally referred to pluralism in denominations within Christianity. A shift occurred, however, when faiths outside of Christianity began to influence Western moral thinking.

As people began to dispose of the central tenets of traditional Christianity, the New Age Movement, Islam, Buddhism, and Hinduism offered alternatives. Among the theologians who embraced pluralism was John Hick, who advocated a shift from a Christ-centered faith to a god-centered faith. His position was that salvation could be reached through Islam, Buddhism, or any other religion. Rather than accepting the absolute truth or superior viewpoint of any particular religion, Westerners began to compare and analyze each religion after they dismissed Christianity's unique ability to offer salvation. Religious pluralism proposed historical relativism, focused on conversations with faiths outside of Christianity, and embraced human liberation and social progressivism. Stating that "all classical religions are relative," the religious pluralist view is that all religions need to deepen their understanding of each other through dialogue that is based on a religious essence. In pluralism, all religions stand on an equal footing.

Globalization

In the time of Jesus, the Roman Empire globalized her boundaries, spanning across Europe, North Africa, Asia Minor, and the Middle East. The government system, culture, law, architecture, road system, and Greek language became common in the Empire. Genghis Khan, the Mongol leader, united many kingdoms in Asia, parts of Europe, and even the Middle East and globalized the area through the empire. The same thing occurred when the Spaniards and Portuguese colonized areas in Latin America, Africa, and some Asian regions in the sixteenth century. European powers proceeded with "protoglobalization," which intensified commercialism through colonial conquest and overseas mission. However, a new type of globalization in the nineteenth century came to light called "the modern globalization," where advanced non-Western worlds colonized areas and legitimized the western culture, education, and system of governance. After the World Wars, indigenous, independent, and autonomous cultures in the Global South contributed to the post-colonial globalization.[1]

Nowadays the global village is drawing people closer to one another, transcending geographical boundaries. Effective tools of connecting people include the Internet, media, films, music, books, sports, art, and other expressions of postmodern culture. The international monetary system has made commercial transactions possible through credit cards in environments as diverse as savannahs in Africa, Middle East desert cities, marts in the Pacific islands, and small Australian aboriginal towns. People and cultures are intermingling and interrelating, and the Global South is growing in the overall picture of world Christianity. Global issues are communicated and fittingly interpreted in local settings—a phenomenon known as *glocalization*. Allen states:

> Everywhere we see the same types. Our missions are in different countries amongst people of the most diverse characteristics, but all bear a most astonishing resemblance one to another. If we read the history of a mission in China we have only to change a few names and the same history will serve as the history of a mission in Zululand. There has been no new revelation. There has been no new discovery of new aspects of the Gospel, no new unfolding of new forms of Christian life.[2]

1. Kalu, *Globalization and Mission*, 25.
2. Allen, *Missionary Methods*, 142.

Globalization took place as Christianity's center of gravity was shifting from the Global North to the Global South. Starting in 1960s, communication technologies accelerated, facilitating the spread of new trends in art, music, movies, and culture, as well as political issues and economic concerns. Theological work being done in Germany at that time influenced the United Kingdom, United States, and eventually the entire world. Evolution theory, liberal theology, secularism, humanism, sexual libertinism, and capitalistic approaches to church programs were all part of this wave of influence.[3]

Revivals that began as singular events in Wales, India, Azusa Street, and Pyongyang grew to be part of a greater and greater phenomenon when news spread to other nations. In the time of George Whitefield, news of revival united the thirteen colonies. Today, global Christian news unites believers with prayer requests and mutual support.[4] Beek and Karamaga affirm, "Through the confessional and ecumenical world bodies of which they are members, the Protestant churches have begun to deal globally with issues such as economic justice and care for the Earth."[5] Kalu states:

> Globalization as a descriptor of contemporary culture has imbued the context of doing mission, supplied the tools and resources, and enormously enlarged the scale and opportunities for doing a different type of mission. . . . The growth of Christianity in the Global South, and in Eastern and Central Europe, combined with the emergence of new cultural trends— all have influenced global processes to scramble the old modes of Christian expressions, ministerial formation, theological education, and missionary structures and strategies.[6]

Mission work is enhanced by a sense of being united to one another and to other cultures. People can receive global news wherever they live and can follow happenings in the world, maintaining a connection with others who are far away. Tennent states,

> Globalization has fostered dramatic changes in immigration, urbanization, and technological connectivity. The result is that the traditional sending structures and geographic orientation that have dominated missions since the nineteenth century

---

3. Kalu, "Globalization and Mission," 25–26.

4. Ibid., 42.

5. Beek and Karamaga, "Protestants, 1910–2010," 89.

6. Kalu, "Globalization and Mission," 35–36.

are no longer tenable. . . . The long-held distinction of "home" missions and "foreign" missions is passing away, not just because of the collapsing center noted above, but also because of forces set into motion by globalization, which have had such a profound effect on all of us.[7]

In the twenty-first century, we will surely encounter new types Christianity not experienced before. Pentecostal Christianity helps believers to develop a strong identity in a global system that can reduce people to stereotypes or statistics. This is crucial since it has been shown that globalization creates an identity crisis on all levels of society through the constant infiltration of new behaviors and convictions. Pentecostalism offers a solution as it shifts the thinking from the individual, personal level and connects it to the global picture.[8]

Urbanization

In the twenty-first century, the urban population is increasing in size and scale. In 1910, the world's largest cities were London, New York, Paris, Berlin, Chicago, Vienna, Philadelphia, Buenos Aires, Ruhr, and Manchester.

TABLE 8.1 1910 LARGEST CITIES

1910 Largest cities				
City	*Country*	*Population*	*Christians*	*%*
1 LONDON	Britain	6,958,000	6,680,000	96.0
2 New York	USA	5,405,000	5,135,000	95.0
3 PARIS	France	3,854,000	3,777,000	98.0
4 BERLIN	Germany	2,966,000	2,906,000	98.0
5 Chicago	USA	2,300,000	2,208,000	96.0
6 VIENNA	Austria	1,739,000	1,670,000	96.0
7 Philadelphia	USA	1,654,000	1,588,000	96.0
8 BUENOS AIRES	Argentina	1,464,000	1,435,000	98.0
9 Ruhr	Germany	1,406,000	1,378,000	98.0
10 Manchester	Britain	1,425,000	1,368,000	96.0

Cities listed in ALL CAPITALS are capital cities

Cities listed in all CAPITALS are capital cities.
Source: Atlas of Global Christianity[9]

7. Tennent, *Invitation to World Mission*, 42.

8. Ibid., 55.

9. Johnson and Ross, *Atlas of Global Christianity*, 238.

Migration can significantly affect the religious composition of urban areas. For example, during the twentieth century, many Chinese migrated to Vancouver, Canada, making them the largest minority group in that city. The seventh largest immigrant group in Canada is the Chinese who practice folk-religions brought over from China.[10] Urban areas, especially the largest one hundred worldwide, typically contain large minority populations that affect the city's religious makeup. Additionally, undocumented immigrants often find their way to large cities; their effect on immigrant demographics (and thus religious adherence statistics) depends on whether or not they are officially recognized and counted. The world's urban areas are meeting places for a variety of religious and spiritual beliefs and practices.[11] Major cities throughout the world have seen an increasing mix of cultures, races, and tribes. Most revivals and awakenings have taken place in major Western cities, including London, Northhampton, Boston, New York, and Los Angeles. Non-Western revivals also took place in major cities, such as Tinnevelli, India, in 1802; Pyongyang, Korea, in 1907; Valparaiso, Chile, in 1909; Buenos Aires, Argentina, in 1954; and Nagaland, northeast India, in the 1960s and 1970s.[12]

Revivals based in urban areas can also affect surrounding rural areas when migrants to the city return to their rural hometowns, bringing the good news of the gospel with them. The dynamic also works in the opposite direction, with rural religious influences affecting cities through migration. For example, in metro Manila, traditional religion from rural origins, especially folk Catholicism, found its way into urban areas.[13] In Brazil, the urban-to-rural pattern is seen in the growth of the Christian Congregation of Brazil. This self-propagating, self-governing, self-supporting and lay-led denomination was founded by Luigi Francescon in 1910. When revival broke out in the city, members were dispatched to rural areas as lay missionaries.[14] Rural/urban migration has affected Pentecostal/charismatic churches in particular. Matviuk points out the great impact seen when poor urban residents

---

10. Statistics Canada, "Population," line 17.

11. Johnson and Ross, *Atlas of Global Christianity*, 238.

12. Backholer, *Revival Fire*, 21–22.

13. Poethig, "The Philippine Urban Family," 228.

14. Westmeier, *Protestant Pentecostalism in Latin America*, 17.

find spiritually dynamic churches, citing examples of Pentecostal and charismatic church growth in Africa, Asia, and Latin America.[15]

The twentieth century Pentecostal movement began in cities worldwide, including Los Angeles, New York, Chicago, and Zion City, Illinois, and cities have been strategic in the promulgation of the gospel around the world.[16] With large populations and systems that facilitate access and communication, cities are places of social change.[17] The church has a particular attraction for urban migrants who miss the extended family they used to enjoy in their rural communities. Those who hunger for security and a spiritual presence in their lives find that the church meets this need as a sort of surrogate family.[18] With large numbers of migrants joining churches, the result has been the formation of megachurches.[19]

Martin believes that Latin America's Iberian culture by means of colonization deferred economic development. Pentecostalism as a pivotal element, Latin America can obtain the cultural underpinning required for modernization and development.[20] Pentecostal church

15. Matviuk, "Pentecostal Leadership Development," 155–56.

16. Poethig, "The Philippine Urban Family," 273. Philip M. Hauser, Urbanization in Asia and the Far East: Proceedings of the joint Un/Unesco Seminar (in Co-Operation with the Internatinoal Labour Office) on Urbanization in the Ecafe Region, Bangkok, 8–18 August, 1956, Tensions and Technology Series (Calcutta: UNESCO Research Centre on the Social Implication of Industrialization in Southern Asia, 1957).

17. Elwood, *Churches and Sects in the Philippines*, 65.

18. Martin, *Pentecostalism*, 161. Hong states, "The difficulty of finding a place to belong and loss of identity can make humans more connected to God, placing more demands on the role of religion. . . . Many people migrating from rural areas to cities usually had animistic religious patterns and affectionate human relations, but experienced the new cold social structures and milieu with culture shock." Hong, "Charismatic Mega-churches in Korea," 106. Martin finds that urbanization has facilitated the growth of Pentecostalism.

19. In Korea, the urban population has increased dramatically: 28 percent in 1960, 41.1 percent in 1970, 57.3 percent in 1980, and 65.4 percent in 1985. Hong points out, "Most large churches and all the mega-churches are centered in and around Seoul. The Korean Protestant church has an urban character, and especially do the charismatic mega-churches." Hong, "Charismatic Mega-churches in Korea," 106.

20. Martin, *Tongues of Fire*, 27–46. Cf. Chesnut, *Born Again in Brazil*, 4–5; Berryman, *Religion in the Megacity*, 3. Protestant church growth in Latin American is closely interrelated with social-cultural factors. One key issue is urbanization that gave people an easy route to emigrate into urban areas. Eventually urban poor and rural origin people who had been practicing spiritual power through folk religions

growth in Brazil correlates with modernization, urbanization, indus-trialization, and the settlement of new land areas.[21] Modernization is defined as the process of social change that affects an entire society, increasing productivity through technological innovations. While Martin believes that social factors have had a greater impact on Latin America than religious ones, he agrees that Pentecostalism has of-fered empowerment and security to those who are victimized by modernization.[22]

Christianity was born in the city of Jerusalem and developed in the major cities of the Roman Empire: Antioch, Ephesus, Corinth, Alexandria, and Carthage.[23] A similar situation exists today in Brazil, where the majority of citizens now live in cities. Studies have been shown that the fastest growing Brazilian churches are in urban centers. Over the past twenty years, the number of inhabitants in Brazil has doubled, and over the same period, the population of urban centers has quadrupled. For many years, Sao Paulo was the fastest growing city in the world.[24]

Between in 1950 and 1960, with the growth of industry, the process of urbanization accelerated. By 1960, almost the half of the Brazilian population was found in cities.[25] The largest churches are in the largest cities, located in coastal areas.[26] As of 1990, one out of every six Brazilians claimed affiliation with a Protestant denomination.

In Brazil's second largest city, Rio de Janeiro, the great major-ity of Christians (91 percent) are Pentecostal. On average, one church per workday has been established since the beginning of the 1990s.[27] Pentecostal churches appeal to those whose extended family networks

---

accepted easily Pentecostal manifestations.

21. Read and Ineson, *Brazil 1980*, 142–43. Pentecostal growth is indeed taking place in urban areas. Developing infrastructure, domestic immigration, industrial-ization and urbanization had attracted people from rural areas. Pentecostal churches attract new urban dwellers.

22. Martin, *Tongues of Fire*, 65–68. Cf. Chesnut, *Born Again in Brazil*, 4–5.

23. Weld and McGavran, *Principles of Church Growth*, 12–2.

24. Ibid., 12–3.

25. For details, see Read, *New Patterns of Church Growth in Brazil*, 130. Cf. Mandryk, *Operation World*, 119.

26. Read, *New Patterns of Church Growth in Brazil*, 130.

27. Chesnut, *Born Again in Brazil*, 3.

have disintegrated and who are newcomers to the cities.[28] A 1992 study in Rio de Janeiro classified 39 percent of churches as historic and 61 percent as Pentecostal. Further, 91 percent (648 of the 710) of new churches established in 1990 through 1992 period were Pentecostal.[29]

Not only is the world's population becoming more urban, but the large cities of the world are also becoming non-Western. In 1910, nine of the ten largest cities were in Europe or the United States. In 2010, only two of the world's twenty largest cities were located in the West.

TABLE 8.2 LARGEST URBAN AREAS BY POPULATION 2010

100 largest urban areas by total population, 2010, 1-25				
			Religions	
	Urban area	Country	Population	Largest	%
1	TOKYO	Japan	35,467,000	Buddhists	56.0%
2	MEXICO CITY	Mexico	20,688,000	Christians	95.3%
3	Mumbai	India	20,036,000	Hindus	69.0%
4	New York - Newark	USA	20,009,000	Christians	65.0%
5	São Paulo	Brazil	19,582,000	Christians	88.5%
6	Delhi	India	16,983,000	Hindus	78.0%
7	Shanghai	China	15,790,000	Chinese folk	30.0%
8	Kolkata	India	15,548,000	Hindus	69.0%
9	JAKARTA	Indonesia	15,206,000	Muslims	65.0%
10	DHAKA	Bangladesh	14,625,000	Muslims	90.0%
11	Lagos	Nigeria	13,717,000	Christians	71.2%
12	Karachi	Pakistan	13,252,000	Muslims	93.0%
13	BUENOS AIRES	Argentina	13,067,000	Christians	91.4%
14	Los Angeles	USA	12,378,000	Christians	80.0%
15	Rio de Janeiro	Brazil	12,170,000	Christians	90.0%
16	CAIRO	Egypt	12,041,000	Muslims	87.0%
17	MANILA	Philippines	11,799,000	Christians	93.8%
18	BEIJING	China	11,741,000	Agnostics	36.0%
19	Osaka-Kobe	Japan	11,305,000	Buddhists	55.0%
20	MOSCOW	Russia	10,967,000	Christians	84.0%
21	Istanbul	Turkey	10,546,000	Muslims	95.0%
22	PARIS	France	9,856,000	Christians	61.1%
23	SEOUL	South Korea	9,554,000	Christians	45.7%
24	Guangzhou	China	9,447,000	Agnostics	36.0%
25	Chicago	USA	9,186,000	Christians	78.0%
Cities listed in ALL CAPITALS are capital cities.				

Cities listed in capital letters are capital cities.
Source: *Atlas of Global Christianity*[30]

In 1999, 120 million people lived in urban areas. The population of just the world's top twenty-five cites totaled nearly 380 million, with 10 to 30 million people in each area. There are thirteen Asian, four

28. Glazier, *Perspectives on Pentecostalism*, 135. Glazier analyses the reason of modernization for Pentecostals growth that "Pentecostals exist not because they are near to the forces of modernization but precisely because they are so marginal to normal social existence. Patronage tends to flow through pre-established social networks such as the extended family."

29. Berryman, *Religion in the Megacity*, 18.

30. Johnson and Ross, *Atlas of Global Christianity*, 238.

Latin American, and two African cities among the largest, and these cities are still growing rapidly, gaining 100,000 people every day. In 2010, urbanites numbered 1.3 billion and constituted 40 percent of the global population. This is quite a contrast to 1910, when only 16 percent of the world's population lived in cities.[31]

MAP 8.1 100 LARGEST CITIES BY RELIGIOUS ADHERENCE, 2010

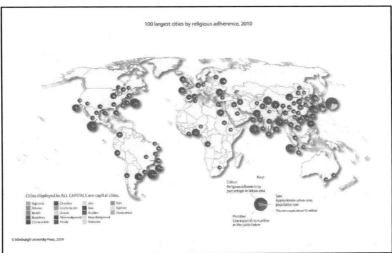

Source: Atlas of Global Christianity[32]

Today, urban areas are replete with mission opportunities. Among the people living in cities are minority groups, unreached people, and unengaged people from remote areas. Both native people and immigrants live together in close proximity with access to transportation and communication systems that can be used to facilitate the spread of the gospel. For global Christianity, urban mission will be the best chance to share the gospel of Jesus Christ in the twenty-first century.

Mirana-Feliciano finds that South Korea, Brazil, the Philippines, and Colombia have the most urban evangelistic activity.[33] In Brazil, the United States, Canada, Australia, Columbia, India, Indonesia, Nigeria, South Korea, and the Philippines, urban areas have housed the nation's mission agencies, short-term training schools, vacation

31. Miranda-Feliciano, "Christianity in Cities, 1910–2010," 240–41.

32. John and Ross, *Atlas of Global Christianity*. 238–239.

33. Ibid., 240–41.

Bible schools, and church-planting organizations. As we have seen, the growth of the Pentecostal church in Brazil is attributable to the use of urban resources for sharing the gospel.[34] If urban areas are touched by the Holy Spirit, revival will spread to the entire society.

According to Willems, Protestantism in Latin America, as it was instituted in urban areas, turned into in an exceedingly restricted approach "as a factor contributing to sociocultural change. Then industrialization, urbanization, internal migration, and the opening of rural frontiers not only generated conditions increasingly favorable to the growth of Protestant denominationalism but also gradually reinforced its active role in the process of sociocultural transformation . . . ."[35]

In the same way, rapid Pentecostal expansion is taking place in religiously pluralistic cities in Asia, the Middle East, and the West. Drawing from non-Western traditions, culture, worship styles, and ecclesiastical systems, the global church at the end of the twentieth century includes a mixture of traditions, races, nationalities, ages, and social classes in urban environments. Traditional churches in Myanmar, Thailand, Malaysia, Vietnam, and Singapore have become Pentecostalized.[36] Similarly, in Latin America, most Protestant evangelical churches are actually Pentecostal in practice, and Pentecostals represent 75 percent of all Protestants.[37]

Throughout the world and throughout history, urban church growth has facilitated the spread of the gospel. God has used revivals and awakenings to draw people to himself in urban areas from the time of the First Awakening to the classical Pentecostal revivals, from the outpouring of the Holy Spirit in Jerusalem to cities throughout the globe. "You heavens above, rain down my righteousness; let the clouds shower it down. Let the earth open wide, let salvation spring up, let righteousness flourish with it; I, the Lord, have created it" (Isa 45:8 NIV).

---

34. Read and Ineson, *Brazil 1980*, 142–43.

35. Willems, *Followers of the New Faith*, 13.

36. Anderson, "Pentecostalism in East Asia," 117.

37. C. Peter Wagner found that "the Assemblies of God, has become the largest or second largest in denominational membership in Argentina, Bolivia, Brazil, Costa Rica, Cuba, Dominican Republic, Guatemala, Honduras, Nicaragua, Panama, Peru, Puerto Rico, Uruguay, Venezuela or 13 (excluding Puerto Rico and Portuguese-speaking Brazil) of the 18 Spanish-speaking republics of Latin America." Petersen, "The Formation," 32–33.

Migration

Eleanor Wilmer wrote in her poem, "There are always in each of us these two: the one who stays, the one who goes away."[38] Immigration generates theological and missiological concerns, and today's advanced communication and transportation make it possible for more people to migrate from one place to another. People from the Global South can migrate to the Global North, leading to multicultural communities, diaspora missions, second-generation education, and interracial and interfaith issues for local churches.

GRAPH 8.1 APPROXIMATE SPREAD OF IMMIGRANTS IN THE PAST
FIFTY YEARS (TOTAL 191 MILLION)

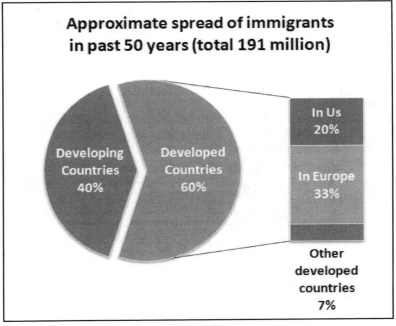

Source: Global Issues[39]

In 2008, there were 191 million immigrants worldwide. This number has doubled in the last fifty years. Twenty percent of immigrants, or 38 million people, live in the United States, 33 percent live in Europe, and 7 percent live in other developed nations, totaling 60

38. Wilnor, "Emigration," lines 1–3.
39 Shah, "Worldwide Immigrants Statistics," line 1.

percent. The other 40 percent of global immigrants live in developing nations. Three out of four immigrants live in just 28 nations.[40]

The United Nations reports that there were 213,944,000 immigrants in 2009. A total of 127 million immigrants live in developed nations and 86 million in developing nations.[41] There were 42.8 million immigrants to the United States, followed by the Russian Federation with 12.3 million. These numbers "challenge old trends and traditional thinking that the West is the destination of all migrants. The specific intake of migrants by continent in 2005 (Europe, 34 percent; North America, 23 percent; Asia, 28 percent; Africa, 9 percent; Latin America, 3 percent; and Oceania, 3 percent) actually shows Asia receiving more migrants than North America."[42] Still, the United States is deeply impacted by immigration: "[T]he Census Bureau predicts that minorities will account for half of the U.S. population by 2050."[43]

GRAPH 8.2 INTERNATIONAL MIGRATION, 2009

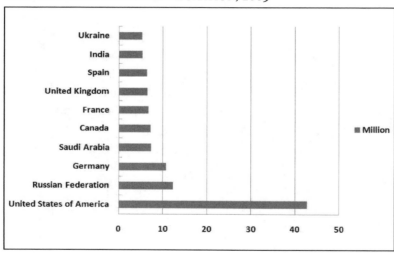

Source: United Nations, Department of Economic and Social Affairs, Population Division (2009). International Migration, 2009 Wallchart (United Nations publication, Sales No. E.09.XIII.8)[44]

40. Women represent half of all immigrants, or 95 million people. Between 1990 and 2005, there were 36 million migrations. Ibid., line 1–5.

41. United Nations, "International Migration 2009," lines 3–5.

42. Cruz, "Expanding the Boundaries," 71–72.

43. Ibid., 72.

44. Population Division, International Migration, 2009" §1.

Immigrant communities become mixtures of different faiths. There are Muslims living in Europe; Asian workers in the Middle East; Hispanics, Asians, Africans, and Europeans in the U.S.; Polynesians in Australia and New Zealand; and so on. In communities around the world, many languages and races are learning to communicate with each other. This creates an opportunity for a sort of reverse mission. While European countries and other nations are turning to Islam and eastern religions, evangelized immigrants from the southern hemisphere—mostly Pentecostals and Charismatics from Latin America, Africa, and some Asian countries—are reinvigorating dwindling Western churches.[45]

Latin American immigrants, for example, are not simply moving to the northern hemisphere, but are bringing with them the spiritual and cultural elements and the pastoral methodology compatible with the Pentecostal worship they experienced in their nations of origin. This situation is the same for people from Asia and Africa.[46] Immigrants who have experienced the Pentecostal revival can share that experience with their Western neighbors through shared church buildings, a common marketplace, and through school and prayer meetings.[47]

In the case of domestic migration, an interchange between rural and urban areas gives rise to a sort of hometown mission. Those who hear the gospel in the city bring it back to the rural areas. Immigrants are great sources of evangelism and church planting around the world. The emergence of strong native church leadership by means of migration contributes to the growth of Christianity everywhere.[48]

---

45. Lee, "Future of Global Christianity," 104.

46. Escobar describes several factors contributing to the growth of Pentecostal and charismatic churches: "the free action of the Spirit, hunger for God, a need for security and community in a hostile world, lay participation, freedom of worship and emotion, and the use of folk music and instruments." Escobar, "Latin America: An Evangelical Perspective," 247; cf. Núñez and Taylor, *Crisis in Latin America*, 156.

47. Tuggy and Toliver, *Seeing the Church in the Philippines*, 81.

48. Tuggy and Toliver descibe seven characteristics of Pentecostal/charismatic expansion: "a nationwide strategy of evangelism; strong emphasis on evangelism and church planting; close ties between churches and institutional work, especially Bible schools; a multilevel ministry for churches; a low missionary-to-communicant-member ratio; and emphasis on both centrifugal (strong central churches) and centripetal (rural evangelism) growth. Pentecostal expansion was achieved not by "forced growth" tied to the presence of missionaries, but by spontaneous growth where indigenous people carry the major burden of expansion." Ibid., 83–84.

The population of Europe has continued its steady decline: "[W] hen the European Union was founded, it collectively represented approximately 14 percent of the world's population. Currently, those same European countries represent about 6 percent of the world population, and by 2050 it will be down to 4 percent. . . . Thus, one of the major trends in Western Europe over the last sixty years has been the collapse of Christendom and the rise of Islam."[49] The United States population is expected to grow to 400 million in 2050 from 300 million in 2010 and 258 million in 1993. Growth will be greater among people of color; the Hispanic/Latino immigrant community will be second in size only to the Anglo-American community. Africans, Filipinos, Koreans, Chinese, and others will collectively become the majority as nonwhite groups continue to grow at higher rates.[50]

GRAPH 8.3 PERCENT OF THE POPULATION BY RACE AND HISPANIC ORIGIN, 1990, 2000, 2025, AND 2050

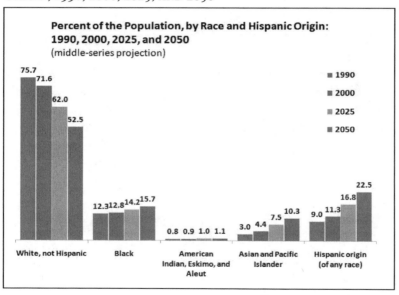

Source: U.S. Census Bureau[51]

49. Tennent, *Invitation to World Mission*, 43.

50. Ibid., 43–44.

51. United States Census Bureau, "National Population Projections," line 33.

With the population of the West declining, is increasing immigration the only solution? If Christianity is strong in the West, non-
Christian immigrants will be affected by the Christian environment.
If not, then the West needs immigrants as missionaries: "Despite the
recent anti-immigration sentiment in the United states, Christians
should understand that immigration represents the most important
hope not only for the ongoing viability of our society but also for the
re-evangelization of the West."[52] Mission field and mission force are
no longer defined by geography, but by the presence of Christians who
are willing to live in a way that offers a witnessing for the gospel.

AGE OF HOLY SPIRIT

The flourishing global Christianity demonstrated an unprecedented
diversity in form, worship, doctrine, and church system amongst traditional mainline churches, independent churches, and fairly indigenous churches. Winning new converts and filling church seats with
enthusiastic believers can be observed in the Global South. It is quite
striking for Westerners who have been accustomed to empty seats
with a handful of gray-haired people worshipping in old cathedrals.
The Western church has forgotten the important thing that provides
the life of the church, the outpouring of the Holy Ghost. Worship
gatherings in the savannas of Africa, the highlands of South America,
and the rainforests in Borneo, as well as the repetitive hymnal singing
by Afro-Caribbeans, the small house prayer gatherings in China, and
the open air services in India all have one thing in common, and that
is the outpouring and anointing of the Holy Spirit in the twenty-first
century.

Pentecostal Age

The twentieth century has brought many opportunities for church
growth. The global church is more diverse denominationally, racially,
ethnically, culturally and geographically. Communication and travel
technologies have increased accessibility, and more denominations
have demonstrated a spiritual openness. Dynamic movement can be
seen among conservative Protestants in Latin America; Presbyterian
churches in South Korea; converts from Islam in the world's largest

---

52. Tennent, *Invitation to World Mission*, 44–45.

Muslim country, Indonesia; Christians experiencing revival in com-
munist-controlled China; witnesses for Christ even in the most fundamentally Islamic country, Iran; and many more. In the scope of just
one hundred years, the gospel of Jesus Christ has made monumental
progress in the Global South. Many African nations have become
more strongly Christianized, and sub-Saharan African missionaries from Nigeria, Kenya, Uganda, and Ghana are now being sent to
Islamic regions in the north. All of these phenomena come from the
outpouring of the Holy Spirit in the twentieth century. For example,
in Ghana,

> [T]he nature of Ghanaian Christianity has subtly changed.
> Proportionately, Ghana's mainline churches, according to reli-
> able surveys, are losing members. Spectacular real growth lies
> with newer Pentecostal churches: these must be distinguished
> from traditional AICs [African Initiated Churches], which
> are themselves suffering a far greater decline than the main-
> line churches. The Pentecostal explosion has not only taken
> members from the mainline churches, but Pentecostalised
> these churches themselves. The new churches stand for a Faith
> Gospel focusing on this-worldly blessings, and increasingly for
> a deliverance theology which, though built on African tradi-
> tional conceptions, is expressed strongly in terms of modern
> Western charismatic thinking. Some of the most educated
> and articulate church leaders display considerable creativity,
> and are relating Pentecostal Christianity to Ghana's particular
> circumstances.[53]

As the charismatic movement has influenced major traditions
and denominations, a spirit of unity has increased interdenominational efforts in evangelism and missions.[54] In areas where revivals
have taken place, a spiritual dynamism and fervent prayer movements
continue—among them Kashia Hills and Nagaland in Northeastern
India, Chin state in Myanmar, the Chilean Methodist Episcopal
Church, Aladura Church in Nigeria, Zion Christian Church in South
Africa, and house churches in China. Over the years, the tradition of
revival became contagious and affected neighboring denominations
and churches. Growth came sometimes in spite of opposition from
traditional churches in areas such as Azusa Street in Los Angeles,

---

53. Gifford, *African Christianity*, 306.
54. Tennent, *Invitation to World Mission*, 423–24.

United States; Sunderland, United Kingdom; Mülheim in Germany; Sweden; Norway; Zion City in South Africa; India; and Korea.

One revival in Korea has transformed entire nations over a hundred-year period. The Great Revival in the Pyongyang Changdaehyun Presbyterian church in 1907 marked the beginning of traditions that persist today, including early-morning prayer, annual Bible conferences, revival meetings, and Spirit-filled overnight prayer meetings. This great revival was an interdenominational effort of Presbyterian, Methodist, Holiness, and Baptist churches that together experienced the outpouring of the Spirit on the day of "the Korean Pentecost." The subsequent Pentecostalization of each denomination led people to seek the outpouring of the Holy Spirit and established an overall trend among Korean Protestants to practice revival-oriented Pentecostal worship and prayer.[55] The Pyonyang revival led to the widespread practice of corporate prayer, known as unison prayer or *tongsung kido* in Korean, which includes shouting and praying aloud with chanting and spontaneous outcries. Like the Wesleys, Moravians, and Evan Roberts in Wales, many Korean Christians practice sunset and sunrise prayers. More than 700 prayer mountains exist in South Korea for those seeking solitude or for prayer in times of fasting, crisis, or spiritual restoration. Whether conservative Presbyterians, enthusiastic Wesleyan Holiness churches, liberal Korean Methodist churches, or dispensational Baptists, these Christians are considered strong Pentecostal believers. Almost all churches have an annual Bible conference (usually a weeklong period twice a year) and youth camps (regularly twice a year). Massive prayer rallies and "crusades" are organized regularly. Still, the Pentecostal fervor in Korea has cooled with increasing economic prosperity, and because some churches are focusing on this-world prosperity and presenting Christian faith in a cause-and-effect way.

Pentecostals in Brazil, Nigeria, India, Chile, the Philippines, and South Korea have experienced upward mobility from poor to middle-class, as did the Methodists and Baptists in the United States and United Kingdom. Korean Christians have experienced social advancement and have become leading figures in business, politics, and

---

55. The Korean Pentecost did not have any link with American classical Pentecostalism. Protestant churches became Pentecostalized in an indigenous Korean way.

education.[56] This social lift increases their ability to affect society and to witness to the gospel.

If an outpouring of the Spirit leads to a great number of conversions, church growth will naturally follow. A high percentage of people who experienced conversion are practicing Pentecostal worship and prayer in Latin America, sub-Saharan Africa, and many countries in Asia and Oceania today.[57] The twentieth century phenomenon of Pentecostalism has greatly affected existing denominations and revitalized their congregations.

> Because Pentecostals see themselves as reviving the apostolic faith rather than breaking off from or emerging out of any existing movements, it allows them, even if naively, to provide a basis for ecumenism around their common commitment to the biblical witness in Scripture and their shared experience of the Holy Spirit. Though most Pentecostals deride the word ecumenical and, quite frankly, have exhibited as much sectarianism and theological controversy as any other Christian group, it is nevertheless remarkable to see how Pentecostalism actually has contributed positively to ecumenism. The Pentecostals learned the principle of *sola scriptum* from the Reformation but then used it as a basis for celebrating a supernatural, apostolic faith that predated the historical divisiveness of denominationalism. The result was a new basis for cooperation and collaboration in missions, which facilitated the rapid spread of Christianity around the world. The growth of the global church in the wake of Pentecostal witness was so profound that Henry Van Dusen rolled the expression "Third Force" to describe it.[58]

In one Brazilian case, the expansion of Pentecostal churches is the result of evangelistic actions to address poverty.[59] Many Brazilian church members experienced social advancement from their previ-

56. In Korea, Hong reports that Pentecostal/charismatic churches mainly consist of the lower classes and middle-class people who recently moved up the economic ladder from lower rungs. Hong, "The Background and Characteristics," 111, 115.

57. Hong's research shows that 42.5 percent of megachurch attendees in Korea in 1998 had experienced a charismatic conversion from a variety of religious backgrounds including no religion, Buddhism, Confucianism, Shamanism, and folk religion. This is a contrast to the Philippines, where 70 percent of megachurch attendees stated their previous background as Roman Catholic. Ibid., 111–12.

58. Tennent, *Invitation to World Mission*, 424.

59. Generally in the Global South, particularity in Brazil, early Pentecostal believers were considered the "poorest of the poor." Chesnut, *Born Again in Brazil*, 17.

ous environment: the urban slum.[60] When low-income Brazilians sought out the church in response to a sense of neglect, powerlessness, and loneliness, they found themselves well accepted by the congregations.[61] The Pentecostalization of existing churches has been powerful for the underprivileged and marginalized classes in India, Indonesia, Latin America, and Africa as well. For instance in Brazil, Pentecostal churches are full of racial-minority women, children, and the poor encountering the Spirit's outpouring.[62] The appeal of Pentecostal churches to those who live on the fringes is undeniable. In Colombia, most upper-class citizens are Pentecostals, but the majority of congregants come from marginalized groups.[63] Social promotion of church members is occurring in Brazil, Argentina, Latin America, and sub-Saharan Africa as well; Pentecostals are now joining the upper classes around the world.[64]

In Brazil and elsewhere, high church growth rates are correlated with divine healing or deliverance.[65] Chesnut has studied the attraction of faith healing to the Brazilian lower classes.[66]

> Thus, this study posits that the dialectic between poverty-related illness and faith healing provides the key to understanding the appeal of Pentecostalism in Brazil and much of Latin America. Although somatic maladies predominate over other forms of affliction in the life histories of my informants, I expand the concept of illness beyond its physical social distress present on the urban periphery. Pentecostalism's message of healing power reverberates among the popular classes, particularly women, whose already precarious household economies are further debilitated by alcoholism, unemployment, and domestic strife.[67]

60. Vásquez, *The Brazilian Popular Church and the Crisis of Modernity*, 76.

61. Cook, *New Face of the Church in Latin America*, 73.

62. Burdick, *Blessed Anastacia*, 132.

63. Chesnut, *Born Again in Brazil*, 3–4.

64. Read, *New Patterns of Church Growth in Brazil*, 130.

65. The Pentecostal revivals broke out attracting the masses like the poor, women, and underprivileged. Ethnically its followers were diverse such as urban dwellers and converts who had Afro-Brazilian cults backgrounds. Parker, *Popular Religion and Modernization*, 144–48, 155. See also Vásquez, *The Brazilian Popular Church and the Crisis of Modernity*, 76.

66. Some of the factors to the phenomenal Pentecostal growth are divine healing and the prosperity gospel.

67. Chesnut, *Born Again in Brazil*, 6.

In Asia, people have a deep sense of the spiritual world. Whereas in the West, any form of religion can be minimized by the attraction of modernism, this is far from the case in the Global South, especially in Asia. Wonsuk Ma says, "No matter how modern a society may look, basically Asian minds are animistic in orientation."[68] Yung explains the receptiveness of Asians to the supernatural, "The picture in the non-western world was rather different. Most non-westerners possess a supernaturalistic worldview, which even a modern western scientific education could not fully eradicate easily. It is so much part and parcel of their cultural backgrounds. Consequently, a truly indigenous Christianity in Asia has to be supernaturalistic, and therefore Pentecostal!"[69]

Charismatic Manifestations

Who could have foreseen the worldwide impact of Pentecostal and charismatic Christianity? It has had profound effect in Africa, Asia, and Latin America; less so in North America and Europe.[70] The humble beginnings of the movement by Charles Parham and William Seymour were the first strands of a new tapestry of global Christianity that includes a variety of manifestations of the Holy Spirit, new models of leadership, heartfelt praise and worship, powerful prayer, spiritual experiences, new cultural expressions of the Christian faith, and church governance systems that represent a radical change from that of nineteenth century evangelicalism. According to Hayford, the Pentecostal and Charismatic movements contributed tremendously to the growth of Christianity in the Global South, which he defines as the "charismatic century." He indicates that the historic momentum did not take place in a famous church building but in a lowly, small clapboard house at 312 Azusa Street. The mixture of African Americans, white Holiness groups, Mexicans, and a few Pacific Asians mingled together, praying aloud, groaning, repenting, crying, and experiencing the great outpouring of the Holy Spirit with manifestations of speaking in tongue. Hayford calls this small congregation the new beginning of the New Testament church in the early twentieth century. This dramatic Pentecostal revival contributed to the worldwide

68. Ma, "Asian (Classical) Pentecostalism," 7.
69. Yung, "Pentecostalism and the Asian Church," 11.
70. Yong, *The Spirit Poured Out on All Flesh*, 59.

missionary movement and the growth of the Global South changing Christian worship, prayer, music, and theology.[71]

The difference between the Pentecostal revival at Azusa and the evangelical awakenings and revivals drew theological attention in seeing the true manifestation of the Holy Ghost and the conversion experience. The Puritan awakening, First and Second Awakenings, and the Holiness revivals until the late nineteenth century had been focused on personal conversion, rebirth, sanctification, healing, baptism of the Holy Spirit, and the expectation of the Second Advent of Christ. The early Pentecostal revival had no doctrinal differences from the previous evangelical revivals and awakenings, yet they directly experienced healings and the baptism of the Holy Spirit among individual lives whereas the evangelical revivals and awakenings had not experienced such things. The Classical Pentecostal movement known as the early Azusa Revival in the early twentieth century disseminated throughout the entire world and reshaped the face of Christianity into the new Christian world such as the Global South. When the Pentecostal movement grew together along with the charismatic movements, the size, style, hierarchy, worship, and religious tapestry of the Global South could be recognized as a greater part of the Christian body worldwide. The Pentecostal movements also brought new theological issues like spiritual gifts, particularly speaking in tongue, the manifestation of the Holy Spirit, church government system, worship style, and an imminent calling and response to world mission.

Above all the differences between the previous evangelical revivals and awakenings, and the early Classical Pentecostal Revival, is the issue on the baptism of the Holy Spirit.[72] Pentecostals who agreed on the baptism of the Holy Spirit formed different classical denominations, and furthermore, the Pentecostal Fellowship of North America as the United Pentecostal body was formed to give their own voice with a unified alliance of the Pentecostal denomination. They declared, "We believe that the full gospel includes holiness of heart and life, healing for the body, and baptism in the Holy Spirit with the evidence of speaking in other tongues as the Spirit gives the utterance."[73] Classical Pentecostalism has always recognized speaking in tongues

71. Hayford, *The Charismatic Century*, 1–26.

72. Williams, "Baptism in the Holy Spirit," 40.

73. Ibid., 40–41.

as "initial evidence"—an immediate sign of Spirit baptism.[74] Classical Pentecostals believed that Holy Spirit baptism is principally demonstrated through glossolalia.[75]

The early Pentecostal theology on the baptism of the Holy Spirit caused a great schism among evangelicals. Most mainline churches in North America where they rejected the Pentecostal theology and the manifestation of the Holy Ghost stuck to the fundamental or liberal theology. However, Pentecostal theology grabbed most evangelicalism, particularly the fundamental theology, yet they added the theology of the Holy Spirit, or pneumatology. For several decades before the mid twentieth century the churches in North America were divided into Pentecostals, Evangelicals, and liberals. When the mainline churches were able to accept the Pentecostal manifestation in their churches a new wave of the renewal movement was about to begin. This was called the charismatic renewal movement that began around 1960. This movement was ignited by Episcopal priest Dennis Bennett. Major traditions such as the Episcopal, Lutheran, Roman Catholic, and Orthodox churches came to accept charismatic experiences as normative. This led to indigenous, cross-denominational revival that was geographically dominated by the developing world and Pentecostal in theology. This movement was widely accepted, and Spirit baptism was seen as bringing power into the lives of individuals. Once a person experiences Spirit baptism, other spiritual gifts and the power to live a renewed life will follow.

J. Rodman Williams, the father of modern renewal theology from a reformed theological background, reflected on the relationship between Pentecostalism and reformed theology:

> A profile of the charismatic movement within the historic churches would include at least the following elements: (1) the recovery of a liveliness and freshness in Christian faith; (2) a striking renewal of the community of believers as a fellowship (*koinonia*) of the Holy Spirit; (3) the manifestation of a wide range of "spiritual gifts," with parallels drawn from 1 Corinthians 12–14; (4) the experience of "baptism in the Holy Spirit," often accompanied by "tongues," as a radical spiritual renewal; (5) the reemergence of a spiritual unity that essentially transcends denominational barriers; (6) the rediscovery

---

74. This theory was dominant in the Apostolic Faith movement.

75. Williams, "Baptism in the Holy Spirit," 44.

of a dynamic for bearing comprehensive witness to the Good
News of Jesus Christ; and (7) the revitalization of the eschatological perspective.[76]

Williams stated that the Pentecostal elements such as vitality,
fellowship, spiritual gifts, baptism in the Holy Spirit, spiritual unity,
dynamic evangelism, and end time revivals became key issues that
spread to the Global South. In due course these Pentecostal theological issues and manifestations became more common. One of the
greatest factors leading to tremendous church growth in the Global
South is the manifestation of divine healing and speaking in tongues
within Pentecostal and Charismatic congregations. Even though holiness tradition declared divine healing as one aspect of the fourfold
gospel in the nineteenth century, it was hardly ever practiced until
the Pentecostal revivals of the early twentieth century.[77] As healing
power was manifested, other gifts of the Spirit also began to permeate
Pentecostal and charismatic worship, including prophecies, dreams,
trances, and speaking and interpretation of tongues.[78]

The ministry of a Trinitarian God was now being seen more fully
as the work of the Holy Spirit became widespread. For a long time, in
traditions such as Orthodox, Catholic, and Reformed, the focus was
on the Father and the Son, with the work of the Holy Spirit limited to
liturgical sacraments alone and not part of everyday believers' prayer
and worship. Now, modern people were learning that the Trinitarian
God of creation could, through the Holy Spirit, lead people to become
a new creation. As Jesus performed miracles, signs, and wonders, any
person now willing to receive the Holy Spirit's gifts can now do the
same. Droogers states "because of the totality of this experience, it is
primarily expressed through metonymy, with the partial experience
of the single subject standing for the immeasurable totality of God's
omnipresence. In reflecting on this experience, and testifying to it,
the believer also appeals to metaphor, if only because it is difficult to
directly express the totally different experience of God's presence."[79]

The Trinitarian view of the Holy Spirit encompasses the evangelical and Pentecostal theological spectrum. This widened their views

---

76. Williams, "The Charismatic Movement and Reformed Theology," lines 8–16.

77. Warrington, *Pentecostal Theology*, 265–66.

78. Droogers, "The Normalization of Religious Experience," 33.

79. Ibid., 46.

and worship service and Christian life became more dynamic than ever before. Outward, supernatural signs of the Holy Spirit—healing, miracles, tongues, and prophecies—are attractive to new converts, which helps explain much of the growth of Pentecostal and charismatic churches. Droogers states,

> Healing, prophecy, dreams, and visions, expressions of the physical experience of wholeness, are actor-centered bodily experiences. As individuals, Pentecostals are confident actors, not afraid to occupy their own position within their society. . . . Thus, they create their own version of the dialectical relation between the actor and his society or culture. The dynamism of this relation, ideally nourished by the Spirit's presence, demands an emphasis on praxis in the social science appraisal of Pentecostalism.[80]

The classical Pentecostal revival was followed by speaking in tongue in the early twentieth century. However the miracles and signs and wonders were manifested more in the time of the charismatic movements. The experience of the Spirit brings the supernatural into the everyday life of the believer. Experiencing miracles, healings, and baptism in the Holy Spirit opened Pentecostals to a new life far beyond their formal and traditional ways. In addition to the experiential manifestation of the Holy Ghost, Pentecostals believed the outpouring of the Holy Spirit was a sign that Jesus will return soon. Pentecostals believed the baptism of the Holy Spirit opened the way to become sanctified. Even though they lived in the world, they could attain the sacred life. Droogers states, "The transcendental and the real intermingle, breaking down the theological and cultural barriers between the sacred and the profane. This intermingling of the transcendental and the quotidian in Pentecostalism has the immediate effect of giving plausibility to the hostile world in which the poor live."[81]

Those who had crossed over from the traditional Christian ways to the dynamic and experiential Pentecostal traditions were attuned to the outpouring of the Holy Spirit and experienced a transformation in individual life. This would often happen not in the Global North, in the Global South, but mostly among the masses and the poor. Why do Pentecostal and charismatic movements gain more adherents in

80. Ibid., 46.
81. Cesar, "From Babel to Pentecost," 27.

the Global South than in the Global North? Among the reasons are preexisting beliefs in the supernatural and in the afterlife. The practice of witchcraft and consultation of spiritual mediums historically have provided a window to the supernatural, which can also create openness to Pentecostal and charismatic manifestations. In addition, Droogers points out, Pentecostalism is a better fit with the non-Western sense of wholeness:

> Pentecostal acceptance of religious experiences to restore an individual's sense of wholeness represents a critique of Western culture. . . They tend to be particularly uncomfortable with the attitude of favoring one of a pair of opposites above the other; for example, reason above emotion, the profane above the secular, the mind above the body, and society above the individual. It is this Western tendency to emphasize one of these poles above the other that is responsible for the fragmentation or pluralization of experience. For example, the sacred may be experienced in church (a defined space), and on Sunday morning (a defined time), but not in the restaurant, bedroom, or university. In North America, the secularization of healing is only stopped during revivals. Dreams and visions are assigned to the field of psychotherapy. Modern medicine isolates body from mind, the individual from her social context, and the patient's religious convictions from medical treatment. Morality and ethics are contextualized, theology and preaching rationalized, and clergy and laity divided.[82]

The decline of Christianity in the Global North is not a matter of simple quantitative demise but a matter of decline of authentic beliefs such as the afterlife, biblical principles, the supernatural, and signs and wonders. Intellectual and liberal thinkers criticized the authentic beliefs in the bible and the supernatural as a byproduct of the age of myth propagated by August Comte and other secularists. However, the work of the Holy Spirit was clearly seen in the early church and early twentieth century to today. Pentecostal revivals ignited the fire among the low class, poor, uneducated, and indigenous and independent people in the Global South. Pentecostal and Charismatic movements take on the local flavor of the communities where they are located. North American Pentecostal and charismatic phenomena

---

82. Droogers, "The Normalization of Religious Experience," 34.

have become localized in South Africa and elsewhere.[83] Apart from classical Pentecostals, charismatic churches have taken root: "new church charismatics . . . neo-Pentecostal churches, or new independent churches" since the 1960s.[84]

Belief in the supernatural such as glossolalia, trance, dreams and visions, divine healing, signs and wonders, and prophecy became very common as the Global South exponentially grew. At this point it is clearer why those supernatural manifestations were easily accepted in the Global South. Many scholars agree that primal cultures, folk religious practices and beliefs, and an indigenous worldview on the supernatural provided the platform for those in the Global South to easily accept the Pentecostal message and phenomena. When the Global South experienced several stages of indigenization, contextualization, and eventually inculturation, the people were able to adjust themselves to receive the outpouring of the Holy Spirit from an indigenous standpoint and worldview.

> The functional continuity between Pentecostalism and its more traditional, or popular, predecessors also seems to point in the direction of a common human basis, beyond specific times and places. It may well be that the Pentecostal gifts ought to be seen as a specific use and interpretation of a global human body language, doubly adapted to Pentecostal theology and the local cultural context in which it is sometimes helped, as in the African, Brazilian and Korean contexts, by a tradition of similar experiences, albeit critically used and interpreted. The Pentecostal repertoire has coloured human potentialities through the role attributed to the Holy Spirit, thus giving them a unique and exclusive flavor.[85]

Latin American Pentecostal and Charismatic phenomena have taken on a local flavor that reflects spiritual views and practices that have long been in place in the culture.[86] We have often observed that the local flavor of the Pentecostal phenomena developed into global phenomena. The early Pentecostal revival in Azusa Street, India, Chile, South Korea and others were individually unique, but when the Pentecostal revival became common in one locality or country

83. Hexham and Poewe, "Charismatic Churches in South Africa," 50.

84. Ibid., 58–59.

85. Droogers, "Globalisation and Pentecostal Success," 55–56.

86. Martin, "Evangelical and Charismatic Christianity in Latin America," 73.

the local flavor has the ability to influence the global village through migration, media, mission networking, and scholarship report. For example, Martin illustrates, "There are many elements of affinity between Pentecostalism and traditions already existing in Latin America. Pentecostalism expels evil spirits, engages in miraculous healing, offers ecstatic release, insists on ascetic discipline, and arouses millenarian expectation. Brazil, in particular, has harbored millenarian movements and Afro-Brazilian movements for spiritual health and healing."[87]

Although Pentecostalism takes on local flavor, each community also has a sense of its place in the worldwide movement. The classical Pentecostal movements as a local flavor in the America eventually became a global phenomenon because the early Pentecostal movements were able to attract several global elements such as race, traditions, systems, class, languages, and culture. Likewise, the Pentecostal manifestations such as speaking in tongue, interpretation, and healing became very common in Latin America, sub-Saharan Africa, and some Asian countries, contributing to the local flavor of each nation. For instance, prayer for the sick in Africa and Latin America can be easily adapted anywhere among the Pentecostals in the Global North. The prayer movements from South Korea and South Africa became well known to the whole world. As Corten and Marshall-Fratani state:

> It is with this shift that we see the enormous growth of transnational networks, the privileging of transnational connections and experiences in the operation and symbolism of local organizations, and the embracing by converts of the representation of a transnational Pentecostal community. It is by a closer examination of the implications of this shift for doctrine, practice and organization that we may begin to sketch out the ways in which Pentecostalism is articulated within, and responds to, the context of globalised "late modernity."[88]

The centrality of the Holy Spirit remains a common theme throughout all expressions of Pentecostalism. There are various manifestations of the Holy Spirit in styles, cultures, and countries yet the outcome is the same. We see genuine conversion, life-changing expe-

---

87. Ibid., 77–78.
88. Corten and Marshall-Fratani, *Between Babel and Pentecost*, 6.

rience, Spirit-filled worship, yearning for sanctification, and expecting the imminent return of Jesus.

REDISCOVERING THE GLOBAL SOUTH CHRISTIANITY

Christianity was considered the major player of world religion by the Western world. Simply put the non-Western world was considered recipients of the Christian gospel and her culture from the West. But as soon as churches in the West no longer supported their missionaries Westerners left the mission field, leaving behind their bases after the Second World War. When post-colonial missions began, without Westerners, the locals, natives, and indigenous peoples were able to see explosive church growth. When the whole world saw this fast growth in the Global South, their eyes and conception began to turn to the indigenous in the Global South. The culture, religiosity, and locality of the people, language, and history began to be respected by observers and students of revival.

Indigenous Christianity

The gospel of Jesus Christ is most readily understood and accepted when it is accessible to indigenous culture. However, the embodiment of the gospel, without a doubt, is susceptible to pagan and non-Christian culture where the gospel had never been preached. The gospel message is communicated through the messenger and hearers' individual cultural settings. This is what Leslie Newbigin claims, "the gospel does not come as a disembodied message, but as the message of a community which claims to live by it and which invites others to adhere to it, the community's life must be so ordered that it 'makes sense' to those who are so invited."[89] Paul Davies calls attention to the messenger and the hearer of the Gospel and states, "the [gospel] message must be incarnated. This means that the messenger must live out the message and identity with the hearers. This raises the question between identity and identification, which is a problem that always faces the church in mission."[90]

The preaching of the gospel as perceptibly mandatory must be in tuned with the indigenous context since the messenger and the

89. Leslie Newbigin, *The Gospel in a Pluralistic Society*, 141–42.
90. Davies, *Identity and Identification*, 1.

indigenous natives may have different perspectives from each other. John Nevius designates this point, and says, "While the circumstances of the missionary furnish the strongest motives to induce him to multiply native agents as fast as possible, the circumstances of the natives naturally and very strongly lead to the same result."[91] In this context, rendition of the gospel into local culture necessitates indigenous understanding. Sanneh calls it "indigenous discovery" of the gospel rather than "Christian discovery of the indigenous societies." Through language and culture, the gospel can permeate the local way of life. Sanneh says, "Bible translation has thus helped to bring about a historic shift in Christianity's theological center of gravity by pioneering a strategic alliance with local conceptions of religion."[92] As Europeans and Americans indigenized the gospel in the past, global expansion of the faith followed. Now, the gospel as indigenized by Global South cultures is impacting the Global North.[93]

What are the characteristics of an indigenous church? In the early days of Western modern missions, the policy of Henry Venn,[94] Rufus Anderson,[95] and William Taylor[96] was to encourage planting indigenous churches with the *three-self* principle: self-governing, self-supporting, and self-propagating. It took several decades until this was realized. One of best examples of the three-self principle has been accomplished in Korea, where missionary John Nevius encouraged Korean leaders to follow this model, with great success. This is the case with underground churches in China, and with indigenous churches in Africa, Latin America, India, Indonesia, and elsewhere.

Among the Pentecostal and charismatic churches that became indigenous, whether begun by foreign missionaries or by locals, are those started by Willis Hoover in Valparaiso, Chile; Gunnar Vingren

91. Nevius, *Method of Mission Work, 1886/1895*, 3.

92. Sanneh, *Whose Religion Is Christianity?*, 11.

93. Ibid.,10–11.

94. Henry Venn, an Anglican priest, evangelical leader, and chief secretary of the church missionary society, is acknowledged as the father of the indigenous church principle: self-supporting, self-governing, and self-propagating.

95. Rufus Anderson was senior secretary of the American Board of Commissions for Foreign Missions. He believed that a strategy of "scriptural self-propagating" would help the gospel flourish under native ministry.

96. William Taylor was a Methodist bishop for Africa and founder of Taylor University in Upland, Indiana.

and Daniel Berg in Brazil; Pandita Ramabai in South India; and Kil Sunjoo in Pyongyang, Korea. There was fruitfulness in the missionary works in Latin America. The common phenomena of the early Pentecostal revivals were ignited and disseminated by indigenous churches and leaders. In this manner Roland Allen agreed that indigenous church leaders became effective instruments in receiving more outpouring of the Holy Spirit. In the early era of Pentecostal mission, native churches were interrelated with the United States directly or indirectly.[97] As Pentecostalism reached each particular context, it became localized or contextualized.[98]

Most Brazilian Pentecostal churches fall into one of two categories: independent or autochthonous churches, and mission- or missionary-originated churches that later became local and totally independent of financial or organizational support from foreign countries.[99] The International Church of the Foursquare Gospel is the most notable exception because even though the denomination is of American origin, Brazilian Foursquare churches manage themselves. The same case extists in Chile, where Pentecostalism developed concurrently with that of America, but did not originate from it. The Brazilian case is similar, though not identical.[100] Brazilian native Pentecostalism developed largely independently of world Pentecostalism, a "national Protestantism" non-dependent on foreign finances and organization.[101] The Brazilian churches flourished under native leadership

97. Petersen, "The Formation of Popular, National, Autonomous Pentecostal Churches in Central America." 29. Peterson states, "the allure of Pentecostalism for modern Latin Americans no longer can be satisfactorily explained within the older traditional theories that espoused that Pentecostalism was 'foreign' or 'a penetration of something that came from outside.'" Cf. Dempster et al., *Called and Empowered.*

98. McGee, *Miracles, Missions, and American Pentecostalism*, 163–70.

99. Read, *New Patterns of Church Growth in Brazil*, 162–64.

100. D'Epinay, *Heaven of the Masses*, 13. In 1910, Chilean Pentecostalism was born within local Methodism led by Willis Collins Hoover, an American Methodist medical missionary at the Methodist Episcopal Church of Chile. It eventually broke away from the Chilean Methodist Church. This schism led to Hoover start the Indigenous Methodist Pentecostal Church in Chile based on the three self principles without foreign support or intervention. d'Epinay says, "While there is no possible doubt that the birth of Chilean Pentecostalism is due to his [founder Willis Collins Hoover] influence, once the initial impulse had been given, the movement would doubtless survived had he disappeared."

101. Cook, *New Face of the Church in Latin America*, 69.

and have preserved an autochthonous character up to the present.[102] Although there were Pentecostal missions from North America, and to a lesser degree from Europe,[103] these churches were already fairly institutionalized and their doctrines well defined. Many Pentecostal churches initiated by North American or European efforts have gone on to achieve autonomy and now have a more autochthonous leadership style.[104] This leadership transfer of authority and responsibility for the work is at the hands of local leaders.[105]

Some indigenous, independent churches result from the work of foreign missionaries who planted new churches, brought them to self-support, and then turned them over to native pastors.[106] For instance, participation in Brazil by missionaries from North American Assemblies of God churches did not occur until 1934, twenty-three years after the founding, of the Assemblies of God (Assembléias de Deus) in Brazil.[107] Indigenous churches also tend to be rooted among the common people, while the historical Protestant churches had been confined to the middle class.[108]

In Korea, the nature of the church is indigenous, yet it fits comfortably within the evangelical and Pentecostal traditions. This is also the case in most of Latin America, China, some parts of India and Indonesia, most independent churches in Africa, and in the Philippines.[109] The Christian gospel is presented by indigenous

102. Ibid., 69.

103. Read, *New Patterns of Church Growth in Brazil*, 20–44, 117–43. They include the Swedish American Pentecostals Daniel Berg and Gunner Vingren, and Christian Congregation founder Luigi Francescon, an Italian American.

104. Cook, *New Face of the Church in Latin America*, 69.

105. Weld and MacGavran, *Principles of Church Growth*, 14–22.

106. Read, *New Patterns of Church Growth in Brazil*, 159.

107. Wilson, "Passion and Power." 91. According to statistics compiled by Everett A. Wilson, in 1988, the "Assemblies of God, Springfield, Missouri, the largest North American Pentecostal mission in three of the four countries emphasized in his study, supported only four couples in El Salvador, five in Guatemala, ten in Chile, and eleven in Brazil." See Read, *New Patterns of Church Growth in Brazil*, 121–22.

108. Núñez and Taylor, *Crisis in Latin America: An Evangelical Perspective*, 157. In Latin America Pentecostals attempt to understand the great needs of local "leadership, education," and realizing the problem of "division and social alienation," yet still display great hope for Christianity in the respective countries.

109. Petersen, "The Formation," 23. In El Salvador, the Assemblies of God church has been established through indigenous efforts with little external assistance or missionary control by the United States.

churches in a way that makes sense within the worldview of those who have pre-Christian beliefs. Jeyaraj indicates that believers' "dual identity as Christians and Africans instills in them a positive pride, self-respect and self-confidence."[110] Worship and prayer take forms that fit within the context of local customs in Latin America, Asia, and Africa.[111] Korea "is exposed to religious and cultural radiation from the U.S.,"[112] but nevertheless modifies the influences of American conservative evangelicalism, contextualizing and indigenizing them.[113]

A difference between theoretical indigenization[114] and true contextualization is seen perhaps in the traditional attitude of evangelical missions toward native Indian cultures in Latin America and the new missionary approach to these communities.[115] Michael Frost and Allan Hirsh point out that "To contextualize is to understand the language, longings, lifestyle patterns, and worldview of the host community and to adjust our practices accordingly without compromising the gospel."[116] When the gospel message is clothed in vernacular culture, language and worldview, the masses are attracted. In the Brazilian case, according to John Medcraft,

> The music is no Anglo-Saxon durge. 'The Pentecostal hymns are sung in the unadulterated rhythm of the samba and other folk dances.' Autochthonous musical expression with 'genuine rumba, cha-cha and samba compositions, accomplished by indigenous accompaniments' fill the air. The hymns often use the imagery and key words of popular songs, and apply them all

---

110. Jeyaraj, "The Re-Emergence of Global Christianity, 1910–2010," 54.

111. Dempster et al., *Called and Empowered*, 29–30.

112. Martin, *Tongues of Fire*, 135.

113. Anderson, "The Contribution of David Yonggi Cho," 86. Anderson observes, "The extent of Pentecostalism and Charismatic forms of Christianity in the religious diversity of East Asia is seldom recognized. Indeed, many forms of Pentecostalism in much of the world are fundamentally different from these movements in the western world, and are no importation of American Christianity."

114. Núñez and Taylor, *Crisis in Latin America*, 313. The methods of John L. Nevius, missionary to China, became a model for indigenization. Pioneer missionary thinkers like Henry Venn and Rufus Anderson popularized the concept of indigenous churches that would be self-governing, self-supporting, and self-propagating, but not self-theologizing.

115. Ibid., 315.

116. Frost and Hirsh, *The Shaping of Things to Come*, 85.

to one true friend. The end result is genuine Brazilian enjoyed by all."[117]

Most scholars on Latin American Protestantism agree that the growth of Protestant churches is related to socioeconomic, popular religious, and demographic elements and changes that encouraged people to emigrate from the rural to urban areas to experience the rapid transition from the Catholic monopoly to a religiously diverse context. This growth can also be attributed to urbanization, industrialization, and rationalism. In many countries in Latin America urban dwellers brought their popular traditional religious activities and beliefs into the new urban settlements, which played a large role in giving contextualization to the traditional beliefs with a new Protestant and Pentecostal movement.[118]

As we look at the political, social, religious, and economic crisis in Latin America, they can be viewed as the social state of anomie within the periphery of the demographic situation. Latin American Pentecostalism's prevailing predisposition, as observed by Lalive d'Epinay, "would replicate the social structure of the hacienda, with the pastor taking up the role of the *patrón* and the religious lay workers acting as his lieutenants. [Due to the conventional popular religious and egalitarian system of the hacienda Pentecostalism in Latin America, particularly in Chile, a system was developed and contextualized,] on a dualist paradigm, emphasizing the primacy of spiritual over material values."[119] Through these series of events Protestant religious groups eventually played a role in modifying the "hacienda" model. d'Epinay discerned the process of the acculturation of Protestantism and explained the spread of the faith in terms of how it fit with the values of popular religion and culture.[120]

117. Medcraft, "The Roots and Fruits of Brazilian Pentecostalism," 85.

118. Willems, *Followers of the New Faith*. 73, 88.

119. Steigenga and Coleman, *Protestant Political Orientations and the Structure of Political Opportunity*, 468.

120. Denominations, sects and religious groups in Latin America were deeply indebted to d'Epinay's typology, who tried to classify the broad spectrum of Protestantism. In general, Latin America had always been in the periphery of Catholic monopoly until dozens of Protestant religious groups began to emerge. Hence Catholicism and Protestantism can be referred to as a church, but denominations and religious groups may be referred to as sects. Many Protestant and evangelical churches and denominations are considered as part of the Protestant sectarian

In the late 1940s and 50s the Presbyterian church in Latin America researched and studied each mission agency and denominational mission society in order to identify what type of churches were aligned within each culture and context. One particular denomination is the Presbyterian Church in Latin America that is closely related with the church system of the US and the local context. But they found a serious concern on the synthesis of the popular forms of Protestantism that deeply seeped into the political culture, church system and Christian behavior.[121] At one point the Protestant Churches in Brazil functioned in two roles, from being a liberating force for the underprivileged to an oppressive force born from its many brushes with the culture.[122] On the other hand, Bastian believes that the expansion of Pentecostalism corresponds neither to a reform of popular Catholicism nor to an acculturation of Protestantism to the values and practices of popular Catholic culture.[123] According to Bastian, Pentecostalism is a substitute for Catholicism and is filling a vacuum: "Surely this radical Protestantism, without dogmatic demands, entirely centered on inspiration, wholly subject to the divine presence is ultimately closer to the priestless Catholicism of a section of the masses?"[124] For instance in Brazil, in the nineteenth century, one Roman Catholic priest had to pastor over 100,000 parish adherents. Today the global average for priests is 1,344 parish members, yet in Europe the average falls to 1,067. Statistics in Brazil in late twentieth century, however, indicate one priest is in charge of 7,692 parish members. As stated before, this is due to the fact that Latin Americans are so religious with the majority practicing folk Catholicism.[125]

---

movement.

121. Bastian, "Protestantism in Latin America," 341.

122. Alves, *Protestantism and Repression*, 107–114.

123. Bastian, "Protestantism in Latin America," 341. "During the 1970s, when the theme of popular religion was fashionable, several scholars stressed the autonomy of popular Catholic religious practices vis-à-vis hierarchical controls. They remarked on juxtaposition of practices, which are articulated but not integrated."

124. Ibid., 342. In the Latin American context there had always been an imbalance in the number of priests who were able to take care of the parishes. There are many parishes that do not have sufficient number of priests, which are referred to as priestless Catholic churches.

125. Medcraft, "The Roots and Fruits of Brazilian Pentecostalim," 78.

The relationship between the culture and the gospel becomes a critical issue in giving different hypotheses such as indigenization, contextualization, adaptation, enculturation, and eventually inculturation. The gospel message is the core of salvation for every human being. However, the way the gospel penetrates into lives has to deal with that society's cultural issues. In other words, what Catholic missiologists have called accommodation to culture. However, the Protestants took up the idea of adaptation to the existing cultures. Reformed traditions have opted for the possession of culture. Pentecostal and charismatic movements observed indigenous religiosity integrated in their contextual elements. And contemporary evangelicals opt for the transformation of culture. Their indigenization produced exponential church growth because the masses such as the underprivileged, poor, and urban dweller are attracted by seeing the Pentecostal manifestation from the eyes of the common cultural setting.[126] Pentecostalism in an indigenous setting demonstrates how each coherent cultural issue is intertwined in producing a contextualized spiritual byproduct.[127]

A great number of Pentecostals in Latin America are still practicing Shamanistic rites that were observed by many scholars to indicate that their religious activity became a veritable syncretism. In 1946, the Mennonite Board of Mission and Charities created a firsthand report of the historical, economic, and socio-political issues and cultural integration of the Toba Indians of the Argentine Chaco." Above all, the outstanding survey indicates that remnants of Shamanistic rites remain among the Toba Christians.[128] Chesnut has found that Brazilian Pentecostalism is acculturated for the popular classes, and particularly, for women.[129] Another approach contextualized for the urban poor has been tried by Berryman and Burdick.[130] For centuries, Catholicism in Latin America was tied to colonialism; today it is largely a neo-Christendom absorbed by modernity. But Roman

126. Núñez, "Doing Theology in Latin America," 114.

127. Bastian, "Protestantism in Latin America," 342.

128. Mennonite Board of Missions and Charities, 1954. Cf. Reyburn, *The Toba Indians of the Argentine Chaco.*

129. Chesnut, *Born Again in Brazil,* 6. "Pentecostalism's message of healing power reverberates among the popular classes, particularly women, whose already precarious household economies are further deliberated by alcoholism, unemployment, and domestic strife."

130. Burdick, *Looking for God in Brazil,* 1–15.

Catholic Christianity of a mestizo, indigenous, and black nature has grown from other social and cultural worlds.[131] Only when there is a truly critical symbiosis, and the Christian experience is really integrated into the local culture, can we speak of incarnation.[132]

It is worth looking at how the Protestant, evangelical, and Pentecostal churches had been producing various outcomes of indigenization and contextualization in the case of Latin America." The non-Protestant model that implanted their style of worship, theology, and church hierarchy originated from Mormon and Jehovah's witness missionary works. However, La Luz del Mundo in Latin America, particularly in Mexico, demonstrates a glimpse of syncretistic indigenous religiosity in the local leadership with a popularist approach and folk religious system.[133] When La Luz del Mundo disseminated into Mexico and into neighboring countries, similar movements were found in parts of South America such as thaumaturges, or miracle-workers, who embedded completely alien practices among folk religious beliefs where shrines provide a place for rituals, and millenarianism, which absorbed popular culture and myths during the colonial conquest, particularly in Brazil. The millenarian movement has been used at times as a political tool, such as when the backlanders utilized it to oppose the modernization of the church and state.[134] Having found syncretic popular and indigenous religious movements like Brazilian millenarianism, Martin discovered strong similarities between Pentecostals and Catholics and how they behave in society.[135]

131. Vatican II realized existing cultures from indigenous and local people could become mutual partners of God to missionaries who came from Christianized areas. Shorter, *Toward a Theology of Inculturation*, 11.

132. Ibid., 12–13. The term acculturation was favored by Pope Paul VI.

133. La Luz del Mundo ("The Light of the World") was founded in Guadalajara, Mexico by Eusebio Joaquín Gonzalez in 1964. Now his son, Samuel Joaquín Flores, succeeds in his place. This ministry has spread throughout South America.

134. Bastian, *Protestantism in Latin America*, 339. Millenarian movements generally are found in Latin America, particularly Brazil. Its impact has been felt among Catholic members. The founder Antonio Conselheiro was believed to be the second coming of Christ who wanted to build a holy city in the late 1800s. Followers saw millenarianism to not only enhance religious beliefs and practices but also help gain political ground. Today the sertão of Northeastern Brazil attracts the most followers but other countries, particularly Mexico, holds many followers as well.

135. Martin, *Tongues of Fire*, 70. Martin states that the political leadership of base communities is more left-leaning than the Pentecostal leaders. He states that Pentecostal and community leaders lean to the right and left correspondingly yet followers stay in the middle.

The various processes of indigenization and contextualization in South America can be observed in Asia and sub-Saharan Africa as well. Africans can rediscover the values, worldview, culture, notion, and indigenous religion forced aside during colonial times. The statement of Kwame Kkrumah, Ghana's first president, that, ""In the last century, the Europeans discovered Africa. In the next century, the Africans will rediscover Africa," serves as a reminder for the rediscovery of African values."[136] Scholars from around the world had significantly rediscovered African culture and worldview in accordance with the Vatican's declaration of giving heed to the ideas of indigenization along with inculturation. It was certain that preexisting African worldviews and religious behaviors and practices proactively created a new version of indigenous African Christianity that flourished in a new growth of Christian churches in the African setting after colonial powers ended. Post-colonial Christianity brought enormous amounts of revivals with African indigenous religiosity.

Evangelical and Pentecostal growth have drawn a following from all social classes in tune with pre-existing popular religious beliefs and practices, ancient worldviews, and supernatural beliefs and practices. Exponential growth of Christian churches in the Global South has come primarily from indigenous leaders reaching out to populations of non-Westerners. In 1948, when communist China became closed to the outside world, 25 percent of leaders were indigenous Chinese Christians. After the expulsion of all Western missionaries, virtually all leadership positions were held by indigenous leaders.[137] Indigenization and contextualization not only produce the rapid growth of Christianity in the Global South but also produce indigenous theology, contextualized systems, worship styles, and leadership that has been made available to implement in other parts of the world.

Inculturation

To bring the gospel to any community, it is necessary to understand the context of the people, including culture, language, and history. When the gospel first came to countries in the Roman Empire, to Europe, and to North America, it was interpreted for Christian living in each

136. Okolo, "The African Experience of Christian Values: Dimensions of the Problematic." No pages.

137. Robert, "The Great Commission," 13.

cultural environment. Now, non-Western nations must do the same. In addition to the terms *contextualization* and *indigenization* is the term *inculturation*, used most frequently by the Vatican to describe the adaptation of the gospel to non-Christian settings.

Inculturation means the reclamation of cultural sensitivity in the spread of the Christian gospel, and it has had increasing influence as part of the Vatican's direction.[138] The term was used in Manila at the Asian bishops' conference in 1971, "Soon after the holding of the Second Vatican Council in the mid-sixties, terms like "radical adaptation" to the culture, indigenisation" and "localization" became commonplace within [the] theological circles. The meetings of the Asian bishops in Manila in 1971 during Paul VI's visit gave birth to the word "inculturation.""[139]

Six years later, in 1977, the Pan African Congress of Majority World Theologians which was held in Accra coined the term inculturation.[140] Two years later, a 1979 papal letter by Pope John Paul II to the Pontifical Commission first officially used the term inculturation.[141] Phan defines inculturation as "a double process comprising insertion of the gospel into a particular culture, and introduction of the culture into the gospel."[142] It is likely recognized by Tano as obsolescent.[143] The terms *accommodation* and *adaptation* were commonly used before Vatican II,[144] and Vatican II documents often mentioned the "adaptation" of liturgy to local culture and circumstance.[145] Inculturation, in-

---

138. Shorter, *Toward a Theology of Inculturation*, 4, 10–13; Irarrazaval, *Inculturation*, 4–5, 34–35.

139. He states, "The Synod of 1974 and Evangelii Nuntiandi were convinced that 'evangelization loses much of its force and effectiveness if it does not take into consideration the actual people to whom it is addressed, if it does not use their language, their signs and symbols, if it does not answer the questions they ask, and if it does not have an impact on their concrete life." Zialcita, "Culture and Inculturation," 14.

140. Healey and Sybertz, *Towards An African Narrative Theology*, 26.

141. Inculturation is the process of cultural discourse bringing inventive and energetic correlation between the gospel message and each individual culture.

142. Phan, *In Our Own Tongues*, 6.

143. Tano, *Theological Issues in the Philippine Context*, 8. Filipino theologian Rodrigo Tano describes four types of indigenization: (1) "nature of culture viewed anthropologically and theologically," (2) "the relationship between the Gospel and culture," (3) "the mechanics of indigenization," and (4) "the danger of syncretism."

144. Shorter, *Toward a Theology of Inculturation*, 10–11.

145. Mercado, *Elements of Filipino Theology*, 5. The Asian bishops also suggested

digenization, and contextualization can be considered as evangelistic/apologetic notions.[146]

The World Council of Churches Theological Education Fund defines the term *contextualization* as follows:

> Contextualization means all that is implied in the familiar term "indigenization" and yet seeks to press beyond. Contextualization has to do with how we assess the peculiarity of third [Majority World] world context. Indigenization tends to be used in the sense of responding to the Gospel in terms of a traditional culture. Contextualization, while not ignoring this, takes into account the process of secularity, technology, and the struggle for human justice, which characterize the historical moment of nations in the Third World [Majority World].[147]

Historically, Catholicism and Protestant churches attempted one uniform gospel translation and interpretation based on Western culture. Some cultures resisted the gospel while others accepted it; nations Christianized long ago with Catholicism tended to accept Pentecostalism quickly. Latin American, Iberian, and Filipino cultures are already cultivating the new type of Pentecostal development and growth. Matviuk points to "the importance of the aspects of the Latin American culture that permeate Latin American Pentecostalism."[148] Martin indicates that Latinos tend to adopt "Anglo" values into Pentecostalism. He perceives that the flourishing movement of Pentecostalism in Latin America is greatly indebted to the European Protestant values such as Puritanism, Methodism, and early American Pentecostalism. He sees that Anglo Protestant evan-

---

indigenization.

146. Costa, *One Faith, Many Cultures*, xii. Costa states, "Inculturation and indigenization . . . are focused on the translation or interpretation of a received text for a given culture. . . . Contextualization sees this translation/interpretation as a dialectical process in which text and context are interdependent."

147. Ibid., xii. See also Fleming, *Contextualization of Theology*, 52; and Núñez and Taylor, *Crisis in Latin America*, 314. After a long debate on indigenization in the late nineteenth and twentieth century, mainline Protestant church missiologists suggested a new hypothesis, contextualization. In 1972, the World Council of Churches proposed the idea of contextualization in order to reform theological education.

Dussel, *The Church in Latin America*, 315.

148. Matviuk, "Pentecostal Leadership Development and Church Growth in Latin America," 162.

gelical influence permeated into the periphery of the Latin American Pentecostal expansion. Martin states the North American influence of Pentecostalism in Latin American churches is derived from the contribution of the Methodist holiness revival origin. Over time, Latin Americans would attain the cultural groundwork needed for attaining modernity.[149] This could be the "Holiness-Methodist-Puritanical Anglo-American value" contributing to the growth of Pentecostal/charismatic movements in Latin America, the Philippines, and other Catholic nations.

There have always been different cultures, so homogeneous Christian culture is difficult to accomplish. In order to take the gospel to different cultures, the groundwork must be laid not on Western cultural settings of Christianity, but on the transcendent Christ present in every human community. Having the view that no culture is superior to another, the gospel message has to be instituted at the outset of any missionary enterprise in appreciation of local cultural settings.[150] Unfortunately, for the past several centuries, particularly to Latino Roman Catholic countries, Protestantism has been considered a religious heterodoxy to Catholic predominance. The resulting Pentecostal phenomenon is seen as a classic "church of the disinherited."[151] Scholars on Latin American Christianity are provoked to conduct more comparative studies on the broad concept of Christianity not only in its Protestant forms, but its Catholic ones as well. The American Presbyterian mission in Brazil attempted to appreciate the cultural elements of the locals to be channels of gospel acceptance. They attempted to adapt local culture, language, and system so as to catechize the locals in their cultural context.[152]

Some may ask why Christianity in the Global South looks different from the Global North. That question brings us to the cultural issue of indigenization, contextualization, and inculturation because for many centuries the Western culture had been the means for the gospel message to the non-West. The culture of the West is inseparable from the message of the Gospel. In the past, up to World War II, Western

---

149. Martin, *Tongues of Fire*, 9–46. Cf. Chesnut, *Born Again in Brazil*, 4–5; Berryman, *Religion in the Megacity*, 3.

150. Irarrazaval, *Inculturation*, 29.

151. Norman, *Christianity in the Southern Hemisphere*, 67–68.

152. Irarrazaval, *Inculturation*, 52.

countries colonized non-Western countries through missionary work influencing them culturally. The Christian Gospel was clothed with the face of Western culture so that non-Westerners, having no other alternatives at the time, adapted Western culture with the Christian Gospel. When colonialism came to a halt, the first era thereafter unveiled the value of norms, worldview, and religiosity of indigenous people in the Global South. The Gospel message became intertwined with the local culture free from Western influence. The relationship between culture and the Christian Gospel must be re-visited or re-packed. Indigenous worldview and norms and values of the Global South can and should be recognized while coexisting with those of the West. In this respect inculturation can uphold a balance between culture and the Gospel.

Acculturation

Different cultural adaptations to the Global North's unprecedented and unseen aspects of non-Western Christian culture had been generated in the past century. The non-Western cultural elements of the Global South are intriguing scholars of the world to study the cultural issues of various Christian facets in the Global South. Many cultural elements are intertwined differently while accepting or integrating the essence of the Gospel. Several critics on Christianity in the Global South sounded an alarm as to whether they are genuine Christians as a result of seeing alien cultural elements, also known as syncretic acculturation.

The word *acculturation* is closely associated with the theological concept of inculturation. Acculturation is the adoption of a culture's traits and values by an outsider encountering that culture—an encounter between two cultures. This is perhaps the principal cause of cultural change.[153] Acculturation can sometimes lead to syncretism, where illegitimate symbiosis happens and the core values of the gospel are compromised. As indicated earlier South American Protestant, Evangelical, and Pentecostal worship service and religious life integrated with popular forms of Protestantism and participated in a syncretic religious culture where "transitions from one church to another are frequent; and members of the Assembly of God often go

---

153. Shorter, *Toward a Theology of Inculturation*, 6–7.

to the Umbanda terreiro [meeting place of folk religion practitioners] and less often the Catholic church."[154]

Trends show that Latin America is de-Catholicizing. In 1994, 400 Latin Americans were joining Pentecostal or the Protestant evangelical churches every hour. One-eighth of the region's 500 million people, i.e., 65 million, belong to Pentecostal or Protestant churches.[155] In 2010 in Latin America, there were 156 million Pentecostals and charismatics, constituting 26.3 percent of all renewalists worldwide.[156] The rapid expansion of Pentecostalism and, to a lesser extent, spiritism, has transformed the Catholic Church's attitude of how greatly they prohibited the Protestant and Pentecostal growth by sending pastoral letters to the many parishes throughout the country requesting they refrain from being involved in those circles.[157] Evangelical Protestantism, and Pentecostalism in particular, has substituted Catholicism as the principal figure of popular religion in most urban areas. The "*ciudades perdidas* (shanty towns) of Tijuana to the *favelas* (slums) of Rio de Janeiro" serve as examples. In Brazil, more than 60 percent of Pentecostals live in urban areas. And the average number of Protestants churchgoers exceeded the number of Catholic adherents.[158]

Looking at most Pentecostal denominations in Latin America most have adapted a sectarian way of worship and religion since the 1960s. d'Epinay described this kind of movement as "acculturation to corporatism." The point is that he did not classify this movement as a branch of former Protestant churches or syncretic Protestant religious groups. However, in his analysis and description surely the Protestant sectarian group had been working in the Protestant format within the "panorama of popular religions, alongside animisms, spiritisms, Afro-American religions, messianic religions, [and] popular forms of

154. Bastian, "Protestantism in Latin America," 342.

155. Haynes, *Religion in Third World Politics*, 109–115.

156. Johnson and Ross, *Atlas of Global Christianity*, 103.

157. Chesnut, *Born Again in Brazil*, 33–34. In 1939, the Catholic authority, particularly the Brazilian Plenary Council, researched and collected data about contemporary Protestant church activities through a department known as the Defense of the Faith (Defesa da Fé) against the fast growing Protestant groups, mostly Pentecostals who are disrespectfully referred to as crentes.

158. Ibid., 3. Home to three-fifths of Ibero-America's Protestants, Brazil has seen its Protestant population almost quadruple from 1960 to 1985.

Catholicism which have grown up around shrines."[159] There are many syncretic activists of evangelical and Pentecostal branches, with nearly 30 million Brazilians practicing the Afro-based religion.[160] Umbanda as a cultic movement of similar provenance offers the greatest single challenge to Pentecostalism. Typical syncretic practices are found in Umbanda, a well-known Afro-Brazilian religion that is practiced among the poor. Since the twentieth century Umbanda began to grow all over southern Brazil even in Uruguay and Argentina. It combines a supreme creator, Catholic saints, and spirits from the deceased who remain in the world, with some the elements coming from French intellectualism. Their belief can develop through a medium to gain a better life.[161] Although Pentecostal believers are no longer practicing 'saint veneration,' 'Mary adoration,' and other folk Catholic practices, those folk beliefs and practices paved the way for them to easily accept the supernatural, miraculous signs, and divine healing.[162]

Acculturation occurs over time in a dynamic way.[163] Pentecostals in Brazil have identified spiritual needs among migrants who find themselves repeatedly uprooted and transplanted due to innumerable economic and religious factors such as job opportunities, famines in rural areas, inflation, education and idolatry. The church helps to fill the sociological space created by continuous migration.[164]

We must ask whether it is relevant still to talk of forms of Pentecostalism, and whether it is not rather a matter of new syncretic religious movements providing effective resistance and offering the chance of survival to sectors of the population dependent on syncretic religiosity.[165] Other Christian churches have had to "Pentecostalize"

---

159. Bastian, "Protestantism in Latin America," 341. Nevertheless, d'Epinay addresses the role of "sectarian Protestantism in regards to the continuity and redevelopment of a popular religious culture, and asks whether these forms of Protestantism "should not be interpreted as a reform of popular Catholicism as much as a type of renewal within Protestantism itself.""

160. Dempster et al., *The Globalization of Pentecostalism*, 143.

161. Martin, *Tongues of Fire*, 68–69. Umbanda combines spiritism in folk religion and Kardecist spiritism in which more intellects stick to "a belief in the survival of the spirit after death."

162. Medcraft, "The Roots and Fruits of Brazilian Pentecostalism," 78.

163. Shorter, *Toward a Theology of Inculturation*, 7–8.

164. Read, *New Patterns of Church Growth in Brazil*, 130.

165. Bastian, "Protestantism in Latin America," 343.

to survive the fierce competition of the new religious marketplace in Brazil. Many members of the mainline Protestant churches, such as the Presbyterian, have seceded from their parent congregations. In so doing, they preserve much of their denominational heritage while integrating the Pentecostal gifts of the Spirit.

So we need to reconsider the place of Latin American history in world history in order to revalue the oppressed peoples—the Indians, the African slaves, and the peasants and workers, with women as doubly oppressed in all periods and classes.[166] The most important work on Brazilian identity is considered to be the Brazilian Indian novel *Iracema*, written by Jose de Alencar and published in 1865, depicting a love story between a native woman and a Portuguese colonist.[167] The cultural and racial issues of Brazilian society played a very critical role in the Protestant church growth. Racial issues between Portuguese, Europeans, Africans, and Indians provided a distinctive racial and ethnic identity as a "logical and effective strategy in the struggle to create a meaningful and complete national history, to establish a consciousness of national separateness and worth and to defend that new identity against powerful cultural pressures from abroad."[168]

Today people are recognizing Brazilian Indians as the original inhabitants of the country and their role in creating a new Brazilian race consisting of Indian and European blood. Having seen the various mixed races in Brazilian society, the declaration of equality of all races played a factor in the rapid growth of Pentecostal churches at the national level intermingling aboriginal religious practices. Syncretic acculturation may be observed in most parts of North and Latin America, for example in Brazil, according to Lanternari's careful research, "Among the indigenous populations of Brazil, the impact of European civilization has given rise, even in recent times, to prophetic manifestations which have affected certain aborigines more than others."[169] Lanternari provides such examples as The Tukunas of the Brazilian Amazon jungle, the Tupi-Guarani in South America, and

---

166. Bochio, "The Native Protestant in Brazil," 16.

167. Lemaire, "Re-Reading Iracema," 1.

168. Ibid., 13.

169. Lanternari, *The Religions of the Oppressed*, 141. Cf. Bochio, "The Native Protestant in Brazil," 14.

New Messianic Movements amongst Brazil Negroes.[170] In addition to racial democracy, liberty in religious activities originated from native *indios*, where African religious practices and European Catholic and Protestant beliefs can freely be exercised through Pentecostal manifestations. According to Brumanna and Martinez, "Certainly, the presence of blacks in positions of institutional authority, as well as their access to the charismatic gifts of healing and prophecy, have helped to erode the racism of at least some light-skinned *crentes*."[171]

In Latin America, for the second half of the twentieth century, scholars have noted that the unparalleled expansion of the Pentecostal movement, in reality, was indebted to the political turmoil which took place in agrarian society, particularly at the setting with "cacique."[172] Those who belonged to the "cacique," who enjoyed a position of authority in rural barrios whether they were "traditional indigenous or mestizo elites," had gained more influence in society. A long-standing collaboration of the "cacique-type-control" leadership with the Catholic Church provided a monopolistic sustainable economic and trade relationship. When Pentecostal movements arose, they broke this type of monopoly between the Catholic Church and cacique leadership.[173] When Pentecostal and other popular religious movements broke out they became a way of breaching this type of traditional relationship.

Acculturation amongst Protestants, evangelicals, and Pentecostals has manifested different methods of cultural implementation in South

170. Ibid., 141–143 (Tukunas), 143–150 (Tupi-Guarani), 153–160 (New Messianic Movements).

171. Brumana and Martinez, *Spirits from the Margins; Burdick, Looking for God in Brazil*, 173–74.

172 Dodson, "Pentecostal, Politics, and Public Space in Latin America, 32. The Pentecostal pastor in the Latin American setting is viewed as a "cacique" or "cadillo" who is the absolute master. Several case studies have shown an increasing cacique-type control by traditional indigenous or mestizo elites. The agrarian society in Brazil played an important role in terms of providing a Catholic medieval style of paternal agricultural community that was a display of the "hacienda model." The hacienda model was a system of large land holdings aimed at developing a self sufficient community based off the vast farmland. Pentecostal churches were able to penetrate the stronghold of authoritarian and traditional communities such as the hacienda model where Catholicism and politics were closely co-related to draw the masses, farmers, and low class people. A cacique was the term "for the pre-Columbian chiefs or leaders of tribes in the Bahamas, Greater Antilles, and the northern Lesser Antilles."

173. Bastian, "Protestantism in Latin America," 343.

America. There are four types of cultural church models: foreign origin that has been localized, foreign origin that is still dominant, local origin that grows faster to the neighboring countries, and a mixed model that blends foreign and domestic elements. Therefore the author cannot judge which is better or worse since each culture holds its own distinctive value. The focus should be on the elements of the salvific gospel of Jesus as the Lord and Savior, the Holy Trinity, the cardinal pillars of the Christian doctrines, and the advent of Jesus. It is time to look at each culture outside of the Western lens without bias, prejudice, or theological judgments. However, the author sees potential dangers amongst syncretic believers who cannot discern the harmful rituals, practices, and unacceptable folk religious activities.[174]

Folk Religion

Translating the gospel into the vernacular language is not an easy task. It requires evaluating customs, perceptions, worldviews, and mindsets and choosing the ways that best represent the truth of the gospel to communities in Africa, Latin America, and Asia. These regions have rich cultural heritages that include religion and perception of other religions. Most pre-Christian cultures include religious beliefs and practices, among them animism, shamanism, totemism, or worship of ancestors. These preexisting beliefs can become associated with the Christian faith, including beliefs in heaven and hell, miracles, healing, exorcism, incarnation, and supernatural manifestation. Existing beliefs in supernatural power can easily lead people to accept supernatural manifestations of the Holy Spirit, such as healing and exorcism, and other Christian beliefs and practices including baptism ,the afterlife, and eternal life.[175]

Folk religion is an ethnically or regionally oriented belief system that has an association with a major world religion, yet has incorporated other elements into that religion. Examples include Christianized Irish Celts, Filipino spiritists who identify with Catholicism, and

---

174. Ibid., 345.

175. Petersen, "The Formation," 23–24. For example, in El Salvador, "Religiously inclined persons contextualized Pentecostalism, adapting features appropriate to their circumstances, to make their churches not only the religion's largest expression of Protestantism, but also one of its most important grass-roots social movements."

African Kimbanguists.[176] Popular religion is a form of folk religion that uses mysterious beliefs and practices, such as astrology, occult practices, or pseudo-scientific activities. Marzal has described four groups in Latin America: "syncretic Catholicism,[177] Mestizo Catholicism,[178] transplanted Catholicism,[179] and emergent popular religion."[180] For example, in Brazil, 93.5 percent of Brazilians identified themselves with the Catholic Church in 1950. As indicated earlier in the previous chapters, belonging does not mean real attendance because believing brings one's life to religious activity. A 1958 religious survey revealed that the average attendance at Catholic mass was only ten percent. Where had all the Catholics gone? The answer is that most Catholics participated in 'folk Catholicism' meaning they practiced things such as saint veneration and shrine worship.[181]

Controversy surrounds the question of whether Pentecostal and charismatic churches should prohibit or compromise folk and popular religious rituals and beliefs. Because African, Asian, and Latin American spiritual history includes animistic and shamanistic beliefs, it is easy for them to blend that historical belief with Christian teachings about supernatural power, life after death, healing, trances, visions, mediations, and blessings. Many who have recently accepted Christ in these regions follow modified and adapted versions of their longtime folk and popular religious traditions. Westerners tend to accuse them of syncretism.[182] Nonetheless, it is easy to see how folk reli-

176. Simon Kimbangu is the founder of this church in the Democratic Republic of Congo.

177. Marzal, "Daily Life in the Indies," 72. Marzal gives some examples of tribes such as Indians from the Andes and Mesoamerica, the "aliplano" from Bolivia, Indians from Maya in Mexico, Afro-Haitians, and Afro-Brazilians in central Brazil who came together and mixed their cultures after initially encountering strong resistance for a compromise.

178. The native or black religious traditions from Chile and Paraguay encountered less conflict in the assimilation of their cultures making a new culture to be called mestizo Catholicism.

179. This group consists mostly of European immigrants who do not need cultural adaptation. Germans, Italians, and Iberians are found in the already-independent Argentina, Uruguay, and Brazil.

180. Marzal, "Daily Life in the Indies," 71–73. Marzal states that most Latin Americans belong to emergent groups that they created out of Indio cultures to form a new Catholic expression.

181. Medcraft, "The Roots and Fruits of Brazilian Pentecostalism." 78.

182. Ma, "Asian (Classical) Pentecostalism," 4–5.

gion dovetails with the supernatural manifestations of Pentecostal and charismatic worship. Pentecostals have occasionally tried to espouse folk religious liturgical forms and styles in Latin America and the Philippines.[183] Kärkkäinen states, "In some parts of the area, Christian churches in general and Pentecostal/Charismatic churches in particular are growing in an amazing way while in most Asian/Pacific countries traditional religions are still in control."[184] Medcraft states, "Popular Catholicism has in a number of ways provided the stage for the attraction of Pentecostal doctrines and characteristics which the large masses of rural low-class people encounter upon their arrival in the fast-growing urban centres."[185]

Early missionaries in Africa, Asia, and Latin America intentionally squelched folk and popular religious practices and attempted education, Christian discipline, Bible study, and medical missions.[186] Still, concepts of God or gods, spirits, angels, heaven and hell, demons, and witchcraft persist and cannot be ignored. There is no difficulty for these communities to believe accounts of the Holy Spirit or healing or other spiritual manifestations.[187] Common denominators among Pentecostals and charismatics in Africa, Asia, and Latin America include healing, exorcism, prophesy, etc. In particular, the Philippines and Latin America share common historical, religious, and cultural factors from Iberian folk Catholicism.[188] According to Harper, "The

183. Matviuk, "Pentecostal Leadership Development," 170. Matviuk also points out the vitality of folk religion: "Folk religion does not mean a low quality/low standards religion; this means a religion profoundly rooted in the essential aspects of the local culture. This is one of the reasons for the Pentecostal success in Latin America."

184. Kärkkäinen, "Truth on Fire," 36.

185. Medcraft, "The Roots and Fruits of Brazilian Pentecostalism," 79.

186. Harper, "Philippine Tongues of Fire?," 226.

187. Alvarez, "The South and the Latin American Paradigm," 141–42. Alvarez summarizes similarities between the Philippine and Latin American Pentecostal/charismatic beliefs: (1) a background of Christian knowledge already acquired in the Roman Catholic tradition; (2) a worldview that accepts the supernatural and is not over-rationalized: Latin American Pentecostals accept the baptism in the Holy Spirit as an event that unveils a new reality; (3) disenchantment with the Roman Catholic church as a fallen religious system; conversion occurs when the individual understands the gospel as revealed by the Scripture and the Holy Spirit and joins the Pentecostal family, followed by the new paradigm of the community of believers and the life in the Holy Spirit.

188. Harper, "Philippine Tongues of Fire?," 226–27.

two regions have many things in common, but there are many things
that set them apart as well. For example, Filipinos showed more resil-
ience in the process of Hispanization than did the Aztecs, Incas and
other aboriginal American peoples."[189]

Korea, was "marked by schism and the canalization of spiritual
power through rival charismatic leaders."[190] Korean folk religious practices resemble Shamanistic activities, and I believe that Koreans modify folk religious practices when they encounter the gospel. Without
exception, nations in Europe, North and South America, Asia, and
Africa, have absorbed folk and popular religious beliefs and practices.
The church can deal with them in three different ways: indigenization,
contextualization, and inculturation.[191]

Chinese folk religious practices and beliefs related to the supernatural and spirit world easily blend with Christianity. In 1920s
and 1930s, with influences from both Chinese spiritual beliefs and
foreign missionaries, two Chinese Pentecostal denominations were
established: the True Jesus Church and the Jesus Family. Numerous
Chinese house churches practice Pentecostal and charismatic types
of worship.[192]

There should be some concern about popular culture's effects
on the contemporary Pentecostal and Charismatic movements. Kalu
identifies some areas for attention:

> [F]irst, the religion in culture model emphasizes the use of
> religious themes, languages, images, characters, and subjects
> in film or music, sports or television. It supports the rebuttal
> that entertainment appears crucial for the survival of religion

189. Ibid., 251. In addition to Iberian culture, now American culture is a magnet
for Filipinos and Latin Americans.

190. Martin, *Pentecostalism*, 161.

191. Ibid., 162. Martin comments, "It is with regard to shamanism that the ambi-
guities of indigenization are most obvious. The issue can be argued in several ways,
so that shamanism can be positively valued as a female practice or as an expression of
'the oppressed,' and from such perspectives one would expect the Pentecostal adoption of (for example) pilgrimages to the prayer mountain to be applauded. Another
aspect of indigenization is the distinctly Confucian interest in examination success,
in mutual care and wellbeing, and the evident reverence for pastors. Of course,
Pentecostalism is noted for its ability to 'inculturate' but in the Korean case the ap-
plause of other Korean Christians has been rather muted, even though they have
themselves extensively adopted many features of the Pentecostal style."

192. Ma and Anderson, "Pentecostals (Renewalists)," 101.

in the marketplace of culture. It is an inculturating pathway for touching youthful audiences, who are already enmeshed, wired in the electronic culture, and bored with the equally packaged institutional religion. Religion and popular culture must be geared to attract youth, just as mainline churches experiment with new liturgies and music.[193]

The popular culture has effective means of communication which, when used by religion, along with sports and entertainments, can affect people enormously.[194] Kalu again voices concern about the perception that

secular corporate interests have taken over spirituality to subvert individuals and seduce them into consumerism, and that advertisements utilize religious cultural cachet and brand products by associating them with personal fulfillment, inner peace, happiness, and success in relationships. Management efficiency is packaged as providing religious paths to enlightenment. . . . All communication production is under the economic control of the production and orchestration of consumption, whether used by Christians or others. Should Christian missionary strategies contest and avoid electronic media as a satanic realm?[195]

The preeminent twentieth century accomplishments of Pentecostal and charismatic movements are indebted to secular and popular technology. Charles Finney, Billy Sunday, Aimee Semple McPherson, and Billy Graham used human technology and popular tools to reach people for Christ. It is not my role to make judgments about the problems of those who make use of popular movements or folk religious culture. There has always been controversy when large numbers of people have accepted Jesus Christ because of popular approaches. If the internet, entertainment, sports, and the media are indeed effective tools to share the gospel of Jesus Christ—why not make the most of them? However, there has been a syncretic, unbiblical, secular minded, materialistic, and spiritist approach intermingled into the popular format and folk religiosity. Those movements require us to discern what to take on in order to keep the purity of belief in

193. Kalu, "Globalization and Mission," 39.
194. Ibid., 39–40.
195. Ibid., 40.

the gospel of Jesus and living in holiness that may not be affected by external elements of popular folk religious practices.

POWER AND UNITY

As mentioned earlier in this book, there are 38,000 Protestant denominations in the world, displaying the diversity of Christian cultures from around the world. The praying in tears of the Yoruba people in Nigeria, the repetitive hymnal singing of the Chinn people in Myanmar, and the Samba dancing with praise of the people in Brazil express the depth and width of cultural and ethnic differences. Local expressions of the indigenous Christian voice were heard after colonialism had ended. Expressing Christian practices and beliefs in various languages and cultures spawns sundry adaptations of culture and beliefs. Now is the time to turn our eyes to unite and collaborate together despite our differences whether in church polity, denominational lines, or political agendas.

Postcolonialism

The World Wars were a turning point in history. Europe had been known as a Christian continent, but Christians killed other Christians, as well as six million Jews, by manipulating Christian ideology to justify their actions. Many theologians, priests, ministers, and Christian thinkers were left speechless by the church's weak response to enormous injustices. Leading up to the World Wars, there had been lustful colonial expansion characterized by economic greed and territorial ambition. For centuries, the developing world was ravaged by Western colonial powers that depicted native people as uncivilized and uneducated savages who needed to be taught literacy with the Bible and exploited for their commercial potential. After the World Wars, a correction occurred. The West sent missionaries who took a more culturally sensitive approach and planted the seeds of revival, which would later yield a global harvest. Postcolonialism begins with a reawakening of things that the West had ignored or forgotten.

When China came under the control of the communists, the regime banned Western missionaries because they believed these missionaries were trying to westernize China with Christianity. Before the communists took control, there were one million Protestants and two million Catholics in China. The communists began a policy of severe discrimination against Christians. During the Cultural Revolution, between 1966 and 1976, if Chinese Christians were found to have any Western connections, they were imprisoned or executed to keep the People's Republic a pure socialist state. This persecution resulted in martyrdoms and drove the church underground, paving the way for future revivals in China. The communist government established the Three-Self Patriotic Movement among Protestant and Catholic churches in order to establish control and to delegitimize unregistered Christian groups, such as the Jesus Family.

Turning this deplorable situation into an opportunity, Chinese Christians received strength to testify to the gospel in prisons, agricultural work camps, and prison camps. Underground churches multiplied, and leaders were educated in prisons and camps without the benefit of Western theological training and curriculum. Jeyaraj affirms, "Chinese religious oppression strengthened Chinese Christian mission both inside and outside of China, and Chinese Christianity experienced significant growth."[196]

Similar outpourings of revival were seen in Indonesia, Korea, the Philippines, Latin America, and Africa during this time period. The postcolonial era was a chance for Christians in the developing world to grow. "Non-Western Christian leaders were no longer restrained by Western colonial masters, who for economic and political gains had overtly been supporting the interests of non-Christian counterparts."[197] Post-colonial Christianity is now expressed in their own styles within their own indigenous, independent, and local flavors.

Socio-Political Changes

The early twentieth century image of Pentecostals was synonymous with the poor, underprivileged, outcast, and marginalized while mainline Protestant denominations have progressively moved up in social status in identifying themselves as mostly middle class. We now see that image in transition. In the latter part of the twentieth century, Pentecostal church leadership actively entered secular poli¬tics in Colombia, Brazil, Guatemala, the Philippines, Burundi, Chile, and Argentina. The secularization thesis predicts a separation of the religious and political spheres, but, in several Latin American

196. Jeyaraj, "The Re-Emergence of Global Christianity," 54.
197. Ibid., 54.

countries, a fresh connection is being made between church and politics. According to Bastian, "the Pentecostalist leadership in certain countries has become a political leadership in the traditional sense of corporatist mediation."[198] When liberation theology helped left wing activists in Latin America, Pentecostal church leaders played the role of peace (corporatist) mediators between right and left wing political leaders. In the dominantly Catholic Philippines, Eddie Villanueva, the Pentecostal leader of the largest church, Jesus Is Lord, ran for the presidency twice. Sociopolitical interactions between Pentecostal and political leaders frequently occur. There is dialogue with ecumenical leaders on the issues of social liberation, injustice, equality, environmental policy, and human trafficking. The agenda of Pentecostal leaders goes beyond the commonality of manifestations of the Spirit to touch the social, economic, political, and educational spheres.[199] Wonsuk Ma finds:

> Unlike liberation theology, Minjung theology (its Korean cousin), or Dalit theology (the Indian attempt), has a starting point in the idea of a change in structure. The Pentecostal movement brought a spiritual dynamic to deprived lives. . . . It is powerfully illustrious that a Latin American Pentecostal leader answered, when asked what is the Pentecostal social program: "We are the program." It is no wonder that many reports indicate change in life style among Latin American Pentecostals, and this pattern is replicated in Asia.[200]

With their humble beginnings, Pentecostals today are no longer seen as outcasts in society. A local revival can swiftly be acknowledged by the world through the Internet, global communications, transportation, and worldwide ethnic and racial networks.[201] These interactions, coupled with an interest in renewal movements, also focus on challenging social, economic, and ecological issues.[202] For example, in

198. Bastian, "Protestantism in Latin America," 345. In Latin America Pentecostal church leaders act as mediators between the left and right wings in non-governmental organizations. They are called corporatist mediators.

199. Minjung means "people." The Korea Assemblies of God joined the Korean National Council of Churches and caused some debate on participation in the social gospel and the relationship to Minjung theology.

200. Ma, "Asian (Classical) Pentecostalism," 5.

201. Alvarez, "The South and the Latin American Paradigm," 140.

202. Ibid., 152. Alvarez states, "At the end of the twentieth century Pentecostals

the Philippines, religious organizations such as the Iglesia Ni Cristo play a crucial role in rallying support for some winning Presidential candidates. Vigorously political Protestant churches have limitations in influencing their communities because they are in the minority. Political involvement differs widely among different denominations and leaders. More active involvement is found in Latin America and Africa, less in Asian countries. Pentecostal politicians focus on issues such as the war on terror, drugs, pornography, human trafficking, prostitution, corruption, injustice, gambling, and immorality. Conservative circles tend not to take a political stance, seeing the separation between church and state as justified. Others make their voices heard around the world. Regarding the influence of the United States in this phenomenon, Martin says, "There are, of course, particular parts of the world, such as Liberia, Puerto Rico, and the Philippines, with a long history of American political involvement which presumably continues. The precise role of evangelicals in all the geopolitics of the Pacific is unclear."[203]

The theological spectrum of renewalists is quite diverse. Wesleyan Holiness, Reformed Calvinist, classical Trinitarian, Canadian Oneness, and dispensational Baptist leaders and churches all helped shape the Pentecostal movement. Premillenialists and others from the African indigenous, Latin American grassroots, and Asian independent renewalist traditions have voiced many different theological opinions. These varied theological stances allow Pentecostals to be political or apolitical.[204]

> In his magisterial survey of literature on this topic up to 1986, Terence Ranger argued that the powerless have often found in religion a means of altering their situation and even reversing their status in both symbolic and social terms. Religions can therefore become ideological and symbolic aspects of resistance to power. He cites the Watchtower in Zambia and

were faced with the trends of a postmodern society. Relativism, liberalism, materialism, secularism and individualism became the common denominator of a world in continuous and accelerated change. On the one hand, there is no doubt the world started to experience a major spiritual revival as the millennium ended. Most members of the Christian church were experiencing unusual levels of concern with the natural eschatological implications of the times."

203. Martin, *Pentecostalism*, 164.

204. Westmeier, *Protestant Pentecostalism in Latin America*, 24.

Zionism in South Africa as illustrations. Such rural resistance, cultural and therefore political, can be resistance even though it is not armed conflict.[205]

Gifford finds that Pentecostal or born-again Christian leaders were responsible for the maintenance of dictatorship in Benin:

> That this "born-again" Christianity has political ramifications is undeniable. Striking confirmation of this came in March 1996 when Mathieu (or from 1980, Ahmed) Kerekou, the Marxist military strongman and archetypal kleptocrat who had bankrupted Benin in his seventeen years of brutal repression (1972–1990) and been the first African dictator to fall in the second liberation struggle, was re-elected to power—this time not as a Marxist but as a born-again Christian. In 1996 there was no political mileage in Marxism, but a great deal in Pentecostalism.[206]

Sociological research in Pentecostal and Charismatic church growth has been conducted on the political and social structural changes in Brazil. As a result of the study, several findings were discovered such as the shift from an agrarian, conventional, and authoritarian (feudal) society to one that is urban, industrial, modern, and democratic.[207] Shifting from the pre-modern to a modern society in the twentieth century, society encountered social change and religious transformation that brought about new issues and new technology such as highway infrastructure, communication, technology, information technology, and media. Rapid social change in the Global South in Africa, Asia, and particularly Latin America saw an advance in their way of life and saw the quality of manufactured goods increase through the renovation of social organizations by the process of modernization that overarches the entire population.[208] Willems regards Pentecostalism in Latin America, especially in Brazil, as a sociocultural change:

> In the course of our field work it became abundantly clear that Protestantism, particularly its sectarian varieties, were thriving in those areas . . . where exposure to cultural change had

205. Gifford, *African Christianity*, 31–32.

206. Ibid., 34.

207. Cook, *New Face of the Church in Latin America*, 70.

208. Ineson, *Brazil 1980*, 143.

been long and intensive. Statistical data on the distribution of Protestants confirmed that industrialized modern metropolitan area and, to a lesser extent, rural frontiers had indeed the largest Protestant population . . . thus a seemingly contradictory possibility began to take shape: Protestantism "causing" cultural change and "being caused" by culture change.[209]

As Protestant churches experienced growth in other parts of the world, followers acted to contribute to the social, economic and cultural changes in society. Infrastructural developments in rural areas, domestic immigration, urbanization, industrialization, modernization, and eventually globalization afforded a more positive atmosphere for the expansion of Protestant churches in underpinning effective procedures for sociocultural transformation."[210] Whether intentional or not a growing number of Pentecostals have affected the reshaping of existing classes as well.[211] Berryman affirms, "Evangelical Protestantism has almost certainly replaced Roman Catholicism as Brazil's most widely practiced faith."[212]

Diversity in Unity

According to Operation World 2010, an estimated 38,000 Renewalist Christian denominations[213] exist worldwide, with more than 426 million Renewalists.[214] Continent by continent, region by region, nation by nation, differences among the denominations can be found, yet they find common ground in their Charismatic manifestations. And though there may be differences in the style of manifestation among the different mainline Protestant churches and faith mission agencies they all demonstrate a common evangelical theology. Out of the many different denominations, Pentecostal diversity in charismatic unity is multifaceted in Latin America due in part to the wide-range of origins. Independent and Pentecostal churches, even charismatic churches, share a common classical Pentecostal origin through the work of mis-

209. Willems, *Followers of the New Faith*, 510.

210. Ibid., 13.

211. D'Antonio and Pike, *Religion, Revolution, and Reform*, 93.

212. Berryman, *Religion in the Megacity*, 3.

213. Johnstone, *The Future of the Global Church*, 124.

214. Mandryk, *Operation World*, 3.

sionaries in conjunction with the locals which added a local flavor that contributed to the quilt work of Pentecostal diversity.[215]

Most Christian churches in the world are divided into three categories, Orthodox, Catholic, and Protestant, but Charismatic influences can be found in all three traditions. Latin American Catholics, especially in Brazil, are inclined to categorize Protestants into historic churches or faith missions. In reality, several Protestant denominations are interrelated with the ecumenical movement. Otherwise they cooperate with other local churches in terms of ministerial association. Denominations can also choose to go the independent route as well.[216] Pentecostal churches in Brazil may be separated into those whose origins date from the US in the early twentieth century (e.g. Assemblies of God) and those formed more recently. The following is a rough categorization:[217]

CHART 8.1 PROTESTANT CHURCHES IN BRAZIL

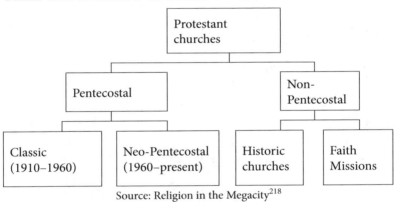

Source: Religion in the Megacity[218]

There are two major divides between the Pentecostal and non-Pentecostal church by issues such as class, education, and history. Many evangelical and Pentecostal churches draw attention in public from the low class. However, when we look closely at the churches

215. Cook, *New Face of the Church in Latin America*, 69.

216. Brumana and Martinez, *Spirits from the Margins*, 34. The Roman Catholic Church today in Brazil recognizes Pentecostal churches as sectarian movements. Brumana and Martinez say Pentecostalism is seen as "a cult with an ample doctrinal and practical spectrum which can be represented as being marked out by three poles."

217. Berryman, *Religion in the Megacity*, 3.

218. Ibid., 169.

we may find many differences in terms of church hierarchy, doctrine, management, and evangelism. Non-Pentecostal churches also consist of two major players. First, mainline denominations from the US and second, from faith missions which contributed a great number of churchgoers. To an outsider, evangelical churches in low-income communities may look much alike, but seen from within, differences are significant. The clearest dividing line is between Pentecostal and non-Pentecostal churches. The latter include the historic churches (mainline denominations in the United States) "Presbyterians, Baptists, and Methodists," and others including those from faith missions, "such as the Dios Admirable church in Caracas."[219] In mainline churches the similarity is small in terms of doctrine and implementation of governance as well as church system. Pentecostal churches usually adopt the doctrine of traditional evangelical churches but the leadership and government may be extremely diverse. Evangelical and Pentecostal churches may look similar in terms of putting their energies into evangelism but preaching and practices of the supernatural may differentiate them.[220]

Pentecostal and non-Pentecostal churches have experienced tremendous social lift, although Pentecostal churches have seen the majority remain in the lower class. Charismatic Pentecostal leaders have attracted the masses, poor, and urban dwellers. On the other hand, non-Pentecostals, mainly historic mainline churches, attract both low and middle class people. For example, we see this in the God is Love church and the Universal Church of the Kingdom of God. These churches with charismatic leadership practice divine healing, deliverance, and the effective usage of the media. Church leadership is centered on "cadres of preachers and a caudillo (authoritarian) leaders."[221] Furthermore, so much effort has been put forth in uniting the churches and denominations in South America. In Brazil, Catholic and Protestant, Pentecostal and non-Pentecostal, independent and sectarian groups have tried to join together but have been unsuccessful. The God is Love congregation has never attempted to

219. Ibid., 168. One of the fastest growing church movements comes from faith mission, the Dios Admirable church in Caracas.

220. The hot issues between the two groups include their social attitudes such as dress code.

221. Berryman, *Religion in the Megacity*, 170.

recognize other churches because their system and leadership refuse to align with other denominations due to differences. Many churches have been attempting to unite, such as the Brazil for Christ ministry that has engaged church leaders and their movements into the evangelistic and political agenda, yet not all religions accept it.[222] Bastian explains:

> Passive conformism, far from proving a kind of self-reflection of the religious counter-society, is in fact a major characteristic of the corporatist dynamics of contemporary form of Protestantism in Latin America. For this reason over the last twenty years the Pentecostalist leadership in certain countries has become a political leadership in the traditional sense of corporatist mediation.[223]

The Assemblies of God (AG) in Brazil is the largest national denomination amongst Assemblies of God in the world, and it is self-governed, self-managed, and self-supported. The church has influenced other countries in Latin America and to some degree at the global level. Therefore, the influence of the AG in Brazil gives a voice for the unity movement amongst diverse churches and denominations in Latin America.[224] In the Latin American family system, paternalism and male dominance is still strong, though the feminine preacher is partially recognized. However, there is an exception, as thirty-five percent of Foursquare church ministers are women.[225]

The division into historic and Pentecostal churches is an oversimplification. Some churches profess biblical inerrancy, but focus on biblical preaching and do not accept the Pentecostal conviction that the gifts of the Holy Spirit are available now and manifest in divine healing and deliverance. Pentecostal practices have been making advances in historic churches, where they are usually referred to as charismatic.[226] Most historic churches feel there is no salvation out-

222. Many pastors serve as state senators, mayors, governors and political party members and are called vereadores municípas. See Read, *New Patterns of Church Growth in Brazil*, 154–55.

223. Bastian, "Protestantism in Latin America," 345.

224. The Assemblies of God requires that their ministers receive seminary training. In both God Is Love and the Universal Church, ministerial formation is very much in-house, and becoming a minister is like being initiated into a guild.

225. Berryman, *Religion in the Megacity*, 170.

226. Cook, *New Face of the Church*, 18. Many Latin American churches from

side their own church, and so follow a policy of non-association with other evangelical churches, even other Pentecostal churches.[227] The Assemblies of God is also criticized by Read, who says, "their theology is wrong: they interpret Bible literally." But, a Bible-centered approach is one of the strongest points of Pentecostalism.[228]

CONCLUSION: FULFILLING THE GREAT COMMISSION IN THE GLOBAL VILLAGE

In the contemporary global village Christianity has encountered a new global trend not seen before. Migration and urban issues are enormous, as people are able to leave their countries and urbanites occupy more than half the global population. Cultural issues such as indigenization, contextualization, inculturation, syncretistic acculturation, and folk religiosity have permeated into everyday Christian beliefs and practices in all areas of the world. There are great diversities amongst all Christian members of denomination, sects, organizations, and independent churches throughout the world. There are more non-Western global elements among the Global South yet the Global North holds power in leadership, teaching, education, culture, traditions, and history. It seems the Global North and Global South can work to complement each other and support each other. But Christianity in the Global North and Global South have encountered strong resistance from religious blocks such as Islam, Hinduism, Buddhism, and folk religions in the 10/40 window. In reformed and dispensational theological circles the restoration of Israel was not given much thought. However, when the nationhood of Israel was restored in 1948, it changed how people would interpret the relationship between Israel and church. Peace and reconciliation issues between Palestine and Israel are an ongoing concern for Christians throughout the world. Evangelical bodies through Renewal Movements are getting stronger, growing faster, and encouraging churches to do the task of evangelism. In this sense the mainline, evangelical, Pentecostal

---

historical traditions—Baptists and Presbyterians, for example—are far more conservative than their counterparts elsewhere in the world.

227. For instance, the Christian Congregation, founded by Brazilian Oscar Chaves, said that Presbyterians have some of the same practices and methods used by spiritism in Brazil.

228. Read, *New Patterns of Church Growth in Brazil*, 139–42.

and Charismatic churches should endeavor together for the Great Commission. Therefore, denominational lines, ethnic boundaries, and cultural diversities should not hinder the unity of the body of Christ in completing the Great Commission. The challenges arising in the twenty-first century is to fulfill the Great Commission to every tongue, people, tribe, and language confess that Jesus is Lord.

Bibliography

Abercrombie, Nicholas, and Alan Warde, eds. *Contemporay British Society: A New Introduction to Sociology*. Cambridge: Polity Press, 1988.

Abrams, Mark, et al. *Values and Social Change in Britain: Studies in the Contemporary Values of Modern Society*. Basingstoke, Hampshire: Macmillan, 1985.

Acquaviva, Sabino S. *The Decline of the Sacred in Industrial Society*. Translated by Patricia Lipscomb. Oxford: Basil Blackwell, 1979.

———. "Some Reflections on the Parallel Decline of Religious Experience and Religious Practice." In *Secularization, Rationalism and Sectarianism: Essays in Honour of Bryan R. Wilson*, edited by Eileen Barker et al., 47–58. Oxford: Clarendon Press, 1993.

Adams, George P. "The Interpretation of Religion in Royce and Durkheim." *The Philosophical Review* 25, no. 3 (1916): 297–304.

Adeney, Walter F. "The Relation of New Testament Theology to Jewish Alexandrian Thought." *The Biblical World* 26, no. 1 (1905): 41–54.

———. *From Christ to Constantine; Christianity in the First Three Centuries*, Normal Studies for Sunday School Teachers. London: General Books, 1884.

Ahlstrom, Sydney E. *A Religious History of the American People*. New Haven: Yale University Press, 1972.

Alexander, Gallus. "A Biofunctional Theory of Religion." *Current Anthropology* 13, no. 5 (1972): 543–68.

Alexandria, Clement of. *The Stromata*. Translated by William Wilson. Edited by Kevin Knight et al. Book I, Chapter 7. New York: Christian Literature Publishing, 1885.

Allen, Ethan. *Reason: the Only Oracle of Man: Or a Compenduous System of Natural Religion. Alternately Adorned with Confutations of a Variety of Doctrines Incompatible to It; Deduced from the Most Exalted Ideas Which We Are Able to Form of the Divine and Human Characters, and from the Universe in General*. Bennington, Vermont: Haswell & Russell, 1784.

Allen, Roland. *Missionary Methods: St. Paul's or Ours?* Grand Rapids: Eerdmans, 1962.

Allen, William. *The History of Revivals of Religion*. Issue 7 of Revival series vols: Revival Publishing, 1951.

Allix, Pierre. *Some Remarks Upon the Ecclesiastical History of the Ancient Churches of Piedmont*. Gallatin, TN: Church History Research & Archives, 1989.

Altizer, Thomas J.J. *The Gospel of Christian Atheism*. Philadelphia: Westminster Press, 1966.

Alvarez, Miguel. "The South and the Latin American Paradigm of the Pentecostal Movement." *Asian Journal of Pentecostal Studies* 5, no. 1 (2002): 135–53.

Alves, Rubem A. *Protestantism and Repression: A Brazilian Case Study*. Maryknoll, NY: Orbis Books, 1985.

Anderson, Allan H. "The Contribution of David Yonggi Cho to a Contextual Theology in Korea." *Journal of Asian Mission* 12, no. 1 (2003).

———. *An Introduction to Pentecostalism: Global Charismatic Christianity*. Cambridge: Cambridge University Press, 2004.

———. "Pentecostalism in East Asia: Indigenous Oriental Christianity?" *Pneuma: The Journal of the Society for Pentecostal Studies* 22, no. 1 (2000).

Anderson, Michael H. "The Nicene Creed." (2008) No pages. Online: http://www .creeds.net/ancient/nicene.htm.

Anker, Roy M. *Self-Help and Popular Religion in Modern American Culture: An Interpretive Guide*. London: Greenwood Press, 1999.

Ankerberg, John. "The Concept of God in Islam and Christianity." In *Islam vs. Christianity debate* edited by John Ankerberg. Chattanooga, TN: The Ankerberg Theological Institute.

Antolinez, Jesus M. Merino. "Primal Religions and Primal Religion in the Dialogue between Faith and Culture." *Philippiniana Sacra* XXXIII, no. 97 (1998): 95–104.

Armstrong, Anthony. *The Church of England, the Methodist and Society 1700–1850*. London: University of London Press, 1973.

Ashford, Sheena, and Noel Timms. *What Europe Thinks: A Study of Western European Values*. Aldershot, VT: Dartmouth Publishing, 1992.

Askew, Thomas A. "The Founding Colleges, 1820–1860." In *Eerdmans' Handbook to Christianity in America*, edited by Mark A. Noll et al., 225–27. Grand Rapids: Eerdmans, 1983.

Bacchiocchi, Samuele. *From Sabbath to Sunday : A Historical Investigation of the Rise of Sunday Observance in Early Christianity*. Rome: Pontifical Gregorian University, 1977.

Backholer, Mathew. *Revival Fire: 150 Years of Revivals, Spiritual Awakenings and Moves of the Holy Spirit Days of Heaven on Earth*. LaVergne: By Faith Media, 2010.

Badone, Ellen, ed. "Pilgrimage and Popular Religion at a Greek Holy Shrine." In *Religious Orthodoxy and Popular Faith in European Society*, 113–36. Princeton: Princeton University Press, 1990.

Bainbridge, William Sims. *The Sociology of Religious Movements*. New York: Routledge, 1997.

Baker, G.P. *Constantine the Great and the Christian Revolution*. New York: Cooper Square Press, 1992.

Bamaiyi, Pwabeno H. "The Effect of Syncretism on Christian Spirituality: A Seminar Paper Presentation." In *The Effect of Syncretism on Christian Spirituality*, edited by P.H. Bamaiyi, 1–25. Mubi, Nigeria: Adamawa State Unversity.

Barna Group "America's Faith Is Changing – but beneath the Surface " The Barna Reaserch Group. No pages. Online: http://www.barna.org/barna-update /article/5-barna-update/117-americas-faith-is-changing-but-beneath-the -surface?q=religious+beliefs.

———. "Barna's Annual Tracking Study." No pages. Online: http://www.barna.org /congregations-articles/103-barnas-annual-tracking-study-shows-americans -stay-spiritually-active-but-biblical-views-wane.

———. "Barna's Annual Tracking Study Shows Americans Stay Spiritually Active, but Biblical Views Wane." No pages. Online: http://www.barna.org/barna-update /article/18-congregations/103-barnas-annual-tracking-study-shows-americans -stay-spiritually-active-but-biblical-views-wane?q=religious+beliefs.

Barrett, David B. "The Twentieth-Century Pentecostal/Charismatic Renewal in the Holy Spirit, with Its Goal of World Evangelization." *International Bulletin of Missionary Research* (1988): 119–29.

Barrett, David B., and Todd M. Johnson. "Annual Statistical Table on Global Mission: 2003." *International Bulletin of Missionary Research* 27, no. 1 (2003).

Barrett, David, et al. "Missionmetrics 2008: Reality Checks for Christian World Communications." *Interanational Bulletin of Missionary Research* 32, no. 1 (January 2008): 29.

Barrett, David, et al. eds. *World Christian Encyclopedia: A Comparative Survey of Churches and Religions in the Modern World.* Vol. I. Oxford: Oxford University Press, 2001

Barrow, Mandy. "What Is the Population of Britain?." No pages. Online: http://www .woodlands-junior.kent.sch.uk/customs/questions/population.html.

Bastian, Jean-Pierre. "Protestantism in Latin America." In *The Church in Latin America 1492-1992*, edited by Enrique Dussel, 313–50. Kent: Burns & Oates, 1992.

Bebbington, David W. *Evangelicalism in Modern Britain: A History from the 1730s to the 1980s.* London: Routledge, 1989.

———. "Evangelical Social Influence in North Atlantic Societies." In *Evangelicalism: Comparative Studies of Popular Protestantism in North America, the British Isles, and Beyond, 1700-1900*, edited by Mark A. Noll et al., 113–36. Oxford: Oxford University Press, 1994.

Beebe, Keith Edward. "Touched By The Fire: Presbyterians and Revival," *Theology Matters*, A Publication of Presbyterians for Faith, Family and Ministry, Vol. No. 2 (Mar/Apr 2000) 1, 1–8.

Bellah, Robert N. "Civil Religion in America." In *Religion in America*, edited by William G. McLoughlin and Robert N. Bellah, 3–23. Boston: Beacon Press, 1968.

Belloc, Hilaire, Europe and the Faith, Rockford: Tan Books and Publishers, 1992.

Beltran, Benigno S.V.D. *The Christology of the Inarticulate: An Inquiry into the Filipino Understanding of Jesus Christ.* Manila: Divine Word Publications, 1897.

———. *The Christology of the Inarticulate: An Inquiry into the Filipino Understanding of Jesus Christ.* Manila: Divine Word Publications, 1997.

Bentley, James. *Cry God for England: The Survival and Mission of the British Churches.* London: The Bowerdean Press, 1978.

Bercovitch, Sacvan. *The American Jeremiad.* Madison: University of Wisconsin Press, 1978.

Berger, Peter L. "The Desecularization of the World: A Global Overview." In *The Desecularization of the World: Resurgent Religion and World Politics*, edited by Peter L. Berger, 1–18. Grand Rapids: Eerdmans, 2005.

———. "Epistemological Modesty: An Interview with Peter Burger." No pages. Online: http://www.findarticles.com/p/articles/mi_m1058/is_n30_v114/ai20013864.

———. *The Noise of Solemn Assemblies: Christian Commitment and the Religious Establishment in America.* Garden City, NY: Doubleday, 1961.

———. *The Sacred Canopy; Elements of a Sociological Theory of Religion.* [1st ed. Garden City, NY: Doubleday, 1967.

Berger, Peter L., and Thomas Luckmann. *The Social Construction of Reality: A Treatise in the Sociology of Knowledge.* New York: Anchor Books, 1967.

Bernard, L.L. "Religion and Theology." *The Monist* 32, no. 1 (1922): 61–88.

Berryman, Phillip. *Religion in the Mega City: Catholic and Protestant Portraits from Latin America.* Maryknoll, New York: Orbis Books, 1996.

———. *Religion in the Megacity: Catholic and Protestant Portraits from Latin America.* Maryknoll, NY: Orbis Books, 1996.

Bidegain, Ana Maria. "Christianity in Latin America, 1910–2010." In *Atlas of Global Christianity*, edited by Todd Johnson and Kenneth R. Ross, 174–75. Edinburgh: Edinburgh University Press, 2009.

Birtwhistle, N. Allen. "Methodist Missions." In *A History of the Methodist Church in Great Britain, Volume Three*, edited by Rupert Davies et al., 1–116. London: Epworth Press, 1983.

Blackburn, William Maxwell. *History of the Christian Church from Its Origin to the Present Time.* Cincinnati: Walden and Stowe, 1879.

Blackwell, Dean. "The Plain Truth about the Waldensians: A Handbook." MA diss., The Great Ambassador College Graduate School of Theology, 1974.

Blumhofer, Edith Waldvogel. *The Assemblies of God: A Chapter in the Story of American Pentecostalism.* Vol. II. Springfield, MO: Gospel Publishing House, 1989.

Bob Jones University, The, "Preface to John Gilles's Historical Collections of Accounts of Revival." No pages. Online: http://greatawakeningdocumentary.com/items /show/14.

Bochio, Fernando Clemente. "The Native Protestant in Brazil: Its Origins, Development, and Identity, " An Attempt to Brazilianise Protestant Church History"." MPhil diss., University of Birmingham, 1993.

Bonk, Jonathan J. "The Council on African Studies and the Macmillan Center African Studies Lecture Series " Dictionary of African Christian Biography. No pages. Online: http://www.dacb.org/xnmaps.html#top .

———. "Ecclesiastical Cartography and the Invisible Continent: The Dictionary of African Christian Biography " In *African Studies Lecture Series* The Council on African Studies and the MacMillan Center 2008.

Brandes, Stanley. "Conclusion: Reflections on the Study of Religious Orthodoxy and Popular Faith in Europe." In *Religious Orthodoxy and Popular Faith in European Society*, edited by Ellen Badone, 185–200. Princeton: Princeton University Press, 1990.

Bréchon, Pierre. "Integration into Catholicism and Protestantism in Europe: The Impact of Moral and Political Values." In *Religion in Secularizing Society: The Europeans' Religion at the End of the 20th Century*, edited by Loek Halman and Ole Riis, 114–61. Leiden: Brill, 2003.

Brierley, Peter. *"Christian" England: What the 1989 English Church Census Reveals.* London: MARC Europe, 1991.

———. *Vision Building: Knowing Where You're Going.* London: Hodder & Stoughton, 1989.

———. *Future Church: A Global Analysis of the Christian Community to the Year 2010.* Crowborough: Monarch Books, 1998.

Brierley Peter, and Heather Wraight, ed. *UK Christian Handbook: Religious Trends 1998/99*: Christian Research Association, 1997.

Brierley, Peter, et al. *UK Christian Handbook: Religious Trends No.1, 1998/1999 Edition.* London: Christian Research Association, 1999.

Briggs, John H.Y. "Beyond Membership—Christianity—Common Understanding and Vision: Continuing the Discussion." No pages. Online: http://www.findarticles .com/p/articles/mi_m2065/is_n3_v50/ai_21152627/.

British Humanist Association, The. "Religion and belief: some surveys and statistics." No pages. Online: http://www.humanism.org.uk/campaigns/religion-and-belief-surveys-statistics.

Broadbent, E.H. *The Pilgrim Church*. London: Marshall Pickering, 1931.

Brown, Callum G. "The Secularisation Decade: What the 1960s Have Done to the Study of Religious History." In *The Decline of Christendom in Western Europe, 1750-2000*, edited by Hugh McLeod, 29–46. Cambridge: Cambridge University Press, 2003.

———. *The Death of Christian Britain: Understanding Secularisation 1800-2000*. London and New York: Routledge, 2001.

Brown, Callum G., and M.F. Snape. *Secularisation in the Christian World: Essays in Honour of Hugh Mcleod*. Farnham: Ashgate, 2010.

Brown, Colin. *Christianity and Western Thought: A History of Philosophers, Ideas & Movements, from the Ancient World to the Age of Enlightenment*. Vol. 1. Downers Grove, IL: IVP Academic, 1990.

Brown, Harold O.J. *Heresies: Heresy and Orthodxy in the History of the Church*. Peabody, MA: Hendrickson Publishers, 2007.

Brown, P.R.F. "Constantine Invented Christianity: A Thesis in the Field of Ancient History." Mountain Man Dot Com, Australia, Web Publications Index, http://www.mountainman.com.au/essenes/thesis.pdf.

Bruce, F.F. "John Wycliffe and the English Bible." *Churchman* 98, no. 4 (1984): 1–11.

Bruce, Steve. *God Is Dead: Secularization in the West*, Religion in the Modern World. Malden: Blackwell Publishers, 2002.

———. *Religion in Modern Britain*. Oxford: Oxford University Press, 1995.

———. *Religion in the Modern World: From Cathedrals to Cults*. New York: Oxford University Press, 1996.

Brumana, Fernando Giobellina, and Elda Evangelina Gonzalez Martinez. *Spirits from the Margins: Umbanda in Sao Paulo/Students* Acta Universitatis Upsaliensis. Uppsala Studies in Cultural Anthropology, 12: Uppsala University 1989.

Burdick, John. *Blessed Anastacia: Women, Race and Popular Christianity in Brazil* London: Routledge, 1998.

———. *Looking for God in Brazil: The Progressive Catholic Church in Urban Brazil's Religious Arena*. Berkeley: University of California Press, 1993.

Burckhardt, Jacob. *The Age of Constantine the Great*. Translated by Moses Hadas. Berkeley and Los Angeles: University of California Press, 1993.

Burgess, Stanley M., et al. *Dictionary of Pentecostal and Charismatic Movements*. Grand Rapids: Regency Reference Library, 1988.

Burnaby, John. *The Belief of Christendom: A Commentary on the Nicene Creed*. London: S.P.C.K., 1959.

Butler, Jon. *The Huguenots in America: A Refugee People in New World Society*, Harvard University Press, Cambridge, MA, 1983.

Butterfield, Herbert. "England in the Eighteenth Century." In *A History of the Methodist Church in Great Britain*, edited by Rupert Davies and Gordon Rupp. London: Epworth Press, 1965.

Calhoon, Robert M. "Separation of Church and State." In *Eerdmans' Handbook to Christianity in America*, edited by Mark A. Noll et al., 271–73. Grand Rapids: Eerdmans, 1983.

Calhoun, David. "Calvinism in Nineteenth-Century America." In *Reformation & Modern Church History*. No pages. Online: http://worldwidefreeresources.com /upload/CH320_T_30.pdf.

Callerder, J.P. *Illustrations of Popery, The "Mystery of Iniquity" Unveiled: In Its "Damnable Heresies, Lying Wonders, and Strong Delusion*. New York: The Clerk Office of the District Court of the Southern District of New York, Francis F. Riplep, 1838.

Calver, Clive, ed. *Hope for the Future*. Edited by John Wolffe, Evangelical Faith and Public Zeal: Evangelicals and Society in Britain 1780–1980. London: SPCK, 1995.

Cameron, Euan. *Waldenses: Rejections of Holy Church in Medieval Europe*. Oxford, UK: Blackwell Publishers, 2000.

Carden, Allen. *Puritan Christianity in America: Religion and Life in Seventeenth-Century Massachusetts*. Grand Rapids: Baker Book House, 1990.

Carwardine, Richard. "The Second Great Awakening in the Urban Centers: An Examination of Methodism and the 'New Measures'." *The Journal of American History* 59, no. 2 (1972): 327–40.

———. *Trans-Atlantic Revivalism: Popular Evangelicalism in Britain and America 1790–1865*, Contributions in American History, Number 75. Westport, Connecticut: Greenwood Press, 1978.

Casanova, José. *Public Religions in the Modern World*. Chicago: University of Chicago Press, 1994.

Case, Shirley Jackson. "Christianity and the Mystery Religions." *The Biblical World* 43, no. 1 (1914): 3–16.

Castelli, David. "The Future Life in Rabbinical Literature." *The Jewish Quarterly Review* 1, no. 4 (1889): 314–52.

Castleman, Graeme. "Golgotha, Athens and Jerusalem: Patristic Intimation of the Religio Perennis." *Eye of the Heart: A Journal of Traditional Wisdom* 47, no. 1 (2008): 47–79.

Caughey, James and Daniel Wise. *Earnest Christianity illustrated: or, Selections from the Journal of the Rev. James Caughey*. Boston: J.P. Magee, 1855.

César, Waldo. "From Babel to Pentecost: A Social-Historical-Theological Study of the Growth of Pentecostalism." In *Between Babel and Pentecost: Transnational Pentecostalism in Africa and Latin America*, edited by André Corten and Ruth Marshall-Fratani. Bloomington, Indianapolis: Indiana University Press, 2001.

Chadwick, Owen. "Great Britain and Europe." In *The Oxford Illustrated History of Christianity*, edited by John McManners, 341–83. Oxford: Oxford University Press, 1990.

———. *The Secularization of the European Mind in the 19th Century*. Cambridge: Cambridge University Press, 1975.

———. *The Victorian Church*. First ed. Part I. London: Adam & Charles Black, 1966.

Chappell, Paul G. "Healing Movements." In *Dictionary of Pentecostal and Charismatic Movements*, edited by Stanley M. Burgees and Gary B. McGee, 353–74. Grand Rapids: Zondervan, 1988.

Chaves, Mark. "Americans Have Lost Faith in Religious Leaders and Church Attendance." No pages. Online: http://www.huffingtonpost.com/2011/08/21 /religion-trends-clergy-church-attendance_n_929963.html.

———. "Secularization as Declining Religious Authority." *Social Forces* 72, no. 3 (1994): 749–74.

Chesnut, R. Andrew. *Born Again in Brazil: The Pentecostal Boom and the Pathogens of Poverty*. New Brunswick, NJ: Rutgers University Press, 1997.

———. *Born Again in Brazil: The Pentecostal Boom and the Pathogens of Poverty*. London: Rutgers University Press, 1997.

Cheyney, Edward P. "The Recantations of the Early Lollards." *The American Historical Review* 4, no. 3 (1899): 423–38.

Christian History, The. "Charles Finney: *Father of American revivalism*." No pages. Online: http://www.christianitytoday.com/ch/131christians/evangelistsandapo logists/finney.html?start=2.

Church of the Holy Trinity v. U.S., 143 U.S. 457(1892). No pages. Online: http://supreme.justia.com/us/143/457/case.html.

Clymer, Kenton J. *Protestant Missionaries in the Philippines, 1898–1916: An Inquiry into the American Colonial Mentality*. Urbana and Chicago: University of Illinois Press, 1986.

Commager, Henry Steele. "The American Mind: An Interpretation of American Thought and Character since the 1880's." New Haven: Yale University Press, 1950.

Cook, Guillermo. *New Face of the Church in Latin America: Between Tradition and Change*. Marknoll, New York: Orbis Books, 1994.

Corten, Andre, and Ruth Marshall-Fratani. *Between Babel and Pentecost: Transnational Pentecostalism in Africa and Latin America*. Bloomington, IN: Indiana University Press, 2000.

Costa, Néstor Da. "Secularization and Sacralization: Situated Reflections around the "Secularization" Concept," Globalization, Values, and Pluralism Conference." In *Globalization and Religious Pluralism*, edited by the Study of United States Institutes Alumni, 1–16. Shanghai, China: The Department of Religious Studies, Univeersty of California, Santa Babara, 2010.

Costa, Ruy O., ed. *One Faith, Many Cultures: Inculturation, Indigenization, and Contextualization*. Maryknoll, NY: Orbis Book, 1988.

Costen, M.D. *The Cathars and the Albigensian Crusade*. Manchester: Manchester University Press, 1997.

Couper, W.J. *Scotland Saw His Glory: A History of Revivals in Scotland*. Edited by Roberts, A Compilation of Materials Gathered From the Work of W.J. Couper. Wheaton, IL: International Awakening Press, 1995.

Cox, Harvey. *Fire from Heaven: The Rise of Pentecostal Spirituality and the Reshaping of Religion in the Twenty-First Century*. London: Cassell, 1996.

———. *The Secular City: Secularization and Urbanization in Theological Perspective*. London: SCM Press LTD, 1965.

Crawford, Michael J. "Origins of the Eighteenth-Century Evangelical Revival: England and New England Compared." *The Journal of British Studies* 26, no. 4 (1987): 361–97.

Croft, Steven. *Transforming Communities: Re-Imagining the Church for the 21st Century*. London: Darton, Longman and Todd, 2002.

Crompton, James. "Leicestershire Lollards." *Leicestershire archeological and historical society* XLIV, no. 3 (2007): 11–44.

Cross, F.L., ed. *The Oxford Dictionary of the Christian Church*. London: Oxford University Press, 1958.

Cruz, Gemma Tulud. "Expanding the Boundaries, Turning Borders into Spaces: Mission in the Context of Contemporary Migration." In *Mission after*

Christendom: Emergent Themes in Contemporary Mission, edited by Obgu U. Kalu et al., 71–83. Louisville: Westminster John Knox Press, 2010.

Cultural Research Service, The. *The Pagan Saviours: Pagan Elements in Christian Ritual and Doctrine*, Monograph Series No. 38. London: The Instistute for Cutural Reseach, 2000.

Curran, John R. *Pagan City and Christian Capital : Rome in the Fourth Century*, Oxford Classical Monographs. Oxford; New York: Clarendon Press; Oxford University Press, 2000.

D'Antonio, William V., and Frederick B. Pike. *Religion, Revolution, and Reform; New Forces for Change in Latin America*. New York: Praeger, 1964.

D'Aubigne, J.H. Merle. *History of the Reformation of the Sixteenth Century, Book One*. Edited by Hnery White. Author's Revision ed. London; Edinburgh: Religious Tract Society ; Oliver & Boyd, 1846.

Davenport, John. "Religion in the Public Sphere: How Deliberate Democracy Offers a Middle Road." In *Rethinking Secularization: Philosophy and the Prophecy of a Secular Age*, edited by Herbert De Vriese and Gary Gabor, 287–325. Cambridge, UK: Cambridge Scholars Publishing.

Davie, Grace. "Europe: The Exception That Proves the Rule?" In *The Desecularization of the World: Resurgent Religion and World Politics*, edited by Peter L. Berger, 65–83. Grand Rapids: Eerdmans, 1999.

———. *Religion in Britain since 1945: Believing without Belonging*. Oxford: Blackwell Publishers Ltd, 1994.

Davies, Paul. *Identity and Identification: The Latin American Protestant Church*, Encounter Mission Ezine, Issue 10: February 2006

Davies, Rupert E. *Methodism*. London: Epworth Press, 1963.

Day, Jenifer Cheesesman. "National Population Projections." No pages. Online: http://www.census.gov/population/www/pop-profile/natproj.html.

Dayton, Donald W. *Theological Roots of Pentecostalism*, Studies in Evangelicalism. No. 5. Peabody: Hendrickson, 1987.

DeMar, Gary. *America's Christian Heritage*. Nashville: Broadman & Holman Publishers, 2003.

Dempster, Muray A.H., et al. *Called and Empowered: Global Mission in Pentecostal Perspective*. Peabody, MA: Hendrickson, 1991.

———. *The Globalization of Pentecostalism : A Religion Made to Travel*. Oxford, UK ; Irvine, CA: Regnum Books Intl., 1999.

Department of Economic and Social Affairs, Population Division "International Migration 2009." New York: United Nations (UN), 2009.

D'Epinay, Christian Lalive. *Heaven of the Masses: A Study of the Pentecostal Movement in Chile*. UK: Lutterworth Press, 1969.

Diesto, Jr., Genaro Depakakibo. "The Effects of Colonial Mentality on the Religious Consciousness of Filipinos." PhD thesis, Fuller Theological Seminary, 1998.

Ditchfield, G.M. *The Evangelical Revival*, Introductions to History. London, Bristol, PA: UCL Press, 1998.

Dobbelaere, Karel. "Church Involvement and Secularization: Making Sense of the European Case." In *Secularization, Rationalism and Sectarianism: Essays in Honour of Bryan R. Wilson*, edited by Eileen Barker et al., 19–36. Oxford: Clarendon Press, 1993.

———. *Secularization: An Analysis at Three Levels*. Brussels: P.I.E.-Peter Lang, 2002.

Dobson, Ed, et al. *The Fundamentalist Phenomenon: The Resurgence of Conservative Christianity.* 2nd ed. Grand Rapids: Baker Book House, 1986.

Dobschütz, E. von. "Christianity and Hellenism." *Journal of Biblical Literature* 33, no. 4 (1914).

Dodson, Michael, "Pentecostals, Politics, and Public Space in Latin America." In *Power, Politics, and Pentecostals in Latin America,* edited by Cleary, Edward L.and Hannah W. Stewart-Gambino. Boulder, CO: Westview Press, 1997.

Draskoczy, Julie. "Ritual as an Amalgam of Allegiance: Spiritually and Death in Early Kievan Rus." *Ritual: Studies in Slavic Cutlures* V (2006): 95–108.

Droogers, Andre. "Globalisation and Pentecostal Success." In *Between Babel and Pentecost: Transnational Pentecostalism in Africa and Latin America,* edited by André Corten and Ruth Marshall-Fratani, 41–61. Bloomington: Indiana University Press, 2001.

———. "The Normalization of Religious Experience: Healing, Prophecy, Dreams, and Visions." In *Charismatic Christianity as a Global Culture,* edited by Karla Poewe, 33–49. Columbia: University of South Carolina Press, 1994.

Drummond, Andrew Landale. *Edward Irving and His Circle: Including Some Consideration of the 'Tongues' Movement in the Light of Modern Psychology,* James Clarke & Co., Ltd, Carter Lane, 153, 168.

Duffield, Guy P., and Nathaniel M. Van Cleave. *Foundations of Pentecostal Theology.* Los Angeles: Foursquare Media, 2008

Durant, Will. *Caesar and Christ: A History of Roman Civilization and of Christianity from Their Begining to A.D. 325.* Vol. III, The Story of Civlization: Part iii. New York: Simon and Schuster, 1972.

Durasoff, Steve. *Bright Wind of the Spirit: Pentecostalism Today.* London: Hodder and Stoughton, 1973.

Durkheim, Émile. *The Elementary Forms of the Religious Life.* Translated by Joseph Ward Swain. London: George Allen & Unwin Ltd, 1976.

Dussel, Enrique D. *The Church in Latin America, 1492–1992,* A History of the Church in the Third World V. 1: Comisión De Estudios De Historia De La Iglesia En Latinoamérica. Tunbridge Wells; Maryknoll, N.Y.: Oates & Burns; Orbis Books, 1992.

Editorial Introduction, The. "After Secularization (Special Double Issue)." *The Hedgehog Review* 1, no. 8 (2006): 1–2.)

Edman, V. Raymond. *Finney on Revival.* Minneapolis, Minnesota: Bethany House Publishers, 2000.

Edwards, Brian H. *Revival: A People Saturated with God.* Durham: Evangelical Press, 1990.

Edwards, Jonathan. *A Faithful Narrative of the Surprising Work of God.* Edited by Eye-Kyoung Choi. Ames, Iowa: The International Outreach, 2011. No pages. Online: http://www.jonathan-edwards.org/Narrative.html.

Edwords, Fred, et al., eds. "Humanism and Its Aspirations: Humanist Manifesto iii." *American Humanist Association* (2003). Online: http://www.americanhumanist .org/who_we_are/about_humanism/Humanist_Manifesto_III.

Eliade, Mircea, ed. *The Encyclopedia of Religion.* Vol. 11. New York and London: Macmillan Publishing Company and Collier Macmillan Publishers, 1987.

Elliott-Binns, L.E. *The Early Evangelicals: A Religious and Social Study.* Greenwich, Connecticut: The Teabury Press, 1953.

Ellis, Ieuan. "The Intellectual Challenge to 'Official Religion.'" In *The British: Their Religious Beliefs and Practices 1800–1986*, edited by Terence Thomas, 48–71. London and New York: Routledge, 1988.

Elwood, Douglas J. *Churches and Sects in the Philippines: A Descriptive Study of Contemporary Religious Group Movements*, Siliman University Monograph Series a (Religious Studies), No. 1. Dumaguete City, Philippines: Silliman University, 1968.

Emerton, Ephraim. "The Religious Environment of Early Christianity." *The Harvard Theological Review* 3, no. 2 (1910): 181–208.

Escobar, Samuel. "Latin America: An Evangelical Perspective." *Missiology: An International Review* 20, no. 2 (1992): 241–53.

European Commission. "Social Values, Science and Technology." *Special Eurobarometer 225 / Wave 63.1 – TNS Opinion & Social* (2005): 1–334.

Evans, Don. "Humanism and Religion." *In Humanism: Historical and Contemporary Perspectives*, Washington Area Secular Humanists, Washington D.C., 1999.

ExLibris. "Lollards." *English Dissent* (2008), No pages. Online: http://www.exlibris.org/nonconform/engdis/index.html.

Fields, Clive. "British Religion in Numbers." No pages. Online: http://www.brin.ac.uk/news/?p=1407.

Finke, Roger, and Rodney Stark. *The Churching of America, 1776–1990: Winners and Losers in Our Religious Economy*. New Brunswick: Rutgers University Press, 1992.

Finney, Charles G. *Revival Lectures*. Old Tappan, NJ: Fleming H. Revell Company Publishers, 1868.

Fish, Henry Clay. *Handbook of Revivals*. Boston: Congregational Board, 1855.

Fishwick, Marshall W. *Great Awakenings: Popular Religion and Popular Culture*, Haworth Popular Culture. New York: Harrington Park Press, 1995.

Fleming, Bruce C.E. *Contextualization of Theology: An Evangelical Assessment*. Pasadena: William Carey Library, 1980.

Forbush, William Byron, ed. *Foxe's Book of Martyrs: The History of Lives, Sufferings and Deaths of the Early Christian and Protestant Martyrs*. Grand rapids, Mich.: Zondervan Publishing House, 1967.

Forrester, Duncan B. "Christianity in Europe." In *Religion in Europe: Contemporary Perspectives*, edited by Sean Gill, Gavin D'Costa and Ursula King, 34–45. Kampen: Kok Pharos Publishing House, 1994.

Fowler, Charles Smith, et al. *A Rocky Mountain Sailor in Teddy Roosevelt's Navy: The Letters of Petty Officer Charles Fowler from the Asiatic Station 1905–1910*, History and Warfare. Boulder, CO: Westview Press, 1998.

Freeman, Charles. *A.D. 381: Heretics, Pagans, and the Dawn of the Monotheistic State*. New York: The Overlook Press, 2009.

Freke, Timothy, and Peter Gandy. *The Laughing Jesus : Religious Lies and Gnostic Wisdom*. New York: Three Rivers Press, 2005.

Gabriel, Ralph Henry. *Religion and Learning at Yale: The Church of Christ in the College and University, 1757–1957*. New Heaven, CT: Yale University Press, 1958.

Galilea, Segundo. *The Challenge of Popular Religiosity*. Quezon City: Claretian Publications, 1988.

Gallup Jr., George, and D. Michael Lindsay. *Surveying the Religious Landscape: Trends in U.S. Beliefs*. Harrisburg: Morehouse Publishing, 1999.

Gary, Jay. "Ten Global Trends in Religion." (1997).

Gaustad, Edwin S. *Historical Atlas of Religion in America*. New York: Harper & Row, 1962.

———. *A Religious History of America*. New York: Harper & Row, 1974.

George, A.C. "Pentecostal Beginnings in Travancore, South India." *Asian Journal of Pentecostal Studies* 4, no. 2 (2001): 215–37.

Gerloft, Roswith, and Abraham Ako Akrong. "Independents, 1910–2010." In *Atlas of Global Christianity*, edited by Todd M. Johnson and Kenneth R. Ross, 76–77. Edinburgh: Edinburgh University Press Ltd, 2010.

Gibbon, Edwrad. *The Decline and Fall of the Roman Empire*. London: Chatto and Windus Ltd, 1960.

Gibbs, Eddie, and Ian Coffey. *Church Next: Quantum Changes in Christian Ministry*. Downers Grove: Inter-Varsity Press, 2001.

Gifford, Paul. *African Christianity: Its Public Role*. Bloomington: Indiana University Press, 1998.

Gill, Robin. *Beyond Decline: A Challenge to the Churches*. First ed. London: SCM Press Ltd, 1988.

———. *The 'Empty' Church Revisited*, Explorations in Practical, Pastoral, and Empirical Theology. Aldershot: Ashgate, 2003.

———. *The Myth of the Empty Church*. London: SPCK, 1993.

Gallup Jr., George, and D. Michael Lindsay. *Surveying the Religious Landscape: Trends in U.S. Beliefs*. Harrisburg: Morehouse Publishing, 1999.

Gabriel, Ralph Henry. *Religion and Learning at Yale: The Church of Christ in the College and University, 1757–1957*. New Heaven: Yale University Press, 1958.

Gaustad, Edwin Scott. *Historical Atlas of Religion in America*. New York: Harper & Row, 1962.

———. *A Religious History of America*. New York: Harper & Row, 1974.

Glazier, Stephen D., *Perspectives on Pentecostalism: Case Studies from the Caribbean and Latin America*. Washington: University Press of America, 1980.

———. *The 'Empty' Church Revisited*, Explorations in Practical, Pastoral, and Empirical Theology. Aldershot: Ashgate, 2003.

———. *The Myth of the Empty Church*. London: SPCK, 1993.

Glock, Charles Y., and Rodney Stark. *Christian Beliefs and Anti-Semitism: A Science Study of the Ways in Which the Teachings of Christian Churches Shape American Attitudes toward the Jews*1966.

———. *Religion and Society in Tension*. Chicago: Rand McNally & Company, 1965.

Gorski, Philip S., and Ateş Altinordu. "After Secularization?" *Annual Review of Sociology* 34 (2008): 55–85

Gruen, Erich S. *Heritage and Hellenism : The Reinvention of Jewish Tradition*, Hellenistic Culture and Society 30. Berkeley, California: University of California Press, 1998.

Grund, Francis J. *The Americans in Their Moral, Social, and Political Relations*. London,: Longman, Rees, Orme, Brown, Green, & Longman, 1837.

Guder, Darrell L., et al. *Missional Church: A Vision for the Sending of the Church in North America*, The Gospel and Our Culture Series. Grand Rapids: William B. Eerdmans Publishing Company, 1998.

Guinness, Os. "A World Safe for Diversity: Religious Liberty and the Rebuilding of the Public Philosophy, an Address to the American Assembly." In *Religion in American Public Life: Living with Our Deepest Differences*, edited by Martin E. Marty, 137–52. New York: W. W. Norton & Company, 2001.

——. *The Gravedigger File: Papers on the Subversion of the Modern Church*. Downers Grove, IL: InterVarsity Press, 1983.

Guthrie, Stewart. "A Cognitive Theory of Religion." *Current Anthropology* 21, no. 2 (1980): 181–203.

Hadden, Jeffrey K. "Desacralizing Secularization Theory." In *Secularization and Fundamentalism Reconsidered: Religion and the Political Order*, edited by Jeffrey K. Hadden and Anson Shupe, 3–26. New York: Paragon House, 1989.

——. "Secularization and Fundamentalism Reconsidered." In *Religion and the Political Order V. 3*, edited by Jeffrey K. Hadden and Anson D. Shupe, 3–26. New York: Paragon House, 1989.

Haddock, Doris. "The Lollards and Social and Religious Reform." *History* 1, no. 2 (1998).

Hall, Douglas John. *Confessing the Faith: Christian Theology in a North American Context*. Minneapolis: Fortress Press, 1996.

Halman, Loek, and Theoleif Pettersson. "Differential Patterns of Secularization in Europe: Exploring the Impact of Religion on Social Values." In *Religion in Secular Society: The Europeans' Religion at the End of the 20th Century*, edited by Loek Halman and Ole Riis, 48–75. Leiden: Brill, 2003.

Halsey, A.H. "On Methods and Morals." In *Values and Social change in Briatain*, edited by M. Abrams, et al. London: Marc Europe, 1985.

Halman, Loek, and Ole Riis. "Contemporary European Discourses on Religion and Morality." In *Religion in Secularizing Society: The Europeans' Religion at the End of the 20th Century*, edited by Loek Halman and Ole Riis, 1–21. Leiden: Brill, 2003.

Hambrick-Stowe, Charles E. *Charles G. Finney and the Spirit of American Evangelicalism*, Library of Religious Biography. Grand Rapids: Eerdmans, 1996.

Hamilton, M. "Secularisation: Now You See It, Now You Don't." *Sociology Review* 7, no. 4 (1998): 28.

Hammond, Peter. "The Reformation." No pages. Online: http://www.frontline.org.za /articles/thereformation_lectures.htm.

——. *The Protestant Presence in Twentieth-Century America: Religion and Political Culture*, Suny Series in Religion, Culture, and Society. Albany: State University of New York Press, 1992.

Hammond, Phillip E. *The Protestant Presence in Twentieth-Century America: Religion and Political Culture*, Suny Series in Religion, Culture, and Society. Albany: State University of New York Press, 1992.

Hammond Phillip E., and Mark A. Shibley. "When the Sacred Returns: An Empirical Test." In *Secularization, Rationalism and Sectarianism: Essays in Honour of Bryan R. Wilson*, edited by Eileen Barker, James A. Beckford and Karel Dobbelare, 47–58. Oxford: Clarendon Press, 1993.

Handy, Robert T. *A Christian America: Protestant Hopes and Historical Realities*. Oxford: Oxford University Press, 1971.

Hardy, Edward R. *Athanasius' Writings on Arianism: A Brief Essay*. Edited by Rihard T. Nolan. New Haven, CT: Berkely Divinity School, 1960.

Hartford Institute for Religion Research, The. "How many people go to church each Sunday?" No pages. Online: http://hirr.hartsem.edu/research/fastfacts/fast_facts .html#numcong.

Harper, George W. "Philippine Tongues of Fire? Latin American Pentecostalism and the Future of Filipino Christianity." *Journal of Asian Studies* 2, no. 2 (2000): 225–59.

Harrel, Jr., David Edwin. "Book Review." *American Historical Review* (2001).

Hartford Institute for Religion Research, "How many people go to church each Sunday?" No pages. Online: http://hirr.hartsem.edu/research/fastfacts/fast_facts.html#numcong.

Hastings, Adrian. *A History of English Christianity 1920–1985.* First ed. London: Collins, 1986.

———. "Turning Points in Religious Studies." In *Christianity in Africa*, edited by Ursula King. Edinburgh: T. and T. Clark, 1990.

Hauser, Philip Morris. *Urbanization in Asia and the Far East: Proceedings of the Joint Un/Unesco Seminar (in Co-Operation with the International Labour Office) on Urbanization in the Ecafe Region, Bangkok, 8–18 August, 1956,* Tensions and Technology Series. Calcutta: UNESCO Research Centre on the Social Implications of Industrialization in Southern Asia, 1957.

Hayford, Jack W., and S. David Moore. *The Charismatic Century: The Enduring Impact of the Azusa Street Revival.* New York: Faith Words, 2006.

Haykin, Michael A.G. " Constantine and His Revolution, Fellowship for Reformation and Pastoral Studies." *Fellowhip for Reformation and Pastoral Studies* 27, no. 6 (1999): 1–14.

———. "Calvinism and Revival," 1–22. Online: http://www.andrewfullercenter.org/files/calvinism-and-revival.pdf.

Haynes, Jeffrey. *Religion in Third World Politics*, Issues in Third World Politics. Boulder, CO: L. Rienner, 1994.

Healey, Joseph, and Donald Sybertz. *Towards An African Narrative Theology*, Nairobi: Pauline, 1996.

Hempton, David. "Evangelicalism and Reform, C.1780–1832." In *Evangelical Faith and Public Zeal: Evangelicals and Society in Britain 1780–1980*, edited by John Wolffe, 17–37. London: SPCK, 1995.

———. *Methodism and Politics in British Society, 1750–1850.* London: Hutchinson Education, 1984.

———. *The Religion of the People: Methodism and Popular Religion C. 1750–1900.* London: Routledge, 1996.

Hernandez, Albert. "Re-Discovering Medieval and Early Modern Conceptions of Pentecost in the Twenty-First Century." In *Consultation Paper: Pentecost and the New Humanity, Revitalization Consultation* edited by Steve O'Malley, 1–27. Wilmore, KY: Center for the Study of World Revitalization Movments, Asbury Theological Seminary, 2009.

Hill, Louis. "Martin Luther." In *Truth Matters* Vol. 2, Issue 4 (2002). No pages. Online: http://www.rdm.org/TruthMatters/tm1002.pdf.

Hill, Michael. *A Sociology of Religion.* New York: Basic Books, Inc., Publishers, 1973.

Hitchcock, James. *What Is Secular Humanism?: Why Humanism Became Secular and How It Is Changing Our World.* Harrison, NY: RC Books, 1982.

Hocken, Peter. *Streams of Renewal: The Origins and Early Development of the Charismatic Movement in Great Britain.* Exeter: Paternoster, 1986.

———. "A Survey of the Worldwide Charismatic Movement." In *The Church Is Charismatic*, edited by Arnold Bittlinger, 117–54. Geneva: The World Council of Churches, 1980.

Hoge, Dean R., and David A. Roozen, eds. *Understanding Church Growth and Decline: 1950–1978*. New York: The Pilgrim Press, 1979.

Holman, Loek, and Thorleif Pettersen. "Three Differential Patterns of Secularization in Europe: Exploring the Impact of Religion on Social Values." In *Religion in Secularizing Society : The Europeans' Religion at the End of the 20th Century*, edited by Loek Halman and Ole Riis, 48–75. Leiden Boston: Brill, 2003.

Holmes, Janice. *Religious Revivals in Britain and Ireland 1859–1905*. Dublin; Portland, OR: Irish Academic Press, 2000.

Hong, Young-gi. "The Background and Characteristics of the Charismatic Mega-Churches in Korea." *Asian Journal of Pentecostalism* 3, no. 1 (2000).

Houtman, Dick, and Stef Aupers. "The Spiritual Turn and the Decline of Tradition: The Spread of Post-Christian Spirituality in 14 Western Countries, 1981–2000." *Journal for the Scientific Study of Religion* 46, no. 3 (2007): 305–20.

Howie, John. *The Scots Worthies*. Edited by W.H. Carslaw. Edinburgh: The Banner of Truth, 1995.

Hudson, Winthrop S. *The Great Tradition of the American Churches*. New York: Harper & Row, Publishers, 1963.

Hulbert, Henry Woodward. "Profanity." *The Biblical World* 54, no. 1 (1920): 69–75.

Hull, John M. "Can One Speak of God or to God in Education?" In *Dare We Speak of God in Public?: The Edward Cadbury Lectures, 1993–1994*, edited by Frances Young, 22–34. London: Mowbray, 1995.

Humphrey, Heman. *Revival Sketches and Manuel*. New York: The American Tract Society, 1859.

Humphrys, John. "YouGov Survey Results." No pages. Online: http://www.yougov .co.uk/extranets/ygarchives/content/pdf/Humphrys%20Religion%20Questions .pdf.

Hunt, Chester L.,et al, ed. *Sociology in the Philippine Setting: A Modular Approach*. Quezon City: Phoenix Publishing House, 1987.

Hurlbut, Jesse Lyman. *The Story of the Christian Church*. Grand Rapids: Zondervan, 1967.

Hutchinson, Caitlin. "The Pagan Influences on Christian Art in Ireland." *Meeting of Minds* (2010): 1–8.

Hyatt, Eddie L. *2000 Years of Charismatic Christianity*. Lake Mary: Charisma House, 2002.

IndexMundi. "United Kingdom Demographics Profile 2011." (2011) No pages. Online: http://www.indexmundi.com/united_kingdom/demographics_profile.html.

Irarrazaval, Diego. *Inculturation: New Dawn of the Church in Latin America*. Maryknoll, New York: Orbis Books, 2000.

Irenaeus. "Against Heresies." Text Excavation 2011. No pages. Online: http://www. textexcavation.com/irenaeusah.html.

———. "Against Heresies." Buffalo, NY: Christian Literature Publishing Co., 1885. No pages. Online: http://www.newadvent.org/fathers/0103506.htm.

Jackson, Bob. *Hope for the Church: Contemporary Strategies for Growth*. London: Church House Publishing, 2002.

Jenkins, Philip. *The Next Christendom: The Coming of Global Christianity*. Oxford: Oxford University Press, 2002.

Jevons, Frank Byron. "Hellenism and Christianity." *The Harvard Theological Review* 1, no. 2 (1908): 169–88.

Jeyaraj, Daniel. "The Re-Emergence of Global Christianity, 1910–2010." In *Atlas of Global Christiantiy*, edited by Todd M. Johnson and Kenneth R. Ross, 54–55. Edinburgh: Edinburgh University Press, 2009.

Johansen, Geir Are. "The Transition from Paganism to Christianity: A Perspective from the Borg Site, a Chieftains Farm in Northern Norway." 1–11. Lofotr, 2003.

John, Thomas Nichol. *The Pentecostals*. Plainfield, New Jersey: Logos International, 1966.

Johns, Jeremy. "Christianity and Islam," ed., John McManners, *The Oxford Illustrated History of Christianity*, Oxford University, New York, 1990.

Johnson, Edward A. "Constantine the Great: Imperial Benefactor of the Early Christian Church." *JETS* 22, no. 2 (1979): 161–69.

Johnson, Todd, et al. eds. *World Christian Encyclopedia: A Comparative Survey of Churches and Religions in the Modern World*. Vol. I. Oxford: Oxford University Press, 2001.

Johnson, Todd, and Sun Young Chung. "Christianity's Centre of Gravity, AD 33–2100." In *Atlas of Global Christianity*, edited by Todd Johnson and Kenneth R. Ross, 50–51. Edinburgh: Edinburgh University Press Ltd, 2009.

Johnson, Todd M., and Kenneth R. Ross. *Atlas of Global Christianity 1910–2010*. Edinburgh: Edinburgh University Press, 2009.

Johnstone, Patrick. *The Future of Global Christianity*. Colorado Springs: Biblica, 2011.

Johnstone, Patrick, and Jason Mandryk, eds. *Operation World 21th Century Edition*. Cumbria: Paternoster, 2001.

Jones, Adam. *Genocide: A Comprehensive Introduction*. New York: Routledge, 2011.

Jones, Jeffrey. "U.S. Clergy, Bankers See New Lows in Honesty/Ethics Ratings: Police officers' image recovers," No pages. Online: http://www.gallup.com/poll/124628 /clergy-bankers-new-lows-honesty-ethics-ratings.aspx.

Jones, William. *The History of the Christian Church, from the Birth of Christ to the Eighteenth Century Including the Very Interesting Account of the Waldenses and Albigenses*. 3rd American from the 4th London ed. Louisville: E.A. Smith, 1831.

Joseph, Valdimir Immanuel. *Paraclete: The Holy Spirit as a Person*. Makati City: SOLT, 1998.

Justia.com. "United States V. Macintosh, 283 U. S. 605 (1931)" US Supreme Court Center. No pages. Online: http://supreme.justia.com/us/283/605/case.html.

Kaase, Max, and Kenneth Newton. *Beliefs in Government*, Beliefs in Government Vol. 5. Oxford: Oxford University Press, 1995.

Kahn, Herman, and Wiener, Anthony J. *The Year 2000: A Framework for Speculation on the Next Thirty-Three Years*. New York: Macmillan, 1967.

Kalu, Ogbu U. "Globalization and Mission in the Twenty-First Century." In *Mission after Christendom: Emergent Themes in Contemporary Mission*, edited by Ogbu U. Kalu, Peter Vethanayagamony and Edmund Kee-Fook Chia, 25–42. Louisville: Westminster John Knox Press, 2010.

Kärkkäinen, Veli-Matti. ""Culture, Contextualization, and Conversion": Missiological Reflections from the Catholic-Pentecostal Dialogue (1990–1997)." *Asian Journal of Mission* 2, no. 2 (2000): 261–75.

———. "Truth on Fire: Pentecostal Theology of Mission and the Challenges of a New Millennium." *Asian Journal of Pentecostal Studies* 3, no. 1 (2000): 33–60.

Kasibante, Amos. "Beyond Revival: A Proposal for Mission in the Church of Uganda into the Third Millennium." In *Anglicanism: A Global Communion*, edited by

Andrew Wingate, Kevin Ward, Carrie Pemberton and Wilson Sitshebo, 363–68. London: Mowbray, 1998.

Keane, John. "Secularism?" In *Religion and Democracy*, edited by David Marquand and Ronald L. Nettler, 5–19. Oxford: Blackwell Publishers.

Keenan, William. "Post-Secular Sociology: Effusions of Religion in Late Modern Settings." *European Journal of Social Theory* 5, no. 2 (2002): 270–90.

Kelley, Dean M. *Why Conservative Churches Are Growing: A Study in Sociology of Religion.* San Francisco: Harper & Row, 1977.

Kitano, Koichi. "Spontaneous Ecumenicity between Catholics and Protestants in the Charismatic Movement: A Case Study." PhD diss., Centro Escolar University, 1981.

Knight, Kevin. "Secularism." *Catholic Encyclopedia.* No pages. Online: http://newadvent.org/cathen/13676a.htm.

Knox, R.A. *Enthusiasm: A Chapter in the History of Religion with Special Reference to the Xvii and Xviii Centuries.* London: Collins Liturgical Publications, 1987.

Kosmin, Barry A., and Egon Mayer. "American Religious Identification Survey 2001." 1–46. New York: The Graduate Center of the City University of New York, 2001.

Kosmin, Barry A., et al. "American Religious Identification Survey 2001." The Graduate Center of the City University of New York. No pages. Online: http://www.gc.cuny.edu/studies/aris.pdf.

Kreis, Steven. "Heretics, Heresies and the Church." In *Lecture 27, The History Guide Lecture on Ancient and Medieval European History.* No pages. Online: http://www.historyguide.org/ancient/lecture27b.html.

Krueger, Robert. "The Origin and Terminology of the Athanasian Creed." In *Western Pastoral Conference of the Dakota-Montana District*, 1–6: the Wisconsin Lutheran Seminary Library, 1976.

Kurian, George Thomas, ed. *Nelson's Dictionary of Christianity: The Authoritative Resource on the Christian World.* Nashville, Tenn.: Nelson, 2005.

Labaree, Leonard W. "The Conservative Attitude toward the Great Awakening." *The William and Mary Quarterly, 3rd Ser.* 1, no. 4 (1944): 331–52.

Laermans, Rudi, and Bryan Wilson. "The Secularization Thesis." In *Secularization and Social Integration : Papers in Honor of Karel Dobbelaere*, edited by Rudi Laermans, et al., xvi, 338. Leuven, Belgium: Leuven University Press, 1998.

LaHaye, Tim F. *Faith of Our Founding Fathers.* Green Forest, Arkansas: Master's Books, Inc., 1994.

Lalonde, Gerald V. "Pagan Cult to Christian Ritual: The Case of Agia Marina Theseiou." *Greek, Roman, and Byzantine Studies* 45 (2005): 91–125.

Lanternari, Vittorio. *The Religions of the Oppressed; a Study of Modern Messianic Cults.* [1st. American ed. New York,: Knopf, 1963.

Latourette, Kenneth Scott. *A History of Christianity.* Vol. I: to A.D. 1500. Peabody, MA: Prince Press, 2003.

———. *A History of Christianity.* Rev. ed. Vol. II: A.D. 1500–A.D. 1975. Peabody, MA: Prince Press, 2007.

———. *A History of Christianity.* London: Eyre and Spottiswoode Limited, 1955.

———. *A History of the Expansion of Christianity: Three Centuries of Advance A.D. 1500-A.D. 1800.* Vol. III. New York: The Paternoster Press, 1971.

————. "Christianity through the Ages: Revival and Involvement in Medieval Europe, A.D. 950–1350." ed Richard Heard. New York: Harper & Row and Ted and Winnie Brock, 1965.

Laughton, Ariel Bybee. "Virginity Discourse and Ascetic Politics in the Writings of Ambrose of Milan." PhD diss., Duke University, 2010.

Lechner, Frank J. "The Case against Secularization: A Rebuttal." *Social Forces* 69, no. 4 (1991): 1103–19.

Lee, Jae-Won. "Religion." In *Sociology: Themes and Perspectives*, edited by Sarah Pearsall, 430–501. London: HarperCollins Publishers Limited, 2000.

Lee, Moonjang. "Future of Global Christianity." In *Atlas of Global Christianity*, edited by Todd M. Johnson and Kenneth R. Ross, 104–05. Edinburgh: Edinburgh University Press Ltd, 2009.

Lehmann, Hartmut. "'Community' and 'Work' as Concepts of Religious Thought in Eighteenth-Century Württemberg Pietism." In *Protestant Evangelicalism: Britain, Ireland, Germany and America C.1750-C.1950 Essays in Honour of W. R. Ward*, edited by Keith Robbins, 79–98. Oxford: Basil Blackwell Publisher Ltd, 1990.

Lemaire, Ria. "Re-Reading Iracema: The Problem of the Representation of Women in the construction of a National Brazilian Indentity," Luso-Brazilian Review, Vol. 26, No. 2, Winter 1989

Lewis, Abram Herbert. *Paganism Surviving in Christianity*. New York: The Knickerbocker Press, 1892.

Loetscher, Lefferts A., ed. *Twenties Century Encyclopedia of Religious Knowledge: An Extension of the New Schaff-Herzog Encyclopedia of Religious Knowledge*. Grand Rapids: Baker Book House, 1955.

Lugo, Luis. "Islam and Christianity in Sub-Saharan Africa: Preface." The Pew Forum on Religion and Public Life. No pages. Online: http://www.pewforum.org /uploadedFiles/Topics/Belief_and_Practices/sub-saharan-africa-preface.pdf .

————. "Tolerance and Tension: Islam and Christianity in Sub-Saharan Africa." 1–324: Pew Forum on Religion and Public Life, 2010.

————. "Overview: Pentecostalism in Asia." (2006) No pages. Online: http://pewforum. org/Christian/Evangelical-Protestant-Churches/Overview-Pentecostalism-in -Asia.aspx.

Love, Dane. *Scottish Covenanter Stories: Tales from the Killing Time*, Neil Wilson Publishing, Glasgow, Scotland, 2009.

Lloyd-Jones, Martin. *Revival*. Wheaton: Crossway Books, 1987.

Lyon, D.G. "Judaism and Christianity." *The Old Testament Student* 12, no. 6 (1891): 367–73.

Ma, Julie, and Allan Anderson. "Pentecostals (Renewalists)." In *Atlas of Global Christianity*, edited by Todd M. Johnson and Kenneth R. Ross, 100–1. Edinburgh: Edinburgh University Press Ltd, 2010.

Ma, Wonsuk. "Asian (Classical) Pentecostalism: Theology in Context." Paper presented at the International Conference on Asian Pentecostalism, George Breeze Hall, Fircroft College, Birmingham, 17–20 September 2001.

McGee, Gary B. *Miracles, Missions, & American Pentecostalism: American Society of Missiology Series, No. 45*. Maryknoll: Orbis Books, 2010.

McGiffert, Arthur Cushman. "The Influence of Christianity Upon the Roman Empire." *The Harvard Review* 2, no. 1: 28–49.

McGrath, Alister E. *Evangelicalism and the Future of Christianity*. Downers Grove: InterVarsity Press, 1996.

———. *The Future of Christianity*, Blackwell Manifestos. Oxford: Blackwell, 2002.

McLeod, Hugh. "Introduction." In *The Decline of Christendom in Western Europe, 1750–2000*, edited by Hugh McLeod, 1–26. Cambridge: Cambridge University Press, 2003.

———. "The Privatization of Religion in Modern England." In *Dare We Speak of God in Public?: The Edward Cadbury Lectures, 1993–1994*, edited by Frances Young, 4–21. London: Mowbray, 1995.

———. *Religion and the People of Western Europe 1789–1989*. Oxford: Oxford University Press, 1997.

———. *The Religious Crisis of the 1960s*. Oxford ; New York: Oxford University Press, 2007.

———. *Secularisation in Western Europe, 1848–1914*, European Studies Series. Basingstoke: Macmillan, 2000.

McLoughlin, William G. *Revivals, Awakenings, and Reform: An Essay on Religion and Social Change in America, 1607–1977*. Chicago: The University of Chicago Press, 1978.

McManners, John. "Enlightenment: Secular and Christian (1600–1800)." In *The Oxford Illustrated History of Christianity*, edited by John McManners, 267–99. Oxford: Oxford University Press, 1990.

———, ed. *The Oxford Illustrated History of Christianity*. Oxford: Oxford University Press, 1990.

MacMullen, Ramsay. *Christianity and Paganism in the Fourth to Eighth Centuries*. New Haven: Yale University Press, 1997.

Maggay, Melba P. "Towards Sensitive Engagement with Filipino Indigenous Consciousness." *International Review of Mission* LXXXVII, no. 346 (1998): 361–73.

Mandryk, Jason, ed. *Operation World: 7th Edition*. Colorado Springs: Biblica Publishing, 2010.

Markus, Robert. "From Rome to the Barbarian Kingdoms (330–700)." In *The Oxford Illustrated History of Christianity*, edited by John McManners, 62–91. Oxford: Oxford University Press, 1990.

Marsden, George M. *Fundamentalism and American Culture: The Shaping of Twentieth-Century Evangelicalism 1870–1925*. New York: Oxford University Press, 1982.

———. *Understanding Fundamentalism and Evangelicalism*. Grand Rapids: Eerdmans, 1991.

Martin, David. *Christian Language in the Secular City*. Hants, England: Ashgate Publishing Company, 2002.

———. *A General Theory of Secularization*. London: Blackwell Pubishers Ltd, 1978.

———. *Pentecostalism: The World Their Parish*, Religion and Modernity. Oxford: Blackwell, 2002.

———. *A Sociology of English Religion*. First ed. London: Heinemann Educational Books Limited, 1967.

———. *Tongues of Fire: The Explosion of Protestantism in Latin America*. Oxford, UK; Cambridge, Mass., USA: B. Blackwell, 1990.

———. *The Future of Christianity*. Surrey and Burlington: Ashgate, 2011.

———. "Evangelical and Charismatic Christianity in Latin America." In *Charismatic Christianity as a Global Culture*, edited by Karla Poewe, 73–86. Columbia: University of South Carolina Press, 1994.

Martin, William. "How the Fundamentalists Learned to Thrive." *Christian Century*, (Sep. 23–30 1998) 872–75.

Marty, Martin E. *The Modern Schism: Three Paths to the Secular*. New York: Harper & Row, 1969.

———. "Religion in America since Mid-Century." In *Religion and America: Spiritual Life in a Secular Age*, edited by Mary Douglas and Steven Tipton, 271–87. Boston, MA: Beacon Press, 1982.

Martyr, Justin. *The First Apology of Justin*. Translated by Roberts-Donaldson. Edited by Peter Kirby. Vol. Chapter 46, Eraly Christian Writings2011.

———. "The Second Apology of Justin Martyr for the Christians." Edited by Peter Kirby. No pages. Online: http://www.earlychristianwritings.com/text /justinmartyr-secondapology.html.

Marzal, Manuel Maria. *Daily Life in the Indies: Seventeenth and Early Eighteenth Centuries*. Edited by Enrique Dussel, The Church in Latin America 1492–1992. Kent: Burns & Oates, 1992.

Mather, Cotton. *Magnalia Christi Americana; or, the Ecclesiastical History of New England, from Its First Planting, in the Year 1620, Unto the Year of Our Lord 1696, . . .The Sixth Book of the New-English Hisotory: Wrrtten Very Many Illustrious Discoveraries and Demonstrations of the Divine Prodidence in Remakabale Merceis and Judgements on Many Particular Persons*. Translated by Lucius F. Robinson. Hardford: Silas Adrus & Son, 1853.

Matviuk, Sergio. "Pentecostal Leadership Development and Church Growth in Latin America." *Asian Journal of Pentecostal Studies* 5, no. 1 (2002): 155–72.

May, Henry F. "The Decline of Providence." In *Ideas, Faiths, and Feelings: Essays on American Intellectual and Religious History 1952–1982*, edited by Henry F. May, 130–46. New York: Oxford University Press, 1983.

———. *The Enlightenment in America*. New York: Oxford University Press, 1978.

———. *Ideas, Faiths, and Feelings: Essays on American Intellectual and Religious History, 1952–1982*. New York: Oxford University Press, 1983.

———. "The Problem of the American Enlightenment (1970)." In *Ideas, Faiths & Feelings: Essays on American Intellectual & Religious History 1952–1982*, edited by Henry F. May, 110–29. New York: Oxford University Press, 1983.

———. "The Recovery of American Religious History (1964)." In *Ideas, Faiths & Feelings: Essays on American Intellectual & Religious History 1952–1982*, edited by Henry F. May, 65–86. New York: Oxford University Press, 1983.

May, Henry Farnham. *The Enlightenment in America*. New York: Oxford University Press, 1976.

M'Crie, Thomas. *History of the Progress and Suppression of the Reformation in Spain in the Sixteenth Century*. Edinburgh: Edinburgh & Company, 1829.

———. *The Revival at Stewarton and Kirk of Shotts: From the Reformation to Disruption*. London: Blackie & Son, 1875

Mead, Sidney E. "American Protestantism since the Civil War-from Denominationalism to Americanism." In *Lively Experiment: The Shaping of Christianity in America*, 134–55. New York, 1963.

Medcraft, John. "The Roots and Fruits of Brazilian Pentecostalism," Vox Evangelica 17 (1987): 66–94.

Mercado, Leonardo N. *Elements of Filipino Theology*. Tacloban City: Divine Word University Publications, 1975.

Merlini, Cesare. "A Post-Secular World?" *Survival* 53, no. 2 (2011): 117–30.

Merriam-Webster. "Revivalist." No pages. Online: http://www.merriam-webster.com /dictionary/revivalist.

Meyer, F.W.C., " The Formal Principle of the Reformation," The Old and New Testament Student, 15, (1892) 31–39.

Miller, Perry, and Thomas H. Johnson, eds. *Puritans: A Sourcebook of Their Writings, Two Volumes Bound as One.* Mineola, New York: Dover Publications, 2001.

Miranda-Feliciano, Evelyn. "Christianity in Cities, 1910–2010." In *Atlas of Global Christianity*, edited by Todd M. Johnson and Kenneth R. Ross, 240–41. Edinburgh: Edinburgh University Press, 2009.

Moore, R. Laurence. *Selling God: American Religion in the Marketplace of Culture.* New York: Oxford University Press, 1994.

Moorman, John R.H. *A History of the Church in England.* London: Adam and Charles Black, 1953.

Morrill, John. "The Stuarts (1603–1688)." In *The Oxford Illustrated History of Britain*, edited by Kenneth O. Morgan, 284–351. Oxford: Oxford University Press, 1986.

Mugambi, J.N. Kanyua, and Laurenti Magesa. *The Church in African Christianity: Innovative Essays in Ecclesiology*, African Challenge Series No. 1. Nairobi, Kenya: Initiatives Ltd., 1990.

Mullin, Robert Bruce. "North America." In *A World History of Christianity*, edited by Adrian Hastings, 416–57. Cambridge: William B. Eerdmans Publishing Company, 1999.

Munro, Dana C. "The Popes and the Crusades." *The American Philosophical Society* 55, no. 5 (1916): 348–56.

Murray, Andrew, et al., eds. *Healing: The Three Great Classics on Divine Healing.* Edited by Jonathan L. Graf. Camp Hill, PA: Christian Publications, 1992.

Murray, Iain Hamish. *Revival and Revivalism: The Making and Marring of American Evangelicalism, 1750–1858.* Carlisle, PA: Banner of Truth, 1994.

Murray, Stuart. "Christendom and Post-Christendom." (2011), No pages. Online: http: //missionalchurchnetwork.com/wp-content/uploads/2010/04/christendom -murray.pdf.

Nash, H.S. "The Idea of the Logos in Relation to the Need of Law in the Apostolic Age." *Journal of Biblical Literature* 21, no. 2 (1902): 170–87.

Nash, Ronald. "Was the New Testament Influenced by Pagan Religions?" 1–7. Online: http://www.equipresources.org/atf/cf/%7B9C4EE03A-F988-4091-84BD -F8E70A3B0215%7D/DB109.pdf

Neill, Stephen. *A History of Christian Missions.* Vol. 6. London: Penguin Books, 1964.

———. "Secular, Secularism, Secularization." In *Concise Dictionary of the Christian World Mission*, edited by Stephen Neil et al., 545–47. London: Lutterworth Press, 1970.

Nettles, Thomas J. "A Better Way: Reformation and Revival," Reformation and Revival, A Quarterly Journal for Church Leadership, 1 (1992) 23–64

Newbigin, Lesslie. *The Gospel in a Pluralist Society.* London: SPCK, 1989.

Nevius, John L. *Method of Mission Work.* Valuable comments on new-believer/ catechetical classes & starting new congregations. 1886/1895.

Newport, Frank. "More Than 9 in 10 Americans Continue to Believe in God: Professed Belief Is Lower among Younger Americans, Easterners, and Liberals." (2011). No pages. Online: http://www.gallup.com/poll/147887/americans-continue -believe-god.aspx.

Nichol, John Thomas. *The Pentecostals.* Plainfield, NJ: Logos International, 1966.

Noll, Mark A. "Christianity in Northern America, 1910–2010." In *Atlas of Global Christianity*, edited by Todd Johnson and Kenneth R. Ross, 190–91. Edinburgh: Edinburgh University Press Ltd, 2009.

———. et al, eds. *Eerdmans' Handbook to Christianity in America: The Varied and Inspiring Story of the Christian Faith in America from the Colonial Period to the Present Day.* Grand Rapids: Eerdmans,1983.

———. *The Rise of Evangelicalism: The Age of Edwards, Whitefield and the Wesleys,* History of Evangelicalism Series. Downers Grove: InterVarsity Press, 2004.

———. *The Scandal of the Evangelical Mind.* Grand Rapids: Eerdmans, 1994.

———. et al. *The Search for Christian America.* Colorado Springs: Helmers & Howard, 1989.

———. Nathan O. Hatch, and George M. Marsden. *The Search for Christian America.* Colorado Springs: Helmers & Howard, 1989.

Norman, Edward R. *Christianity in the Southern Hemisphere: The Churches in Latin America and South Africa.* Oxford: Clarendon Press, 1981.

Northcott, Michael S. *The Church and Secularisation: Urban Industrial Mission in North East England.* Frankfurt am Main: Verlag Peter Lang, 1983.

Núñez, Emilio Antonio. "Doing Theology in Latin America." In *Crisis in Latin America: An Evangelical Perspective,* edited by Emilio A. Ñuñez, 311–47. Chicago: Moody Press, 1989.

Núñez C, Emilio Antonio, and William David Taylor. *Crisis in Latin America.* Chicago: Moody Press, 1989. (confirm name)

———. "Critical Issues for Evangelicals in Latin America." In *Crisis in Latin America: An Evangelical Perspective,* edited by Emilio A. Núñez C and William D. Taylor. Chicago: Moody Press, 1989.

O'Brien, Susan. "A Transatlantic Community of Saints: The Great a Wakening and the First Evangelical Network, 1735–1755." *The American Historical Review* 91, no. 4 (1986): 811–32.

O'Connor, Daniel. "The Society in Changing Times." In *Three Centuries of Mission: The United Society for the Propagation of the Gospel 1701–2000,* edited by Daniel O'Connor, 1–231. New York: Continuum, 2000.

Okolo, Chuckwudum Barnabas. "The African Experience of Christian Values: Dimensions of the Problematic." No pages. Online: http://www.crvp.org/book /Series02/II-3/chapter_xi.htm.

Olds, Mason. *American Religious Humanism.* Minneapolis: Fellowship of Religious Humanists, 1996.

———. "John H. Dietrich: Religion without God? 1878–1957." Notable American Unitarians/Harvard Square Library Home. No pages. Online: http://www .harvardsquarelibrary.org/unitarians/dietrich.html.

Orchard, G.H. *A Concise History of Foreign Baptists: Taken from the New Testament, the First Fathers, Early Writers, and Historians of All Ages; Chronologically Arranged; Exhibiting Their Distinct Communities, with Their Orders in Various Kingdoms, under Several Discriminative Appellations from the Establishment of Christianity to the Present Age. With Correlative Information, Supporting the Early and Only Practice of Believers' Immersion: Also Observations and Notes on the Abuse of the Ordinance, and the Rise of Minor and Infant Baptism Thereon Intended for Juvenile Branches of Their Churches.* London: George Wightman, 1838.

Orr, J. Edwin. *Campus Aflame: Great Awakenings in Collegiate Communities.* Ventura: Regal Books, 1971.

———. *Evangelical Awakenings in Latin America*. Minneapolis: Bethany Fellowship, 1978.

———. *The Re-Study of Revival and Revivalism*. Glendale: Church Press, 1981.

———. *The Second Evangelical Awakening in Britain*. London: Marshall, Morgan & Scott, 1949.

Ostwalt, Conrad Eugene. *Secular Steeples: Popular Culture and the Religious Imagination*. Harrisburg, PA: Trinity Press, 2003.

O'Sullivan, Brian. *Parish Alive*. London: Sheed and Ward, 1979.

O'Sullivan, John. "Is Europe Losing Its Faith? Third World Christians Are Increasingly Devout, but Many Western Churches Have Fallen Victim to Secularization." Online: FindArticles, http://www.findarticles.com/p/articles/mi_m1571 /is_31_18/ai_90990424/.

Oxford American Dictionary. New York: Oxford University Press, 1980.

Ouseley, Gideon. *A Short Defense of the Old Religion, Against Certain Novelties, recommended to the People of Ireland*. Dublin, Ireland: J.C. Ball, 1821.

Parker, Cristián. *Popular Religion and Modernization in the Latin America: A Different Logic*. Maryknoll, NY: Orbis Books, 1996.

Parsons, John J. "Olam Hatorah: Mercy Triumphs over Judgment." (2011), http://www.hebrew4christians.com/Articles/Olam_Hatorah/OlamHaTorah.pdf.

Petersen, Douglas. "The Formation of Popular, National, Autonomous Pentecostal Churches in Central America." *Pneuma: The Journal of the Society for Pentecostal Studies* 16, no. 1 (1994).

Perrin, Jean Paul, et al. *History of the Ancient Christians Inhabiting the Valleys of the Alps: i. The Waldenses. ii. The Albigenses. iii. The Vaudois*. Philadelphia: Griffith and Simon, 1847.

Pettifer, Julian, and Richard Bradley. *Missionaries*. London: BBC Books, 1990.

Phan, Peter C. *In Our Own Tongues: Perspectives from Asia on Mission and Inculturation*. Maryknoll, NY: Orbis Books, 2003.

Phelan, John Leddy. *The Hispanization of the Philippines: Spanish Aims and Filipino Responses 1565–1700*. Madison: The University of Wisconsin Press, 1959.

Pickering, W.S.F. *Durkheim on Religion*. Translated by Jacqueline Reddiing and W.S.F. Pickering. London and Boston: Routledge Kegan & Paul, 1975.

Pirouet, Louise, ed. "Introduction: The Background to Modern Missions." In *Christianity Worldwide: AD 1800 Onwards*, 1–2. London: SPCK, 1989.

Plaisted, David. "Lost Records of Religious History." 2010.

Poethig, Richard P. "The Philippine Urban Family." In *Acculturation in the Philippines: Essays on Changing Societies, a Selection of Papers Presented at the Baguio Religious Acculturation Conferences from 1958 to 1968*, edited by Peter G. Gowing and William Henry Scott, 222–34. Quezon City: New Day Publishers, 1971.

Popescu, Bogdan. "Constantine the Great and Christianity: Church and State Commingled." *States, Globalisation and Economic Justice* 1 (2004): 86–93.

Price, John. *America at the Crossroads: Can America Escape National Decline, Economic Collapse, and Devastating Conflict?*. Wheaton: Living Books, 1979.

Prince, Thomas, and Nathan Hale. *A Chronological History of New-England in the form of Annals:… from the Discovery of Capt. Gosnold, in 1602, to the Arrival of Governor Belcher, in 1730*. Boston: Cummings, Hilliard, and Co., 1826.

Prosman, Hendricus Johannes. "The Postmodern Condition and the Meaning of Secularity: A Study on the Religious Dynamics of Postmodernity." Universiteit Utrecht, 2011.

Putnam, Robert D. *Bowling Alone: The Collapse and Revival of American Community.* New York: Simon & Schuster, 2000.

Qualben, Lars P. *A History of the Christian Church.* New York: Thomas Nelson and Sons, 1942.

Rack, Henry D. "Survival and Revival: John Bennet, Methodism, and the Old Dissent." In *Protestant Evangelicalism: Britain, Ireland, Germany and America C.1750-C.1950 Essays in Honour of W.R. Ward*, edited by Keith Robbins, 1–23. Oxford: Basil Blackwell Publisher, 1990.

Read, Frank A., and William R. Ineson. *Brazil 1980: The Protestant Handbook.* Monrovia, CA|: MARC, 1973.

Read, William R. *New Patterns of Church Growth in Brazil.* Grand Rapids: Eerdmans, 1965.

Reed, Bruce. *The Dynamics of Religion: Process and Movement in Christian Churches.* London: Darton, Longman and Todd, 1978.

Reeves, Thomas C. *The Empty Church: Does Organized Religion Matter Anymore?* New York: A Touchstone Book, 1996.

Rémond, René. *Religion and Society in Modern Europe.* Translated by Antonia Nevill. Oxford: Blackwell Publishers, 1999.

Rennie, Bryan S. "Mircea Eliade and the Perception of the Scared in Profane: Intention, Reduction, and Cognitive Theory." *Temenos* Vol. 43, No. 1 (2007): 83–208.

Reyburn, William David. *The Toba Indians of the Argentine Chaco: An Interpretive Report* Mennonite Board of Missions & Charities 1954.

Richards, Julian D. "Pagan and Christians at the frontier: Viking Burial in the Danelaw." In *Carver, M.O.H., (ed). The Cross Goes North: Processes of Conversion in Northern Europe, AD 300–1300*. York/Woodbridge: York Medeival Press in association with Boydell & Brewer, 383–395.

Richardson, Cyril C., et al. *Early Christian Fathers.* Edited by John Bailie et al., The Library of Christian Classics. Philadelphia: Westminster Press, 1953.

Riis, Ole. "Religion and the Spirit of Capitalism in Modern Europe." In *Religion in Secular Society: The Europeans' Religion at the End of the 20th Century*, edited by Loek Halman and Ole Riis, 22–47. Leiden: Brill, 2003.

Riss, Richard M. *A Survey of 20th-Century Revival Movements in North America.* Peabody: Hendrickson Publishers, 1988.

Roberts, Dana L. "The Great Commission: In an Age of Globalization." In *Antioch Agenda: Essays on the Restoration Church in Honor of Orlando E. Costas*, edited by Daniel Jeyaraj, Robert W. Pazmino and Rodney L. Petersen, 1–22. New Delhi: Indian Society for the Promotion of Christian Knowledge for Andover Newton Theological Knowledge and the Boston Theological Institute, 2007.

Robinson, Martin, and Dwight Smith. *Invading Secular Space: Strategies for Tomorrow's Church.* London: Monarch Books, 2003.

Roozen, David A. "The Efficacy of Demographic Theories of Religious Change: Protestant Church Attendance, 1952–68." In *Understanding Church Growth and Decline 1950–1978*, edited by Dean R. Hoge and David A. Roozen, 123–43. New York: The Pilgrim Press, 1979.

Ruiz, Teifilo F. *Spanish Society, 1400–1600.* Essex: Pearson Education Limited, 2001.

Runia, Klaas. "The Decline of Faith?: Christians in Europe." In *The Quiet Revolution*, edited by Robin Keeley, 197–217. Oxford: a Lion Book, 1985.

Russello, Gerald J., ed. *Christianity and European Culture: Selections from the Work of Christopher Dawson*. Washington, D.C.: Catholic University of America Press, 1998.

Sanneh, Lamin. *Whose Religion Is Christianity?: The Gospel Beyond the West*. Grand Rapids: Eerdmans, 2003.

Schaff, Philip. *History of the Christian Church: Christianus Sum. Christiani Nihil a Me Alienum Puto*. New ed. Vol. VI The Middle Ages: From Boniface VII., 1294, To the Protestant Reformation, 1517. Grand Rapids: Eerdmans, 1994.

———. "The Development of Religious Freedom" *The North American Review*. Vol. 138. No. 329 (Apr., 1884), 351–352. (349–361)

Schlesinger, Arthur Meier. *The Rise of the City, 1878–1898*, A History of American Life. New York: Macmillan, 1933.

Selfe, P.L. *Sociology*. First ed. London and Sydney: Pan Books, 1987.

Sellars, Roy Wood. *The Next Step in Religion; an Essay toward the Coming Renaissance*. New York: Macmillan, 1918.

Semmel, Bernard. *The Methodist Revolution*. London: Heinemann, 1974.

Shah, Anup. "Introduction." No pages. Online: http://www.unfpa.org/swp/2006/english/introduction.html.

———. "Introduction-Worldwide Immigrants Statistics." No pages. Online: http://www.globalissues.org/article/537/immigration.

———. "Introduction-Worldwide Immigrants Statistics." No pages. Online: http://www.globalissues.org/article/537/immigration#IntroductionWorldwideImmigrantsStatistics.

Sheehan, Jonathan. "Enlightenment, Religion, and the Enigma of Secularization: A Review Essay." *The American Historical Review* 108, no. 4 (2003): 1061–80.

Sheldrake, Philip. "Placing the Sacred: Transcendence and the City." *Literature & Theology* 21, no. 3 (2007): 243–58.

Shiner, L.E. *The Secularization of History: An Introduction to the Theology of Friedrich Gogarten*. Nashville: Abingdon Press, 1966.

Shorter, Aylward. *Toward a Theology of Inculturation*. Maryknoll, NY: Orbis Books, 1988.

———. *Toward a Theology of Inculturation*. London: Geoffrey Chapman, 1988.

Simms, P. Marion. *The Bible from the Beginning*. New York: Macmillan, 1929.

Sin, Jaime L. *Guidelines of the Catholic Charismatic Renewal Movement in the Archdiocese of Manila*. Manila: Archdiocesan Office For Research and Development, 1983

Smeeton, Donald Dean. *Lollard Themes in the Reformation Theology of William Tyndale*, Sixteenth Century Essays & Studies, Vol 6. Kirksville, MO: Truman State University Press, 1986.

Smith, Christian. "American Evangelicalism Embattled." In *Global Religious Movements in Regional Context*, edited by John Wolffe, 225–46. Hants: Asgate Publishing, 2002.

———. *American Evangelicalism: Embattled and Thriving*. Chicago: University of Chicago Press, 1998.

Smith, George. *History of Wesleyan Methodism*. 3 vols. London: Longman, Brown, Green, Longmans, and Roberts, 1857.

Smith, Graeme. *A Short History of Secularism*. London: I.B. Tauris, 2008.

Smith, Oswald J. *The Revival We Need*. New York: The Christian Alliance Publishing Company, 1925.

Smith, Page. "The Expansion of New England." In *American Urban History*, edited by Alexander B. Callow Jr., 83–93. Oxford: Oxford University Press, 1969.

Spence, Lewis. *Boadicea, Warrior Queen of the Britons*. London: R. Hale, 1937.

———. *The History and Origins of Druidism*. New York: Rider, 1949.

———. *Legendary London: Early London in Tradition and History*. London: R. Hale, 1937.

———. *The Mysteries of Britain: Or, the Secret Rites and Traditions of Ancient Britain Restored*. London: Rider, 1928.

———. *Mysteries of Celtic Britain*. Bristol: Siena, 1998.

Spickard, Paul R., and Kevin M. Cragg, eds. *A Global History of Christians: How Everyday Believers Experience Their World*. Grand Rapids: Baker, 1994.

Spickard, Paul R., et al. *A Global History of Christianity: How Everyday Believers Experienced Their World*. Grand Rapids: Baker Academic, 2005.

Spurgeon, Charles H. "What Is a Revival?" *Sword and Trowel* (1866). No pages. Online: http://www.spurgeon.org/s_and_t/wir1866.htm.

Squires, Josephine E. "The Significance of Religion in British Politics." In *The Secular and the Sacred: Nation, Religion and Politics*, edited by William Safran, 82–100. London: Frank Cass, 2003.

Stark, Rodney. *The Rise of Christianity*. San Francisco: Harper, 1997.

———. "Secularization, R.I.P.—rest in peace." No pages. Online: http://findarticles .com/p/articles/mi_m0SOR/is_3_60/ai_57533381/.

Stark, Rodney, and William Sims Bainbridge. *The Future of Religion: Secularization, Revival and Cult Formation*. Berkeley: University of California Press, 1985.

Statistics Canada. "Population by selected ethnic origins, by province and territory (2006 Census)." No pages. Online: http://www40.statcan.gc.ca/l01/cst01 /demo26a-eng.htm.

Steigenga, Timothy J., and Coleman, Kenneth M. "Protestant Political Orientations and the Structure of Political Opportunity: Chile, 1972–1991." Polity, Vol. 27, No. 3 (Spring, 1995), 465–82.

Stibbe, Alison Heather. 'Hans Nielsen Hauge and The Prophetic Imagination' PhD Thesis, University of London, February 2007

Stibbe, Mark. *Revival*. England: Monarch Books, 1998.

Stoll, David. *Is Latin America Turning Protestant?: The Politics of Evangelical Growth*. Berkeley: University of California Press, 1990.

———. *Protestantism, Capitalism, and Nature in America / Mark Stoll*. 1st ed. Albuquerque: University of New Mexico Press, 1997.

Strayer, Joseph Reese. *The Albigensian Crusades*. Ann Arbor: University of Michigan Press, 1992.

Strong, Roy. *The Story of Britain: A People's History*. London: Random House, 1998.

Sturtevant, David Reeves. *Popular Uprisings in the Philippines, 1840–1940*. Ithaca: Cornell University Press, 1976.

Sun, Benjamin. "Assemblies of God Theological Education in Asia Pacific: A Reflection." *Asian Journal of Pentecostal Studies* 3, no. 2 (2000): 227–51.

Swatos Jr., William H., and Kevin J. Christiano. "Secularization Theory: The Course of a Concept." *Sociology of Religion* 60, no. 3 (1999): 209–28.

Synan, H.V. "Evangelicalism." In *The New International Dictionary of Pentecostal Charismatic Movements*, edited by Stanley M. Burgess and Eduard M. Der Maas, 613–16. Grand Rapids: Zondervan, 2002.

Tano, Rodrigo D. *Theological Issues in the Philippine Context: A Case Study in the Contextualization of Theology*. Quezon City: New Day Publishers, 1981.

Taylor, John. "The Future of Christianity." In *The Oxford Illustrated History of Christianity*, edited by John McManners, 628–65. Oxford: Oxford University Press, 1990.

———. *The Go-Between God: The Holy Spirit and the Christian Mission*. London: SCM Press, 2004

Tcherikover, Victor. *Hellenistic Civilization and the Jews*. Peabody, MA: Hendrickson Publishers, 1999.

Tennent, Timothy C. *Invitation to World Mission: A Trinitarian Missiology for the Twenty-First Century*. Grand Rapids: Kregel Publications, 2010.

Tertullian, *Ad Scapulam*. Grand Rapids, MI: Christian Classics Ethereal Library, 1885. No pages. Online: http://www.ccel.org/ccel/schaff/anf03.pdf.

———. *On the Veiling of Virgins*. Translated by S. Thelwall. Vol. Chapter 1: Christian Classic Ethreal Library, A.D. 204. No pages. Online: http://www.ccel.org/ccel /schaff/anf04.iii.iv.i.html.

Thomson, T. Jack. "Some Reflections on Popular Religiosity in Britain." *International Review of Mission* LXXXII, no. 327 (1990): 375–81.

Tidball, Derek J. *Who Are the Evangelicals?: Tracing the Roots of Today's Movements*. London: Marshall Pickering, 1994.

Tocqueville, Alexis de. *Democracy in America*. Vol. 2. New York: Random House, 1945.

Townroe, Christopher, and George Yates, ed. *Sociology for Gcse*. Essex: Longman, 1987.

Towns, Elmer, and Douglas Porter. *The Ten Greatest Revivals Ever: From Pentecost to the Present*. Ann Arbor: Vine Books, 2000.

Trace, Arther. *Christianity: Its Rise and Fall*. Philadelphia, PA: Xlibris Corporation, 2000.

———. "Methodism in England 1900–1932." In *A History of the Methodist Church in Great Britain, Volume Three*, edited by Rupert Davies, et al., 309–61. London: Epworth Press, 1983.

Trainor, Brian. "Augustine's 'Sacred Reign-Secular Rule' Conception of the State; a Bridge from the West's' Foundational Roots to Its Post-Secular Destiny, and between 'the West' and 'the Rest.'" *HeyJ LII* (2011): 1–15.

Tuggy, Ralph, and Leonard A. Toliver. *Seeing the Church in the Philippines*. Manila: O.M.F. Publishers, 1972.

Turner, John Munsey. *Conflict and Reconciliation: Studies in Methodism and Ecumenism in England 1740–1982*. London: Epworth Press, 1985.

Uhlhorn, Gerhard. *The Conflict of Christianity with Heathenism*. Translated by Egbert C Smyth and C.J.H. Ropes. London: Sampson Low, 1882.

United Nations, The, " International Migration, 2009 Wallchart." New York: United Nations, Department of Economic and Social Affairs, Population Division, 2009.

———. "International Migration 2009." No pages. Online: http://www.un.org/esa /population/publications/2009Migration_Chart/ittmig_wallchart09.pdf.

U.S. Census Bureau. "National Population Projections." Population Profile of the United States, 2010. No pages. Online: http://www.census.gov/population/www /pop-profile/natproj.html.

Villari, Pasquale, *Life and Times of Girolamo Savonarola*, Vol 2. Translated by Linda Villari. New York: Scribner and Welford, 1890.

Van Beek, Huibert, and Andre Karamaga. "Protestants, 1910–2010." In *Atlas of Global Christianity*, edited by Todd M. Johnson and Kenneth R. Ross, 88–89. Edinburgh: Edinburgh University Press, 2009.

Van Buren, Paul Matthews. *The Secular Meaning of the Gospel, Based on an Analysis of Its Language*. New York: Macmillan, 1963.

Vásquez, Manuel A. *The Brazilian Popular Church and the Crisis of Modernity*, Cambridge Studies in Ideology and Religion. Cambridge: Cambridge University Press, 2008.

Voas, David, and Rodney Ling. "Religion in Britain and the United States." In *British Social Attitudes: The 26th Report*, edited by Alison Park, John Curtice, Katrina Thomson, Miranda Philips, Elizabeth Clery and Sarah Butt, 65–86. Thousand Oaks, CA: Sage Publications Inc., 2010.

Wagner, C. Peter. *Look Out! The Pentecostals Are Coming*. Carol Stream, IL: Creation House, 1973.

Walker, Larry J., *Standing Fast in Freedom: history, organization and principles of the Association of Free Lutheran Congregations*. Minneapolis: Association of Free Lutheran Congregations, 1996.

Walls, Andrew. "Christianity Across Twenty Centuries." In *Atlas of Global Christianity*, edited by Todd M. Johnson and Kenneth R. Ross, 48–49. Edinburgh: Edinburgh University Press, 2010.

Walsh, Michael J. *Dictionary of Christian Biography*. London: Continuum, 2001.

Walther, Daniel. "Were the Albigenses and Waldenses Forerunners of the Reformation? 178–02. Online: http://www.auss.info/auss_publication_file.php?pub_id=431&journal=1&type=pdf.

Ward, Kevin, and Brian Stanley, eds. *The Church Mission Society and World Christianity, 1799–1999*. Cambridge: Eerdmans, 2000.

Ward, W.R. "Missions in Their Global Context in the Eighteenth Century." In *A Global Faith: Essays on Evangelicalism and Globalization*, edited by M. Hutchinson and O. Kalu. New South Wales: The Centre for the Study of Australian Christianity, Macquarie University, 1998.

Wand, J.W.C. *A History of the Early Church to A.D. 500*. 4th ed. London: Methuen & Co., 1965.

Warfield, Benjamin Breckinridge. *Counterfeit Miracles*, Thomas Smyth Lecture. London: Banner of Truth, 1972.

Warner, Tim. "Tertullian." No pages. Online: http://pfrs.org/foundation/Tertullian.pdf.

Warren, Robert. *Being Human, Being Church: Spirituality and Mission in the Local Church*. London: Marshall Pickering, 1995.

Warrington, Keith. *Pentecostal Theology: A Theology of Encounter*. London: T & T Clark, 2008.

Webster, Daniel. *Webster Unabridged Dictionary*. New York: Simon and Schuster, 1983.

Weir, John. *Irish Revivals. The Ulster Awakening: Its Origin, Progress, and Fruit*. London,1860.

———. *The Ulster Awakening: An Account of the 1859 Revival in Ireland*. Edinburgh: Banner of Truth, 2009.

Weld, Wayne, and Donald A. MacGavran. *Principle of Church Growth*. Pasadena: William Carey Library, 1974.

Wessels, Anton. *Europe: Was It Ever Really Christian?: The Interaction between Gospel and Culture*. Translated by John Bowden. First British ed. London: SCM Press, 1994.

Westmeier, Karl-Wilhelm. *Protestant Pentecostalism in Latin America: A Study in the Dynamics of Missions*. Madison, NJ: Fairleigh Dickinson University Press, 1999.

Wiegele, Katharine Leone. "Transforming Popular Catholicism: The El Shaddai Movement of the Philippines." PhD diss., University of Illinois, 2002.

Wilken, Robert Louis. *The Christians as the Romans Saw Them*. 2nd ed. New Haven, CT: Yale University Press, 2003.

Willaime, Jean-Paul. "Secularism at the European Level: A Struggle between Non-Religious and Religious Worldviews, or Neutrality Towards Secular and Religious Beliefs?" In *Debating Secularism in a Post-Secular Age*, 1–13. St. Louis, MO: Religious Studies Conference, Washington University, 2010.

Willems, Emilio. *Followers of the New Faith: Culture Change and the Rise of Protestantism in Brazil and Chile*. Nashville, TN: Vanderbilt University Press, 1967.

Williams, J. Rodman. "Baptism in the Holy Spirit." In *Dictionary of Pentecostal and Charismatic Movements*, edited by Stanley M. Burgess and Gary B. McGee, 40–48. Grand Rapids: Zondervan, 1988.

———. "The Charismatic Movement and Reformed Theology." *A Theological Pilgrimage* (2003). No pages. Online: http://www.renewaltheology.net/A_Theological_Pilgrimmage/tp07.htm /.

Wilson, Bryan. "New Images of Christian Community." In *The Oxford Illustrated History of Christianity*, edited by John McManners. Oxford: Oxford University Press, 1990.

———. "Religion and the Churches in Contemporary America." In *Religion in America*, edited by William G. McLoughlin and Robert N. Bellah, 73–110. Boston: Beacon Press, 1968.

———, ed. *Rationality: Key Concepts in the Social Sciences*. New York: Harper Torchbooks, 1970.

———. *Religion in Sociological Perspective*. Oxford: Oxford University Press, 1982.

———. *Religion in Secular Society*. Baltimore: Penguin Books, 1969.

Winslow, E., ed. *Jonathan Edwards' Writings*. New York: New American Library, 1966.

Woodbridge, John D., et al. *The Gospel in America: Themes in the Story of America's Evangelicals*. Grand Rapids: Zondervan, 1979.

Wostyn, Lode. *Doing Ecclesiology: Church and Mission Today*. Quezon City: Claretian Publications, 1990.

———. "The Significance of Catholic Charismatics in the Philippines." Paper presented at the International Conference of Asian Pentecostalism, George Breeze Hall, Fircroft College, Birmingham, 17–20, September 2001.

Wright, Christopher J.H. "The Christian and Other Religions: The Biblical Evidence." *Themelios* 9, no. 2 (1984): 4–15.

Wuthnow, Robert. *The Crisis in the Churches: Spiritual Malaise, Fiscal Woe*. New York: Oxford University Press, 1997.

———. *The Struggle for America's Soul: Evangelicals, Liberals, and Secularism*. Grand Rapids: Eerdmans, 1989.

Wylie, J.A. *History of the Waldenses*. London: Cassell, Petter, Galpin, 1860.

Wilner, Eleanor. "Emigration." The Poetry Center at Smith College. No pages. Online: http://www.smith.edu/poetrycenter/poets/emigration.html.

Yong, Amos. *The Spirit Poured out on All Flesh: Pentecostalism and the Possibility of Global Theology*. Grand Rapids: Baker Academic, 2005.

Yount, David. *The Future of Christian Faith in America*. Minneapolis: Augsburg Books, 2004.

Yung, Hwa. "Pentecostalism and the Asian Church." Paper presented at the International Conference on Asian Pentecostalism, George Breeze Hall, Fircroft College, Birmingham, 17–20 September 2001.

Zaide, Sonia M. "The Centennial of Biblical Christianity." *Evangelical Today*, Centennial Issue 1998, 31–33.

Zialcita, Fernando N. "Culture and Inculturation." Paper presented at the Symposium: Culture and Inculturation, De La Costa Auditorium, Loyola School of Theolgy, 1995.

Zukeran, Patrick. "Pagan Connection: Did Christianity Borrow from the Mystery Religions?" (2011), http://www.evidenceandanswers.org/articles/Pagan%20Connection.pdf.

Subject/Name Index

Numbers in *italics* indicate figures.

accommodation, 317, 399, 402
acculturation, xxiii, 397, 398, 400n132,
    405–10
Act of Uniformity, 210
Adamson, James, 291
adaptation, 297, 343, 399, 402, 405,
    411n179, 415
Adonis religion, 82–83
Advent, 105
Adversus Haereses (*Against Heresies*;
    Irenaeus), 187–88
Africa
    Christianity in, 4, 19–21, *22*
    Muslims in, 19–20
African independent (indigenous)
    churches, 21, 401
African-initiated churches, 21, 380
African values, rediscovering, 401
Afro-Brazilian religion, 407
afterlife, xxvi, xxx, 7, 49n22, 54, 134,
    137, 157, 173, 178, 329, 389, 410
Age of Reason, 109, 136, 172, 232,
    326–27
aggiornamento, 35, 119
agrarian society, 360, 409, 419
Ajobard of Lyons, 201
Albigensians(Albigenses), 189, 191,
    193-194,196, 205-206, 214
Alencar, Jose de, 408
Alexander V, 202
Alexander VI, 27, 109, 204
Allen, Ethan, 329
Allen, Roland, 394
Allen, William, 193, 203

All Saints' Day, 112
America. *See also* American
    Christianity; Americans; United
    States
    Christian culture and tradition of,
    263
    denominational variety in, 261,
    314, 315
    disestablishment in, 307, 317, 319,
    321, 322, 323–26, 340
    evangelical Protestantism, 284, 300,
    311, 319, 322, 324, 331, 406, 420
    five factors contributing to church
    growth in, 259
    generating its own style of religion,
    316
    mission mandate of, 304
    Reformed traditions in, 263
    religion of, 303, 311–12, 321, 344
    religious minority groups seeking
    refuge in, 264–65
    religious perspective, 14
    secularity of religion in, 307
    secularized theology of, 306
American Baptist Churches in the
    U.S.A., 257, 258
American Christianity, xxviii–xxix
    divergence of, from Great Britain,
    263
    five key factors in growth of, xxxi
    flourishing in secularized
    environment, 312
    more likely to adapt to secular
    society, 316
    pulled in different directions,
    345–46
    secularization of, 316, 339

American Christians, discarding
    secularist ideas, 336
American Enlightenment, leading to
    secular humanism, 296, 350–51
American evangelicalism, 239, 302, 345,
    346. *See also* evangelicalism
American Humanist Association,
    353–55
American intellectualism, opposing
    biblical foundation for
    Christian values, 337
Americans. *See also* America; United
    States
    advancing the kingdom of God, 277
    as Calvinist-leaning Christian
        Pietists, 343
    common beliefs among, 263
    demonstrating Christian practices
        in daily life, 243
    developing an identity of demo-
        cratic individualism and self-
        worth, 296
    evaluating churches, as spiritual
        lighthouses, 318
    having more religious experiences
        than the British, 55
    identifying with cultural religion,
        296
    mixing politics and Christian
        vocabulary, 319
    percentage believing in God, 48
    on religious leaders in politics,
        262–63
    religion, 313, 315, 316
    respect of, for clergy members and
        ministers, 261–62
    trusting churches more than secular
        institutions, 261
Anabaptists, xxviii, 112, 170, 204, 205,
    303
Anderson, Rufus, 393, 396n114
Andover Theological Seminary, 286
Anglican, 21, 64, 68, 72, 77, 114, 122,
    154, 166, 215, 216, 218, 221,
    228, 232, 236, 237, 241, 344
Anglican Church, attendance at, 64

Anglicanism, 114, 211, 226, 233, 301,
    328, 344
Anglicans in colonial America, 263,
    265, 266, 271, 281, 299, 317, 323
Anne (queen of Bohemia), 202, 212,
    268
anticlericalism, 147
antisecularization, 224–25
antisupernaturalism, 147, 149
Apostles' Creed, 186, 352
Apostolic, 83, 184, 185
Apostolic Faith Mission, 11, 382, 386
Arianism, 92–93
Arius, 92, 186n24
Arminianism, xxvii, 226–27, 241, 327
Arnold of Brescia, 201
Asbury, Francis, 278, 285, 287, 298
Asia
    Christianity's growth in, 22–26
    indigenization and
        contextualization in, 401
    Pentecostals in, 7
    receptivity in, to the supernatural,
        384
    revivals in, 23
Assemblies of God, xxvii, 3, 6, 14, 30,
    112, 258, 259, 374n37, 395n107,
    395, 395n109, 417n199
Assemblies of God, Hot Springs,
    Arkansas, 11, 11n32
Assemblies of God, Springfield,
    Missouri, 395n107
Assemblies of God in Brazil, 421, 423,
    423n224, 424
Assemblies of God in the United
    Kingdom, 11
Athanasian Creed, 93n78, 187
Athanasius, 186
Atlas of Global Christianity, 4
Auer, J. A. C. Fagginger, 353
Augustine, 131, 140–43, 192
Australia, 11, 14, 45n13, 118, 234, 235,
    295, 366, 373, 377
Australia, religion in, 57
awakenings, 3, 181–82. *See also* Great
    Awakenings; revivals; spiritual
    awakenings

common beliefs of, 224

correlated with national political events, 292

source of, 185

Azusa Street Revival, xxviii, 6, 10–11, 14, 18, 26, 30, 304, 363, 367, 380, 384–85, 390

Babylonian religion, 98

Backus, Isaac, 319, 319n54

Balokole movement, 237

Bank of Amsterdam, 223

Bankin, John, 286

baptism of the Holy Spirit, 10–11, 15, 17, 30, 34, 35, 298, 363, 385–86, 387, 388, 412n187

Baptist Missionary Society, 236

Baptists, xxvii, 36, 196, 204, 205, 215, 216, 229, 230, 234, 254, 255, 259, 261, 267, 277, 279, 285, 288, 301, 302, 303, 311, 313, 323, 324n71, 381, 422, 424n226

democratic church system of, 297

growth of, 256–57, 324

revival among, 210–11

Bar Kochba rebellion, 97

Barrett, David, 30, 32n104, 36, 60

Bartleman, Frank, 11

Bauer, Bruno, 307

Beck, Wilhelm, 219

Beebe, Keith E., 207–8

Beecher, Henry Ward, 345

Beecher, Lyman, 290

Beets, Nicolaas, 291

belief in God

in Great Britain, *247*, 248

in North America and the U.K., 246

in Northern Ireland, *247*

in the U.S., *247*, 248–49

belief systems

changes in, 49–50

continuity between, 137

Belloc, Hilaire, 80–81

Benin, dictatorship in, maintained by Christians, 419

Bennett, Dennis, 13, 34, 35, 386

Bentley, James, 44, 129, 152n105

Bercovitch, Sacvan, 266–67, 266n114

Berg, Daniel, 394, 395n103

Berger, Peter, 156, 158, 159, 159n141, 162, 163, 167, 177, 240–41, 316

Bernard, L. L., 175–76

Beyond Decline (Gill), 44

Bible

authority of, challenged, 166, 190, 199, 201, 222n219, 334, 337, 349

reading of, 190, 191–92

revivals in, pattern of, 129, 179, 191

translation of, 190–96, 198, 200, 201–2, 393

viewing differently after Christendom, 145

Bible believers, searches for, 192–93

Bible-believing movements, 201

biblical criticism, 122, 166, 332, 333, 344, 358

biblical literalism, 294

Blasphemy Act of 1698, 114

Blumhardt, Johann Christoph, 291

Boardman, W. E., 221

Boehm, Anton Wilhelm, 268

Bohemian Brethren, 213

Böhler, Peter, 214

Book of Common Prayer, 211

Bradlaugh, Charles, 134

Bradley, Richard, 237–38

Bragg, Raymond, 352

Brainerd, David, 299

Brazil

equality of races in, 408

gospel message delivered in vernacular culture, 396–97

Pentecostal churches in, 394–95

Pentecostal expansion in, 382–83

Protestant churches in, 421–22

religious marketplace in, 408

syncretic practices in, 407

traditions in, similar to Pentecostalism, 391

urbanization in, 371–72

Brazil for Christ, 423

Brazilian Plenary Council, 406n157

Bréchon, Pierre, 46

Bredesen, Harald, 34

Brierley, Peter, 66, 68, 70, 71, 75, 76, 78,
    122n224, 128n258
British church, decline of, 43–44
Brothers, Jeffery, 11
Brown, Callum G., 42–43, 43n1, 44,
    45, 45n11, 65–66, 70n89, 119,
    119n212, 120, 123, 124, 150,
    172–73
Brownists, 265–66
Bruce, F. F., 197–98
Bruce, Robert, 207, 207n136
Bruce, Steve, 13, 44, 46, 49–50, 56, 64,
    67, 74, 77, 79, 108, 120, 121,
    147, 150, 167, 170
Bruys, Peter, 201–2
Bryce, James, 317, 317n47
Burgess, Stanley, 13
Burtt, Edwin A., 353

cacique, 409, 409n172
Caesar worship, 82
caesaropapist, xxix, xxxii, 80, 92, 140,
    143, 175, 313, 314,
calendar, Roman, shift to, 99–100
Calhoon, Robert, 318, 318n48, 326
Calvin, John, 146, 190, 206, 214,
    263n93, 327
Calvinism, xxvii,176, 180, 183, 194,
    227, 214, 287, 289, 301, 324,
    324n71, 356
Calvinism, Puritanism and, 265, 268
Calvinist Baptist churches, 210–11
Calvinist congregation in France, 206
Calvinist dissents, 227
Calvinist evangelicalism, 227
Calvinist Methodists, 212, 271,
    271n137
Calvinist Presbyterians, 3
Calvinists, 206, 263, 271, 327, 328, 343,
    344, 418
Cambridge Inter-Collegiate Christian
    Union, 236, 237
Cambridge University, 221, 236, 237
Cambuslang Work, 217, 275
camp meetings, 228n248, 257, 278, 286,
    287, 294, 301
Campbell, Alexander, 275–76

Campbell, Duncan, 184
Campbell, Thomas, 275–76
Campos, Bernardo, 35
Canada
    belief in God in, 246, 248, 250
    Chinese migration into, 369
    Christianity, 118, 220, 234, 240,
        295, 373
    declining religious influence in, 57
canonical law, 133, 154
capitalism, 157, 268
capitalism, as secularized Calvinism,
    176
Caputo, John, 171
Carbonnier, Jean, 214
Carey, William, 236
Carolingian formula, 143
Cartwright, Peter, 285
Casanova, Jose, 162, 307, 308, 309, 314,
    316, 319–25, 321n71, 324n71,
    327–28, 356
Case, Jackson Shirley, 82, 83
Castelli, David, 132
Cathar movement, 191, 196
Catholic Church, xxxiii, 3
    assuming political power, 140
    banning the masses from reading or
        reproducing the Bible, 192–93
    beginning of, 90
    cacique leadership, 409
    charismatics in, 35–36, 40
    condemning Christians as heretics,
        189–90
    distinguishing between the secular
        and the clergy, 133
    inquisitions and crusades of,
        144–45
    institutionalization of, 3, 174, 185,
        363, 364
    mass killings by, 189–90
    medieval solidarity of, 122
    persecuting Wycliffe and his
        followers, 200–201
    problems in, stemming from its
        hierarchy, 191
    trying to enforce power over sacred
        and secular areas of life, 145

sex abuse scandal in, 262n90

viewing Pentecostal churches as sectarian movements, 421n216

violent reaction to sectarian groups, 191

Catholicism. *See also* folk Catholicism

distinguished from folk Catholicism, 110–11

popular, 98

Catholic mysticism, 110, 112, 225, 311

Caughey, James, 220

Celtic rites, 104–5

Census of Religion (Great Britain; 1851), 63–64

Chadwick, Owen, 152

Chalcedon Council, 93, 93n81, 187, 187n33

Charismatic belief, 412n187

Charismatic leadership, 422

Charismatic manifestation, 384, 389, 420

charismatic movement, xxxii, xxvi, 5–9, 15, 16, 19, 20, 30, 31, 33, 34–36, 170, 304, 340, 369, 370, 380, 384–92, 399, 409, 412, 413, 414

Catholics, 40

Churches, xxxi, 8, 43, 77, 165, 387, 388, 390, 411, 419, 420, 425

decline of, 119, 126, 129, 147, 164, 165, 378

distinguished from Pentecostals, 40

in Africa, 19, 21

in Asia, 23, 25, 370n18, 370n19, 382n56, 382n57, 396n113

in Europe, 241

influence of, 380, 421

in Latin America, 26, 377, 377n46, 377n48, 390n86, 393, 404, 420, 421

in North America, 13, 15, 16, 17, 263, 316

popular culture's effect on, 413–15

revivals, 179

sociological research into, 419–20

worldwide growth of, 17–18

worship, 413

charismatic renewal movement, 12, 15, 32, 32n104, 35, 41, 386, 387, 406

Charlemagne, 105

Charles I, 265

Charles II, 208

Chaves, Mark, 164

Cheyney, Edward, 197, 199, 200–201

China

Christianity growing in, 416

discrimination in, against Christians, 415–16

folk religious practices in, 413

Pentecostal denominations in, 413

Christ, transcendent, 404

Christendom, xxxii–xxxiii

between Judaism and Paganism, 81–89

Christianity not dependent upon, 164–65

corruptness of, 142

crumbling of, in the Medieval era, 146

distinguished from Christianity, 95

dominating Northern, Eastern, and Western Europe, 80, 103, 240

evidence of, in the U.S. today, 244

expansion to the New World, 109

formation of, 80, 89–95, 97, 98, 139, 140, 142, 145

idea of, 113

in Great Britain, 113

injustices and abuses of power in, 145

in the medieval, 115, 138n44, 146, 171, 190, 201, 244, 303, 352

in Reformation, 113

inseparable from Greco-Roman culture and civilization, 96

pagan rituals in, 95, 102–8

secular and ecclesiastical power working together for, 106

secularization's effects on,

shift of, during Charlemagne's time, 94, 134, 149n90

Christendom state, 175, 3140Christ
　followers, percentage growth
　in, xiii
Christian, definition of, xiv–xv
Christian America, rise of, 239
Christian beliefs
　applying democratic principles to,
　　348
　commonly held, even by the
　　nonchurched, 338
Christian cell group, 232
Christian Congregration (Brazil), 369
Christian culture,
　in America, 182, 241, 263
　in Europe, 95, 104, 117, 138
　in non-Western, 404, 405, 415
Christian denominations, assuming
　moralist character, in the U.S.,
　337
Christian doctrine, fading belief in,
　122, 166, 351–52
Christian education, 68, 69
Christian fundamentalism, 239
Christian idealism, 309
Christian identity, 158
Christianity
　absorbing prehistoric religious
　　practices, 102–3
　adherents in major traditions and
　　movements, 39
　adopting existing religious
　　practices, 84, 98
　adopting paganism, 88, 91–92, 102
　adoption of, made easier by cultural
　　continuity, 98
　aggressive expansion of, in Iberian
　　countries, 109
　alternatives to, 365–66
　American, xxviii
　as Americanized faith, 303–4
　center of, moved to non-Western
　　regions, xxiii, xxiv
　Constantine's conversion to, 89
　as cultural religion, 175–76
　decline in, xxv, xxx, 43–45, 59, 108,
　　114–15, 118
　definition of, xiv–xv

depoliticization and demystification
　of, 154–55
differences in, between America
　and Europe, 267–68
dismissive attitude toward, 135
distinguished from Christendom,
　95
diversity of, in the Global South, 41
doctrines of, 48–49, 56
elite, 109
entering Roman Empire with
　salvific message, 84
European way of, 237
expansion into non-Western
　nations, local perception of, 115
forces in America antagonistic to,
　305
future of, 165
Gentile customs infiltrating, 84
gloomy outlook for, in the West,
　130
Greco-Roman philosophy
　intermingled with, 83
growth of, xxxii, 1, 22–26
Hellenization of, 96, 97
holidays and festivals celebrated,
　98–99
humanistic characteristics of, 350
indigenous, 392–93, 395–97
influencing a nation's culture and
　economy, xxiv–xxv
institutionalization of, 2, 364
integral part of Africa today, 19–21
linked with *Pax Romana* and
　Romanitas, 94
as living organism, 95
low form of, 109
major eras of, 130
major traditions of, as percentage of
　global population, *38*
moving in multi-faith direction, 44
new expressions of, 340
new face of, xiv
New Testament church's difference
　from Constantine 139
1960s as most important period
　in, 124

not dependent on Christendom,
    164–65
official recognition of, 81, 84
in postcolonial era, 415–16
in post-secular historical context,
    175–76
predicted ends for, because of
    modernity, 155
pre-Reformation, 108
prevalence of, in American society,
    244
principles of, established at
    educational institutions, 355
replacing with other belief systems,
    16
role of, in the West, 12
shifting to the non-West, 363
symbols of, 91, *108*
synthesizing Jewish monotheism
    and Greco-Roman polytheism,
    88–89
taking the place of pagan rituals
    and Hellenistic elements, 96
three present categories of, xxxiii
traditions of, 49
understanding the history of, 80
viewing through lens of Global
    North and Global South, 45–46
Western, Eurocentric mentality
    of, 4
Christianity Not Mysterious, 154–55
Christian radicalism, 193
Christians. *See also* church attendance
adopting Greco-Roman literature,
    95–96
beliefs of, less influential on their
    practices, 46
church-related behavior, in past
    seven days, *253*
by continent, *5, 18*
increasingly in the Global South,
    4–5
majority of, in non-Western
    regions, 2
numbers of, 61
spiritual gifts of, 187–88
Christian Scientists, 339

Christian student movement, 236
Christian symbols, appropriation of,
    103
Christian Union, 294n258
Christian worship, early existing
    records of, 95
Christmas, origins of, 99, 100–101
church
becoming a political mechanism,
    140
decoupling from state, 122, 138
institutionalization of, 185
losing interest in society after the
    Reformation, 146
monopoly of, disintegrating, 167
as polarizing force in Western
    Europe, 117
secularization of, 169, 306–7of,
    312–13
theological legitimacy for its
    involvement in the secular
    world, 141–42
Church, Joe, 237
church activity, international rates of,
    58
church adherence, 254n58
Church of Agia Marina Theseiou, 104
church attendance, 47
compared to sense of spiritual
    presence, 55
in Europe, 56, *73*, 74
in Great Britain, 65, *66*, 68, 70–73,
    77
historic indicators of, 63
in Ireland, 73
linked with religious beliefs, 53–54
measuring, 67
in Northern Ireland, 73
in Scandinavia, 56–57, 73, 121n219
in the U.S., 55
in the U.S. and the U.K., 55, 65,
    246, 251
church of the disinherited, 404
Church of the East, 19
churched culture, 241
Church of England, 113

churches
accepting Eastern religions and new
religious movements, xxx
aging congregations of, 128
becoming a matter of choice, xxv
becoming Pentecostalized, 374, 383
building of, in the Roman Empire,
91
challenges to, 111–12
declining attendance in, xxvii
disappearance of, predicted, 78
embracing evangelical
characteristics, 230
experiencing prosperity following
the Great Awakenings, 306
losing their moral standing, 129
Pentecostalizing, 407–8
as primary moral influence on
society, 68
responding to decline with secular
solutions, 121
secularization of, xxx, 335–36,
340–42
Churches of Christ, 258
Churches of God, 259
Church of God in Christ, 258
Church of God Ministry of Jesus Christ
International, 28–29
church governance
applying democratic principles to,
348
congregational form, 265
church growth
correlated with divine healing or
deliverance, 383
following conversions, 382
opportunities for, 379–80
opposition to, 380–81
church membership, 65
decline in the 1960s and 1970s,
126–27
in the United Kingdom, 74–78
measuring, 67, 74
in the U.S., 251–55, *260*
Church Missionary Society (CMS), 18,
236, 237

church organization, secular
rationalism affecting, 339
church-state relationship, 45, 91, 140–
45, 175. *See also* Christendom
church-state separation, 146, 307
allowing Christian revivals to
flourish, 313
allowing free exercise of religion,
317–20, 340–41
American Christianity remaining
strong in spite of, 321
linked to the church's decline, 122
paving the way for America's
secularization, 311, 315
viewed negatively in Europe, 319
Church of Uganda (Anglican), 237
Cistercians, 198n88
cities
becoming more non-Western,
372–73
growth of, 372–73
largest, by religious adherence, *373*
largest, with percentage of
Christians (1910), *368*
by total population (with majority
religion), *372*
City of God (Augustine), 141–43
civil unity, through public Christian
profession, 94
Civil religion, 15, 176, 309, 319, 324,
337
Civil War, undoing positive aspects of
Christian revival, 292
Clapham Sect, xxvii, 226, 236
Claudius of Turin, 201
Cleave, Nathaniel, 218
Clement of Alexandria, 86
clergy
influence of, in educational
leadership positions, 356
responding to religion's decline
with secular solutions, 121
CMS. *See* Church Missionary Society
colleges, 356–57
Colman, Benjamin, 282, 282n188
colonialism, end of, effect on the gospel
message, 405

coming age, expectation of, 131–32
Commager, Henry Steele, 306
communitarianism, 286
comparative religion, 333
Comte, Auguste, 116, 137, 148, 155–56, 158, 351, 352, 354, 389
Congregational Church, role of, in New England, 313
Congregationalism, 275, 324
Congregationalists, in the U.S., 255–56
Connecticut Valley Awakening, 275
Conselheiro, Antonio, 400n134
conservative Protestantism, 345
conservatives
    acting more like independents, 347
    causing their own downfall, 347
    great exodus of, 347
    theological, realizing need for unity, 346, 347
Constantine, 2, 81, 88, 89
    Christianity under, different from the New Testament church, 139
    conversion of, 138–39
    integrating the Roman Empire's religious and cultural spheres, 91
    officially recognizing Christianity, 98
    playing role of religious leader, 92–93
    ruling the western empire, 90
    using religious symbols to unite his constituents, 139
contextualization, xxvi, 396, 403
conversion experience, 233, 274–75, 385
Cooper, William, 282n188
Copeland, Kenneth, 296
Coptic Church, 19
corporate prayer, 381
corporatism, acculturation to, 406
corporatist mediators, 417
Costen, Michal, 196
Council at Arles, 92, 93
Council of Chalcedon, 187
Council of Ephesus, 93, 187
Council of Nicaea, 92, 93

Council of Tarragona, 192
Council of Toulouse, 192
Counter-Reformation, 27
Couper, William, 207
covenanters, 208–9
covenant theology, 324n71
Crawford, Michael, 224–25
Crévecoeur, Michel de, 266
critical mythography, 173
Croft, Steven, 72
Cromwell, Oliver, 196
crucicentrism, 222n221
Crumpe, Henry, 198–99
Crusades, 189, 364
Cry God for England (Bentley), 44
cults, 127–28
cultural change, cause of, 405
cultural church models, types of, 410
cultural religion, 175–76, 241, 296
cultural secularization, 175
culture, relating the gospel to, 399
Cybele/Attis cult, 82
cyclical theory of institutional religion, xxvi

Dalit theology, 417
Darney, William, 216n186
Darwin, Charles, 116
Darwinism, 166, 332–34, 344, 345
Davenport, John, 173
Davie, Grace, 48, 124, 126–28
Davies, Paul, 392
Davison, John, 207
Death of Christian Britain, The (Brown), 42–43
Death of God movement, 43n1
death-and-resurrection stories, 100–101
de-Christianization, xxvii, 3, 12, 95
Defense of the Faith, 406n157
Deism, 327
deliverance, 383
demythologization, 344
denomination, adherents to, and their beliefs, *51*
denominational competition, between Methodist and Baptists, 288

denominationalism, 14, 229–30, 314
denominational pluralism, 314, 315, 340
denominational prestige, 319–20
denominations
    competing with each other, 261, 340–41
    expressing spiritual openness, 379–80
    homogenization of, 319–20
    Pentecostalization of, 381
    plurality of, 307
    political involvement by, 418
d'Epinay, Lalive, 397, 406
deposito martyrum, 99n113
devil, belief in, 54
devotional religious societies, 279
Dewey, John, 353
Dickson, David, 208
Dictatus Papae Gregorii VII, 144
didactic Enlightenment, 330–31
Dietrich, John H., 351–52, 353
differentiation, 162
Dionysius, 100
disenchantment, 157
disestablishment. *See* church-state separation
dissenters, 182, 365
    in America, 311
    attracting artisan groups, 217
    first communities of, 277
    leaving for the New World, 264–65, 303
    new groups of, in Great Britain, 216–17
    zeal of, burning out in Great Britain and Europe, 264
dissenting churches, 65, 152
divine healing, 2, 383, 387, 390, 407, 422, 423
divorce, 127
Dobbelaere, Karel, 54, 72, 73, 122, 123, 125–26, 162, 168–69
Doddridge, Philip, 212
Dominumet Vivificantem (John Paul II), 35
Donatists, 92, 93

double sitting, 64
Duffield, Guy, 218
Durkheim, Émile, 136–37, 156, 158
Dutch Reformed Church of New York, 269
Dutton, Ann, 283
Dwight, Timothy, 278, 286, 356

early church, ignoring the Holy Spirit in practice, 185–86, 187
East African Revival movement, 237
Easter, celebrations of, 100
Eastern Orthodox Church, 3
East India Company, 223
ecclesiastical hypochondria, 121
ecumenical councils, 92, 96
ecumenical movement, 229
ecumenism, Pentecostalism contributing to, 382
Edict of Milan, 90–91, 99
Edict of Nantes, 215, 303n289
Edman, V. Raymond, 183
Education Act (Great Britain; 1944), 68
educational institutions, secularization of, 334
Education Reform Act (Great Britain; 1988), 69
Edwards, Jonathan, xxvii, xxviii, 182–83, 212, 214, 216, 268–69, 271, 274–75, 277–78, 281–84, 298, 300
    spreading the gospel through schools, 356
    utilizing the reason of the Enlightenment, 328–29
Eliade, Mircea, 173
Elim Church, 11
Engels, Friedrich, 156
Enlightenment, the, xxix, 115–18, 148–51, 167, 225
    affecting relationship of church and society, 328
    challenging the mystery of the sacred in Europe, 32
    different expressions of, throughout Europe, 148–49
    evangelical embrace of, 329

ideas of, restricted, 331
implications of, for the Great
Awakenings, 327–32
intellectuals of, revivalists
interacting with, 329
types of, in the U.S., 330
waning influence of, 331
Wesley's knowledge of, 226
Episcopal Church, 258, 259
Err, Edwin, 231
Erskine, John, 282
Erving, Edward, 220
eschaton, 131
Ethical Union of Britain (EUB), 352
Europe
allegiance in, to the church, 54
anti-God sentiments in, 49
architecture in, affected by de-
Christianization, 44, 91, 120–21
attraction in, to non-Christian
faiths, 176
Christianity's decline in, 43–44,
124–25, 168–69
Christianization of, 81
church attendance in, *73*, 74
church decoupling from state in,
138
church's decreasing geographical
presence in, 44
civilization in, formed around
Christianity, 94–95
common Christian identity of, 89
de-Christianization's effects in, 120
decreasing church attendance in,
xxx
definitive period of decline in,
xxix–xxxi
different expressions of the
Enlightenment in, 148–49
divided among different
denominations, xxvii–xxviii
evangelicalism in, 222–30
faculties in, comprising
independent scholars, 357
growing minority population in,
xxx–xxxi

growth in Christianity coming from
Pentecostal and charismatic
revivals, 179
Islam's influence in, xxxi
mid-20th-century religious decline
in, 119–20, 121, 123–24
needed re-evangelization, 80–81
political upheavals in, 231
population of, 378
rejuvenation of Christianity in, 177
religious affiliations in, 125–26
religious belief in, 50–55
religious differences among
generations, 59
revivals in, 211–15, 271–72, 291
secularization in, xxvi, xxix, xxx,
12, 57, 309, 355
social and economic progress in,
152–53
superficially Christianized, 138
three foundational worldviews of,
89
views in, on church-state
separation, 319
younger generations in, lacking in
religious foundation, 59
Europe: Was It Ever Really Christian?
(Wessels), 80
European churches
growth in, from immigrants, xxvi
opposition to, 1
European Value Systems Study Group
(EVSSG), 72, 125
Eusebius, 88, 141
Eutyches, 187n33
evangelical awakening, 181, 182
evangelical church, xxxiii
evangelical churches
roots in American Calvinistic
Puritanism and pietism, 265
sustaining growth, 254
evangelicalism, 30, 204, 205
American, 239, 301–2
Anglo-Saxon flavor of, 235
appeal of, to the poor and working
class, 231
becoming mainline, 223–24

evangelicalism–continued
  beginnings of, 223–24
  broad spectrum of, 301–2
  denominationalism and, 229–30
  emergence of, 179
  in Europe, 222–30
  flourishing in America, 257–58, 345
  four elements of, in the U.K., 222
  Great Awakenings leading to,
    300–303
  historical contributions of, in Great
    Britain, 226
  message of, appealing more to
    British and American citizens
    than Europeans, 279–80
  morality of, seen as detrimental and
    oppressive, 342
  Pietism and, 224–25
  popular, 226–28
  success of, 230
evangelical revivals, 205–11, 363
evangelicals
  adding to growth of Protestant
    denominations, 255
  American, aligning with main
    cultural currents, 331
  articulating fundamental beliefs to
    confront liberalism, 346
  biblical experientialism of, 222
  connected to awakening
    movements, church growth
    for, 344
  conservative, losing ground, 342
  division among, on baptism of the
    Holy Spirit, 386
  establishing new educational
    institutions, 358
  growth in numbers of, 220
  increasing political participation,
    260–61
  keeping distance from religious
    pluralism, 365
  receiving less attention than
    liberals, 346
  seeking to declare the U.S. a
    Christian nation, 325–26
  self-identification of, 245

  taking leadership positions in
    mainstream schools, 357–58
  withdrawing from the secular
    world, 359
evangelism
  as focus of Methodism, 218
  modern, Finney as the father of,
    289
  shared responsibility for, xxxiv
  simplistic models of, 118
  transdenominational, 320
  in urban areas, 373–74
evangelists, replacing parish priests and
    pastors, 298
evolution, 116
experiential faith, xxv

faith
  called into question, xxvii
  god-centered, 365
  relegated to the private sphere, 162
*Faithful Narrative of the Surprising
    Work of God in the Conversion
    of Many Hundred Souls, A*
    (Edwards), 183, 275, 283–84
Falwell, Jerry, 296
Far Eastern faiths, 352–53
Ferry, Jean-Marc, 148
Finke, Roger, 163
Finney, Charles Grandison, xxviii,
    183–84, 220, 221, 259, 274, 278,
    289, 293, 298, 300, 322, 414
  spreading the gospel through
    schools, 356
  starting a new type of revivalism,
    290–91
First Great Awakening, 270, 271–84,
    363, 385
  causing national sense of harmony
    and unity, 280
  creating spirit of American
    independence, 277
  elements of, 275
  initiating the repentance and regen-
    eration movement, 285
  lay leadership in, 274
  met with resistance, 295

Five Mile Act, 210
Fletcher, John, 9
folk Catholicism, 103, 108, 109–13, 235, 369, 398, 407, 411, 412
folk religion, 110, 112, 122, 169, 296, 369, 390, 410–15
folk religious movements, 111–13
Forrester, Duncan, 81
Fosdick, Harry Emerson, 351
Foursquare church, 423
Fourth Great Awakening, 270–71, 278
Fourth Lateran Council, 189
Fox, George, 209
Foxcroft, Thomas, 282n188
France
    religious enthusiasm in, 214–15
    Saxons massacred in, 105
    secularization in, 153
Francescon, Luigi, 369, 395n103
Francke, August Hermann, 212–13, 268, 269
Frederick I, 212
free churches, 65, 113, 152, 182, 324n71
freedom, replacing the sacred, 125
freedom of religion, 146
freethinking, achieving through reason, 331
Frelinghuysen, Theodore Jacobus, 269, 273, 282
French Revolution, 117, 147, 225, 237, 319, 332, 343
Freud, Sigmund, 116, 156, 166
Frontier Revival, 283. *See also* First Great Awakening
Frost, Michael, 396
functionalist fallacy, 174
fundamentalism, 15, 239, 302
    and evangelicalism, 302, 322, 350
    basic doctrines of, 346, 347
    emergence of, 322, 324, 325
    flourishing in America, 257
    confronting liberal theology, 343, 345, 346–47
    increasing political participation, 261
    maximizing areas of agreement, 346

Fundamentals, The: A Testimony of Truth, 346

Gary, Jay, 8
Gaustad, Edwin Scott, 259, 284–85, 293
Genghis Khan, 366
Gentile church, xxxiii, 364
German higher criticism, 358
Germany
    national aggrandizement as dominant religion in, 175–76
    secularization in, 153
Ghanaian Christianity, 380
gifts of the Spirit, 387–88
Gill, Robin, xxvi, 13, 44, 64, 64n68, 118, 118n209
Gillies, John, 283
Glasgow Missionary Society, 236
global church, greatest need for, xxiii–xiv
globalization, 366–68
Global North
    abandoning Christianity, 46
    affected by gospel as indigenized in the Global South, 383
    Christianity's decline in, linked to decline in authentic beliefs, 389
Global South
    adjusting to receive gifts of the Holy Spirit, 390
    Christianity in, 17, 41, 404–5
    church growth resulting from gifts of the Spirit, 387–88
    embracing Christianity, 46
glocalization, 366
glossolalia. *See* speaking in tongues
God
    belief in, 47–48, 50, *51*, 52–53, 56
    conventional view of, 246
    disbelief in, *51*, 55–56
    personal relationship with, 222–23, 224, 225
    traditional Christian view of, 50, 220
God Is Love, 422, 423
Godman, dying and resurrecting, 100
Gogarten, Friedrich, 335

gospel
    preaching of, in indigenous context,
        392–93, 395–97
    reclaiming cultural sensitivity in
        spread of, 402
    relating to culture, 399
    spreading in multiple directions,
        3–4
    Western culture wrapped up with
        404–5
Gould, Frederick M., 351
government, implementing Christian
    principles, 321
Graham, Billy, 32, 259, 296, 414

Great Awakenings, xxvi–xxvii, xxix,
        181–82, 216, 270–95, 363
    affecting mission work, 294,
        299–300
    effects of, 285–303
    Enlightenment and, 327–32
    leading to emergence of
        evangelicalism, 300–303
    occurring every 50 years, 277
    paralleling political developments,
        277n168
    people involved in, wanting
        sociopolitical change, 271
    role of, in confronting America's
        social problems, 279
    significance of, in American
        history, 277
    transatlantic nature of, 272, 273–75
    transforming the cultural system
        during, 276
Great Britain
    belief in God in, 47–48, 50, 247, 248
    as case of Christian decline,
        xxix–xxx
    Christendom in, 113
    Christianity in the 1930s, 120
    Christian population growth in, 75
    church attendance in, 65, 66, 68,
        70–73, 117–18, 77, 123, 251
    church membership in, 75, 76
    congregation sizes in, 72
    crisis of the church in, 42–44

denominations and class system
    in, 216
divorce in, 127
erosion of Christian convictions
    in, 129
growing more secular through the
    Victorian age, 152
Methodism's increasing power in,
    227–30
mid-20th-century religious decline
    in, 119–20, 121, 123–24
as mission field, 45
people in, losing reverence for the
    sacred, 127
Pietistic religious societies in, 215
religious attitudes in, 43, 124, 250
Restoration period in, 154–55
revivals in, 215–18, 221, 271, 275,
    293
revolution of 1688, 210
secularization of, 124
society moving away from
    Christian beliefs, 124
Sunday school in, 68, 69
theories of religion in (1800–1963),
    150
young adults less involved in
    church activities, 72
Great Commission, xxiii, 184, 424, 425
Great Revival, Pyongyang
    Changdaehyun Presbyterian
    church, 381
Greco-Roman philosophy, 83
Greece, popular religion in, 104
Greek mystery religions, 96
Greek Orthodox Church, 103–4
Greek philosophy, early church fathers
    familiar with, 86
Gregorian Reform, 143–44
Gregory VII, 144
Grimshaw, William, 216
Grund, Francis, 320
Guilds of Piety, 212n168
Guinness, Os, 340
Guthrie, Stewart, 137
Guyse, John, 275

Habermas, Jürgen, 171
hacienda, 397, 409, 409n172
Hadway, Kirk, 251–52
Haldane, Robert, 219, 275
Haldane, James Alexander, 275
Hall, Douglas J., 240
Hampden-Sydney College, revival at, 285–86
Hans Nielson Hauge, 235
Haraldsson, Olaf, 107
Harris, Howell, 212, 215, 216n186, 276, 283
Harvard, 263n93, 281, 353, 355, 356, 358
Hastings, Adrian, 126
Hauge, Hans Nielsen, 219
Haydon, A. Eustace, 353
Hazard, Samuel, 283
healing, 9, 11, 16, 17, 21, 30, 96, 104, 111, 170, 187, 190, 218, 222, 279, 383, 385, 387, 388, 389, 391, 399n129, 409, 410, 411, 412
heaven, belief in, 249
Hegel, G. W. F., 148–49
hell, belief in, 249
Hellenism, 97–98, 364
Hellenization, 82, 96, 97
Hempton, David, 218
Henchman, Daniel, 283
Henry IV, 144, 201
Henry of Lausanne, 201
Heraklitus, 85
Hick, John, xxxv, 365
Higher Christian Life, The (Boardman), 221
Hill, Michael, 12
Hindus, numbers of, 60, 61
Hirsh, Allan, 396
Historical Atlas of Religion in America (Gaustad), 259
historical relativism, 365
History of English Thought into the Clear Light of the Day, A (Stephen), 166
Hodges, William, 286
Holiness movement, 9–11, 218, 239, 278, 294, 294–95, 325, 363

Holiness revival, 385
Holy Grail, story of, 105
Holy Spirit, 182
    baptism in. *See* baptism in the Holy Spirit
    descent of, giving birth to a Jewish-centered church, 363
    in Ghana, 380
    giving birth to the church, 184–85
    manifestations (gifts) of, 2, 10, 190, 209, 387–88
    nature of, 186–87
    origin of all revivals and awakenings, 185
    outpouring of, in the 21st century, 379
    practically ignored by the early church fathers, 185–86, 187
    secularization theorists omitting the spiritual dynamics and manifestations, 177
    sought by renewal movements, 279
    Tertullian witnessing the works of, 188
    transforming power of, 184
    Trinitarian view of, 387–88
Holyoake, George Jacob, 134, 156
Honest to God (Robinson), 126
Hoover, Willis Collins, 393, 394n100
house churches, 127, 412
Howie, John, 209
Hughes, Ray H., 13
Huguenots, xxxiii, 116, 170, 189, 205, 206, 214, 215, 264, 303, 303n289
humanism, xxxv–xxxvi, 305
    as new type of religion, 137, 352, 353
    religious, 351–55
    replacing religion, 171
    running contrary to Christianity's basic tenets, 354–55
    running counter to the biblical worldview, 178
    secular, 350–51
    types of, 351
Humanist Fellowship, 352

humanist manifestos, 352–54
Hume, David, 148, 330
Humphrey, Heman, 184
Humphrys, John, 50
Hus, Jan, 202–3
Hussites, xxxiii, 179, 193, 197, 200, 203, 205, 213
Hussite Unity of the Brethren (Unitas Fratrum), 213
Hutcheson, Francis, 330
Hutchinson, Mark, xiii
Huxley, Thomas Henry, 166

Iannaconne, Laurence, 163
Iberia, aggressive expansion of Christianity in, 109
Iberian Peninsula, church in, 116
identity crisis, 368, 370n18
Iglesia Ni Cristo, 418
immediatism, 298
immigrants
    communities of, mixing different faiths, 377
    effect of, on American religion, 261, 333–34
    increasing number of, 375–76
    as missionaries, 379
    spread of, *375*
incarnation, 399–400
inculturation, xxv, xxvi, 390, 399, 401– 5, 402n141, 403n146, 413, 424
independent (autochthonous) churches, 36–41, 394–95
Independent Church, 216
independent traditions, largest, *40*
indigenization, xxiii, xxvi, 27, 390, 396, 399, 400, 401, 402, 403, 404, 413, 424
indigenous Christianity, 392–93, 395–97
indigenous churches, 393–94
indigenous discovery, 393
Indigenous Methodist Pentecostal Church (Chile), 394
indigenous religion, 110
individualism, 150, 298
individual secularization, 165–71

industrialization
    accelerating rationalism and secularization, 150–51
    leading to secularization, 113, 114
Industrial Revolution, xxv
Innocent III, 189, 192–93
Innocent VII, 202
institutional crisis, 58
institutional religion
    cyclical theory of, xxvi
    decline in, 118
International Church of the Foursquare Gospel, 394
investiture controversy, 144
invisible religious revolution, xxvii
Iracema (Alencar), 408
Ireland
    Christianity and pagan/Celtic traditions fused in, 104–5
    church attendance in, 73
    revival in, 221
Irenaeus, 187–88
Isis/Osiris/Serapis cults, 83
Islam, xxxiv, 364
    in Africa, 19–20
    growth of, 78, 364–65
    spread of, into Europe, xxxi, 191
Israel, reestablishment of, xxxiii–xxxiv, 364
itinerants, 276, 300–301
    replacing parish priests and pastors, 298
    uncomplicated message of, 296

Jackson, Andrew, 319
Jackson, Bob, 113
Jefferson, Thomas, 148, 312, 318
Jehovah's Witnesses, 339
Jenkins, Philip, xiii
Jerusalem, destruction of, 97, 99
Jesus
    belief in, as Son of God, 251
    dual nature of, 93, 186, 187
    identifying the *logos* with, 87–88
Jesus Family, 413, 416
Jesus Is Lord, 417
Jesus movement, 15, 278

Jews
  living disconnected from the
    Western church, 364
  uniting with Gentiles, 364
John Paul II, 35, 402
Johnstone, Patrick, 8
Jones, Adam, 189
Jones, Griffith, 212, 215, 216n186, 236
Judeo-Christian
  belief, 56, 305, 351
  institutions, 241
  monotheism, 89
  religion, 52, 248
  tradition, 351
Justin Martyr, 86–87, 187

Kant, Emmanuel, 148
Kasibante, Amos, 237
Keane, John, 133, 134, 144, 147
Kelley, Dean M., 257
Keswick Convention, 221, 237
Killing Time, 209
Kim, Elijah, xiii–xiv
Kkrumah, Kwame, 401
Knapp, Jacob, 291
Knox, John, 207
Korea
  folk religious practices in, 413
  indigenous church in, 395
  revival in, 381–82
  urban population in, 370n19
Korean Christians, 381–82
Korean Pentecost, 381
Kurtz, Paul, 353
Kuyper, Abraham, 138–39

Labadie, Jean de, 212
laïcité, 135–36
laicization, 135
La Luz del Mundo, 400
Lanphier, Jeremiah C., 291
Latin America
  alignment in, of churches and
    cultures, 398
  Catholicism established in, 110
  Christianity in, 4, 26–29

churches in, producing varieties
  of indigenization and
  contextualization, 400
de-Catholicizing of, 406
immigrants from, 377
native Indian cultures in, new
  missionary approach to, 396
Pentecostalism in, 9, 398, 406
Protestantism in, 370–71n20, 374,
  397
revaluing oppressed people in, 408
syncretism in, 399
traditions in, similar to
  Pentecostalism, 391
latitudinarianism, 327, 344
Latourette, Kenneth, 288, 299
Latter-day Saints (Mormons), 258–59,
  339
Lausanne Covenant, 359
Lausanne Movement, xxiv
lay leaders, in revivals, 220, 274
Laymen's Prayer Revival, 220
lay missionaries, 369
lay preachers, 233
Lectures on the Revivals of Religion
  (Finney), 220, 289–90
Lewis, John, 283
liberalism, xxix, xxxiv–xxxv
  influencing American Christianity,
    346
  points of similarity with secularism,
    348–49
  political, 348
  religious, 347–49
liberal theology, xxv, xxxiii, 257–58,
    305, 334, 343–44
  gaining adherents, 345
  influence of, in seminaries, 345
  taking root in academic circles, 351
liberation theology, 417
Liber Generationis, 98–99
Licinius, 90
Ling, Rodney, 47
Livingston, John, 208
Lloyd-Jones, Martin, 206, 206n125, 296
Locke, John, 148, 330
Lockean philosophy, 344

Logos, 84–88, 186n24
Lollard Bible, 198
Lollards, 190, 197–201, 202, 205
London Missionary Society, 236
Louis XIV, 303n289
Luckmann, Thomas, 163
Luther, Martin, 146, 190, 203, 204, 224
Lutheran Church, 211, 212

Ma, Wonsuk, 417
Madison, James, 312, 317–18n48, 318
Mahan, Asa, 221
mainline denominations
    decline in, 121, 254, 256–58, 260,
        306–7, 342, 344
    growing until 1960, 259
    replaced with newer ones, 325
    secession from, 286
majority world, xiv, xv, xvi, xvii, xxiii,
        xxiv, xxxii, xxxiv, 1, 3, 4, 403
Majority World Christianity, xiv–xv
Manifest Destiny, xxvii, 243, 265,
        277n168, 322, 361
Manifeste des Camisards, Le
        (Carbonnier), 214
Marler, Penny, 251–52
Marsden, George, 244–45
Mar Thoma church, 18
Martin, David, 26, 34, 57, 117–18, 138,
        156, 159–60, 177
Marx, Karl, 148
Mason, Charles H., 13
Mason, Samuel, 283
materialism, 120, 131
material wealth, 305
Mather, Cotton, xxviii, xxxii, 13, 128,
        166n171, 167, 180, 212, 266,
        268, 330, 418n202
Matthew of Janov, 202
Max Weber, 156–58
May, Henry, 14
McCulloch, William, 216–17, 282
McGrath, Alister, 223–24
McGready, James, xxviii, 278, 286
McLeod, Hugh, 119, 127, 152, 164–65
McLoughlin, William G., 209–10, 267,
        278

McPherson, Aimee Semple, 13, 414
M'Crie, Thomas, 192, 208
Medcraft, John, 396–97, 412
Medieval Church, xxxiii, 103, 112,
        112, 113, 190, 192, 195, 218,
        218n200
Mediterranean, regional worship
        practices in, 96
megachurches, 15–16, 370, 382n57
membership, defining, 74
Mennonite Board of Mission and
        Charities, 399
Mennonites, 196
Merton, Robert, 156
Messiah, coming of, 132
Messianic age, 132
Mestizo Catholicism, 411
Methodism, 205, 226, 232
    dominant characteristics of (18th
        cent.), 222–23
    growth of, 219–20, 301
    increasing power of, in English
        society, 227–30
    revival movement, 180, 211n162,
        217–18, 220, 279–80, 287, 301
    teachings of, 228
Methodist Church
    assimilating to secular culture, 325
    democratic system of, 397
    flexibility of, 288–89
    growth of, in the U.S., 257, 285,
        287–89
Methodist Revolution, The (Semmel),
        226
Middle Ages
    continuous growth in, of pagan
        activities, 103–4
    secularization in, 133–34
migration
    affecting religious composition of
        urban areas, 369–70
    domestic, 377
    international, *376*
    theological and missiological
        concerns of, 375
Milic, John, 202
Mill, John Stuart, 166

millenarianism, 286, 400
millennialism, 290n235
millennium, 11, 35, 115, 322, 345, 418n202
Miller, William, 290
Millerites, 290
Mills, C. Wright, 158
ministries led by lay leadership, 286
Minjung theology, 417
miracle workers, 400
missionaries
expanded work of, 234, 235–37
proclaiming a variety of gospels, 115
sent from North America, 241–42
working in cultural isolation from one another, xv
mission field, changing notion of, xxiii
mission-originated churches, 394, 395
missions
lay missionaries, 369
linked with imperialism, 237–38
globalization's effect on, 367–68
international, 297–300
new basis for collaboration in, 382
post-colonial, 392
in urban areas, 373–74
Mithra, 96, 100, 101n124
M'Laurin, John, 282
moderate Enlightenment, 330
modernism, 346
modernity
birth of, 148
effecting a redistribution of believing, 174
relationship of, to religion and transcendence, 360
rise of, 151
secularization linked to, 359–60
time period of, 359–60
modernization, 157, 158–59, 170, 371
leading to secularization, 165–66
role of, in marginalizing Christianity, 165
modern scientific perspective, birth of, 149–50
monastery, sacred space of, 134

monastic revival, 191
monophysitism, 93n81, 187n33
Moody Bible Institute, 297
Moody, Dwight L., xxviii, 31, 221–22, 236, 259, 274, 278, 292–94dy, 297, 298, 322, 345, 356
moral perfection, 294
moral pluralism, growing, 127
Moravians (Moravian Brethren), 213–14, 205, 235
Morrill, John, 155
Morris, Colin, 129
multifaith worship, 69
Murray, Iain, 180
Muslims, numbers of, 60, 61
mystery religions, 83, 84, 96, 97, 100
mysticism, Catholic, 112, 225
mythography, 173

national churches, 65
nation states, increasing predominance of, 152–53
Native Americans, mission to, 299
Neo-Christendom, 399
neo-Pentecostalism, 9, 40
Nestorian Schism, 93n80
Nestorius, 93, 187
Netherlands, secularization in, 153
Nettles, Thomas J., 206
Nettleton, Asahel, 289
Nevius, John, 393, 396n114
New Age movement, 342
Newbigin, Lesslie, 392
new differentiation theory, 174–75
New Humanist, 352
New Lights, 271
New Messianic Movements, 409
new religious movements, 127–28, 260, 340
New Testament church, settling differences in, 84
Newton, Isaac, 330
New World
awakening in, during the Enlightenment, 269
housing the first dissent Christian communities, 277

New World–continued
    Puritanism in, 265–68
    religious minority groups seeking
        refuge in, 264–65
New York Prayer Revival, 270, 363
New Zealand, declining religious
    influence in, 57
*Next Christendom, The: The Coming of
    Global Christianity* (Jenkins),
    xiii
Next Step in Religion, The (Sellars), 352
Nicene Creed, 93n79, 186, 186n26
Niceo-Constantinopolitan Creed, 93
Nicholas of Hereford, 200
Nine O'clock in the Morning (Bennett),
    34
Noble, Thomas, 283
Noll, Mark, 16, 257, 267, 315, 327, 328,
    330–31, 337–38, 349–50
Nordic countries, church in, 116
North America. *See also* America;
        Canada; United States
    belief in God in, 246
    Christianity's upward and
        downward trends in, 13–15
    church in, paradox of, 240–41
    future of Christianity in, 16
    religious belief and practice in, high
        levels of, 245
    religious influence in, 240–41
    religious revival in, 13–14
    secularization in, 239
Northampton (MA, USA), revival in,
    183, 269, 274, 280
Northern Ireland
    belief in God in, 47–48, *247*
    church attendance in, 73
Northfield Conferences, 297
Norway, revival in, 219
NRMs. *See* new religious movements

O'Connor, Cormac Murphy, 44
Odin, 107
Old Lights, 271
ontological secularity, 172
Oriental religions, 342
Origen, 86

Origin of Species (Darwin), 116, 332
Orr, J. Edwin, 182
Osiris, 100
Ostwalt, Conrad Eugene, 15, 16, 169,
    313, 316, 326, 341
Oxford University, 236
Ozman, Agnes, 10

pagan, 82
pagan-Christian feasts, 95–103
pagan-Christian syncretism, 104–8, 112
paganism
    assimilation of, into Christian
        worship, 91–92
    burial rituals, 106
    fertility rituals, 106
    neutralization of, 102
    rituals of, in medieval
        Christendom, 102–8
    transition of, to Christianity, 102
pagan religions, 90, 96, 97, 102, 103
Palmer, Phoebe, 221
Pan African Congress of Majority
    World Theologians, 402
Pancasila (Sukarno), 162
Parham, Charles, 10, 384
Parsons, John J., 132
Parsons, Talcott, 156
Paul, shifting the faith from Israel to
    Europe, 363
Paul VI, 402
Pax Romana, 94
Pelagianism, 337
Pentecost, 105, 106, 100
Pentecostal Century, 5–6, 384-392
Pentecostal churches, xxxiii
    growth in, sociological research
        into, 419–20
    differences between, 422
    independent churches, 41
    reasons for growth of, 377n46
    sustaining growth, 254
Pentecostal Fellowship of North
    America, 385
Pentecostalism, xxv–xxvi, xxxii, 5–9,
    30–32
    in Africa, 380

American evangelism leading to, 302

appealing to people on the fringes, 383

beginning in cities, 370

better fit with non-Western sense of wholeness, 389

contextualization of, 410n175

contributing to ecumenism, 382

diversity in unity, 420–21

dominant force in global Christianity, 1

elements of, 387

expansion of, 377n48

global phenomenon of, 391

growing in urban areas, 371n21, 374

growing with charismatic movement, 385

helping people victimized by modernization, 371

impact of, 14, 16

Holy Spirit's centrality to, 391–92

in Latin America, indebted to European Protestant values, 403–4

leading to personal transformation, 388

making advances in historic churches, 423–24

message of healing power, 383

missionary nature of, 32

offering solution to identity crisis, 368

paving the way for worldwide revivals, 33–34

political advantage of, 419

popular culture's effect on, 413–15

projected growth of, in Latin America, 29

rapid expansion of, 406

reformed theology and, 385–86

revitalizing congregations, 382

revivals and, 239, 385

as sociocultural change, 419–20

spreading in Brazil, 371–72

substituting for Catholicism in Latin America, 398, 406

taking on local flavors, 390–91

theology of, 386

worldwide growth of, 17–18

worship style of, 30–31

Pentecostals

in Africa, 21

in Asia, 23, 25

church leadership of, entering secular politics, 416–17

classical origins of, 421

espousing folk religious forms, 412

experiencing upward mobility, 381–82

in Latin America, 26

politicians among, issues of, 418

varied theological stances among, 418–19

Pére Hyacinthe, 201

personal conversion, 277–78, 294

Pettifer, Julian, 237–38

Philadelphia Prophetic Convention, 346

Philippines, Pentecostalism in, 412–13

Phillips, John, 212

Philo, 84–86

Pia Desideria (*The Piety We Desire*; Spener), 212

Pietism, xxvi, 211–13, 214, 215, 232, 234

emotional aspects of, 225

evangelicalism and, 224–25

Puritanism and, 225, 268–70

resurgence of, 273

Pietists, 204, 205, 269

Pilgrims, 266

Plaisted, David, 189

Plessis, David du, 35

Pliny, 95

pluralism, xxxiv–xxxv, 365

pneumatology, 386

political action, biblically motivated, 234

political liberalism, 348

politico-ecclesiastical hierarchy, 137

polytheism, 83

popular evangelicalism, 226–28
popular religion, 31, 104, 109, 111, 121,
    169, 176, 288, 296–98, 341, 411
popular religious movements, 111–12
Portugal, totalitarian faith in, 109
positivism, 155–56
post-Christendom, 146n78
post-Christianization, 1
postcolonialism, 415–16
postmillennial faith, 322
postmillennialism, 324n71
postmodernism, 120
postmodern secularity, 171–72
post-secular age, 171
Potter, Charles Francis, 353
poverty, evangelistic actions to address,
    382–83
prayer movements, 380, 391
pre-Christian cultures, beliefs of, 410
prehistoric religious practices,
    Christianity's absorption of,
    102–3
premillennialism, 297, 322
pre-Reformation, 112
Presbyterian Church, USA, 258
Presbyterianism, 114, 207
Presbyterians, 205, 208–9
Price, Hugh, 233
Price, John, 277
Primitive Methodists, 228
Prince, Thomas, Sr., 282, 282n188
Princeton, 358
privatization, 162, 167–69
profane, 137
Prosman, Hendricus Johannes, 143,
    144, 146–54, 171–72
prosperity gospel, 383n66
Protestant churches, growth of,
    preceding sociocultural
    changes, 420
Protestant denominations
    church attendance among, linked
        with religious beliefs, 53–54
    foreign missionary enterprise of,
        235
    growing in the U.S., 255
    homogenization of, 319–20

internal secularization among, 325
    segregating themselves from each
        other, 323–24
*Protestant Ethic and the Spirit of
    Capitalism, The* (Weber), 157
Protestantism
    altering the religious culture of
        Western Europe, 116
    American, 243–45, 324, 345
    authority of, attacked, 337
    as civil religion in America, 337
    considered religious heterodoxy,
        404
    establishment of, 114
    opposition to, 27
protoglobalization, 366
public schools, 67, 68–69, 357
Puritan Awakenings, 270, 385
Puritanism, 207, 209–10, 211, 227
    breaking with the Church of
        England, 265–66
    foundations of, 266
    holding contrasting elements of
        faith and rationalism, 310
    influencing generations of
        American life, 266
    legacy of, in the U.K. and the U.S.,
        245
    in the New World, 265–68
    Pietism and, 225, 268–70
    preserving orthodoxy, 310
    rationalistic approach of, 310–11
    spread of, 264–65
    theological influence of, 267
Puritans, 204, 205
    losing original vision, 270, 276
    moving to the New World, 269
    Old Lights and New Lights, 271
Purvey, John, 200, 201

Quakers, 204, 205, 209
quasi-religion, 12

Ramabai, Pandita, 394
Randall, John Herman, Jr., 353
Ranger, Terence, 418
rational enlightenment, 330

rationalism, xxv, 122, 157, 166, 269
    setting the tone for faith in the U.S.,
        312
    without spiritual inclination,
        310–11
Raymond Earl of Foxe, 191
Raymond Earl of Toulouse, 191
reason
    achieving freethinking through, 331
    applying to society and theology,
        328
    as source of happiness, xxvii
    becoming the dominant force, 146
    effect of, on religion, 160
    replacing the divine, 115–16, 125
    used in judging the Bible, 343
    used to oppose religious mystery,
        117
Reason: The Only Oracle of Man
    (Allen), 329
Reasonableness of Christianity, The,
    154–55
Reed, Bruce, 103
re-enchantment, 175
Reese, Curtis W., 352, 353
Reformation, xxxiii, 3, 145, 363
    breaking link between the sacred
        and the secular, 146–47
    changing Christendom in the
        minds of Europeans, 113
    church losing interest in society,
        146
    contrasting results of, in Northern
        and Southern Europe, 156–57
    cradle of, in South of France, 191
    feeding anticlericalism and
        antisupernaturalism, 147
    impetus for, 145
    as revival, 204–5, 206
    revivals serving as forerunners of,
        205–6
Reformed churches, 113–14
Reformed Church, 211, 275, 363
Reformed theology, 324n71, 385–86
Reformed tradition, 3, 6, 206, 215, 228,
    399
Reid, Thomas, 330

reincarnation, belief in, 53, 249
relativistic secularism, 337–38
religion
    aiding in social evolution, 173
    alienating the working class,
        168–69
    arising from primitive communal
        awareness, 136
    becoming a way of life, 327
    cultural, 175–76, 241
    death of, 159
    decline of, 16, 130, 131, 158, 159,
        161, 164, 167, 168, 171, 172
    definitions, 12, 119, 122, 136–37
    deinstitutionalization of, 174
    evolutionary future of, 130
    expressed in different venues, 118
    functions of, transferred to secular
        society, 151, 153–54
    individualistic, 167
    influence of, 290
    marketing of, 288, 414–15
    as memory chain, 173–74
    multiple choices in the marketplace
        of, 167
    mystery and sacredness of,
        vanishing, 335
    non-theistic philosophy of, 352
    perceived influence of, 251
    privatization of, 168
    rationality's effect on, 160
    replacing, with secular alternatives,
        136
    return to, in postmodern era, 172
    secularized, 176
    separation from, as part of
        evolutionary change, 174–75
    serving a social function, 308–9
    sociological view of, 326
    spirituality of, diminishing, 309
    surviving in the private sphere,
        158–59
    viewed as resistance to power,
        418–19
    working with secular systems, 309
Religion Coming of Age, A (Sellars), 352
religion in culture model, 412–13

Religion in Modern Britain (Bruce), 44
Religion in Latin America, xv
Religion in the West, xvii, xviii
religious adherence, 255, 256
religious belief, 46–50, 250
    in Europe, xxix, 27, 50–55, 89
    interrelated with religious
        experience, 55
    linked with denomination, 51, 53
    religious practice aligned with, 53
    in the East, xxx, 13, 56
    in the West, 55–57
    in the world, xxv, 12, 62
Religious Crisis of the 1960s, The
    (McLeod), 119
religious enthusiasm, 118
religious establishment, marginalization
    from, 117
religious humanism, 351–55
religious liberalism, 347–49
religiousness, expansion of, 158
religious persecution, deaths resulting
    from, in Europe, 189
religious pluralism, xxxiv–xxxv, 245
    Evangelicals keeping distance from,
        365
    favorable environment for, in North
        America, 240
religious practice
    different in Great Britain and North
        America, 245–46
    linked with belief, 46
religious sects, 339–40
religious symbols, Constantine's use
    of, 139
religious tolerance, 118, 210, 334–35,
    339–40
renewal, waves of, 33, 34
renewalists, 6–9. *See also* charismatics;
        Pentecostalism; Pentecostals
    in Asia, 25
    in Latin America, 26, 27, 28, 29
    numbers of, 420
    theological spectrum of, 418–19
    term, 32n104
    traditions of, by number of
        adherents, 28

renewal movements, xxxiii, xxxvi, 8,
    9, 10, 13, 25, 29, 386. *See also*
    spiritual renewal movements
repentance, 363
Restoration period (Great Britain),
    154–55
revival advocacy, 286
revivalism, 32, 180–83, 181n7, 230, 285,
    286, 290, 293, 301, 302, 318,
    322, 356
revivals, xxiii, xxiv, xxxvi
    in Asia, 23
    Baptist, 210–11
    based in urban areas, 369
    in the Bible, 179
    characteristics of, 385
    commonality among, 206
    contemporary, reasons for, 360
    in continental Europe
        (1600s–1700s), 211–15
    declines and, xxvi
    definitions and characteristics of,
        180–84
    distinguished from awakenings,
        181–82, 270
    distinguished from non-Western
        church growth, xxv
    domino effect of, 238
    effects on Western Europe (18th
        cent.), 231–32
    in Europe, 271–72, 291
    evangelical, 205–11
    following patterns of New
        Testament churches, 185
    in Great Britain, 215–18, 221, 271,
        275, 293
    impacts of, 14, 230
    influencing American Christianity,
        345–46
    influencing the Christian student
        movement, 236
    international, 274, 275, 367, 417–18
    in Ireland, 221
    in Korea, 381–83
    Methodist, 211n162, 217–18, 220.
        See also Methodism, revival
        movement

in the Middle Ages, 189–204
missionary in character, 193
New Testament model for, 362
in New Zealand, 57
non-Western, xxvi
in Norway, 219
occurring in midst of spiritual
    discouragement, 173
origins of, 9–11
patterns of, 362
Pentecostal, 239
in the post-Reformation era,
    204–22
preparing believers for the trials
    they will face, 185
producing missions, 234, 235–37
Quakers, 209
reasons for beginnings of, in
    England and New England, 279
Reformation as example of, 204–5,
    206
resembling New Testament
    patterns, 185
schisms within, 3
in Scotland, 207–8, 221, 271, 275
source of, 185
supporters of, 345
three points of, 206
transatlantic, 269–70, 272, 273–75
in the U.S., xxix, 220, 228n248,
    269–303, 384–85
worldwide results of, xxvi–xxvii
revivalists, 180, 276
    challenging rationality, 329
    interacting with intellectuals of the
        Enlightenment, 329
revolutionary Enlightenment, 330
Rigge, Robert, 200
rights, as blessings of Jesus Christ, xxxvi
Rise of the City, The (Schlesinger), 333
Ritzema, Helperus, 219
Robe, James, 282
Robert, Dana, 4
Roberts, Evan, 10, 11
Roberts, Oral, 13, 296
Robinson, A. T. John, 126

Roman calendar, eclipsing Sabbath
    observance and the Hebrew
    calendar, 99–100
Roman Catholic Church. *See* Catholic
    Church
Roman Catholics, church attendance
    among, linked with religious
    beliefs, 53–54
Romanitas, 94
Rome, converted to Christianity, 93–94
Roosevelt, Franklin Delano, 243
Rosenius, Carl Olof, 219
Rousseau, Jean-Jacques, 115, 148
Rowland, Daniel, 215
Rowland (Wales), revival in, 10, 14,
    215–16, 221, 280
Ruotsalainen, Paavo, 219
Russello, Gerald, 114–15
Ryder, Henry, 220n210

Sabbath observance, 99
sacral society, 139–40
sacred, as essential component of
    religion, 136
sacred history, 140–41
sacred/secular duality, 132–33
saeculum, 131–32
salvation, 140–41, 337, 424
    achieving, through any religion, 365
    assurance of, 225
    discovered within the universal
        religions, 160
    gospel message at core of, 399
    personal, 271
    preached by the apostles, 185
    Whitefield's message of, 282
sanctification, 9–10, 294, 388
Sankey, Ira D., 221, 293
Savonarola, Girolamo, 203–4
Scandinavia
    church attendance in, 73, 121n219
    religious belief and practice in,
        56–57, 107
Schaff, Philipp, 192–93
Schleiermacher, Friedrich, 343
Schlesinger, Arthur, 333

schools
adopting secular tendencies,
356–58
promoting liberalism and
revivalism, 356
religious influence on, 357
scientism, 334, 344
Scotland
revivals in, 207–8, 221, 271, 275
shrinking denomination size in, 77
Scottish Enlightenment, 330
Scottish Missionary Society, 236
second blessing teaching, 294
second disestablishment, 325
second establishment, 322
Second Great Awakening, 228n248,
270, 278, 284–91, 363, 385
evangelicals establishing new
educational institutions, 356,
358
reshaping American religious life,
284–85
resulting in many denominations'
unparalleled growth, 285
Second Vatican Council, 126
second-wave renewal movement, 34
sectarian movements, 260
secular
contemporary meaning of, 135
defined, 131–32
distinguishing from spiritual, 145
used in reference to clergy, 144
secular abbot, 144–45
secular canopy, 316
secular clergy, 133
secular culture, mainline churches'
compromise with, 260
secular education, 355–59
secular history, 140–41, 175
secular humanism, xxxv–xxxvi, 350–
51, 358
secularism, 257–58
connecting difference replacements
for Christianity, 338
definitions of, 134
disproportionate influence of, on
social and religious life, 336

influence of, 331–32, 335–36, 343,
357–58
introduced into churches, 112, 169
as latest expression of Christian
religion, 172
points of similarity with liberalism,
348–49
Protestant crisis of, 231
relativistic, 337–38
transforming the face of European
history, 145
in the U.S., 334–38
secularity, 171, 172
secularization, xxv–xxvi, xxxv, 135, 137
affecting people's private lives,
167–68
Americanized, 342–61
and revivalism, 338–342
beginning of, 167
catastrophic effects of, 150
crisis of, 126
cultural, 175
as decline in spiritual authority, 172
different in the American and
European contexts, 163
different levels and dimensions of,
161–62
different meanings of, 154
dismantling monopoly between
church and state, 151
distinguished from laicization, 136
effects of, in North America, 239
effects on the educational system,
153–54
of Europe, xxix, xxx, 12, 355
following revivals and awakenings,
178
in Great Britain, 124
historical, 309–16
historical and theological
perspectives on, 171
individual, 162, 165–71
inevitability of, 161
meaning a separation from or
rejection of religion, 134,
163–64
in the Middle Ages, 133–34

penetrating the churches, 127
process of, 162–63
as product of Western, Christian
civilization, 149n90
as reason for decline of Western
church, 365
after the Reformation, 138
resulting from modernization,
165–66
self-limiting nature of, 340
societal, 163
spatial connotation of, 134
spreading around the world's major
cities, 120
study of, 172–73
taking different paths in each
country, 146
theories of, contradicted, 172
two causes of, in the West, 308
in the U.S., 305–8, 323
secularization thesis, 56, 119, 131, 161,
170–71, 178, 359–60, 416–17
discarding, 177
misconceptions about, 177
in a post-secular age, 172–75
secular rationalism, informing church
organization, 339
secular religion, 331–32
secular societies, 166n171
segregation, among Protestant
denominations, 323–24
Sellars, Roy Wood, 352–53
Semmel, Bernard, 226
Separatists, 265–66
sertão, 400n134
sexual ethics, changes in laws relating
to, 127
Seymour, William, 10, 384
Shamanistic activities and rite, 399, 413
Sheldrake, Philip, 136, 142–43
Simpson, A. B., 9
Simpson, Matthew, 244
skeptical Enlightenment, 330
skepticism, 358
slavery, 291
Smale, Joseph, 11
Smeeton, Donald D., 201

Smith, Adam, 330
Smith, Christian, 301
Smith, George, 180
Smith, Hannah Pearsall, 221
Smith, John Blair, 286
Smith, Robert, 221
Smith, Stanley, 237
Snape, Michael, 172–73
social Darwinism, 344
social gospel movement, 323, 341
social power, as substitute for old
religion, 137
societal secularization, 163
Societies for Reformation of Manners,
236
Society for Promoting Christian
Knowledge, 235
Society for Propagating Christian
Knowledge, 235
Society for the Propagation of Christian
Knowledge (SPCK), 236
Society for the Propagation of the
Gospel (SPG), 235, 280–81
Society for the Propagation of the
Gospel in Foreign Parts, 235
society, stages of development in,
155–56
Society of Friends, 209n148
sociopolitical change, sought by those
in the Great Awakenings, 271
Sol Invictus, 88, 99
sola scriptum, 382
soul winning, 218, 284, 288, 289, 297,
301
South America, uniting churches and
denominations in, 422
Southern Baptist Convention, 259
Southern Baptists, 302
Spain, religious atmosphere in, 109–10
speaking in tongues, 10, 15, 30, 34, 35,
387–88, 390
initial evidence, 41
and baptism of the Holy Spirit, 386
Spence, Lewis, 102, 112
Spener, Philipp Jakob, 212, 269
Speroni, Hugo, 196

Spirit Bade Me Go, The: An
    *Astounding Move of God in the
    Denominational Churches* (du
    Plessis), 35
Spirit baptism. *See* baptism of the Holy
    Spirit
spiritual awakenings, outliving
    indoctrinations and church
    programs, 179. *See* awakenings;
    revivals
spiritual gifts, 187–88
spirituality, 169–71
spiritual movements, influence on
    social issues, 338
spiritual renewal movements, xxxiii,
    xxxv–xxxvi
Spurgeon, Charles Haddon, 184
Stark, Rodney, 163
state-recognized churches, 94
Stephen, Leslie, 166
Stewart, Dugald, 330
Stibbe, Alison, 219
Stibbe, Mark, 180, 184
Stickna, Conrad, 202
Stiles, Ezra, 255
Stoddard, Solomon, 274n153
Stoll, David, 26
Stone, W. Barton, 286
Story of the Grail, The (Troyes), 112
Stott, John, 296
Stout, Jeffery, 172
Studd, C. T., 236
Student Volunteer Movement for
    Foreign Mission, 31, 297
sub-Saharan Africa, indigenization and
    contextualization in, 401
Suenens, Leon-Joseph, 13
Sumner, Charles, 220n210
Sumner, John, 220n210
Sunday Sabbath observance, 99
Sunday school, 68, 69
Sunday, Billy, 32, 293, 296, 414
Sunjoo, Kil, 394
supernatural
    Asians' receptivity to, 384
    belief in, 172, 389, 390
superstitions, 103

Swaggart, Jimmy, 296
syncretic acculturation, 405–6
syncretic Catholicism, 411
syncretism, 83, 399, 400, 405–8, 410–12
Système de politique positive (Comte),
    155

Taylor, Charles, 177
Taylor, John, 215
Taylor, William, 393
technology, aiding the Pentecostal and
    charismatic movements, 414–15
10/40 Window, xiii–xiv
Tennent, Gilbert, 269, 273, 282, 283
Tennent, Timothy, 34
Tertullian, 86, 188
Tewahedo Church, 19
thaumaturges, 400
Themistius, 88
Theodosius, 82, 88, 186–87
theological Darwinism, 344
theology
    liberal criticism of, intensified, xxvii
    secularization of, 306
Theophilus, 86
third disestablishment, 324
Third Great Awakening, 270–71, 278,
    292
third-wave renewal movement, 41
third-world church, growth of, 59–60
Thomas, Edward, 244n19
Three-Self Patriotic Movement, 416
three-self principle, 393
Tidball, Derek, 116
Toba Indians, 399
Tocqueville, Alexis de, 307–8, 320
Toleration Act (1689), 114
tongsung kido (unison prayer), 381
Trainor, Brian, 141–43
transcendence
    different concepts of, 360
    importance of, in modern life, 361
transplanted Catholicism, 411
Trinity, the, 185–87, 387–88
Troeltsch, Ernst, 156
Trollope, Frances, 320
Troyes, Chrétien de, 112

True Jesus Church, 413
Tukunas, the, 408
Tupi-Guarani, the, 408
Turner, John Munsey, 232–33
Twelve Days of Christmas, 105–6
Tyndale, William, 201

Uhlhorn, Gerhard, 184–85
Ulster Revival, 291
Umbanda, 407
unison prayer, 381
Unitarian Church, 331
Unitarianism, xxv, 286, 327
Unitarian Universalism, xxv
United Church of Christ, 258
United Kingdom. *See also* Great Britain
    belief in God in, 246
    church membership in, 74–78
United States. *See also* America
    belief in God in, *247*, 248–49
    Catholic settlers in, 311
    as a Christian nation, 242–44, 361
    Christian denominations in,
        assuming moralist character,
        336
    Christian faith in, identifying with
        Christianity, 303
    Christianization of, 361
    church in, secularization of, 312–13
    church attendance in, 55, 251
    church membership in, 251–55, *260*
    church's rise and decline in, xxxi–
        xxxii, 125, 239, 242, 341–42
    Constitution of, 314–15, 318–19,
        331
    Declaration of Independence of,
        315
    denominational pluralism in, 340
    entering post-secular stage, 176
    evangelical camp losing influence
        in the judiciary, 326
    faith in, rationalism setting the tone
        for, 312
    founding of, including elements of
        faith and secularism, 310
    free market for churches in, 316–17
    future of, 361
        influence of, on worldwide
            missions, 299–300
        liberal-conservative divide in, 344
        measuring secularization in,
            316–17
        political influence of, 418
        population of, 378
        producing a new religious culture,
            xxviii
        Protestant identity of, 243–45
        Puritanism's legacy in, 242
        rapid transition to a secular
            mindset, 342
        relationship in, between church and
            culture, 240
        religion's strength in, 240, 297
        religious affiliation in, 254, *256*
        religious beliefs in, *250*
        religious landscape in (19th–20th
            cent.), 307
        religious pluralism in, 245
        revivals in, 220, 228n248, 269–303,
            384–85
        second disestablishment in, 321–22
        secularism in, 334–38
        secularization in, 305–8, 323,
            342–61
        secular religion in, 331
        smaller and younger churches
            overtaking mainline churches,
            258–59
        third disestablishment in, 324
        types of Enlightenment in, 330
        vigorous religious culture in, 123
        white Protestant church attendance
            in, *258*
Universal Church of the Kingdom of
    God, 422
Universal Church of the Reign of God
    (Igreja Universal do Reino de
    Deus), 28
University of Georgia, revival at, 287
University of Halle, 212–13
urban areas
    containing a variety of religious and
        spiritual beliefs, 369
    mission in, 373–74

urban areas–continued
  Pentecostal growth in, 371n21, 374
  Pentecostal movement beginning
    in, 370
urban church growth, 374
urban ministry, xxv
urbanization, xxv, 285, 339, 368–74

Valdo, Peter. *See* Waldo, Peter
Van Dusen, Henry, 382
Vatican, 402
Venn, Henry, 393, 396n114
Victorian era, religion during, 123–24
Villanueva, Eddie, 417
Vingren, Gunnar, 393, 395n103
Virgin Mary, adoration of, 99
Vitagliano, xiii
Vitry, Jacques de, 191
Voas, David, 47
Voltaire (François-Marie Arouet), 115,
    148, 155
voluntary church syndrome, 285

Wagner, C. Peter, 374n37
Waldensians (Waldenses), 189, 193–97,
    202, 204, 205
Waldo, Peter, 190, 194–96
Wallace, Anthony F. C., 130, 156
Walls, Andrew, 2
Walther, Daniel, 214
Watts, Isaac, 212, 275, 284
Weiner, Anthony J., 307
Weiner, Herman, 307
Weinstein, Jacob K., 353
Weir, John, 221
Welch, John, 207
Wesley, Charles, 214
Wesley, John, xxvii, 9, 182, 213–16, 218,
    219, 226–28, 234, 236, 268, 274
  in context of his time, 232–33
  Edwards's influence on, 275, 283–84
  visiting the colonies, 275
  knowledge of the Enlightenment,
    226
  methodical system of, 228
  using Enlightenment principles,
    329

Wesleyan Methodist Missionary
    Society, 236
Wesleyans, 213
Wessels, Anton, 80
West
  Civilization, 115, 116, 149n90
  de-Christianization of, 3
  mission, xv
  needing immigrants as
    missionaries, 379
  religious belief in, 55–57
  secularization in, two causes of, 308
Western
  Church influence, xxv, 12
  Christianity, xiii, xiv, 3
  decline of, xxiv, xxv, xxxii, xxxv, 1,
    44, 45, 57, 59, 77, 79n120, 121,
    136, 154, 159, 176, 365
  leadership, xxiii, xxiv
  missionaries, xv. Xxvii, 45, 115
  mission shift, xxiii, 1, 2, 14, 17, 27,
    363
thought, xiii,
religious belief, 55
revivals, xxv
Western Europe
  Christian culture's diminished role
    in, 16, 117, 118
  Christian ethics and values
    predominating in, 45
Western theology, decreasing influence
  of, xxiii,
Westminster Confession, 275
Whiston, William, 214
Whitefield, George, 214, 215–17, 219,
    227, 228, 234, 274, 275, 298,
    300–301
  critical of unspiritual clergy and
    church leaders, 281
  extent of his preaching, 283
  impact of, 280
  keeping in touch with other
    ministers, 282–83
  leading people to personal
    conversion, 277–28
  public response to, along the U.S.
    eastern seaboard, 280–82

Wieman, A. N., 351
Wilberforce, William, xxvii, 226, 236
Wilkerson, David, 13
Willaime, Jean-Paul, 135–36
William of Ockham, 145
Williams, J. Rodman, 386–87
Williams, Roger, 311
Williams, William, 215
Wilmer, Eleanor, 375
Wilson, Bryan, 150, 156
Wilson, Edwin H., 352, 353
Wilson, Everett A., 395n107
Wilson, Woodrow, 242
Winthrop, John, 266
Woolston, Thomas, 155
Worcester (South Africa), Spirit of God
        in, 291
World Council of Churches, xxiv,
        403n147
World Evangelical Alliance, xxiv
world evangelism, 359, 364
world missions movement, 298
world population, 378
world religions
        comparative growth of, *60*
        global changes in, *61*
        by nation, *63*
        by proportion, *62*
        ranked by global adherents, *61*
Worldwide Evangelization Crusade,
        236
Wuthnow, Robert, 261, 344
Wycliffe, John, 145, 190, 197–201, 202
Wycliffe Bible, 198, 200

Yale, 355, 358
Yount, David, 251, 254, 259
Youth with a Mission, 359

Zinzendorf, Nicolaus von, xxvii, 213,
        234
Zulehner, Paul M., 137–38